THE HALF-VANISHED STRUCTURE

Magnus Ullén

# THE HALF-VANISHED STRUCTURE

## Hawthorne's Allegorical Dialectics

PETER LANG
Bern · Berlin · Bruxelles · Frankfurt am Main · New York · Oxford · Wien

**Bibliographic information published by Die Deutsche Bibliothek**
Die Deutsche Bibliothek lists this publication in the Deutsche Nationalbibliografie; detailed bibliographic data is available on the Internet at ‹http://dnb.ddb.de›.

British Library and Library of Congress Cataloguing-in-Publication Data:
A catalogue record for this book is available from *The British Library,* Great Britain, and from *The Library of Congress,* USA

Cover Illustrations: The menorah on the arch of Titus, as reproduced in Leon Yarden, The Spoils of Jerusalem on the Arch of Titus: A Re-Investigation *(Stockholm: Skrifter utgivna av svenska institutet: Rom, 1991). Reprinted with permission of the Board of Publication at the Swedish Institutes in Rome and Athens.*

Cover design: Thomas Jaberg, Peter Lang AG

ISBN 3-03910-200-1
US-ISBN 0-8204-6868-1


Hochfeldstrasse 32, Postfach 746, CH-3000 Bern 9, Switzerland
info@peterlang.com, www.peterlang.com, www.peterlang.net



Printed in Germany

Contents

# Acknowledgements

It is with pleasure that I renew my thanks to the people who assisted me during the course of writing this study. I am indebted in particular to Professor Torsten Pettersson and Dr. Arne Axelsson at Uppsala University, both of whom attended to the many versions these chapters have gone through with patience and care before they reached their present shape.

I am grateful also to Professor Roland Lysell of Stockholm University, Dr. Brian Harding of the University of Birmingham, and Professor Samuel Coale, for offering critique of various aspects of the study, and to Frederick Newberry for helpful advice. I thank Buford Jones for sharing his extensive knowledge of Hawthorne's life and letters with me in conversation during my time at Duke University. My thanks also to Fredric Jameson, who encouraged me to develop my theoretical approach, and from whose teachings on allegory and dialectics I have greatly profited.

While at Duke, David Anderson and Catherine Shreve, with their children Jake and Sally, showed my family and myself the best of American hospitality, receiving us into their home with great warmth and generosity, greatly contributing towards making our year in North Carolina one of our most treasured memories.

My friend David Herron kindly took the time to check the language of part of the dissertation; needless to say, all remaining errors are attributable only to myself. Neither Roger Solax nor Mikael Byström have read as much as a line of this study, but I could not have written it without our innumerable conversations on every conceivable aspect of life. My mother, Dorothy Ullén, has sustained me throughout my life with her love and warmth, and has helped me in so many ways that it almost seems petty to thank her for reading my first attempts to write about Hawthorne in English. My gratefulness extends to my father, Olle Ullén, who passed away quietly while this work was still in its early stages.

My research has been supported by generous grants from the Swedish Fulbright Commission, the Swedish Institute, the Helge Ax:son Johnson

Foundation, Karl and Betty Warburg Fund, the Anders Karitz Foundation, and the Magnus Bergvall Foundation. I acknowledge these sources with gratitude.

Substantial portions of chapter one contains material that originally appeared in *New Literary History* 32 (2001), under the title "Dante in Paradise: The End of Allegorical Interpretation." I am grateful for permission to reprint.

I am grateful to my children, Linn, Henning, and Alice, for reminding me that some things are even more important than poking about in books, and for giving me more than I can ever hope to return.

My greatest debt is to my wife Lisa, for her ceaseless support and affection, and for reminding me daily what love can be.

M. U.

Solna, June 2003

# Abbreviations

| | |
|---|---|
| CE | *The Centenary Edition of the Works of Nathaniel Hawthorne.* 23 vols. Edited by William Charvat, Roy Harvey Pearce, Claude M. Simpson, Thomas Woodson, et al. Columbus: Ohio State UP, 1962–1997. |
| SL | *The Scarlet Letter* |
| HSG | *The House of the Seven Gables* |
| BR | *The Blithedale Romance* |
| MF | *The Marble Faun* |
| *Study* | Waggoner, Hyatt Howe. *Hawthorne: A Critical Study.* Cambridge: Harvard UP, 1955. Rev. ed. 1963. |
| *Tragic* | Roy R. Male, *Hawthorne's Tragic Vision.* Austin: University of Texas Press, 1957. |
| *Practicing* | Richard Millington, *Practicing Romance: Narrative Form and Cultural Engagement in Hawthorne's Fiction.* Princeton: Princeton UP, 1990. |
| PU | Fredric Jameson, *The Political Unconscious: Narrative as a Socially Symbolic Act.* Ithaca: Cornell UP, 1981. |

In the Notes, full bibliographical details are provided only at the first entry of any given work. Subsequent references are made only by name, or, where necessary, by name and a condensed form of the work's title.

# Introduction

In one of the travel sketches collected in *Our Old Home*, Hawthorne describes his reaction to the Gothic cathedral of Lichfield, England:

> The traces remaining in my memory represent it as airy rather than massive. A multitude of beautiful shapes appeared to be comprehended within its single outline; it was a kind of kaleidoscopic mystery, so rich a variety of aspects did it assume from each altered point of view, through the presentation of a different face, and the rearrangement of its peaks and pinnacles and the three battlemented towers, with the spires that shot heavenward from all three, but one loftier than its fellows. Thus it impressed you, at every change, as a newly created structure of the passing moment, in which yet you lovingly recognized the half-vanished structure of the instant before, and felt, moreover, a joyful faith in the indestructible existence of all this cloudlike vicissitude. A Gothic Cathedral is surely the most wonderful work which mortal man has yet achieved, so vast, so intricate, and so profoundly simple, with such strange, delightful recesses in its grand figure, so difficult to comprehend within one idea, and yet all so consonant that it ultimately draws the beholder and his universe into its harmony. It is the only thing in the world that is vast enough and rich enough. (5: 124–25)

The passage thus represents Hawthorne's account of the ideal qualities of a work of art. Appearing always "newly created," yet retaining within itself "the half-vanished structure of the instant before," the Gothic cathedral succeeds in fusing the temporal with the eternal, and thus provides a passageway from the real to the ideal. Equally important, by switching focus from the cathedral itself to his own reaction to it in the very next paragraph, Hawthorne also gives us an account of himself as a reader of this ideal work of art:

> Not that I felt, or was worthy to feel, an unmingled enjoyment in gazing at this wonder. I could not elevate myself to its spiritual height, any more than I could have climbed from the ground to the summit of one of its pinnacles. Ascending but a little way, I continually fell back and lay in a kind of despair, conscious that a flood of uncomprehended beauty was pouring down upon me, of which I could

> appropriate only the minutest portion. After a hundred years, incalculably as my higher sympathies might be invigorated by so divine an employment, I should still be a gazer from below and at an awful distance, as yet remotely excluded from the interior mystery. But it was something gained, even to have that painful sense of my own limitations, and that half-smothered yearning to soar beyond them. The Cathedral showed me how earthly I was, but yet whispered deeply of immortality. After all, this was probably the best lesson that it could bestow, and, taking it as thoroughly as possible home to my heart, I was fain to be content. (5: 125)

Citing the above passage, Herbert Read aptly claims that it is expressive of a "sense of an almost giddy vertiginous gulf between human finiteness and the infinity of the Absolute, whether in art or religion."[1] No matter how long he will contemplate the cathedral, Hawthorne recognizes that he will always remain "a gazer from below and at an awful distance, as yet remotely excluded from the interior mystery." Yet he does not lament this circumstance; instead, he turns this recognition of his own inherent imperfection, this acknowledgement of a lack within himself that must always keep him at a distance from the ideal, into a prerequisite for gaining a sense of the ideal, if not the ideal itself. The cathedral "showed me how earthly I was, but yet whispered deeply of immortality," and "this was probably the best lesson that it could bestow." Paradoxically, then, the distance which separates us from the ideal, is also the medium whereby a sense of the ideal may be attained.

Like so many other passages of his later works, the extracts cited above may be read as metatextual comments by Hawthorne on his own art, the literary form he termed "romance."[2] It is universally acknowledged that the Hawthornean romance is a form of writing that attempts to fuse the imaginary with the actual, the ideal with the real. In the famous moonlight scene of "The Custom-House," the room described by Hawthorne becomes emblematic of the conceptual space of the romance, "a neutral territory, somewhere between the real world and fairy-land, where the Actual and the Imaginary may meet, and each imbue itself with the nature of the other" (36). I will be arguing throughout this study that Hawthorne strives to effect this fusion not, as is commonly held, by conflating these two categories, but on the contrary by making the reader aware of why and in what sense they must necessarily remain distinct from each other, in order that there may remain a passageway from the Actual to the Imaginary—the real and the ideal—that affirms the existence of the latter realm, without suppressing the essential feature of the former: the sense of guilt which is a sign of man's radical imperfection. Furthermore, I shall argue that the desire to deny this imperfection—this gap between the Imaginary and the Actual—produces symbolism, while the effort to retain the gap is a distinctive feature of allegory.

Broadly speaking, the present study sets out to do two interrelated things: to renew our conception of Nathaniel Hawthorne as an allegorical writer, and to revitalize allegory as an interpretive method. It is an explicit assumption of this study that every narrative is an allegory of its own mediation. The opening theoretical chapter argues that this is the founding principle from which any properly allegorical interpretation must proceed. Throughout this study, the claim for the universality of this version of *allegoresis* will be accompanied by a more specific claim: namely, that Hawthorne consciously made use of this metatextual allegory—in other words, that he always wrote about the artist and his audience, and, most importantly of all, about the medium through which these two actants (artist and audience; writer and reader) establish a relation. If Hawthorne's works are allegorical in any other sense than other literary works must be said to be so, it is primarily in that they demand of us that we reflect upon our own activity as readers. Writing and reading, Hawthorne's narratives would have us see, could be conceived as a dialectical process, the structural paradigm of which is to be found in the notion of the Fortunate Fall. This paradoxical formula provides the theoretical means by which an individual may bridge the gap between the real and the ideal, in all its manifestations; and it does so by insisting on the importance of mediation, of the need for the individual to recognize his or her insufficiency to establish a direct relation with God—or, if we prefer a more profane formulation, with that totality that enables us to feel, think, and speak. In insisting upon the need for mediation, the formula of the Fortunate Fall thus requires of us to look to distance rather than presence as a sign of divinity in life. Hawthorne's allegory, I will argue, is designed to retain a concept of spirituality which is incompatible with the insistence on presence characteristic not only of the Transcendentalist thinkers of his society, but of his, and our, historical context in general.

## 1. Critical Background

As should be clear from the above, the present study argues the importance of highlighting the theological aspects of Hawthorne's writings. In this it owes much to F. O. Matthiessen's influential discussion of Hawthorne in *American Renaissance* (1941), who submits that Hawthorne's conception of life "is built on the experienced realization that man is radically imperfect."[3] A number of important studies of the nineteen-fifties solidify this view, most rewardingly, perhaps, H. H. Waggoner's *Hawthorne: A Critical Study* (1955), and Roy R. Male's *Hawthorne's Tragic Vision* (1957).[4] Indeed, it seems safe to say that the centrality of Hawthorne's Christianity was more or less taken for granted until Frederick Crews openly attacked it in his psychoanalytic study of Hawthorne, *The Sins of the Fathers* (1966). Crews forcibly argues the case against the tendency implicit in the critical strategy of Waggoner, Male, and other critics to smooth over the contradictory traits of Hawthorne's texts. "Hawthorne's keynote," Crews writes, "was neither piety nor impiety, but ambivalence. [...] In the typical Hawthorne tale there is a jarring dissonance between the 'sweet moral blossom' that is served up with an obliging flourish and the 'human frailty and sorrow' that compose the story. Hawthorne's ambiguity—to which every critic pays lip-service before going on to build a tower of allegory—is not a didactic strategy but a sign of powerful tension between his attraction to and his fear of his deepest themes." Crews' own position is (or at any rate, was, since he has since renounced psychoanalysis) that Hawthorne's writings can be seen as a practical precursor to Freudian psychoanalytical theory: "In Hawthorne's fiction [...] *suppression* always has the psychological consequences of *repression*: the denied element surreptitiously reappears in imagery and innuendo.[5]

Ten years later, Nina Baym in *The Shape of Hawthorne's Career* (1976) dealt another blow against the established view of Hawthorne as a Christian writer. Rather than being an example of Christian man's dilemma, in Baym's reading the Hawthornean hero (who, as we have said, is almost invariably in some sense an artist figure) is a creative individual in conflict with a repressive society. Hawthorne's "controlling preoccupation," in Baym's view, is to define "a way of writing that could embody the imagination and justify it to a skeptical, practical-minded audience." In this, Hawthorne's "romantic vision was allied to that of Coleridge, Wordsworth, and particularly the American transcendentalists."[6] Baym has since become one of the most quoted Hawthorne scholars, and there is no denying that her study, in tandem with that of Crews, has been pivotal in sharpening our sense for the importance of the sexual themes in Hawthorne's writing. Yet more is involved in this downplaying of the relation between Hawthorne's writings and Christian faith than a mere change of critical emphasis from spirituality and metaphysics to sexuality and psychology. To lose sight of the concept of faith in Hawthorne is to lose sight of the key to the ideological implications of his writings, to willingly reduce their scope to the psyche of the author, for as Matthiessen puts it, we will "be in a position to test" Hawthorne's ideological prerogatives "against what we ourselves may believe to be primary forces in the universe" only "if, instead of discounting his views as part of a world gone by, we try to experience to the full what he thought and felt about human destiny."[7] The present study does not pretend to make any definitive assertions about whether Hawthorne entertained genuine religious beliefs or not, but it takes as its point of departure the undeniable fact that his writings are deeply informed by cognitive patterns deriving from Christianity. Whether Hawthorne believed or not, he made use of those patterns to express his understanding of how the existential conditions of man are refracted through politics, history, and art.

It would be unfair to say that the psychological reductionism that is characteristic of the studies of Crews and Baym has not been challenged in the plethora of critical studies of Hawthorne that has followed in the eighties and nineties. Yet with one or two significant exceptions, renewed attempts to historicize Hawthorne's writings have nevertheless largely ignored the issue of their relation to Christianity.[8] More importantly, studies that do take his use of the concept of faith seriously have tended to look upon it as determined by the historical context, rather than considering it as the vehicle whereby Hawthorne attempted to resist the ideological fabric of this context. In *The Office of The Scarlet Letter* (1991), for instance—one of the most compelling studies of Hawthorne to have emerged in the last two decades—Sacvan Bercovitch shows how the rhetorical strategies employed by Hawthorne in his most famous romance are related to the "distinctive social-symbolic outlook" that Bercovitch traces back to the Puritan settlers in *The Puritan Origins of the American Self* (1975), and *The American Jeremiad* (1978).[9] As Bercovitch shows, the seeds of symbolism are present already in the rhetorical strategies of the Puritans, a circumstance that I shall get back to in the conclusion of the present study. It seems to me, however, that Bercovitch's analysis fails to consider some very important points at which Hawthorne's understanding of faith contrasts with that of the Puritan settlers, as well as with that of their descendants. It is well-known that Hawthorne's conception of Christianity allowed him to see the world in a very different way from the optimistic conception of the Transcendentalist movement, one of the leading intellectual groups of mid-nineteenth century New England. As Millicent Bell has shown, "Hawthorne gave conscious assent to the transcendental view of art: a presentation of that ideal of which the visible world is but an imperfect expression." However, despite the profusion of scattered remarks in Hawthorne's writings affirming such a view, Bell nevertheless maintains that "the transcendental view of the artist represents only part of Hawthorne's thinking on the subject, and actually its less vital part—a sort of passive residue which in his art he seems continually to struggle against."[10] While verging rhetorically towards the transcendental, then, Hawthorne's stories ultimately present a deeply sceptical view of transcendentalism as such. But *how* does his idealism differ from that of the Transcendentalists? And how is this difference manifested in his writings? How are we to conceive of his project today? I will be arguing that Hawthorne's writings are rooted in an allegorical conception of life which projects an imperative that is social as much as spiritual, with political implications much more radical than were those of the openly reformative tenets propounded within Unitarianism as well as Transcendentalism. In order to see this, it will be necessary to reconsider the relation between Christianity and allegory.

## 2. Allegory and Symbolism

To this end, the opening chapter of this book is devoted to a discussion of allegorical hermeneutics. There is a distinctive difference, the discussion assumes, between the allegorical hermeneutics of Medieval Christianity, and the hermeneutical tradition that dates back to Goethe and Coleridge, at the very least. I will refer to this tradition, which has dominated literary criticism for the last two centuries, as a symbolistic hermeneutics, or simply as symbolism, one of its constitutive traits being the valorization of the symbol at the expense of allegory that is codified in the Coleridgean distinction between allegory and symbolism. As will be seen, this valorization is replicated in Hawthorne criticism as well. This is not to say that all the critics who have expounded Hawthorne's "symbolism" have been entirely wrong: there is in Hawthorne a tension between symbolism and allegory which is not nearly as apparent in, say, Bunyan or Spenser. But this tension, I will argue, is one that Hawthorne has designed his narratives to resolve, by actively engaging the hermeneutical desire of the reader, who is invited, as it were, to become a second parent of the narrative. Or rather, it is demanded of us that we assume some such role in relation to the narrative, or it will refuse to consummate the interpretive desire it arouses in us. Hawthorne's project, then, could be described as an attempt to nurture the reader's allegorical sensibility, to educate the reader in an allegorical mode of perception. Which is to say that he tries to make us aware of how the significance of the part is always dependent upon the whole, even though the significance of the whole would seem to be generated by its parts.

Hawthorne's method for doing so, as I have already suggested, is to turn his narratives into allegories of his own vocation, figurative representations of the interaction between audience and artist. Traditionally, the artist figure in Hawthorne has been equated with the leading male character of each romance.[11] I will argue, in contrast, that in three of Hawthorne's four mature romances the role of the artist figure is assigned to a female character—Hester in *The Scarlet Letter*, Zenobia in *The Blithedale Romance*, and Miriam in *The Marble Faun*.[12] Furthermore, I will argue that with the exception of Holgrave in *The House of the Seven Gables*, the male characters who have traditionally been assigned this role are more rewardingly looked upon as a reader, a secondary creator. The allegorical "reader" that I identify in Hawthorne's fictions is invariably in some sense a representative of society, whereas the "artist" represents the individual. This is the key to the metatextual allegory that I will trace in my analyses of the romances: as the fate of the artist figure's art can be seen to be dependent upon the way society responds to it, so the fate of Hawthorne's fictions are dependent upon how we as readers conceive of our relation to them. As will be seen, the figure of the artist/individual is distinguished by what I will refer to as a *symbolistic* desire, a desire to refashion the norms of society in accordance with his or her private emotional experiences. In representing the communal norms of society, the reader, in contrast, represents an allegorical stance. Hawthorne's writings can thus be said to enact a conflict between the private experiences of the individual and the public norms of society. In the terms of this study, this is a conflict between a symbolistic and an allegorical attitude towards the world. Ultimately, I will argue, Hawthorne strives to transcend this conflict by conceiving of his chosen fictional mode—the romance—as the medium for a dialectical interaction between writer and reader.[13]

Although Hawthorne makes frequent use of many rhetorical devices traditionally associated with allegory as a genre, my interest is not primarily with personification or any other such device, but rather with allegory and symbolism as distinct conceptual modes.[14] In allegory and symbolism alike, the relation between part and whole is that between the concrete manifestation of the signifier and the ideal totality ascribed to the signified. Yet as modes of perception, as well as literary strategies, allegory and symbolism differ from each other in that symbolism assumes that it is possible to make the leap from the real to the ideal immediately, without the aid of any mediating agency above the symbol itself. The structure of the allegorical image, in contrast, displays allegory's inherent recognition of the necessity of mediation. In contrast to the symbol, the allegorical image is not already a part of the meaning it signifies, but an entity of a completely different status. In allegory, that is, there is no internal relation between signifier and signified, wherefore the move between signifier and signified can be accommodated only by means of an act of translation. This mediating act of translation, however, is not in itself sufficient to complete the move from signifier to signified: since the signified per definition is the totality, it follows that no set of signifiers can ever fully express it. This entails that instead of arriving immediately at the signified, as in symbolism, in allegory the signifier of one discourse can at best be translated into the signifier of another, and so forth. As we shall see in chapter one, this does not entail that allegorical interpretation is endless. Whereas symbolism posits the presence of an ineffable meaning, allegory insists on translating the ineffable into a rationally comprehensible discourse, while at the same time acknowledging that no rational discourse can ever hope to express the irrational that must also be included in a totality of meanings. Symbolism thus almost by necessity must constantly repeat its assertion of the presence of the ineffable by a potentially endless production of metaphors. Allegory, in contrast, by highlighting its own inadequacy, implicitly acknowledges that its true meaning is not be sought in any specific translation of the ineffable, but rather in the very inability of any translation to represent its true signified. By thus implicitly rejecting the notion of mimesis, allegory presents the very impossibility of representation as its true signified. Allegory, then, is a discourse which is always directed at an ideal which it cannot arrive at except as an absence, wherefore negation necessarily becomes the key to the ideal in the allegorical discourse. While allegory and symbolism alike strive for the presence of a totality, allegory, in contrast to the latter mode of perception, recognizes that this desire can be consummated only by means of a paradoxical strategy which substitutes absence for presence as the mode of experiencing this ideal totality. Eternity is not won through life, but death.

In the analyses of Hawthorne's works that comprise the bulk of this book, I hope to show that the recurrence of the motif of death in the romances must be seen in relation to the paradoxical nature of allegory. Medieval exegetes of the Bible assumed that meaning is not an indefinite concept, but that meanings are always constricted by God, who acts, as it were, as an epistemological boundary for the world. Although unable to take the assumption of God as boundary for granted, Hawthorne's allegorical practice nevertheless displays a similar recognition of the necessity of constraining the signifying potential of his works within a definite boundary. Within the narratives themselves, this can be seen by their recurrent preoccupation with death. Ultimately, however, the reader must function as such a boundary, for the romances are designed to make evident that it is the way we interpret their plots that determine the significance of the recurrent death-motif. By thus invoking the reader as a boundary, I will argue, Hawthorne's allegory strives to re-contain its own symbolistic momentum, and hence to reintegrate the artistic desire to transgress the norms of society as a vital contribution to these norms. But it also seeks to make clear that the reader will be able to hold the position of such an epistemological boundary only if we in turn are willing to accept the writer as our own boundary, by acknowledging that the vision expressed by the writer/artist is just as inviolable as are the norms of society. The outcome of this dialectical relation—if ideally consummated—could thus be looked upon as a social imperative of long-standing authority: do unto others as you would have them do unto you. Hawthorne's version of the Golden Rule, however, places the reader in a somewhat paradoxical situation, for it entails that we must both actively engage the text, and passively subject ourselves to its ideological prerogative. We are invited to generate the figurative sense of the text, as many commentators have sensed, but only on the condition that we do not violate the literal sense of the text. My methodological procedures, sketched below, have been fashioned with this end in view.

## 3. Method and Outline

All of Hawthorne's full-length writings, I will argue, are structured on what could perhaps be termed a principle of chiastic inversion, to the effect that the second half of the narrative in question subtly but significantly repeats the events of the first half in inverted order.[15] The technique is by no means original with Hawthorne—a similar principle for arranging the material of the narrative can be found in *The Odyssey*, for instance, and, in a considerably more elaborated form, in *The Aeneid.* What is involved is the tying together of textual sequences, temporally separated from each other, in such a manner that the reader comes to recognize an inherent relationship between them. There is no end to the varieties the symmetrical principle may produce, but in Hawthorne it habitually—though not exclusively—takes the form of arranging the material around one central chapter. This central chapter is comparable to a stone dropped in water: the remaining chapters will spread around it in symmetrical configurations, much like the ripples that can be seen spreading over the water into which the stone was dropped, lending a spatial impression to the temporal dispersion of the narrative.[16]

The imposition of spatial structures upon the text is a strategic if not absolutely necessary step towards reinserting the allegorical gap or distance that the symbolistic insistence on immediacy represses. By taking a detour over a spatial construction of the text, we automatically introduce a distance between the reading experience and our conceptualization of this experience. The spatial form of the text, one must be careful to observe, is something which can only be recovered, never instantaneously apprehended. While we read, the form is not present; it can be sensed only by reflecting upon our reading experience. Having thus generated a sense of the spatial aspects of the text, we may discern a sense in which the Truth of the literary work of art can be said to be fixed by its form, a sense in which it transcends the conditions of its own enunciation. This transcendental quality of art, I will be arguing, allows it to fulfil a mediating office equivalent to that fulfilled by Christ in Christianity. Like Christ, the work of art can make the realm of Absolutes available to man, but it cannot by itself negate the cleavage that is a consequence of the Fall. Ultimately, the meaning of Hawthorne's narrative works of art must be decided by each reader, upon whom it falls to look to the narratives as means to re-establish a bond to their creator, or to turn them into symbolic vehicles for his own self-expression. In the terms of this study, this is a choice between allegory and symbolism, for allegory entails the recognition of the importance of subjecting oneself to an interpretive grammar which stresses the communal nature of hermeneutics, whereas symbolism, conversely, marks the attempt to break out of the strictures that such a grammar must inevitably impose upon the individual. Ideally, then, the structure of the text should somehow repeat or comment on the act of reading that the reader must perform in order to produce it. It may thus be seen, in a sense, as the antitype which the reading process itself suggests as a type. However, this typological structure must not be conceived of as the end of the reading process in anything but an instrumental sense: the generation of this type of structure is our end, only because it allows us a vantage point from which the narrative may be read all over again.

The analyses of the individual romances are undertaken against the background of having recovered these structural patterns. Allegory, I have posited, is a dialectical mode of perception, and I have tried to fashion the interpretive chapters in accordance with this conviction, in order to apply concretely my theoretical suppositions. The remaining chapters on the individual romances all conform to roughly the same pattern. After an initial general discussion, I discuss the structure of each romance, focusing especially upon the way individual chapters are related to each other through the recurrence of words, phrases, and situations. On the basis of this analysis of the narrative discourse, I form a notion of the narrative as a spatial whole, and then proceed to investigate how different chapters, or sequences of chapters, function within this spatial totality. In the terminology that will be fully explained in chapter one, we could say that I make the literal sense of the text my starting point, whereupon I move from part to whole, and back to the parts again. However, as the literal sense that marks the ostensible starting point of my interpretive enterprise is in truth always already situated in—or determined by—its anagogical sense (that is, the hermeneutic space—which is strictly speaking no space at all, but a temporal process—in which the act of interpretation takes place), the interpretive effort can be brought to a close only if we are able to find a way back to this unacknowledged starting point. The interpretive process can thus be described in terms of a movement emanating from the anagogical sense, which must traverse the literal, the allegorical, and the moral senses, before it can be brought to a halt once more in the anagogical sense, which can not be named until the other three senses have already been engaged.

I will argue in the analytical chapters of this study that Hawthorne tried to resuscitate allegory as a natural conceptual mode by privileging the aesthetic dimension of life. The spatial conception of the romance enforces that the reading process which it facilitates is invested with a doubleness which is parallel to that of Christ, in that it can be seen to be made up of a static as well as a temporal dimension. This section of the study starts in chapter two with an analysis of "Rappaccini's Daughter," which brings out the symmetrical structuring device of Hawthorne's fictions that plays a central role in my analyses of the subsequent romances. In "Rappaccini's Daughter" the structural component of the tale is hardly a primary feature—the brevity of the story necessarily makes the question of structure seem subordinate. In the longer narrative form that he was to engage a few years later, however, it will be seen that Hawthorne consciously developed what was perhaps originally merely a compositional aid into one of the most important formal elements by which he intended his fictions to convey their meanings.[17]

Before we move on, it is necessary to make one further point of clarification. In speaking of Hawthorne's intentions, as I shall often do in this study, I do not, as a rule, intend a reference to the private psychology of the author, but rather to the specific *direction*, the Husserlian *Gerichtetsein*, of the discursive universe we know by the author's name. As Paul de Man has shown, the New Critics' critique of what Wimsatt and Beardsley made known as "the Intentional Fallacy,"[18] is based upon a confusion of a philosophical and an everyday understanding of the concept of intention. In the latter sense, the concept involves a person's conscious or unconscious purposes for doing or saying something. In the former, philosophical, sense, however, the concept simply designates the fact that the consciousness of a subject is always a consciousness *of* something, that it is directed at something beyond itself. What is in the latter sense a strictly epistemological concept, in the former sense is expressive of the assumption that the relation between psychology and physiology must be structured in terms of cause and effect. "This is to ignore," de Man points out,

> that the concept of intentionality is neither physical nor psychological in its nature, but structural, involving the activity of a subject regardless of its empirical concerns, except as they relate to the intentionality of the structure. The structural intentionality determines the relationship between the components of the resulting object in all its parts, but the relationship of the particular state of mind of the person engaged in the act of strucurization to the structured object is altogether contingent. The structure of the chair is determined in all its components by the fact that it is destined to be sat on, but this structure in no way depends on the state of mind of the carpenter who is in the process of assembling its parts. The case of the work of literature is of course more complex, yet here also, the intentionality of the act, far from threatening the unity of the poetic entity, more definitely establishes this unity.[19]

From this perspective, then, the concept of intentionality designates the *activity* that goes into the making of an object, not the posited origin of this activity, such as the mental states of the author. Furthermore, since a text is written with the intent that it be read, it must be seen as an activity comprising writing *and* reading. As the intention of the text is immanent to this activity, a writer can be said to have shaped his materials in order to convey a certain meaning, to have intended the words to be understood in a certain way, quite regardless of whether he ever conceptualized his project in any such manner. This circumstance does not entail that we must refrain from invoking empirical evidence in making our arguments: while this structural definition of intentionality holds that the relationship between the state of mind of the creating subject and the function of the created object is contingent, it nevertheless insists that the relation between the *activity* of the creating subject and the created object is fundamental. Insofar as empirical concerns of the subject can be related to this activity, then, they are most certainly admissible.

The intention of the text is thus something we create rather than something we uncover, somewhat in the same manner as the "truth" which is "uncovered" in psychoanalytic practice is more properly viewed as a joint creation of analyst, analysand, and context, than as an objectively verifiable fact. *What* a text explicitly says must therefore be looked upon as less important than in *what way* it is said. By shifting the focus from the meaning of a statement to the way in which the statement communicates its meaning, literary analysis thus implicitly acknowledges the necessity of transforming figurative into literal sense in order properly to understand a text. In *Allegories of Reading*, de Man has shown that such a transformation must inevitably take the form of an infinite regress.[20] It is my conviction that this regress can be transcended only on the condition that we stipulate the existence of a medium capable of inverting the significance of negation. The medium to that purpose should be a paradoxical one: it should be both present and absent, both perfect and imperfect, and, most importantly, it should make evident how the literal and the figurative aspects of reality interact to create the complexity of history. It should, in short, have all the characteristics of Hawthorne's romance.

I elaborate on these considerations in the chapter that follows, which outlines the theoretical framework that informs this study. In an attempt to go beyond the symbolistic interpretive tradition, I discuss the medieval fourfold system of interpretation, which divided the text into a literal, an allegorical, a moral, and an anagogical sense, at some length in this section. By means of a critical discussion of Fredric Jameson's attempt to revitalize this model, it is argued that the allegorical key we insert into the model in place of the life of Christ must be the reading process itself. The investigation proper begins in chapter two, which, as I have said, sketches my conception of the structural principle of Hawthorne's romances by means of an analysis of "Rappaccini's Daughter," and suggests how the writer-reader relation that I am concerned with throughout is related to the paradoxical formula of the Fortunate Fall. Chapter three approaches *The Scarlet Letter* as a working through of the problematic relation between allegory and symbolism. Taking issue with Sacvan Bercovitch's conception of Hawthorne's writings as a form of symbolism, I argue that Hawthorne rejects the petrified version of allegory represented by the Puritan society as well as the symbolistic stance of Hester, by having the romance enact a dialectical formula which is modelled on the actual transference that takes place between writer and reader in the process of reading. The subsequent chapters trace how each of the succeeding romances varies this formula. *The House of the Seven Gables*, it is argued in chapter four, like *The Scarlet Letter* achieves a redemptive conclusion by valorizing art. Tracing the closely entwined themes of sexuality and economics, I argue that the much debated ending of the romance must be understood as an illustration of the notion of Providential Irony, which involves the individual in the mediation between the past and the future in a way that is analogous to the way art mediates between the Actual and the Imaginary.

In chapter five Hawthorne's two collections of Greek stories for children are read as allegorical representations of the individual's development from childhood innocence to adult maturity. The first of these books, I argue, enacts a successful version of the allegorical dialectics involved in the romances as well; the latter, in contrast, provides us with an example of how this allegorical formula may be displaced into a form of symbolism, if confronted with a reader who refuses to recognize the paradoxical nature of the medium whereby writer and reader are united. The chapter ends with a slight biographical excursion, suggesting that certain circumstances in Hawthorne's relation to his wife may have precipitated the more complex narrative strategies mounted in *The Blithedale Romance* and *The Marble Faun.* Instead of portraying ideal scenarios in which the romance performs its redemptive office successfully, I argue in chapters six and seven, these narratives depict the mechanisms that may obstruct the romance from achieving its ideal end. If *The Scarlet Letter* and *The House of Seven Gables* alike could be said to typologically prefigure the reading process by presenting us with a figure of the reader whose attitude the actual reader is encouraged to emulate, the figure of the reader presented by *The Blithedale Romance* and *The Marble Faun* must be characterized, rather, as something of an anti-model, whose attitude towards the romance we must be careful not to replicate. These later romances show us not only how we as readers must act to bring the romance to a redemptive close, but also how we must not act. The difficulty of reading them, I will be arguing, stems from the fact that they do not instil their lesson explicitly, but rely on the reader's propensity for sympathy to communicate their message. In this, I will argue, they are exemplary instances of Hawthorne's allegorical dialectics, which relies on the sympathetic response of the reader to perform its office. In the study's conclusion, finally, I address the political ramifications of Hawthorne's conception of the Fortunate Fall, and end by tentatively suggesting why Hawthorne's allegorical project should be seen as a reaction against, rather than an outgrowth of, a symbolistic impulse inherent in much American thinking, briefly sketching the evolution of this impulse from Puritanism, over Unitarianism, to Transcendentalism.

## CHAPTER ONE
# In Defence of Allegory

[...] we find him monotonous at decidedly the worst of all possible points—at that point which, having the least concern with Nature, is the farthest removed from the popular intellect, from the popular sentiment and from the popular taste. I allude to the strain of allegory which completely overwhelms the greater number of his subjects, and which in some measure interferes with the direct conduct of absolutely all.

*Edgar Allan Poe,* "Tale Writing—Nathaniel Hawthorne"

All of Hawthorne's major fictions, critics agree, revolve around the problematic relation between the individual and society. If this is a common enough motif in literature, Hawthorne's willingness, in the midst of Transcendentalist enthusiasm for reform, to approach the relation as an aporia, an unsolvable contradiction, is all the more noteworthy. His conception of this aporia is perhaps most explicitly brought to the fore in a passage from the opening sketch of *Our Old Home*, "Consular Experiences." Expatiating on the difficulties he had had in dealing with cases of reported mutiny, or conversely, alleged brutality, on board the ships trafficking the sea between England and the U.S., Hawthorne neatly concentrates the paradoxical double moral standard informing his writings:

> The origin of the evil lay in the character of the seamen, scarcely any of whom were American, but the off-scourings and refuse of all the sea-ports of the world, such stuff as piracy is made of, together with a considerable intermixture of returning emigrants, and a sprinkling of absolutely kidnapped American citizens. Even with such material, the ships were very inadequately manned. The shipmaster found himself upon the deep, with a vast responsibility of property and human life upon his hands, and no means of salvation except by compelling his inefficient and demoralized crew to heavier exertions than could reasonably be required of the same number of able seamen. By law he had been intrusted with no discretion of judicious punishment; he therefore habitually left the whole matter of discipline to his irresponsible mates, men often of scarcely a superior quality to the crew. Hence ensued a great

> mass of petty outrages, unjustifiable assaults, shameful indignities, and nameless cruelty, demoralizing alike to the perpetrators and the sufferers; these enormities fell into the ocean between the two countries, and could be punished in neither. Many miserable stories come back upon my memory as I write; wrongs that were immense, but for which nobody could be held responsible, and which, indeed, the closer you looked into them, the more they lost the aspect of wilful misdoing, and assumed that of an inevitable calamity. It was the fault of a system, the misfortune of an individual. (5: 33)

"The origin of the evil lay in the character of the seamen;" nevertheless, it was "the fault of a system, the misfortune of an individual." Hawthorne does not go so far as to denying the individual agency (and hence, responsibility), yet he nevertheless makes clear that the agency of the individual is constricted by a web of relations that ultimately involve society as a whole. The individual is thus held morally responsible for his actions, even while being declared incapacitated on epistemological grounds. The problem, then, is not to determine whether guilt belongs more properly to the individual or to society, but rather how to accept that the individual and society alike are equally guilty: that guilt is a necessary feature of existence, and not some accidental contingency that could be displaced upon the opposite party.

Hawthorne thus conceives of guilt in terms of Original Sin. Indeed, it is now almost half a century since Roy Harvey Pearce argued the case for one of Hawthorne's early tales—"My Kinsman, Major Molineux" (1832)—as a kind of socio-religious Ur-myth, the implication of which is that "Something like Original Sin becomes the prime fact of our political and social history. Adam's Fall and the Idea of Progress become not two myths but one. For—so the argument of the tale runs—if to become more than we are, we must destroy something in ourselves, then we cannot forget what it is we destroy." Yet as Pearce perceptively points out, for such a story to be completely successful, it must not only voice this moral, but also "manifest dramatically the burden of historical responsibility" placed upon the protagonist of the tale. According to Pearce, this is precisely what Hawthorne's best stories do:

> These [...] deal with historical themes in such a manner as to give us perspective upon our own involvement with those themes. They treat history as a continuum joining author, actor, and reader. Therefore, as they focus upon the quality of life as it exists at any given point on the continuum, they focus on the mutual involvement

> of the three parties in that continuum. The problem of composition in a work of this sort is complex and involved; for it entails at once portraying an historical episode, making the protagonist in the work come to see his relationship to the episode, and also making the reader aware of his relationship to the episode. The reader, that is to say, must be brought into some sort of direct relationship with the protagonist, so that what he takes from the story is, above all, an awareness of his own responsible involvement in the protagonist's actions.

In Pearce's view, however, the dialectical interaction between writer, narrative, and text, which the above quote is suggestive of, is fully realized only in a small part of Hawthorne's fiction. Ultimately, this complex interaction between writer and reader was something Hawthorne was unable to sustain: subsequent to *The Scarlet Letter*, Pearce concludes, Hawthorne's "understanding of history failed him, or he failed it."[1]

Although Hawthorne's writings have been valorized in many important respects during the past fifty years, the notion that Hawthorne's later romances fail his historical understanding has proved remarkably resilient. Michael J. Colacurcio, for instance, argues persuasively in *The Province of Piety* that Hawthorne's career can be seen as an attempt to depict the "moral history" of his country, and suggests that all of the romances develop the theme of the relation between past and present, in conjunction with his second and equally important major theme—the aesthetic theme of the relation between art and reality. Despite his perceptiveness, however, Colacurcio confines *The Marble Faun*, Hawthorne's last completed romance, to "the literary wreckage of Hawthorne's 'Last Phase'," and describes it disparagingly as "a sort of 'May-Pole of Merry Mount' writ large: a factitious American fable of innocence, guilt, and partial redemption was recast as a structural myth of all possible experience. The result was, philosophically speaking, only too successful. For once in his life Hawthorne really did work though the historic back to the essential. But when he did, his own literary project seemed to collapse."[2]

As I hope to show in a later chapter of this study, *The Marble Faun* can be seen to "collapse" only if we allow that Colacurcio's case for granting pre-eminence to the historical themes of Hawthorne rather than his psychological themes is completely convincing.[3] I will be arguing in this study that in Hawthorne history and psychology allegorically suggest each other. Hawthorne's interest in history must be seen in relation to his employment of Christian faith, in accordance with which he conceives of the History of mankind as metaphorically repeated in the life of individual man.[4] That is to say, something like Original Sin becomes the prime fact not only of "our political and social history," as Pearce suggests, but of human psychology as well: from the point of view of Hawthorne's conception of Christianity, history and human psychology alike begin with the Fall of Man. I will argue, furthermore, in contradistinction to Pearce, that Hawthorne never gave up on his attempt to join author and reader by means of his romances, and that the difficulties we have had in seeing how this is done in the romances following *The Scarlet Letter*, is testimony not to a betrayal of his historical understanding, but to an unswerving faith in it.

It is perhaps not surprising that Pearce, writing in the mid-fifties, came to a different conclusion, for to be able adequately to accommodate Pearce's outline of the writer-reader relation in our readings of Hawthorne's fictions, those readings must be informed by a theoretical framework that allows us to explain how the transitions over this continuum take place, and it must account, moreover, for what is involved in those transitions. The New Critical apparatus that Pearce, despite his historicist bent, was still working within, provided excellent tools for making sense of texts as long as these were considered as autonomous objects; but the very notion of art as a somehow autonomous universe clearly incapacitates New Criticism when it comes to accounting for the transition between art and reality which Pearce rightly identifies as a vital component of Hawthorne's method.

Art and reality are not the same thing, nor are they completely separate from each other. Hawthorne's best work insists upon the importance of remembering the latter circumstance without erroneously assuming the former; which, in the terminology of our investigation, is equivalent to warning against the dangers of giving in to symbolism, while recognizing the need of allegory. I will be concerned in the present chapter to suggest the importance of maintaining the distinction between allegory and symbolism. I begin by sketching the way it has been brought to bear on Hawthorne's writings, an application that can be seen to be governed by the long-standing valorization of symbolism at the expense of allegory. The aim of the subsequent discussion, which traces the concept of allegorical interpretation from the middle ages to poststructuralism, is to counter this prejudicism in favour of symbolism, and to show how a renewed conception of allegorical hermeneutics may aid our understanding of the relation between literature and history.

## 1. Hawthorne Criticism and Allegory

Though Hawthorne's age was in many ways anti-allegorical, Hawthorne himself was nevertheless deeply steeped in the allegorical tradition: the influence of Bunyan, Spenser, and Milton upon his writing is pervasive.[5] Yet despite Hawthorne's well-documented appreciation of allegory, critics have argued throughout the twentieth-century that Hawthorne's own artistic practice is in truth a form of symbolism. The most thorough discussion of the relation between allegory and symbolism in Hawthorne remains that of F. O. Matthiessen in *American Renaissance* (1941).[6] Matthiessen wisely insists on the importance not to exaggerate the contrast between these two concepts, claiming that his aim is rather "to suggest that a refreshed understanding of both modes may be gained by examining here the real ground that they hold in common." Nevertheless, it quickly becomes apparent that the critics Matthiessen draws upon—Huizinga, Croce, and Robert Penn Warren, among others—make him prejudiced in favour of symbolism from the outset of his discussion. The "differentiation between symbolism and allegory," in Matthiessen's view, corresponds to that "between Melville and Hawthorne at their most typical" and is "allied to Coleridge's fundamental distinction between imagination and fancy," the former being an expression "of the reconcilement of the general with the concrete, of the fusion of idea and image," whereas the latter is a category in which "the abstract, the idea, is often of greater interest than its concrete expression."[7]

When Matthiessen turns to Hawthorne's allegorical practice it becomes clear that to him, Hawthorne can be seen to transcend "the stiff layers of allegory" precisely to the extent that it becomes the vehicle for a psychological realism that points towards the symbolical practice of Henry James, or even T. S. Eliot. Thus Matthiessen speaks approvingly of "the device of multiple choice" in Hawthorne's fictions, because it shows, he maintains, that Hawthorne "does not literally accept his own allegory, and yet he finds it symbolically valid because of its psychological exactitude." Succinctly put, while "both allegory and symbolism can arise from the same thinking," allegory, in Matthiessen's view, is an inferior mode of symbolic expression, because a "created symbol, in contrast with allegory, is dynamic; 'its components, not to be equated with anything else, function in their own right'."[8]

Despite the proliferation of critical perspectives that has since been applied to Hawthorne, on the issue of Hawthorne's allegory critics have not swerved far from the position of Matthiessen.[9] In countering Matthiessen's bias towards Melville, Hawthorne scholars as a rule have not thought to re-examine the basis for the valorization of symbolism at the expense of allegory, which lies at the heart of his argument. Instead, it has become standard practice to conceive of Hawthorne as "symbolist in spite of himself." This line of reasoning was first presented by Charles Feidelson's *Symbolism and American Literature* (1953), wherein Hawthorne's allegorical method in effect is rephrased as a form of symbolism. Allegory, Feidelson declares, is not really central to the imagination that produced the "inconclusive luxuriance of meaning" in *The Scarlet Letter*; on the contrary, it "was the brake that Hawthorne applied to his sensibility," a brake which "imposes the pat moral and the simplified character."[10] This hostility to Hawthorne's allegorical tendencies has, as critics of Hawthorne are well aware, a considerable genealogy. Beginning with Edgar Allan Poe, who used a review of the second edition of *Twice-Told Tales* as an excuse to set out his own symbolistic aesthetics, praise of Hawthorne's genius has almost always been tempered by some censuring comments concerning what Hawthorne himself referred to as "an inveterate love of allegory" (10: 91). Picking up the corrective stick from Poe, Henry James, in his monograph, claims that "Hawthorne, in his metaphysical moods, is nothing if not allegorical, and allegory, to my sense, is quite one of the lighter exercises of the imagination."[11] If subsequent critics have spoken more approvingly of Hawthorne's metaphysics, they have been equally prone to denigrate allegory as such. Thus Richard Harter Fogle claims that Hawthorne fulfils the "crucial requirement, which divides *mere* allegory from literature." This requirement is specified by Fogle as Wellek and Warren's definition of the symbol as "an object which refers to another object but which demands attention also in its own right, as a presentation."[12] Fogle's understanding of this conception points to an underlying ideological position which emphasizes the individual at the expense of the collective or relational. "The symbol must be interesting in itself, not merely as it points to something else," Fogle states, winding up his discussion by stating that "Hawthorne's symbols are broadly traditional, drawn from the main stream of Western thought. [...] Created as they are of old materials, these symbols are yet fresh from Hawthorne's imagination. He invests them with a new vitality and suggestiveness."[13] The symbol is thus at once eternal ("broadly traditional") and unique ("fresh from Hawthorne's imagination"); it is, in a word, a-historic.

Hawthorne himself does not seem to have made any significant distinction between "allegory" on the one hand and "symbolism" on the other—for him, apparently, allegory was symbolical and symbols allegorical. But this circumstance does not invalidate the critical discussion which hinges upon the distinction. If anything, it lends further weight to the issue, since it implies that in approaching his writings, literary critics of the twentieth century have been guided by a distinction that Hawthorne himself never thought to make. While most Hawthorne scholars agree that his writings are, in some sense, allegorical, this concession is usually immediately qualified by maintaining that they are so in a vastly different manner than the allegories of his favourite authors, Spenser and Bunyan.[14] In a thesis from 1962, Peter Berek attempts to codify this difference by arguing that the allegory of the earlier writers "can be called 'objective;' that is, the doctrine it proposes is public property." That of Hawthorne, in contrast, is subjective, since "in place of the corporate beliefs of *The Faerie Queene* and *The Pilgrim's Progress* [...] Nathaniel Hawthorne gives us the 'psyche of the author'." If this view may seem outdated by today's standards, what is most striking about it in my view, is the extent to which it is still embraced. Berek's substitution of psyche for doctrine implies at least two things: firstly, that values—meanings—in Hawthorne's time are tied less to a community than to an individual, which entails that the values expressed by the writer are in possession of a greater immediacy than those expressed by Spenser or Bunyan; that they represent the writer's "private feelings, his private emotions," as Berek puts it, rather than some intersubjectively expressible content at some remove from the author's immediate phenomenal experiences. And secondly, that the price the writer and reader must pay for accessing the immediacy of this new form of allegorical writing is ambiguity, since the dichotomization of the allegorical proposition into "story" and "meaning" "imply a clarity" that Hawthorne "simply does not—could not—have."[15]

The ambitious attempt to historicize Hawthorne anew in the nineteen-nineties has in many ways modified our conception of his writings, yet rather than questioning the notion of Hawthorne's ambiguity it has tended to view ambiguity as the unconscious product of ideology rather than of psychology. Writing of *The Marble Faun*, for instance, Jenny Franchot in typical new historicist mode displaces the centre of attention from the novel under study, to the ideological context in which it was written. Since this ideological context is constructed largely in terms of the tension between Hawthorne's Protestantism and the Catholic environment he was living in while writing the book, it becomes practically interchangeable with biographical context. As a result, the 'text' again becomes equatable with the "psyche of the author." Hence Franchot's claim that while *The Marble Faun* as aesthetic object "is dead, there is a vital cultural life behind it that partially remedies its awkward impairments." In effect, the argument of Berek has been inverted: because Hawthorne's feelings are *not* immediately available to him but always mediated through a language and overdetermined by a cultural context, his intended meanings must always be secondary to the ideological ramifications of these meanings, that are available only to the cultural analyst. Franchot goes so far as to assert that *The Marble Faun* is so severely overdetermined by the cultural anxieties of its historical context that it would seem that Hawthorne was incapable "to release his materials into an interactional space of representation, to allow them to *become aesthetic*." The ambiguity cherished by Berek (and the New Critics before him) is thus resolved by denying that the text operates on an aesthetic plane at all, or, at the very least, that the aesthetic level is always secondary to the historical context in which it was produced. [16]

The belated reappraisal of allegory that has taken place in the last two or three decades has not substantially altered this situation. On the contrary, there are signs suggesting that this reappraisal does not mark the return to a mode of understanding long held in abeyance, but rather the consummation of the tendency to eradicate the notion of collectivity conceptualized in the medieval Christian exegetical tradition, that I will return to below. In Deborah Madsen's *Allegory in America*, for instance, allegory is resuscitated by blurring rather than emphasizing the distinction between allegory and symbolism, while introducing a distinction between typology and allegory in place of the old one: "All typology is allegorical. But not all allegory is typological." Madsen ascribes all the negative associations traditionally attributed to allegory to typology, while subsuming under the notion of non-typological allegory precisely the qualities we have grown accustomed to associate with symbolism:

> Modern allegory confronts us with the unknowability of transcendent categories of experience and restricts our sphere of questioning to the subjective. The entire issue of national spiritual destiny is displaced into the issue of *whether any meaning can ever carry an objective authority and collective significance.* Postmodernist allegory, then, asks whether we can ever separate the perception of meaning from the subjective projection of significance and, if we cannot, whose interests are served by this ambiguity.[17]

Madsen achieves this displacement of the values traditionally assigned to the terms we are dealing with by simply ignoring that what she terms allegory has, for the last fifty years or so, been known to us as symbolism; Feidelson is a conspicuous non-presence in her book, figuring only in the bibliography as an epitaph to the resourceful forgetfulness of the critic.[18]

These are not fringe phenomena: the devalorization of allegory is traceable throughout the history of Hawthorne criticism. Although Hawthorne himself confessed to writing allegories, from Feidelson onwards most critics have agreed that Hawthorne is at his best when he transcends the limitations of the role he identified with and becomes instead a symbolist. Alternatively, critics have argued that Hawthorne makes use of allegorical methods to turn them against allegorical intentions. While there is undoubtedly some truth in this view, it is equally unquestionable that allegory remains a contested mode in Hawthorne criticism. The issue is of course complicated by the fact that there is no real consensus as to how the concept of allegory is to be understood. One may feel, as I do, that much of the finest criticism in the field is in truth a form of allegorical interpretation, which might perhaps explain why Hawthorne scholars eager to launch new critical paradigms have often accused their precursors of allegorizing Hawthorne. Thus Crews complained in the sixties that "every critic pays lip-service" to Hawthorne's ambiguity "before going on to build a tower of allegory." A decade later, Kenneth Dauber argued, more elaborately but to the same effect, that the historical phases of Hawthorne criticism thus far could be seen as corresponding to the different senses of the medieval fourfold model of interpretation.[19] Though little more than an ingenious analogy, Dauber's argument nevertheless suggests that one of the primary limitations of Hawthorne criticism is that it has not been able, or willing, to provide a totalizing model of interpretation, that is, a model that would allow us to account not only for the various levels of meaning in Hawthorne's fictions, but also, and more importantly, for how these levels interpenetrate. For if it is indeed the case, as Northrop Frye remarks in *Anatomy of Criticism*, that in some sense "all commentary is allegorical interpretation," it is not a flaw of previous criticism that it has indulged in allegorizing Hawthorne, but rather an inevitable outcome of the practice itself.[20] On the contrary, from this perspective the general fault of Hawthorne criticism is not that it has been allegorical, but that it has not been allegorical enough. Before taking on the romances themselves, then, it will be necessary to make a theoretical detour, in order to suggest the outline of an allegorical mode of interpretation that will allow us a better view of how Hawthorne's writings join author, actor, and reader into the historical process we call a *text*.

## 2. The Disparagement of Allegory

The sharp opposition between symbol and allegory which is a predominant feature of much twentieth-century criticism is a relatively recent phenomenon—it is commonly traced back to Goethe.[21] Goethe, of course, did not invent the distinction, even if he may be the first prominent person in the history of Western literature to place much emphasis on it. In Anglo-Saxon criticism, it is perhaps most famously expressed by Coleridge:

> Now an allegory is but a translation of abstract notions into a picture-language, which is itself nothing but an abstraction from objects of the senses; the principal being more worthless even than its phantom proxy, both alike unsubstantial, and the former shapeless to boot. On the other hand a symbol [...] is characterized by a translucence of the special in the individual, or of the general in the special, or of the universal in the general; above all by the translucence of the eternal through and in the temporal. It always partakes of the reality which it renders intelligible; and while it enunciates the whole, abides itself as a living part in that unity of which it is the representative. The other are but empty echoes which the fancy arbitrarily associates with apparitions of matter, less beautiful but not less shadowy than the sloping orchard or hill-side pasture seen in the transparent lake below.[22]

Despite dating back no further than to the turn of the eighteenth century, it is a distinction that has carried—and still carries—great weight in American literary criticism. Although the literary criticism of the last two decades nominally rejects the censure of allegory that is such a characteristic trait of a work like Feidelson's *Symbolism and American Literature*, it seems to me that the dichotomization is still at work to a large degree, and that allegory is still held to be, in some sense, intolerable.

It should be noted in this context, that Feidelson's important study blurs the line between dialectics and symbolism: the former, in Feidelson's view, is merely an incompletely wrought-out form of the latter. "In the very act of resolving an opposition," Feidelson writes, dialectic "must always respect the law of opposition, the 'either-or' of logic. In symbolism no 'either-or' can arise. [...] Unlike the structure of symbolism, which presents opposed elements in absolute unity, the structure of dialectic asserts the unity as a logical proposition, thereby continually undermining itself." But if this is so, there seems little reason to maintain, as Feidelson does, that the "dialectician closely approaches the symbolistic point of view."[23] In truth, the difference between dialectics and symbolism, slight as it may appear, is fundamental. As Feidelson's phrasing implicitly acknowledges, dialectic thinking is a supreme form of deconstruction. The Hegelian scheme of thesis-antithesis-synthesis, we should remember, is not a closed system, since the status of the synthesis is radically double: it is not that of a simple ending, but of an ending and a new beginning—bringing together thesis and antithesis, it is also a thesis in its own right, already projecting an antithesis. While this projection may be said to be inherent in the thesis, it is not strictly speaking simultaneous to it, since the realization of the antithesis which is present in the thesis in potential form is something that evolves in time; in other words, it is dependent upon the constitution of a temporal distance between thesis and antithesis. There is no end to the dialectical process; but there is—and this is equally important to keep in mind in order to distinguish it from various forms of symbolism—always a form of metaphorical closure built into the very structure of the scheme. In dialectics properly conceived the end is an immanent rather than imminent position; and this, I will argue, is a feature that dialectics has in common with allegory.

It would be quite misplaced, then, to make a case for the open-endedness of dialectical thinking and hence to confuse the *deferral* of absolute meaning with the *dissemination* or *dissolution* of absolute meaning. Far from espousing any such view of textual meaning as an endless process of production, the dialectician must insist that the ending is present at all times, as the final point which determines the textual process in which meaning is generated. But it is present only in a paradoxical way, neither fully present nor wholly absent, but encompassing both presence and absence by promoting a sense of the distance that must always keep these concepts separated from each other, but which in so doing also becomes the means to bridge the gap between them.

It is of the utmost importance, then, that for Coleridge, allegory and symbolism are distinguished by their capacity for representational immediacy: the symbol supposedly gives us privileged access to the concept represented, whereas the allegorical expression is merely the abstract purveyor of a concrete thought or truth that always remains at one remove. It is not, then, that the symbol shares a materiality with the concept that it represents that makes it preferable to allegory, but that it is able to relate the spirituality of the represented concept more directly than can allegory.[24]

> The Symbolical cannot perhaps be better defined in distinction from the Allegorical, than that it is always itself a part of that, of the whole of which it is representative.—"Here comes a sail," (that is a ship) is a symbolical expression. "Behold our lion!" when we speak of some gallant soldier, is allegorical. Of most importance to our present subject is this point, that the latter (allegory) cannot be other than spoken consciously;—whereas in the former (the symbol) it is very possible that the general truth may be unconsciously in the writer's mind during the construction of the symbol; and it proves itself by being produced out of his own mind,—as the Don Qui-

> xote out of the perfectly sane mind of Cervantes, and not by outward observation or historically. The advantage of symbolic writing over allegory is, that it presumes no disjunction of faculties, but simple dominance.[25]

Coleridge, in short, writes "symbol" where we would write "synecdoche" (or, possibly, "metonymy"), and "allegory" where we would have "metaphor."

This valorization of the symbol must of course be seen in conjunction with the redefinition of selfhood that takes place at the dawn of Romanticism. By associating the symbol with synecdoche, Coleridge in effect paves the way for an understanding of the world *parte totum*, so to speak. In so doing he provides the philosophical foundation for the notion—widely held by the transcendentalists of Hawthorne's New England—that there need be no gap between temporal and eternal existence, and that it is possible to return "to a mode of knowledge prior to that separation of the knower from the known which Emerson called 'the Fall of Man'."[26] Historically a neutral term, allegory is hereby made suspicious, as being a form of representation that is somehow disassociated from the individual subject. Allegorical writing presumes a "disjunction of faculties," a distribution or dissemination of the power of understanding that has the unwonted effect of making the individual unable to grasp the significance of what is written, unless he is aided by conceptual faculties other than his own senses—for instance, the ideological framework of a religious or political creed, or some other system of norms codified by a social collective.

We do well to bear this in mind when we consider the resurgence of interest in the concept of allegory that has taken place during the last three decades or so. Having fallen out of grace at the end of the eighteenth-century, allegory has remained in disrepute throughout the major part of the twentieth-century, but has now, it seems safe to say, been restored as a central concept of critical and theoretical discourse. Whether we agree that allegory is reductive or not, we must grant that there is a finality to allegory wholly lacking in symbolism: the symbol knows no limit, it makes us swoon—allegory in contrast, always has an end, albeit a provisional one. This, it seems to me, is what makes allegory—both as writing and as interpretation—indispensable: it imposes a limit upon desire, which in symbolism goes unchecked. Desire in symbolism works only one way: symbolical interpretation is always capable of generating new avatars of the symbol that it flaunts—indeed, it is compelled to do so. Allegory, on the other hand, turns desire into a relational concept: it defuses the disseminating potential of desire, in a sense, by investing it into a specific signified, which becomes a mirror of the interpreting subject.

It is the aim of the following discussion to interrogate the attempts that have been made to transpose a conception of allegory into our own time, in order to determine how the end that allegory assumes, as a consequence of its reflective nature, must be understood today. I start by addressing the distinction between allegory and *allegoresis*, that is, between allegory as a mode of writing, and allegory as a mode of reading. I will attempt to show that this is a distinction that cannot, on closer scrutiny, be upheld, but that the intentional structure of a text must always be conceived of as a dialectical interaction between two fundamental positions, both of which an allegorical model of interpretation must be able to account for if it is to avoid lapsing into some form of symbolism. For this purpose, I avail myself of the medieval fourfold scheme of interpretation, which both Frederic Jameson and Northrop Frye have suggested might fulfil the office of totalizing our conception of textual interpretation. It is the central point of my own adaptation of this scheme that we must conceive of its fourth—anagogical—sense in performative rather than eschatological terms. That is, rather than looking upon the anagogical sense as a sense prophesying the end of the world, I suggest we conceive of it as the hermeneutic space in which the reader effects the end of the text, by pronouncing its meaning. I end by sketching very briefly how the model I propose will be applied in my own analyses of Hawthorne's writings.

## 3. Allegory and *Allegoresis*

The classical definition of allegory as a genre, or more precisely, as a mode of writing, is that of Quintilian: "Allegoria [...] aut aliud verbis aliud sensu ostendit aut etiam interim contrarium." ["*Allegory* [...] either presents one thing in words and another in meaning, or else something absolutely opposed to the meaning of the words."][27] Concentrated to its first half, this has become the traditional definition of allegory; in the simplest terms, as Angus Fletcher puts it, "allegory says one thing and means another." But if this is the case, almost any verbal message would have to be recognized as being more or less allegorical: "in discussing literature generally we must be ready to discern in almost any work at least a small degree of allegory."[28] This definition, then, threatens to make allegory an all-inclusive term, and hence useless for the purposes of critical discourse.

Partly in order to obviate this difficulty, some critics have attempted to argue the case for allegory as a distinct genre. Maureen Quilligan, for instance, holds that punning is the defining generic characteristic of allegory, in combination with the essentially ethical argument the allegorical text confronts the reader with: "Language does or does not lie." Both of these features are indeed vital components of allegory; we will have reason to get back to them both below. For Quilligan, however, these features are distinctive of allegory as a genre, as opposed to allegory as *allegoresis*, that is, as a form of (over)-interpretation. Allegories, as she puts it, "do not need *allegoresis*."[29]

The allegorical nature of language, however, derives precisely from the impossibility of establishing a clear distinction between word and object, and between text and interpreter. Therefore, as long as the fundamental structural device of the binary opposition is left intact, we have in fact implicitly denied the utility of allegory. Such, at least, is the upshot of Paul de Man's crucial redefinition of the concept. For de Man, Coleridge's distinction between allegory and symbol in *The Statesman's Journal* is not the "unqualified assertion of the superiority of the symbol over allegory" that it appears to be at first sight. The difference between symbol and allegory, de Man argues, is not that the former allows for a synthesis of the perceived image and its inherent signified, while the latter does not, as is usually taken to be the case, since the notion of translucence introduced by Coleridge into the definition of the symbol has the effect of spiritualizing this concept to such an extent "that the moment of material existence by which it was originally defined has now become altogether unimportant: symbol and allegory alike now have a common origin beyond the world of matter." The difference is, rather, that whereas "the symbol postulates the possibility of an identity or identification, allegory designates primarily a distance in relation to its own origin, and, renouncing the nostalgia and the desire to coincide, it establishes its language in the void of this temporal difference. In so doing, it prevents the self from an illusory identification with the non-self, which is now fully, though painfully, recognized as a non-self."[30]

The means by which this painful recognition may be alleviated is that of irony. The irony in question is the specific romantic irony, which "splits the subject into an empirical self that exists in a state of inauthenticity and a self that exists only in the form of a language that asserts the knowledge of this inauthenticity;" the paradigm case, of course, is that of a fictional character aware of its own fictionality, as in, say, Pirandello's *Six Characters in Search of an Author*. The inauthenticity of the empirical self thus corresponds to the inauthenticity of the (temporal) symbol's identification with the eternal, whereas the ironic view of the self as a mere rhetorical construction corresponds to allegory's affirmation of the necessary distance between its language (what is said), and the origin of this language (what is meant). Irony, then, shares with allegory a certain structural trait, "in that, in both cases, the relationship between sign and meaning is discontinuous, involving an extraneous principle that determines the point and the manner at and in which the relationship is articulated. In both cases, the sign points to something that differs from its literal meaning and has for its function the thematization of this difference." Irony, de Man concludes, "is a synchronic structure, while allegory appears as a successive mode capable of engendering duration as the illusion of a continuity that it knows to be illusionary." The temporality generated by allegory, then, is fictitious (hence the *rhetoric* of temporality referred to by the title of de Man's essay), because in positing a continuity between the points of the temporal flow, allegory tacitly assumes that the diachronicity of this flow is nevertheless governed by an inherent synchronicity. Which is to say that allegorical time is properly speaking not time at all, but a specific kind of space: it is a text wherein every letter is already written, and therefore acquires its meaning from its position in relation to the other letters, which must be understood as the temporal moments of the text.[31]

As we shall see below, this conception of time is analogous to the Biblical conception of history. According to de Man, however, what emerges in the Romantic period (and even more decisively, perhaps, in the Pre-romantic period), is the awareness that this continuity is strictly speaking illusory: that it is made possible by the structuring movement of the ironic principle, which allows us to traverse the moment, so to speak, thereby tying what is in truth a discontinuous moment to other moments equally discontinuous. It might appear, then, as if irony became yet another foundational principle, on the stable basis of which a logical epistemology could be raised anew. But because irony allows the individual to take an "outside" view of herself from a position within herself, irony also reveals this self to be a fiction: if it is possible for me to take an external view of myself from an internal vantage point, the space designated by this "internal" point must itself be fictitious. Thus if fiction is conceived of as a space from which a threatened reality may be regained, then this reality must itself be illusory.

The deconstructive practice of de Man thus confronts us with a double negativity: an allegorical time which is not time, but time as a space; and an ironic Self, which is not the indubitable spatial consciousness of Descartes' *cogito*, but space as time. It is on the basis of this double negation that our notions of both self and world are constructed. Therefore, the only way to escape the lack, or blindness, which is bound to plague our investigations (since it is inherent in the very concepts which make the investigation possible) is to make the lack itself the *telos* of our investigations. Allegorical readings, then, must proceed on the assumption that what they finally uncover is the utterly contingent nature of their own practice.

The case for allegory as a genre rather than a mode of interpretation rests on the assumption that there exists a set of distinctive textual features, such that it is possible for us to determine whether or not a text deserves to be labelled an allegory. Historically, however, it is a well-documented fact that allegory begins as *allegoresis*: "allegorical interpretation, chiefly of the Homeric epics, began well in advance of any sustained allegorical works and played a significant role in their emergence."[32] Originally, then, allegory is a way of reading, a systematic way of understanding the text that is based upon an intersubjectively determined norm. It is not difficult, in this light, to see why allegory has been accused of being reductive; indeed, of being a promulgator of specific power structures: typically that of God, or rather, that of the Church. From the conception of the world as a text written by God, confirming his supreme power, it is of course but a short step to the notion of the writer as a vicarious God, who by writing the text creates it and thus bestows a meaning upon it. It is hardly surprising, then, that the concept of allegory has traditionally been associated with the notion of the writer as the origin of the literary work; in this perspective, a text can be a an allegory only insofar as the writer has intended it as such.[33]

Needless to say, the notion of unconscious allegories that has developed during the twentieth century with the emergence of psychoanalysis, radically challenges this traditional linking of allegorical meaning with authorial intent. The notion of the unconscious as such implies a change in interpretive emphasis, from the act of writing to the act of reading. If there is such a thing as the unconscious, meaning can no longer be seen as something that is determined once and for all in the creative act, but must be seen, rather, as a process in which a previously hidden (or even non-existent) meaning, at a subsequent stage may be taken as an explanation to a sense of the text that has not existed before. The allegorical layer that is thus exposed, the interpreter will insist, was really there from the beginning, yet it remained unacknowledged until it received its retrospective enunciation. History no longer *is* what it *was*; instead, history *becomes* according to how it is read, that is, interpreted. In a way, the assertion of unconscious allegories marks a return to the medieval appropriation of the Hellenistic conception of allegory as *allegoresis*. In this practice, any text could be taken as the holder of a hidden meaning (God), as God was seen as the ultimate Writer of every text. Twentieth-century hermeneutics repeats this assumption, merely substituting Society or Historical Context for God.

The principle at work here is that which Freud calls "Überdeterminierung" ("overdetermination"), or "mehrfache Determinierung" ("multiple determination").[34] One of the most challenging attempts to systematize the application of this principle in literary analysis is the case mounted by Fredric Jameson in *The Political Unconscious*, which "conceives of the political perspective [...] as the absolute horizon of all reading and all interpretation."[35] Jameson supports this bold claim by introducing his book with a long chapter delineating the nature of interpretation. The fundamental premise of his argument is suggested by the title of his book, namely that the true significance of literary works—and, indeed, of any cultural artefact—can be revealed only when they are seen "as socially symbolic acts" (*PU*, 20). This entails that interpretation is conceived of as an essentially allegorical operation, a translation of literal into hidden meaning. Thus, while noting that the critique against various modes of twentieth century hermeneutics could be seen as a denunciation of "a system of allegorical interpretation in which the data of one narrative line are radically impoverished by their rewriting according to the paradigm of another narrative, which is taken as the former's master code or Ur-narrative and proposed as the ultimate hidden or unconscious *meaning* of the first one" (*PU*, 22), Jameson claims his own project is less to dismantle or deconstruct this kind of allegorical interpretation, than to provide an alternative to it in the form of an "immanent or antitranscendent hermeneutic model" (*PU*, 23).[36]

As Jameson explains, the hermeneutic tradition that he simultaneously turns against and continues is that of "the Christian philosophy of history" (*PU*, 18), as elaborated by Augustine and others. The Christian view of history arguably derives much of its philosophical and political force from encompassing a total conception of history—in the transition between Genesis, the Gospels, and the Revelation, the Bible presents us with a complete narrative, one that is in possession of all the necessary constituents listed by Aristotle in the *Poetics*: a beginning, a middle, and an end. At first sight, this may not seem very original: most mythologies, after all, come with an account of the birth and death of the world. What makes Christianity unique, however, is the way in which origin and end are connected through the middle, that is, by the story of the Life of Christ, which becomes the locus not only of the temporal mediation between the past and the future, but also of the spatial mediation between the individual and God, whose very omniscience allow us to look upon him as an embodiment of the collective. The life of Christ, it is important to observe, does not end with the Gospels: in providing the type of the Present, the coming of Christ has made available a space that did not exist prior to his birth. Prior to the Life of Christ the present was a moment ceaselessly fading away; subsequently, it has become the site of an ongoing temporality in which every person re-enacts the original type, thereby lending to history a continuous presence.

In order to replace the Christian narrative—the significance of which I have sketched above—Jameson looks primarily to Marxism, which in his view is the only philosophy of history which is able to recover the urgency of the political struggles of the past "within the unity of a single great collective story" (*PU*, 19). Citing "The Communist Manifesto" on the history of "all hitherto existing society" as "the history of class struggles,"[37] Jameson adds: "It is in detecting the traces of that uninterrupted narrative, in restoring to the surface of the text the repressed and buried reality of this fundamental history, that the doctrine of a political unconscious finds its function and its necessity" (*PU*, 20).

As this passage makes clear—and as is signalled by the title of Jameson's study—in order to present an efficient alternative to the Christian view of history, Marxism has to be supplemented by the central concept of Freudian psychoanalysis, the unconscious, which comes to fulfil in the Marxist paradigm a function parallel to that which the story of the Life of Christ performs in the Christian paradigm. Somewhat in the same manner as in the early writings of Wilhelm Reich, Jameson transposes the concept of the unconscious from the locus of the individual into that of the social sphere at large.[38] This is a seminal move; particularly illuminating is Jameson's revivification of the medieval fourfold scheme for interpreting the Bible. This highly suggestive interpretive methodology is the acme of the typological tradition, which grew out of the need to relate the truth of the Old Testament to that of the New. In other words, its express purpose was to retain a past truth while simultaneously transforming its significance in the light of a future projected by the present.[39]

Jameson illustrates the function of this scheme by recounting what has become its archetypal example: the interpretation of the Exodus as a prefiguration of the Life of Christ (including his death and final resurrection). Dante advances the same example in his letter to Can Grande in explaining the allegorical mode of *The Divine Comedy*:

> And this mode of treatment, for its better manifestation, may be considered in this verse: 'When Israel came out of Egypt, and the house of Jacob from a people of strange speech, Judaea became his sanctification, Israel his power.' For if we inspect the letter alone the departure of the children of Israel from Egypt in the time of Moses is presented to us; if the allegory, our redemption wrought by Christ; if the moral sense, the conversion of the soul from the grief and misery of sin to the state of grace is presented to us; if the anagogical, the departure of the holy soul from the slavery of this corruption to the liberty of eternal glory is presented to us.[40]

To recapitulate: in the literal sense of the biblical text, the exodus marks a historical event, something that has really happened. In the allegorical sense of the text, this historical event signifies the Life of Christ. In the moral sense of the text, the same event represents the individual's psychological experience of the truth of the allegorical signified, in observing how his life repeats the pattern provided by the Life of Christ. And in the anagogical sense of the text, finally, the historical event points forward to the final referent of the allegorical key, namely the Apocalypse.

In Jameson's appropriation of this scheme, the allegorical sense, or level (which is the term Jameson uses), is designated as the "allegorical key or interpretive code" (*PU*, 31): it is, in other words, the site of the political unconscious. One should bear in mind, however, that what attracts Jameson to this model is "the closure of the scheme as a whole" (ibid.), rather than the possibility that it might function as an exhaustive model of interpretive practice.[41] The importance of the anagogical level, in Jameson's version of the scheme, comes down to it constituting a "political reading" of the text, a reading in which the "collective 'meaning' of history" (ibid.) is revealed. This seems to me a somewhat reductive conception of the function fulfilled by the anagogical sense in the medieval scheme, and indeed, in the Marxist scheme substituting for it. We cannot automatically associate collectivity and politics in this manner—after all, the fully realized communism that Marx projects as the final stage of his philosophy of history marks the end of politics as much as its consummation.[42] As a result, the fourfold scheme comes to take on the aspect of an ingenious parable rather than a systematic interpretive operation by means of which one could arrive at a mode of interpretation, "such that not only the content of the analysis, but the very method itself, along with the analyst, then comes to be reckoned into the 'text' or phenomenon to be explained" (*PU*, 47).

While Jameson is surely right in remarking that "the relationship the Christian scheme projects between anagogical and moral is not available to us today" (*PU*, 31), it is notable that his appropriation of the model does not remedy this complication. In Jameson's hands the Christian paradigm is simply displaced by a Marxist paradigm, the functionality of which is as dependent upon an article of faith as is that of the Christian scheme. To associate the anagogical level with a collective experience, in other words, is to posit the primacy of the social totality, a presupposition which seems defensible only if we are willing to take the Marxist perspective that Jameson propounds for granted, as something of a given. The arrival at a collective destiny can only be termed an ultimate end if we have already decided in favour of the pre-eminence of the collective over the individual, of the universal over the particular, of the Idea over its concrete embodiment. While such presuppositions may be valid within a particular interpretive framework, they are obviously insupportable when it is the very validity of this foundation that is in dispute. It is not that Jameson is mistaken in associating the anagogic with the collective—on the contrary, the anagogic must be able to account for the mediation between the particular and the general, and hence must embrace a totality. However, the arrival at the collective sphere merely marks the recognition of *spatial* totality. This must be complemented by a notion of temporal totality if we are to be able to grasp the functionality of the anagogic as such. Jameson's revival of the medieval fourfold system of interpretation, although interesting, is therefore clearly not sufficient for our purposes. In order to benefit from the deconstructive critique of the last decades, we must reject the temptation of positing the anagogical sense of the text as yet another sense to be found *within* the text, and conceive of it instead as the very conceptual framework which makes possible a conception of the text as an activity comprising writing *and* reading.

## 4. A Performative Conception of Anagogy

I have argued above that it is impossible to maintain a strict distinction between allegory and *allegoresis*, or loosely speaking, between intended and unintended allegories, that is, between allegories originating in the writer and allegories originating in the reader. Nevertheless, I think a valid distinction could be made between what we could term natural and contrived allegories, respectively. Contrived allegories are those that are dependent upon some sort of interpretive manual. As no allegory can be completely independent of such, all allegories are in a sense contrived. However, given the appropriate dissemination of the tenets governing the interpretive manual in question, any contrived allegory can come to seem a natural one, as if arising by itself. Natural allegory, then, involves a certain kind of circularity: there must be an ideological correspondence between the individual and society in order for it to emerge—hence the prevalence of allegory in the Middle Ages, and the aversion to it that sets in during the Enlightenment and is strengthened in the Romantic and post-Romantic periods. By this I mean that it must be possible for the individual to give vent to his private desires in a discourse which is equally valid in a social and political context, as when Dante is able to combine in the figure of Beatrice his erotic and his religious desires, and by extension of the latter, his political desires as well. Or, to take a more recent example, as happens in American soul music during the nineteen-sixties, wherein erotic, religious, and political desires could be expressed as if they were one. Natural allegory thus conceived constitutes a kind of layering of discourses, wherein one can move effortlessly from the one layer to the other. If the prerequisite for natural allegory is the presence of a shared ideological space, the dissolution of this normative system will by necessity entail the dissolution of allegory as a conceptual mode as well, even if there may remain remnants of it within less comprehensive normative systems (hence the validity of, say, psychoanalytical allegories in the more limited context of a psychological discourse).

But this also means that allegory as a conceptual mode can always be reasserted, provided that its contextual parameters are made sufficiently wide. In Hawthorne's New England, as in present society, allegory had lost its ground as a natural conceptual mode. The Puritan society of the seventeenth century had provided a doctrine which, in theory if not in practice, was capable of regulating every aspect of society. By the mid-nineteenth century, however, religious sentiment had long been in the process of liberating itself from successively attenuated versions of this doctrine, and no matter how beneficial this might have been in some respects, it also meant that religion was no longer capable of sustaining a system of norms through which the individual could automatically perceive how she or he was related to the rest of society. I do not want to play down the very substantial differences between Hawthorne's New England and our own culture, yet it seems fair to say that both are periods in which the notion of allegory as a viable conceptual mode has largely been abandoned. As I indicated in the Introduction, the analytic chapters of this study will argue that Hawthorne attempts to revivify allegory as a mode of perception by valorizing the aesthetical dimension of life. I am suggesting now, that it is precisely such a highlighting of the aesthetic aspect of discursive practices that is necessary in order to make the medieval fourfold system of interpretation our primary model for textual analysis. While Jameson's adaptation of the system rewardingly makes clear why interpretation must necessarily be a social activity, I have complained that it does not adequately account for the temporal dimension of hermeneutics. In order to do so, it is necessary to transform our notion of the anagogical sense of the text, and to understand it as a performative rather than eschatological category.

The primary importance of the anagogical sense is that it projects an ending: an end that, because it involves mankind in its totality, determines the meaning of the narrative sequences of the other levels. We do well to remember that according to Scriptures the final victory of Yahweh that was supposed to coincide with the coming of the Messiah, was associated with a notion of the end of history. As Henri de Lubac has pointed out, from the book of Daniel onwards the expected triumph of Yahweh "appears as the end of human history."[43] Christ did not, of course, effect the promise of an everlasting kingdom that the Book of Daniel holds forth. Nevertheless, as Jean Daniélou has demonstrated, the main purpose of apostolic preaching was to show that the Messianic typology of the Old Testament prophets "had been fulfilled in Jesus Christ."[44] To do so, is to argue that the promise of the Messiah has been fulfilled not as an actual condition, but as a prophecy: as a type of what is still to come. It is not a supplementary prophecy, however; on the contrary the prophecy is instrumental in bringing about the end which it looks forward to. (Again, the structural similarity between the Christian and the Marxist narrative is readily apparent: like Christianity, Marxism has the character of an instrumental prophecy.) This points to the importance of the moral sense of allegorical interpretation, as it is through the individual that a relation between past, present, and future is established; which is also why we must conceive of history as a *drama*, rather than the tedious unveiling of a story whose outcome is already known. We know how it will end, but we have still to find out what this end will mean to *us*. The allegorical sense of the text, which makes history intelligible to the individual, will come to nought unless the individual is willing to acknowledge the ethical imperative of the allegorical key. This circumstance is highlighted by A. C. Charity, who argues persuasively that "the intellectual claim of typology is nothing without the existential claim, and demand, which accompany it." He continues:

> The proposition "Jesus Christ is history's fulfillment, to which all history is related in as much as in him it finds its norm, its perfector and judge," is not a proposition to which one can assent without affirming also "Christ is my perfector and my judge." We may believe that it is valid to make the claim, in some such form as this, almost abstractly, as a dogmatic statement; but it exists as genuinely true [...] only as confession and as self-surrender, here and now.[45]

Just as is the case with the "applied typology" of the Bible, allegorical interpretation, in order to be genuine, must involve the interpreter in the object or event he or she is interpreting.

The anagogical sense of the text thus constitutes what might legitimately be called the master plot of the text; it is only in relation to this plot that the plot of Christ's death on the cross acquires its significance. The essence of allegory, we should keep in mind, is always relational: it facilitates the transition from one plot to another. The problem with Jameson's Marxist adaptation of the fourfold scheme of interpretation is that it does not account for how, and why, we are able—or, rather, compelled—to hierarchize the systematization of plots inherent in the medieval fourfold scheme. Hence it is unable to restrain the process of *allegoresis*: just as the Marxist paradigm may substitute for the Christian paradigm as the master plot of the text, the Marxist narrative may itself be displaced by some other interpretive paradigm—whatever plot we come up with as the true significance of the literal plot, this plot could always be substituted by yet another, and so forth, *ad infinitum.* This dilemma must necessarily occur if we evade the essential question of the individual reader's involvement with the text; that is, if we fail to account for how readings are *produced.*

It will be helpful, in this context, to consider briefly Northrop Frye's appropriation of the medieval scheme in *Anatomy of Criticism*, and the critique Jameson directs at it. In Frye's Theory of Symbols, the four senses of the medieval scheme (literal, allegorical, moral, and anagogic) corresponds to four phases (descriptive, formal, mythical, and anagogic), to which Frye adds an additional first phase, which he calls—much to the chagrin of the reader who may feel matters are quite sufficiently complicated already—the literal, by which he means the "letters" of a poem, "its inner structure of interlocking motifs" its "rhythm or movement of words."[46] While commending Frye's identification of a Mythical or Archetypal phase which "looks at poetry as one of the techniques of civilization," and hence is concerned "with the social aspect of poetry, with poetry as the focus of a community,"[47] Jameson faults him for recontaining and ultimately privatizing this social aspect of literature by subsuming it under the image of "the libidinal body" that Frye advances in his delineation of the final, anagogic phase. In other words, Jameson accuses Frye of reversing the terms of the medieval scheme, to the effect that the finality this scheme associates with the collective, becomes associated, for Frye, with "the category of individual experience" (*PU*, 74). Jameson supports his view by quoting Frye as stating that his "fourth level [...] is the third medieval level of moral and tropological meaning." There is no incongruence between Frye and the medieval scheme on this point, however, since the fourth level of Frye is not the anagogic, but the formal. Nor does it seem quite fair to say that the anagogic phase privatizes the social aspect of life, since for Frye, man in this phase already embraces the collective:

> When we pass into anagogy, nature becomes, not the container, but the thing contained, and the archetypal universal symbols [...] are no longer the desirable forms that man constructs inside nature, but are themselves the forms of nature. Nature is now inside the mind of an infinite man who builds his cities out of the Milky Way. This is not reality, but it is the conceivable or imaginative limit of desire, which is in-

> finite, eternal, and hence apocalyptic. By an apocalypse I mean primarily the imaginative conception of the whole of nature as the content of an infinite and eternal living body which, if not human, is closer to being human than to being inanimate.

An infinite and eternal living body—what else could this be but the collective human race throughout its historical existence?[48]

Nevertheless, there is some justification for maintaining that the anagogical phase becomes a weak spot in Frye's system, although for a somewhat different reason; in fact, the weak spot of Frye's system is reproduced in Jameson's adaptation. In Frye's conception, the anagogic phase is associated with the "conception of a total Word" which in analogy with Aristotle's notion of the unmoved mover "is the postulate that there is such a thing as an order of words;" but also with the feeling that, from the circumference of this total Word, "we have moved into the still center of the order of words." This phase, then, marks the reestablishment of a connection between origin and end, a return to "the centripetal aspect of meaning" designated by the literal phase, in which a poem belongs neither to society nor to the individual, but simply "to the class of things called poems, which in their turn form part of the larger class known as works of art." Literature, then, is ultimately concerned only with itself—a view which would have seemed less unsatisfactory if Frye had specified the principle of mediation by which literature passes from the still centre of the order of words to the apocalyptic circumference which embraces all mankind and all history. As it stands, his Theory of Symbols is more of a monument over the New Critical conception of the autonomy of the literary work of art, than the grand refutation of this view that it strives to be.[49]

This shortcoming is the direct outcome of Frye's modification of the medieval fourfold scheme; that is, of the redefinition of the literal sense of literature that he undertakes on the grounds that one must maintain an absolute distinction between literary and non-literary texts. When this centripetal sense of the text is assigned an autonomous phase, it is in effect cut off from the interpreting subject. In order to re-establish the relation between the reader and the literality of the text, this dissevering must be undone. Such a restoration is most purposefully achieved by reintegrating the literal with the descriptive phase, carefully pointing out that while there is some justification for holding that these two phases are temporally distinct, they are nevertheless spatially identical.

When Frye insists on the necessity of distinguishing between the literal and the descriptive phases, he is overlooking the dual status of the literal sense in the medieval scheme, where it functions at once as a designation of a historical fact, and as a prophecy, that is to say, as signified and signifier respectively. Frye rightly senses that this poses a problem, since if we are to be able to maintain that it is the signifying capacity of the text that is the point of departure for literary criticism, this literal level must not already be contaminated with history, so to speak. As Jameson senses, however, the consequence of Frye's solution to the problem is that the literal phase is completely voided of historicity.

Jameson's own appropriation of the fourfold scheme could hardly be faulted on this account. Like Frye's version, however, it replicates the notion of the text as an autonomous object in which the four senses of the medieval scheme are somehow contained, and as we have already pointed out, this entails that it is unable to impose a limit upon *allegoresis*. The force of the medieval scheme, we must bear in mind, hinges upon the universality of its allegorical key: the fact, that is, that the story of the Life of Christ is potentially the story of Everyman. If we want to refashion this scheme to our own purposes, the allegorical key we make use of must be such that it can be applied to any text: it must be able to annihilate the differences between, say, *Pet Sematary* and *The Aeneid*, or *The House at Pooh Corner* and Kant's *Critique of Pure Reason*. Allegory in the medieval sense is a means to impose a sense of universality: when read through the allegorical key, every text should potentially tell the same story, regardless of its historical and rhetorical specificities, just as every life potentially re-enacts the allegorical paradigm in the medieval scheme. Jameson's assertion that the notion of the political unconscious may function as the allegorical key to any text is an ingenious move; but it stops short of explicating the textual features of this political unconscious, and as a result is laid open to doubt. The question how the private act of reading a text can—and indeed, must—be said to involve a collectivity goes unanswered.

It seems to me that we can avoid this undesirable consequence, only if we are willing to acknowledge that an adequate appropriation of the medieval scheme must embrace a conception of the text as consisting of an outside and an inside, and that this conception must simultaneously be able to specify how outside and inside are interconnected. Such a conception is in fact suggested by the tripartite division of the text into *narrative discourse*, *narrating agent*, and *story* that is nowadays customary in most narratological models of the text.[50] These terms, however, cover only the first (literal), second (allegorical), and third (moral) levels of the medieval scheme. The narratological terminology thus refers to what we will call the "inside" of the text, or more appropriately, its intranarrative aspects. The anagogical sense of the text, conversely, covers the "outside," or extranarrative, aspects of the text.

To say that the literal sense comprises the narratological categories of narrating *and* narrated (or, as some may put it, of narrator and story), is to acknowledge the doubleness inherent in the literal sense or phase, while simultaneously insisting that the integration of the signifying potential of the literal phase with its potential for signification is always in truth deferred until we have already traversed the anagogical sense of the text: the literal sense of the text can be infused with a descriptive (or historical) sense only once it has already been subject to interpretation. In other words, we may insist on the "emptiness" of the literal sense of the text as long as we acknowledge that the literal sense is not the origin of the reading process, although we approach it *as if* it were such a starting point. This is important: it goes to show that far from being neutral, the literal (and/or descriptive) sense of the text is in truth the most heavily overdetermined of all of the four senses our scheme allows, since in order to arrive at the descriptive or historical aspect of the literal sense we must already have traversed the hermeneutic system in its entirety.

I submit, then, that the anagogical sense of the text must be equated with *the act of interpretation* itself. There is, after all, one relation which is present in all texts: that between the writer and the reader, or, in other words, the relation between an absent origin and a present end, of which one must paradoxically say that the absence is intrinsic to the narrative discourse, while the presence is extrinsic to it. It is the existence of this relation that enables us to generate the other three senses through an act—or, rather, a series of acts—of interpretation. Once these senses have been constituted, they will each in turn point toward their origin, which is also their end, thereby creating the self-reflexive quality of the text which is essential to all reading and writing.

The anagogical sense of the text thus constitutes the space in which interpretation takes place: it is a space in which the temporality governing the other three senses of the narrative is annulled, or rather, compressed into one single moment. By dividing the text into four different senses, the allegorical interpreter may look upon each moment as shot through with temporality. If, as the allegorical interpreter holds, the moment in itself is virtually a negative moment, an instance of nothingness and meaninglessness, it may nevertheless be a key to transcendence. For if the moment itself is nothing, it will take on substance only insofar as the past and the future will be operating on it, that is, only insofar as the past and the future are already present in the moment. Thus the very nothingness of the moment allows us to transform temporality into a form of presence. The anagogical sense, then, is a space that is determined by an end that is not available through any of the other senses of the text, except in the form of figural prefigurations of this end. This end cannot be determined in advance, independently of an active engagement with the signified senses of the narrative in which the act of reading consists, yet it has a name: it is what we call "the meaning of the text." To assert such an end is to perform an allegorical as opposed to a symbolical act of interpretation. Yet by conceiving of this meaning as something that belongs to the act of reading rather than something that is produced by the narrative independently of such an act, we have designed a strategy for deferral, which allows us endlessly to postpone the final revelation of this meaning.

The act of reading thus conceived structurally repeats the revisionism that Frank Kermode has shown to be inherent in apocalyptic pronouncements.[51] The Apocalypse, Paul Ricoeur notes in discussing Kermode's valuable book, "offers the model of a prediction that is continually invalidated without ever being discredited, hence of an end that is itself constantly put off."[52] The upshot of this strategic deferral is that the end becomes a matter of immanence rather imminence; it is transposed from a temporal into a spatial aspect of narrative, from a concept to which we are predominantly metonymically related, to a concept to which our relation is predominantly metaphorical. This is the meaning of the text, we say; time will prove us right. That time frequently disproves our bold assertions of having unveiled the anagogical signified of the text is of little or no matter to the allegorical interpreter, since in having asserted this meaning we have already achieved our goal, which is to impose a sense of meaningfulness upon the text by transforming what is essentially a temporal process into an imaginary object, to which a specific force is attributable.

We come up, then, with an understanding of the four senses of the text that can be summarized in the following way:

| | |
|---|---|
| LITERAL | The narrative discourse. |
| ALLEGORICAL | The universal story of the narrative as a *mise en abyme* of the mediation of the narrative itself. |
| MORAL | The plot. |
| ANAGOGICAL | The meaning of the narrative as determined by the reader. |

Each sense thus constitutes an enactment of another sense. The written text, or discourse, is an enactment of the anagogical sense; the story is the allegorical enactment of the discourse; the plot is the moral enactment of the allegorical sense; and the meaning of the text, finally, is the anagogical enactment of the significance of the plot. While there are four senses, the circularity of the scheme prevents us from privileging any one sense at the expense of the others: it is a closed system in perpetual movement.

The circularity of our definition of allegory, entails that in the fourfold hermeneutical scheme drawn above, history is understood as an exclusively intratextual concept. The narrative itself is the local history in question; through the allegorical interpretation of this narrative as a *mise en abyme* of the act of reading itself, local history is transformed into a kind of prophecy. This prophecy is manifested as moral history in the plot, the significance of which is ultimately dependent upon how it is understood, that is, anagogically determined by the reader. This is not to say that the intratextual history of the narrative is not related to what we refer to as "real" history. But this "real" history enters into the narrative only through its anagogical sense, which is the conceptual space occupied by writer and reader alike. The anagogical sense of the text, then, is an extranarrative spatial site embracing two distinct positions or functions (the writer and the reader), and has as its counterpart the intranarrative spatial site constituted by the two temporally distinct functions of narrated and narrating (that is, the narrative discourse itself, in which the narrating agency is inherent). These two spaces—the anagogical and the literal—are separated by a temporal gap, which is constituted by the other two senses of the text. These are the senses or levels traversed by writer and reader alike, although in inverted directions: for the writer, this traversal effects his transformation into a reader, whilst for the reader the traversal transforms him into a writer—at any rate, the passage makes possible such textual gender-switching. Which is to say that "real" history always enters the text as a function that already belongs to the "inside" of the text. History is never exterior to the text, because insofar as it enters into the text at all, it does so in the form of the actual writer and the actual reader, both of whom function as intratextual principles of the text (not to be confused with the intranarrative principles of the text expounded in narratology), rather than exterior performers of this text. Rather than an ontological object, then, the text is more properly seen as a process involving both writer and reader, and hence as a performance by some extraneous principle—God, Being, Language, whatever we want to call it; but at any rate, a transcendental (collective) subject in relation to which writer and reader alike must be construed of as objects. The dialectical movement of allegory, then, cannot be conceived in terms of a movement between subject and object, since the literal and the anagogical position alike are already destabilized, both being made up of dialectical relations in their own right, between signifier and signified, and between writer and reader, respectively.

*

On the definition of allegorical interpretation sketched above, the master plot—or determining signified—of any narrative concerns the parameters of its own enunciation. Any genuine allegorical interpretation, then, must proceed on the assumption that what the interpreted text is ultimately about is the way it is read, but it must also acknowledge its paradoxical foundation: that *language does and does not lie.* It lies, in pretending to set free a meaning it cannot deliver; and it does not lie, in making itself out to be simultaneously the source of constraint and of emancipation, of allegory and *allegoresis*. This insistence upon the importance of the self-reflective aspect of literature, however, does not mark a turn away from the historical and psychological realities seemingly made available to us by the interpretive matrixes employed in other forms of criticism focusing upon the ideological ramifications of literature. On the contrary, it is only by facing up to the blindness that the deconstructive insight condemns us to that we may be said to truly engage these realities; which is to say that we do allow a place for the matrixes of these realities—if not the realities "themselves"—in our fourfold scheme of interpretation. Only, we insist that they must be taken to express the anagogical sense of the text, which is always tied up with the specific interpretive moments we call writing and reading. The narrative discourse which expresses the literal sense of the text mediates between these moments by means of introducing a parallel universe which, rather than reflecting history, must be said to bring the concept of history as such into being by engendering our understanding of it.[53]

To argue, as I do, that any text is an allegory of its own mediation is to stipulate that the extranarrative triad made up of writer, reader, and discourse, must necessarily be duplicated at the level of the narrated, where it appears as a *mise en abyme* of the textual process as such. That is, any story is reducible to an allegory involving three functions: writer, reader, and discourse, the fictional medium by means of which the writer and the reader are able to establish a deferred intercourse. From this perspective, allegorical interpretation thus must identify the discursive counterparts of these three functions. In "Rappaccini's Daughter," for instance—somewhat to forestall my analysis in the next chapter—Rappaccini holds the position of the Writer (or the Artist, as I will refer to it in order to distinguish it from Hawthorne himself), Giovanni that of the Reader, and Beatrice that of the Discourse, which in Hawthorne's case is of course identical to the Romance. Or so I will argue; I wish to emphasize, however, that it is certainly possible that one or all of these functions could be enacted by more than one character, and/or that the role of portraying an allegorical function could pass from one character to another within a given narrative, somewhat in the manner, say, of how the characters of Poe's "The Purloined Letter" are assigned different functional positions in Lacan's well-known reading of the story. Given the importance of plot—and hence of action—in narrative discourse, it is more likely than not that the allegorical embodiments of the writer-, reader-, and discourse-functions will be characters, but this is of course not necessarily the case. Indeed, it will be seen that in Hawthorne at least, the discursive embodiment of the romance-discourse is always duplicated: it is enacted both by a character, and an object to which this character somehow has privileged access. Thus Rappaccini's daughter is not only Beatrice, but also the purple shrub she refers to as her "sister," and Pearl is "the scarlet letter in another form" (SL, 102). In *The House and the Seven Gables*, Judge Pyncheon is linked to the House—he is an individual who "builds up, as it were, a tall and stately edifice, which, in the view of other people, and ultimately, in his own view, is no other than the man's character, or the man himself" (HSG, 229)—and in *The Blithedale Romance*, similarly, Priscilla in her capacity of the Veiled Lady is associated with the veil, that book's leading image. *The Marble Faun*, finally, makes the identification of character and object as explicitly as does *The Scarlet Letter*. Donatello, we are informed in the opening chapter of the romance, "is the very Faun of Praxiteles" (MF, 7) which provides the book with its title. There may, then, be more than one allegorical reader in a narrative, more than one allegorical writer, more than one figure of the discourse, but there must always be all three, since the function of any allegorical figure is wholly a matter of its relation to the other functions in the system we have posited. What is more, these intranarrative functions must in turn be read as somehow mimicking the relation between the extranarrative relation between the writer and the reader that is mediated by the narrative discourse. If we are to avoid performing yet another example of unwonted *allegoresis*, we must, in a word, approach the allegory of the text as a system.

Throughout this study, it is with the anagogical perspective as defined above—that is, as a performative rather than eschatological category—that we will ultimately be concerned, although in engaging it we must inevitably bring the other aspects of the texts into play as well. Needless to say the issue is a convoluted one. Before taking on the romances themselves, therefore, I will consider some of Hawthorne's earlier writings, and sketch the methodological principles of my procedure in an analysis of "Rappaccini's Daughter," a tale in which all the central elements of the allegory I will trace in the four mature romances are already present: the Artist attempting to negate the consequences of the Fall by means of his art, itself an ambiguous emblem of sin and divinity, and the Reader, torn between a faith in the ideal essence of this art, and sceptic misgivings brought on by its imperfect appearance.

## CHAPTER TWO

# "This Fearful Sympathy:" Hawthorne's Allegory of the Fortunate Fall

The allegorical has its existence in abstractions; as abstraction, as a faculty of the spirit of language itself, it is at home in the Fall.
Walter Benjamin, *The Origin of German Tragic Drama*

In 1840 and 1841, Hawthorne published three history books for children, *Grandfather's Chair*, *Famous Old People*, and *Liberty Tree*, subsequently collected under the title *The Whole History of Grandfather's Chair*. Between them they tell the history of New England, each book dealing with a phase of its history—the Puritan period proper, generally taken to be 1630–1692, during which period the governor of the colony was appointed not by the king but the people of New England; the ensuing period of British governorship, and finally the events leading up to and including the Revolution. The structure, then, owes much to the quasi-typological arrangement of historical events characteristic of George Bancroft's *History of United States*, a work for a mature audience with which Hawthorne was well acquainted—Bancroft was Hawthorne's superior officer at the Boston Custom House at the time the *Whole History* was written, which might explain why Grandfather refers to it in the first volume of the work.[1] Much as the early Puritan settlers had interpreted their colonial endeavour as the typological fulfilment of certain Biblical prophesies, Bancroft's History paints a picture of the colonists' break with England as the fulfilment of an underlying providential agency, in which the early Puritan settlers typologically prefigure the heroes of the American Revolution.

However, as Frederick Newberry points out in one of the few discussions we have of the work, Hawthorne intentionally problematizes this typological pattern, by having Grandfather's narrative repeatedly focusing on the violence and suffering that accompany its realization. Much in the same way as his early tales dramatize what Newberry calls

Hawthorne's "divided loyalties" (to the aesthetics of an English tradition, and to the revisionism of American democracy), the book therefore undercuts the popular historical ideology of his day: "The inconsistencies and contradictions in Grandfather's narrative [...] substitute for the irony Hawthorne employs so extensively in the seventeenth- and eighteenth century tales. The result is a countervailing pattern of intolerance, bigotry, and violence encroaching upon and all but obliterating what typological design exists."[2]

I will not quarrel with Newberry's insightful discussion of the main outline of Hawthorne's history, which leaves little to be desired. But to draw attention to the pain associated with the typological design is not necessarily to deny its general validity, even though Newberry is certainly correct in suggesting that Hawthorne consciously problematizes the typological conception of history. In the framing narrative of the three books, Grandfather relates the history of the chair he is sitting in to an audience of four children, Alice, Charley, Clara, and Laurence. In the story-telling situation, then, the chair becomes the mediating principle between past and present, and also between the immediate surroundings of the children and the broader interrelations of society; as Colacurcio appositely puts it, "to know about 'the old chair' is, in the symbolism of the whole work, to know about the moving center of historical significance in early Massachusetts."[3] The different reactions of the children—or at least of the two boys, since little Alice, "hardly five years old" (6:10), principally figures as an emblem of childhood innocence, and cousin Clara is little but a name in the text—record different attitudes towards history. The set-up is typical of Hawthorne: Charley is a belligerent and rambunctious little boy who wants to hear of battles and heroic adventures, Laurence a thoughtful and sensitive person with a highly developed moral susceptibility. The very presence of this oppositional pair amply demonstrates that the contradictory tendencies that run through Grandfather's account of New England's history by no means are absolved in the present in which the union of a delivered America is an established fact. But as Newberry helpfully argues, the principal aim of Hawthorne's early historical fictions is to envision "the role of mediating or synthesizing extremes, the role that grandfather resuscitates and performs in his own narrative."[4] Such a role, I would insist, is not in itself contradictory to a reading of history as developing typologically along the lines of a providential scheme. *The Whole History of Grandfather's Chair* is one of the clearest examples we have of how Hawthorne conceives of narrative as a medium capable of linking the past to the future, and how this mediating process allows for the pain associated with the past to be transformed into a future good by passing through the act of narration that takes place in the present. Such a transformation may come about, however, only if the typological design is not perceived as something already completed, but as a continuous dialectical process, the future end of which is not determined in the future but in the present. Thus it seems to me that Hawthorne is not so much questioning the view of history as developing in accordance with a typological design, as making a point of emphasizing that the significance of this typological design is ultimately dependent upon how the individual (including the reader) responds to it in a present that is itself transient and impermanent, but which nevertheless holds a central position in the historical continuum made up of past, present, and future.

What is more, it is a noticeable trait of Grandfather's rendition of the typological scheme that loss and pain are typically portrayed as incurred by the individual, whereas social progress and increasing liberty are rendered as beneficial on a collective plane of society. Intolerance, then, would seem to be a burden for the individual, freedom a grace for society. Grandfather's history makes practically no attempt to reconcile this contradiction. This is what lies behind Grandfather's acknowledgement, towards the end of the first volume, that he is merely recounting the outward appearance of history:

> "But, after all," continued Grandfather, "any other old chair, if it possessed memory, and a hand to write its recollections, could record stranger stories than any that I have told you. From generation to generation, a chair sits familiarly in the midst of human interests, and is witness to the most secret and confidential intercourse, that mortal man can hold with his fellow. The human heart may best be read in the fireside chair. And as to external events, Grief and Joy keep a continual vicissitude around it and within it. Now we see the glad face and glowing form of Joy, sitting merrily on the old chair, and throwing a warm, firelight radiance over all the household. Now, while we thought not of it, the dark clad mourner, Grief, has stolen into the place of Joy, but not to retain it long. The imagination can hardly grasp so wide a subject, as is embraced in the experience of a family chair."
>
> "It makes my breath flutter—my heart thrill—to think of it," said Laurence. "Yes; a family chair must have a deeper history than a Chair of State." (6: 65)

It is the office of the romance, as opposed to the history book, to record that "deeper history," and thus to function as the principle of mediation not merely between past and present, but between private and public as well. I will return to this issue towards the end of this chapter, when we will be in a better position to grasp the complexities of Hawthorne's artistic endeavour. For now it must suffice to maintain that because of the additional requirement of the romance that it mediate between public and private as well as between past and present, the question of aesthetics must be much more pressing in relation to the romance than to the history lesson.

I do not mean to imply that Hawthorne had been unaware of this in his preceding literary career; all of his most important early pieces testify to the contrary—after all, Hawthorne introduces the concept of the romance already in the head notice to "Roger Malvin's Burial," written in 1832. Nevertheless, it seems to me that *The Whole History* can be seminally seen as a summing up, in some ways, of the themes that had occupied him through the better part of a decade, an attempt to be rid of materials that were beginning to stifle him. At any rate, the lack of historical themes is almost as conspicuous in Hawthorne's writings of the forties as they were prominent in the thirties: none of his fictions after 1840 are set in Puritan New England until *The Scarlet Letter* was written, with the exception of "Main-street," which was conceived at around the same time.

We will only have time to perform an in-depth analysis of one of those tales, in which I shall try to outline the parameters of Hawthorne's project in the romances, the aim of which, I will argue, is to reconcile the recognition of the inevitable loss and pain in the present with a religiously inspired faith in the future. I shall refer to this project as an allegorical dialectics, by which I understand a dialectics that achieves the closure of fulfilment inherent in typological hermeneutics, without cancelling the processual nature of dialectics that ensures that the fulfilment achieved can be final only in relation to a posited anagogical end. As I have argued in the previous chapter, the typological pattern is already built into the patristic fourfold scheme. Yet Hawthorne does not conceive of the anagogical end in eschatological terms. In his writings the anagogical perspective is not associated with the end of the world, but with the terminating point of each individual life: death. This reinterpretation of anagogy, not as the ending point of time, but as a point altogether beyond time, is of absolutely vital importance for our understanding of Hawthorne, for if we ignore it, we will be prone to mistake Hawthorne's allegory for a version of the social-symbolic outlook that Sacvan Bercovitch has taught us to associate with America's Puritan origins.[5] I will attempt to demonstrate in this chapter, that by focusing on the privileged role of the reader in Hawthorne's writings, we may understand how Hawthorne's allegorical practice entails that the narrow understanding of typology as a correlation between two historical facts must be abandoned; or rather, that it must be expanded to include once more a spiritual fact or vantage point from which the two historical facts are understood. The allegorical fourfold scheme of interpretation provides such a vantage point by tying the moral sense to the anagogical sense, to the effect that the moral sense could be said both to determine and to be determined by the other senses. As we will see below, the moral sense, in being tied to the present, has the power to determine the significance of the past. In our case, this is equivalent to the plot being able to determine the significance of the narrative discourse created by the author. Yet while the present (plot) can thus be seen to have the power to determine the meaning of the past (discourse of the writer), the meaning of this moral present is itself determined by its future anagogical fulfilment, which is acted out by the reader.[6] I will discuss this understanding of the anagogical sense of the text at greater length towards the end of this chapter, before confronting Bercovitch's argument directly in my discussion of *The Scarlet Letter* in chapter two. I will begin, however, by sketching the components of Hawthorne's allegorical practice.

## 1. Hawthorne's Tales: History and Sexuality

The tales that Hawthorne wrote in the second major creative phase of his career and published as *Mosses from an Old Manse*, in many ways constitute a new departure for him. All of his most profound earlier pieces are concerned with historical subjects. In the words of one of his most astute critics, "what the best of Hawthorne's early tales offer us, again and again, is some explicitly fictional moment of conflict or choice, derived from and referable back to some actuality, but generalized and dramatized in such a way as to stand for the limits of perception or experience at a certain critical moment in the historical past."[7] The stories of the Old Manse period, in contrast, all but abandon historical themes, and are marked by an increasingly meta-reflexive tendency. This is not to say that history ceases to be an issue in the tales of this period. Indeed, as the very same critic has argued, these later stories could well be described as "the History of His Own Times."[8] But even if this is the case—and I for one believe that it is—it will not do to explain the aestheticist bent of the later stories merely as a convoluted critique of various Transcendentalist tenets. No one who reads the best of these stories—say, "The Artist of the Beautiful," "The Birth-Mark," or "Rappaccini's Daughter"—can doubt that the question of the problematic relation between the Actual and the Ideal that they incessantly return to, is one which carries the greatest weight for Hawthorne himself, not as a contingent historical problem, but as the founding problem of historical experience as such.

If it is true to say, then, as Colacurcio argues, that the Provincial tales and sketches manifest the attitude of a moral historian, in the Old Manse stories we nevertheless witness a shift from stories probing the problems of history to stories probing the difficulties of telling stories of history.[9] Admittedly, this had been a central concern for Hawthorne from a very early stage of his writing career (witness "Alice Doane's Appeal"), but this circumstance cannot hide the fact that *Mosses from an Old Manse* offers a much larger selection of tales in which the role of the artist is an explicit concern than does *Twice-Told Tales*. For some critics, this turn away from history has been advanced as a crude explanation of what they perceive as the comparative failure of his later tales; abandoning history, so the argument goes, Hawthorne abandons the substance matter that sustains his imagination. *The Scarlet Letter*, then, is almost a priori defined as a masterpiece, and the alleged "failure" of the subsequent romances to repeat its success is equally conveniently explained away as the natural outcome of the author insisting, pigheadedly, on doing once more something other than the critic knows that he was good for.[10] This argument, of course, assumes that history was Hawthorne's major subject; his writings of the eighteen-forties, however, suggest otherwise. Increasingly self-reflective, the tales produced in this decade seem to have incorporated the framing narratives that Hawthorne had projected for so many of his early tales into themselves, clearly indicating that for the later Hawthorne, at least, history is less interesting in itself, than in the interpreted form we call art.

If the Old Manse tales abandon historical themes, they nevertheless develop the veiled subject matter of many of his most important earlier pieces: sexuality.[11] This subject, be it observed, is intrinsically related to Hawthorne's concern for history, for from the point of view of Christian dogma it is precisely the recognition of sexuality that marks the birth of historical consciousness as such: in psychological as well as in metaphysical terms, the recognition of sexuality signals the individual's entrance into temporality. "Roger Malvin's Burial," "Alice Doane's Appeal," "Young Goodman Brown," "The Minister's Black Veil," "The May-Pole of Merry Mount"—in all of these tales sexuality is depicted as the very medium the individual must traverse in order to become part of the community. The tales collected in *Mosses from an Old Manse* thematize the difficulty of transcending the tragic vision of sexuality that is such a distinctive mark of tales such as "Young Goodman Brown" and "The Minister's Black Veil," without simply replacing it with an ideal conception of sexual love in which women are unstained by desire, but therefore also unreal. In the third story proper of the collection, "A Select Party"—strategically inserted between "The Birth-mark" and "Young Goodman Brown"—a Man of Fancy invites an array of his fantasies "for the sake of observing how they would compare [...] with the real characters to whom his maturer life had introduced him." Among these "shadowy people," we find, significantly, "a sort of wax figure of an angel—a creature as cold as moonshine—an artifice in petticoats, with an intellect of pretty phrases, and only the semblance of a heart—yet, in all these particulars, the true type of a young man's imaginary mistress" (10: 63). This creature the Man of Fancy now dismisses, claiming to "have learned to love what Nature makes, better than my own creations in the guise of womanhood." The effect of this confession, is immediate and fatal: "Ah, false one!" shrieks the dream-lady dissolving, "your inconstancy has annihilated me!" The Man of Fancy shows little emotion, however. "So be it," he comments tersely on her dying words, "and a good riddance, too!" (10: 64).

The tone of this sketch is humorous, and as so often in Hawthorne, vaguely self-ironic. In truth, however, the scene dramatizes the difficulty of holding on to the Ideal in the face of the Real. The comical tone of the sketch could easily make us as dismissive of the Man of Fancy's former acquaintances as he is himself, and thus to see the substitution of Natural for Ideal womanhood as something that Hawthorne wholeheartedly supports. But Hawthorne is careful to disassociate himself from the Man of Fancy he so clearly resembles. "Alas!" he exclaims, "it is not good for the full grown man to look too closely at these old acquaintances, but rather to reverence them at a distance, through the medium of years that have gathered duskily between" (10: 63).

If the Man of Fancy exhibits too little faith in the ideal conceptions of his youth, the fault of the male protagonist of the tale that precedes "A Select Party" in *Mosses from an Old Manse* is the opposite. In "The Birth-mark," Aylmer, another one of Hawthorne's artist figures clothed as a "mad scientist," attempts to purge his wife Georgiana of a birthmark, in which he perceives "the fatal flaw of humanity, which Nature, in one shape or another, stamps ineffaceably on all her productions, either to imply that they are temporary and finite, or that their perfection must be wrought by toil and pain" (10: 38–9). Aylmer is successful in his attempt, only to find that the fulfilment of his desire is a source of tragedy rather than joy: ridded of her birthmark, Georgiana dies in his arms. The closing paragraph of the tale leaves no doubt that Hawthorne looks upon Aylmer's desire for perfection as misguided: "had Aylmer reached a profounder wisdom, he need not thus have flung away the happiness, which would have woven his mortal life of the self-same texture with the celestial." The ideology advocating heavenly perfection in a domestic society is replaced in the tale by an ideology of hope, in which imperfection is not seen as an illness to be cured, but rather as a scar which rips through the ostensible presence of reality (the realm of Becoming as opposed to that of Being, in the apposite diction of James K. Folsom), opening up a gap through which the individual may find the means to "look beyond the shadowy scope of Time, and living once for all in Eternity, to find the perfect Future in the present" (10: 56). Hawthorne, in other words, acknowledges what the transcendentalist tries to suppress: that the perfect future can be found in the present only if it is absent from it; that for the perfect future to remain it must always be held at a distance from the present. Instead of transcending desire, Hawthorne consequently seeks to sustain it, as it is only by denying its immediate fulfilment that desire can remain an incentive to better the world.

As these tales suggest, the problem that Hawthorne was concerned with was principally that of envisioning a dialectics capable of mediating between the Ideal and the Real. How affirm the Ideal without violating the Real, as does Aylmer? How stay true to the Real without compromising one's faith in the Ideal, as does the Man of Fancy? These are intimately interrelated questions, and they are addressed as one in "Rappaccini's Daughter," in which the two extremes of Aylmer and the Man of Fancy find their respective counterparts in the form of two scientists, Rappaccini and Baglioni. It is a tale about a young man's encounter with the ambiguous nature of sexual love, and although it ends tragically it nevertheless presents the reader with the possibility of realizing an alternative vision. In so doing, I will argue, it constitutes a paradigm of Hawthorne's allegorical dialectics.

## 2. *Rappaccini's Daughter*: The Allegory of Romance

"Rappaccini's Daughter" is introduced by a fictional notice in which Hawthorne playfully presents himself as the translator of a typical piece of the French writer M. de l'Aubépine, whose writings are said to be tainted by the author's "inveterate love of allegory" (10: 91). We are given an abundance of titles—*"Contes deux fois racontées," "Le Voyage Céleste à Chemin de Fer," "Le nouveau Père Adam et la nouvelle Mère Eve," "Roderic: ou le Serpent à l'estomac," "Le Culte du Feu," "La Soirée du Chateau en Espagne," "L'Artiste du Beau; ou le Papillon Mécanique"* (10: 92)—all easily identifiable as allusions to previous works by Hawthorne himself. Critics have been puzzled by the playful and apparently self-derogatory tone of this opening piece; what it suggests, however, is that the ensuing tale is precisely an allegorical depiction of the plight of the artist who insists on working through the form of allegory. The density of the tale has provoked more than one critic to pronounce it obscure. As always in Hawthorne, however, one should be careful not to mistake artistic complexity for epistemological ambiguity. The moral thrust of the tale is evident through the overt moralizing of its narrator, and it is only if we have overdosed on twentieth century theories of unreliable narration and focalization that we can doubt that his words are to be taken seriously.[12]

The allegorical bias of the tale is suggested already in its first paragraph, where the references to Dante serve to remind us that the action takes place in a fallen world, which should also call to mind that the only way to re-establish contact with unfallen Reality (with God, that is) is via the mediation of Love, or Beatrice. In disentangling the other allegorical strains of the story, we must be careful to observe how painstakingly precise Hawthorne is in his use of classical and Christian intertexts. When the garden is first presented to us, we are informed that it contains a statue of Vertumnus. Vertumnus was a Roman deity, a god of seasonal change; etymologically, his name means "turner." But it is not the literal, but the literary connotations that merit our attention in this case. Hawthorne's source for this figure, Thomas F. Walsh Jr. has shown, "is the story, told by Ovid in his *Metamorphoses* (XIV. 623 ff.), in which Vertumnus, vying with Sylvanus, Pan, and other satyrs and fauns, entered the garden of Pomona and won the heart of the desirable nymph, who, like Beatrice, excelled in her love and cultivation of the garden." As Walsh points out, this is not the only time "Hawthorne uses fauns and nymphs to portray a pre-Adamite world of innocent animal spirits—an amoral world, untroubled by the knowledge of good and evil;" he does so already in "The Maypole of Merry Mount" and returns to it with much elaboration in *The Marble Faun*. It is therefore surely not insignificant that Giovanni's appearance, as Walsh observes, "is remarkably similar to Donatello's"—he has, the narrator of the tale specifies, "rather a Grecian than an Italian head, with fair, regular features, and a glistening of gold among his ringlets" (10: 104). Indeed, Milton, too, Walsh reminds us, alludes to Ovid's treatment of Vertumnus and Pomona in *Paradise Lost*, book IX (393–95), the very book in which Adam and Eve fall from grace.[13]

It is no coincidence, then, that "Rappaccini's Daughter" explicitly presents us with the equatability of the artist with that of Adam, fallen man. "Was this garden, then, the Eden of the present world?" Giovanni wonders when first seeing Rappaccini, "and this man, with such a perception of harm in what his own hands caused to grow, was he the

Adam?" (10: 96). This inaugural conundrum is echoed, at the end of the tale, by another set of questions: "Oh, was there not, from the first, more poison in thy nature than in mine?" the dying Beatrice asks Giovanni who dumb-stricken watches the effects of the antidote he has administered to her. While critics have almost unanimously answered Beatrice's question in the affirmative, surprisingly few critics have been willing to affirm Giovanni's first tentative identification of Rappaccini with Adam. Instead the received opinion would seem to coincide with that of Deborah L. Jones: "If this garden is indeed 'the Eden of the present world' then Rappaccini is the false deity. He has sought to create through his art a new Adam and Eve."[14] Jones, like many other critics of the last two decades, reads the story as a meditation and affirmation of the indeterminacy of signs. But the questions are not mere rhetorical flourishes; on the contrary, our understanding of the tale, and consequently of Hawthorne's art, hinges upon the way we decide to answer these questions, which are in fact merely the prolegomena to the question which literally ends the tale: "Rappaccini! Rappaccini! And is *this* the upshot of your experiment?"

Why does the tale end on a question? Beatrice is dead; Rappaccini, who had attempted to endow his daughter "with marvellous gifts, against which no power nor strength could avail an enemy" (10: 127), stands thunder-stricken at the outcome of his experiment; Baglioni, his competitor in the world of science, arrives just in time to deliver the last words "in a tone of triumph mixed with horror" (10: 128). So why does Hawthorne have the tale end on the evasive figure of a question mark rather than opting to maximize the emotional impact of the story by ending it on an exclamation mark, as Poe, say, surely would have done?[15] He does so because he wants us to understand that the story does not end with this signifier, for this signifier points towards a signified, which will be made up of the way the reader decides to answer the questions raised by the story. *Is* the death of Rappaccini's daughter the upshot of Rappaccini's experiment? And is the death of "Rappaccini's Daughter" the upshot of Hawthorne' experiment in allegoric art? This is what we are called upon to decide, for it is the predicament of Hawthorne, just as it is the plight of Rappaccini, that the significance of his art is ultimately dependent upon the response of the reader.[16]

The allegorical connotations that we have outlined above should thus all be seen as subservient to (yet modifying) the primary allegory of the tale, in which Rappaccini is a figure of the artist, Beatrice is his beloved creation (the romance, that is, or the tale itself), and Giovanni, finally, is a figure of the reader. In this light, it may be worth recalling that according to his son Julian's biography, Hawthorne read an unfinished version of the tale to Sophia, who asked how it would end—was Beatrice to be a demon or an angel? Hawthorne, Julian claims, responded "with some emotion" that he had "no idea!"[17] This report may seem to clash with the very openly moralistic pronouncements of the narrator, and hence suggest that there would be some grounds for the contention that Hawthorne was not, after all, quite sure of what he was doing when he wrote this story.[18] Under the assumption that Hawthorne deliberately attempted to make the reader conceive of Rappaccini's project as parallel with that of the author, however, it makes perfect sense, even down to accounting for the emotion Sophia's question reportedly aroused in him. For if such a gentle reader as Sophia Hawthorne could doubt the nature of Beatrice, how could Hawthorne have envisioned the outcome of the story as anything but a failure?

To substantiate the above argument, we should observe at this point, that while Rappaccini is merely tentatively aligned with Adam, he is quite unequivocally likened to an artist by the narrator in the second half of the story—approaching Beatrice and Giovanni at the very moment at which his daughter puts the fatal antidote to her lips, he seems "to gaze with a triumphant expression at the beautiful youth and maiden, as might an artist who should spend his life in achieving a picture or a group of statuary, and finally be satisfied with his success" (10: 126).[19] As so often in Hawthorne, we must read this passage in conjunction with the earlier passage in which he is tentatively identified with Adam in order to understand it properly: Rappaccini is the type of the artist precisely because he is a second Adam, the creative plight of whom has been suggested to us in a subordinate clause that we have already quoted, which states that his destiny is to be constantly plagued with "a perception of harm in what his hands caused to grow." Rappaccini, like Hawthorne himself, realizes this. Significantly, the means by which he would try to transcend the imperfection of this world is not to reject this imperfection, but on the contrary to make imperfection the source of perfection. As Rappaccini's opponent, doctor Pietro Baglioni, explains to Giovanni: "It is his theory, that all medicinal virtues are comprised within those substances which we term vegetable poisons" (10: 100). This paradox is the key to Beatrice's doubleness. Her outward beauty hides an inner blight, but given the appropriate response, this blight might give way to greater beauty still. Hawthorne is not invoking a clear-cut inner/outer dichotomy; his point is the very opposite, namely that Beatrice's beauty is her poison, just as her poison is her beauty. There is—in this Eden of a fallen world—no way to separate the one from the other without killing both.[20]

It has been suggested that Beatrice is analogous to Duessa in *The Faerie Queene*, "in which Duessa's apparent beauty hides a monstrous (and eventually unmasked) inner evil," but this analogy falters considerably, as do all other conceptions of Beatrice that conceive of her beauty and her poison as forming an oppositional pair. The split in Beatrice, or in Giovanni's perception of her, is not between "her apparent spiritual beauty and her real spiritual toxicity."[21] Rather, it is a split between her real physical and spiritual beauty and her equally real physical toxicity. In other words, in her physical appearance, Beatrice is both beautiful and toxic, while in her spiritual appearance she is beautiful through and through. Rappaccini's aim—the project of his art, as it were—is to make Giovanni (the reader of his creation) share the radically double experience that Beatrice embodies, but which has its origin in Rappaccini himself. Because Rappaccini, as Beatrice does not fail to inform Giovanni, has two daughters that are obviously metaphorically united: "at the hour when I first drew breath, this plant sprang from the soil, the offspring of his science, of his intellect, while I was but his earthly child" (10: 123).[22] Thus the story's title—"Rappaccini's Daughter"—denotes a doubleness not only in the figurative sense of Beatrice being simultaneously beautiful and poisonous, but also in the literal sense of designating both Beatrice and the flower shrub which she refers to as "my sister" (10: 97).[23]

Rappaccini is often reduced to the diabolic figure of one of Hawthorne's "mad scientists," yet his project is ultimately governed by an idealistic impulse.[24] After all, his hope is that Giovanni will not only share the physical attributes of Beatrice, but that he will accept them, as they are a prerequisite for his continued intercourse with Beatrice, whose spirit is pure. Had Giovanni accepted this burden, he would have cleansed himself of the poison which Beatrice's last words suggest have been present, from the first, more fully in his nature than in her own. Considering that Beatrice's physical appearance is poisonous as fully as her spiritual appearance is pure, this is a fine way of saying that in Giovanni, the poison has infected his spiritual essence. It may appear a circumstantial route, but if Giovanni is in any way representative of mankind in general, Rappaccini is, by means of his theory of the medical virtues of poison, in truth trying to save the world by the only means possible.

## 3. Hawthorne's Structural Principle of Chiastic Inversion

Just as significant as these thematic considerations is the way that these materials are arranged. It may be argued, indeed, that "Rappaccini's Daughter" already bears in itself the embryo of the structural principle of the longer romances that were to follow within five or six years. In the simplest statement of its form, we could say that the story consists of two halves, the second repeating the first half in inverted sequence. Having presented us with Giovanni, whose initiation into the hermeneutics of a fallen world the reader comes to share, the tale proceeds by sketching the garden with the marble fountain and the purple shrub. We watch Rappaccini at a distance and Giovanni wonders if he might be Adam; then Beatrice is presented and we see her tending the purple shrub, affectionately addressing it "my sister" (10: 97). This first section of the story ends with Giovanni retiring to his bed, dreaming a dream in which "Flower and maiden were different and yet the same, and fraught with some strange peril in either shape" (10: 98). The next day, which coincides with our second section, Giovanni pays a visit to Baglioni, who informs him of Rappaccini's theory concerning the "medicinal virtues" of "vegetable poisons" (10: 100). Disconcerted by what his father's friend has told him, Giovanni returns to his chambers, buying "a fresh bouquet of flowers" (10: 101) on his way home. From his window he sees Beatrice a second time in the garden, and gets a first indication that Beatrice may be poisonous when he sees first a lizard, and then an insect, die in her presence, and seems to see the bouquet of flowers he has thrown down to her "beginning to wither in her grasp" (10: 104).

The following section comprises a longer time-span although it is actually shorter than the preceding ones. It is now obvious that Giovanni is affected by Beatrice in an unhealthy manner; she has "instilled a fierce and subtle poison into his system" which is neither love nor horror, "but a wild offspring of both" (10: 105). By chance, Giovanni meets with Baglioni on the street when doctor Rappaccini happens to pass by. Judging from the look on the scientist's face, Baglioni announces that Rappaccini must have made Giovanni the subject of one of his experiments. Unwilling to listen to the older man, Giovanni breaks away, but the reader is allowed to hear Baglioni pronounce his intention to thwart his competitor: "Perchance, most learned Rappaccini, I may foil you where you little dream of it!" (10: 108).

Returning to his lodgings, Giovanni is greeted by his landlady who shows him the way into the garden where he finally comes to stand face to face with Beatrice. This is the central section of the tale. Significantly, the interview between the prospective lovers touches the matter of Beatrice's double nature. "Forget whatever you may have fancied in regard to me," she begs him. "If true to the outward senses, still it may be false in its essence. But the words of Beatrice Rappaccini's lips are true from the depths of the heart outward. Those you may believe!" (10: 112).

Back in his chamber again, Giovanni falls to sleep convinced that Beatrice "was worthiest to be worshipped" (10: 114). Yet on waking up, there is another indication that he has been infected by her poison: at the very spot where Beatrice had touched him, warding him off from the purple shrub, there is "a purple print, like that of four small fingers, and the likeness of a slender thumb upon his wrist" (10: 115). But we are also reminded of the shallow nature of Giovanni's feelings for Beatrice, as the narrator implies that it might not be love that makes him disregard this sign, but "that cunning semblance of love which flourishes in the imagination, but strikes no depth of root into the heart" (10: 115). Again a considerable amount of time passes in the matter of a few paragraphs, whereupon Baglioni pays a visit to Giovanni in his room, in what is the second section of the second half of the story. Baglioni now confirms what was only suggested in the second section of the first half of the story, namely that Beatrice is poisonous: "Yes; poisonous as she is beautiful!" (10: 118). Leaving a vial with what he claims to be an antidote on the table, Baglioni departs, and Hawthorne again allows the reader to overhear him scheming against Rappaccini: "'We will thwart Rappaccini yet!' thought he, chuckling to himself, as he descended the stairs" (10: 119). Recalling the incidents that made him suspect that Beatrice might indeed bear some monstrous secret—"the lizard, the insect, and the flowers" (10: 120)—Giovanni decides to settle the matter once and for all by presenting another flower bouquet to Beatrice, but before he has the chance to put his plan into action he finds that the flowers of the bouquet, "which he had never once laid aside from his hand" (10: 121) have already started to droop, and realizes that he has been contaminated by Beatrice.

In a rage, he storms down into the garden to meet with Beatrice. Walking silently together, they stop by "the marble fountain, and to its pool of water on the ground, in the midst of which grew the shrub that bore gem-like blossoms" (10: 123), where Giovanni finally accuses Beatrice of having wilfully instilled him with her poison. Horrified by his accusations, Beatrice accepts the antidote, at which moment Rappaccini emerges and is likened to a triumphant "artist," only to see his daughter die.

For illustrative purposes, I shall condense the motifs we have sketched above into a series of patterns, the first of which reads "Garden; marble fountain, Rappaccini = Adam?; Beatrice." This will be A. Our second pattern condenses the next section of the tale into: "Baglioni; flower bouquet; Beatrice poisonous;" this is B. C reads as follows: "Giovanni poisoned?; his heartless love; Baglioni slights Rappaccini." Then follows the central scene, Giovanni's first meeting with Beatrice in the garden. The second half of the tale repeats the patterns of the first half with slight variations, merely inverting their order: C, B, A.[25]

I am, it should be admitted, slightly exaggerating the symmetry of the composition; but only slightly, as can be readily seen if we take a more inclusive view of the motifs that run through the tale:

A (Arrival of Giovanni.) The garden, marble fountain, Rappaccini = Adam?, Beatrice.
B Baglioni, Rappaccini's theory (virtues in poison), flower bouquet, Beatrice poisonous.
C Giovanni poisoned?, his heartless love, Baglioni slights Rappaccini.
D Meeting in garden.
C Giovanni poisoned?, his heartless love.
B Baglioni slights Rappaccini, flower bouquet, Giovanni poisonous.
A The garden, marble fountain, Rappaccini = artist!, Beatrice.

This symmetrical way of arranging the material into a structural "rhyme scheme," as it were, provides the formal backbone of Hawthorne's dialectical aesthetics. This may seem a surprising claim, as the scheme we have outlined above may appear to substantiate Richard Fogle's view "that there is no synthesis in Hawthorne's thinking, only thesis and antithesis in balance,"[26] rather than suggest any form of Hegelian progression from thesis to antithesis coming finally to rest in synthesis. But this is to ignore the pragmatic thrust of Hawthorne's art; that is to say, to be blind to the importance he attaches to the reader. Roy R. Male has described Hawthorne as belonging to the expressive group of critical theories, as defined by M. H. Abrams in *The Mirror and the Lamp*, that is to say, as being primarily concerned with "the relation between the speaker or writer and his language."[27] As is well documented in Abrams' classic study, the turn towards the expressive paradigm as an aesthetic norm is a characteristic trait of romanticism. But Hawthorne does not fit easily into the mould of the romantic artist, as is indicated by his predilection for the Augustans. Even more revealing is a passage from a letter to his then fiancée Sophia, in which he explicitly assumes a homology between his heart and his art:

> I am glad to think that God sees through my heart; and if any angel has power to penetrate into it, he is welcome to know everything that is there. Yes; and so may any mortal, who is capable of full sympathy, and therefore worthy to come into my depths. But he must find his own way there. I can neither guide him nor enlighten him. It is this involuntary reserve, I suppose, that has given the objectivity to my writings. And when people think that I am pouring myself out in a tale or essay, I am merely telling *what is common to human nature, not what is peculiar to myself.* I sympathize with them—not they with me. (15: 612–13; my emphasis.)

Poised between romantic conceptions of art as a vehicle for unveiling a private self, and enlightenment notions of art as a mirror of universal truths, Hawthorne manages to wed the romantic predilection for self-expression with a classicist emphasis on objectivity and didacticism. This interlocking of two seemingly incompatible aesthetical paradigms provides us with a key to Hawthorne's narrative practice. The reader must find his own way to the heart of the romance, which is also the heart of the artist. We find this way, we may surmise, by looking into our own heart: there is the synthesizing agency capable of bringing together the contradictory aspects of the romance. What must be emphasized, is that because the heart of the romance is both that of the writer and that of the reader, this act of introspection must not be understood as a withdrawal from the larger concerns of the community, but on the contrary must be recognized as the only way to open up a true intercourse with the social world that embraces the individual.[28] What is more, because the act of sympathy thus conceived involves an act of conscious introspection, the Heart cannot be understood exclusively as an emotional metaphor in Hawthorne's writings, but must be accredited an intellectual office as well.[29]

It may be objected, of course, that all of the correspondences noted above could have been observed without the additional argument that they are arranged in such a way as to compose a more or less symmetrical structure. This is undeniably true, and it must also be admitted that the correspondences we have highlighted by no means exhaust the possibilities of tying one textual segment to another. Yet much is achieved by this way of structuring the material. For one thing, we may become aware, by generating structures like this, of relations that may otherwise seem obscure, if at all noticed, as the identification of Adam and the artist, for instance. More importantly, however, it shows in what sense the intention of the text must be construed as the product of a dialectical interaction of writer and reader. It is we as readers who generate the structure of the narrative, but we do so on the assumption that our activity is warranted by the writer's preceding attention to his own act of composing the discourse. In so doing, our capacity for sympathetically engaging the artist's work is brought directly to bear on this work, to the effect that our sympathy (or lack thereof) becomes an integral part of the very romance we read. As a consequence, the intricate question of the accuracy of the intended structure hereby revealed loses some of its urgency. Once we have sensed that the artist *might* have entertained an Imaginary conception of some such structure as we seem to have seen, what matters is primarily whether we are willing to retain our faith in its Actual existence. "Nobody," as Hilda says in *The Marble Faun*, "ought to read poetry, or look at pictures or statues, who cannot find a great deal more in them than the poet or artist has actually expressed" (MF, 379).

## 4. The Allegory of Love: Sexuality and the Fortunate Fall

So far, I have almost entirely refrained from commenting upon the subject matter I have already suggested is at the heart of the tale we are considering: sexuality. There is no denying the heavily erotic overtones in the description of the Garden; it is a sensuous paradise, but as these places tend to be in epic literature, it is a perverted paradise.[30] What makes "Rappaccini's Daughter" such a dense tale is primarily the way that the metatextual allegory that we have explicated above is inextricably interwoven with the sexual allegory that it can also been seen to suggest. The point of intersection for these two allegories is the biblical story "Rappaccini's Daughter" so emphatically invokes, that of the Fall of Man.

The centrality of the theme of the Fall to Hawthorne's thinking has long been a commonplace in criticism. More specifically, Hawthorne's writings repeatedly invoke the notion of the Fall as a prerequisite for attaining a greater good, an interpretation of the story of the Fall commonly known as the paradox of the Fortunate Fall. It is a concept of considerable genealogy; Hawthorne, however, would have derived it from Milton.[31] From our present perspective it is important to observe that Milton's representation of the immediate consequences of Adam's disobedience provides a suggestive illustration of the interconnection between desire, allegory, and symbolism. Having tasted the forbidden fruit, Adam is overcome by the awakening of sexual lust, that he and Eve waste little time in gratifying:

Her hand he seized, and to a shady bank,
Thick overhead with verdant roof embow'red
He led her nothing loath; flow'rs were the couch,
Pansies, and violets, and asphodel,
And hyacinth, earth's freshest softest lap.
There they their fill of love and loves disport
Took largely, of their mutual guilt the seal,
The solace of their sin, till dewy sleep
Oppressed them, wearied with their amorous play. (IX: 1037–45)

It may seem tempting, thus, to characterize the Fall as a fall into sexuality, but as Adam and Eve make heavenly love already in book IV (736–775), this cannot be the case. What is involved, rather is the transformation of spiritual into carnal desire; by eating of the forbidden fruit, the first parents become aware of their bodies: "Carnal desire enflaming, he on Eve/ Began to cast lascivious eyes, she him/ As wantonly repaid; in lust they burn" (IX: 1011–34). The eating of the fruit makes it possible for Adam and Eve to experience sexuality as a thing in itself rather than as an integral part of a greater whole: it performs the dissevering operation of transforming sexuality into a separate issue, an experience isolated from all other concerns in life. While this may account for the heightened sense of pleasure temporarily experienced by Adam and Eve, it also explains their subsequent feelings of guilt, since it cuts sexuality off from God, making it a space of self-fulfilment rather than of praise of God, as are all their other actions. It is precisely this dissevering quality of lust that makes it evil: it performs a partializing office, isolating part from whole.[32]

Importantly, Milton represents the Fall as a series of events, rather than as one all fatal moment. In fact, the poem refers to a number of falls in its course. Not only is the Fall of man preceded by that of Satan (who is in a sense its primary cause), but when it actually takes place in book IX it is divided into two distinct scenes: the temptation and fall of Eve (lines 733–83), and Adam's fatal decision to repeat her transgression (960–1016). At the beginning of book X, we learn that in "not obeying" (14) God's "high injunction not to taste that fruit" (13), Adam and Eve "deserved to fall" (16), a formulation that may seem to imply a distinction between the Fall and the deed that brings it about, as if the Fall were not the act of disobedience itself, but the punishment of guilt inflicted upon the first parents as a result of their disobedience. Indeed, it is not until the end of book X, when Adam and Eve have repented of their transgression, that we learn that "they forthwith to the place/ Repairing where he judged them prostrate *fell*/ Before him reverent" (1098–1100; my emphasis). The Fall, in other words, is not completed until Adam and Eve have repented their sinful act, and this act of repenting takes the form of a process, which involves the transformation of a figurative fall into a literal fall.

The reader must be brought to see how these seemingly distinct episodes are really parts of a greater whole. And the means by which the reader is initiated into the mysterious interrelation between the literal and the figurative is that of typology. For if the Fall is a fall into partialization—that is, into a state of spatial absence—it is also a fall from temporal presence (eternity) into temporal absence, that is to say into history. Having let Death into the world, the first parents are directly responsible for the transformation of a circular conception of time into a linear conception of time, wherein the individual life will make up a discrete unit rather than a synecdochical part. God's omnipresence fills the whole of the world, Michael tells Adam in book XI, and then goes on to explain how Adam could have been related to God's totality:

> All th' earth he gave thee to possess and rule,
> No despicable gift; surmise not then
> His presence to these narrow bounds confined
> Of Paradise or Eden: this had been
> Perhaps thy capital seat, from whence had spread
> All generations, and had hither come
> From all the ends of th' earth, to celebrate
> And reverence thee their great progenitor. (XI: 339–46)

These lines suggest that it might have been Adam's destiny, had he not fallen, to become the spatial centre of the world, and thus to be metaphorically related to God. With the Fall, however, this possibility is undone: "this preeminence thou hast lost, brought down/ To dwell on even ground now with thy Sons" (XI: 347–48). The spatial dispersal, for which Adam could have functioned as the centre, is displaced by a temporal dispersal, in which every individual, including Adam, may inhabit merely a moment of history.

This would have been a purely negative outcome, had not Christ offered his own life in place of that of man. By becoming a man, Christ in effect reinstates the metaphoric unity which the original sin had dissolved: through the mediation of Christ man becomes Man, partaker of the holy trinity. The means by which this is done, is a striking instance of reversal through repetition, since in order that Christ be born as a man, God must enter into an incestuous relation with his own offspring, "Mary second Eve" (X: 183). While superficially mimicking Satan's intercourse with Sin described in book II (761–67), the immaculate conception of Christ in truth undoes it, since it reinstates the possibility of sexual intimacy cleansed from lust, and thus marks a kind of reinscription into the world of the heavenly intimacy of the "wedded Love" (IV: 750) that Adam and Eve engage in prior to the Fall. Milton emphasizes that the first parents are not devoid of knowledge prior to eating the fruit in the very lines that depict Adam's fatal act of transgression: "he scrupled not to eat/ Against his better knowledge, not deceived,/ But fondly overcome with Female charm" (IX: 997–99). That Adam is fully aware that in eating the fruit he is disobeying the one limit God has set for man in Paradise is wholly in line with Milton's beliefs concerning free will. But it resonates oddly with the section in book III, in which God explicitly declares that man, in contrast to the revolting angels, will find grace because "man falls deceived/ By the other first" (III: 130–31). This is not some extreme expression of misogynism, implying that Eve must somehow be aligned with Satan. On the contrary, the passage serves to underscore the metaphoric unity of unfallen man and woman in Paradise, and hence of the two seemingly distinct episodes of the crisis depicted in book IX. Adam may be fully aware that he is doing something wrong when he eats of the fruit, but Eve was not, and in deceiving her, Satan may be said to deceive Adam as well: "Our State cannot be severed, we are one,/ One Flesh; to lose thee were to lose myself" (IX: 958–59). *Paradise Lost* is designed to make the reader sense that the crisis depicted in book IX forms a metaphoric unity with the judgement that the Son of God pronounces upon them in book X, which is, figurally speaking, its consummation. The poem itself could thus be said to function as an educator in the form of typological perception that the fact of the Fall has made necessary.

In Milton, then, the coming of Christ mends the rupture of eternal time, shattered by the Fall into the distinct moments of a history, since the totality of the life of Christ (birth-life-death) provides the type for history as such. As we saw in the previous chapter, the life of Christ effects a kind of spatialization of time: in providing the type of Everyman, the life of Christ makes available a moral space that did not exist before he was born. The function of this moral space is to wed the present with the eternal. As a consequence of the Life of Christ, as we have said, the present has become the site of an ongoing temporality in which every person re-enacts the original type, thereby lending to history a continuous presence. Thus the partialization of the world that is the immediate consequence of the Fall is undone through the Providential working of typology.

The literal fall's ability to invert the consequences of the figurative fall thus hinges upon the mediating agency fulfilled by Christ. In Hawthorne, however, the mediating office performed in Milton by the Son of Man is supplanted by that other offspring of human labour: art. This circumstance necessarily displaces the typological structure that is inherent in the concept of the Fortunate Fall. Typological interpretation depends upon identifying the internal connection between a set of historical events, the paradigm case being the relationship between the figurative death of Man in the Fall of Adam, the literal death of man that awaits us all, and finally, inserted between these two events, the death and resurrection of Jesus Christ, which is able to invest the latter event with the power to transform Adam's Fall into a Fortunate Fall. There is no automatism in this transformational process: the outcome depends upon whether the third event is related to the second. The Fall, that is, becomes fortuitous only if the individual interprets the life of Christ as relating to himself; if the relevancy of the Christian narrative is rejected and Christ is denied, the Fall remains unfortunate.

In Hawthorne this redemptive agency of Christ is transferred to the romance, the efficacy of which, however, is wholly dependent upon our willingness to suspend our disbeliefs and accept it as a medium which expresses a truth about ourselves. In contrast to the life of Christ, however, the romance is not a historical event but a fiction. Nevertheless, the romance can perform the office of mediating between two historical events—writing and reading—because the temporal world of history is tied to the spiritual world of Eternity through the faculty of the human imagination, which is like Christ in that it partakes both of the secular realm of Becoming and the divine realm of Being. This displacement of the typological scheme from history to imagination is of great importance, for it entails that there is no conflation of the spiritual and the historical in Hawthorne, as there is in the writings of a symbolist such as Emerson, to pick a contrasting example not entirely at random. In Hawthorne's allegorical dialectics, the two realms are kept distinct from each other, and although the romance provides a "neutral territory [...] where the Actual and the Imaginary may meet, and each imbue itself with the nature of the other" (SL, 36), the ability of his writings to perform a redemptive office depends upon the reader's recognition that the two realms must nevertheless be kept apart.

It is to this end that Hawthorne's stories invoke sexuality. While not sinful in itself, in Hawthorne sexuality is a sign of sin, in that the recognition of sexuality entails the recognition of sexual *desire*: as signifier if not as signified, sexuality connotes sin. "The Paradise of Children" that Hawthorne invokes in one of his stories for children is entirely mythical: children are not the innocent creatures they were held to be by the norms of Victorian society, but are stained with sin even before they commit any sinful acts.[33] The original wrong resides in the human Heart, as Hawthorne stresses in "Earth's Holocaust" and other stories, making sin virtually interchangeable with the very symbol of human love. In inadvertently suggesting sin, sexuality introduces an irrevocable distance between the state of innocence and the state of guilt. It is the attempt to close this gap that accounts for the aporetic structure of the double moral standard in Hawthorne: society and the individual alike are found guilty of attempting to deny the reality the gap. Society does so by outlining a set of conditions under which desire need no longer be perceived as sinful; the individual, in contrast, attempts to repress the recognition of this gap by denying the validity of the very norms society has advanced in order to bridge the gap in the first place. Unlike the history books which he wrote for children, the romances are designed to record that "deeper history" (6: 65) which involves not only the relation between past and present, but the aporetic relation between private and public as well. But in order to do so, Hawthorne's writings must attempt to recover the gap between innocence and guilt without either unduly prescribing what emotional experiences are to be open to the individual (as does society), or allowing the individual to set his own emotional experiences above the norms of society. Hawthorne's art, then, sets out to envision an alternative path which manages to circumvent repression and isolation alike.

In "Rappaccini's Daughter," the contradictory attitudes of society and the individual towards the problem of guilt, or imperfection, are suggested by the contrasting attitudes towards science of Baglioni and Rappaccini, respectively. The former would purge Beatrice by a concoction "distilled of blessed herbs" (10: 126). Rappaccini, in contrast, rejects the very norms of society that stipulates that innocence is preferable to the experience of guilt, and attempts to redeem his daughter by accentuating the very traits within her which society (in the form of Baglioni) would extinguish altogether. In a sense, this stance of the individual—of the Artist—comes closer to a correct understanding of the human plight than does the law-making machinery of society which implicitly suggests that guilt could be legislated away. Rappaccini is correct in assuming that this is impossible, that guilt is an inherent feature of existence and that the attempt to suppress it must therefore inevitably backfire. This is why his chosen course is to wed Giovanni to Beatrice, his work of art, by exploiting the natural sympathy that must exist between all guilty creatures: "My science," he explains to Beatrice, "and the sympathy between thee and him, have so wrought within his system, that he now stands apart from common men, as thou dost, daughter of my pride and triumph, from ordinary women" (10: 127). Hawthorne, however, distances himself from the Artist figures that people his stories by underscoring that the success of the artistic venture depends upon a factor over which he has no control: it depends upon whether or not the reader (or artist's audience) can be brought to accept "this fearful sympathy" by which the Artist attempts to unite the reader and the work of art.

Hawthorne's conception of "sympathy" is thus informed by a paradoxical response of active passivity.[34] Just as the individual is obliged to understand her fellow man, the "Gentle Reader" (MF, 1) is obliged to understand the author, who "addresses, not the many who will fling aside his volume, or never take it up, but the few who will understand him, better than most of his schoolmates and life-mates" (SL, 4); that is, "that one congenial friend—more comprehensive of his purposes, more appreciative of his success, more indulgent of his short-comings, and, in all respects, closer and kinder than a brother—that all-sympathizing critic, in short, whom an author never actually meets, but to whom he implicitly makes his appeal, whenever he is conscious of having done his best" (MF, 1). To retain such a notion of sympathy, artist and reader alike must refrain from giving in to the symbolistic impulse to transform meanings into images of emotional states: they must acknowledge the primacy of allegory, that is to say, subject themselves to a conception of the world as a system of meanings. Contrary to the opinion of a great many of Hawthorne's twentieth-century interpreters, then, interpretive freedom is not depicted as a desired *telos* in Hawthorne: it marks rather the existential state that the individual is condemned to as a consequence of the Fall.

But the "openness" seemingly suggested by Hawthorne's rhetoric—all the "mays," "mights," and "perhapses" that pervade his every story—is not a sign of epistemological ambiguity as twentieth century criticism commonly assumes, but testifies to the *ethical* openness of his fictions. That "Rappaccini's Daughter," like Hawthorne's writings in general, may be said to bestow the interpretative authority upon the reader does not mean that there is no privileged way of reading it. Hawthorne is careful to point out in the introductory note that M. de l'Aubépine's works are likely to be enjoyed, only "if the reader chance to take them in precisely the proper point of view," else "they can hardly fail to look excessively like nonsense" (10: 92). In 1851, when his first collections of tales were republished, Hawthorne repeated the injunction in the Preface: "The book, if you would see anything in it, requires to be read in the clear, brown, twilight atmosphere in which it was written; if opened in the sunshine, it is apt to look exceedingly like a volume of blank pages" (9: 5). Yet having delivered this methodological imperative, he immediately goes on to insist upon the accessibility of his stories:

> The sketches are not, it is hardly necessary to say, profound; but it is rather more remarkable that they so seldom, if ever, show any design on the writer's part to make them so. They have none of the abstruseness of idea, or obscurity of expression, which mark the written communications of a solitary mind with itself. They never need translation. It is, in fact, the style of a man of society. Every sentence, so far as it embodies thought or sensibility, may be understood and felt by anybody, who will give himself the trouble to read it, and will take up the book in a proper mood.

> This statement of apparently opposite peculiarities leads us to a perception of what the sketches truly are. They are not the talk of a secluded man with his own mind and heart, (had it been so, they could hardly have failed to be more deeply and permanently valuable,) but his attempts, and very imperfectly successful ones, to open an intercourse with the world. (9: 6)

Hawthorne's fictions can be termed ambiguous only in that they deliberately demand of us that we approach them "in a proper mood," which is exactly the same requirement that Giovanni is seen to miserably fail in the tale we have considered. Somewhat incisively, we may say that there are only two options available for the reader of Hawthorne's fictions: either we approach them as they ask to be approached, with sympathetic faith, or we come to them with cold and incredulous curiosity, at which the narrative, like Beatrice must die. The outcome, however, is not dependent upon epistemological circumstances; it involves, rather, an ethical choice, which the narrative is designed to enforce upon the reader.[35] In opposition to the received view, therefore, we must not yield to the temptation to describe Hawthorne's allegorical practice as a form of symbolism.

I have attempted to show above that the tale of Giovanni's encounter with ambiguous Beatrice replays the drama of the Fall not only as an allegory of sexual love, but equally importantly, as an allegory of reading. In accordance with the example of Milton's epic, the ending that Hawthorne's allegory projects is ultimately a potentially felicitous one; over and over again he restates the theme of the Fortunate Fall. Unlike Milton's epic, however, Hawthorne's romances never reach the point of *Paradise Regained*, albeit projecting this end as a possibility. The allegorical sequence spanned by his narratives could thus be written:

1. Epistemological innocence ->
2. Transgression ->
3. Guilt ->
4. (True innocence regained)

The Fall is felicitous in that it provides the means for transforming the epistemological innocence of childhood, in which innocence is equivalent to not knowing the difference between good and evil, into the true innocence of a future state of being, which coincides with the shedding of our earthly garments, that is, with death. But the final position of the narrative sequence cannot be *represented* in the romances, since that would require the existence of a comprehensive external system of norms, such that the ending of the scheme could be taken for granted, as the indubitable consequence of a certain moral stance. It is precisely the lack of such a stable, external authority that Hawthorne's romances constitute a response to, and that requires that the anagogical level of the text which for Dante and the medieval exegetes could be identified with the ending of a historical narrative already known, must be transformed into a conception of an ending incessantly forestalled. And in this, we are of course Hawthorne's heirs.

## CHAPTER THREE
# *The Scarlet Letter*: The Office of Art

Other religions, as the pagan, are more popular, for they consist in externals. But they are not for educated people. A purely intellectual religion would be more suited to the learned, but it would be of no use to the common people. The Christian religion alone is adapted to all, being composed of externals and internals. It raises the common people to the internal, and humbles the proud to the external; it is not perfect without the two, for the people must understand the spirit of the letter, and the learned must submit their spirit to the letter.

Pascal, *pensée* 251

There is at least one question which arises out of reading *The Scarlet Letter* that no reader can avoid tentatively forming an answer to: what does the scarlet letter signify? Over the years there has been such an abundance of attempts to answer this particular question that the most likely answer would seem to be *Anything*. The apparent impossibility of pinpointing the meaning of the letter has led Millicent Bell to suggest that *The Scarlet Letter* "is, as much as any work of fiction can be, an essay in semiology. Its theme is the obliquity or indeterminacy of signs." True to her initial suggestion, she ends her own discussion of this theme on an indeterminate note: "Hawthorne may have felt that it was his only stay against skepticism to believe in an ultimate revelation, an ultimate deciphering of what is beyond our comprehension in this life. But he may also have entertained the suspicion that no ultimate meanings exist."[1] In an essay critical of readings that, like Bell's, celebrate the openness of the novel, Jonathan Arac argues more provokingly that in *The Scarlet Letter* "'indeterminacy' functions as a closure." In Arac's view, accepting the openness of the novel, as Bell and many others have done, is to refrain from questioning the ideological bias of the book, to fail to highlight one of its most important features, namely "the very status of his writing as art, of his identity as an artist, that Hawthorne established to defend himself against implication in the political embroilments of Salem." Reading *The Scarlet Letter* in tandem with Hawthorne's campaign biography of his friend and former schoolmate Franklin Pierce, Arac argues that the apparent ideological openness of *The Scarlet Letter* depends on a substitution of stability for change which is embodied by "a literature that suppresses the overtly ideological plotting of action and prefers investment in character." To prove his case Arac generates a four-part matrix on the example of Fredric Jameson's application of Greimas' semiotic rectangle which "offers a way of interpreting characters as projections of ideological possibilities." The possibilities within this scheme are passion and principle; passion but not principle; not passion but principle; and finally the double-negative position of neither passion nor principle. Within the book, Arac, claims, these positions are aligned with Hester, Dimmesdale, the Puritan society, and finally, to Chillingworth.[2]

Arac's mapping out of the logical possibilities inherent in the text strikes me as a seminal move in our efforts to understand this elusive narrative; his own configuration of these possibilities, however, seems to me less satisfactory—in fact, he misrepresents each of these possibilities by assigning them to the wrong characters. For one thing, society can hardly be said to be one of the book's principal actants. Its presence may be felt much more directly in *The Scarlet Letter* than in the other romances, but it remains in the background, almost as if it were part of the scenery. Governor Bellingham, Reverend Wilson, various people of the crowds—all contribute to the texture of this backdrop, but their views are not necessarily consistent with each other. More importantly, Arac's decision to include "society" as a representative of one of the logical possibilities suggested by the book entails that he is forced to refrain from affording Pearl such a status. Once we have realized the necessity of reinscribing Pearl into the Greimasian model, the need to reassign the other characters to their proper places immediately becomes apparent.

Hester, to begin with, is clearly not intended as an example of the ideal possibility of the union of passion and principle. Arac himself concedes as much, but his axiomatic supposition that *The Scarlet Letter* is a work of symbolism forces him to become a champion of the romantic notion of Hester as Heroine almost in spite of himself: "We all construct this figure in our readings and then must confront Hawthorne's failure to actualize her in his text. [...] Only to the extent that the ideal Hester exists can Hawthorne be considered a fundamentally subversive writer; otherwise, we must value the hope he offers in his openness to our interpretive energies but must recognize his own limitations within a 'framework'."[3] In truth, of course, Hester's is an ideology of love, not of law, and the narrative consistently reminds us of this imbalance between passion and principle in her character. Nor is Chillingworth quite the monster Arac's consignment of him to the double negative position of neither passion nor principle would imply, though he is indeed the structural counterpart to Hester, as his is an ideology of law but not of love. The double negative position must be reserved for Dimmesdale, on the grounds that he is equally untrue to his lover and his congregation, thereby offending the ideology of love and that of law in equal measures. The ideal position, finally, belongs to the very character whom Arac leaves out: Pearl, "the scarlet letter endowed with life" (102). Only in her, Hawthorne would have us see, can the ideal of passion and principle be realized.

Arac's argument rests on the assumption that Hawthorne consciously elaborated his text in such a manner that it would evade final analysis, thereby confirming the autonomous status of art.[4] Such a reading seems to me duplicitous in that it makes out to reject a notion of Hawthorne's writings which derives from the New Critical movement of the forties and fifties, while it is in truth dependent on some such notion of Hawthorne as a symbolist or a promulgator of *l'art pour l'art* in order to make its case. The whole point of making a case for Hawthorne as a symbolist was to save the New Critics from the embarrassment that one of their canonized authors was, and always will remain, essentially an allegorist—and the standard critique of allegorical fiction is not that it lends itself to endless rereadings, but that it lends itself too readily to being reduced to a specific meaning. Needless to say, art for the allegorical artist can never be understood in isolation, allegory being essentially a relational concept, a means of conceptualizing a distance between an experience felt and an experience expressed, a distance, that is, between content and form. To insist that Hawthorne's writings are allegories, then, is to conceive of them as inviting us to explicate their truth by establishing their meaning.

I will attempt to demonstrate, in the present chapter, that the very basis of the conflict enacted in *The Scarlet Letter* can be reduced to an allegorical representation of the relation between the artist, the art of the artist, and society, hence circumventing the normative thrust of Arac's argument, yet avoiding the equally questionable course of insisting upon the openness of the text. In so doing I will be developing an argument launched by Joel Porte, in agreement with whom I hold that "in writing *The Scarlet Letter* [Hawthorne] was preoccupied generally with the very nature of his chosen fictional genre," and that it is much to the benefit of our understanding of the romance if we grant that Hester Prynne is a "type of the artist" and that Pearl may be looked upon as a virtual embodiment of the art of romance.[5]

Several times in the narrative, Hawthorne makes use of a notion of the scarlet letter which does not try to specify its purport, but which looks upon it, rather, as an agent, the function of which is to perform an office, to fulfil the role "as a messenger of anguish" (256). The romance may be read as an extended attempt to delineate what is required for a letter to fulfil such a role, as Bercovitch has convincingly argued in *The Office of The Scarlet Letter.* It seems to me, however, that Bercovitch misconstrues the nature of the office Hawthorne has designed his romance to fulfil. Bercovitch's argument turns on the authorial silence concerning Hester's return to Boston in the Conclusion, wherein she is seen to resume the letter "of her own free will" (263). By neglecting to explain why she returns, Bercovitch argues, Hawthorne "mystifies Hester's choice by forcing us to represent it through the act of interpretation" (*Office*, 92). Of the canonized authors of the American renaissance, Bercovitch admits, Hawthorne "was the most resistant" to the view of America as a symbol that "transformed radicalism itself into a mode of cultural cohesion and continuity" (*Jeremiad*, 205). Much is at stake, then, if Hawthorne too, despite his resisting tendencies, can be shown to have celebrated and represented "the same ideal of liberal community" (*Office*, 92) in his most famous work.

In an effort to reclaim *The Scarlet Letter* to the ranks of works bearing truly radical implications, several critics have attempted to refute Bercovitch's argument, but few, if any, have succeeded in doing so. In fact, it may well be that one of the greatest contributions of Bercovitch's book to our understanding of Hawthorne lies in its exposure of how difficult it is to tell radicalism from forces working for the perpetuation of social status quo. Paul K. Johnston, for instance, in a characteristic rebuttal, insists that at the end of the novel "Hester does affirm that in some future time such a new truth [as she envisions] will be revealed, that such a transformation will take place. A reader in 1850, or indeed in 1995, might reasonably think, in the framework Hawthorne has provided, that the future might well be now."[6] But this is precisely Bercovitch's point: *The Scarlet Letter*, in his view, represents contradiction as an ambiguity in the process of resolving itself. In other words, it is by transforming social tensions into epistemological ambiguities that Hawthorne's romance defuses revolutionary tendencies in the present and redirects our energies to a common future goal. In the process of doing so, we inevitably must consent to the prevailing norm which looks to America as a self-fulfilling prophecy of the New Jerusalem. To argue Hawthorne's radicalism by making a case for his progressive faith in the future is thus merely unwittingly to confirm Bercovitch's argument. But if that is the case, how can it be countered?

It is crucial that we observe the common ground that Bercovitch's argument shares with that of Arac: for both, the ideological closure that *The Scarlet Letter* achieves is an outcome of its symbolic structure, which—in their view—is paradoxically a means to evade closure by enforcing that the narrative remains open to endless reinterpretation. "Hawthorne's strategy of negation," as Bercovitch puts it, "posits a perpetual tension between means and ends—continually forces a gap between process and closure" (*Office*, 147). In arguing the necessity of reading Hawthorne allegorically, the present chapter attempts to demonstrate in what respect Bercovitch misrepresents the nature of the "gap" in Hawthorne. This gap, it seems to me, must be measured against the yardstick of Hawthorne's understanding of Christian faith. If we do so, we find that the gap between process and closure is not, for Hawthorne, as for the Puritans and their ideological descendants, a temporal gap, and hence—in theory if not in practice—bridgeable, but an absolute gap: death. Death is an absolute gap, because it is a gap between realms, not between moments in history. I will argue that Hawthorne invokes death as such an absolute gap, and that this entails that in contrast to "the social-symbolic outlook" Bercovitch sees him as a representative of, he does not conflate secular and sacred history. It is only in relation to this insight, it seems to me, that we can fully understand how Hester's prophetic vision that the romance makes room for before it ends is related to the office of art. *The Scarlet Letter* does indeed strive towards closure; but this closure is not, as Bercovitch holds, the openness of symbolism. Symbolism is merely one of two possibilities that Hawthorne's fictions always offer us, the other possibility being the allegorical closure which can be effected only if we prove willing to open an intercourse with the artist, and accept full responsibility for the meaning of the romance thus generated.

## 1. Through "The Custom-House"

As a preliminary to our main discussion in this chapter, it will be helpful to inquire as well into the office fulfilled by the sketch that opens *The Scarlet Letter*. "The Custom-House," appropriately enough, is a description of Hawthorne's experience in office, as Surveyor of the Salem Custom-House, a position he held between April 1846 and June 1849, when he was removed from the post, following election of Whig President, Zachary Taylor, in 1848. His "true reason for assuming a personal relation with the public," Hawthorne declares, is merely "a desire to put myself in my true position as editor, or very little more, of the most prolix among the tales that make up my volume" (4); critics, however, have wisely judged that if not exactly false, this declaration is highly loaded.[7] As many commentators have observed Hawthorne in "The Custom-House" is concerned with justifying his own chosen career as a "writer of story-books!" (10). In other words, he is anxious to define a space in his culture in which his occupation will not be sneered at but will be recognized as performing a vital task for the well-being of the community. *The Scarlet Letter* may be read as an allegorical rendition of the artist's plight.[8] In the very first sentence of "The Custom-House", the narrator points out that this is not the first time that he finds himself overtaken by "an autobiographical impulse;" as he goes on to inform us, when *Mosses from an Old Manse* had been published, it too had been prefaced by an autobiographical sketch.

In contrast to the later piece, "The Old Manse" does not depict days of drudgery and a concomitant spiritual decay, but a time of almost Arcadian blissfulness. According to its subtitle, the sketch is one in which "The Author Makes the Reader Acquainted with his Abode"—but as it turns out the Author can barely keep himself from getting out of doors: we are afforded long descriptions of the river, the battlefield, the orchard, and the garden in the vicinity of the Old Manse, and are taken on walks and fishing-excursions to such an extent that the Old Manse itself is almost forgotten. And yet we have been informed in the second paragraph of the sketch that in entering this abode the Author had entertained great hopes of a professional nature: "In the humblest event, I resolved at least to achieve a novel, that should evolve some deep lesson, and should possess physical substance enough to stand alone" (10: 5). But the three years of happiness spent at the Old Manse "hastened away with a noiseless flight," and the Author is left without the "treasure of intellectual gold" he had so much hoped to find: "No profound treatise of ethics—no philosophic history—no novel, even, that could stand, unsupported, on its edges. All that I had to show, as a man of letters, were these few tales and essays, which had blossomed out like flowers in the calm summer of my heart and mind" (10: 34).

In "The Custom-House," the situation is the reverse: while the Author informs us that life in the Custom-House had left his literary faculty "suspended and inanimate within me" (26), it is within the same Custom-House that the Scarlet Letter is found; "the story that points the way out of 'The Custom-House' is found within it," as Millington aptly notes (*Practicing*, 65)—although, as one should be careful to observe, in "the second story of the Custom-House" (28). The transition from the ground floor to this second story may perhaps be said to signify "Hawthorne's withdrawal from external reality into the private reality of his own mind," as Baym argues.[9] But more importantly, it bespeaks the existence of a private sphere in the seemingly public world of the Custom-House; that is, a sphere which is in principle open to any individual frequenting the public building. Furthermore, it implies that in any official account of the events of the world there is such a "second story" which is set off from the official story by its association with the private sphere of the individual. By taking us into the Custom-House, Hawthorne shows how the origin of the letter is tied to the public life of the community: the official sphere of the Custom-House is the origin of the Scarlet Letter both in the sense of an emblem of the individual's guilt (the scarlet letter as worn and embroidered by Hester), and as the romance in which Hawthorne thematizes this emblem. Yet it is found by the individual in the story of the Custom-House which the individual stalks out by his own accord, the story in which the individual may find the means to change his perception of the present by relating it to the past.

In fact, by the time we are led on to this second story, the narrator has already demonstrated in what way the inhabitants of the Custom-House may themselves be said to frequent such stories. The portraits of the inmates of the house suggest that there exists for each of them a more substantial reality in their personal past. The Inspector, the narrator informs us, still had "flavors on his palate, that had lingered there not less than sixty or seventy years, and were still apparently as fresh as that of the mutton-chop which he had just devoured for his breakfast" (19); and of the Collector, a retired General, it is stated, similarly, that: "It might be, that he lived a more real life within his thoughts, than amid the unappropriate environment of the Collector's office. The evolutions of the parade; the tumult of the battle; the flourish of old, heroic music, heard thirty years before;—such scenes and sounds, perhaps, were all alive before his intellectual sense" (23). For the Surveyor himself, who is an earlier embodiment of the narrator, the central experience is his recognition that "it lay at my own option to recall whatever was valuable in the past" (26), to acknowledge that "the past was not dead" (27). The only person apparently untouched by the past (and, presumably, for this very reason "thoroughly adapted to the situation which he held" [25]) is a man who has been "Bred up from boyhood in the Custom-House," who strikes the narrator as "the Custom-House in himself; or, at all events, the main spring that kept its variously revolving wheels in motion." Significantly, it is only to this embodiment of the Custom-House that "the many intricacies of business [...] presented themselves [...] with the regularity of a perfectly comprehended system" (24). What this serves to emphasize is that the relation to the past must be conceived as vital on the private level of the individual rather than on the official level of the community: while the system as such may dispense with the past, the individuals that make up the system cannot.

Ironically, then, the three years of happiness at the Old Manse produced nothing, while the three years of unhappiness in the Custom-

House produced *The Scarlet Letter*, which suggests that the artist, too, is dependent upon being imprisoned in order to find his or her "treasure of intellectual gold;" through being thus confined the artist comes to discover the importance of the past, and the necessity of recovering the past in order to restore hope in the future. To be truly happy, happiness must be denied; or rather, real—or should we say, material—happiness must be superseded by a spiritual happiness, a happiness which is not founded upon the presence of Actual happiness but upon the Hope of the possibility of a happiness to come. In a word, the Actual must be supplanted by the Imaginary. This is what the three years in the Custom-House teaches Hawthorne, and this, as we will see, is likewise what the scarlet letter teaches its wearer. Yet this lesson is brought home to the author, it is important to observe, only once he has been ousted from office. Thus figuratively decapitated, Hawthorne announces himself "a politically dead man," and asks that the whole of his volume "be considered as the POSTHUMOUS PAPERS OF A DECAPITATED SURVEYOR" (43). Death, in other words, is shown to be a prerequisite for restoring enough spiritual life to the author to enable him to write *The Scarlet Letter*. Having submitted this moral, "The Custom-House" has done its office, proleptically suggesting that of *The Scarlet Letter* as well.

## 2. The Paradoxical Structure of *The Scarlet Letter*

Like Hawthorne's other works, *The Scarlet Letter* is informed by what I have referred to in chapter one as a double moral standard. The clearest statement of this double standard in the book appears at the end of chapter 14, when Hester implores her husband to forgive her the ill-treatment he has suffered. Chillingworth, however, will hear nothing of it:

> "Peace, Hester, peace!" replied the old man, with gloomy sternness. "It is not granted me to pardon. I have no such power as thou tellest me of. My old faith, long forgotten, comes back to me, and explains all that we do, and all we suffer. By thy first step awry, thou didst plant the germ of evil; but, since that moment, it has all been a

> dark necessity. Ye that have wronged me are not sinful, save in a kind of typical illusion; neither am I fiend-like, who have snatched a fiend's office from his hands. It is our fate. Let the black flower blossom as it may!" (174)

Chillingworth, it would seem, is anxious to lift the burden of guilt from Hester yet at the same time situates the cause of guilt with her, as if blaming her without holding her personally responsible—or, less sympathetically put, as if delivering her from responsibility yet blaming her all the same. She and Dimmesdale "are not sinful, save in a kind of *typical illusion*," that is, emblematic illustration, yet "the germ of evil" is attributed to Hester's "first step awry."

If we are to consider to what extent Hester may or may not be blameworthy, then, it is imperative that we determine precisely what this "first step awry" consists in. But this is the very question the novel refuses to answer; or, rather, it gives two conflicting answers and refrains from privileging either one. Ostensibly, there may seem to be no ambiguity on this point: Hester's first step awry is the act of adultery she commits with Dimmesdale. Unquestionably, this would seem to be the implication of Chillingworth's statement. Hester herself, unsurprisingly, takes another view of the matter. Musing upon her former relation with her husband, it is made clear that she looks upon her consent to marry him as her first mistake: "She marvelled how she could ever have been wrought upon to marry him! She deemed it her crime most to be repented of, that she had ever endured, and reciprocated, the lukewarm grasp of his hand, and had suffered the smile of her lips and eyes to mingle and melt into his own" (176). These sentiments trigger a significant reaction from the narrator:

> Let men tremble to win the hand of woman, unless they win along with it the utmost passion of her heart! Else it may be their miserable fortune, as it was Roger Chillingworth's, when some mightier touch than their own may have awakened all her sensibilities, to be reproached even for the calm content, the marble image of happiness, which they will have imposed upon her as the warm reality. (176–77)

As this passage suggests, Hester's crime is a revolt against a role that the norms of society enforce upon the individual. The ideal of domesticity in nineteenth-century America, T. Walter Herbert points out, "proposed womanhood and manhood as complementary opposites," that were "conventionally regarded [...] as a law of nature and of nature's God, a matter of universal essences that were at once universal and ethereal."[10] To the essence of Woman, domesticity ascribed purity, a lack of sexual desire which was to function as "a psychic contraceptive."[11] To be a Woman then, becomes incompatible with entertaining sexual desire: the marble image imposed upon Hester "as the warm reality" is one that serves to exclude her awareness of "all her *sensibilities*,"—an obvious euphemism for the realm of passions in which the individual's sexual desire resides. Because this image is a "reality" *imposed upon* woman, it must inevitably shatter if her "sensibilities" are aroused, as Hester's have been. In short, Hester's discovery of a love in which sexual passion forms an integral part negates the concept of love propounded by the Puritan community, which—in keeping with the ideology of domesticity pervading the community of Hawthorne's own day and age—purges the concept of love from sexual desire.

Privately rejecting the norms of society, Hester nevertheless remains locked within the model of polar opposites which is their underlying philosophical foundation. Retaining society's dichotomization of love and guilt into an oppositional pair, Hester merely changes its emphasis. Her public announcement of "guilt," is privately interpreted as "love:"

> What she compelled herself to believe,—what, finally, she reasoned upon, as her motive for continuing a resident of New England,—was half a truth, and half a self-delusion. Here, she said to herself, had been the scene of her guilt, and here should be the scene of her earthly punishment; and so, perchance, the torture of her daily shame would at length purge her soul, and work out another purity than that which she had lost; more saint-like, because the result of martyrdom. (80)

Hester is, in her own eyes, a martyr, one who suffers innocently for her faith. She becomes in effect a mirror-image of society, an inverted reflection of its norms, in which public guilt is private love, and public love (marriage) conversely private guilt, "her crime most to be repented of" (176). Hester recognizes that she has broken the norms of society, but as Chillingworth's claim on her seems inextricably entwined with those norms, she is able to formulate her mistreatment of her husband as a justified revolt against an unjust regime: "He betrayed me! He has done me worse wrong than I did him!" (176). This is an attitude the very opposite of Chillingworth's: Hester situates the "germ of evil" in the constricting norms of society, while her husband attributes the planting of this germ to the individual. This contradiction is fully in accordance with the double standard of moral reasoning at work throughout Hawthorne's writings: the cause of the individual's guilt is "the fault of a system;" yet the "origin of the evil" lies "in the character" (5: 33) of the same individual. It is the office of *The Scarlet Letter* to make us understand this paradox.

It is worth recalling in this context that the description of the circumstances under which Surveyor Pue's original manuscript documenting the story of Hester Prynne are found serves to emphasize that Hester is in many ways the character of the story who forms the closest parallel to Hawthorne himself. As Baym puts it, within "this romance, *The Scarlet Letter* figures both as an autobiographical event and as an example of Hawthorne's art. The scarlet letter that Hawthorne puts to his breast symbolizes that romance and stands to Hawthorne in the same relation that the letter A, in the romance, stands to Hester."[12] This does not allow us to say, as Baym does, that the description which accompanies the scene in which the manuscript is found "creates an image of Hester as an unambiguous heroine;"[13] Hawthorne's view of his own profession is far more complicated than that. And even though this scene makes perfectly clear that the story of *The Scarlet Letter* concerns "the life and conversation of one Hester Prynne" (32), this does not allow us to look upon her as the principal protagonist of the novel. There can be little doubt, however, that she is an allegorical representation of the artist, as we are informed that the letter is "a specimen of her delicate and imaginative skill," and that Hester "possessed an art that sufficed, even in a land that afforded comparatively little scope for its exercise, to supply food for her thriving infant and herself" (81). Hester may very well be the most memorable character of Hawthorne's fictions, but *The Scarlet Letter* like the other romances is concerned less with individual characters than with the structural relations of these characters. Despite the parallels between Hester and Hawthorne, we do well to repeat that Hester is a figure of the artist, not of the author: Hawthorne's writings leave little doubt that the former is a type which the author is anxious to disassociate himself from—all the more so, perhaps, because he perceives and exploits the correspondences between that type and himself.

Equally important, the artist figure tends to become for Hawthorne a metaphor for the individual in general, which partly explains, I think, why it is so much easier to feel sympathy for Hester than for Dimmesdale, as is attested to by the shift in critical emphasis from Dimmesdale to Hester that has taken place during the last four decades. To many of the critics of the fifties, Dimmesdale is the true protagonist of the narrative. From the early seventies onwards, however, Dimmesdale's character has been so radically reassessed that in some recent readings he seems more of an antagonist to Hester than her beloved.[14] This tendency bespeaks how critics are prone to overlook Dimmesdale's allegorical function, and the extent to which they tend as a result to reduce the conflict at hand to a collision of the private moralities of two individuals, Hester and Dimmesdale.[15] Yet while Dimmesdale is certainly an individual, he is also in his capacity of minister a representative of the legislative authorities of the Puritan society, a role he entertains throughout the romance. This makes him doubly responsible for the letter worn by Hester as an emblem of guilt: not only has he generated that other "token of her shame" (52)—Pearl—with Hester, he is also seen to preside with the authorities who have sentenced her to wear the letter as an emblem of her guilt in the first scene. Dimmesdale, then, as a private individual is the father of Pearl, while as a public representative of society he is a father of the letter, a circumstance that bespeaks his a-moral position within the structural configuration we have appropriated from Arac: publicly he disowns his private fatherhood, while privately he refuses to acknowledge the significance of the letter fastened upon Hester's breast that he has publicly fathered. Yet the question that the reader must ultimately provide an answer to is not whether the letter is more appropriately assigned to Hester or to Dimmesdale. We are challenged, rather, to understand how the transference of the letter from the one to the other and back again, invites us to become, as it were, participants of the drama enacted. The structure of *The Scarlet Letter* suggests that the movement of the narrative is one way in which the romance outlines the conditions of this dialectical process of transference, which it is the office of art to perform.

Critics have long admired the symmetrical conception of *The Scarlet Letter*, in which the development of the plot is given artistic form by progressing through the three scaffold-scenes. The first critic systematically to pursue the formal aspects of Hawthorne's writings was Leland Schubert, who perceives in *The Scarlet Letter* "a structural pattern of seven parts:" the chapters between the scaffold-scenes, located at the beginning (chapters 1–3; section A1), the middle (chapter 12; A2), and the end (chapters 21–3; A3) of the book, may themselves be divided into groups of five and three chapters each, consisting respectively of chapters 4–8 (B1) and 16–20 (B2), and 9–11 (C1) and 13–15 (C2).[16] This seven-phase division relies on the perception of a fairly general correspondence between the structural units identified. Of these the internal relation between the opening, the central and the closing scenes is so obvious that it does not require any additional comments at this stage: it has never been questioned. While neither the criteria for setting the other units (B1, C1, B2, and C2) apart nor the internal relations between these units are quite as transparent, it is still, I believe, quite accessible. The five chapters of unit B1 all concern Hester (and Pearl), especially her relation to the community. Hester is equally prominent in the five chapters of unit B2, with the marked difference that the narrative in this section focuses on her relation to Dimmesdale. In both units, the final chapter involves a change of focus—partial in the first instance, complete in the second—from Hester to Dimmesdale, a change indicated in the chapter-titles as well, in both of which "the Minister" is mentioned. In unit C1, Chillingworth and Dimmesdale are in focus. More specifically, the three chapters focus in turn upon Dimmesdale's relation to the community, to Chillingworth, and finally to his own guilt. This pattern is repeated in unit C2, though this time the focus is upon Hester: the chapters focus in turn upon Hester's relation to the community, to Chillingworth, and finally to Pearl, who, of course, embodies Hester's guilt.[17]

Following Schubert's lead we may look upon *The Scarlet Letter* as falling into two halves, divided by Dimmesdale's nightly ascension of the scaffold described in chapter 12. In both, the first section (A1 and C2) focuses on Hester, while in the second (B1 and B2) there is a shift in emphasis from Hester to Dimmesdale, to the effect that the third (C1 and A3) is clearly perceived as focusing upon the latter. This effect, it is well to observe, is achieved not by placing Dimmesdale at the centre of each chapter of the third section, but by having it subtly repeating the structural movement of the larger segment of which it is a part. Thus the focus in section C1 is first upon Chillingworth (chapter 9), then upon Chillingworth and Dimmesdale (chapter 10), and, finally, upon Dimmesdale himself in chapter 11; in section A3, similarly, the focus moves from Hester (chapter 21), to Hester and Dimmesdale (chapter 22), settling finally upon the minister in chapter 23, the last chapter of the unit. This repetition corresponds to a large-scale replication, as the scaffold-scenes themselves follow the same pattern: in the first Hester is seen to mount the scaffold, in the second she and Dimmesdale mount it together, and while this joint ascension is repeated in the third scene, it is nevertheless Dimmesdale who is seen finally to appropriate our attention.

The structure of *The Scarlet Letter* can thus be said to amount to a chiastic pattern, summarized in the following table:

| (D1) | (D2) |
|---|---|
| The Custom-House; Surveyor Pue's manuscript. | 24. Conclusion; Surveyor Pue's manuscript. |
| **A1** | **A3** |
| 1. The Market-Place; focus on Puritan community. | 21. The Market-Place; focus on Puritan community. |
| 2. Hester is focus of public attention. | 22. Dimmesdale is focus of public attention. |
| 3. Dimmesdale asks Hester to reveal the father of Pearl. | 23. Dimmesdale reveals that he is father of Pearl. |
| **B1** | **B2** |
| 4. Hester promises Chillingworth to keep his secret (154). | 16. Hester is "constant in her resolve" (124) to break promise to Chillingworth. |
| 5. Hester dreams of being reunited with Dimmesdale "before the bar of final judgement" (80). | 17. Hester reunited with Dimmesdale in forest. |
| 6. Pearl (the fruit of Hester's and Dimmesdale's love). | 18. Hester's and Dimmesdale's renewed moment of love. |
| 7. Pearl points to the scarlet letter mirrored in breastplate. | 19. Pearl points to disappearance of the scarlet letter, and her gesture is reflected in brook. |
| 8. Mistress Hibbins approaches Hester. | 20. Mistress Hibbins approaches Dimmesdale. |
| **C1** | **C2** |
| 9. Dimmesdale's relation to the community. | 13. Hester's relation to the community. |
| 10. Dimmesdale's relation to Chillingworth. | 14. Hester's relation to Chillingworth. |
| 11. Dimmesdale's relation to his own guilt. | 15. Hester's relation to Pearl (Hester's guilt). |

A2

12. Pearl asks Dimmesdale to stand on the scaffold in public with her and Hester.

Thus the movement of the novel is one that goes *from* Hester *to* Dimmesdale: this is how the plot repeatedly foregrounds the characters, even though the narrative finally returns to Hester in the Conclusion. This is not to say that Dimmesdale, rather than Hester, is the true protagonist of the romance.[18] On the contrary, to make this movement an issue of such a debate is to lose sight of the much more interesting possibility that the movement itself may very well be the central point the romance is making. The structure of the narrative, which the links or correspondences that I have delineated above allow us to establish, implies that the same thing happens twice, but in reverse order, and with reversed results. I will argue below that the movement inherent in this structure is suggestive of a complex system of transference which is seen to be vital for the subsistence of individual and society alike.[19]

## 3. The Allegorical Chain

Already in the first half of the narrative both Hester and Dimmesdale confess to their sin, yet in different manners, Dimmesdale speaking it from the pulpit, Hester showing it on her breast. In both cases, moreover, the confession takes a form which allows the sinner to transform it into a strategy for suppressing the truth. Hester, publicly guilty, in private remains unrepentant; Dimmesdale, officially stainless, is privately plagued by an awareness of his falseness. In short, both confess by the letter; but for the letter to fulfil its office it must be made to communicate the spirit as well. The plot, built on reversal, thus turns on the concealment of the secret of Dimmesdale's complicity in Hester's sin, progressing towards its disclosure. The case is complicated by the circumstance that the secret in question is a secret of the heart: not only have Hester and Dimmesdale sinned, they are, perhaps unconsciously, hoping to do it again. Hence the truth is, if not ineffable, then at least impossible to put directly into words, for neither Hester nor Dimmesdale is fully aware of the ramifications of the secret they are concealing. The truth of the romance, likewise, is a truth that needs to be experienced to be fully revealed. The meaning of the romance, then, is not one that can be condensed into a statement, but must be seen as the product of the interplay of the various sections of the narrative.

In this sense it is certainly true, as Waggoner puts it, that the philosophical content of Hawthorne's writings is best described as a form of "*thinking in terms of image and situation, character and action*" (*Study*, 73; emphasis in the original). One way of understanding this statement would be to say that Hawthorne discovers meaning as he goes along, in the process of writing. There is probably some truth in this, yet the careful revision that each romance seems to have undergone before he submitted it for publication must make us careful not to underestimate the conscious effort that lies behind the finished result as we know it.[20] Another, and probably better, way of expounding Waggoner's suggestion is to say that meaning, for Hawthorne, is always relational: it is something that can be grasped only by perceiving how a multitude of different ideas converge and are related to each other. What Hawthorne said of his method in the Preface to *The House of the Seven Gables* is equally valid for each of the romances:

> When romances do really teach anything, or produce any effective operation, it is usually through a far more subtile process than the ostensible one. The Author has considered it hardly worth his while, therefore, relentlessly to impale the story with its moral, as with an iron rod—or rather, as by sticking a pin through a butterfly—thus at once depriving it of life, and causing it to stiffen in an ungainly and unnatural attitude. A high truth, indeed, fairly, finely, and skilfully wrought out, brightening at every step, and crowning the final development of a work of fiction, may add an artistic glory, but is never any truer, and seldom any more evident, at the last page than at the first. (2–3)

It is this conviction, more than anything else, that lies behind the way Hawthorne handles the principal symbol of *The Scarlet Letter*, which made Henry James complain that the symbolism of the book "is overdone at times, and becomes mechanical; it ceases to be impressive, and grazes triviality."[21] If Hawthorne overelaborates, as James suggests, it is because he is concerned to establish a system of meanings, joining images and scenes together by refracting them onto the central symbol. This makes of the scarlet letter a highly complex image, but not necessarily an ambiguous one: we are asked to see how the Scarlet Letter (the symbol as well as the romance which it represents) is capable of holding a multiplicity of significances which nevertheless are suggestive of one all-embracing meaning, much as was the Bible in the hermeneutical fourfold scheme.

To see this practice in action, consider the moment when Pearl approaches her mother, who, in the presence of Dimmesdale, has just rid herself of the letter. The child, Hawthorne explains, "had been offered to the world, these seven years past, as the living hieroglyphic, in which was revealed the secret they so darkly sought to hide,—all written in this symbol,—all plainly manifest,—had there been a prophet or magician skilled to read the character of flame!" (206–7). The "character of flame," of course, is a pun on the scarlet letter, the "scorching property" of which James felt Hawthorne had made "too much" of.[22] As to make sure that this point does not escape us, we have been informed at an earlier point of the narrative that Hester has dressed up her Pearl in such a fashion as to "create an analogy between the object of her affection and the emblem of her guilt and torture." In the romance itself, this "analogy" is strengthened into identity: "It was the scarlet letter in another form; the scarlet letter endowed with life!" The pun, likewise, hardens into identity, for Pearl is not only the letter, but also "the very brightest little jet of flame" (102).

The significance of these elaborations become evident if seen in connection with what Male pronounced the "guiding metaphor" (*Tragic*, 100) of the book, "the Tongue of Flame" (142).[23] As Male points out, Hawthorne derives this metaphor from Acts 2: 3–4: "And there appeared unto them cloven tongues like as of fire, and it sat upon each of them. And they were all filled with the Holy Ghost, and began to speak with other tongues, as the Spirit gave them utterance." Hawthorne alludes to this passage when discussing the fame Dimmesdale has won "in his sacred office" (141). Many other clergymen, Hawthorne explains, exceed the Pastor in erudition and saintliness, but they lack

> the gift that descended upon the chosen disciples, at Pentecost, in tongues of flame; symbolizing, it would seem, not the power of speech in foreign and unknown languages, but that of addressing the whole human brotherhood in the heart's native language. These fathers, otherwise so apostolic, lacked Heaven's last and rarest attestation of their office, the Tongue of Flame. (141–42)

This last attestation, we infer, is precisely what Dimmesdale has "won [...] by his sorrows" (141). Again, this underscores the similarity between his situation and that of Hester, for she, too, has acquired "a sympathetic knowledge of the hidden sin in other hearts" (86). Yet neither to Dimmesdale nor Hester does this almost "preternatural" "power of experiencing and communicating emotions" (141) bring a sense of relief amid their feelings of anguish.

Thus both Hester and Dimmesdale, in their own ways, have an ability to speak the language of the heart with tongues of flame. It is doubtful, however, that they fully understand what they are saying, since they are unable, as we have seen, to *read* "the character of flame." Dimmesdale most certainly does not, for in the central chapter, Pearl—who is, I repeat, the character of flame embodied—offers to inform him of the identity of Chillingworth, but her words leave him in confusion, since she has spoken "in a tongue unknown to the erudite clergyman" (156). Hester, we may feel, has a deeper understanding of the language of the heart, than has the minister. Yet even though Hester wears the scarlet letter throughout the romance it is not her understanding of the letter as a symbolic purveyor of the emotions of the individual that finally wins out. Instead, Dimmesdale's revelation of a letter written in flesh outpowers the suggestiveness of that worn by Hester, by reducing her letter to the mere emblem of that which is displayed upon his own chest, unambiguously signifying guilt.

The scene which effects the reversal of positions between Hester and Dimmesdale which culminates in chapter 23, is made up by what is quite literally the central chapter of the story, chapter 12. The chapter is set apart from the rest of the novel by its very tone, the dense, almost phantasmic texture of which is given further emphasis through the frequent underscoring of the dreamlike character of the whole scene. Openly signalled in its very first sentence which declares that Dimmesdale walks to the scaffold "in the shadow of a dream" (147), it is made explicit again on page 149, and once more towards the end of the chapter where Dimmesdale leaves the scene in custody of Chillingworth "like one awaking, all nerveless, from an ugly dream" (157).

The scene is a dream partly because it is an extravaganza of wish-fulfilment on the part of the minister: Dimmesdale, Hester and Pearl holding hands to form "an electric chain" (153); the meteoric letter lighting up the sky "to give another moral interpretation to the things of this world than they had ever borne before. [...] as if it were the light that is to reveal all secrets, and the daybreak that shall unite all who belong to one another" (154). The narrator, it is true, would seem to question the reality of this dream by aligning Dimmesdale's perception of "the appearance of an immense letter" (155) in the sky, with the reports of meteoric sightings as supernatural events, the credibility of which "rested on the faith of some lonely eyewitness, who beheld the wonder through the colored, magnifying, and distorting medium of his imagination, and shaped it more distinctly in his after-thought" (155). Yet this is exactly the kind of distortion of reality and reflection after the fact that Hawthorne in his capacity of narrator of "The Custom-House" has made clear is necessary in order to bring out the "deeper import" of the "page of life;" although declaring himself unable to transcribe that "better book" of "the reality of the flitting hour," the author points out that it may be possible at a future date to "*remember* a few scattered fragments and broken paragraphs, and write them down, and find the letters turn to gold upon the page" (37; my emphasis). For reality to be truthfully represented, it *requires* to be distorted by the medium of imagination. Chapter 12 in its entirety makes up such a distortion, and for this very reason holds the centre position of the romance.

While immediately ineffectual, Dimmesdale's mounting of the scaffold in the light of the Romance proves vital in that it is through this act that Hester comes to see the extent to which she has wronged him by attempting to reserve the letter as her own personal property. In fact, this chapter performs a function within the romance parallel to that which Hawthorne would seem to have hoped that the Romance would be capable of performing within society: although apparently of little or no value it does in fact make up a cathartic space which enables both Hester and Dimmesdale to change their understanding of their relation to society.

We learn in the very next chapter that Hester's "whole soul was moved by the shuddering terror with which [Dimmesdale] had appealed to her,—the outcast woman,—for support against his instinctively discovered enemy" (159); as a direct result of this appeal Hester resolves to break her promise given to Chillingworth, finally doing so in the forest scene. From this point onwards, Hester is no longer capable of using the letter for her own ends, as she was seen to do in the first half. This change in Hester's relation to the letter is bespoken by the title of chapter 13, "Another View of Hester," wherein her inability to retain control of the letter is signalled by the fact that the original signification attached to the letter is seen to give way to the view amid groups of the society that the letter stands for "Able" (161). This is one of the circumstances usually heralded as a sign of Hester's capability of effecting a small but nevertheless important change in the community she belongs to.[24] One must observe, however, that this reinterpretation of the letter is the very opposite of what Hester desires. Hester clearly wants to remain an outcast: when she is accosted, "she laid her finger on the scarlet letter, and passed on." But her command of the letter is no longer what it was in the first half of the book, and consequently "society was inclined to show its former victim a more benign countenance *than she cared to be favored with*, or, perchance, than she deserved" (162; my emphasis).

*

While Hester is depicted as being true to her letter for the greater part of the novel, she is false to almost everyone else; functionally, as we have said, her position is that of love and not law. By failing to inform Dimmesdale of Chillingworth's identity, she is indirectly responsible for aggravating the minister's sufferings. More seriously still, in withholding the identity of her lover from Chillingworth and the authorities—ostensibly a magnanimous act—she effectively robs Pearl of a father. In the end it becomes apparent that such insincerity threatens to make her false to the one thing that is dearer to her than Dimmesdale: Pearl. The paradox of Hester's situation is thus revealed to us by one of those reversals so characteristic of the romance: it is precisely by staying true to the letter of her spirit (which dictates that love extinguishes guilt), that she is false to the spirit of the letter. For the spirit of the letter insists that love and guilt are identical, that the contradiction between the individual's private emotional interpretation of the letter and its public communal significance must not be negated, but accepted as an existential condition of life. If we can remain sympathetic to Hester despite the narrative's exposure of her inability to grasp the spirit of the letter, this is because the romance does not fault her for it. On the contrary, the whole point of its plot is to demonstrate the necessity of Dimmesdale rectifying her partial understanding of the letter, by revealing that he is the father of Pearl in such a way that its spirit is made manifest.

Throughout *The Scarlet Letter* Dimmesdale's actions, as a number of critics have stressed, are contingent upon a concern for himself rather than for his worldly family (Hester and Pearl).[25] But the only way he can escape the torments of his own soul is to accept responsibility for the letter worn by Hester, by turning her guilt into his. This act of accepting responsibility is equivalent to displacing the guilt of Hester in the eyes of the community, and by so doing, Dimmesdale simultaneously, if inadvertently, displaces Hester's understanding of the letter. In revealing that he is the father of Pearl, he also reduces her signifier into a rather flat signified: Arthur—this was what her mysterious letter told of all the time. As one critic points out, "it is a convenient coincidence that the 'A' she wears is the initial of her lover's first name."[26] Her passion, then, has not, after all, been all that different from that of the other members of the Boston community: the congregation as a whole idolizes Dimmesdale. What is specific about Hester's experience is that in contrast to the rest of the community's members, she has been forced to find the means to wed her perception of what is holy to her perception of what is sinful; just like Rappaccini, Hester has been forced to create an alloy of light and dark, good and evil.

Yet despite being founded upon what may be termed an allegorical experience of the doubleness of human existence, Hester's "writing" of the letter, in contrast to the literary practice of Hawthorne himself, is an exercise in symbolical rather than allegorical art. Whereas the doubleness of Beatrice is brought out by Hawthorne/Rappaccini with the ultimate aim of allaying the imperfection of the world by marrying the public appearance of imperfection (poison) to a private recognition of perfection, Hester's insistence on the doubleness of the letter is an attempt to keep the private and public meanings of the letter strictly separated from each other. By investing the letter with her own emotions, Hester is able to wrestle the interpretive authority from that of the community and make the letter speak of a signified over and above that which the Puritan authorities intended it to convey. This is the prerogative of the artist, so to speak; the emotional power Hawthorne invests in the figure of Hester no doubt bespeaks the extent to which he can identify with her situation. Yet her attitude through the bulk of the book—until the very last chapter, in fact—is one which he is careful to extricate himself from. What Hawthorne seeks to do is not to subsume an allegorical mode of thinking under a symbolistic one, but rather to envision a way in which symbolism can be adjusted to allegory, without the one form having to give in entirely to the other. Like the romantics, Hawthorne recognizes the need to acknowledge the passionate response of the individual to the surrounding world; unlike a Blake or a Shelley, however, he is unwilling to grant pre-eminence to the feelings of the individual at the cost of the norms of society.

The point of Hawthorne's undertaking, in short, is to envision, and ideally, to make available, the means whereby the community may make room for both passion and principle, love and law. Hester's dilemma is a parallel to the larger question of whether the individual or society is to be granted interpretive pre-eminence; in fact, the struggle for pre-eminence between symbol and allegory that takes place in the history of literature in the romantic period is itself a symptom of this question. This might sound like an abstruse phrasing of her situation, depicted with such admirable concreteness in the romance itself. Yet it seems to me necessary in order to bring out the universality of Hester's plight: as a consequence of society's foundation in language, one can resist playing an unwonted part in it only by investing the signs informed with a public significance with a private ditto, making them speak with a symbolic vocabulary that evades the censuring strictures of its authorities. Within the sphere of such a symbolic language the individual is free to express herself. As the narrative of *The Scarlet Letter* makes clear, however, this freedom is in truth merely another prison, since it is won by curtailing one's ability to communicate with the rest of society: it is a freedom which consists in locking oneself up in one's own emotions, in a house of passions, where meanings are gloriously and immediately available, but also despondently ineffable.

Thus the letter is used as a protective shield of sorts in the first scaffold-scene, when Hester displays her luxuriously embroidered letter before the Boston community, which has "the effect of a spell, taking her out of the ordinary relations with humanity, and inclosing her in a sphere by herself" (54). The rest of the romance depicts the reintegration of Hester, the artist, into society, which it is the office of art to perform. But it also makes clear that this reintegration is something that Hester resists, something that she tries her best to escape. To maintain her subversive force, her embroidery of the letter must remain inconsistent with the received notion of what her letter stands for in the Puritan community. If the radical discrepancy between image and word (between her letter and her character) which this embroidery is expressive of would be negated, the radical dichotomization of the world into private and public which sustains her would also be annulled. For Hester, to accept the community's interpretation of her letter would entail becoming reduced to a symbol within an allegorical structure in its own right: "she would become the general symbol at which the preacher and moralist might point, and in which they might vivify and embody their images of woman's frailty and sinful passion" (79). By questioning the allegorical significance the community attaches to her letter, Hester is able to resist this epistemological reification, but the price is her expulsion from the realm of allegorical signifieds altogether. Her option at the outset, then, is that of accepting an already designated place in a larger whole, or simply evading this larger whole altogether.

This is why Hester's situation is aggravated rather than relieved in the latter half of the novel, when the people of the community begin to accommodate an interpretation of the signified of her letter—reading it as "Able" (161)—which allows the gap between symbolical image and allegorical word to close: it is the other significance of the letter, its ability to connote something which goes beyond any significance that can be accommodated by the norms of the community, that prevents Hester from becoming a moral statue, a mere image of the community's moral norm. When the norm is sufficiently displaced to be able to pacify the apparent contradiction between the ignominious signified of her letter and the luxurious signifier expressing it, the foundation of her creative vitality is in peril, entailing that her aspect takes on a "marble quietude," her face becoming "like a mask; or rather, like the frozen calmness of a dead woman's features" (226).

Like Dimmesdale before her, Hester comes to experience the pain rather than the relief that being unable to make the community distinguish between appearance and being may involve. The community's tendency "to look upon the scarlet letter as the token, not of that one sin, for which she had borne so long and dreary a penance, but of her many good deeds since" (162) thus is a sign not of Hester's reformative powers, but of her having become, belatedly, the slave of the letter. While this leads to "a kind of sacredness" (163) being attributed to her, it also exacts the price of taking on the aspect of "marble coldness" (164), of seeing one's private character subjugated under a public image: "there seemed to be no longer any thing in Hester's face for Love to dwell upon; nothing in Hester's form, though majestic and statue-like, that

Passion would ever dream of clasping in its embrace; nothing in Hester's bosom, to make it ever again the pillow of Affection" (163).

Finding herself unable to insist upon the letter's dual function as an emblem both of her "happiness" and her "torture, none the less" (113) (as she states her case before the authorities in chapter 8), Hester also begins to realize the extent to which she has wronged not only Dimmesdale but Chillingworth too. Seeking out her husband, Hester cannot avoid acknowledging her share in his transformation "into a devil:" "The scarlet letter burned on Hester Prynne's bosom. Here was another ruin, the responsibility of which came partly home to her" (170). That she proceeds to question his right to seek vengeance upon Dimmesdale, nonetheless underscores that Hester has "climbed her way [...] to a higher point" since the beginning of the story, whereas her husband has "brought himself nearer to her level, or perhaps below it, by the revenge which he had stooped for" (167). As this circumstance certainly indicates, Hester's ability to influence the ways of the community is gradually increasing. But as a consequence of this increasing social influence, Hester has to face her decreasing ability to insist upon the radically double nature of the letter. That is, the symbolical aspect of the letter under which it has become an image of her private emotions, is gradually giving in to the weight of its allegorical aspect, under which its significance is determined by the community rather than by herself.[27]

Concurrently with this shift from the letter as symbol to the letter as allegory, there is a change in the functional offices performed by Chillingworth and Pearl respectively in relation to Hester. Whereas in the first half of the book it is the former who plagues her with his inquiries into the significance of the letter, in the second half her daughter performs this inquisitive role. Again and again in the latter half of the narrative, Pearl asks Hester to specify the meaning of the letter, until Hester finally is provoked to tell a lie, just to silence her daughter. This, the narrator makes clear, is a matter of some importance: "In all the seven bygone years, Hester Prynne had never before been false to the symbol on her bosom" (181). Yet she lies to no avail, as Pearl keeps on pestering her with questions, until Hester is desperate to make her stop: "'Hold thy tongue, naughty child!' answered her mother, with an asperity that she had never permitted to herself before. 'Do not tease me; else I shall shut thee into the dark closet!'" (181).

This desperate attempt of Hester to retain her ability to communicate her understanding of life through the letter is given an equally violent expression in the ensuing forest scene, in which Hester finally reveals to Dimmesdale that Chillingworth is her husband. When Dimmesdale at first refuses to forgive Hester for not having told him this before, she half appeals, half commands him to give in to her will, much as she was seen to do in chapter 8 at the threat of having Pearl taken away from her by the authorities of the community: "Look thou to it!" she then demanded of Dimmesdale. "I will not lose the child! Look to it!" (113). Now she repeats this imperative stance:

> "Thou shalt forgive me!" cried Hester, flinging herself on the fallen leaves beside him. "Let God punish! Thou shalt forgive!"
>
> With sudden and desperate tenderness, she threw her arms around him, and pressed his head against her bosom; little caring though his cheek rested on the scarlet letter. He would have released himself, but strove in vain to do so. Hester would not set him free, lest he should look her sternly in the face. (194)

Again her appeal takes the imperative form; again the road to Dimmesdale's submission goes via the letter. Only this time, it has grown apparent that Hester must revert to violent means in order to force Dimmesdale into compliance with her understanding of the letter as a mark of love rather than a mark of guilt. Hester would have the letter stand for Affection rather than Adultery, but as these scenes make evident, the letter no longer is capable of transferring her private understanding of it to her loved ones in unadulterated form: her brand of Affection has become something she must impose upon Dimmesdale and Pearl alike, much as the "marble image" of love was originally imposed upon her by Chillingworth.

Such is the position she entertains when she unclasps the letter in the forest scene:

> The stigma gone, Hester heaved a long, deep sigh, in which the burden of shame and anguish departed from her spirit. O exquisite relief! She had not known the weight, until she felt the freedom! By another impulse, she took off the formal cap that confined her hair; and down it fell upon her shoulders, dark and rich, with at once a shadow and a light in its abundance, and imparting the charm of softness to her features. There played around her mouth, and beamed out of her eyes, a radiant and tender smile, that seemed gushing from the very heart of womanhood. A crim-

> son flush was glowing on her cheek, that had been long so pale. Her sex, her youth, and the whole richness of her beauty, came back from what men call the irrevocable past, and clustered themselves, with her maiden hope, and a happiness before unknown, within the magic circle of this hour. (202)

What is portrayed in this scene is the dream of the individual being free to be at one with her own passions, to be free to affirm herself as a sexual creature. The fact that this momentary fulfilment of the dream takes place in the forest, outside the confines of society, suggests that this desire to affirm sexuality coincides with the dream of the artist to reject the crippling norms of society and follow a path of her own. To find a sphere of freedom in the realm of one's sexual passions one must reject the stigmatization of extramarital sexuality performed by society. In *The Scarlet Letter*, this stigmatization is expressed in the form of an axiomatic proposition concerning signifier and signified: A = Adultery. Signifiers always point to their conceptual referents: this is the principal tenet of allegorical interpretation, and it is this principle that is threatened when Hester has the audacity to give her letter the sheen of glory. For while she is unable to cancel the ostentatious principle as such, the "gorgeous luxuriance of fancy" (53) which she invests in the signifier is enough to subvert the transparency of the allegorical formula. "A" still stands for Adultery, but "Adultery" all of a sudden is no longer a transparent concept. As long as Hester wears the letter she entertains a kind of middle position, halfway between the allegorical constrictions of society and the symbolic freedom of the individual. In other words, while being the means whereby she makes manifest her departure from the norms of society, the letter is nevertheless at the same time her principal bond to this society.

Casting off the letter thus is an act equivalent to denying or even cutting off this bond, as it is precisely by delimiting the individual's symbolistic capacities within an allegorical framework of transparent signifiers that society is built. Passion, Puritan society stipulates, is sinful unless exercised within the confines of Marriage, wherein it no longer connotes "sin" but "love." Within this society, then, Love does not translate into Passion or Sexuality, but into Marriage. It may be worth remembering in this context, that sexuality itself was not seen as sinful by the Puritans or their descendants; Adam and Eve, as we recall, do enjoy sex before the

Fall in Milton's paradise. It is against what is added to sexuality in post-lapsarian existence that Puritanism—like Christianity in general—enforces strictures: desire. Since desire betokens the recognition of a lack within oneself, the censure of desire is not difficult to explain; its presence makes for the potential upheaval of the allegorical view of language according to which words are transparent signifiers that automatically enable us to see through to their signifieds: Erotic Love = Marriage = Woman and Man = Man and Church = Church and God. If erotic love must not necessarily entail Marriage, as the introduction of desire into this chain of signifieds suggests, the transparency of the chain can no longer be taken for granted. In this petrified version of an allegorical conception of language one is always supposed to be able to move from one signifier to another, and, regardless of where one started, end up at the same ultimate point of assurance, signified, of course, by the presence of God.

Much, then, is at stake in Hester's artistic endeavour to represent her own feelings, her own private truth, in the very letter she has been sentenced to wear as a punishment for having transgressed Puritan law: the assurance of the presence of God, that is, of some power capable of guaranteeing the meaningfulness of language and hence of existence. On a collective level of society, the loss of such a power cannot be compensated for, no matter how great is the private gain of the individual. Hawthorne realizes as much, and accordingly censures the "freedom of speculation" (164) that Hester assumes after having worn the letter for seven years, and refuses to allow her to fulfil the ideal logical possibility of passion and principle that some critics fault him for.[28]

The narrative implicitly reveals as much when Hester unclasps the letter in her explicit attempt to undo the past: her claim to "undo it all" (202) by discarding the scarlet letter which she has worn as a symbol of her emotions, betrays that she has found out that it is no longer in her power to maintain the radical dichotomization of private and public which has sustained her through her seven years of ignominy, but which has also prevented the letter from doing its office, an office that must embrace at once the communal and the private spheres of life. Because even if Hester publicly concedes the ambiguous nature of her daughter ("She is my happiness!—she is my torture, none the less!" [113]), the narrative leaves little doubt that she secretly pretends that Pearl would lose this unsettling ambiguity once her parents are reunited. Hester believes, in other words, that Pearl could be transformed into an unambiguous emblem of love from the vantage point of her parents' romance. This is the symbolical (that is, partial) office that Hester as a figure of the artist would seem to hope that the letter would fulfil.

And it is as a symbol of such unadulterated Affection that Hester, having discarded the letter and let down her hair, hopes to present the child to its father: "Thou must know Pearl!" (203). Once again, however, the imperative form of her statement contradicts the image of Affection it is intended to convey. And Pearl herself violently resists her mother's attempt to separate private love from public guilt by discarding the letter:

> [...] Pearl, not a whit startled at her mother's threats, any more than mollified by her entreaties, now suddenly burst into a fit of passion, gesticulating violently, and throwing her small figure into the most extravagant contortions. [...] Seen in the brook, once more, was the shadowy wrath of Pearl's image, crowned and girdled with flowers, but stamping its foot, wildly gesticulating, and, in the midst of all, still pointing its small forefinger at Hester's bosom! (209–10)

In a figural prolepsis of the conclusion the minister implicitly admonishes Hester to resume the letter she has attempted to cast off: "I know nothing that I would not sooner encounter than this passion in a child. In Pearl's young beauty, as in the wrinkled witch, it has a preternatural effect. Pacify her, if thou lovest me!" (210).

What Hester is offering Dimmesdale in this scene is what the Transcendentalist writer is offering the reader: an art unstained by the imperfections of the artist, art as a direct effluence of divinity. Dimmesdale's reaction confirms that Hawthorne rejects this conception of art on account of it being untrue to the experience of the artist, and hence unable to act as mediator between artist and society. And it is here that I would claim that it becomes possible to trace the analogy that the text establishes between the human (sexual) romance of Hester and Dimmesdale, and the fictitious (textual) romance of Hawthorne and the reader. We look to Hester's relinquishing of the letter as a "moment of possibility," as one critic has called it,[29] because her desire to negate the contradiction between love and guilt is paralleled by our desire for the coming together of passion and principle in the figure of Hester Prynne, as we saw Jonathan Arac argue in the opening section of this chapter. Much like Hester wants Dimmesdale to subject himself to her view of the letter as a letter of love, we want the text to yield to our desire for relief, and invest all our hopes in the construction of Hester as the character with the potential to perform such an office. But as Arac observes, Hester does not hold up to such a conception: the force we have ascribed to her character is displaced by that of Dimmesdale, the character we had hoped she would prove capable of saving. Instead we must face the troubling circumstance that he is seen to save her, by transforming the character she has nurtured at her bosom through seven long years into a person. Despite all the toil that Hester has had with raising her Pearl, the fate of the child is seen to depend ultimately on one who has never publicly known her. More precisely, it hinges on how this person reacts at the crucial moment when the letter has been transferred from its mother to its father; that is, from artist to society, from writer to reader. In the last three decades, many critics have been prone to conceive of Dimmesdale's actions in the latter half of the novel in almost entirely negative terms.[30] I would insist, in contrast, that he provides us with an exemplary reaction; a model for us as readers to emulate. Ultimately, *The Scarlet Letter* exposes as futile Hester's attempt to escape the imprisoning norms of society by converting Dimmesdale to her own religion of love. As we have seen, from the point of view of the artist, the romance, which issues from the prison-door along with Hester, must itself be seen as an attempt to break free from the norms of society. Nevertheless it must be the reader's role to guide the straying romance back into the confines of society. Thus the reader's role must in an important sense be parallel to that performed by Dimmesdale within the story, that is, essentially a role of closure.

By admonishing Hester to resume the character she would fain discard, Dimmesdale resists her attempt to repress the spirit of the letter. While Hester's longing to negate her allegorical experience of life, by effecting the separation of the emblem of her guilt from the emblem of her love, is thus thwarted by her lover, it is nevertheless not wholly ineffectual. Her attempt to rid herself of her Character makes manifest an urge which is latent in Dimmesdale as well, and by so doing Hester makes it possible for Dimmesdale to approach a better understanding of himself, to recognize *his* true character. Dimmesdale up to this point has sustained himself by adhering to a private/public dichotomy the inverse of

Hester's, but no less radical for that. Emerging from the forest revitalized by his spiritual intercourse with Hester, he muses to himself on the happy circumstance that he shall still have time to perform the Election Sermon before she elopes with him, which the narrator looks upon as irrefutable evidence "of a subtle disease, that had long since begun to eat into the real substance of his character. No man, for any considerable period, can wear one face to himself, and another to the multitude, without finally getting bewildered as to which may be the true" (216). Dimmesdale is no exception: over the course of his seven long years of religious devotion he has come to mistake the purity of his public appearance for the adulteration of his private character. But the renewal of his sin in the forest makes it increasingly difficult for him to uphold the appearance of purity over his character of sinfulness, which has been so newly restored to strength. Over and over again in chapter 20, the character of sinfulness threatens to explode the image of purity as Dimmesdale is repeatedly tempted to perform some petty vicious act during the passage from the forest to his chamber, a vivid illustration of the moral point Hawthorne is making: "Another man had returned out of the forest; a wiser one; with a knowledge of hidden mysteries which the simplicity of the former never could have reached. A bitter kind of knowledge that!" (223).

When Hester picks up the letter at Dimmesdale's imploring, she in effect transfers the control of the letter upon her lover, who, once he has the letter in his power, proceeds to compose the Election Sermon. In an indirect way, however, her understanding of the letter still informs its conception. Dimmesdale's experience in the forest is a concrete lesson in the contradictory premises of human existence, and having taken this lesson to heart, it provides the impetus for the double sense that runs through his sermon. The letter of his sermon is fired by his acquiescence to Hester's symbolistic negation of the doubleness inherent in her letter, and accordingly prophesies the glory of a future New England. The spirit of his sermon, in contrast, is informed by his memory of how he had to impose the letter upon the breast of Hester, that is, by his recognition that there is a limit to human desire that cannot be transgressed. Dimmesdale, in short, has learned, if yet unconsciously, that the whole truth of the scarlet letter must involve spirit and letter alike, that it must accommodate passion and principle, love and law. He has learned, moreover, that the whole truth of the letter can be grasped only if society is willing to incorporate the individual's recognition of how guilt and love are inextricably entangled with each other. It is precisely such an incorporation of the artistic truth which is allegorically depicted through Dimmesdale's spectacular revelation of "a SCARLET LETTER [...] imprinted in the flesh" (258), the sight of which the narrator declines to expatiate upon on the grounds that "it were irreverent to describe that revelation" (255), a phrasing which subtly bespeaks the narrator's endorsement of the religious sentiment that Dimmesdale has invested into his revelation. This silence is highly suggestive; it implies that the letter revealed by Dimmesdale is one that the reader is expected to find in his own society, in his own body. *This* letter, Hawthorne is suggesting, is one that the artist is not authorized to describe, since this would entail representing a letter which in contrast to that of the artist (that is, that of Hester) has not been transformed through the medium of artistic faith which makes the letter of the artist a letter of beauty as well as of pain. To describe such a letter would be equivalent to picturing the letter as it must seem when it is *not* viewed through the transcendent desire of the artist, that is, to behold guilt without being able to see within it the path leading through guilt to God, which in Hawthorne is the same path—and this strikes me as true even if we are unable to entertain a religious conception of God—that leads to a communion with other human beings, a path that allows us to conceptualize our feelings of insufficiency at other people's sufferings, yet to find redemption in an acknowledgement of guilt. In short, to give a description of such a revelation would be tantamount to committing the sin of Chillingworth, that of violating "the sanctity of a human heart" (195). By withholding Dimmesdale's letter from the reader's view, Hawthorne ensures that the reader must believe in the existence of the letter without being exposed to its material expression.[31]

## 4. The Deferring Office of Art

I have argued above that through the major part of the romance, Hester occupies a middle position, somewhere between allegory and symbolism. We must be careful, however, not to mistake this for a confirmation of Fogle's view of Hawthorne's art as a case of thesis and antithesis in balance. Hawthorne clearly does not look upon this middle position as a viable solution to the paradoxical situation, but only as a temporary, if necessary, step in a dialectical process whereby the complications inherent in allegory as well as symbolism may be transcended. As I have said, the Puritan conception of allegory can be described as a chain of signifiers that leads to an ultimate signified: God. Such a conception is untenable, Hester shows us, because it contradicts human experience. No rational discourse can adequately express the phenomenal life of an individual, tainted as it inevitably is, by postlapsarian desire, and therefore incapable of experiencing the transparency of the signifier. Like Hester, we may know that passion is sinful, but cannot help that our experience of passion tells us otherwise, given the appropriate circumstances. Like Hester again, the symbolist may subvert the allegorical chain by transforming the signifier into an image of his own private emotions. But the plight of the symbolist is that he cannot go beyond the symbol itself: all of a sudden the image has become an end in itself, a mode of communication which ends before it begins, since to express the symbol in another way would be to succumb to the epistemological precepts of allegory. The symbol must mean everything and nothing, all at once.

Hawthorne's way of manoeuvring between this semantic equivalence of Scylla and Charybdis involves generalizing the sphere of the aesthetic so that it becomes coequal to the sphere of religion (which was in turn coequal to the political sphere in Puritan society). Furthermore, it involves the substitution of absence for presence as the means by which the assurance of God is accomplished. To see how Hawthorne accomplishes this widening of the field of aesthetics it is necessary to return to the beginning of *The Scarlet Letter.* In the first scaffold scene, there is a short but highly significant passage that deserves to be quoted in full:

> Had there been a Papist among the crowd of Puritans, he might have seen in this beautiful woman, so picturesque in her attire and mien, and with the infant at her bosom, an object to remind him of the image of Divine Maternity, which so many illustrious painters have vied with one another to represent; something which should remind him, indeed, but only by contrast, of that sacred image of sinless motherhood, whose infant was to redeem the world. Here, there was the taint of deepest sin in the most sacred quality of human life, working such effect, that the world was only the darker for this woman's beauty, and the more lost for the infant that she had borne. (56)

The point of this effusion is not to establish a parallel between Mary and Hester, but, rather, to establish the possibility of arriving at a point of allegorical closure by tracing the connotations of a chain of signifiers that are hereby suggested. "There is no Christ in *The Scarlet Letter*," Woodberry once claimed, and there is some truth in this.[32] But while Hawthorne refuses to succumb to the transcendentalist tenet that art is a direct effusion of divinity, the romance nevertheless performs a mediating office by placing in our hands the most precious product that human sensibilities (imaginative as well as physical) is capable of. The paradoxical strategy of the romance is to insist that this imperfect product is nevertheless suggestive of Christ, if "only by contrast." As we saw in the previous chapter, Rappaccini's theory "that all medicinal virtues are comprised within those substances which we term vegetable poisons" (10: 100) is in effect an attempt to make the ideal available by accepting rather than denying the imperfection of man. In similar fashion, the romance itself acquires its redemptive potential not by synecdochically embodying the ideal in symbolistic fashion, but on the contrary by emphasizing how distant it is from the ideal it suggests.

The concept of mediation is central to all dialectical thinking, and in Christian thought, as we saw above, the mediating agency is fulfilled by Christ (see chapter one, section 4). In making possible the transition from a state of absolute wretchedness to one of absolute redemption, Christ fulfils a function of mediation that must be characterized as allegorical, in that it involves the translation of one seemingly self-contained level of meaning to another. What allows Christ to perform this office is his double nature: he is at once wholly of this world, and wholly divine. It is notable, however, that in Unitarian and Transcendentalist preaching of early- to mid-nineteenth century America, in contrast, the divinity of

Christ is almost entirely subsumed under his human aspect: Christ is seen as the brother of man, rather than the Son of God.[33] As a consequence, the figure of Christ comes to fulfil a symbolical rather than allegorical function, being metonymically rather than metaphorically related to humanity; that is, seen as a *part* of humanity, rather than a being of an altogether different status.

The figure of Christ, in other words, is privatized, and while this enables the individual to establish a direct relation with God, it also means that this relation no longer automatically involves the notion of a social totality that is implicit in an allegorical conception of Christianity. This is why the metatextual allegory that we have traced in *The Scarlet Letter* becomes such a crucial trait of Hawthorne's writings. Faced with a de-allegorized conception of Christ, Hawthorne is forced to refrain from directly invoking the figure of Christ as mediator between the individual and God, or, to put the matter in more secular terms, between self and community. But in order to retain a comparable notion of totality, the mediating function of Christ in Hawthorne is relocated to the very medium through which he attempts "to open an intercourse with the world:" the romance. This is not to say that art displaces the importance of religion to Hawthorne; rather, it replicates it: Hawthorne relies upon the romance to perform the mediating role once occupied by Christ.

If Pearl is suggestive of Christ, she is also "the scarlet letter in another form" (102). Significantly, it is as such that she announces to Governor Bellingham that she "had been plucked by her mother off the bush of wild roses, that grew by the prison door" (112). This rose-bush is introduced already in the first chapter, "so directly on the threshold of our narrative," as Hawthorne puts it, that "we could hardly do otherwise than pluck one of its flowers and present it to the reader. It may serve, let us hope, to symbolize some sweet moral blossom, that may be found along the track, or relieve the darkening close of a tale of human frailty and sorrow" (48). In accordance with his view of *The Scarlet Letter* as a promulgator of the kind of "symbolic analysis" (*Jeremiad*, 178) that he sees as the foundation of the American "ideal of liberal community" (*Office*, 92), Bercovitch claims that this rose "is obviously symbolic and obviously impossible to explicate." Yet while it is certainly true, as Bercovitch argues, that the rose "is either one thing or another or still another," and that "it *may* function [...] for one of several different purposes," this does not entail that its significance is indeterminate.[34] To hope, as Hawthorne does, that the rose may symbolize a moral that may be found along the narrative track, is another way of saying that it will symbolize this moral *if* it is found. If it is not found, the rose (which is Pearl, the Scarlet Letter—and by extension *The Scarlet Letter*, too—in another form, and thus suggestive of Christ by contrast) may still relieve the darkness of the narrative's close.

Whether the moral is found or not thus depends upon the response of the reader, for Hawthorne makes clear already in the very first paragraph of "The Custom-House" that in contrast to "Some authors," the author of "The Custom-House" has not indulged "in such confidential depths of *revelation* as could fittingly be addressed, only and exclusively, to the one heart and mind of perfect sympathy" (3; my emphasis), but has been careful to "keep the inmost Me behind its veil" in order to "be autobiographical, without violating either the reader's rights or his own" (4). As we saw in the previous section, Hawthorne is careful to veil Dimmesdale's revelation in a similar manner, by merely suggesting the presence of "a SCARLET LETTER—the very semblance of that worn by Hester Prynne—imprinted in the flesh" (258) of Arthur Dimmesdale, without exposing it directly to the reader's view. Thus we are implicitly invited to transform the letter through the medium of our own imagination.

The Conclusion, nevertheless, affords a number of possible explanations for the origin of the letter that most of "the spectators testified to having seen, on the breast of the unhappy minister" (258). In considering these divergent accounts, we must bear in mind that Matthiessen advances them as one of his paradigm examples of Hawthorne's "device of multiple choice." As I pointed out in chapter one, for Matthiessen this is a device whereby Hawthorne transcends the "mechanical delimitation" inherent in his allegorical practice, a means to rewrite allegory as a form of psychological symbolism; Hawthorne, "does not literally accept his own allegory, and yet he finds it symbolically valid because of its psychological exactitude."[35] In line with his general argument that epistemological openness may function as a form of ideological closure, Bercovitch argues that this description of Hawthorne's use of ambiguity as a "device of multiple-choice" is acceptable only on the condition that "we recognize it as a device for enclosure and control" (*Office*, 18), a device which "tells us that meaning, while indefinite, is neither random nor arbitrary; rather, it is gradual, cumulative, and increasingly comprehensive" (*Office*, 19). From this perspective, Bercovitch importantly observes, "to interpret is willfully, in the interests of some larger truth, *not to choose*" (*Office*, 22). These are perceptive comments, but they present the case in somewhat too tendentious a manner to be wholly correct.

In the Conclusion, we are initially afforded three different explanations:

1. the letter was inflicted by Dimmesdale as "a hideous torture on himself;"
2. Chillingworth "caused it to appear, through the agency of magic and poisonous drugs;" and
3. "those best able to appreciate the minister's peculiar sensibility" conclude that "the awful symbol was the effect of the ever active tooth of remorse" (258).

"The reader," in Hawthorne's words, "may choose among these theories." Then, after having encouraged this freedom of speculation as to the possible origin of Dimmesdale's letter, he adds yet a fourth view, which derives from a set of "highly respectable witnesses" who simply deny "that there was any mark whatever on his breast" or that he had acknowledged having any part in Hester's guilt. In this view, Dimmesdale "had made the manner of his death a parable, in order to impress on his admirers the mighty and mournful lesson, that, in the view of Infinite Purity, we are sinners all alike. It was to teach them, that the holiest among us has but attained so far above his fellows as to discern more clearly the Mercy which looks down, and repudiate more utterly the phantom of human merit, which would look aspiringly upward." Having accounted for this version, Hawthorne immediately undermines its authority, by considering it "only an instance of that stubborn fidelity with which a man's friends—and especially a clergyman's—will sometimes uphold his character; when proofs, clear as the mid-day sunshine on the scarlet letter, establish him a false and sin-stained creature of the dust" (259).

By chance or by intent the four explanations presented above correspond to a literal, an allegorical (since Chillingworth embodies Dimmesdale's feelings of guilt), a moral, and an anagogical way of accounting for the revelation of the Scarlet Letter. We need not press this point too emphatically (though considering his acquaintance with Dante, it seems highly unlikely that Hawthorne was unaware of the technicalities of the fourfold scheme) to register its implication: we may choose among the different versions, because it makes little difference which version we choose—they are all different ways of rendering one and the same truth. But if this is the case, the reservations that Hawthorne mounts in relation to the fourth, anagogic, explanation, take on added interest. On the one hand, the amount of elaboration bestowed upon this version suggests that it holds some special interest to Hawthorne; on the other hand, it is the only version which he rejects on account of its not corresponding to facts. Even so, he rejects it "Without disputing a truth so momentous" (258); it is not the spiritual meaning that these witnesses read into the scene that Hawthorne refutes, but their allowing it to extinguish the historical fact. "I do not censure those who may have been able to carve out some spiritual interpretation from every historical fact recounted [in the Bible]," Augustine explains in *The City of God* 16: 3, "so long as they take good care first and foremost to adhere to the historical fact."[36] This is the exact template of Hawthorne's attitude. Spiritual truths are in a sense the most important ones, in that they belong to the realm of absolutes and thus are concerned with ultimate ends, but they must not be allowed to substitute for the literal events from which they are derived. Historical fact and spiritual truth are not wholly different phenomena, nor must they be conflated into one to the effect that the former is merely read as the signifier to the latter's signified. The point is that they form a system, that the meaning is only fragmentarily manifested in each of the four explanations we are offered, and that we can approach a full understanding of this meaning only by relating them to each other. One might thus say, with Bercovitch, that to interpret is not to choose; but a more precise way of putting it is to say that to interpret is to *choose* not to choose between a historical explanation on the one hand, and a spiritual on the other hand. In choosing to refuse such a choice, we acknowledge that there are two, not one, fundamental categories involved in our experience of the world. Yet even while stressing the importance not to conflate secular history with the spiritual realm of eternity, we may nevertheless insist—and Hawthorne does—that the interpenetration of these two realms (or distinct experiential categories), yield only one truth. But this is a truth born by our affirmation of the distance that separates the one realm from the other, a truth that cannot survive any attempt to negate this distance.

As Bercovitch has shown more persuasively than anyone else, the Puritan project in its entirety is fuelled by precisely this ambition: to fuse secular and sacred history, to make of New England a city on the hill.[37] Hawthorne, too, of course, was well aware of this circumstance, and he consciously exploits it in the final scaffold scene in order to offset his allegorical conception of Christianity against the symbolistic tendencies inherent in the Puritan society that provides the back-drop for his story. The subject of Dimmesdale's sermon,

> it appeared, had been the relation between the Deity and the communities of mankind, with a special reference to the New England which they were here planting in the wilderness. And, as he drew towards the close, a spirit as of prophecy had come upon him, constraining him to its purpose as mightily as the old prophets of Israel were constrained; only with this difference, that, whereas the Jewish seers had denounced judgments and ruin on their country, it was his mission to foretell a high and glorious destiny for the newly gathered people of the Lord. But, throughout it all, and through the whole discourse, there had been a certain deep, sad undertone of pathos, which could not be interpreted otherwise than as the natural regret of one soon to pass away. (249)

The antithesis between communal triumph and individual hardships that the juxtaposition of the final two sentences of the above passage highlight, brings us back to the paradox inherent in the view of history as structured along the lines of typological fulfilment that Hawthorne drew attention to already in his history books for children. As we noted earlier, Dimmesdale is in fact communicating on two planes at the same: he is preaching both by the letter and by the spirit. Notably, these two modes of communication do not congeal. The letter of his sermon prophesies the glory of New England; but the spirit, which is communicated "by the mere tone and cadence" (243) of his voice, suggest that we may look forward to a glorious society only if the individual is willing to suffer a tremendous price for its achievement: death. The full implication of this spiritual message may not be immediately evident, but when Dimmesdale dies in the arms of Hester a few pages further on, thwarting her hopes of reuniting with her lover, the moral should be clear: the promise of a bright future destiny is not to be fulfilled in this world, but the next. Death, in other words, is not the price exacted of us for having had the privilege to live in a glorious society, it is the very entrance ticket to our "high and glorious destiny."

Hester's final vision in the Conclusion, which Hawthorne elaborates for us in the penultimate paragraph of the book, must also be understood in the light of the paradoxical fusion of letter and spirit that Dimmesdale accomplishes in his sermon. For here again there is a hidden subtext that contradicts the overt significance of the words of which it is composed:

> She assured them, too, of her firm belief, that, at some brighter period, when the world should have grown ripe for it, in Heaven's own time, a new truth would be revealed, in order to establish the whole relation between man and woman on a surer ground of mutual happiness. Earlier in life, Hester had vainly imagined that she herself might be the destined prophetess, but had long since recognized the impossibility that any mission of divine and mysterious truth should be confided to a woman stained with sin, bowed down with shame, or even burdened with a life-long sorrow. The angel and apostle of the coming revelation must be a woman, indeed, but lofty, pure, and beautiful; and wise, moreover, not through dusky grief, but the ethereal medium of joy; and showing how sacred love should make us happy, by the truest test of a life successful to such an end! (263)

In a sense, this is the very dream Hester has entertained throughout her seven years of public ignominy. Yet the conditions under which she is able to assert her dream of establishing "the whole relation between man and woman on a surer ground of mutual happiness" have changed. In the first half of the romance she is willing to imagine the bond between man and woman as one that is forged in hell: "a union, that, unrecognized on earth, would bring them together before the bar of final judgement, and make that their marriage-altar, for a joint futurity of endless retribution" (80).[38] In the forest-scene, this radically subversive phrasing has changed to the considerably less provocative claim that the act of adultery she committed with the minister "had a consecration of its own" (195). The final phrasing, quoted in full above, finds Hester's desire completely transformed into the religious, and hence socially acceptable, conception that Dimmesdale's revelation of the letter amounts to. The new order will come about "in Heaven's own time," it is no longer conceived of as an attempt of the self to assert itself but as a "mission of divine and mysterious truth" that is to be carried out by an "angel and apostle" inculcating the "sacred" aspect of love, asserting instead the principle of the absolute primacy of "the ethereal medium of joy" before that of "dusky grief" that it was originally Hester's aim to overturn. Thus the individual's subjective experience of guilt is purged of its threatening revolutionary elements and comes to function instead as a means of transforming her transcendental desire to escape from the temporal conditions of the realm of Becoming into a religious faith in a better existence to come.

It is all too easy to mistake this for mere escapism, or to argue alternatively, as Bercovitch does, that this is a vision which in redirecting revolutionary sentiment in the present towards a future consummation, is all of a piece with the social-symbolic outlook that American culture has inherited from the Puritans. Bercovitch's argument, however, hinges on the assumption that the letter does not perform its office until Hester returns to Boston, and resumes the letter "of her own free will" (263). The narrative would have it differently, for we are told already in the final scaffold scene, that with Dimmesdale's revelation of the letter, "Pearl's errand as a messenger of anguish was all fulfilled"—"Towards her mother, *too*" (256; my emphasis). In fact, we are allowed to choose among the theories of the origin of Dimmesdale's letter, because, Hawthorne says, "We have thrown all the light we could acquire upon the portent, and would gladly, *now that it has done its office*, erase its deep print out of our own brain; where long meditation has fixed it in very undesirable distinctness" (259; my emphasis).

Hawthorne, then, allows for Hester's concluding vision only *after* the scarlet letter has already performed its office; performed it, we should observe, by showing how Hester's attempt to realize it in the present was misjudged. In fact, the vision itself is immediately tempered by two sentences which present the moral of the book in a beautifully understated manner: "So said Hester Prynne, and glanced her sad eyes downward at the scarlet letter. And, after many, many years, a new grave was delved, near an old and sunken one, in that burial ground beside which King's Chapel has since been built" (264). Thus Hawthorne suggests that Hester, at the end, is as fully aware as is he of the limit which must inevitably impose itself upon all human endeavours. She knows that her vision will never be fulfilled in our world: the presence of death makes it impossible. Yet Hawthorne, like Hester, recognizes the beauty of the vision, and offers it as a spiritual truth. It is this spiritual truth, I submit, that constitutes the sweet moral blossom that stands out of the sombre heraldic motto which closes the romance—"ON A FIELD, SABLE, THE LETTER A, GULES"—which is "relieved only by one ever-glowing point of light gloomier than the shadow" (264); it is the recognition that the only thing that makes the pain of the sable field of life bearable, is the conviction that this very pain is a promise of a better life to come. Yet even should the flower that Hawthorne plucked and handed over to us in the very first chapter fail to blossom in such manner, it may yet bring relief. For if we find the truth of the human heart too dark to face, we may take Hester's vision literally, in order to "relieve the darkening close of a tale of human frailty and sorrow" (48). In truth, however, the vision is one that can live—like the Unfortunate Lover of Marvell's poem, from which the closing motto is adapted—"in Story only:" it is a truth that needs to be mediated through the Romance, the artistic form which shares with erotic love the ability to make us realize how our imperfections must be acknowledged if we shall have any hope of ever attaining the ideal we long for.[39]

*

We have seen above how Hester is presented as a flawed ideal in *The Scarlet Letter*. As the artist figure of the romance, she alone owns the insight necessary to transform the sign she has been sentenced to wear as an emblem of guilt into an emblem of love. The artistic act of creation is thus seen to be tantamount to taking joy in an activity that society deems sinful. More specifically, it is linked to the adulterous sexual act which ties Hester to Dimmesdale, a representative of the very society which condemns her. To move beyond this flawed position, Hester is dependent upon the aid of Dimmesdale, who is himself as radically flawed as Hester. *The Scarlet Letter* is thus informed by an aporetic conception of guilt, according to which the germ of sin is to be located in the individual and society alike. Hester and Dimmesdale represent these positions, yet while they are imperfect to equal measures, the community recognizes the mark of guilt only upon the former, while shutting their eyes to that which is present upon the representative of their community.

*The Scarlet Letter* is designed to encourage the reader to adopt a relational conception of meaning, by taking a holistic view of the romance. None of the three scaffold scenes by itself expresses the final significance of the contradictory qualities of the letter. To arrive at an adequate understanding of the office of the scarlet letter, rather, we must view the scenes as a system, studying them in relation to each other. The structure of the romance shows us how the letter is transferred from the individual to society via the mediation of romance, how it goes from Hester to Dimmesdale via Pearl. This movement reflects the letter's shifting status in the book: from being primarily the symbolistic vehicle whereby Hester expresses her contradictory emotions, it gradually takes on the aspect of an allegorical sign expressing a set of moral values that the community ascribes to Hester, under the weight of which she threatens to be petrified into the "marble coldness" (164) of a moral statue. Symbolism expresses the spirit, allegory the letter: the problem is how to fuse the former with the latter without violating either.

The romance achieves such a fusion by making plain that the literal sense of history must not be obliterated by our spiritual modes of interpreting it, but that the Actual aspects of history must rather be seen to form a system with the Imaginary ways in which history may be interpreted. Within this system, the romance makes evident, negation—in the form of death, but also in the form of fiction, of the romance itself—fulfils a key mediating function. Like death, fiction fulfils a deferring office: it is capable of consummating our desires on the proviso that we agree to transfer that consummation from the Actual to the Imaginary, from the here and now to a realm to which we can have access only through the figurative mediation of imagination, and the literal mediation of death.

The primary perceptual mode of *The Scarlet Letter* thus is not that of symbolism, as so many critics have assumed, but that of allegory. Unlike symbolism, allegory does not conflate the secular with the eternal. It may well be the case that allegory in analogy with "the American Puritan jeremiad" feeds "on the distance between promise and fact" (*Jeremiad*, 14), but in contrast to the jeremiad, allegory nevertheless remains a discursive practice which makes evident that this distance can be overcome only by substituting an epistemological distance for the temporal distance originally invoked. Unlike the deferral of closure that takes place in symbolism, the deferral of closure in allegory is primarily of a spatial rather than temporal order. In allegory, Actual closure (that is, temporal fulfilment) is recognized as something that will never be achieved, whereas Imaginary closure (spiritual fulfilment), on the other hand, is permanently available to us. In allegory, in short, the notion of an ending is displaced from the realm of the Actual into the realm of the Imaginary.

It is vital that we bear this in mind when we now turn to the writings that followed on the one universally recognized master-piece of Hawthorne's oeuvre. Ostensibly, these works may seem to confirm Bercovitch's thesis even more emphatically than might *The Scarlet Letter*—even if they, in contrast to the latter romance, must be said "to expose (rather than reconcile) ideological contradictions." For Bercovitch, as for so many commentators before him, Hawthorne's unwillingness to close "the gaps between process and closure" in the later works is suggestive of the writer's inability to accept changes in the American political climate, an "incapacity" so serious that it "drained him of crucial intellectual and moral resources" (*Office*, 104). Essentially, then, Bercovitch's argument at this point simply reruns Pearce's contention that the comparative failure of Hawthorne's works from *The House of the Seven Gables* onwards is attributable to the posited "fact" that Hawthorne's "understanding of history failed him, or he failed it."[40] Bercovitch is of course aware that this view has long since been questioned by a number of critics. He acknowledges as much in a footnote, but only to dismiss such attempts as unconvincing: "critics have sought to convert narrative weaknesses into authorial strengths by assuming that Hawthorne *intended* the weaknesses—planted these as clues by which he meant for us to demystify cultural myths" (*Office*, 104; emphasis in the original). Without saying it in so many words, the passage implies that this is more than Hawthorne can plausibly be credited with.

I will attempt to demonstrate in the chapters that follow, that Bercovitch writes off the possibility of Hawthorne having intended the complex narrative strategies that a few critics have argued are at work in the later romances too easily. It is my conviction, too, that what Bercovitch and many other critics have deemed the narrative weaknesses of the fictions Hawthorne produced after *The Scarlet Letter*, are in truth narrative strengths. I will support this line of reasoning by arguing that each of these romances can be seen to be intentionally structured on some version of the principle of chiastic inversion, which we have already seen at work in *The Scarlet Letter*. Like the latter, in other words, I will be arguing that the romances that we now turn to are designed to show how true fulfilment—be it aesthetical, spiritual, or political—is possible only if the reader is willing to follow the artist's example by Imaginatively making Actual shortcomings into the very prerequisite of hope.

# CHAPTER FOUR
# *The House of the Seven Gables:* Pictures Out of Sunshine

The right of purchase is the only safe one. This is a world of bargain and sale and no absurdity is more certain to be exposed than the attempt to make it anything else.

Hawthorne to Caroline Sturgis Tappan, Sept. 5$^{th}$, 1851.

If *The Scarlet Letter* depicts an ideal version of Hawthorne's allegorical dialectics, it is part of its triumph that it manages to do so without in any way compromising its aesthetic impact: readers may debate its significance, but very few question that it is a great book. The case of Hawthorne's second full-length romance is rather different. Like its predecessor, *The House of the Seven Gables* presents us with an ideal fashioning of the office performed by the romance, but it ends not on a melancholy note of faith in a better world to come, but in a sparkle of sunshine that could easily make us believe that Hawthorne did not, after all, rule out the possibility that spiritual and material fulfilment might quite possibly be achievable in the here and now—for once, it would seem, Hawthorne proved unable to resist the temptation of bringing the romance to what he himself described as a "prosperous close" (16: 421). There is no question that Hawthorne consciously strove to write a book that would be more "characteristic" of his mind, "more proper and natural" (16: 461) for him to have written than the "h-ll-fired story" (16: 311) of *The Scarlet Letter.* We know as well that in a letter to James T. Fields, his publisher, Hawthorne wrote of *The House of the Seven Gables* that the book "darkens damnably towards the close, but I shall try hard to pour some setting sunshine over it" (16: 376).

It is perhaps not surprising, then, that the conclusion of the story has often been looked upon as being at odds with the thematic drift of the romance—and hence, as an artistic flaw. This mode of response dates back to E. P. Whipple, who complained upon the book's publication that "the conclusion departs from the integrity of the original conception, and interferes with the strict unity of the work."[1] The censure was repeated by Anthony Trollope in 1879, and codified in 1941 when Matthiessen expressed a similar view in *American Renaissance*: "in the poetic justice of bestowing opulence on all those who had previously been deprived of it by the Judge, Hawthorne overlooked the fact that he was sowing all over again the same seeds of evil."[2] Through the years, various attempts have been made to explain this "failure" of the ending. It has been argued, for instance, that it is an outcome of Hawthorne's semi-unconscious desire to meet the demands of the reading audience of his day. In this view, *The House of the Seven Gables* is best seen as a compromise, the record of a writer shying away from his own deepest convictions. Thus Michael Bell states "that the ending of *The House of the Seven Gables*—endorsing sunshine, healthy normalcy, novelistic realism, in a word, Phoebe—seeks to leave behind" the "understanding of the link between guilt and fantasy" that "lies at the heart of Hawthorne's writing from the 1830s down to *The Scarlet Letter*."[3] Alternatively, a number of critics have argued that the ending must be read as intentionally ironic: the very fact that the happy ending *is* a prosperous close, jars suspiciously with the author's announcement in the Preface that "he would feel it a singular gratification, if this Romance might effectually convince mankind (or, indeed, any one man) of the folly of tumbling down an avalanche of ill-gotten gold, or real estate, on the heads of an unfortunate posterity, thereby to maim and crush them, until the accumulated mass shall be scattered abroad in its original atoms" (2).[4]

Taking a somewhat different course, Waggoner—whose reading remains one of the most rewarding discussions of the book—argues that the ending of *The House of the Seven Gables* can be seen as a failure only from an anachronistic point of view that fails to observe the symbolic structure of the work, in which the conflict between the linear and cyclical conception of history is ultimately synthesized. The figure for that synthesis in the book is that of the ascending spiral curve, advanced by Clifford in the train-scene. In Waggoner's view, the "structure of the novel as a whole, with the departure from the house and the marriage combining to make a happy ending, would seem to suggest that Hawthorne approves of Clifford's understanding of history as figured on an ascending spiral curve, even if he does not approve of the reasons Clifford gives for his hopeful view." But at the same time, Waggoner maintains, Hawthorne "also believes that no great wrong is ever set right." In so doing, "Hawthorne demonstrates a Keatsian sort of 'negative capability' in entertaining sympathetically two opposed views." Nevertheless, the author provides "a partial resolution of the conflict both on the level of belief and on the level of feeling and imagination" (*Study*, 179). The figure of the ascending spiral curve thus comes to imply "that both change and permanence are real, and that we are not to think of them as being one good and the other bad. Instead, we must think of them in terms of the necessary distinctions between superficial and profound, external and internal, physical and moral" (*Study*, 186). This is hardly a satisfactory conclusion, seeing as it is in effect merely to substitute one positive-negative dichotomy for a set of others, a fact that Waggoner's switching of positions of the negatively and positively loaded terms he employs can but insufficiently cover.[5]

Nevertheless, Waggoner's view that the romance projects an ending which ultimately must be something we hope for rather than something that can be fulfilled in the present is one that I hope not so much to refute as refine in the following pages. In so doing, I will be implicitly questioning a way of reading the romance which is parallel to Bercovitch's analysis of *The Scarlet Letter* in that it sees in *The House of the Seven Gables* a romance that confirms the American vision which attempts to turn the real historical conflicts generated by the American ideal into a self-dissolving rhetorical ambiguity. "The point of the plot in *The House of the Seven Gables* is to erase and undo all action," Jonathan Arac has argued. "The key to redemption in that book is replacing all human action, which is guilt-ridden, with the beneficent process of nature."[6] This is a perceptive comment, but it requires us to conceive of *The House of the Seven Gables* in wholly negative terms: by erasing action, *The House of the Seven Gables* would seem to erase guilt. The brightness of *The House of the Seven Gables* would then rest on the suppression of the very negation that provides the momentum for the rest of Hawthorne's oeuvre. Such a conception of the romance is closely allied to the quite widespread opinion that the most troubling aspect of *The House of the Seven Gables* is that it seems to deny that guilt is an essential feature of life. The argument this romance seems to be making—in sharp contradistinction to that of Hawthorne's other major works—is that the guilt of the past need *not* spill over into the present, and that therefore the future *can* be built anew, from an untainted position in the present.

If this was really the case, we would have to look upon *The House of the Seven Gables* as the supreme embodiment of the symbolistic version of the dialectical formula according to which a sense of balance between spirituality and materiality can be achieved by conceiving of these concepts as pure presence and absence respectively. This would indeed be making *The House of the Seven Gables* an anomaly in Hawthorne's canon, an unprecedented outburst of optimism which it would seem very difficult to account for, especially when we consider that *The House of the Seven Gables* is preceded by the sombre landscape of *The Scarlet Letter* and followed by the grim and almost nihilistic *The Blithedale Romance*, all written within three years. Some critics have argued that this is precisely what *The House of the Seven Gables* is. I will argue, in contrast, that Hawthorne's second romance is as firmly set in an allegorical conception of life as is *The Scarlet Letter*. As in the latter, *The House of the Seven Gables* is informed by an allegorical conception of religious faith, which it promotes as a substitute to political activism. In order to see why this does not make the romance into an instrument of suppression, it will be necessary once again to conclude by considering the valorization of art upon which the efficacy of the romance's redemptive vision rests. As we saw in the previous chapter, *The Scarlet Letter* effects the involvement of writer and reader with the actors of its narrative, by demonstrating how the intranarrative romance of Hester and Dimmesdale is homologous to that of the extranarrative relation between Hawthorne and the reader, and furthermore, by insisting that the outcome of the intranarrative romance is ultimately determined by the way that we conceive of the extranarrative relation in which we are ourselves involved. *The House of the Seven Gables*, like the romances that Hawthorne was still to write, constitutes a version of this formula. Again, we shall see, the key to the redemptive vision the romance projects must be sought in the dialectical interplay it facilitates between the reader and the writer.

## 1. The Dissipation of Guilt: Sexuality and Economics

Despite the marked differences between the two books, the opening of the present day narrative of *The House of the Seven Gables* in chapter 2 does in a sense mimic that of the opening scaffold scene in *The Scarlet Letter*. Once again we are presented with a female protagonist—Hepzibah Pyncheon—who has to confront a moral reality that she longs to transcend.[7] Her moment of crisis is consummated in chapter 3, when she finally accepts payment for one of her gingerbread cookies. Although the tone throughout is jocular, the representation of this scene is nevertheless indubitably designed to underscore the importance of this act:

> The new shopkeeper dropped the first solid result of her commercial enterprise into the till. It was done! The sordid stain of that copper-coin could never be washed away from her palm. The little schoolboy, aided by the impish figure of the negro dancer, had wrought an irreparable ruin. The structure of ancient aristocracy had been demolished by him, even as if his childish gripe had torn down the seven-gabled mansion. Now let Hepzibah turn the old Pyncheon portraits with their faces to the wall, and take the map of her eastern-territory to kindle the kitchen-fire, and blow up the flame with the empty breath of her ancestral traditions! What had she to do with ancestry? Nothing;—no more than with posterity! No lady, now, but simply Hepzibah Pyncheon, a forlorn old maid, and keeper of a cent-shop! (51)

What should be observed in this scene, is that the coin which Hepzibah accepts fulfils a function that is largely analogous to that performed by the letter in the scaffold scene of the previous romance. Through the agency of the coin, Hepzibah is dissevered from the past, as it were; a circumstance that is subtly underscored by the fact that the tense of the two sentences containing the word "now" in the above passage is neither that of the present or the past. (We will return to the importance of Hawthorne's manipulation of the narrative's tense in section 3.) Instead she is isolated in the insuperability of the present moment, just as Hester finally comes to reduce the world to her present situation in her moment of crisis upon the scaffold: "She clutched the child so fiercely to her breast, that it sent forth a cry; she turned her eyes downward at the scarlet letter, and even touched it with her finger, to assure herself that the infant and the shame were real. Yes!—*these were her realities,—all else had vanished!*" (SL, 59; my emphasis.)

In Hepzibah's case moral reality thus is intricately tied to economics, much like moral reality for Hester is tied to sexuality: economy seems to have acquired the function which in Hawthorne's version of the Puritan past was fulfilled by sexuality, namely as the one aspect of life which is both sinful and necessary. This intermixing of economy and sexuality is something we are reminded of throughout *The House of the Seven Gables*. To begin with, it is suggested in the scene we are already considering. Hepzibah's endeavour to set up shop in chapters 2–4 is conveyed in terms which suggest that this project of the old maiden is in some opaque sense parallel to a sexual act, as if handling money were somehow analogous to allowing oneself to be penetrated by the desire that pervades society. We "have stolen upon Miss Hepzibah Pyncheon, *too irreverently*, at the instant of time when the patrician lady is to be transformed into the plebeian woman" (38; my emphasis); the tinkling of the shop-bell "set every nerve of her body in responsive and tumultuous vibration" (42); and when she finally accepts a "potent" copper-coin which operates both on her "body and spirit" (52), she acquires a "sordid stain" that "could never be washed away from her palm" (51). No wonder, then, that Hepzibah begins "to fear that the shop would prove her ruin, in a moral and religious point of view, without contributing very essentially towards even her temporal welfare" (55).

The representation of Colonel/Judge Pyncheon (two temporally distinct signifiers denoting an identical signified in the moral space of the romance), too, is suggestive of some sort of correlation between money and sex, for just as the avatar of the Colonel is marked by an excessive desire for wealth, it is suggested that he is guilty of similar sexual excesses. "The Puritan," we learn, "had worn out three wives," and although the "Judge had wedded but a single wife" she had survived only three or four years of marriage, and is supposed to have "got her death-blow in the honey-moon" (123). Finally, there is the Italian organ grinder's monkey, who is explicitly presented as an "image of the Mammon of copper-coin, symbolizing the grossest form of the love of money." Marked by an "excessive desire for whatever filthy lucre might happen to be in anybody's pocket" and an "enormous tail, (too enormous to be decently concealed under his gabardine,)" (164), the representation of this monkey suggests an ineluctable connection between money and sexuality, that is to say, between the social and the private spheres of life.

But if there is indeed a parallel of sorts between sexuality on the one hand and economics on the other in *The House of the Seven Gables* (and the recurrence of the intertwining of the subjects in *The Blithedale Romance* strengthens the hypothesis that there is), then what are the grounds of this homology? What is it about money that compels us to associate it with sex?

To answer this question, we must first take note of how the transition of the setting of the romance from the past to the present is accompanied by a kind of dissemination of the symbolic centre of the romance. In *The Scarlet Letter*, Hawthorne was able to exploit the letter A as a metaphor for all of the ideological ramifications of the Puritan past, functioning both as symbol for the individual's emotions and as an allegorical sign of the norms of the community. The abundance of symbols in *The House of the Seven Gables*, on the other hand, suggests that the universe of the present is no longer capable of being metaphorically expressed in one all-encompassing image. The narrative is almost overwrought with symbols and emblems of various kinds—the House itself (the anthropomorphic description of which certainly lends credibility to the view of the romance as something of a present-day psychomachia);[8] the garden, with Maule's Well, the Pyncheon-elm, the Pyncheon-hens, and the cat that stalks upon them; Alice Pyncheon's harpsichord; the blighted white roses of the garden and the crimson-spotted Alice's Posies growing from the roof of the house itself; Colonel Pyncheon's portrait, the miniature of Clifford, and Holgrave's daguerreotypes; the Italian organ-grinder with his monkey and organ figures that emblematically portray how all mortals "dance to one identical tune, and, in spite of our ridiculous activity, bring nothing finally to pass" (163); symbolically significant characters like Uncle Venner and Ned Higgins. All this ornamentation—most of which we will have reason to get back to in the following—suggests that the move to the present is a dislocating one; a side effect, perhaps, of the author seeing himself pressed to rewrite the drama of guilt and retribution publicly enacted in the past as one enacted privately in the present. As a consequence, there is no longer *one* symbol to express the bonding of the individual and society through guilt, since society has in a sense rejected the possibility of publicly branding its members with its mark. The House may be as recurrent a symbol as the letter, but society has not fixed the purport of the House the way it had that of the letter.[9]

The prominence of the House in *The House of the Seven Gables*, suggests, rather, that the most decisive consequence of the shift from the romance of the past (*The Scarlet Letter*) to that of the present, is the inevitable internalisation of the problem of guilt. *The House of the Seven Gables* identifies the suppression of guilt in the present, and attempts to envision a possible means of retribution in a society which no longer recognizes the need to collectivize the experience of guilt. It seems to me that this is one of the main reasons economics becomes a central concern in this romance: money, Hawthorne seems to be suggesting, is capable of functioning as a symbol that may effect the transformation of a private experience of guilt into a kind of social cement that allows us to see how the individual is related to society. In order that it may perform such an office, however, it is vital that one does not look to money as a means to its own end, but that one recognizes how its accumulation is necessarily linked to a series of transgressions, hence how the handling of money must inevitably involve feelings of guilt. If money is recognized as such a guilt-laden medium, monetary transactions may be looked upon as the social equivalent of Hester's public confession of guilt, wherefore guilt and joy must hence be in some sense the same. On the other hand, if the link between money and guilt is not recognized, it can only serve to isolate the individual from the rest of society, to contain him or her in a structure which does not allow even distinguishing between exterior appearances and interior essences.

Hence the prominence of the House: it is the very emblem of such a constricting structure. Once again we are presented with a situation in which the figure of the artist is seen to ascribe a private significance to an object which is to be openly displayed. The House is built by a Maule (from whom Holgrave, "the artist," as he is habitually designated in the story, descends), but it is commissioned and paid for by a Pyncheon: money thus right from the start links Maule to Pyncheon in much the same way that the letter links Hester to society in *The Scarlet Letter*. As the Artist is required to fashion the edifice to the taste of its owner, he is in no position to stamp his creation with a mark whereby the owner could recognize his own true character. Nevertheless, Maule buries a secret in the structure of the House, which is ultimately responsible for lending an ambiguity to the pompous edifice which is highly reminiscent of Hester's letter. In *The House of the Seven Gables*, in short, guilt no longer occupies a central space in the public consciousness of the community: guilt has been displaced into an outward show of respectability and wealth. This is disquieting, as *The Scarlet Letter* shows that there can be no redemption from guilt unless there is a signifier in which public guilt may be rewritten as private joy. To effect the transformation of guilt into hope, guilt must first be written, brought out into the open from its confinement within the structure of the House where it has been hidden.

Once again we are thus dealing with a chain of signifiers that are somehow intrinsically related to each other. As we saw in the previous chapter, *The Scarlet Letter* is not so much a critique of the notion of meaning as a chain of allegorical signifieds, as an attempt to supplant an apparently transparent instance of such a chain with a decidedly more oblique variant, which—unlike the repudiated version—will not unduly simplify the question of how the individual is caught up in the chain. *The House of the Seven Gables*, too, can be approached in terms of substituting a complex allegorical chain for a transparent but untenable one. The House is an emblem of Colonel Pyncheon's wealth, and this wealth in turn is connected both to the written "Indian deed" (18) upon which the family's territorial claims are founded, and upon the "deed of sin" (21) that the Colonel committed in order to lay his hands upon the property of the Maule family. The chain which is implicitly put in question when the story picks up in chapter 2 thus runs something like this: money = the House = the Indian deed = wealth. Hepzibah's situation in the opening narrative must necessarily complicate this chain, as it makes evident that money may be a sign of poverty as well as of wealth, and that the allegorical chain could thus be read: money = the House = the deed Hepzibah commits in opening the shop = poverty.

This pun on the double meaning of "deed" receives considerable emphasis in the book.[10] Within the historical sequences of events invoked in *The House of the Seven Gables*, deed as document is repeatedly transformed into deed as act. Gervayse Pyncheon's attempt to find the missing written deed, fictively represented by Holgrave in chapter 13, has as its outcome Matthew Maule Jr.'s deed, his violation of Alice's integrity, which ultimately causes her death. In the present narrative sequence, similarly, the deed is transformed from the testament of Uncle Jaffrey, to Jaffrey's false accusation of his cousin, only to materialize once more as "the schedule, the documents, the evidences, in whatever shape they exist, of the vast amount of Uncle Jaffrey's missing property" (235), before it is finally transformed again into Holgrave's and Phoebe's joint decision to reveal the corpse of Judge Pyncheon that they discover in the House. What is more, despite the variations of the pattern, it is notable that the original deed is not recovered in the book until its properties have undergone a radical transformation. In the case of the written deed, when it is finally found "it has long been worthless" (316); in the case of the act—Clifford's alleged murder of Jaffrey (Uncle *and* Cousin, a doubling which brings us back to the pattern of fraternal/paternal homicide present already in "Alice Doane's Appeal," which is to get its most profound formulation in *The Marble Faun*, in the shape of the relation between Donatello and the Model)—this act is ultimately revealed to be the natural outcome of "an hereditary liability" (311). In both cases, then, the value of the deed is shown to be merely apparent. As a consequence, the deed is something which can exert a decisive influence upon the world only on the condition that its true nature, its "secret character," is not disclosed.

Holgrave alone is in possession of the secret that the deed is locked up under the image of Colonel Pyncheon; he openly admits in the final chapter that "the secret [...] is the only inheritance that has come down to me from my ancestors" (316). Yet when Phoebe asks him, in chapter 14, if he is aware of any new trouble facing her relatives, he insists that he is not. "Believe me, if I were really aware of any secret, the disclosure of which would benefit your friends [...] you should learn it, before we part. But I have no such knowledge," he claims, "no secrets, but my own" (217). In thus refraining from disclosing the secret of the deed, he has in a way repeated the stance of his forefather, who also claimed not to know where the deed was to be found. By claiming the secret of the deed as his own, then, Holgrave plays a key part in history repeating itself in the death of the Judge, and he is faced with the prospect of being responsible, albeit indirectly, for Clifford being once more falsely accused of murder.

This, then, is presented as the difficulty facing the present-day artist: he must find a way of disclosing the secret he conceives of as a private inheritance, his sole property, to a society which clings to the notion that the deed is the key to happiness. It is worth noting that it is not only the Judge who covets the deed—Hepzibah does so as well, though she is less assured than is her cousin of its existence. Even more pertinently, Holgrave himself is a believer in the deed, although in his case this belief manifests itself as a belief in the deed as act rather than as document:

> His error lay, in supposing that this age, more than any past or future one is destined to see the tattered garments of Antiquity exchanged for a new suit, instead of gradually renewing themselves by patchwork; in applying his own little life-span as the measure of an interminable achievement; and, more than all, in fancying *that it mattered anything to the great end in view, whether he himself should contend for it or against it.* Yet it was well for him to think so. (180; my emphasis.)

It was well for him to think so, but this belief in the deed nevertheless represents a delusion from which Holgrave must be purged.[11] For it is precisely the secret of the deed, the secret that Holgrave denies to be in possession of at the end of chapter 14, that ties him (and Phoebe) to the death of Judge Pyncheon; not as murderer, but as someone who—much like Judge Pyncheon himself—has withheld "the one decisive explanation" (312).

Hawthorne, in contrast, does not withhold the explanation of his narrative as much as he veils it. Indeed, the explanation for his conception of history is suggested by the very names of the two families figuring in the romance: Pyncheon and Maule. "Types were engraved with an instrument called a puncheon ('an instrument driven so as to make a hole or impression', says Johnson's *Dictionary*) and one tapped it with a mallet or maul," Frank Kermode helpfully points out, in a rewarding discussion of the nature of Hawthorne's typology.[12] Despite the Pyncheons' greater wealth, it is suggested that they are at the hands of the Maules: "The Pyncheons, if all stories were true, haughtily as they bore themselves in the noonday streets of their native town, were no better than bond-servants to these plebeian Maules, on entering the topsyturvy commonwealth of sleep" (26). The Maules drive the Pyncheons: tapped by Maule's curse, Colonel Pyncheon dies; so, too, does Alice, tapped by Maule's gaze. Both families are thus shown to be instruments employed by the Creator (artist and God) to create the text we know as the world. This notion of man as an instrument in God's hands, is one that Hawthorne himself explicitly endorses in a letter to Elizabeth Peabody: "Vengeance and beneficence are things that God claims for himself. His instruments have no consciousness of His purpose; if they imagine they have, it is a pretty sure token they are *not* His instruments. The good of others, like our own happiness, is not to be attained by direct effort, but incidentally. All history and observation confirm this" (18: 116). Although written in 1857, the notion of an absolute limit to the efforts of mankind that these words convey is central to *The House of the Seven Gables* as well, as is made explicit in the passage in chapter 12 that we are considering, in which the narrator goes on to foresee how, when Holgrave's "early faith should be modified by inevitable experience,"

> it would be with no harsh and sudden revolution of his sentiments. He would still have faith in man's brightening destiny, and perhaps love him all the better, as he should recognize his helplessness in his own behalf; and the haughty faith, with which he began life, would be well bartered for a far humbler one, at its close, in discerning that man's best-directed effort accomplishes a kind of dream, while God is the sole worker of realities. (180)

Hawthorne, we should note, does not entirely reject the value of human deeds. What the above passage underscores, rather, is that belief in the deed must be tempered by the *sense of distance* that must inevitably separate the revolutionary fervour of youth from the maturity won by age.

*

His possession of the secret of the hidden deed gives to the Artist, of which Holgrave is the main representative, the advantage of knowing how the guilt of his employer is linked to his fortune, how the deed as act is equivalent to the deed as document upon which the Pyncheons' claim to wealth rests. But it also implicates the Artist in this guilt, as he shows himself willing to suppress his knowledge in exchange for money. The problem, then, is almost the inverse of that of *The Scarlet Letter*, which turns on an emblem of guilt which the Artist dresses up as an emblem of fortune. *The House of the Seven Gables*, in contrast, is built around an object that society mistakes for an emblem of wealth, within which the Artist has hidden a secret which, if divulged, would prove this emblem's true significance to be guilt. This repression, the romance suggests, amounts to a kind of dissipation of guilt, which causes it to enfold the very crust of reality to the effect that what becomes guilty is no longer a specific deed, but rather the very surface of reality itself: our inability to tell appearances from reality thus comes to function as an all-pervading signifier of guilt.

What has been lost, then, is a specifically allegorical consciousness, as it is a distinctive mark of the allegorical sign that it always points to something else as being the meaning that provides it with its significance. The symbol, in contrast, tends to internalize the ostentatious quality of the allegorical image; that is, it tends to *point to itself* as the ultimate arbiter of its own significance. It can do this, as we saw in *The Scarlet Letter*, by rewriting, as it were, the meaning which is tied to the allegorical image as a phenomenal experience. The symbol, in other words, transforms rationality into emotions, or more precisely, words into images, as images in contrast to words need have no rational content in order to be experienced in such a way that their "truth" may be intuitively felt yet pronounced ineffable, and hence by definition transcending the realm of rational discourse. While it is true that the letter itself is repeatedly being pointed to in *The Scarlet Letter*, what is hereby brought forth is not the essentially ineffable emotional quality of the symbol, but rather its relational nature: Chillingworth points to Hester, Dimmesdale points to Chillingworth, Hester points to herself, and at the very end, the narrative points to Dimmesdale yet refuses to represent the letter it implies is inscribed upon him, in order that we might perceive how Dimmesdale's death consigns the letter upon ourselves.

This tendency of symbolism to turn back upon itself and conceive of itself as a self-contained whole is echoed in the very plot of *The House of the Seven Gables*. For as the narrative progresses it becomes clear that the conflict between Pyncheons and Maules that is invoked in the opening chapter, now involves only the former family. Holgrave's story of Alice Pyncheon in chapter thirteen shows how the transgression of the Pyncheons is given a new direction, how it is given an incestuous bent, as it were. Where Colonel Pyncheon's transgression afflicted Matthew Maule, Gervayse Pyncheon's transgression afflicts a member of his own family: in his desire for the deed, he is willing to barter his own daughter. The main narrative repeats this incestuous turn of the conflict: it is not

Holgrave whom Judge Pyncheon violates, but his own cousin Clifford. While this circumstance underlines the structural similarities between the story told by Holgrave, and the larger story told by Hawthorne, it also makes quite clear that Phoebe is not the structural counterpart of Alice in the present that she is easily mistaken for, given the parallel that is established between these two characters through her being hypnotized by Holgrave's story much as Alice is mesmerized by Matthew within that story. In the present day manifestation of the drama, Gervayse Pyncheon's part is acted out by the Judge, who looks to Phoebe to get at the deed no more than he looks to Holgrave. Instead, Alice position in the present is held by Clifford.

As the matter stands on the present level of the narrative, then, the drama of the House has long since degenerated into an internal conflict, a conflict not between Maules and Pyncheons, but between members of the same family. What used to be a social conflict involving a real dialectic between the individual and society, has degenerated into a private conflict within the individual himself, and hence the potentially productive aspects of the conflict have been lost. This, I take it, is the allegorical significance of the Pyncheon-hens, those "pure specimens of a breed which had been transmitted down as an heirloom in the Pyncheon family" (88), though it has now "degenerated [...] in consequence of too strict a watchfulness to keep it pure" (89).[13] In order to break out of the incestuous rut that the conflict has taken through Gervayse Pyncheon's willingness to barter his daughter for the secret of the deed, the bond between the Artist and Society needs to be re-established. This is why the route to redemption must go through Phoebe, who is an outsider, a visitor to the House, just as is the reader, albeit in a different sense. Holgrave's refusal to take advantage of Phoebe in her mesmerized state is an important first step towards the reconciliation which is ultimately brought about within the narrative of *The House of the Seven Gables*, yet it marks only a partial and incomplete movement toward a merging of the historical and present plot of the book, not the one decisive moment in which "the historical plot and the present plot merge completely," as is sometimes mistakenly held.[14] Holgrave refrains from violating Phoebe the way Matthew violated Alice, it is true, but then in contrast to his forefather he is under no pressure from the present avatar of the "Evil Genius" (21) of the Pyncheon family: the situations are not parallel, and hence cannot possibly in itself suffice to link the future to the past. What is more, even if Holgrave refrains from taking control of Phoebe the way his ancestor took control over Alice, he nevertheless repeats the stance of his forefather in that he keeps the secret of the hidden deed to himself. The garden scene in chapter 14 can therefore at most mark a partial remedy of the sins of the past.

But if this is not the one turning point of *The House of the Seven Gables* it may easily be mistaken for, then what is it? On the face of it, it may simply seem as if the question of guilt which should be a concern for the younger generation of the future, were displaced upon the older one of the past. But how can such a displacement of guilt be consonant with a view that insists upon the importance of recognizing guilt as a vital inheritance of the past in the present? In order to find out, the reader, like the characters of the romance, must come to understand how Past, Present, and Future are interconnected. In the reader's case, this is tantamount to grasping how the plotline of Holgrave and Phoebe is interrelated with that of Clifford, Hepzibah, and the Judge. As a first step towards doing so, we may re-examine the structure of the romance.

## 2. The Structure of *The House of the Seven Gables*

While the structural outline of *The Scarlet Letter* has long been widely perceived, the same cannot be said of that of Hawthorne's second romance, and yet *The House of the Seven Gables* is in fact as ambitiously constructed as its predecessor. [15] As its very title suggests, the twenty-one chapters of the romance can be divided structurally into seven groups of three. To a considerable degree, the chapters of the romance arrange themselves naturally into groups of three: 2–4, 5–7, 8–10, 12–14, 15–17, and 18–20. These six groups are themselves framed, so to speak, by the first, the eleventh (literally the central), and the final chapter, that together may be said to form the temporal arch of the romance, in that chapter 1 literally deals with the past, chapter 21, "The Departure," clearly implies a reference to the future, and chapter 11, finally, subtly implies a reference to the Present, itself a transparent arch through which past and future are connected.[16] In other words, these three chapters functionally correspond to the temporal span of Past, Present, and Future.

Significantly, chapters 2-4 constitute the opening of the *narrative* of *The House of the Seven Gables*, which is solemnly announced in the last sentence of chapter 1: "And now—in a very humble way, as will be seen—we proceed to open our narrative" (29). They are acted out within the span of a single day, and all concern Hepzibah setting up shop. The structural coherence of chapters 5–7 is not quite as self-evident, for while chapters 5 and 6 take place during one day, the latter is temporally separated from chapter 7 by one night, just as chapter 5 is set off from chapter 4 by one night. As chapter 8 follows immediately upon chapter 7, the latter might seem more closely connected to the former then the two chapters with which I maintain that it forms a group, or gable, of *The House of the Seven Gables*. However, whereas the break between chapters 4 and 5 also involves a change of focus, from Hepzibah to Phoebe, no such change of perspective is involved in the night that marks the break between chapters 6 and 7. On the contrary, the last paragraph of chapter 6 finds Phoebe in the bed of her chamber, where she wakes up in the first paragraph of chapter 7. Thus chapters 5–7 focus primarily on Phoebe, just as chapters 2–4 focus primarily upon Hepzibah.

Between chapters 7 and 8, on the other hand, there is again a marked change of focus, as chapter 7 ends with a dialogue between Hepzibah and Clifford and chapter 8 returns to Phoebe by means of an analepsis—the technical term for what is commonly known as a "flashback"[17]—bringing us back to the point in the story where she left the elderly pair in order to answer the call of the shop-bell. Chapters 8–10 present the most disparate group of the romance. In contrast to the majority of the chapters of the book, chapters 9 and 10 are primarily set in a diegetic rather than mimetic mood, to speak with Genette. What is more, they are temporally much more diffuse than the other groups of the romance. These chapters nevertheless form a unit in that Judge Pyncheon's intrusion into the shop in chapter 8 underscores the frail nature of Clifford's present situation, the relative calm and well-being of which is the subject of the following two chapters, especially highlighting his relation to Phoebe.

The second half of the book follows a similar pattern. Chapters 12–14 depict the interview and dawning romance of Holgrave and Phoebe in the Pyncheon garden, with 41 out of a total 50 pages taking place on a single evening (including the whole of chapter 13, as this apparent excursion into the past is in fact read to Phoebe by Holgrave on the night in question). Chapters 15–17 concern the figurative departure of the Past from the House in the form of Hepzibah and Clifford's flight from it; and again, the action is confined to a single day and night. The last section, finally, comprising chapters 18–20, reverts to the House on the night of Hepzibah's and Clifford's departure and ends on the following day with their return. The narrative of the book thus begins with six chapters acted out in three days, and ends with six chapters acted out in two. It is preceded by one chapter recounting the events of some 170 years, and followed by one chapter recounting the events of a week or two, but opening up a vista to a future of indefinite extension. Which leaves us with the central seven chapters of the romance, that recount the passing days of a summer in which nothing much seems to happen. Indeed, it seems to me that it is the very failure of this section to contribute much to the plot besides "a kind of irrelevant whimsicality for the most part," as one critic complains,[18] that suggests how it functions within the romance as a whole: it is just there, a long stretch of presence which seems almost to dissolve into nothing if one looks upon it from the point of view of the plot, much like "this visionary and impalpable Now, which, if once you look closely at it, is nothing" (149).

As in *The Scarlet Letter*, the various sections of the book are rewardingly looked upon as forming sets of symmetrically interlocked sequences: chapters 2–4 interlock with chapters 18–20, 5–7 with 15–17, and 8–10 with 12–14.[19] The parallels and contrasts are most significant to our understanding of the romance in the first case; between the other chapters they are of a more general nature. For instance, the title of chapter 5 ("May and November") sets up an opposition between Phoebe and Hepzibah, and chapter 15 similarly sets up an opposition between Hepzibah and the Judge ("The Scowl and the Smile"); the evocation of the Pyncheon hens in chapter 6 (88–90) is contrasted by the evocation of their absence in chapter 16 (247); and while chapter 7 marks Clifford's first appearance in the house (he enters it already at the end of chapter 6, but only as a voice heard by Phoebe), chapter 17 shows his departure from it. The middle sections could also be conceived of in terms of such parallels and contrasts, chapters 8–10 revolving primarily around the relation between Phoebe and Clifford, while chapters 12–14 are principally concerned with the relation of Phoebe and Holgrave. It is hardly by chance that the scene between the latter pair is acted out in the Pyncheon-Garden, which is the title and principal subject of chapter 10. As Alice Pyncheon's harpsichord is alluded to in five of the romance's twenty-one chapters, it may be purely incidental that it is referred to in chapters 9 and 13 alike, but one should observe that it is also referred to in chapters 5 and 15 that are similarly symmetrical counterparts, wherein the allusion to this instrument comes with the specification that its music heralds death in the Pyncheon family. (The fifth and final evocation of the harpsichord is in the last paragraph of the book.) Whatever the case might be, there is a further parallel in that Phoebe is likened to a flower in chapter 9 (142), as is Alice in chapter 13 (191), the relevance of which is underscored by Clifford looking between a flower and Phoebe "as if the garden-flower were the sister of the household-maiden" (147) in chapter 10, observing in chapter 14 that her maiden days are over by declaring that "the bud is a bloom!" (220).

Important as these correspondences are for establishing the structure as such, it is the correlations between chapters 2–4 and 18–20 that may help us elucidate the subject of the romance. We have already pointed out the sexual connotations of Hepzibah's venture to set up shop in chapters 2–4. Though Hepzibah is initially "stained" through her contact with money in the opening chapters, Phoebe in contrast handles business transactions as if it were her second nature, retaining her innocence throughout. Yet Phoebe, too, eventually is stained by a kind of sin, but not until chapter 20. The sexual imagery implicit in chapters 2–4 should therefore be seen in conjunction with the union of Holgrave and Phoebe that takes place in the gable of the book which is comprised of chapters 18–20. This closing section of the narrative inverts its opening section in another respect as well, for whereas Hepzibah must find the courage to come out of the House, Phoebe must venture to enter it. In both cases, as we shall see in section 3, the House is emblematic of Death.

Before we expound this assertion, we may note some of the other correspondences between the two sections. Chapter 3 is the first time inside the House we hear the tinkling of the shop-bell (42); in chapter 19, it is heard for the last time (288), now from a position outside the House. The two men on the street, Dixey and his friend, enter in chapter 3, and reappear in chapter 19, compressing their views on the business of cent-shops in phrases that remain almost identical from chapter to chapter:

> "[...] My wife kept a cent-shop, three months, and lost five dollars on her outlay!"
> "Poor business!" responded Dixey, in a tone as if he were shaking his head.—"Poor business!" (47)

> "[...] My wife tried it, and lost five dollars on her outlay!"
> "Poor business!" said Dixey, shaking his head.—"Poor business!" (291)[20]

Ned Higgins, the little urchin who is Hepzibah's first customer, also makes his first appearance in chapter 3 (49–51), and is present again in chapter 19. To conclude our inventory of chapter 3, we might wish to observe that Holgrave tries to comfort Hepzibah by insisting that her feelings of anxiety will soon turn out to be "as unreal as the giants and ogres of a child's story-book" (44). In chapter 19, significantly, the news that Judge Pyncheon might be murdered make the children take to their heels, "as if some giant or ogre were in pursuit" (296).

In sum, the chiastic pattern of *The House of the Seven Gables* is the following.

| D1 | D3 |
|---|---|
| 1. The Old Pyncheon Family (the past). | 21. The Departure (the future). |
| **A1** | **A2** |
| 2. The activities of a single character, Hepzibah, rendered largely in the present tense. | 18. The non-activities of a single character, Judge Pyncheon, rendered in the present tense. |
| 3. Dixey and friend comment on Hepzibah's shop (47). | 19. Dixey and friend comment on Hepzibah's shop (291). |
| 4. Hepzibah's "crisis" (64)—her day in the shop— "is like death" (67). | 20. Phoebe's and Holgrave's "crisis," in which "there is no Death" (317). |
| **B1** | **B2** |
| 5. Alice's harpsichord prefiguring death (83–4). | 15. Alice's harpsichord "prelusive of death in the family" (225). |
| 6. The Pyncheon hens (88–90). | 16. The Pyncheon hens absent (247). |
| 7. Clifford appears in the House. | 17. Clifford departs from the House. |
| **C1** | **C2** |
| 8. "The Pyncheon of Today;" the pres-ent avatar of Colonel Pyncheon. | 12. "The Daguerreotypist;" the present avatar of Matthew Maule. |
| 9. Phoebe likened to a flower (142). | 13. Alice likened to a flower (191). |
| 10. Clifford urged to grasp likeness of happiness in the moment (158); garden compared to "Eden of a thunder-smitten Adam" (150). | 14. Holgrave has "never felt anything so very much like happiness as at this moment;" House compared to "bower in Eden" (214). |

D2

11. The Arched Window (a symbol for the Present).

Thus the principal structural device of *The House of the Seven Gables* is a form of repetition by inversion, just as is the case in *The Scarlet Letter*. The same thing happens twice, but under conditions so altered as to almost amount to a reversal. The method is less readily identifiable in *The House of the Seven Gables* largely because its cast of characters has grown larger, and because there is the added difficulty of comprehending how the figures of the present relate to those of the past.

But there is another aspect of the structure of *The House of the Seven Gables* that renders it more complicated. I have already argued that chapters 1, 11, and 21 stand for Past, Present, and Future, in the overarching structure of the romance. However, there would seem to be an alternative past-present-future pattern in the book, which is more intimately concerned with the figure of the Colonel/Judge. Although he appears in six chapters of the romance, Judge Pyncheon enters into the House only in two, chapters 8 and 15. To these two should be added chapter 1, seeing that the Judge is a veritable avatar of the Colonel: "putting aside his steel-hilted broadsword to take up a gold-headed cane, the Colonel Pyncheon, of two centuries ago, steps forward as the Judge, of the passing moment!" (120). The character of the original founder of the Pyncheon race thus is present in the House in three chapters, neatly separated by seven chapters each.[21] What is more, the titles of the first two of these chapters ("The Old Pyncheon Family," and "The Pyncheon of To-Day") are suggestive of the temporal theme of the romance, its preoccupation with the interrelation of "a mysterious and terrible Past [...] a blank Future," and "this visionary and impalpable Now, which, if you once look closely at it, is nothing" (149). In view of how effortlessly these chapters respectively suggest the Past and the Present, we might expect the title of the third chapter in which the Judge enters the House to complete the sequence by implying a reference to the Future, but "The Scowl and Smile" clearly does not.

However, the narrative sequence of past, present and future is not so much disrupted as deferred by this circumstance, because the Judge does in fact keep house in one additional chapter where the future is definitely, if ironically, implied by the title: "Governor Pyncheon"—a reference to a future unrealized, mocking the ambitions of the dead Judge that now belong irrevocably to the past. Like chapter 8, chapter 18 is subtly set off from the linear progression of the narrative through the means of an analepsis. There are, in fact, only three instances of analepses in *The House of the Seven Gables.* The first, of course, is the complete analepsis of chapter 1. The other two (both of them partial) occur significantly at the beginning of chapter 8 and chapter 18 respectively: when Phoebe enters the shop at the beginning of chapter 8, the narrative moves back approximately a page; when it turns back on itself at the beginning of chapter 18, it moves back perhaps a chapter. The temporal distance covered by these analepses is in itself a trifling matter; what matters is that they are there, that each of these three chapters mark a sort of turning back to a point closer to the origin.[22] Thus the circumstance that the very frame of the romance may be said to imply a past-present-future pattern must not make us dismiss the alternative past-present-future paradigm indicated by the titles of chapters 1, 8 and 18, which seems, if anything, even clearer than that of the chapters to which we have already ascribed it. One must perhaps conclude, then, that *The House of the Seven Gables* contains two mutually incompatible structures. But in that case one must also say, I think, that the temporal paradigm represented by chapters 1, 8, and 18, is incapable of executing the providential work Hawthorne has designed *The House of the Seven Gables* to fulfil. How fully—if at all—this double structure is wrought out in *The House of the Seven Gables* is an open question; but as will be seen, this strategy of a double structure is one that we can certainly identify in *The Marble Faun*.

Regardless of how we decide on this matter, chapter 18 is in many ways the key chapter of the romance. As I have already pointed out above, chapters 15–17 emblematically portray how the Past departs from the House in "The Flight of Two Owls," while chapters 19–20 show us how the House is temporarily reappropriated by the Future in the form of Phoebe and Holgrave, after which it is definitely abandoned by the Past and the Future alike, in "The Departure." But in order to arrive at this conclusion, the narrative must pass through chapter 18, in which Judge Pyncheon sits dead in the House; it is through traversing this death that the Past can be married to the Future, and thus be enabled to leave the premises of the House. Hepzibah and Clifford, we recall, despite their age are frequently referred to as "children." While their departure temporarily startles Clifford "into manhood" (258), chapter 17 significantly ends with Hepzibah's prayer that they may continue to lead their lives as children: "'Oh, God!'— ejaculated poor, gaunt Hepzibah—then paused a moment, to consider what her prayer should be—'Oh, God—our Father—are we not thy children?'" (267). While Phoebe is also at some points referred to as a child, this designation is reserved for the first half of the romance. As has not gone unnoticed, in chapter 14 Clifford explicitly states that for Phoebe, "Girlhood has passed into womanhood" (220). This marks the sexual awakening of Phoebe, to be sure; but the significance of this awakening is lost on us if we fail to observe that on Phoebe's part this awakening is accompanied by "an odd kind of motherly sentiment" (216) towards her older relatives.[23] Clifford, too, is repeatedly designated as a "child," in marked contrast to Holgrave, who despite being a young man is plagued by the past to such an extent that much like the chicken of the Pyncheon-hens he seems "to have aggregated" into himself "the ages, not only of these living specimens of the breed, but of all its forefathers and foremothers" (151). Yet in chapter 20, we learn that Holgrave and Phoebe "were like two *children* who go hand in hand, pressing closely to one another's side, through a shadow-haunted passage" (305; my emphasis). For a brief moment, then, Holgrave and Phoebe are in the position occupied by Clifford and Hepzibah through the major part of the romance: but the "children" of chapter 20 take the passage through the House of Death which the "children" of chapter 17 fled from. It is this *passing through* which enable the young ones of the past to be figuratively reborn as the parents of the future. The offspring of the parents, however, is not the Future, but the Past, because once Judge Pyncheon has joined the ranks of real ghosts, Hepzibah and Clifford might materialize, so to speak, out of their former existence as figurative ghosts. Holgrave and Phoebe may become such parents, because they acknowledge the paradoxical circumstance that to be a parent of the future one must first deliver the past.

The importance of this view of life as the traversal of a moment of grief is subtly underscored in the very first paragraph of the romance, where the narrator claims seldom to "fail to turn down Pyncheon-street, for the sake of *passing through the shadow* of [...] the great elm-tree, and the weather-beaten edifice" (5; my emphasis). It is repeated in more explicit form at the beginning of chapter 16, when the Judge has forced Hepzibah to get Clifford: "Thus it is, that the grief of the *passing moment* takes upon itself an individuality, and a character of climax, which it is destined to lose, after a while, and to fade into the dark gray tissue, common to the grave or glad events of many years ago. It is but for a moment, comparatively, that anything looks strange or startling;—a truth, that has the bitter and the sweet in it" (241; my emphasis). The whole of *The House of the Seven Gables* is in a sense a passing affair; to understand why this is a circumstance that has both the bitter and the sweet in it, we must try to understand how time, wealth, and love are interconnected. In this, I believe, the implications of the romance's structure outlined above will prove helpful.

## 3. The Presence of Death: The Use of the Present Tense

In contradistinction to all other chapters of the romance, chapters 2 and 18 focus exclusively on the activity—or lack thereof—of only one character, Hepzibah, and the Judge, respectively. Both of these characters are in a sense dead; the Judge, of course, quite literally so. But Hepzibah, too, is dead, if only in a figurative sense. As Holgrave explains to Phoebe at one point, "Miss Hepzibah, by secluding herself from society, has lost all true relation with it, and is in fact dead; although she galvanizes herself into a semblance of life, and stands behind her counter" (216). The impression that we are in a sense dealing with a ghost in chapter 2 is underscored in the chapter itself, where it is stated that Hepzibah comes out of her chamber sighing, "like a gust of chill, damp wind out of a long-closed vault, the door of which has accidentally been set ajar" (32).

Another feature that these two chapters have in common is that they are marked by the narrator's manipulation of the narrative's tense to a greater degree than any other chapters of the book. Approximately a third of chapter 2 is set in the present tense, large parts of which is set in a transcendent mode of the present which allows the narrator to bring the character of the narrative into the immediate presence of the reader. Below is a representative passage:

> The maiden lady's devotions are concluded. Will she now issue forth over the threshold of our story? Not yet, by many moments. First, every drawer in the tall, old-fashioned bureau is to be opened, with difficulty, and with a succession of spasmodic jerks; then, all must close again, with the same fidgety reluctance. There is a rustling of stiff silks; a tread of backward and forward footsteps, to-and-fro, across the chamber. We suspect Miss Hepzibah, moreover, of taking a step upward into a chair, in order to give heedful regard to her appearance on all sides, and at full length, in the oval, dingy-framed toilet-glass, that hangs above her table. Truly! Well, indeed! Who would have thought it! Is all this precious time to be lavished on the matutinal repair and beautifying of an elderly person, who never goes abroad—whom nobody ever visits—and from whom, when she shall have done her utmost, it were the best charity to turn one's eyes another way! (31)

As employed by Hawthorne in *The House of the Seven Gables*, the effect of this technique is to expose the pettiness of human dilemmas, to demonstrate how ridiculous all human endeavours must seem, unless they are viewed from a distance that allows us to make out a greater picture, to view man as a part of the greater whole which is Mankind.[24]

This feature is even more pronounced in the "Governor Pyncheon" chapter, that takes the dearth of action distinctive of the whole of *The House of the Seven Gables* to an extreme: throughout, Judge Pyncheon sits dead in the chair of his ancestor. The events of the chapter are experienced by none of the characters of the narrative, and bear no significance whatsoever to the further development of the plot. Strictly speaking, there are no events in the chapter, as the narrator stresses that the ghosts that file in front of the "defunct nightmare" (252) of the Judge "must by no means be considered as forming an actual portion of our story" (281). Within the structure of *The House of the Seven Gables*, then, "Governor Pyncheon" does not only take death as its subject matter, it constitutes a death in its own right: it is in a sense a Nothing, yet a Nothing spread out over sixteen pages.[25]

The present tense is thus indubitably tied to the representation of death, or at least, of death-like states of being, in the book. Symptomatically, the book's other principal "ghost," Clifford ("another dead and long-buried person" [216], as Holgrave puts it), is repeatedly addressed in this transcendent mode of the present tense. Witness for instance the narrator's apostrophe of Clifford at the end of chapter 10:

> Alas, poor Clifford! You are old, and worn with troubles that ought never to have befallen you. You are partly crazy, and partly imbecile; a ruin, a failure, as almost everybody is,—though some in less degree, or less perceptibly, than their fellows. Fate has no happiness in store for you; unless your quiet home in the old family residence, with the faithful Hepzibah, and your long summer-afternoons with Phoebe, and these Sabbath festivals with Uncle Venner and the Daguerreotypist, deserve to be called happiness! Why not? If not the thing itself, it is marvellously like it, and the more so for that ethereal and intangible quality, which causes it all to vanish, at too close an introspection. Take it, therefore, while you may. Murmur not—question not—but make the most of it! (157–8)

Or the ridiculing of him in the following chapter:

> Behold him, therefore, at the arched window, with an earthen pipe in his mouth! Behold him, with his gray hair, and a wan, unreal smile over his countenance, where still hovered a beautiful grace, which his worst enemy must have acknowledged to

> be spiritual and immortal, since it had survived so long! Behold him, scattering airy spheres abroad, from the window into the street! (171)

Holgrave and Phoebe, in contrast, are almost completely spared the doubtful honour of being rendered in this representational mode. Only on one occasion is Phoebe implicated by the death-in-life signified by the transcendent present. Tellingly, this is in chapter 19, when she is on the verge of entering the House in which sits the corpse of Judge Pyncheon:

> Yet we feel it to be a questionable venture, even for Phoebe, at this juncture, to cross the threshold of the seven gables. Is her healthful presence potent enough to chase away the crowd of pale, hideous, and sinful phantoms, that have gained admittance there, since her departure? Or will she, likewise, fade, sicken, sadden, and grow into deformity, and be only another pallid phantom, to glide noiselessly up and down the stairs, and affright children, as she pauses at the window?
>
> At least, we would gladly forewarn the unsuspecting girl, that there is nothing in human shape or substance to receive her, unless it be the figure of Judge Pyncheon, who—wretched spectacle that he is, and frightful in our remembrance, since our night-long vigil with him!—still keeps his place in the oaken chair. (297)

Phoebe's re-entrance into the House is thus described by the narrator in terms which, like those employed when relating Hepzibah's entrance into the shop, makes it an occasion of suspense, a moment of great matter. As if to further underscore the parallels between the situations, the narrator looks upon the circumstances surrounding Phoebe's entrance into the house in chapter 19 as an instance of the "intermingling of *tragedy with mirth*" which "happens, daily, hourly, momently" (295; my emphasis), just as Hepzibah's situation in chapter 2 is seen as exemplifying the precept that "Life is made up of *marble and mud*" (41; my emphasis) and as an illustration of a drama constantly re-enacted in the present ("In this republican country, amid the fluctuating waves of our social life, somebody is always at the drowning-point" [38]).

The use of the transcendent present at this juncture thus serves to underscore the implication that Phoebe, as a result of her imminent confrontation with Death, might turn into another avatar of Hepzibah. The Pyncheons, we should remember, are characterized by "an absurd delusion of family importance," which "caused the poorest member of the race to feel as if he inherited a kind of nobility, and might yet come into the possession of princely wealth to support it." It is important to note that Hawthorne does not repudiate this "absurd delusion" in itself. On the contrary, it is made clear that "this peculiarity" of the species is accountable both for what is best and for what is worst in them. "In the better specimens of the breed," we are informed, it "threw an ideal grace over the hard material of human life, without stealing away any truly valuable quality;" in "the baser sort," however, "its effect was to increase the liability to sluggishness and dependence, and induce the victim of a shadowy hope to remit all self-effort, while awaiting the realization of his dreams" (19). These are the two positions that Hepzibah is torn between in the book; the terminology employed in this sequence (race, specimen, breed) implies that they are universal categories, and hence the Pyncheon predicament is, in a sense, the problem of Everyman, Man being both a partaker of the divine, and the basest of sinners.

And this is why, I think, the representation of Hepzibah's endeavour to open a cent-shop contains such strong sexual undercurrents: this is Hawthorne's way of suggesting that we can come into possession of the wealth we are under the impression of having inherited only if we are willing to acknowledge our sexuality. Hepzibah, the Maiden Lady, prides herself on a fortune—her virginity—that she has never really possessed, as she has never been willing to barter it for something else. In conceiving of the concept of virginity as something which immediately embraces the concept of wealth, Hepzibah thus displays another version of the symbolistic stance which Hawthorne's romance rejects by insisting that the concept of wealth can be wedded to the concept of virginity only through the mediation of the concept of sexual love. Thus Phoebe, too, might squander the inheritance (innocence) that this romance suggests that every person is endowed with through birth, by refusing to trade her virginity, the signifier of this inherited innocence, for a greater signified: love. That is why the narrator wonders whether her presence will be "potent enough" in the passage from chapter 19 that we have quoted above; the copper-coin received by Hepzibah in chapter 3 (the symmetrical counterpart of chapter 19), although "as potent [...] as a galvanic ring" (52), was not. The price one has to pay to attain this greater fortune is a high one indeed: one pays by allowing one's consciousness of innocence to be extinguished by a consciousness of guilt, by accepting that one's mortal frame is but an earthly flower that is bound to wilt and die. But by thus recognizing Death as the inevitable end (in a functional as well as temporal sense) of mortal existence, one may come to see that this transaction is less disadvantageous than it may first appear. In fact, by refusing to engage in such a transaction one squanders the fortune one has inherited, as this fortune is in fact merely the reminiscence of a *future* wealth that can be attained in the present only in a fragmentary and imperfect manner.[26]

That Phoebe does not turn into such an avatar of the Maiden Lady is of course due to the outcome of chapter 20, which is, as is widely acknowledged, obviously designed to constitute the emotional climax of the romance. Yet most readers have been reluctant to accept the success of the redemptive office that Hawthorne must have hoped that the chapter would be capable of fulfilling. I am the first to admit that if looked upon with expectations dictated by the realistic norm of the novel, the emotionally overcharged sentimentality of the chapter seems utterly unconvincing. I am speaking out of my own experience, as I still retain a distinct recollection of how ludicrous the scene appeared to me the first time I read the book. It is true that critics have been known to argue the plausibility of the love scene from a realistic point of view as well. Yet even though it is certainly true that the scene is not unprepared for, the awkwardness of the scene strikes me as a deliberate device to make the reader inclined to interpret it in a way that is not dictated by the realistic paradigm of the novel. It seems to me, in short, an attempt to defamiliarize the conventional love scene of the sentimental novel. As we argued in our discussion of "Rappaccini's Daughter," in Hawthorne's concept of the romance the Heart is not merely a repository for the emotions, but fulfils an intellectual office as well. Hawthorne never trusts his fictions to perform their office by overpowering the emotions of the reader the way such diverse writers as Poe and Maria Cummins both, in their own ways, can be said to do. The emotional charge might be quite as pronounced in Hawthorne, but in his case the impact of this emotional charge does not arise so much out of the scene itself, but is dependent, rather, upon the reader sensing how the scene in question is related to other passages of the narrative. Which is to say that the emotional impact of Hawthorne's stories can be fully experienced only if we prove able, and willing, to distance ourselves from the emotions represented, by grasping them by way of our intellect as well as by our emotions.

# Errata

This index supersedes the one printed on pages 441–450.

*Magnus Ullén: The Half-Vanished Structure. Hawthorne's Allegorical Dialectics.*
ISBN 3-03910-200-1 / US-ISBN 0-8204-6868-1

Hochfeldstrasse 32, Postfach 746, CH-3000 Bern 9, info@peterlang.com, www.peterlang.com, www.peterlang.net

# Index

Like the concluding scaffold scene in *The Scarlet Letter*, the love-scene between Holgrave and Phoebe is designed to defy realism, and hence to be impervious to an exclusively figurative mode of reading: it is a scene which demands to be read literally, to be examined word by word. Superficially, the redemptive outcome of "The Flower of Eden" hinges only on the union of Phoebe and Holgrave that takes place in the chapter. The scene becomes more interesting, however, if we observe that this moment of love marks the symmetrical contrast to Hepzibah's desultory first day in business, recounted in chapter 4. Significantly, both these situations are said to constitute a "crisis" (64 and 307) for the characters involved. More importantly, the situations provide contrasting pictures of the character's experience of time. Hepzibah's venture marks a belated re-entrance into history: by one of those co-incidents that says so much about Hawthorne's allegorical method, Ned Higgins, her first customer, just happens to be "the very emblem of old Father Time" (115). Yet despite thus having taken a step towards that realm of "the very Present that is flitting away from us" (2), Hepzibah is unable to come fully alive in the moment; and her difficulties with handling her job are represented as a consequence of this inability:

> There is sad confusion, indeed, when the spirit thus flits away into the past, or into the more awful future, or, in any manner, steps across the spaceless boundary betwixt its own region and the actual world; where the body remains to guide itself, as best it may, with little more than the mechanism of animal life. It is like death, without death's quiet privilege; its freedom from mortal care. (66–7)

In stark contrast to this state of death in life, Phoebe and Holgrave cancel Death altogether by living entirely in the moment:

> "Do you love me?" asked Holgrave. "If we love one another, the moment has room for nothing more. Let us pause upon it, and be satisfied. Do you love me, Phoebe?"
>
> "You look into my heart," replied she, letting her eyes droop. "You know I love you!"
>
> And it was in this hour, so full of doubt and awe, that the one miracle was wrought, without which every human existence is a blank. The bliss, which makes all things true, beautiful, and holy, shone around this youth and maiden. They were conscious of nothing sad nor old. They transfigured the earth, and made it Eden again, and themselves the two first dwellers in it. The dead man, so close beside

> them, was forgotten. At such a crisis, there is no Death; for Immortality is revealed anew, and embraces everything in its hallowed atmosphere. (307)

These two scenes, then, stand as representatives of the two conceptions of time that the book presents as available to man. On the one hand, Hepzibah's experience of "the intolerable length of time that creeps between dawn and sunset" (67), on the other, "the moment" of love upon which Holgrave and Phoebe pause. Although it is only the first which is explicitly presented in connection with the economic theme of the book, the second, too, if rightly considered must be said to be linked to this theme. After all, it is this moment of love which determines the fortune of the pair: it is their joint decision to make public the news of the Judge's death that constitutes the peripety of the drama of guilt and retribution that their families have been engaged in for some two hundred years. Equally importantly, their decision is made with no thought to what the economic consequences for themselves might be. The scene might therefore be said to mark a point at which the love of gold is transfigured into a love of man.

That some such notion of a transformation of a debased form of desire into a natural form of desire is what the section of the book comprising chapters 18–20 is meant to convey has in fact already been subtly indicated by yet another correspondence between this section and its symmetrical counterpart in the earlier half of the book. At the beginning of chapter 4, Judge Pyncheon enters the scene for the first time, and it is pointed out that he carries himself with an air of opulence, which makes his wealth as indubitable "as if you had seen him touching the twigs of the Pyncheon-elm, and, Midas-like, transmuting them to gold" (57). This transmutation is repeated at the opening of chapter 19, but this time the simile itself is transformed into a figurative fact: one "single branch" of the Pyncheon-elm, we are informed, "by the earlier change with which the elm-tree sometimes prophesies the autumn, had been transmuted to bright gold" (285). The reality of this transformation is not to be doubted, nor that in the value scheme of the book the worth of this "natural" gold far exceeds that of "the big, heavy, solid unrealities," specified in an earlier chapter as "gold, landed estate, offices of trust and emolument, and public honors" (229). Indeed, the golden branch of the Pyncheon-elm, "was like the golden branch, that gained Aeneas and the

Sibyl admittance into Hades" (285). Thus the golden branch that Hawthorne would have us treasure, is the branch whereby one may come to know how death is present in life. We should perhaps recall that Aeneas visit to Hades marks the prophetic moment of *The Aeneid*: by finding one's way to the realm of death from that of life, the epic hero comes to bridge the gap between the Past and the Future, and thus is able to arrive at an understanding of life as a totality. In order to experience the happiness of the moment, one must also be able to experience the pain of the moment, which derives from the very circumstance that the moment always dies, that it is indeed only a "visionary and impalpable Now, which, if you once look closely at it, is nothing" (149). In other words, the present moment is always marked by death.

*The House of the Seven Gables* takes note of this circumstance and develops it by making a case for a kind of movement between temporal perspectives. In order to find happiness, one must be able to live in the present, to enjoy the moment. But in order not to be consumed by the moment, and in order to transcend the pettiness that often adheres to it, the moment must be viewed from a distance. The symbolistic conception of the moment as Presence, must be displaced by the recognition that there is an allegorical Absence built into the moment, in the form of a Presence of Death. As so often in Hawthorne, we are confronted with a paradox: one must both embrace the moment and transcend it. Similarly, one must actively engage the world, yet still come to discern that "God is the sole worker of realities" (180), "that we mortals [...] in spite of our ridiculous activity, bring nothing finally to pass" (163). In effect, however, these seemingly self-contradictory strands serve to cancel each other out, for as Holgrave remarks upon entering the story in chapter 3, there is "nothing so singular in life, as that everything appears to lose its substance, the instant one actually grapples with it" (44). It is thus by engaging the world, rather than evading it, that one may hope to spiritualize it.

Insofar as the moment is truly spiritualized it can be said to partake of Eternity, and it is truly spiritualized, as we have argued above, insofar as it is marked by death. Recognizing the presence of death in life is thus in effect tantamount to incorporating a sense of distance into the moment: it is to conceive of the moment in allegorical rather than symbolistic terms. By seeing how death is a prerequisite for the kind of fullness of the moment that one may experience in erotic love, one comes to see how this fullness of the moment necessarily points beyond itself, to a state of existence that can only be perceived in a fragmentary and paradoxical manner in this world.[27] Thus an allegorical sense of distance is incorporated into the very embodiment of a symbolic moment of presence, creating a Dante-esque effect of symbolism and allegory synthetically interpenetrating each other.[28]

*

As we saw in the previous chapter, *The Scarlet Letter* even in its first chapter explicitly engages the reader in the allegorical chain of signifiers by which it attempts to make its point. Finding the rose-bush on the threshold of the narrative, as Hawthorne puts it, the narrator can "hardly do otherwise than pluck one of its flowers and present it to the reader" (SL, 48). There is a comparable passage in *The House of the Seven Gables*, and even if it is not given nearly as much emphasis as in the earlier book, the similarity of the overall tone of the passages is striking. Significantly, the symbol which is assigned the office of mediating between the realm of the narrative and that of the reader is none other than the golden branch that we have already taken note of above:

> This one mystic branch hung down before the main-entrance of the seven gables, so nigh the ground, that any passer-by might have stood on tiptoe and plucked it off. Presented at the door, it would have been a symbol of his right to enter, and be made acquainted with all the secrets of the house. (285)

We will not expound the rest of the lengthy paragraph that these lines instigate; for our purposes, it is enough to note that we are hereby once again invited to engage in the process of generating the meaning of the romance by partaking in the dialectical process of transference that the romance presents as its ideal end.

At the centre of this process, of course, stand Holgrave and Phoebe, as figures of the Writer and the Reader, the Artist and the Audience, respectively.[29] We must concede, however, that Holgrave and Phoebe only mark one of a whole series of representations of the relation between Artist and Audience. Matthew Maule and Alice Pyncheon constitute another temporal manifestation of this relation, as do Clifford (a personification of "The Artist of the Beautiful" in the guise of someone who never got the chance to effectuate his ideal desires, as several critics observe)[30] and Hepzibah. In each case, furthermore, the relation between Artist and Audience is depicted as being mediated through the work of art itself, metonymically represented by the figure of authority of a previous generation: by the Colonel, Clifford's Uncle Jaffrey, and finally, Judge Jaffrey—or more specifically, by the death of these characters.

In other words, in *The House of the Seven Gables* the figure of the Artist is multiplied to the effect that there is at least one avatar of the Artist at every stage of the historical process under consideration. This series of artist-audience relations allegorically represented in the book, may be seen as a concrete illustration of the image of the "ascending spiral curve" that Clifford expounds on the train:

> You are aware, my dear Sir—you must have observed it, in your own experience—that all human progress is in a circle; or, to use a more accurate and beautiful figure, in an ascending spiral curve. While we fancy ourselves going straight forward, and attaining, at every step, an entirely new position of affairs, we do actually return to something long ago tried and abandoned, but which we now find etherealized, refined, and perfected to its ideal. The past is but a coarse and sensual prophecy of the present and the future. (259–60)

As Waggoner importantly reminds us, there is a certain ambiguity to Clifford's talk of history being "perfected to its ideal"—this phrase need not necessarily be taken to mean "better" or "more desirable," as Clifford would seem to assume, but could in fact mean "that evil as well as good continues, both being gradually 'refined' or rendered more 'spiritual'" (*Study*, 178). Within the narrative of *The House of the Seven Gables* the ascending spiral curve thus moves from an initial hostile relation between Matthew, Jr. and Alice, over the improductive, because incestuous, relation between Clifford and Hepzibah, until it is finally "perfected to its ideal" in the form of the relation between Holgrave and Phoebe—this much the structure of the narrative reveals. What remains undetermined, however, is whether this etherealization must be understood as a positive or a negative process. And the answer to this question, as we have already implied, is dependent upon what response *The House of the Seven Gables* itself elicits from the individual reader.

On the assumption that Holgrave and Clifford must be seen as representing different versions of the artist, the many parallels between them that can be traced in the latter half of the novel seem less inexplicable. As many commentators have observed Clifford's wild speech on the train in chapter 17 in many important respects is closely parallel to Holgrave's railings against the past in chapter 12. What is more, it is Holgrave who recalls Clifford's childhood secret about the hidden deed (315); what Clifford forgets, Holgrave recalls. Even though there is a rational (and hence, realistic) explanation for this, in the more liberal hermeneutic context allowed us by the romance, this is hardly insignificant. In the same scene, Phoebe says to Holgrave that it "is but two or three weeks ago, that you seemed to wish people to live in something as fragile and temporary as a bird's nest!" (315) again clearly invoking Clifford's words on the train about the charm of the early epochs of mankind, when "men dwelt in temporary huts, or bowers of branches, as easily constructed as a bird's nest" (260). In view of these parallels it is surely not coincidental that Holgrave declares in chapter 12 that the Past "lies upon the Present like a giant's dead body!" (182), but that, when the Judge dies, it is Clifford who announces that "The weight is gone" (250), whereas for Holgrave the death of the Judge is, in contrast, a source of anxiety:

> The presence of yonder dead man threw a great black shadow over everything; he made the universe, so far as my perception could reach, a scene of guilt, and of retribution more dreadful than the guilt. The sense of it took away my youth. I never hoped to feel young again! The world looked strange, wild, evil, hostile;—my past life, so lonesome and dreary; my future, a shapeless gloom, which I must mould into gloomy shapes! (306).

Holgrave's expression of a sense of guilt at the Judge's death is one of the more intriguing moments of the narrative, but we do not have to resort to the speculations some critics have engaged in, in order to explain it.[31] It should be seen, rather, in conjunction with the flower imagery emphasized by the titles of chapters 19 and 20, "Alice's Posies" and "The Flower of Eden." "I thought of you both," says Clifford to Holgrave and Phoebe at the very end of chapter 20, "as we came down the street, and beheld Alice's Posies in full bloom. And so the flower of Eden has bloomed, likewise, in this old, darksome house, to-day!" (308).

Significantly, we are informed in the opening chapter that Alice's Posies grow out of death: "the dust of the street and the decay of the roof gradually formed a kind of soil for them, out of which they grew, when Alice had long been in her grave" (28).

As in *The Scarlet Letter*, then, *The House of the Seven Gables* confronts us with an image which is at once Life, a flower, and Death, for Alice's Posies are also invoked as "a mystic expression that something within the house was consummated" (286); and this "something" is not the love of Holgrave and Phoebe, which is not consummated until the end of chapter 20, but the death of Judge Pyncheon. In *The Scarlet Letter*, Pearl is the ideal signified of the material signifier of the letter, a circumstance that heralds the presence of an essential lack in this *ideal*, Pearl being herself a very *material* character. *The House of the Seven Gables* will present a different case only if it is taken for granted that the ideal signified of The Flower of Eden is exclusively associated with the love of Holgrave and Phoebe. Not that it is not made up of this love; but just as the letter in *The Scarlet Letter* which designates the ideal love of Hester and Dimmesdale leaves a material residue in the form of Pearl, the Flower of Eden designating the ideal union of Holgrave and Phoebe comes with the material residue of the corpse of Judge Pyncheon. The truth of the human heart—which is the truth of Romance as well, as the Preface informs us, wherefore it is no coincidence that the House itself is an explicit heart image—is much darker than it might at first appear: the young lovers' present happiness is shown to depend on the death of Judge Pyncheon. Therefore, their happiness is not wholly unstained: despite being formally (publicly) innocent, they are morally (privately) incriminated by the death of Judge Pyncheon. They have not killed him, it is true, but they have been brought together by the wild rapture the circumstances of his death have produced in them.

Phoebe's reaction, then, is quite appropriate: "It seems a sin," she tells Holgrave, "to think of joy, at such a time!" (306); echoing the unwillingness of Dixey's friend to report the suspicious circumstances of Judge Pyncheon's disappearance to the police a few pages earlier: "It seems like a sin to be the first to speak of such a thing" (296). A sin to report a crime, a sin to feel joy in the presence of death: nowhere is Hawthorne's sense of guilt by association keener than in *The House of the Seven Gables*. It seems a sin—but is it? Hawthorne, no doubt, is prone to say "yes" and "no" at the same time, just as he finds Hester both guilty and innocent in *The Scarlet Letter*: once again we are in the presence of the double moral standard that is such a pervasive trait of Hawthorne's writings. *The House of the Seven Gables*, it should be noted, approaches the question of guilt from a perspective very different from that of the former book: it attempts to formulate how and in what sense the individual can (or even must) be said to be innocent and yet guilty at the same time. Thus the problem is not so much how to escape from a paralyzing sense of guilt as how to preserve an animating sense of guilt within a present which is merely *apparently* unstained by guilt. Read superficially, *The House of the Seven Gables* seeks merely to expose the discrepancy between the outward show and internal character of its principal characters, notably Judge Pyncheon. More subtly, the narrative is simultaneously designed to make the reader aware how the *apparently* innocent union of Holgrave and Phoebe, is founded on a recognition of guilt: the purpose of the romance is to bring out this guilt concealed behind the appearance of innocence, in order that it may become an active component in the providential agency of *felix culpa*. Guilt, or at least, guilt transfigured into love, is shown to be the true fortune of mankind. This process of transfiguration is closely connected to the pattern of inversion upon which the formula of the Fortunate Fall operates. In order to prove truly redemptive, however, the pattern of inversion must be supplemented by the mediation of the imagination, which is the faculty through which the individual may come to recognize how guilt involves us all. Such imaginative acts of sympathy effect the transfiguration of guilt by displacing the figurative into the literal, by insisting that what *seems* a sin *is* a sin. It is precisely by thus turning appearance into an essence, an indubitable Reality, that the unreality with which the imperfect moment of the realm of Becoming is marked may be transcended; for it is only if sin is real, that the Hope for redemption can be equally indubitable.

The device which most literally exposes the gap between appearance and reality in *The House of the Seven Gables* is of course the daguerreotype: "There is a wonderful insight in heaven's broad and simple sunshine. While we give it credit only for depicting the merest surface, it actually brings out the secret character with a truth *that no painter would ever venture upon, even could he detect it*" (91; my emphasis). This formulation clearly suggests that there is something transgressive about Holgrave's art. As the daguerreotype looks *through* appearance (the surface) into reality (the secret character beneath it) it allows us to witness the character that is secretly inscribed beneath Judge Pyncheon's appearance of sunshine; a wonderful device, in other words, for the Chillingworths of this world. This preoccupation with sunshine suggests a gap between the artistic practice of Holgrave and that of Hawthorne himself, whose chosen form of expression does not take well to "our own broad daylight," but requires the advantage of being viewed through a "legendary mist, which the Reader, according to his pleasure, may either disregard, or allow [...] to float almost imperceptibly about the characters and events for the sake of a picturesque effect" (2). Why is this? If sunshine provides a medium in which we may look straight through appearance into reality, why does Hawthorne prefer the less clear-sighted medium of moonlight, in which appearance and reality cannot be told apart? If the ideological basis of *The House of the Seven Gables* seems thoroughly conventional, can it be because Hawthorne adopts the strategy of the moon, which "like an ambitious demagogue [...] hides his aspiring purpose by assuming the prevalent hue of popular sentiment" (213)?

In making Holgrave "an artist in the daguerreotype line" (30) Hawthorne is implying that the artist of the present *necessarily* works through the medium provided by present-day society. In *The House of the Seven Gables*, that medium is allegorically represented in Phoebe, whose very name shows her affinity to sunshine. Properly conceived, art is a joint effort, the product of *the relation* between the artist and society (just as Pearl is the product of the relation between Hester and Dimmesdale in *The Scarlet Letter*). As Taylor Stoehr perceptively comments, Holgrave is in part "insulated by his technology, since he cannot be blamed for the 'insights' that the sun itself 'paints'."[32] If we take note of the allegorical significance of this observation, we are provided with a key to the peculiar tone of *The House of the Seven Gables*: the artist cannot be blamed for providing ludicrous, contemptuous, or sentimental representations of the world, as this is how the world reveals itself upon his plates, when filtered through the medium of present day society, when seen, that is, through Phoebe's sunshine.

The artist could, however, be blamed for mesmerizing his audience in his efforts to conjure up a picture of the world before its eyes. We should observe that Hawthorne's description of the mesmerizing process suggests a parallel between his own art and that of Holgrave.[33] Having put Alice Pyncheon into a trance, Matthew Maule tells her father: "Behold your daughter!" (204). Hawthorne uses this pompous verb himself no less than five times, on at least three different occasions (38; 171; 229), thus suggesting that the romance is subject to the author's power, just as is Alice to Matthew's. But it is precisely this power that the Artist must abstain from exercising; and Holgrave—in contrast to Hester—does. Having delivered his tale of Alice Pyncheon, Holgrave makes "a slight gesture upward, with his hand" (212), and thereby releases Phoebe, his impressionable medium, from his control. Hawthorne subtly repeats this gesture in recurrently exposing the fictionality of the narrative by drawing attention to the narrative *performance*; that is, the fact that the narrator's relating of the story is in truth situated in the reader's reading of the story. It is to this effect that the narrator remarks, when disclosing how Phoebe has been overcome with a "certain remarkable drowsiness" upon hearing Holgrave's story of Alice Pyncheon, that it was "wholly unlike that with which the reader possibly feels himself affected" (211): the use of the present tense throughout serves to remind us that the fictitious past is situated in a very concrete present. Through these manoeuvres, the narrative deed (the written text, as well as the act of narration) is tied up with the passing moment.

The felicitous outcome of the romance can hence be said to be dependent upon the willingness of the Artist to disclose to his audience (his reader) "the awful secret of yesterday," an act which is likened to "dragging a hideous shape of death into the cleanly and cheerful space of a household fire" (302). But it is also, and to an equal degree, dependent upon the public/reader responding to this act in such a way that this secret may no longer be hidden from public view. Such a response must include a willingness, on the part of the reader, to take joint custody of the secret the Artist has confided in her; to "throw open the doors" to the House of the Seven Gables, and call all the world "to see the truth" (305) as Phoebe puts it, despite the circumstance that this must inevitably seem to implicate the reader, too, in the secret so long withheld.

For the conclusion to be truly happy, then, Hawthorne is dependent upon the reader responding to him in much the same manner as Phoebe responds to Holgrave, who, as we have said, is innocent of any material transgression, but is implicated in the death of the Judge in that he has withheld the secret of the deed. Like Phoebe, the reader must accept this secret in another form, recognizing it for what it is—Death—yet allowing this recognition to be the foundation of a moment of intimacy rather than dejection. Having shared such a moment with the writer, the reader will already have aligned himself with the writer, thus making the guilt of the latter (which is the refusal to reveal the secret of the deed) his own. *The House of the Seven Gables*, to recapitulate, is designed to prove the deed, in both senses of the word, equally null and void, the deed as document being in the possession of Clifford only as a figment of his imagination, while the deed as act is manifested in the present as the act he never perpetrated. The ramifications of this undertaking becomes clearer if we observe that Hawthorne revives this double meaning of "deed" in the preface to *The Life of Franklin Pierce*, stating that the opinions of his subject "may be read in his straight-forward and consistent deeds" (23: 274). In other words, the deed as act functions simultaneously as a written deed, something which can be read. By acting, then, we are all in a sense writers; hence every individual is an artist of sorts.

And hence Hawthorne's activity acquires at once a typicality which is important to recognize in order to understand why Hawthorne may allow the problem of the artist to become the central concern of his writings: the problem of the artist thus conceived is the problem of Everyman. While writing is therefore in a sense something the individual is condemned to, we may, however, choose to suspend our belief in this writing—just as Hawthorne employs the Preface to ask the reader not to confuse the truth of the Romance with the truth of the Novel.

> The latter form of composition is presumed to aim at a very minute fidelity, not merely to the possible, but to the probable and ordinary course of man's experience. The former—while, as a work of art, it must rigidly subject itself to laws, and while it sins unpardonably, so far as it may swerve aside from the truth of the human heart—has fairly a right to present that truth under circumstances, to a great extent, of the writer's own choosing or creation. (1)

We are asked to replace a mimetic conception of truth with a conception of truth which allows the interpretive agency of the human heart to be built into the very definition of truth.

Therefore, there is unquestionably some truth in the widely held view that Hawthorne's "texts [...] are meant as invitations to co-production on the part of the reader."[34] Yet they are hardly "invitations" so much as attempts to make manifest how the reader is *necessarily* implicated in the romance's production of meaning, its production of types. The role of interpretation in Hawthorne, then, is hardly that of a symbolic site of possibilities, but rather that of an allegorical burden, a possibility from which there is no escape. In fact, it is as an image of this burdened position that Death is presented to us in the book. The whole narrative of *The House of the Seven Gables* strives towards the production of this image, which is presented to the reader in the form of chapter 18, and to Phoebe, in chapter 20, as a daguerreotype of the dead Judge. Having presented this image, the further fate of the artist is dependent upon the response of the reader, who may—like Hepzibah and Clifford—choose to remain a child by invoking the Creator as a Father of this deed; or—like Holgrave and Phoebe—let the recognition of Death engender a joy which makes this moment of recognition "the only point of life, worth living for" (306), rather than anxiously seeking a way to displace this recognition upon an authoritative Father. Because the "secret of Judge Pyncheon's mysterious death" is that although natural, it must bestow a sense of guilt upon whoever attempts to represent it; but also that it is only through such a representation that the Flower of Eden may bloom, that artist and society may be united. This circumstance, more than anything else, suggests a context for understanding Hawthorne's handling of the ending of his second romance.

## 4. The Providential End of Art: The Problem of the Ending

As we pointed out already in the introductory section of this chapter, no one feature of *The House of the Seven Gables* has caused critics more consternation than its ending. As a preliminary to an alternative way of coming to terms with this ending, let us concede that Hawthorne could have dodged much of the criticism that has been directed at his romance simply by refraining from killing off Judge Pyncheon's son along with the Judge, an incident which has been pronounced, with some justification, "quite baldly an auctorial device for forcing a certain kind of conclusion, but one so at variance with the rest of his book that it must be intended as an irony."[35] Had Hawthorne let this son live, we would have been left with an ending that would have seemed much less incongruous within the realist paradigm of the novel: Clifford would have been cleared from the accusations of murder brought against him, and Pyncheons and Maules would have been united through the marriage of Phoebe and Holgrave—but a potential avatar of the Colonel would still have been alive, and the characters would not have had the economic means to depart from the House, but would have been forced to try and build their happiness in a scene in which the reader had already seen sunshine and shadows blend. Surely this would seem to be an ending more consonant with the preceding events than the sudden prosperity of the characters effected by the actual ending. Why, then, did Hawthorne wreck this much more plausible conclusion of his story by bestowing the opulence of Judge Pyncheon upon his characters?

He did so, it seems to me, because the ending of *The House of the Seven Gables* is intended as an illustration of the notion of Providential Irony. Had the romance ended in a blend of sunshine and economic hardships, the whole point of God as "the sole worker of realities" would have gone missing, because in that case, of course, the final outcome of the events *would* have depended upon the actions of the characters, and we would have been forced to conclude that the narrator's disparagement of Holgrave's reformist ambitions in chapter 12 lacked authority, and that *The House of the Seven Gables* would indeed be the radical manifest (in a liberalist sense) some critics have tried to make of it.[36] Instead, *The House of the Seven Gables* as it now stands ends ambiguously: the prosperous close may be a new beginning, but it may also be a return to the starting point of yet another cycle of greed and wrongdoings, in which Holgrave Maule has simply taken the place of Jaffrey Pyncheon as the present avatar of the "model-conservative" (315). Once again, however, it is important to observe that this ambiguity is in a sense merely apparent; that it is of an ethical rather than an epistemological kind, as we put it in our discussion of "Rappaccini's Daughter" in chapter two. What the final outcome of the romance will be is something that can only be determined in the future, but in a future that is tied to the present in the form of the reader, upon whom it falls to determine the final significance of the romance.

This is the key to the "prosperous close" of *The House of the Seven Gables*, for although the ending seems to bestow wealth upon each of the main characters, it is also specified that the cottage that is offered to Uncle Venner in the final chapter "looks just as if it were made of gingerbread" (317). This remark of Phoebe should not be mistaken for evidence of the presence in *The House of the Seven Gables* of a voice of domesticity allowing "the sentimental [...] its say" (*Practicing*, 151). On the contrary, this is one of Hawthorne's habitually ironic gestures, detectable only to the Gentle Reader. The gingerbread figures of Hepzibah's shop, we must remember, are the favourite course of urchin Ned Higgins, who, as we have already pointed out, is also "the very emblem of old Father Time, both in respect of his all-devouring appetite for men and things, and because he, as well as Time, after engulfing thus much of creation, looked almost as youthful as if he had been just that moment made" (115). That Hepzibah is seen to present him "with silver enough to people the Domdaniel cavern of his interior with as various a procession of quadrupeds, as passed into the ark" (318) just prior to the final departure from the house, goes to show that time is left as potent as ever at the end of *The House of the Seven Gables*. Eventually, Time will devour us all, and the fact that Uncle Venner's cottage is "made of gingerbread" clearly implies that the newly found wealth—and happiness—of the leading characters of the romance is not excluded from this prospect. This in turn suggests that we must not mistake the romance's celebration of domestic love for escapism. On the contrary, by turning the House itself both into the principal emblem of guilt but also into the principal scene of domestic bliss, Hawthorne attempts to inscribe the character of guilt upon the most cherished institution of Victorian domesticity: marriage.

But if the happiness of Holgrave and Phoebe will eventually be devoured by time, the philosophy of Uncle Venner, "whose wisdom has not a drop of bitter essence at the bottom" (317), might prove more enduring. This is where it becomes necessary for us to turn the irony of *The House of the Seven Gables* in on itself, so to speak, or to turn from the darkness of the heart to its inner core of perfection to invoke a well-known simile of Hawthorne.[37] According to Uncle Venner, "men make a wonderful mistake in trying to heap up property upon property" (156). As the espousers of an ironical reading of the ending have not failed to point out, it would seem that this is just what Holgrave and Phoebe do when they set out from the House of the Seven Gables to take possession of Judge Pyncheon's estate.[38] But this is to miss the finery of the plot, the point of which is precisely to show that Holgrave and Phoebe, at least, *have not been trying*: the redemption of the leading characters is brought about by their abstention from premeditated actions.

The final appearance of Dixey and his friend in the narrative, which coincide with the leading characters leaving the House, can be seen as the key to the allegorical dialectics projected by the romance:

> "Well, Dixey," said one of them, "what do you think of this? My wife kept a cent-shop, three months, and lost five dollars on her outlay. Old Maid Pyncheon has been in trade just about as long, and rides off in her carriage with a couple of hundred thousand—reckoning her share, and Clifford's, and Phoebe's—and some say twice as much! If you choose to call it luck, it is all very well; but if we are to take it as the will of Providence, why, I can't exactly fathom it!"
>
> "Pretty good business!' quoth the sagacious Dixey. 'Pretty good business!" (318–19)

It is good business, because it is no business; and this is precisely the point that the narrative as a whole is designed to make. This short piece of dialogue marks Hawthorne's final attempt to expose the inability of money to function as an allegorical sign along the lines of the letter in the Puritan community. Because the real fortune of Holgrave and Phoebe is not the inheritance they have come into, but their understanding of death as a presence in life, and the willingness to acknowledge that "the haughty faith, with which [they] began life, would be well bartered for a far humbler one, at its close, in discerning that man's best-directed effort accomplishes a kind of dream, while God is the sole worker of realities" (180).

It is important to underscore, however, that this does not entail that individual agency is wholly extinguished in *The House of the Seven Gables*, as Arac believes. The acts of the male characters of *The House of the Seven Gables*—Clifford's rushed flight from the House, Holgrave's probing of psyches through the means of his art, Judge Pyncheon's constant display of public acts of charity—are indeed all proved equally futile in the end, but these acts are accompanied (in the case of the two artist figures) by the sympathetic response of the female characters. In contrast to Judge Pyncheon and his ancestral avatars, Phoebe and Hepzibah subject themselves to Providence; by this submissiveness they come to enact the role of Providence, and hereby are able to save Holgrave and Clifford from degrading into the type of the Judge, or the Artist of the Beautiful. This is what renders Providence an ironic principle: we become its agents by rejecting the notion of agency as a way to happiness.

I would like to return, at this point, to Waggoner's view that the ambiguity of *The House of the Seven Gables* is only dissolved "on the religious level, in the higher hope motivated by the spectacle of history" (*Study*, 182). As John Gatta argues, *The House of the Seven Gables* "seems to be meditating upon the problem of progress under three different ontological aspects" that have to do "first, with the personal, individual history of the self; second with social history; and third, with a transhistorical, figurative level of narrative recognizable in traditional Christian terms as sacred or visionary history." "If there is any final term of causality linking together all three notions of progress," Gatta continues, "the word that the romance itself suggests, and a word that Hawthorne often uses, is 'Providence'." This is a valuable observation, yet Gatta, too, concludes that "it is only at the level of sacred or visionary history, what we have indicated as the third level of Hawthorne's narrative, that the teleological progress of the race is assured."[39] Such a statement manages to be at once eminently true and to miss the whole point of Hawthorne's project, which is to recast "the level of sacred or visionary history" as a property of "the personal, individual history of the self," and hence to bring it to have a direct bearing on "social history." And for this to happen, politics must be transformed into faith; yet a faith which manifests itself as a reverence for man, rather than for God. Holgrave's development in *The House of the Seven Gables*, as Brook Thomas importantly argues, "is a fall into history and community [...] a fall that is future-oriented;" and for this reason, the outcome of Holgrave's and Phoebe's marriage "is still something to be worked for, imagined, and interpreted."[40] I would add, that Providence fulfils a role in this marriage parallel to that which it fulfils in history as such. Providence mediates between the past and the future, but it does not do so in the form of an autonomous, external agent, but in the form of Phoebe, who conceives of her office in relation to Clifford, to "be, as it were, the Providence of his unconsidered hours" (219). This is a mark of Phoebe's maturity, and the trait which above all else allows her to become a woman in the full sense, while Hepzibah's references to "God's providence" (233) implicitly betrays why she is unable to move beyond the state of a "maiden lady." Providence, in other words, is not to be understood as a metaphysical agent, but rather as a responsibility or product of the actants of society; Providence does not suggest divine interference so much as a concept of mediation that binds the artist to society, that links the writer to the reader. The individual, then, must come to *act the part of Providence in the sphere of humanity*; the conception of Providence as an external agent must be transformed into an understanding of Providence as an internal drive.

And something very similar must be said of art: art is not so much a realm of its own as the medium which enables us to transform our understanding of the relation between the individual and society by means of a dialectical process. Again and again Hawthorne represents the artistic endeavour as a kind of political idealism, although usually misguided. We have already seen examples of this in the representation of Rappaccini, in that of Hester, and in that of Holgrave, and we will see it again in that of Zenobia. It is less pronounced in the case of Miriam, but it reappears more emphatically than ever in the drafts that remain of Hawthorne's Septimius-romance. "One of Septimius's grand objects is to reform the world," Hawthorne wrote on the completion of a first outline of the romance in fifteen scenes, reminding himself a little later that the moral might perhaps "turn out to be, the folly of man in thinking that he can ever be of any importance to the welfare of the world" (13: 529).[41] This suggests that Hawthorne conceives of social idealism as somehow co-equivalent with artistic idealism: the impetus for the artist and the social reformer is essentially the same, as are the dangers that are connected with their respective endeavours. Insisting upon the fullness—or presence—of art, is the artistic equivalent of the reformer's attempt to bring about immediate social change. To be successful, the artistic project, in analogy with society, must be conceived of as a means to enforce a sense of distance, or lack: the work of art must be incomplete in itself in order to fulfil the Providential agency of linking the members of society together, by making them aware of the insignificance of the individual in relation to that greater whole of which he or she is merely a part.

Thus the irony that require us to recognize the end as an inevitable starting point for a renewed spin of life's cyclic patterns, gains its profoundest momentum only when we realize that this is not lamentable, but on the contrary the very prerequisite for allowing the reader to project a sense of innocence beyond the historical cycles that make up the boundaries of human time. The romance, then, does not reach the projected final end that we sketched in our discussion of the Fortunate Fall in chapter two, but suggests rather—as the espousers of an ironic reading of the end are right in pointing out—the return to the already compromised position of an illusory innocence. What Hawthorne would allow us is something which for him must have seemed much more valuable than the temporary satisfaction of seeing the characters of the romance happily off from the House, namely the possibility, for the reader, of conceiving of the present moment from an allegorical perspective and thus to perceive how every moment is in fact all time.[42]

*

As in *The Scarlet Letter*, to sum up, in *The House of the Seven Gables* Hawthorne presents us with an ideal consummation of the romance. It is true that this consummation appears less aesthetically satisfying than in the previous romance, yet one must consider that the move from a historical setting to a contemporary one considerably complicates Hawthorne's artistic venture. In *The Scarlet Letter*, Hawthorne has no difficulty convincing us of the sinful aspect of Hester's and Dimmesdale's union, since there was in Puritan society a norm which they transgress. In *The House of the Seven Gables*, in contrast, Hawthorne has to convince us of the importance of recognizing a sense in which we, as well as the characters of his romance, are guilty, even if the actual guilt may seem to be a thing of the past. Phoebe and Holgrave achieve such recognition, but whether the romance as such will replicate the redemption they hereby achieve, ultimately depends upon the response of the reader.

The whole plot of *The House of the Seven Gables* hinges upon the Maules having hidden a deed at the heart of the House, a circumstance that allegorically suggests the deed hidden in the romance by the artist himself, which, as we have explained, bestows death *and* fortune—in that order—upon its beneficiaries. At the end of the story the reader still has to decide whether or not the new home that Holgrave departs for will also contain a hidden deed. Before he deserts *The House of the Seven Gables*, however, Holgrave exposes the secret of the deed, which is also arguably the secret of art: that the fortune of art, like that of the deed, must be something for which we seek "in vain, while it [is] valuable; and now that [we] find the treasure, it has long been worthless" (316). Art, in other words, amounts to a kind of deferral, a way of postponing the consummation of desire. We dream of fulfilment, and art assists us in our dreaming, as the happy ending of *The House of the Seven Gables* itself makes plain. In truth, however, Actual fulfilment is possible only through the mediation of imagination.

Hence the sexual gratification promised in the Flower of Eden-scene must be accompanied by an image of Death, because it is only through death that the material consummation of sexuality in this realm of Becoming may be transformed into the hope for a spiritual consummation of our desire in the realm of Being. But society—in the form of the reader—like Judge Pyncheon is prone to take "hold of everything as if it were real," that is, to look to art as if it provided Actual fortune, when all it can do is provide "a kind of fairy-tale" (316) of the discovery of the deed. In showing how the discovery of the deed leads to prosperity rather than a sense of guilt *The House of the Seven Gables* enacts this fairy-tale; yet by drawing attention to its own Imaginary status, it also makes evident that this fairy-tale ending is available to us only through the mediation of fiction, and death. Whether the ideal future thus made accessible to us deserves to be called reality, however, is a matter beyond the artist's control: it is a matter of faith.

**CHAPTER FIVE**

# The Wonder Books: The Chimaera of Love

> When the first poet or romancer told these marvellous legends [...] it was still the Golden Age. Evil had never yet existed; and sorrow, misfortune, crime, were mere shadows which the mind fancifully created for itself, as a shelter against too sunny realities—or, at most, but prophetic dreams, to which the dreamer himself did not yield a waking credence. Children are now the only representatives of the men and women of that happy era; and therefore it is that we must raise the intellect and fancy to the level of childhood, in order to re-create the original myths.
>
> Hawthorne, "The Wayside," *Tanglewood Tales*

The bright note of reconciliation on which *The House of the Seven Gables* ends contrasts markedly with the bleak tone of resignation that pervades *The Blithedale Romance*, published a mere fourteen months after the earlier book saw the light of day. In part, no doubt, the differences can be put down to Hawthorne's own sense for marketing strategies. Having completed *A Wonder Book* in the summer of 1851, Hawthorne wrote Bridge on July 22 that should his next project "be a romance, I mean to put an extra touch of the devil into it; for I doubt whether the public will stand two quiet books in succession, without my losing ground" (16: 462). But while this statement may suffice to explain the greater emphasis on intrigue in *The Blithedale Romance*, it hardly accounts for its overall pessimism.[1] Of course, if one views the hopefulness of *The House of the Seven Gables* as an anomaly in Hawthorne's oeuvre rather than an integral part of it, one may want to deny that Hawthorne's outlook undergoes any drastic change at all in this period. In this view, the decidedly darker tone of *The Blithedale Romance* as compared with *The House of the Seven Gables* does not signal a new departure for Hawthorne, but rather a return to what is considered his habitual sombre tone, as exemplified by *The Scarlet Letter*. In opposition to this view, I have been at pains in the two previous chapters to show that despite the significantly different moods of the two books, *The Scarlet Letter* and *The House of the Seven Gables* both project a hopeful vision of the future as a consequence of the romance successfully performing its office of mediation. In the romances that he was still to write, however, Hawthorne turned from portraying the successful course of romance to depicting the obstruction of this course. His children's books offer a unique and hitherto largely ignored opportunity to trace this transformation.

The two collections of children's stories—or "Wonder Books," as Hawthorne designated them—have received comparatively little attention in Hawthorne scholarship. Yet Hawthorne himself professed a great liking for them: "I never did anything else so well as these old baby-stories" (16: 649) he wrote in a letter in 1853.[2] The first of these, *A Wonder Book For Girls and Boys*, was written in six weeks in the summer of 1851, some two months after *The House of the Seven Gables* was published; the second, *Tanglewood Tales For Girls and Boys Being a second Wonder Book*, early in 1853, some ten months subsequent to the completion of *The Blithedale Romance* (in the interval, Hawthorne wrote the campaign biography of Franklin L. Pierce). They thus fall neatly on either side of the partition that separates the tempered hopefulness pervading *The Scarlet Letter* and *The House of the Seven Gables* from the much grimmer tone that is characteristic of his last two romances. As we will see, they offer an excellent vantage point from which to index the nature of the transformation that Hawthorne's vision is subject to between writing *A Wonder Book* and publishing *The Blithedale Romance.*

Baym, who is virtually alone in treating these books in relation to Hawthorne's other fictions, rightly insists upon the marked differences between the two books, despite their common material. *A Wonder Book* is a joyous paean to the good to come out of the relation between man and woman. Several of the stories could be said to involve meditations on the relation between the sexes, and the outcome in all of these is a redemptive assertion of faith in a brighter future. *Tanglewood*, in contrast, presents a much bleaker picture. Baym, however, underestimates the scope of "the aims and intentions" that these works are said to share, which, in her account, are simply "to transcend [Hawthorne's] own temperamental affinity for the dark side of experience and enter into the simple and sunny world view he desired to represent." In Baym's view, Hawthorne turns the Greek myths into "escapist" literature, "products to while away the leisure hours of advantaged children."[3]

It is true that the redressing of the myths is readily observable in the drastic repression of the erotic drive which is often at the very centre of the Greek original.[4] In "The Gorgon's Head" for instance—the opening story of *A Wonder Book*—it is said of King Polydectes that: "As he was not good and kind [...] but extremely wicked, he resolved to send Perseus on a dangerous enterprise, in which he would probably be killed, and then to do some great mischief to Danaë herself" (7: 10–11).[5] Hawthorne, then (or rather, the young man called Eustace Bright relating the stories), retains the wicked character of the king, but censures the motive for his ill-treatment of Perseus: Perseus refusal to let him wed his mother Danaë. It is also true that Hawthorne's preface to *A Wonder Book* betrays what will seem to us a sentimental view of childhood: "Children possess an unestimated sensibility to whatever is deep or high, in imagination or feeling, so long as it is simple, likewise. It is only the artificial and the complex that bewilders them" (4).

But this is not to say that the Wonder Books shun complexity, nor that they are devoid of sexual themes; on the contrary, the erotic undertow is often quite thinly disguised. This is readily acknowledged by Baym in relation to *Tanglewood Tales*, where, she claims, sexuality re-emerges in repressed form.[6] But to recognize the sexual undertow only in *Tanglewood Tales* is to miss the whole point of the Wonder Books, both of which are concerned—like Hawthorne's fiction in general—with the individual's inevitable transition from childhood to adulthood. The structure of both books reflects the child's farewell of childhood innocence, and initiation into the complexity of the adult world. In the first piece of each volume, a young man sets out on a mission; when this is completed, he returns to his mother. The second story is more incidental, in keeping with the playfulness of a childhood existence which is as yet unperturbed by sexual awareness. The third story of each volume disrupts this state, by presenting us with protagonists that are forced to abandon their innocence, and confront a world very different from that which they originally knew. Stories four and five could be said to acknowledge this fall from innocence, without really resolving it. The resolution is left to the final story of each volume. Significantly, in both volumes this story returns us to the paradigm of the story that opened the volume, that is, to a young man setting out to face a great danger. Yet when this quest story is re-enacted, the protagonist has already lost his protective mother. Being unable to fall back on such a figure, the hero instead has to form a union of some sort with a creature that stands in for the missing mother, and which, in contrast to the latter, is not a desexualized image of femininity. In other words, what is left unresolved by the hero-as-child in the first story, in the closing tale must be confronted by the hero-as-adult. Below we will see this pattern repeated in both books, but it will also be seen that the implications of this pattern are very different from the one book to the other.

## 1. *A Wonder Book*

In "The Gorgon's Head," which opens *A Wonder Book*, Perseus slays the Gorgon Medusa, and kills Polydectes by fooling him into looking at her head, which even when severed from her body will turn whosoever lays his eyes upon it into marble, or, as it is put in the story, into "images" (34). Having thus pacified the threat towards his mother (which is, on some level, a threat to the hero's innocence, since it involves having to confront the sexual nature of his mother), the story ends with Perseus going "to tell his dear mother that she need no longer be afraid of the wicked king Polydectes" (34).

Next follows "The Golden Touch," a version of the story of King Midas, who in return for having done Dionysos a favour was granted his wish of having everything he touched turn to gold. Again, Hawthorne's most important change of the myth is to place much more emphasis on the parent-child relation than does the original. Indeed, when we recall that the story of Perseus involves a mother and a son, it might not appear entirely coincidental that this second story of the book involves a father and a daughter. But if this is the case, it is nevertheless clear from the story at hand that it is Midas, rather than his daughter Marygold, who functions as a representative of childhood innocence in the story: having been afforded the Golden Touch, we learn that "his mind was probably in the state of a child's, to whom a beautiful new plaything has been promised" (45).

Hawthorne's version never swerves far from the original, however, and Midas' enthusiasm for his new-won ability quickly turns into the suspicion that what he had imagined a blessing is in truth a curse. The suspicion is confirmed when he accidentally turns his own daughter into "a golden statue." The narrator does not miss out on the opportunity of moralizing the situation: "And now, at last, when it was too late, he felt how infinitely a warm and tender heart, that loved him, exceeded in value all the wealth that could be piled up betwixt the earth and sky!" (53). But as the essentially good-natured child that he represents ("To do Midas justice, he really loved his daughter" [48]), all Midas really needs is a reprimand, and once Dionysos, or "the stranger" as he is referred to in the story, has inculcated the lesson "that the commonest things, such as lie within everybody's grasp, are more valuable than the riches which so many mortals sigh and struggle after" (55), he turns everything right again.

The third story of *A Wonder Book*, "The Paradise of Children," is of greater interest, not just because it constitutes, as I have said, a turning point of sorts in the collection itself, but also because it is the purest statement we have of Hawthorne's affirmation of the notion of *felix culpa*, which is central to the formula of the Fortunate Fall. The story is a rendition of the myth of Pandora, itself seemingly a precursor to the biblical treatment of the Fall: Pandora, the first woman, was sent to earth in charge of a box that she was strictly forbidden to open, but driven by her curiosity she disregarded the instructions of the gods and lifted its lid, at which all the vices and plagues that have pestered mankind ever since immediately flew out. Realizing her mistake too late to shut these woes inside again, only Hope remained in the casket to be let out as some kind of relief to man.[7] As the title of Hawthorne's version of this story indicates, he transforms the myth of an original Golden Age in which there was no evil into a myth of a world in which there are only children. The psychological state of childhood, then, becomes in this myth the locus of innocence. The Golden Age, it is important to observe, is a priori a state of innocence: none of the children of Hawthorne's paradise are evil. How then, one might ask, are we to explain their propensity for wrongdoing which is manifested in Pandora's opening of the box? The answer, it would seem, is that their innocence does not exclude the possibility of their being "ill-tempered" (71), nor of their being "naughty"—indeed, it is explicitly stated that Pandora's is a "naughty little heart," and that she is herself "very naughty, and very foolish" (73), and that Epimetheus (Pandora's husband in the myth, who is assigned the role of Pandora's "playfellow" in Hawthorne's rendition of the tale) is "hardly less naughty" (78) in that he does not prevent his playfellow from opening the box when he perceives that she is about to raise its lid, as he has "his own share of curiosity to know what was inside" (75). Innocence, in other words, does not entail moral goodness, but amorality, a lack of moral concepts altogether.

This amorality is reminiscent of the original state of Adam and Eve in Paradise, as represented by Milton in Book IX of *Paradise Lost*.[8] Just as is the case of Eve, Pandora's innocence cannot ensure her good behaviour because innocence is equivalent to *not knowing* good from bad. But once the box has been opened, once the mystery of what was "inside" has been solved, the naiveté of childhood is lost forever: "The children [...] who before seemed immortal in their childhood, now grew older, day by day, and came soon to be youths and maidens, and men and women by-and-by, and aged people, before they dreamed of such a thing" (77–8), a circumstance that the narrator advances as an illustration of "how a wrong act of any one mortal is a calamity to the whole world" (77). Pandora and Epimetheus, the narrator states, "were in a good deal of pain, which seemed the more intolerable to them, because it was the very first pain that had ever been felt since the world began" (78).

But the story does not end on this note of pain. The lid having fallen back upon the fated box, there is suddenly a tap from within, and a little voice begs to be let out, but the pair is naturally reluctant to open the lid once more. Eventually, however, they give in, and repeat the original misdeed. Only, this time, they commit it together: "with one consent, the two children again lifted the lid" (80), upon which Hope gloriously flies out. It is noteworthy that the narrator does not deplore the circumstances for this outcome as much as he rejoices in the outcome itself:

> And, to tell you the truth, I cannot help being glad—(though, to be sure, it was an uncommonly naughty thing for her to do)—but I cannot help being glad that our

> foolish Pandora peeped into the box. [...] that lovely and lightsome little figure of Hope! What in the world could we do without her? Hope spiritualizes the earth; Hope makes it always new; and, even in the earth's best and brightest aspect, Hope shows it to be only the shadow of an infinite bliss, hereafter! (81)

The case for *felix culpa* could hardly be stated more emphatically. More importantly, the story makes quite clear that for Hawthorne, man can achieve relief from guilt only by *repeating a transgressive act already performed.* As I have suggested above, the Wonder Books themselves structurally repeat this pattern. It is, we might add, repeated throughout Hawthorne's writings; we saw an example of it in *The House of the Seven Gables*, where Clifford is absolved from a crime he did not commit by Phoebe and Holgrave acknowledging their involvement in one for which they are similarly not responsible, and we will see it again in *The Marble Faun*—guilt in Hawthorne is typically incurred not through an actual transgression, but through association. Whether or not an individual actually commits a sin is of secondary importance, as we are guilty by our very propensity for sin. "Man must not disclaim his brotherhood, even with the guiltiest," it is pointed out in "Fancy's Show Box," "since, though his hand be clean, his heart has surely been polluted by the flitting phantoms of iniquity" (9: 226). In other words, although the transgressive act is what makes the characters guilty of a crime, this act need not occur to make them guilty of sin: while the act is criminal, it is the *desire* to perform it which is sinful. It follows, then, that abstention from acting out our desire can never lead to redemption. On the contrary, such a repudiation of the Act can never amount to anything else but a forgery (as is quite literally the case in *The Blithedale Romance*, as we will see in the next chapter), a displacement of the only true means of expiation available to man, which consists precisely in repeating the original crime, and thereby recognizing the pain of guilt which is the inescapable burden of the adult individual.[9]

*

After the turning point marked by "The Paradise of Children," the two stories that follow take on a slightly more melancholy tone. On the evidence of "The Three Golden Apples," it would admittedly seem as if no change had set in, but the penultimate story of the collection, "The Miraculous Pitcher," fits in better with our outline, portraying as it does an elderly pair, Philemon and Baucis, and the happiness granted to them in token of their kind submissiveness. Significantly, they have no children; although it is a story that acknowledges the necessity of growing old, it does not address the concomitant question of sexuality.

If "The Paradise of Children" is the clearest invocation of the notion of the Fortunate Fall in *A Wonder Book*, "The Chimaera"—the final story of the collection—presents us with the most sophisticated rendering of this paradoxical formula. It tells the tale of Bellerophon, who has been sent by King Iobates of Lycia to fight the Chimaera, a terrible monster. Bellerophon has realized that he will not be able to conquer the monster on foot, but will need the assistance of the greatest horse in the world. This, Bellerophon believes, is the winged steed Pegasus, and at the beginning of the story we find Bellerophon at the Fountain of Pirene where he has come in the hope of finding and mounting this mythical creature. Pegasus, as Hawthorne's principal source, Charles Anthon's *A Classical Dictionary,* would have informed him, is "a winged steed, the offspring of Neptune and Medusa, and which sprang forth from the neck of the latter after her head had been severed by Perseus." The well-informed adult reader is thus invited to see in "The Chimaera" a continuation—perhaps even a consummation—of the story of "The Gorgon's Head" that opened the volume; a continuation that must escape the child, but is nevertheless intended to reflect its development. We should remember that Perseus has to defeat Medusa in order to protect his mother from the advances of king Polydectes, advances that were—Hawthorne prudently forgets to inform his young audience, yet certainly expects an adult reader to remember—undoubtedly of an erotic nature: as Anthon informs us, Polydectes "fell in love with Danaë; but her son Perseus, who was now grown up, was an invincible obstacle in his way."[10] In the implicit structural framework of the volume as an allegory of maturation, then, it seems safe to say that Medusa is a representation of the sexuality that Perseus—the hero-as-child—must deny in his mother in order to maintain his relation with her.

Although Hawthorne again suppresses the overt erotic drive of the original story, Bellerophon, the hero of the closing piece, in contrast to Perseus is placed in a postlapsarian landscape in which sexuality can no longer be simply rejected.[11] It should therefore not surprise us to find a double image at the centre of the tale: Pegasus/the Chimaera, its three heads invoking the three Gorgons that Perseus had to encounter. For this double image is emblematic of sexual romance, just as in "Rappaccini's Daughter" we found the romance emblematically portrayed in the twin images of Beatrice and the poisonous flower shrub, in *The Scarlet Letter* as Pearl and the letter with which the Puritan community has branded Hester, and in the *House of the Seven Gables* as the dead Judge Pyncheon and the Flower of Eden.

The structure of the collection as a whole thus subtly repeats that of its central story about the fall of man. Just as in "The Paradise of Children," in *A Wonder Book* redemption is brought about by the repetition of an act already performed. What jumps upon us from under the lid of "The Gorgon's Head" and "The Chimaera" alike is the secret of sexuality, but at the second instance it does so in the form of Pegasus: a figure of Hope, promising that the child's initiation into sexuality, though painful, may nevertheless be the very means by which the pains of this world can be transcended. This figure of Hope, it is important to observe, is also a transfigured embodiment of female sexuality: Pegasus, as I have suggested above, is Medusa in another form. Much as Miles Coverdale assigns the task of mediating between God and Man to Woman, Hawthorne has Eustace Bright present Pegasus as an intermediary figure within the tale: the horse makes possible a transaction between the world of the senses and that presumably higher reality emblematically portrayed in the sky. "Pegasus seemed hardly to be a creature of the earth. Whenever he was seen, up very high above people's heads, with the sunshine on his silvery wings, you would have thought that he belonged to the sky, and that, skimming a little too low, he had gone astray among our mists and vapors, and was seeking his way back again" (146). "Nobody should ever try to fight an earth-born Chimaera, unless he can first get upon the back of an aerial steed!" (152), the narrator warns us: if the evils of this world are to be defeated, the individual must have access to some kind of spiritual medium, something that will allow him to transcend the limitations of this world. This transcending quality is usually reserved for a feminine character in the romances—Beatrice in "Rappaccini's Daughter," Priscilla in *The Blithedale Romance*, and, most markedly of all, Hilda in *The Marble Faun*. (Significantly, in speaking of Priscilla, Coverdale claims that it is "delightful to see a vigorous young girl run a race, with her head thrown back, her limbs moving more friskily than they need, and an air between *that of a bird and a young colt*" [BR, 73; my emphasis].) Despite its masculine sex, then, Pegasus is thus a carrier of values associated with femininity in Hawthorne; given the mythical association of the flying horse with Medusa it seems reasonable to suggest that we could look upon it as a kind of vicarious feminine character within the story.

Bellerophon finds at the Fountain of Pirene a middle-aged man, an old man, a maiden, and a boy—all representing versions of the reader—whom he asks, in successive order, if they have seen the winged horse. The first man laughs him off; the second man recalls believing that there was such a horse in his childhood but claims very seldom to think about it anymore; the maiden, blushingly, admits that she might actually have seen it once, and to have heard another time a neigh that made her heart leap with delight—yet she ran away, as it startled her all the same. Only the child will unreservedly affirm that he has seen the horse, and not only once, but many times. As it turns out, however, it is not the actual horse that the boy has seen; what he has seen is merely "the *image* of the winged horse, in the picture of the sky" (148; my emphasis) reflected in the water. This is a significant fact that I shall return to later, but we may want to note at once that this suggests that the child is structurally the counterpart of Perseus in the collection's opening tale, who escapes the petrifying power of Medusa by looking at her reflection in a shield. Since this is a story for children there is of course nothing surprising about Hawthorne's decision to cast the gentle child in the role of an ideal reader—the epithet "gentle" itself suggests the "Gentle Reader" that Hawthorne evokes in the preface to *The Marble Faun*. The gentle child of the tale represents Hawthorne's depiction of the ideal response he is hoping to call forth in his young audience. Interestingly, the office such a reader is expected to perform is exactly analogous to that performed by Phoebe in *The House of the Seven Gables*: it consists in making manifest one's sympathy with the figure of the artist, and just like Phoebe, the gentle child displays this act of sympathy by putting his faith in the reality of an image. The allegorical Artist of the tale is of course the person who confronts the darker aspects of this world: Bellerophon. And Bellerophon, we are informed, "put his faith in the child, who had seen the image of Pegasus in the water, and in the maiden" (148), and stays by the Fountain in the hope of one day catching and taming the horse. What we are presented with, then, is a pattern of interdependence that suggests a dialectical process of interaction: Bellerophon—the artist—puts his faith in the boy—the reader—who puts his faith in the images evoked, if not created, by the former.

For a long while Bellerophon is unsuccessful, and he is taunted by the inhabitants of the area and their children. But the company of the child makes him persevere: "The dear little fellow, in his play-hours, often sat down beside him, and, without speaking a word, would look down into the fountain and up towards the sky, with so innocent a faith that Bellerophon could not help feeling encouraged" (149); "Every morning, the child gave him a new hope to put in his bosom, instead of yesterday's withered one" (152). When the horse finally does arrive, the child is the first one to perceive it, but once again, only as "an image in the water" (153). The child's reaction on this occasion is reminiscent of that recorded earlier by the maiden. "It makes me tremble!" the child informs Bellerophon, and continues: "I am afraid to look up into the air! It is very beautiful; and yet I dare only look at its image in the water" (153).

The horse comes circling down, and as it descends it is likened to another image associated with Hawthorne's fair-haired women—that of a "dove" (154). Finally it alights and drinks from the waters of the Fountain. Bellerophon, who has hidden in some bushes with the child, peeps forth and watches the horse in its magnificent freedom:

> There never was a more playful creature made, than this very Pegasus. So there he frisked, in a way that it delights me to think about, fluttering his great wings as lightly as ever did a linnet, and running little races, half on earth and half in air, and which I know not whether to call a flight or a gallop. When a creature is perfectly able to fly, he sometimes chooses to run, just for the pastime of the thing; and so did Pegasus, although it cost him some little trouble to keep his hoofs so near the ground. Bellerophon, meanwhile, holding the child's hand, peeped forth from the shrubbery, and thought that never was any sight so beautiful as this, nor ever a horse's eyes so wild and spirited as those of Pegasus. *It seemed a sin to think of bridling him and riding on his back.* (154–55; my emphasis.)

It seemed a sin; as we have seen, the same phrase recurs in *The House of the Seven Gables* at another moment fraught with sexual overtones, the union of Holgrave and Phoebe that takes place in the proximity of the dead Judge Pyncheon: "It seems a sin," Phoebe replies when Holgrave admits to a feeling of exaltation, "to think of joy at such a time!" (HSG, 306).

This expression captures the dilemma, and explains why only the adult man may be a witness to the wild playfulness displayed by the horse: taming the horse entails restraining its freedom, a violation which is aggravated by the fact that it is done with the intention of taking the horse into battle. When Bellerophon mounts Pegasus, the horse fights violently for its freedom; but Bellerophon is in possession of a magic bridle, and once this has been placed in the horse's mouth "Pegasus became as manageable as if he had taken food, all his life, out of Bellerophon's hand" (157). The narrator does not leave this sudden transformation uncommented: "To speak what I really feel, it was almost a sadness, to see so wild a creature grow suddenly so tame" (157). But this is a story for children; that is to say, for the kind of reader who is able to spiritualize the tale by his or her sympathetic capacity. In the presence of such an audience the volume's narrator Eustace Bright, a youth who "had reached [...] the venerable age of eighteen years" (7), is able to transform the violation inherent in the subjugation of Pegasus into an act that the horse consents to. Rather than controlling the horse by force, their relation is depicted as a symbolic marriage. Bellerophon, we are informed:

> was so affected by the gentleness of [the horse's] aspect, and by his beauty, and by the thought of the free life which Pegasus had heretofore lived, that he could not bear to keep him a prisoner, if he really desired his liberty.
>
> Obeying this generous impulse, he slipt the enchanted bridle off the head of Pegasus, and took the bit from his mouth.
>
> "Leave me, Pegasus!" said he. "Either leave me, or love me!" (157–58)

The horse first shoots off into the sky, but soon descends again. From this moment on, they "were friends, and put loving faith in one another" (158).

It is in the battle against the Chimaera that this marriage reaches its consummation. As in *The Marble Faun*, in "The Chimaera" the violent act in which man and woman (or in the present case, hero and horse) are united in order to ward off a greater source of pain and agony functions as a metaphor for sexual intercourse.[12] Some people may think that we are stretching it too far if we read into Bellerophon's exclamation in the midst of battle ("'Dost thou bleed, my immortal horse?' cried the young man, caring less for his own hurt than for the anguish of this glorious creature, that ought never to have tasted pain" [164]) a covert reference to the bleeding associated with lost virginity. As Crews has argued, however, Sophia's editing of Hawthorne's notebooks (at whose hands Hawthorne's "animal desires" became "temperament," "baggage" was transformed into "luggage," "itch" into "fancy," "vent" into "utterance," and "caught an idea by the tail," became "caught an idea by the skirts") bespeaks a "talent for risqué puns" which "was shared by Hawthorne himself and by the whole culture in which he and Sophia moved. In the age of the draped piano leg, even furniture was covertly sexualized."[13] Given such a context, it does not seem unreasonable to me to look upon the Chimaera as an emblem of adult sexuality, which the child will one day have to confront. The monster, in other words, is a representation of the individual's own sexual desire, that he can hope to defeat only if he is able to find someone who is willing to be his partner in crime: "when Bellerophon had won the victory, he bent forward and kissed Pegasus, while the tears stood in his eyes" (165).

It should be noted that the allegory of sexual development that I have ascribed to the structure of the collection, is echoed in the narrative frame in which Eustace Bright relates the stories to a group of children, particularly in the character of Primrose, a twelve year old girl, and hence the oldest member of Eustace's audience. Not only does Eustace suggest to Primrose that Pandora is "the exact picture of yourself" (82), repeatedly referring to her in terms linking them to each other, but her reaction to the story of "The Chimaera" suggests that she is half-consciously aware of its allegorical significance: "In her eyes, there were positively tears; for she was conscious of something in the legend, which the rest of them was not yet old enough to feel" (168). These circumstances have led Lesley Ginsberg to conclude that the sexual allegory of the story turns on the representation of an idealized consent to subjugation: "At the center of 'The Chimaera' is a fiction of emotional consent that legitimates sexuality not by lauding a love between equals but by re-enacting the dramatics of domesticity between tamer and tamed." As this phrasing betrays, Ginsberg conceives of the ideological office hereby performed almost entirely in negative terms; ultimately, the story, and indeed the other stories of the collection as well, "must be read as a narrative of seduction aimed at taming or domesticating nascent female desire through an ideology of love."[14] It seems to me that this reading yields somewhat too easily to the temptation to read the story through the ideological filter of our own day and age. Tellingly, Ginsberg overlooks the story's function for the intradiegetic character of the gentle child, and focuses instead only on its function for the extradiegetic character of Primrose.

While the story up to the point of the successful battle against the Chimaera presents us with an allegorical depiction of the redemption that is to be found in the sexual union of man and woman, when Bellerophon and Pegasus fly back to the Fountain of Pirene, they are emblems not so much of Man and Wife, as of Artist and Art. Up till this moment of the story, the horse has figured for the child only as an "image:" it is only now, when the union of Bellerophon and Pegasus has been consummated in battle, that the "gentle" child is allowed to view the horse directly. Again Bellerophon offers the winged horse its freedom, but the horse will not have it: it is tamed, and desires above all to stay with its master. The child who could not dare to look upon the horse in its state of freedom, is a witness to its consent to subjugation. This child "in after years," the story ends, "took higher flights upon the aerial steed, than ever did Bellerophon, and achieved more honorable deeds than his friend's victory over the Chimaera. For, gentle and tender as he was, he grew to be a mighty Poet!" (167).

These circumstances may seem to corroborate Ginsberg's reading, but this seems to me an area of Hawthorne's thinking where it is wise to proceed with caution: whether or not the story's reification of a character representing femininity into a work of art bespeaks sexism on Hawthorne's part is a difficult question. On the one hand, it must be readily conceded that the sexual allegory of the Wonder Books is unquestionably designed from a male perspective: in both books, the allegorical protagonist is a little boy who has to come to terms with his own sexuality. The role of female characters—or characters associated with femininity—in this allegory is apparently only to function as a medium for male desire. The same could be said of a story such as "Rappaccini's Daughter." But as the artist figure in the novel-romances is more frequently a woman than a man, we must be careful not to jump to the conclusion that this necessarily bespeaks an objectifying attitude towards women on Hawthorne's part. It may be the case that the Wonder Books suggest that Woman is Man's medium for redemption, simply because Hawthorne looks to the two sexes as complimentary to each other: just as Woman is Man's medium for redemption, Man may be Woman's. From the one perspective, Woman spiritualized is Art, from the other, Man spiritualized is Art.[15] In both cases, this etherialization can take place because the individual has recognized that the imperfection seemingly inherent in the object of one's desire, is in truth an imperfection of one's own self: while it manifests itself as a flaw in the object, it really bespeaks an imperfection inherent in oneself, an inability, like that of Aylmer, "to look beyond the shadowy scope of Time, and living once for all in Eternity, to find the perfect Future in the present" (10: 56). The moment of romance, of passion, brings with it the exalted vision that the object of one's desire, in contrast to oneself, is beyond imperfection. This is a vision that is contradicted by empirical reality, and hence it must be modified by experience; but this modification must not take the form of questioning the reality of the ideal image the moment of passion elicited. Instead, it must take place by acknowledging that the ideal image must remain at a distance that can be bridged only by death. We must come to see how the flaw is in truth our own, or commit the fault of Giovanni, when "he fell down, grovelling among earthly doubts, and defiled therewith the pure whiteness of Beatrice's image" (10: 120).

Perseus, the hero-as-child in the first story of the collection, escapes the petrifying gaze of Medusa by looking "at the reflection of her face and figure, in the bright mirror of [his] shield" (29). Through the mediation of such a mirror, the child may view the twisted horror, and beauty, of human desire: "In its surface, he could safely look at the reflection of the Gorgon's face. And there it was—that terrible countenance—mirrored in the brightness of the shield, with the moonlight falling over it, and displaying all its horror. [...] It was the fiercest and most horrible face that ever was seen or imagined, and yet with a strange, fearful, and savage kind of beauty in it" (29). Such is the monster Perseus must kill, in order to remain ignorant of the sexual nature of his mother. In this way, Perseus, the child, circumvents the allegorical experience of the radical ambiguity that pertains to all human emotions. What I have termed the symbolistic desire of the artist—his desire to see the ideal manifested in the present—is thus equivalent to the child's unwillingness to recognize that his desire for his mother bespeaks a lack within himself. If we refuse to confront this lack, we must remain children; this is the moral of both Wonder Books. Yet the belief in the ideal need not be given up, if we come to see how the recognition of the lack is in truth a prerequisite for allowing the Hope for the ideal to subsist in a world of imperfection. As we have seen, "The Chimaera" inculcates this lesson by presenting us with a pattern of interdependence, in which Bellerophon (the Artist) is dependent upon the faith of the gentle child in order to succeed, and the child (the Reader) in turn is dependent upon the former's willingness to confront the ambiguous experience he dare not face himself, in order to be initiated into the allegorical recognition of the doubleness of sexuality without losing his faith in its true ideality.

In "The Chimaera," then, the representation of the transition from childhood innocence to adult maturity by means of a sexual/textual romance still adheres closely to the pattern of *The Scarlet Letter*. That Bellerophon has to violate the freedom of Pegasus in order to defeat the Chimaera is potentially a disturbing circumstance, but the dilemma is resolved by having Bellerophon free Pegasus and the latter return to the hero by its own choice, a choice which echoes the consent to subjugation that we have already seen an example of in Hester's wilful subjugation to the letter, and in Holgrave's relinquishing of his radical desire for renewal. But "The Chimaera" was to be Hawthorne's last glorification of this formula for redemption through subjugation: subsequently, he was to represent the conditions that complicate the dialectical process on which the efficacy of the formula rests, conditions that threaten to transform the formula into an instrument of repression.

## 2. *Tanglewood Tales*

Although following a structural pattern very similar to that of *A Wonder Book*, *Tanglewood Tales* presents us with a very different picture of the possibilities of finding reconciliation through the means of the union between man and woman. The ending of the first tale of the collection,

"The Minotaur," recounts the story of Theseus slaying the bull-headed monster, and replicates the ending of the opening tale of the earlier book: the hero and his mother are reunited. However, as Hawthorne has not expunged the incident of King Aegeus suicide from his version of tale, this reunion of mother and son cannot fully dissipate the melancholy note struck in the original: as Theseus has forgotten to hoist bright sails as a sign of his victory over the Minotaur, his father believes him dead and throws himself into the sea. Thus on stepping ashore Theseus finds "himself king of all the country, whether he would or no; and such a turn of fortune was enough to make any young man feel very much out of spirits. However, he sent for his dear mother to Athens, and, by taking her advice in matters of state, became a very excellent monarch, and was greatly beloved by his people" (212).

Again, the second story of the book, "The Pygmies" (which tells of Hercules encounter with the giant Antaeus and his short-grown brethren), is rather incidental to the theme of maturation that we are tracing, while its third story, "The Dragon's Teeth," is central to it. The story begins with Zeus abduction of Europa, who is out playing with her three brothers, Phoenix, Cilix, and Cadmus. Appearing in the form of "a snow-white bull" (235), Zeus tricks Europa into riding his back and then whisks her off into the sea. Although the colour of the bull is dictated by tradition it is difficult not to read into its whiteness a subtle allusion to that of Pegasus, especially as the bull, too, appears as a "gentle and innocent creature" who is prone to prance around "as sportively as a kitten" (237–38). In this case, however, the appearance of innocence cracks when Europa is abducted, and the bull shows his true character as a "treacherous animal" (238).

Along with their mother and a friend, the three brothers go out to search for their lost sister, but one after the other give the task up as hopeless, until, after their mother's death, Cadmus alone is willing to go on with the search. After having visited the oracle of Delphi, slain a dragon, and planted a city, Cadmus finally meets with a female figure whom he first believes to be his sister. But this proves not to be the case:

> "No, Cadmus!" said the same voice that had spoken to him in the field of the armed men. "This is not that dear sister Europa, whom you have sought so faithfully, all over the wide world. This is Harmonia, a daughter of the sky, who is given you in-

> stead of sister, and brothers, and friend, and mother. You will find all those dear ones in her alone." (263–64)

This story, with its reasonably happy ending, could have functioned as a counterpart to "The Chimaera" by ending the Wonder Book on a note of reconciliation through the union of man and woman. Instead it is placed in the middle of the book, whereby it comes to signal, rather, an awakening to the imperfection of the world: Harmonia is given to Cadmus as a compensation for his loss, just as Hope was bestowed upon Pandora and her friend as a counterweight to the grief that they had let out upon the world in "The Paradise of Children."

The stories that follow would seem to confirm that the child has now been brought to a stage where he must confront the darker shadings of life. "Circe's Palace" retells the episode of the encounter between Ulysses and the enchantress who turned his crew into swine. Ulysses, of course, makes her turn them back into their human forms again, but even so, the story in Hawthorne's hands could hardly be said to be a bright one. Having come of age, so to speak, in the story of Cadmus, the narrative proves unwilling to let the undoing of the enchantress's spell be wholly comforting:

> You must not imagine, however, that the swinish quality had entirely gone out of them. When once it fastens itself into a person's character, it is very difficult getting rid of it. This was proved by the hamadryad, who, being exceedingly fond of mischief, threw another handful of acorns before the twenty-two newly restored people; whereupon, down they wallowed, in a moment, and gobbled them up in a very shameful way. (294)

Circe's magic, in short, only brought out the true nature of these people. Indeed, in the final paragraph of the tale, it becomes clear that to Ulysses, man is not an innocent creature:

> As for the lions, tigers, and wolves, (though Circe would have restored them to their former shapes, at his slightest word,) Ulysses thought it advisable that they should remain as they now were, and thus give warning of their cruel dispositions; instead of going about under the guise of men, and pretending to human sympathies, while their hearts had the blood-thirstiness of wild beasts. So he let them howl as much as they liked, but never troubled his head about them. (295)

While the tone in the following story, "The Pomegranate-Seeds," is considerably less cynical, it remains a story with a somewhat morose subject matter—it tells of Pluto's abduction of Proserpina to the kingdom of Death—and an ending that can be termed melancholy at best: Proserpina's mother is able to deliver her from Pluto, but as she has tasted a pomegranate apple in the realm of shadows, Proserpina must spend six months of the year in the underworld, one for each seed that found its way into her mouth.

In the last story of the collection, "The Golden Fleece" (in which Jason's travel to Colchis and the winning of the fleece is recounted), it becomes evident to the perspicacious reader that the stories of this second Wonder Book have been arranged in a manner that goes a long way toward reinstating the artistic "complexity" which was explicitly denounced in the Preface to the first one. "The Golden Fleece," it turns out, incorporates elements of each of the stories that have preceded it. We are reacquainted with Theseus and Hercules, the heroes of the first and the second stories of the book ("The Minotaur" and "The Pygmies"), both of whom set out with Jason on his quest for the Golden Fleece as two of his Argonauts (345); Jason, like Cadmus of the third story, sows the dragon's teeth (354); in setting out for the court of King Pelias, Jason encounters an old woman with "a pomegranate in her hand" (333), invoking the fruit that was given to Proserpina by Pluto in the previous story, "The Pomegranate-Seeds" (325); and Circe, whom Ulysses encounters in the fourth story, "Circe's Palace," is not only the aunt of Medea whom Jason meets at the court of King Aetes, but the very one who taught her, she informs Jason, to be "an enchantress" (355).[16]

The thread connecting these episodes admittedly is thin. Indeed, it might almost have seemed accidental had not Medea been one of the major characters of the story that opens the book as well: "The Minotaur." When we are reintroduced to Medea in "The Golden Fleece" we have already been presented to her as an unambiguously "wicked" character who tries to have King Aegeus poison his own son Theseus, in order that she might instead give the kingdom to her own son Medus.[17] While the narrator of the latter tale makes it no secret that Medea "was ill-natured, as all enchantresses are" (366), her function in "The Golden Fleece" is nevertheless almost the opposite of that which she fulfils in

"The Minotaur." Whereas, in the earlier tale, she is one of the obstacles the hero must overcome in order to achieve his heroic stature, in the latter tale she proves instrumental to his success. Jason, we remember, would not have been able to steal the Golden Fleece without Medea's assistance, nor would he have been able to escape from Colchis had not Medea come up with the terrible design of tearing her younger brother to pieces, spreading his disjointed limbs among the waves in order that her father might be delayed by gathering up the remnants of his dead body for burial. Hawthorne's version of the story, it need hardly be said, suppresses the latter half of the story. Nevertheless, the way Hawthorne has Eustace tell the story, Medea is not only the helper of Jason, but also a driving force in making him go through with his intention of capturing the Golden Fleece. Medea herself is allowed to make the point to Jason: "Do not you see you are lost, without me as your *good angel*?" (366; my emphasis).

The similarity between the quest for the Golden Fleece and that undertaken by Bellerophon in the final story of the previous Wonder Book is readily apparent; Jason's undertaking, we are informed, "was, of all others, the most difficult and dangerous in the world" (340). This would seem to be underscored by Hawthorne himself when we learn that to the young men who join the venture its attraction stems from the prospect it gives them of "getting astride of a flying serpent, or *sticking their spears into a Chimaera*, or, a least, thrusting their right arms down a monstrous lion's throat" (344; my emphasis). It is notable, however, that in this latter tale, the narrator makes no effort to disguise the extent to which the quest must in itself be characterized as an empty venture. To win the Golden Fleece is not to better the world: it simply symbolizes the wealth associated with material objects. In contrast to Bellerophon's battle against the Chimaera, Jason's quest for the Golden Fleece is not a battle against evil, but simply a task one undertakes because "there is nothing better *in the world*—and one must needs have an object, you know!" (362; my emphasis). It can therefore be characterized as a symbolistic enterprise: it is a quest for immediate gratification, undertaken on the implicit assumption that there need not be a gap between material and immaterial goals, and that figurative meaning may accordingly be reduced to literal manifestation.

Once the Golden Fleece has been won, Jason boards the galley which, interestingly, takes on the attributes of Pegasus: "the galley flew over the water, homeward bound, as if careering along with wings!" (368). The only wings aboard the ship, however, presumably belong to Jason's "good angel," Medea. The story ends abruptly, without being brought to a real close. We are left with a set of disturbing, if implied, questions: what happened to Jason when he got back to the court of King Pelias? Did Pelias keep his word of honour as Jason kept his? And what of Medea? Why is there no mention of what becomes of her although it is clearly suggested that she takes off with Jason? Anyone acquainted with the story knows that it hardly makes a suitable ending for a volume of stories for children (fratricide being one of its key elements), and one might of course argue that the open-ended nature of the story's close arises as a consequence of Hawthorne having to suppress certain incidents in order to support his claim in the introduction that Eustace Bright "does really appear to have overcome the moral objections against these fables" (180).

Even in Bright's hands, however, it is a far cry from the celebration of the redemptive powers of the union of man and woman that "The Chimaera" amounts to; this story would seem rather to imply an inherent emptiness in heroic deeds, including, presumably, the venture of the artist. As we have seen, the design of *Tanglewood Tales* is ostensibly identical to that of *A Wonder Book*. Once again, what is in the first story of the collection an obstacle to the hero, in the concluding story has been transformed into his principal aide. But despite repeating the structural pattern of inversion inherent in *A Wonder Book*, *Tanglewood Tales* does not recapitulate its hopeful conclusion. On the contrary, by ending the latter book with a story that temporally precedes the story which opens the collection, Hawthorne is indicating that the redemptive vision which is projected by the ending of a story such as "The Chimaera" may be subverted by some inherent trait implying a vicious circle. Through Medea's original appearance in the first story of the collection the reader has in fact been informed of what kind of creature it is that Jason is triumphantly bringing back to Athens: an evil enchantress who will utter "precisely such a hiss as one of her own snakes, only ten times more venomous and spiteful" (194–95). Thus the book ends just before the story is to be taken up again in the first story of the collection.

"The Golden Fleece," then, may be read as a bitter reformulation of the dialectical formula rendered in such idealized fashion in "The Chimaera." If, as "The Chimaera" suggests, the development of the child is somehow parallel to the artistic endeavour, "The Golden Fleece" makes quite clear that both of these processes are as likely to end in a constant renewal of the causes of pain, as in redemption. In fact, this must inevitably happen if the dialectical foundation of the process depicted in "The Chimaera" is displaced. The earlier story ends in glory because it shows us a character becoming a Poet by riding—taming—the ambiguous images projected by the artist. In "The Golden Fleece," on the other hand, Jason, the hero, has no sympathetic audience, no gentle child or Gentle Reader, to help him spiritualize the medium—Medea—whereby he gains access to the object of his quest. In "The Chimaera," Pegasus is both the horse and the spiritualized image of the horse as seen through the gentle child's faithful eyes. In "The Golden Fleece", in contrast, Medea is simply an enchantress, who has to pronounce herself Jason's "good angel" in order to make him go through with his quest. The first Wonder Book provides us with an exemplary instance of the benign formula of the Fortunate Fall: the last tale of the collection is able to re-enact the scenario of the opening tale, because the third, mediating story has already drawn attention to the possibility that one and the same act may have two mutually contradictory consequences: opening Pandora's box lets Pain into the world, but also Hope. In accordance with this ambiguous experience the figure of the Romance in the concluding tale is split into a literal and a figurative referent, into the Chimaera and Pegasus.

*A Wonder Book* thus adheres to the pattern of inversion and mediation that we have argued make up the fundamental feature of Hawthorne's application of the formula of the Fortunate Fall. In *Tanglewood Tales*, in contrast, there is inversion but no mediation, a circumstance that is subtly underscored by the fact that Harmonia takes the place of Hope in its third tale, for whereas hope is future-directed, harmony is immediately experienced. Harmony is a mode of presence; hope, in contrast, is a mode of absence: it arises precisely because what we hope for is absent, and it can be sustained only if what we hope for remains at a distance. "The Chimaera" is a tale about transforming the monstrosity of romance (the monster of the title that I have tried to show is a veiled representation of erotic love) into something beautiful: Pegasus, spiritual marriage—a bonding rather than a bondage of man and woman, child and adult. And this bonding becomes possible through the complex function fulfilled by the double image of Pegasus/Chimaera that is to be found in the tale. "The Golden Fleece," in contrast, substitutes the symbol of the golden fleece for the allegorical double image of the earlier tale: with no reader to spiritualize the medium of the artist's quest, its very success is menacingly shown to be a contributing cause of the constant renewal of evil and pain in the world.

## 3. Hawthorne's Marital Crisis of 1852

As no one can fail to notice, the most conspicuous difference between the two Wonder Books is the absence, in the latter book, of a narrative frame within which the stories are related.[18] In *Tanglewood Tales*, then, Eustace is robbed of an audience. As Martin K. Doudna points out, Primrose, the eldest and most talkative of the group of children Eustace tells his stories to in *A Wonder Book*, "is about five years younger than he—just as Sophia Hawthorne was about five years younger than her husband."[19] It should be observed in this context, that the tactics employed in "The Paradise of Children" of securing the innocence of Pandora by ascribing her morally condemnable acts to the "naughtiness" of a child, is one that Hawthorne himself reverted to in his letters to Sophia. In courting his wife-to-be, Edwin H. Miller notes, "he decided to have an ethereal being who was also a sexual being, which he accomplished by dividing her in unspecified proportions into a Dove and a human called quite simply Sophie Hawthorne." The advantage of this division, Miller points out, was that "Sophie, unlike the Dove, could be naughty."[20] What Miller passes over in silence is that by calling the corporeal reality of Sophie Hawthorne "naughty," Hawthorne confers the attribute of a child upon the sexual embodiment of his future wife, thereby allowing her to retain her innocence. By depriving Sophia's sexual side of the *knowledge* of sexuality associated with adulthood in his works, Hawthorne is able to insist on his love for naughty Sophie without compromising the spotlessness of his Dove:

> There is an unaccountable fascination about that Sophie Hawthorne—whatever she chooses to do or say, whether reasonable or unreasonable, I am forced to love her the better for it. Not that I love her better than my Dove; but then it is right and natural that the Dove should awaken infinite tenderness, because she is a bird of Paradise, and has a perfect and angelic nature—so that love is her inalienable and unquestionable right. And yet my wayward heart will love this naughty Sophie Hawthorne;—yes, its affection for the Dove is doubled, because she is inseparably united with naughty Sophie. I have one love for them both, and it is infinitely intensified because they share it together. (15: 400)

Exploiting the culturally encoded double entendre of the term "naughty," Hawthorne is able to circumvent the seemingly self-contradicting circumstance that an axiomatically innocent subject, like the Child or the Dove, is nevertheless ascribed a propensity for entertaining erotic feelings. The recognition of sexuality (which is, as we saw in chapter two, the archetypal mark of the Fall) is suppressed by transforming it into an unconscious trait which is deemed constitutive of the form of the Child and the Dove alike: Sophia's Dove like Child Pandora, reside within the *form* of sexuality (the human body), but can be deemed innocent as long as they do not display any conscious awareness of this form. Naughty Sophie is the imperfect form in which the perfect essence of the Dove resides but, being a child, naughty Sophie need not confront the troublesome implications of her imperfection.

As my discussion of "The Paradise of Children" bears out, the Fall in Hawthorne is always a fall from Childhood into Adulthood, from innocence into recognition of guilt. In other words, the Fall is conceived as a fall into an awareness of the imperfect *form* holding the spiritual essence of the individual. As the above quotation from Hawthorne's letter to Sophia implies, Hawthorne cherishes the recognition of this form not because it gives us the means to transcend its imperfection, but because it proves to be "inseparably united" with its spiritual essence. Hawthorne's heart, like the Heart of mankind, is a "wayward" heart, a heart in which exists already the original wrong. For this reason, the imperfect form of naughty Sophie strikes a chord of sympathy with his heart, and it is this sympathetic chord which inspires a love which encompasses not only Sophia's ethereal essence, the Dove, but also its imperfect corporeal manifestation. To love the ideal essence of the Soul, one must love the Body as well, for one cannot love the Soul exclusively without suppressing an essential feature of one's own self: the lack, or imperfection, of which Man became aware through the Fall.

As we will see in the next two chapters, instead of building his later romances upon scenarios in which this moral is taken to heart, Hawthorne chose to confront the consequences of its suppression. In both of these romances there is a female character who would seem to be a veiled representation of the same type of spiritualized being that Hawthorne referred to as the Dove when speaking of an aspect of Sophia; and rather thinly veiled at that, since both Priscilla and Hilda are explicitly associated with doves—the latter, indeed, is known as "Hilda The Dove" (MF, 56). Correspondences of this kind—of which there is a glaring example in *The House of the Seven Gables* as well, "Phoebe" being another pet name for Hawthorne's wife—suggests the presence of a private allegorical layer in Hawthorne's stories, a layer to be read and understood fully only by Sophia and her husband themselves. I do not wish to make too much of this private allegory, which is no doubt bound to elude us to an even higher degree than many of the other significances that the romances hint at but refuse to spell out explicitly. Nevertheless, it seems to me impossible wholly to ignore this aspect of Hawthorne's writings, to treat it as something of a superfluous embellishment, a quirk on the author's part that should not be allowed to intrude into serious analyses of his works. I am certainly not suggesting that this private allegorical layer represents a deeper or more interesting meaning than that which can be extracted from his fictions without taking recourse to letters and private notebook entries. Yet its presence nevertheless deserves to be recorded, if but for the mere possibility that it may resonate with the dominant writer-reader allegory that I am exploring. The principal difference between *A Wonder Book* and *Tanglewood Tales*, I have argued above, is that the latter book eschews the redemptive conclusion that the former sets forth, choosing instead to represent a kind of communicative breakdown between Artist and Audience. It seems to me that this difference, which is a constitutive trait of *The Blithedale Romance* and *The Marble Faun* as well, may be indirectly connected to changes in the relationship of Hawthorne to his own ideal reader, Sophia.

Before I sketch my hypothesis, it is only fair to say that Laura Laffrado in *Hawthorne's Literature for Children* points to a great number of circumstances that could have contributed to the darker tone of the latter as compared to the former Wonder Book:

> Much had happened to Hawthorne during the months that intervened between his writing of the two books: the Hawthornes had moved across the state from Lenox to Concord; Hawthorne's sister, Louisa, on her way to visit them, had drowned in July 1852; Sophia's mother had died in early 1853; pre-Civil War rumblings were becoming increasingly difficult to ignore; Hawthorne's friendship with Herman Melville, at its peak during the writing of *A Wonder Book*, no longer colored his daily life; and, despite Hawthorne's growing fame as a writer, it was increasingly clear that his writing would provide, at best, a slender means of existence.[21]

Imposing as this list may seem, it is hardly very substantial. First of all, the move back to Concord from Lenox, Berkshire, would seem to be a change for the better, not for the worse: Nathaniel and Sophia alike expressed joy at the prospect, and later confirmed their satisfaction with their new home.[22] Secondly, pre-Civil War rumblings, disconcerting as they must have been, were still not very alarming and are unlikely to have had much influence upon Hawthorne's writing for children.[23] As for the financial argument, it is true that Hawthorne's writings did not earn him the economic rewards he is likely to have hoped for, but the period was not one of financial instability—it was considerably better, at least, than when *The Scarlet Letter* was written in 1849.[24] What is more, having written the campaign biography for his friend Franklin Pierce, who was duly elected president in November 1852, Hawthorne's financial prospects at this point must have seemed brighter than ever.[25] Most importantly, the darker tone of *Tanglewood Tales* is evident already in *The Blithedale Romance*, which was published in April 1852, and hence could have no connection with the deaths of either Sophia's mother or his sister, although it is true that the latter certainly affected him deeply (as the former may also well have done, albeit more indirectly). In short, if critically examined Laffrado's list is reducible to the possible influence of Hawthorne's changed relations with Herman Melville, and although this is something that some of his biographers have made much of, it seems highly unlikely that it could be the principal cause for the darkening vision expressed by his works from *The Blithedale Romance* onwards.[26]

Nevertheless, it remains true that both *The Blithedale Romance* and *Tanglewood Tales* were written and conceived in what was in many ways a turbulent period of Hawthorne's life. Between 1850 and 1853 Hawthorne shot to the firmament of the American literary establishment, and although the financial rewards were not overwhelming, he became America's best-known man of letters almost overnight, it must have seemed, compared to all the years he had been churning out tales whose merits were recognized only in the occasional rave review. In a shrewd move to consolidate the reputation of the man who had written the much acclaimed romance of *The Scarlet Letter*, Hawthorne's American publishers, Ticknor, Reed and Fields, saw to it that no less than eight books bearing his name were published in the period, boosting the creativity of their author by putting out a third edition of *Twice-Told Tales* and issuing a third book of previously uncollected tales as *The Snow Image*. Hawthorne responded accordingly, writing the two collections of children's stories and the campaign biography for Franklin Pierce, over and above *The Scarlet Letter*, *The House of the Seven Gables*, and *The Blithedale Romance*. In the midst of these professional activities, on May 20, 1851, the Hawthornes' third child, Rose, was born in Lenox in a small farmhouse which they rented cheaply from friends of Sophia.[27]

This last circumstance, as incidental as it may seem, is arguably at the root of the darker tone of Hawthorne's later fictions. Not the birth of Rose per se, I should say, but what it practically came to mean to Hawthorne: sexual abstention. According to Herbert the "Hawthornes had discontinued sexual intercourse after the birth of Rose,"[28] a speculation that he substantiates by citing Elizabeth Peabody's claim that Sophia told her, "in the last part of her life, that [Nathaniel] so respected the delicacy of [her] constitution [...] that he proposed they should have but three children, and that there should be two and a half years between the first two, and five years between the second and the third. And this was what happened, for, as she added, 'Mr. Hawthorne's passions were under his feet'."[29] Hawthorne's own comment, in a letter to Pike, July 24, 1851, that Rose is "the last child whom I expect or intend to have" (16: 464) would seem to substantiate this report. Herbert also points out that this decision to abstain from sexual intercourse, apparently took its toll on Hawthorne: "Caresses, expressions of one sort or another, are necessary to the life of the affections, as leaves are to the life of a tree," Hawthorne wrote in his notebook on March 13th, 1853, adding: "If they are wholly restrained, love will die at the roots" (8: 551). Miller argues in a similar vein, that the Hawthornes' 18 months stay at the Berkshires "was no doubt a time of crisis in the marriage which neither was to admit;" and concludes that Hawthorne "apparently pledged himself to chastity at forty-seven," speculating that this might have been a consequence of him having watched Sophia—against her wishes—give birth to Rose.[30] Indeed, considering how flower-imagery in Hawthorne's romances is almost invariably charged with erotic connotations, it may well be that Hawthorne decided on the name for his last child with a view to its allegorical connotations: he knew, the above evidence suggests, that she would be the last offspring of his erotic relation with Sophia. He had, keep in mind, named his firstborn daughter Una, after the heroine of the first book of Spenser's epic.

I am not arguing, be it noted, that sexual abstention per se lies behind the darker tone of Hawthorne's later fictions; after all, if Hawthorne were able to keep his passions under his feet to such an extent that he and Sophia could predict the length of the intervals between their children's births, they are likely to have abstained from sexual intercourse periodically even prior to the birth of Rose. What I am suggesting is simply that Hawthorne's decision to pledge himself to chastity following the delivery of his third child, may have made him prone to explore fictive scenarios in which sexuality is not recognized as a vital, if imperfect, medium whereby a sense of the ideal may be attained in the present. One must of course be wary of assuming speculations for facts, and it must readily be admitted that even if my hypothesis is true, it is almost certainly not the whole truth. Yet it may be a not insignificant part of the truth. It was, after all, through his marriage to Sophia that Hawthorne found the means to merge a conception of perfection with an acknowledgement of imperfection; in her, ideal Dove and real naughty Sophie Hawthorne co-existed and were one. If sexual intimacy between Sophia and her husband *did* cease with the birth of Rose, it would have been tantamount, for Hawthorne, to giving up the medium by which the Ideal and the Real had originally been fused in his life. The loss of such a medium surely would have been enough to make him reflect upon the inestimable value of what he had lost; it may even have suggested to him the idea of fictively trying out how his own life might have turned out, had he never had the good fortune of knowing such a medium.

It is of course impossible ultimately to determine why Hawthorne decided to revert to autobiographical material in writing his next romance. Yet writing to William Pike, a former Custom-House colleague, on July 24, 1851—two months after the birth of Rose—he announced that it was his intention to take "the Community for a subject, and [...] give some of my experiences and observations at Brook Farm." That Miles Coverdale, the first-person narrator of *The Blithedale Romance*, borrows many traits from Hawthorne himself is a well-documented fact, and it seems equally incontestable that the romance is at least in part a study of what "might have been Hawthorne's own fate had he not married Sophia."[31] While the cause of the darker tone of Hawthorne's fictions from this point onwards must necessarily be stated in hypothetical fashion, there is little doubt that the change that sets in primarily concerns the way Hawthorne portrays the relation between the allegorical representatives of Artist and Reader. Where the two previous romances present us with a Reader who is willing to accept the allegorical premise that the Ideal can only be attained through the mediation of an imperfect medium, such as erotic love, the Reader of the romances that followed is a person who for some reason fails to embrace this allegorical premise, with dire consequences—consequences, I have suggested above, that Hawthorne may well have had first-hand experience of. Subsequently to *A Wonder Book*, the interaction between artist and audience in Hawthorne's fictions no longer is brought to a redemptive conclusion, at least not within the narratives themselves. If Hawthorne holds on to his idealism even after this change—and I will be arguing that he does—he is much more sensitive to the circumstances that may bring it to nought from *The Blithedale Romance* onwards. Indeed, I will argue in the following two chapters that it is this heightened sensitivity to the darker shadings of idealism that lies behind the increasingly complex aesthetic strategies of his final works.

## CHAPTER SIX

# *The Blithedale Romance:* Translating the Spirit

I came to this place in one snow-storm, and shall probably leave it in another; so that my reminiscences of Brook Farm are like to be the coldest and dreariest imaginable.

Theodore de l'Aubepine to Sophia Peabody, Brook Farm, October 21st, 1841.

If *Tanglewood Tales* is bleak, *The Blithedale Romance*, published some months earlier, is even more so. Henry James, it is true, pronounced *The Blithedale Romance* "the lightest, the brightest, the liveliest" of Hawthorne's romances, but twentieth century critics have not been prone to agree.[1] Male calls it "Hawthorne's most pessimistic book," and many others have testified to similar views.[2] Male perceptively attributes this pessimism to the way the relation between man and woman is depicted in the book. In contrast to what is the case in *The Scarlet Letter* and *The House of the Seven Gables*, in *The Blithedale Romance*, Male holds, "there is no redemption through tragedy—only an abortive tragedy. In their quest for reformation and refinement, the man and woman of the Western world have sacrificed their normal emotions, including sexual passions" (*Tragic*, 155). While I agree with Male that there is no redemption in the plot of *The Blithedale Romance*, I will be arguing in this chapter that the case may be rather different from the perspective of the anagogical sense of the romance in which we as readers form an integral part of the text. As John Carlos Rowe has perceptively observed, the different idealistic endeavours portrayed in the romance depend "upon extremely general principles, which could lead to radically diverse results if enacted by different personalities."[3] The romance, too, is an idealistic endeavour, and the problem with which the reader is confronted in *The Blithedale Romance*, along with Coverdale and the communitarians, is how to affirm the ideal without rejecting an earthly reality inevitably marked by the Fall.

As we have seen, despite their marked dissimilarities *The Scarlet Letter* and *The House of the Seven Gables* provide essentially the same answer to that question: if the inherent imperfection of our earthly existence is acknowledged, all attempts to realize the ideal immediately, in the present, must be abandoned. The tendency of the individual as Artist, these books argue, is to conceive of the relation between himself and the ideal in symbolistic fashion. Symbolism privileges the individual's emotions as an access to the ideal: the sense of guilt we experience when our emotions conflict with the norms of society can thus be overcome by insisting that any action springing directly from our sensibilities has "a consecration of its own" (SL, 195), as Hester puts it. Hawthorne's romances aim to replace this symbolistic conception of the relation between the real and the ideal, with an allegorical view that does not seek to suppress guilt (the immediate emotional sign of imperfection), but, on the contrary, treasures it as a sign of the distance between the real and the ideal, between individual effort and collective achievement. By conceiving of our individual lives as participating in a dialectical process which one cannot fulfil single-handedly in one's own lifetime, the imperfection inherent in this world need no longer be conceived as obstructing the way to the ideal, but must on the contrary be seen as the very medium whereby the ideal may ultimately be attained. *The House of the Seven Gables* inculcates what *The Scarlet Letter* makes evident: the sign, or letter, of earthly imperfection is sexuality. Erotic love is what makes life potentially beautiful; hence it is figured as a flower, which also serves to suggest that to appreciate its beauty, one must not forget that it is soon to wilt and die. This flower, as we saw in our analysis of *The House of the Seven Gables*, is the key to our earthly fortune, but only on the condition that its transitory nature is recognized. If this is denied, as it is in, but not by, *The Blithedale Romance*, the ground for the dialectical process whereby private psychological stains may be transformed into public political virtues disappears. In the place of such a transformation, *The Blithedale Romance* depicts the translation of public to private and vice versa in symbolistic fashion, as a process which is likened to a distillation of the body into its ideal spiritual essence: to turn the grape (the body) into wine (the ideal essence) is equivalent to separating the soul from the body, to discard the latter in order to enjoy the former perfected.

What Male aptly calls "the sexless outcome" (*Tragic*, 155) of the interaction between man and woman in *The Blithedale Romance* may thus be seen as an expression and negotiation of a sequestering process, an investigation in the consequences of separating the spiritual qualities of a "Dove", from the corporeal qualities of a "naughty Sophie," as I suggested in the conclusion to the previous chapter. This sequestering—emblematically expressed through the doubling of the principal female character of the plot into Zenobia and Priscilla, neither of whom is by herself capable of performing the office of either a Hester or a Phoebe—may very well be the most important element of the plot, but it is far from the only one. *The Blithedale Romance* links this essentially psychological plot with a historical and political plot, a plot which is once more designed to show how the symbolistic desire to conflate the secular and the spiritual, to achieve the Puritan goal of making America a city on the hill, realizing Paradise on earth immediately, must come to a bitter end.

If not his greatest romance, *The Blithedale Romance* might quite possibly be Hawthorne's most complex achievement: feminism, philanthropy, utopianism, mesmerism, hermeneutics—Hawthorne layers these issues one upon the other in the book, making the narrative strive for so much that one may perhaps be excused for holding as one of its main deficiencies, "simply too much plot."[4] Critics have understandably been prone to favour one of these aspects over the others, and hence to argue the primacy of its psychological content over its political purport, or vice versa, or maintained that it is simply a story about the problematics of storytelling. Other critics have argued that *The Blithedale Romance* "gives up the suggestiveness of a symbolic mode for the sake of achieving a new realism of dramatic presentation," and have hence concluded that the fantastic elements of the plot get in the way of its sociological aspects.[5] Yet while it may be necessary, if but for practical reasons, to deal with the different issues raised by *The Blithedale Romance* one at a time, there can be little doubt that Hawthorne intends us to understand these issues as somehow inextricably related to each other: the political aspects of the book cannot be understood in isolation from the love story, nor must its love plot be isolated from its politics.

To better understand the intricately knotted themes of the book, it will be helpful once again to have recourse to an analysis of its structure. It will be helpful to start out, however, by reacquainting ourselves with the specificities of its plot. Critics have frequently vented their dissatisfaction with the "erratic structure" of this plot with its sometimes "chaotic ordering of events."[6] I will argue, in due course, that neither the structure nor the plot of *The Blithedale Romance* are confused. The latter makes sense aesthetically as well as psychologically; yet it can be seen to do so only if we stay sensitive throughout to Hawthorne's allegorical method.

## 1. The Plot and Structure of *The Blithedale Romance*

In comparison with *The House of the Seven Gables*, *The Blithedale Romance* is a marvel of action and intrigue. The night before he is to join the proto-socialist community of Blithedale, Miles Coverdale, the narrator of the book, is approached by an elderly man, old Moodie, who asks Coverdale to do him "a very great favor" (7). Coverdale responds rather reluctantly, which puts Moodie off his original intention, wherefore the precise nature of the favour in question is left indeterminate; however, it is clear from the subsequent development of the plot that Moodie had meant to ask Coverdale to accompany his daughter Priscilla to Blithedale, and to present her to Zenobia. Instead this office is bestowed upon Hollingsworth, a former blacksmith turned philanthropist, whose true motif in joining the Blithedale community is to turn it into a vehicle for his grand scheme of reforming criminals.

Hollingsworth makes a dramatic appearance with Priscilla at Blithedale on the evening of the first day of the enterprise. Coverdale and the other communitarians have already arrived and been welcomed by Zenobia, a writer and feminist. Distinguished by a luxurious flower in her hair, Zenobia's physical advantages are described in some detail by Coverdale. She forms a marked contrast to the "unsubstantial" (26) figure of Priscilla, who immediately approaches her, much to Zenobia's chagrin. In compliance with the wish of Hollingsworth, whom Zenobia is obviously attracted to, she agrees to shelter the younger girl.

The interrelations of these three characters immediately become the focus of Coverdale's attentions, and remain so for the rest of the romance. Only gradually do these become clear: Priscilla and Zenobia are in fact sisters (or half sisters), both being fathered by old Moodie, a formerly wealthy man whom Coverdale in chapter 22 calls Fauntleroy, which suggests that the unnamed crime that he committed in an attempt to save the fortune he squandered, is forgery.[7] Their kinship is known by Priscilla, but not by Zenobia, who believes her father long since to have left the country to escape his crime. Having grown up in poverty, Priscilla is equally unaware that her father has in fact come into a fortune once more, since the death of his wealthy brother—with whom Zenobia has grown up in affluence—leaves him, rather than Zenobia, the sole beneficiary. In an effort, perhaps, to reconcile the two extremes of his life—the wealth associated with Zenobia, and the poverty associated with Priscilla—old Moodie decides to perform a rather cruel experiment: he leaves his youngest daughter in the hands of his older one, in order to see if the latter will treat her with the love and affection that becomes a sister. When he finds, upon visiting Blithedale, that Zenobia's attitude to the younger girl is rather that of "a mistress to a dependant" (88), he promptly decides to disinherit her and bestow the wealth she still believes that she is in possession of upon Priscilla.

The degree to which Hollingsworth is let in on this scheme of the old man is left unspecified, but it is certainly implied that Coverdale, at least, bases his sharp judgement of the other man on the supposition that he has been a confidant of old Moodie all along, as can be ascertained from the fact that Coverdale maintains that he was convinced (at the time) that the "pretty sight" of Priscilla and Zenobia playfully together "must have been purposely arranged by Priscilla, for the old man to see" (88), though his narrative now clearly implies that it was in fact arranged by Hollingsworth. Interestingly, even though Coverdale repeatedly describes her as an actress, Zenobia is unable to conceal her true emotions for Priscilla, and as a result the scene completely fails to convey its intended message: somewhere in her act, resides a truth that will not be covered.

At this point (of the story rather than the narrative discourse, since the intricacies of the plot become clear only once we have already traversed the romance in full) the disagreeable Professor Westervelt emerges upon the scene, seeking an interview with Zenobia. Coverdale, directing him as to where she is to be found, overhears some of their conversation—or at least, imagines in retrospect that he has. Neither the reader nor Coverdale ever finds out how Zenobia and Westervelt are related to each other, although Coverdale concludes that their relation must have been of a sexual nature. What does become clear, is that Westervelt is the very magnetist who has put the Veiled Lady on public display, and that Priscilla is this lady; also, that he has informed Zenobia of the danger that Priscilla constitutes to her, and has suggested that she should be returned to his custody as a way out of the dilemma.

We are now almost halfway through the story; in the following chapter (14)—of which we shall have much to say further on—it is made explicit that Hollingsworth and Zenobia are romantically attached to each other. The peripety of the Blithedale enterprise occurs—for Coverdale, rather than the story—when Hollingsworth proposes that he should join forces with him in turning the whole community into a vehicle for Hollingsworth's own philanthropical project, the economical foundation of which he has secured by his (clandestine) engagement to Zenobia. Coverdale refuses, and in his disillusionment as to the character of his friend, returns to the city, where he soon encounters Zenobia and Priscilla once more, in the company of Professor Westervelt in whose hands Zenobia and Hollingsworth have conspired to return their charge. Coverdale is present on the night when she is again presented to the world as The Veiled Lady upon the stage of a village hall, as is Hollingsworth, who finally delivers her from the mesmeric powers of the Professor, by entering the stage and taking her into his arms.

Two days later Coverdale returns to Blithedale, where he first encounters the other communitarians dressed up as masqueraders in the woods, and then runs into his three friends at the foot of the rock known as Eliot's Pulpit, where they had been in the habit of spending their Sundays together. Zenobia now knows that Priscilla is to inherit the wealth she has thought belonged to her, and Hollingsworth has evidently just broken off his engagement to her, and announced his engagement to Priscilla. Understandably upset, Zenobia admonishes Coverdale to enter Eliot's pulpit, in order that she and Hollingsworth may both plead their cause before him, as before a vicarious judge. Zenobia delivers a passionate speech on the selfishness of Hollingsworth's brand of philanthropy. After having spoken alone with Zenobia, Coverdale falls asleep at the base of the rock, but awakes with frightful premonitions, and after having found Zenobia's handkerchief by the river, wakes Hollings-worth and Silas Foster, the only true yeoman at Blithedale. They go out on the river, eventually recovering Zenobia's body, stiffened in a curious position—kneeling as in prayer, but with her hands "bent before her, as if she struggled against Providence in never-ending hostility" (235). In the penultimate chapter, Zenobia is buried. Encountering Hollingsworth and Priscilla a few years later, Coverdale finds the former a broken man, plagued by the thought of having been the cause of Zenobia's suicide, with "a childlike, or childish, tendency to press close, and closer still" (242), to the side of Priscilla, who has evidently become his caretaker rather than his wife.

This is the story, to which is appended a chapter of barely three pages, in which Coverdale expatiates on the emotionally barren life that he has led since quitting Blithedale, finally revealing a secret that he claims to be "essential to the full understanding" (247) of his story, namely that he was himself in love with Priscilla. I will argue that it is indeed essential to an understanding of the internal coherence of the plot, even if it were added on something of a whim, as evidence that we will observe below suggests.

*

At first reading, the unfolding of the melodramatic intrigue that we have recounted above may certainly strike the reader as little else than the grinding of a rather cumbersome plot machinery. Close attention to detail, however, reveals this romance to be as conscientiously composed as the preceding ones. Critics have had relatively little to say of the structure of *The Blithedale Romance*, barring the important if fairly obvious observation that the action of the romance develops over a period of six months, from April to September.[8] The most ambitious attempt of delineating the spatial form of *The Blithedale Romance* to date is that of Vern B. Lentz and Allen F. Stein, who take note of the fact that the romance contains 29 chapters, "which break," they claim, "into four segments of seven chapters each, with chapter XV, 'A Crisis,' isolated in the center."[9] Given the importance that I attach to the number seven as a structural device in the analyses of the other romances, this is a suggestive argument, especially as the four segments identified by Lentz and Stein form what seems to be naturally self-enclosed units. Chapters 1–7 depict Coverdale's first excursion to Blithedale, chapters 23–29 his second; chapters 8–14 his period of commitment to Blithedale, chapters 16–22 his withdrawal from and disillusionment with it. "Every separate segment," Lentz and Stein claim, "depicts an abortive attempt by Coverdale to move from his condition of passive withdrawal to involvement with the others."[10]

This may be so; it is difficult to dispute the validity of the above account as a general outline of the structure of the book. It is, however, less convincing in detail. For one thing, although Miles Coverdale must indeed in many ways be looked upon as the central character of the romance, we must be careful not to over-emphasize his structural importance. As always in Hawthorne, we can determine the role of the characters only by viewing them in relation to each other.[11] Whether intentionally or not, it must be granted that Hawthorne greatly contributed to facilitating readings that focus on Coverdale, by adding chapter 29, "Miles Coverdale's Confession," to the finished romance, sometime between April 30 and May 14, 1852. But this very circumstance undermines the authority of Lentz's and Stein's analysis, as it would seem that chapter 15 has acquired its position as the centre of *The Blithedale Romance* on the suggestion of an outside party, or possibly on a whim of the author himself; in either case, its centrality would seem to be quite accidental.[12]

A better outline of the structure of the romance can be arrived at by considering it as it must originally have appeared, that is, as being made up of 28 chapters. The centre of these 28 chapters is chapter 14, "Eliot's Pulpit," which ends in a paragraph in which Coverdale looks back "over the long slope of pasture-land," beholding Zenobia and Hollingsworth "standing together, in the light of the sunset, just on the spot where, according to the gossip of the Community, they meant to build their cottage" (127). This central chapter is symmetrically linked to the chapter that was most likely the original ending of *The Blithedale Romance*, namely chapter 28, "Blithedale-Pasture," which begins with a paragraph in which Coverdale reports that he had suggested that Zenobia be buried "at the base of Eliot's pulpit," but that Hollingsworth "made it his request that her grave might be dug on the gently sloping hill-side, in the wide pasture, where, as we once supposed, Zenobia and he had planned to build their cottage" (238).

"Eliot's Pulpit" is thus preceded by 13 chapters, and followed by another 13 before the romance reaches its terminating point. These two groups should each be divided into two main sections. The narrative begins and ends with Coverdale's two sojourns to Blithedale (chapters 2–

5, and 24–27), both of which comprise one full day, and are preceded by a chapter in which Coverdale pays a visit to an exhibition of the Veiled Lady (chapters 1 and 23). This general resemblance between the two sections is greatly reinforced by a number of other parallels: in chapter 3, Coverdale informs us that "the presence of Zenobia caused our heroic enterprise to show like an illusion, a masquerade, a pastoral, a counterfeit Arcadia" (21), yet it is in chapter 24, "The Masqueraders" (from which Zenobia is absent), that the Blithedale enterprise is quite literally transformed into a masquerade. In chapter 4, Priscilla droops to her knees before Zenobia (28), repeating the gesture in chapter 25, where she sinks to her knees "in the very same attitude which she had assumed on their first meeting, in the kitchen of the old farm-house" (219). In chapter 5, Zenobia instructs Coverdale that he "had better turn the affair into a ballad" (33), claiming in chapter 26 to perceive that he is indeed "turning this whole affair into a ballad" (223). Thus we should perhaps not be surprised to find Zenobia drowned in chapter 27, "Midnight," as she announces already in chapter 5 that "this shadowy snow-maiden"—Priscilla, that is—"precisely at the stroke of midnight, shall melt away at my feet, in a pool of ice-cold water, and give me my death with a pair of wet slippers!" (33), one of which, at least, is recovered by Silas Foster in chapter 27 in the form of "a shoe [...] half imbedded in the mud" (231).

The chiastical relationship between chapters of each section is even more rigidly maintained in the two sections that are temporally and thematically quite sprawling. Chapters 6 and 7 concern Coverdale's illness, and in a more general sense, his relation to Hollingsworth, to whom Coverdale confides, in chapter 6, that he has "nothing to do in life" (43). Coverdale's relation to Hollingsworth is thematically the main focus of chapters 15 and 16, as well; significantly, it is in chapter 15 that Hollingsworth offers Coverdale "(what you have told me, over and over again, that you most need) a purpose in life" (133) by joining him in his scheme of turning the Blithedale community into a place "for the reformation of the wicked by methods moral, intellectual, and industrial, by the sympathy of pure, humble, and yet exalted minds, and by opening to his pupils the possibility of a worthier life than that which had become their fate" (131).

In chapter 8 we learn that Coverdale's sickness "had been an avenue between two existences; the low-arched and darksome doorway, through which I crept out of a life of old conventionalisms, on my hands and knees, as it were, and gained admittance into the freer region that lay beyond" (61); in chapter 17 we find "the effeminacy of past days" returning upon him "at once" (145) on his return to the city. In chapter 9, "Hollingsworth, Zenobia, Priscilla," we learn that his three friends stood forth "to my imagination [...] as the indices of a problem" (69), figuring "so largely on my private theatre" (70); in chapter 18, despite having "quitted my three friends" (153) that he has "kept so long upon my mental stage, as actors in a drama" (156), Coverdale finds "the same figures arraying themselves before me, and presenting their old problem in a shape that made it more insoluble than ever" (157).

In chapter 10, old Moodie pays Blithedale a visit in order to find out how Zenobia and Priscilla are getting along, and Zenobia's gentleness towards Priscilla is exposed as an act, with the result that old Moodie decides to disinherit her and bestow his wealth upon Priscilla instead. Chapter 19, again makes Zenobia the object of "a perceptive faculty" (160) trying to ascertain her relation to Priscilla, though this time it is Coverdale who is trying to ascertain "the true character of the woman" (165). In chapter 11 Coverdale meets Westervelt; an encounter that is repeated in chapter 20. Chapter 12 introduces us to "Coverdale's Hermitage," which is situated in a tree which a wild grape-wine has "married" to some neighbouring trees "with a perfectly inextricable knot of polygamy" (98). This private, and natural, hiding place in which Coverdale has "counted the innumerable clusters of my vine, and forereckoned the abundance of my vintage" (99) forms a parallel by contrast to the saloon which forms the public, and artificial, hiding-place of old Moodie, whom Coverdale seeks out "for the purpose of ascertaining whether the knot of affairs was as inextricable, on that side, as I found it on all others" (174). It is here that Coverdale learns from old Moodie the circumstances that form the basis for chapter 22, "Fauntleroy," a story within the story that informs us of the *background* of the twisted relation between the two sisters that leads to the events depicted in the first half of the romance, structurally closely resembling the way the story of the Silvery Veil that Zenobia recounts in chapter 13, "Zenobia's Legend," *anticipate* what follows in the latter half of the romance.

Leaving out chapter 29, the structure of *The Blithedale Romance* can thus be schematized as follows:

| A1 | A2 |
|---|---|
| 1. First encounter with the Veiled Lady. | 23. Second encounter with the Veiled Lady. |
| 2. Coverdale sets out for Blithedale in April. | 24. Coverdale sets out for Blithedale in September. |
| 3. Zenobia makes Blithedale appear as a masquerade. | 25. Zenobia appears in masquerade outfit, accusing Hollingsworth of being "a better masquerader" (218). |
| 4. Hollingsworth enters with the "flower-shrub" (27) of Priscilla. | 26. Hollingsworth exits with "the poor, pale flower" (224) of Priscilla. |
| 5. Zenobia predicts her own death. | 27. Zenobia dies. |
| B1 | B2 |
| 6. Coverdale complains to Hollingsworth of lack of purpose in life. | 15. Hollingsworth offers Coverdale purpose in life. |
| 7. Priscilla gives Coverdale nightcap. | 16. Coverdale asks Priscilla to give him purse. |
| 8. Coverdale enters period of activity at farm. | 17. Coverdale returns to inactivity in town. |
| 9. Hollingsworth, Zenobia, and Priscilla stand forth as indices of problem to Coverdale; Coverdale "would have gone far" to save Priscilla from "catastrophe" (72). | 18. Hollingsworth, Zenobia, and Priscilla present the same old problem to Coverdale; Coverdale begins "to long for a catastrophe" (157). |
| 10. Old Moodie spies on Zenobia; Coverdale is the "one calm observer" (97) of drama staged by Destiny. | 19. Coverdale spies on Zenobia; Coverdale is the "calm observer" (166) of Zenobia's "tragedy" (163). |
| 11. Coverdale meets Westervelt at Blithedale. | 20. Coverdale meets Westervelt in town. |
| 12. Coverdale hides in tree with grapevine. | 21. Old Moodie hides in tavern, drinking wine. |
| 13. Tale within tale predicting events in second half. | 22. Tale within tale explaining events in first half. |
| C1 | C2 |
| 14. Hollingsworth and Zenobia together on the spot of pasture land where they plan to build cottage. | 28. Zenobia buried on the spot of pas-ture land where she and Hollingsworth planned to build cottage. |

More generally, the pattern thus is: A, B, C: B, A, C.[13] There is a build-up to a climax of some sort—an odd climax, perhaps, since chapter 14 is not a very dramatic centrepiece. What we do get in chapter 14 is the possibility of a union; when the climax is repeated in chapter 28, this possibility has been undone by the development of the action in the second half of the book, and instead of the marriage that could have brought the utopian enterprise to fruition, there is a burial, and a marriage which seems destined to be barren.

## 2. The Veil of Allegory

If chapter 14 may seem at first almost incidental to the plot, it is nevertheless of central importance if considered thematically: the introduction of Eliot's Pulpit into the romance serves to establish a direct link between the Blithedale enterprise and New England's Puritan past.[14] The rock derives its name from John Eliot (1604–1690), a Puritan minister who came to Massachusetts in 1631, where he began to preach among slaves and Indians, and undertook the gigantic task of translating the Bible into the Algonquian tongue. We will have reason to return to this circumstance in the concluding section of this chapter. For the moment, it will suffice to observe that the link between Blithedale and the Puritan pilgrims is underscored by the paragraph that opens the chapter: "OUR SUNDAYS, at Blithedale, were not ordinarily kept with such rigid observance as might have befitted the descendants of the Pilgrims, whose high enterprise, as we sometimes flattered ourselves, we had taken up, and were carrying it onward and aloft, to a point which they never dreamed of attaining" (117). The chapter that follows spells out the factors that complicate and, eventually, subvert this enterprise: Hollingsworth's philanthropy (the temptation to turn collective efforts into vehicles for private schemes), Zenobia's feminism (the relation between the sexes), and, finally, hermeneutics, or, as Coverdale refers to it, "a masculine grossness—a sin of wicked interpretation, of which man is often guilty towards the other sex" (47). Of the three complicating factors it is the first which is most immediately responsible for overthrowing the Blithedale enterprise, yet it is the other two factors that are given the most attention in this chapter, and throughout the romance. Indeed, it does not seem amiss to hold that the relation between the sexes is the central aspect of *The Blithedale Romance*, in relation to which the philanthropy of Hollingsworth and Coverdale's interpretive dilemmas alike represent diverging attitudes; attitudes that are spelt out in this chapter in response to Zenobia's impassioned speech "on the injustice which the world did to women, and equally to itself, by not allowing them, in freedom and honor, and with the fullest welcome, their natural utterance in public" (120). Feminism has hardly grown a less pressing issue since *The Blithedale Romance* was written, and the temptation to ascribe our own view to the object of our study is always great. But I think little is gained by consigning Hawthorne to the feminist ranks; Hollingsworth's and Coverdale's attitudes differ substantially from each other, and though neither is what deserves to be called a feminist position, Hawthorne clearly favours the latter.

Both men, we should observe, conceive of woman in religious terms. In Hollingsworth's view, woman "is the most admirable handiwork of God, in her true place and character. Her place is at man's side. Her office, that of the Sympathizer; the unreserved, unquestioning Believer; the Recognition, withheld in every other manner, but given, in pity, through woman's heart, lest man should utterly lose faith in himself; the Echo of God's own voice, pronouncing—'It is well done!'" (122). Woman is a disciple to man, and her office is to help him retain his faith not in God, but in himself. Coverdale is willing to allow woman a more prominent religious function, that of a mediator between God and man:

> Oh, in the better order of things, Heaven grant that the ministry of souls may be left in charge of women! The gates of the Blessed City will be thronged with the multitude that enter in, when that day comes! The task belongs to woman. God meant it for her. He has endowed her with the religious sentiment in its utmost depth and purity, refined from that gross, intellectual alloy, with which every masculine theologist—save only One, who merely veiled Himself in mortal and masculine shape, but was, in truth, divine—has been prone to mingle it. I have always envied the Catholics their faith in that sweet, sacred Virgin Mother, who stands between them and the Deity, intercepting somewhat of His awful splendor, but permitting His love to stream upon the worshipper, more intelligibly to human comprehension, through the medium of a woman's tenderness. (121–122)

At the centre of this outpouring, which occurs roughly at the middle of this central chapter (it is preceded by four and a half pages and followed by another six), we find a reference to Christ, "who merely *veiled* Himself in mortal and masculine shape"—a highly suggestive phrasing, considering the prominent imagery of veils and masks in the book.[15] Other references to the veil in the book suggest that it is operative on a field of considerable extension. Having been rejected by Hollingsworth who has taken up with Priscilla after delivering her from Westervelt, Zenobia in chapter 26 announces her intention "to become a Catholic, for the sake of going into a nunnery. When you next hear of Zenobia, her face will be behind the black-veil" (227–28): itself a veiled announcement of her intention to drown herself in the "black, inscrutable depth" (232) of the river.[16] The veil is shown to be inescapable, a condition of life not to be rid of even in death.

This makes the brief yet central veil image in chapter 14 all the more resonant: if the humanity of Christ is a veil, it is nevertheless this veil that makes it possible for Christ to function as a mediator between man and God. Thus mortality, the veil that seems to constitute the dividing partition between man and divinity, is in truth what makes the reunification of God and man possible. Surprisingly, this explicit association of the veil motif with the figure of Christ has received almost no attention among critics. Tony Tanner, while observing it, writes it off quite casually as suggesting "that corporeality, sheer or mere physicality, is the unreal for Coverdale, an orthodox enough Transcendentalist tenet."[17] But Coverdale's words have nothing to do with transcendentalism; the text that is echoed here is that of Hebrews 10: 20, in which it is claimed that the sacrificial death of Jesus opened for all believers a way into the holiest, "through the veil, that is to say, his flesh." If the veil of flesh is the prerequisite for Christ to perform his mediating function, the romance (both when understood as the sexual relation between man and woman, and as the textual relation between reader and writer), too, must veil its spiritual essence beneath a material façade, so to speak. Tanner is surely right, then, in claiming that "the book is itself a kind of veil," even if he misrepresents the nature of this veil.[18]

But if *The Blithedale Romance* is a veil, it is also a mask. I have as yet left uncommented a misunderstanding that plagues criticism up to this day: the conflation, harking back to an article of Frank Davidson, of the imagery of veils and the imagery of masks.[19] The veil, as we have seen, is presented as an existential condition of life, the mask, in contrast, as something we put on of free will: the veil is imposed, the mask is an adornment. Both serve to disguise the wearer, but in vastly different ways. A notebook entry dating back to the eighteen-thirties suggests the nature of this difference: "An essay on the misery of being always under a mask. A veil may be needful, but never a mask" (8: 23). A veil, we must keep in mind, merely obstructs our view of the thing it hides; the mask, in contrast, presents a different aspect altogether. Thus while the veil may prevent us from seeing the truth, it does not go so far as to replace this truth with something that is false. Yet the contrast between masks and veils is not that of public artifice versus private naturalness: Coverdale's claim that the front of a house "is always artificial; it is meant for the world's eye, and is therefore a veil and a concealment" (149), makes quite plain that a veil may be as artificial as a mask.[20] Rather, the difference is that while the veil signals a gap, or distance, between outward appearance and hidden reality, putting on a mask marks an attempt to eradicate this gap. The veil, then, is an instrument whereby the individual may communicate a truth without disclosing it directly: it is a means to live up to the one explicit moral of *The Scarlet Letter*: "Be true! Be true! Be true! Show freely to the world, if not your worst, yet some trait whereby the worst may be inferred!" (SL, 260). Which is to say that the veil is an allegorical instrument, whereas the mask operates in accordance with the precepts of symbolism. The mask of symbolism presents itself as its own truth; the veil of allegory, in contrast, draws attention to itself only in order to convey that it hides a deeper truth.

There is one specific masque which is particularly interesting for an understanding of *The Blithedale Romance*: Milton's *Comus*. It is explicitly alluded to twice in the narrative, and resonates significantly with the frequent allusions to alcohol that run through the book. Comus is the son of Bacchus and Circe, and is represented by Milton as having inherited the distinctive traits of both of his parents. Like his mother, he transforms men into beasts, but he does so by offering his victims the drought of his father: wine. While his magic is less inclusive than that of his mother—the victims of Comus only have their heads transformed into that of beasts—it is also somewhat more sinister, for the people who fall under his spell are not themselves aware of having been transformed into the shapes of animals, "But boast themselves more comely than before/ And all their friends, and native home forget/ To roll with pleasure in a sensual sty."[21]

Significantly, Milton's masque is an allegorical presentation of Chastity, the "hidden strength" of the Lady of the play.[22] This young woman is fettered in an enchanted chair by Comus, but refuses to taste from his goblet and thus manages to retain her maidenly reserve throughout the drama. The parallel to Priscilla, held captive under the spell of the Silvery Veil by Westervelt, should be obvious, and is greatly reinforced by Coverdale's suggestion that "she has the gift of hearing those 'airy tongues that syllable men's names'—which Milton tells about" (60). In *Comus*, these words are uttered by the Lady:

> [...] A thousand fantasies
> Begin to throng into my memory
> Of calling shapes, and beck'ning shadows dire,
> And airy tongues that syllable men's names
> On sands and shores and desert wildernesses.
> These thoughts may startle well, but not astound
> The virtuous mind, that ever walks attended
> By a strong siding champion, Conscïence.
> O welcome, pure-eyed Faith, white-handed Hope,
> Thou hovering angel girt with golden wings,
> And thou unblemished form of Chastity,
> I see ye visibly, and now believe
> That He, the supreme Good, t'whom all things ill
> Are but as slavish officers of vengeance,
> Would send a glist'ring guardian if need were
> To keep my life and honor unassailed.[23]

The threat is called up only in order for it to be subdued, for as the above quote suggests, and the plot of *Comus* confirms, the spirit of the Lady is sufficiently pure to resist the spirits of Comus.

A similar pun on the double meaning of "spirit" is operative right from the start of *The Blithedale Romance*: coming home to his bachelor's apartments, Coverdale drinks "a glass of particularly fine Sherry" (8). As I suggested in the introduction to the present chapter, Hawthorne is concerned with the problematic nature of authenticity in spiritual experiences throughout *The Blithedale Romance*, focusing especially upon the medium of these experiences. It is particularly striking, then, that there should be a reference to spirits in the two last sentences of the opening chapter, as it is introduced by a sentence identifying the other principal spiritual medium of the book: the Veiled Lady. Coverdale, we are informed, finishes the bottle of Sherry "with a friend, the next forenoon, before setting out for Blithedale" (8), thus quitting his "cosey pair of bachelor-rooms [...] where there was still a bottle or two in the champagne-basket, and a residuum of claret in a box, and somewhat of proof in the concavity of a big demijohn" (10). This must be kept in mind when we consider his account of his first night at the Community. The remainders of a bottle of sherry shared with a friend may not seem an awful lot, but what really counts is not the amount of drinking Coverdale indulges in before setting out for Blithedale, but the amount of references to intoxicating substances that Coverdale makes in recounting the episode. Coverdale, the actor, may have set out with the intention of going back to a way of living that is "true, strong, natural, and sweet" (14), but as narrator Coverdale makes plain that the spirit of modern day civilization is nevertheless demonstrably within him when he arrives.

It should come as no surprise, therefore, that his first encounter with Zenobia is accompanied by the depraved images of a lustful imagination:

> these last words, together with something in her manner, irresistibly brought up a picture of that fine, perfectly developed figure, in Eve's earliest garment. I almost fancied myself actually beholding it. Her free, careless, generous modes of expression often had this effect of creating images which, though pure, are hardly felt to be quite decorous, when born of a thought that passes between man and woman. I imputed it, at that time, to Zenobia's noble courage, conscious of no harm, and scorning the petty restraints which take the life and color out of other women's conversation. [...] One felt an influence breathing out of her, such as we might suppose to come from Eve, when she was just made, and her Creator brought her to Adam, saying—"Behold, here is a woman!" (17)

> As for Zenobia, there was a glow in her cheeks that made me think of Pandora, fresh from Vulcan's workshop, and full of the celestial warmth by dint of which he had tempered and moulded her. (24)

Alcohol, then, is associated with an artificiality from which Coverdale is in some sense reborn after having suffered a figurative death upon arriving at Blithedale.[24] Yet alcohol makes its way into the supposedly natural setting of Blithedale as well. Significantly, the first time we encounter a reference to alcohol at Blithedale is in conjunction with Zenobia, whose inability to prepare a decent bowl of gruel provokes Coverdale to comment that "she should have meddled only with the richest and spiciest dishes, and such as are to be tasted at banquets, between draughts of intoxicating wine" (48). This sour comment is delivered when Coverdale is still in his sickbed, whose sickness is a period of sobering up: a sign of him being severely hung over, in the allegorical scheme of things, with the artificial spiritual experiences he indulges in prior to joining the Community. Tellingly, his return to the city in chapter 17 also marks a return to his "sherry-cobbler" [150].

In the legend of "The Silvery Veil" that Zenobia relates for the amusement of her fellow communitarians, the homology between alcohol and spirituality that is a central motif in the book is again emphasized. Theodore, the young man who wagers that he can find out the identity of the Veiled Lady, seeks her out after having attended a drinking party: "She rose, as it were, with the sparkling effervescence of their wine, and appeared in a more airy and fantastic light, on account of the medium through which they saw her" (108). Even Priscilla is at one point associated with wine during her stay at Blithedale. The young girl, Zenobia asserts, "has never before known what it is to live in the free air, and so it intoxicates her as if she were sipping wine;" it is only in such an inebriated state, Coverdale makes Zenobia imply, that Priscilla could possibly mistake Blithedale for "such a Paradise [...] and all of us, particularly Mr. Hollingsworth and myself, such angels!" (59).

Yet take note of the "as if" in Zenobia's assertion; slight as it may appear, it is of fundamental importance. Wine and other intoxicating substances figure in *The Blithedale Romance* in two senses: a literal (or actual) sense, and a figurative one. Indeed, the story as such could be described as a representation of the problems involved in moving from the former mode of understanding to the latter. As is the case in all of Hawthorne's romances, it is a story of how to transform the literal into the figurative, of how to affirm Imaginary truths, without violating or denying the appearance of imperfection that is a constitutive trait of the Actual. It should be observed in this context, that even in his period of spiritual rebirth at Blithedale, Coverdale never ceases to fantasize about the joys of actual alcoholic spirits. His "hermitage," we are informed, is a "leafy cave" in a tree, into which a "wild grapevine, of unusual size and luxuriance, had twined and twisted itself [...] and, after wreathing the entanglement of its tendrils around almost every bough, had caught hold of three or four neighboring trees, and married the whole clump with a perfectly inextricable knot of polygamy" (98):

> So there I used to sit, owl-like, yet not without liberal and hospitable thoughts. I counted the innumerable clusters of my vine, and fore-reckoned the abundance of my vintage. It gladdened me to anticipate the surprise of the Community, when, like an allegorical figure of rich October, I should make my appearance, with shoulders bent beneath the burthen of ripe grapes, and some of the crushed ones crimsoning my brow as with a blood-stain. (99)

In holding on to his desire for a wine which is actual rather than imaginary, Coverdale looks forward to acquiring a "blood-stain" on his brow. We may determine the significance of this signifier by making a brief excursus over one of Hawthorne's most famous tales, "Young Goodman Brown." While it was written many years prior to *The Blithedale Romance*, it may nevertheless help us clarify some of the issues at hand.

It has long been perceived that Brown's "dark night in the forest is essentially a sexual experience" (*Tragic*, p. 76–80). In the words of Daniel Hoffman, the secret knowledge into which Goodman Brown and Faith are initiated at the witch meeting "is not only knowledge of man's evil nature generally, but knowledge specifically of original sin;" it is "carnal knowledge, sexual sin."[25] It is somewhat misleading to talk of "sexual sin," for Hawthorne would surely agree with Milton that sexuality is not sinful in itself: the sin resides, as we saw in our discussion of Milton's representation of the Fall in chapter two, entirely in carnal *knowledge*, for with this knowledge comes desire, and with desire comes the sinful urge to isolate part from whole; to look upon the object of one's desire as something worth attaining for its own sake, rather than as a means to participate in mankind's united effort to give praise to the creator, that is, to look upon one's desire as a means to achieve a greater common end.

In the context of the veil-imagery so pervasive in *The Blithedale Romance*, it is highly significant that when Brown is brought before the "dark figure" which presides over the witch-meeting, his wife is also brought forward, in "the slender form of a veiled female" (10: 86). When she is unveiled, the dark figure makes plain, Brown will perceive upon his wife's countenance the "one stain of guilt" which makes of the world "one mighty blood spot." Brown and his wife have thus been brought before the altar of evil in order that they might be baptized into the "mystery of sin." Just before the baptism is consummated, however, Brown

> cast one look at his pale wife, and Faith at him. What polluted wretches would the next glance shew them to each other, shuddering alike at what they disclosed and what they saw!
>
> "Faith! Faith!" cried the husband. "Look up to Heaven, and resist the Wicked One!" (10: 88)

At this point the witch meeting dissolves, Brown finds himself alone in the night, and the reader is left to wonder whether he had simply "fallen asleep in the forest, and only dreamed a wild dream of a witch-meeting?" (10: 89). Whatever the case, the resistance against evil that we have seen Brown muster at the very last moment is shown to be of little avail. He lives out the remainder of his life in distrust of others, failing even to appreciate the love of his wife. He has, in short, lost his Faith—not because she attended, or because he believes she attended, the witch meeting, and, unlike himself, failed to "resist the Wicked One." On the contrary, it is precisely because *he* did so resist the baptism into evil, that he is forever left to wonder what "polluted wretches" the next glance would have shown "them to each other, shuddering alike at what they disclosed and what they saw!" Brown has resisted this glance, the moral of this story is, not because he fears what he will see, but because in order to see it, he must disclose his own sinful nature. What he would have realized, had he not resisted the Wicked One, and what Hawthorne invites the reader to see, is that the polluted wretch he would undoubtedly have beheld, was in truth a reflection of his own pollution; the fact that that the tale that follows "Young Goodman Brown" in *Mosses from an Old Manse* is "Rappaccini's Daughter" should be sufficient for us to spell this much out in plain language.

I have taken this detour over the story of Goodman Brown, not only because it shows us that Coverdale's desire for wine, his fantasy about acquiring upon his brow the "blood-stain" that Brown resists, is a sign of his desire for erotic love, but also because it helps us understand what keeps him so long from trying to effectuate his desire. In *The Blithedale Romance*, the complex situation depicted in "Young Goodman Brown" is echoed in the deceptively light-hearted legend that Zenobia stages for the entertainment of her fellow communitarians. In this legend, Theodore—another name suggestive of the private allegorical level of this romance, since Hawthorne himself signed letters to Sophia with the pseudonym "Theodore de l'Aubépine," some of them sent from Brook Farm (see for instance 15: 586 and 592)—is informed by the Veiled Lady that the only way to find out who and what she is, is "to lift my veil" (112). She also declares that what he finds beneath the veil will depend upon whether he approaches her "in holy faith [...] with a pure and generous purpose," or "in scornful scepticism and idle curiosity." In the former case, "all the felicity of earth and of the future shall be mine and thine together," but in the latter, the Lady tells him, "I am doomed to be thy evil fate" (113). Theodore's unwillingness to follow the Veiled Lady's advice—an unwillingness shared by Coverdale for the major portion of the narrative—is in truth a sign of the same kind of fear displayed by Goodman Brown in the earlier tale: a fear to admit that the face one detects behind the veil must in some sense be a reflection of one's own nature. Another text by Milton may perhaps help us suggest the kind of reasoning that lies behind Coverdale's unwillingness to acknowledge his erotic desires:

> if unchastity in a woman, whom St. Paul terms the glory of man, be such a scandal and dishonor, then certainly in a man, who is both the image and glory of God, it must, though commonly not so thought, be much more deflowering and dishonorable; in that he sins both against his own body, which is the perfecter sex, and his own glory, which is in the woman, and, that which is worst, against the image and glory of God, which is in himself.[26]

If these are words that Coverdale the actor would subscribe to, they are implicitly rejected by Coverdale the narrator, or at least by Hawthorne. For the latter, "the image and glory of God" is not be found either in oneself or in the object of one's desire, but in the divinity of the sympathy that will stoop to imperfection for the sake of someone else, that will sacrifice itself for the sake of another. This is what Adam does in *Paradise Lost*, and this is what allows us to look upon the Fall as a Fortunate Fall. For in stooping to the level of Eve, Adam typologically prefigures God's willingness to stoop to the level of mankind by becoming Christ and experiencing mortality. As it happens, the final six lines of *Comus* express this very moral:

> Mortals that would follow me,
> Love Virtue, she alone is free;
> She can teach ye how to climb
> Higher than the sphery chime;
> Or if Virtue feeble were,
> Heav'n itself would stoop to her.

Such, then, is the paradigm that the reader of the romance is admonished to follow: he is to be the Adam to the artist's Eve.

To declare his love for Priscilla, in other words, for Coverdale would be tantamount to admitting to looking at her in the same way he can be seen to look at Zenobia when he first enters Blithedale: with a gaze expressive of erotic desire. It would entail admitting, moreover, that the sensual images that he "at that time" (17) imputed to the way Zenobia carried herself, in fact stem from his own imagination, and hence are a sign of his own inherent sinfulness. He would, in short, have to prove willing to stain the ideal object of his desire with his own desire. It is ultimately his fear of doing so, I will argue below, that brings about the tragic conclusion of *The Blithedale Romance.*

## 3. The Secrets of Zenobia and Coverdale

Just before Hollingsworth abandons Zenobia, she accuses him of having taken her into his plan "as long as there was hope of my being available" (218). As Stoehr importantly observes, this may imply "some revelation about her former life with Westervelt."[27] What it suggests, I submit, is that Coverdale is accurate in surmising that Zenobia has "wreck[ed] herself" (103) on the despicable character of Westervelt, that is, that they are in fact still married. Coverdale's musings on the subject leave little room for doubt that, in his mind at least, Zenobia is in the same predicament as was Hester in *The Scarlet Letter*:

> How many a woman's evil fate has yoked her with a man like this! Nature thrusts some of us into the world miserably incomplete, on the emotional side, with hardly any sensibilities except what pertain to us as animals. No passion, save of the senses; no holy tenderness, nor the delicacy that results from this. Externally, they bear a close resemblance to other men, and have perhaps all save the finest grace; but when a woman wrecks herself on such a being, she ultimately finds that the real womanhood, within her, has no corresponding part in him. Her deepest voice lacks a response; the deeper her cry, the more dead his silence. The fault may be none of his; he cannot give her what never lived within his soul. But the wretchedness, on her side, and the moral deterioration attendant on a false and shallow life, without strength enough to keep itself sweet, are among the most pitiable wrongs that mortals suffer.
>
> Now, as I looked down from my upper region at this man and woman—outwardly so fair a sight, and wandering like two lovers in the wood—I imagined that Zenobia, at an earlier period of youth, might have fallen into the misfortune above indicated. And when her passionate womanhood, as was inevitable, had discovered its mistake, there had ensued the character of eccentricity and defiance, which distinguished the more public portion of her life. (103)

Our suspicion that Zenobia and Westervelt, like Hester and Chillingworth, are indeed married is strengthened by the fact that the narrative makes a brief allusion to Dante in this context; Coverdale, by his own admission, could have made his presence known to the pair "by sending an unearthly groan out of my hiding-place, as if this were one of the trees of Dante's ghostly forest" (103). The reference is not, as most editors of *The Blithedale Romance* have assumed, to the opening scene of Dante's great poem, but to the thirteenth canto of *Inferno*, in which Dante enters the second compartment of the seventh circle: that of the suicides and the spendthrifts, "the first changed into rough and knotted trees [...] the latter chased and torn by black female mastiffs," as Cary summarizes in the Argument of his translation.[28] The combination of these two sins provides us with a key to Zenobia's secret. It is the special distinction of *The Divine Comedy*, Erich Auerbach has taught us, that in it "we are given to see, in the realm of timeless being, the history of man's inner life and unfolding." The suffering souls of *Inferno* are locked within one indefinitely extended moment of time, constantly re-enacted, yet our impression when reading it is not that of having entered a timeless, frozen universe, for Dante is able to show us how this single moment is in fact shot through with temporality. The historical life *as a whole* of the souls

Dante meets prefigure this moment as a type does its anti-type. "The world beyond," in Auerbach's phrasing, "is God's design in active fulfillment. In relation to it, earthly phenomena are on the whole merely figural, potential, and requiring fulfillment."[29] Although Hawthorne does not have access to the after-life of his characters, the allegorical method by which the history of a character or a set of characters is compressed into one all-expressive moment is a trait which his romances share with Dante's Comedy. My point, in the present context, is simply that what literally happens to Zenobia in the latter half of the romance, has already taken place in the former half, albeit merely in figural form. Towards the end of the romance, Zenobia will literally have lost her fortune and become a suicide; and she has lost her literal fortune because she has willingly wasted her figurative fortune—which, as we recall from our analysis of *The House of the Seven Gables*, is passionate love—on the wrong man, not once, but twice. In other words, when Coverdale hears her talking to Westervelt in the wood, she is already a suicide, for she has already committed the suicide's sin, that of violating the union of body and soul.[30] On the same reasoning, she is already a spendthrift, for if she has given her hand to Westervelt, she has squandered her precious love even prior to meeting Hollingsworth.

Like Coverdale himself, we are denied the privilege of overhearing precisely what Westervelt tells Zenobia on their forest ramble, but we are told "that it evidently inspired her with horror and disgust" (104). The import of Westervelt's words, moreover, may be inferred from the legend Zenobia tells in the following chapter, wherein a Magician tells a Lady that "a certain maiden [...] is your deadliest enemy. In love, in worldly fortune, in all your pursuit of happiness, she is doomed to fling a blight over your prospects." The only "possibility of thwarting her disastrous influence," the Magician makes plain, is to return her under the "spell" of "the silvery veil" (115). One could attribute this "disastrous influence" simply to the possibility that the presence of Priscilla might make Hollingsworth—for whom Zenobia, by her own admittance, would have given all, "heedless though it should prove the ruin of my fortune" (217)—fall in love with the young girl. But nothing suggests that he is ever physically attracted to the younger woman. More importantly, the language of the narrative itself suggests that the secret at the heart of the plot must involve marriage: Coverdale's "hermitage," in which he is seated when he overhears the conversation of Zenobia and Westervelt, is a freak of nature owing its existence to a "wild grape-vine, of unusual size and luxuriance" having "caught hold of three or four neighboring trees, and married the whole clump with a perfectly inextricable knot of polygamy" (98); and we learn soon thereafter that Priscilla's "fragile thread of life has inextricably knotted itself with other and tougher threads" (100). Indeed, Coverdale's speculations at the end of chapter 14 suggests that Zenobia intentionally has deluded Hollingsworth:

> In what attitude did Zenobia present herself to Hollingsworth? Was it in that of a free woman, with no mortgage on her affections nor claimant to her hand, but fully at liberty to surrender both, in exchange for the heart and hand which she apparently expected to receive? But, was it a vision that I had witnessed in the wood? Was Westervelt a goblin? Were those words of passion and agony, which Zenobia had uttered in my hearing, a mere stage-declamation? Were they formed of a material lighter than common air? Or, supposing them to bear sterling weight, was it not a perilous and dreadful wrong, which she was meditating towards herself and Hollingsworth? (127)

What is implied, if never plainly stated, is that Westervelt will agree to divorce Zenobia, thereby making her "available" to Hollingsworth, on the sole condition that Priscilla is returned into his custody. Hollingsworth, to continue our speculative reconstruction of the plot, goes along with this scheme, believing Fauntleroy to be dead and Zenobia thus to have inherited the fortune of her uncle. In the climaxing scene before Eliot's Pulpit, Zenobia says that it "is only three days since I knew the strange fact that threatens to make me poor" (216), which entails that Hollingsworth would have heard of her being disinherited precisely one day before Priscilla is again put on display as the Veiled Lady. When he finds out, he as promptly sacrifices Zenobia, as he has previously been willing to sacrifice Priscilla, "whom," as Zenobia tells him, "if God ever visibly showed a purpose, He put into your charge, and through whom He was striving to redeem you!"(218). It is not out of sympathy that he delivers Priscilla from the veil, but out of self-interest.

The alcoholic imagery that pervades the book must be read in conjunction with the knotted intricacies of the plot outlined above. Its importance does not become fully apparent until the very last chapter of the romance proper (chapter 28), when Coverdale extracts a moral out of his narrative in the penultimate paragraph:

> The moral which presents itself to my reflections, as drawn from Hollingsworth's character and errors, is simply this:—that, admitting what is called Philanthropy, when adopted as a profession, to be often useful by its energetic impulse to society at large, it is perilous to the individual, whose ruling passion, in one exclusive channel, it thus becomes. It ruins, or is fearfully apt to ruin, the heart; the rich juices of which *God never meant should be pressed violently out, and distilled into alcoholic liquor*, by an unnatural process; but should render life sweet, bland, and gently beneficent, and insensibly influence other hearts and other lives to the same blessed end. (243; my emphasis)

Coverdale is no direct mouthpiece for Hawthorne, but I think we can rest assured that these are sentiments shared by the author. It is a key passage, in confirming the association between spirit and alcohol, and in reminding us of the dangers of extracting the spiritual essence from the body by means of an unnatural process. It is his fear that Hollingsworth might attempt such a distillation that lies behind Coverdale's concern for Priscilla: "In requital of so rich benefits as he was to confer upon mankind, it would have been hard to deny Hollingsworth the simple solace of a young girl's heart, which he held in his hand, and smelled to, like a rosebud. But what if, while *pressing out* its fragrance, he should crush the tender rosebud in his grasp!" (79; my emphasis).

Furthermore, this distillatory theme resonates uncannily with the allusions to Dante that suggests the nature of Zenobia's flaw. In the central chapter, Coverdale records how he "plainly saw Zenobia take the hand of Hollingsworth in both her own, press it to her bosom, and let it fall again!" (124). This is Zenobia's way of pleading her love for Hollingsworth, but it also clearly suggests that Zenobia desires for herself what Coverdale fears might happen to Priscilla, namely that Hollingsworth might intoxicate himself with her soul. This is further underscored when Coverdale later recalls this incident as the moment "when she so passionately *pressed his hand against her heart*" (167; my emphasis). The bitter irony is that by marrying Westervelt Zenobia has already squandered the rich juices of her heart, and therefore is unable to yield the intoxicating spirit. Deserted by Hollingsworth, who chooses the "pale flower" (224) of Priscilla over the luxurious, yet artificial, hothouse flower Zenobia displays, Coverdale provides us with a sobering picture of her plight: "It was as if a great, invisible, irresistible weight were *pressing* her to the earth. Settling upon her knees, she leaned her forehead against the rock, and sobbed convulsively; *dry sobs, they seemed to be, such as have nothing to do with tears*" (221: my emphasis). Zenobia is dry, there is no spirit left in her: her vitality is altogether artificial.

*

It is important to note that in relating the narrative to the reader Coverdale himself can be seen to perform precisely such a distillation that he explicitly denounces at the end. Likening his own function in the transactions related in the narrative to "that of the Chorus in a classic play," Coverdale specifies that the office of this "calm observer" is "to give applause, when due, and sometimes an inevitable tear, to detect the final fitness of incident to character, and *distil*, in his long-brooding thought, the whole morality of the performance" (97: my emphasis). Tellingly, Zenobia, in her last hour of desperation, teasingly admonishes Coverdale to turn the Blithedale affair into a ballad, predicting as for the moral that "it shall be distilled into the final stanza, in a drop of bitter honey" (224), which, given the way the romance now stands, would seem to indicate Coverdale's stuttering confession that he was in love with Priscilla. The original final sentence is much starker, and much less contrived: "It is because the spirit is inestimable, that the lifeless body is so little valued" (244).

To recapitulate: the Creator never meant that the rich juices of the heart should be "distilled into alcoholic liquor" (that is, into intoxicating emotional experiences that can be immediately quaffed), but intended them to be imbibed in portions throughout life. Yet a distillation of the moral essence of his experience of the Blithedale enterprise is precisely what Coverdale's narrative amounts to, wherein he has detected the final fitness of incident to character. While the authority of Miles Coverdale is thus in some sense undercut, we should be careful not to exaggerate his unreliability as narrator.[31] Hawthorne's fictions consistently undercut the authority of the narrating agency, yet we may always rely on it to provide the means of transcending its partial, but truthful, rendition of the romance. In this respect, Miles Coverdale is no different from the authorial voice that speaks to us from the pages of *The Scarlet Letter* or *The House of the Seven Gables*. In all of these cases, the reader must go beyond the rendition provided by the narrator, in order that the romance may make up what can truly be called a totality; not by striking a balance between its divergent tendencies, but by realizing a way of embracing the contradictions that any notion of totality must necessarily make room for. Much like Giovanni in "Rappaccini's Daughter," the reader must find a way of inhaling the poison of Beatrice, the romance; that is, he must find a way of inhaling its allegorical signified, which adheres to the tenet "that all medicinal virtues are comprised within those substances which we term vegetable poisons" (10: 100). In contrast to Giovanni, however, the reader must refuse the solace of an antidote that "is distilled of blessed herbs" (10: 126), yet come to see with Hawthorne's romance that this does not invalidate the notion of perfection as such: "the words of Beatrice Rappaccini's lips are true from the depths of the heart outward. Those you may believe!" (10: 112). This is the challenge of Coverdale; it is, I will argue in the present section, a challenge he meets, but only when it is already too late. It is, likewise, a challenge which his story transposes upon the reader.

While Coverdale's role throughout the book remains that of an observer, the tragic pathos of the final section of the narrative arguably stems from the fact that it shows him on the brink of entering into a true intercourse with humanity, only to go on to depict how his decision to risk the "deep, deep plunge into the ocean of human life" (HSG, 166)—that Clifford Pyncheon, another of Hawthorne's emasculated aesthetes, considers only to withdraw from—has come moments too late. "Had I been as cold-hearted as I sometimes thought myself," he declares in a passage which is as revealing as it is characteristic, "nothing would have interested me more than to witness the play of passions that must thus have been evolved. But, in honest truth, I would really have gone far to save Priscilla, at least, from the catastrophe in which such a drama would be apt to terminate" (72). This is a reference to a past future unrealized—he "*would* really have gone far to save Priscilla," but he never did, because when he arrives at the critical scene, it is already too late for him to perform what he has set out to do in returning to Blithedale, for "the knot" which involves not only Zenobia and Hollingsworth, but Priscilla too, "had been adjudged an entanglement, and was now violently broken" (216).

So what was it, then, that Coverdale had intended to do? What is the one decisive act which could have transformed the Blithedale romance into reality, had it only been performed? We are never let in on this secret, and the silence, on Hawthorne's part, no doubt is intentional, for there is one conundrum of the plot which virtually stares us in the face, implicitly admonishing us to provide an answer to it: having once left the Community, why does Coverdale go back to Blithedale at all? The cold and critical eye will observe that Coverdale himself provides an answer to that question, and that this answer seems uncomfortably close to a confession on the author's part that his return is simply an excuse for telling the story: Coverdale returns, he tells us, "with a yearning interest to learn the upshot of all my story, and [...] for that sole purpose" (205). A more generous gaze will register that if this is an answer, it must indubitably be a spurious one, since Coverdale nevertheless sees himself obliged to formulate the question a few lines later—and only then:

> Hollingsworth, Zenobia, Priscilla! They glided mistily before me, as I walked. Sometimes, in my solitude, I laughed with the bitterness of self-scorn, remembering how unreservedly I had given up my heart and soul to interests that were not mine. What had I ever had to do with them? *And why, being now free, should I take this thraldom on me, once again?* It was both sad and dangerous, I whispered to myself, to be in too close affinity with the passions, the errors, and the misfortunes, of individuals who stood within a circle of their own, into which, if I stept at all, it must be as an intruder, and at a peril that I could not estimate. (205–206; my emphasis)

If this does not tell us anything else, it does make clear that Coverdale is ready to abandon his role as an observer for that of an "intruder"—and at great peril to boot.

If Coverdale, the narrator, does not let us in on what he was up to, as actor, in returning to Blithedale, he nevertheless presents us amply with hints. He is evidently in a state of great excitement: "amid all my sympathies and fears, there shot, at times, a wild exhilaration through my frame!" (205); "a sickness of the spirits kept alternating with my flights of causeless buoyancy" (206). And when he finally comes across Blithedale again, his reaction makes evident that he has returned to Blithedale with a purpose: "There was my home; and there might be my grave" (206).

Coverdale, not to beat about the bush any further, returns to Blithedale with the one purpose of declaring Priscilla his love. We should recall at this critical juncture, that when Zenobia admits to wondering why "in such Arcadian freedom of falling in love as we have lately enjoyed, it never occurred to you to fall in love with Priscilla," Coverdale replies that he "should have demonstrated myself an ass" (170), had he done so. Given the parallels to Milton's masque that we established in the previous section, this is equivalent to saying that he has resisted tasting Comus' wine for fear of turning into one of his crew. On his return to Blithedale, however, it is evident that Coverdale has overcome such inhibitions. Drinking the "spirit" of the atmosphere "like the sip of ethereal wine" (204), the hermitage is the first place he revisits:

> The grapes, which I had watched throughout the summer, now dangled around me in abundant clusters of the deepest purple, deliciously sweet to the taste, and though wild, yet free from that ungentle flavor which distinguishes nearly all our native and uncultivated grapes. Methought a wine might be pressed out of them, possessing a passionate zest, and endowed with a new kind of intoxicating quality, attended with such bacchanalian ecstasies as the tamer grapes of Madeira, France, and the Rhine, are inadequate to produce. And I longed to quaff a great goblet of it, at that moment! (208)

Coverdale is desperate for this wine of passion, which might bring him the sexual gratification of "bacchanalian ecstasies" that ordinary alcoholic beverages can but function as a tame substitute for. His encounter with the masqueraders shortly thereafter likewise suggests the nature of Coverdale's enterprise. Upon hearing him laugh, someone dressed as "the goddess Diana" announces that she "shall send an arrow through his heart," an "Indian chief" says that he will scalp him, and the witch Moll Pitcher that she will "root him in the earth" so that "the green moss shall grow over him, before he grows free again." With an arrow in his heart, Coverdale must be prepared to die, to embrace the imperfections of an earthly existence from which death is the only means of escape. Finally, as if to confirm that Coverdale is ready to attend the witch-Sabbath from which young Goodman Brown fled in despair, the last masquerader to speak is a figure of the devil himself: "The voice was Miles Coverdale's [...] My music has brought him hither. He is always ready to dance to the devil's tune!" (211).

The confession that concludes the romance ("I—I myself—was in love—with—PRISCILLA!") will therefore go for nothing unless we observe that the disclosure of this "one secret" (247) is designed to elucidate—if one can speak in such terms of a discursive universe which goes out of its way to retain "the clear, brown, twilight atmosphere" (9: 5) of romance—the one other moment of the narrative in which Coverdale has dangled this "one secret" (222) before the eyes of the reader. This is in the scene of Zenobia's despair upon having been rejected by Hollingsworth; and it is a moment that takes on added poignancy when we realize that it is a moment in which Coverdale's plans have been as brutally smothered as have those of Zenobia:

> [...] had it been only a common pity that I felt for her [...] I would have left her to struggle [...]. But, so it happened, I never once dreamed of questioning my right to be there, now, as I had questioned it, just before, when I came so suddenly upon Hollingsworth and herself, in the passion of their recent debate. It suits me not to explain what was the analogy that I saw, or imagined, between Zenobia's situation and mine; nor, I believe, will the reader detect this one secret, hidden beneath many a revelation which perhaps concerned me less. In simple truth, however, as Zenobia leaned her forehead against the rock, shaken with that tearless agony, it seemed to me that the self-same pang, with hardly mitigated torment, leaped thrilling from her heart-strings to my own. (222)

Zenobia has loved and lost, and so has Coverdale. This is why the last section of the romance is informed by such pathos: Coverdale is no longer a mere observer, he has gone from conceiving of his role in the romance as "that of the Chorus in a classic play" (97) to recognizing it as "*my* story" (205; my emphasis).

## 4. The Flower, the Night-Cap, and the Image of Death

To understand the way symbolism is pitted against allegory in *The Blithedale Romance*, we must set Coverdale's final readiness to risk loving in relation not only to Priscilla, but to Zenobia as well. Zenobia, we have seen above, is represented as already having squandered her juices: it makes small difference, then, that she flaunts her voluptuous flower throughout. Zenobia may wear the flower, but it is Priscilla who *is* a flower; no matter how pale, it is she, and not her older sister, who is consistently likened to one. Again, the most revealing passage is to be found in chapter 14: "No doubt, it was a kind of sacrilege in me to attempt to come within her maidenly mystery. But as she appeared to be tossed aside by her other friends, or carelessly let fall, like a flower which they had done with, I could not resist the impulse to take just one peep beneath her folded petals" (125).[32] Priscilla, in short, allegorically embodies what Zenobia merely symbolically suggests: a flower, or, to state what is to be found beneath the folded petals of this signifier, sexuality. The correspondences between *The Scarlet Letter* and *The Blithedale Romance* on this point are worth keeping in mind. Zenobia wears a flower, just like Hester wears the letter; Priscilla is a flower, like Pearl is the letter.[33] The artist figure, then, is shown to be metonymically linked to the central symbol of the romance, while the figure of the romance per se is metaphorically associated with this symbol. Yet if Priscilla metaphorically embodies the romance, unlike Pearl in *The Scarlet Letter* she is not the product of the intercourse between artist and society, but rather the veil which artist and society (writer and reader) alike would seem anxious to reject, tear away.

Instead we find Priscilla producing two highly suggestive artefacts: a silk purse and a night-cap. The sexual connotations of the purse have long been recognized, and need not be doubted. As Von Abele argues, the purse—which Coverdale suggests might be "a symbol of Priscilla's own mystery" (35)—is "as much a symbol of Priscilla's kind of sexuality as the flower is of her older sister's: she wears her sex, as women of her class in her day were intended to do, in a secret place, while Zenobia flaunts it abroad."[34] The significance of the latter object is perhaps more oblique. Priscilla presents it to Coverdale in chapter 7, while the former is still bed-ridden:

> "Do not you need this?" asked she. "I have made it for you."
>
> It was a night-cap!
>
> "My dear Priscilla," said I, smiling, "I never had on a night-cap in my life! But perhaps it will be better for me to wear one, now that I am a miserable invalid. How admirably you have done it! No, no; I never can think of wearing such an exquisitely

> wrought night-cap as this, unless it be in the day-time, when I sit up to receive company!"
>
> "It is for use, not beauty," answered Priscilla. "I could have embroidered it and made it much prettier, if I pleased." (51)

Despite Coverdale's protestations to the contrary, he is very well acquainted with the functional office of a nightcap, as the reader who looks back to chapter 1 will readily recall: "It was nothing short of midnight when I went to bed, after drinking a glass of particularly fine Sherry" (8). The precise temporal reference is hardly as incidental as it may seem: "Midnight," after all, is the title of the chapter in which Zenobia's dead body is recovered from the river, and duly turned over to the group of women who gather round her corpse, whispering about what is to be done while "shaking their night-capt heads" (237).

What is suggested by means of this pun, then, is that Coverdale—like the Blithedalers in general—needs a nightcap in order to recognize the significance of the purse, which is tied to sexuality, not only through its resemblance to the female genitalia, but also through the complex interrelations between sexuality and economics that are suggested by the importance that the question of inheritance has for the plot. Coverdale's reaction to Priscilla's offer of a night-cap, suggests an inability to comprehend a conception of sexuality which does not aestheticize it by looking to erotic love as the ideal essence of the relation between man and woman, but views it more pragmatically as a necessity of life, "for use, not beauty," as Priscilla puts it. Instead, Coverdale asks Priscilla to give him one of her purses; it is hardly by accident that these two events take place in chapters that are chiastic counterparts. Coverdale's desire is thus shown to be consonant, at this point of the narrative, with the symbolistic view of sexuality which conceives of sex as a transcendent signified rather than a mediating signifier; a view, that is, which dictates that sex is both a means and an end. Rather than conceiving of sexuality as the imperfect medium whereby a sense of spiritual perfection may be attained, this symbolistic conception of sexuality as purse rather than night-cap is designed to extinguish the gap between desire and its fulfilment by conflating spiritual ends with material means, to the effect that ends and means can no longer be told apart. From such a perspective, to win Priscilla's love is not so much to win a medium to a higher end, but rather to gain immediate access to her fortune.

As if to emphasize that such is indeed the signified of the purse and the function of the night-cap, the narrative immediately proceeds to inform us that it is "While holding up the night-cap" that Coverdale perceives that Priscilla is in possession of a letter: "As I did not immediately offer to receive the letter, she drew it back, and held it against her bosom, with both hands clasped over it, in a way that had probably grown habitual to her" (51). The mark of sexuality on Priscilla is thus detectable to Coverdale only when his gaze is guided by the night-cap. Our first impulse is surely to conceive of this statement as implying a parallel between Priscilla and Hester; the latter, we remember, when brought out before the crowd at the Boston marketplace, first tries "to clasp the infant closely to her bosom; not so much by an impulse of motherly affection, as that she might thereby conceal a certain token, which was wrought or fastened into her dress" (SL, 39).[35] Priscilla, however, is not the wearer of the letter; her office is simply to deliver it to Coverdale. What is more, the letter is not of her own making, but is from Margaret Fuller, a circumstance that has led many critics to speculate that Zenobia is a veiled portrait of the former.[36] The important point, however, is that this circumstance underlines the mediating office performed by Priscilla: the letter does not belong to her, and although it is her office to deliver it, we cannot hold her responsible for its contents—she is merely a courier, a circumstance that further underscores her resemblance to Pearl, whose "errand," albeit by no choice of her own, is to be "a messenger of anguish" (SL, 256) to her parents.

In an important respect, moreover, Zenobia's artistic practice is parallel to that of Hester: like the latter, she dresses up her charge as an emblem of her own stigma (because this is what her luxurious flower is, even if she wields it so unashamedly that we do not easily recognize it as such), decking her out with a "variety of sylvan ornament," and inserting "among those fragrant blossoms, and conspicuously, too, [...] a weed of evil odor and ugly aspect," which for Coverdale, tellingly, "destroyed the effect of all the rest" (59). Equally revealing is the great importance that Coverdale attaches to Zenobia's own flower, which he conceives of as "a talisman," claiming that if "you were to snatch it away, she would vanish, or be transformed into something else" (45). The wording is hardly incidental, for the chapter in which Coverdale recognizes Priscilla as a flower is entitled "They Vanish," and ends with their temporary disappearance. As we have already pointed out Priscilla metaphorically embodies what Zenobia can merely metonymically figure forth: a flower, and it is this flower—or, rather, Priscilla—that is in truth taken away: "Priscilla—poor, pallid flower!—was either snatched from Zenobia's hand, or flung wilfully away!" (193). What Zenobia does not realize, is that by wilfully flinging Priscilla away, she is in truth allowing her own flower to be snatched away from her; that is why she is "transformed [...] into a work of art" (164) at this point of the narrative.

For Zenobia to disassociate herself from the flower of allegory (Priscilla), thus is tantamount to depriving herself of the sole medium through which she might communicate her symbolistic conception of erotic love as a space of self-fulfilment. For Zenobia, as for Hester in *The Scarlet Letter*, the flower of sexuality is at once her fortune and her misfortune. It was such an emblem of ambiguity for Alice Pyncheon, too, and threatened to become such for Phoebe as well. As we saw in chapter four, however, Phoebe was able to transcend the contradictory qualities inherent in the flower of sexuality by founding her moment of intimacy with Holgrave on the recognition of its connection to a radical lack. By showing death, emblematically figured in the dead Judge Pyncheon, to be the prerequisite for their union, Hawthorne inscribes a sense of distance into his representation of their moment of transcendent love, to the effect that this moment of symbolic presence and fulfilment is nevertheless undercut by an allegorical sense of distance, which signals the recognition of their inability to accomplish this transcendence without the mediation of the "image of awful Death" (HSG, 305) that Holgrave's art has made available.

Coverdale himself concedes in chapter 15 that death is the only thing which can make the enterprise of Blithedale real: "I shall never feel as if this were a real, practical, as well as poetical, system of human life, until somebody has sanctified it by death" (130). Yet when death occurs in *The Blithedale Romance*, it is unaccompanied by any redemptive transcendence:

> For more than twelve long years I have borne it in my memory, and could now reproduce it as freshly as if it were still before my eyes. Of all modes of death, me-

> thinks it is the ugliest. Her wet garments swathed limbs of terrible inflexibility. She was the marble image of a death-agony. Her arms had grown rigid in the act of struggling, and were bent before her, with clenched hands; her knees, too, were bent, and—thank God for it!—in the attitude of prayer. Ah, that rigidity! It is impossible to bear the terror of it. (235)

Zenobia's own transformation into a "marble image" of death lacks the redemptive power of Holgrave's daguerreotype, because it marks an unmediated presentation of death: she "*was* the marble image of a death-agony"—having rid herself of the mediating veil of allegory, the gap between figurative and literal meaning is extinguished, and Zenobia becomes an anti-type of her own type, fulfilling the *figura* of a suicide she has been all along.

In a sense this culminating image of the book must be said to be of Coverdale's own making. Indeed, as narrator, Coverdale may well be aware of this, for he himself concedes that "the aspect of a monster [...] though we can point to every feature of his deformity in the real personage—may be said to have been created mainly by ourselves!" (69). Some critics have argued—with varying degrees of sophistication—that Coverdale is directly responsible for Zenobia's death, but this is hardly the case.[37] If he is indirectly responsible for the concluding image of her death-agony, it is because he has been exposed to images of Zenobia's making at an earlier stage, but failed at that time to respond to them. The description of their very first meeting, as we saw above, suggests Zenobia's propensity for "creating images," images that are of an unmistakingly erotic nature, as we saw above. But these are not the only images Zenobia evokes in Coverdale's imagination; as we have already suggested she also "deck[s] out Priscilla" into "the very picture of the New England spring" (59), making Coverdale compare her to an anemone. When Coverdale encounters the sisters back in town, Zenobia repeats her feat. While wondering "what Zenobia meant by evolving so much loveliness out of this poor girl," Coverdale does not hold back his admiration for her art. "She is a wonderful creature," he tells her. "Ever since she came among us, I have been dimly sensible of just this charm which you have brought out. But it was never absolutely visible till now. She is as lovely as a flower!" (169). It is through the work of Zenobia, the figure of the Artist in this romance, that Coverdale, its Reader, is able to perceive the true beauty of Priscilla.

Priscilla, then, is a veiled flower. Had Coverdale been more susceptible to Zenobia's art, he would not have hesitated to give himself to her in full sympathy, to offer her his love at seeing her "droop" (125) at the sensation of Zenobia making plain her love for Hollingsworth. But Coverdale for a long time is driven by "idle curiosity" rather than "holy faith" (113). Thus, when he is given the opportunity of offering Priscilla his sympathy in "Eliot's Pulpit"—the narrative's structural centrepiece—Coverdale instead gives in to "the impulse to take just one peep beneath her folded petals" (125), by asking her about her relation to Zenobia. In contrast to her younger sister, Zenobia would appear to have rent the veil: she presents her flower openly. As we saw above, however, the Bible makes plain that the veil can be torn asunder only at the price of death: the veil of the tabernacle is torn at the precise moment of Christ's death on the cross (Matthew 27: 50–51, and Mark 15: 37–38). That is why Hawthorne makes a point of stressing the artificiality of the flower worn by Zenobia: "it was a hot-house flower—an outlandish flower—a flower of the tropics" (45), which is later seen to have "undergone a cold and bright transfiguration; it was a flower exquisitely imitated in jeweller's work" (164). Zenobia, in other words, wears the flower like a mask, presenting it—like Hester presents the scarlet letter—as a symbol of her own emotions. To put it in technical terms, her relation to the flower is metonymical; based on contiguity, it is evident but contingent.[38] Priscilla's relation to the flower, in contrast, is metaphorical, as it is based on the veiled identity between herself and the flower, an identity which is fully disclosed only through the mediation of what is the proper meaning of Priscilla and flower alike: fortune.

But Coverdale acts upon this recognition of the true beauty of Priscilla too belatedly for the romance to come to a redemptive conclusion. Priscilla is a flower, but a flower destined never to bloom, for Hollingsworth is not a man capable of true emotional sympathy. Instead of flowering, Priscilla goes from being enthralled behind Westervelt's veil to being wilfully enthralled within the "veiled happiness" she experiences with Hollingsworth, who exhibits "a childlike, or childish, tendency to press close, and closer still, to the side of the slender woman" (242) that Priscilla has become.[39] The "black-veil" taken by Zenobia, then, is not that from which Priscilla has been delivered,[40] but an attempt to put on yet another mask, as Coverdale's reminiscence of Zenobia's mode of dying makes plain:

> A reflection occurs to me, that will show ludicrously, I doubt not, on my page, but must come in, for its sterling truth. Being the woman that she was, could Zenobia have foreseen all these ugly circumstances of death, how ill it would become her, the altogether unseemly aspect which she must put on, and, especially, old Silas Foster's efforts to improve the matter, she would no more have committed the dreadful act, than have exhibited herself to a public assembly in a badly-fitting garment! Zenobia, I have often thought, was not quite simple in her death. (236)

Death, however, will not allow Zenobia to pass away like it befits a "tragic actress" (78), "in lithe and graceful attitudes" (236); in death, the act is all too life-like, "the marble image of a death-agony" all too real.

Zenobia, then, becomes what Hester is represented as standing in danger of becoming in the last scaffold scene of *The Scarlet Letter*, wherein she appears to us "statue-like" (SL, 244), showing us the "marble quietude" which is "like the frozen calmness of a dead woman's features; owing this dreary resemblance to the fact that Hester was actually dead, in respect to any claim of sympathy, and had departed out of the world with which she still seemed to mingle" (SL, 226). By revealing the Scarlet Letter upon his own body, Dimmesdale effectively checks the process whereby Hester is slowly being transformed into a moral statue, by making manifest a sign of his sympathy, a sign which makes evident to all how she has in truth borne his stigma all along. As we saw in the chapter on *The Scarlet Letter*, however, Dimmesdale insists on Hester staying true to her stigma, by making her resume the letter she temporarily discards in the forest. Hollingsworth, in contrast, agrees to Zenobia handing Priscilla over to Westervelt, an act which is structurally equivalent to a scenario in which Dimmesdale would have Hester turn Pearl over to Chillingworth in order that they might elope.

Zenobia's flower, in contrast both to Pearl and Holgrave's daguerreotype of the dead Judge Pyncheon, is not the product of the intermixture of the rays of society and the shadows of the individual, nor is it imposed upon her like Hester's letter; on the contrary, it is something she willingly chooses to adorn herself with. The veil, on the other hand, *is* imposed upon her, in the form of Priscilla. Zenobia's tragedy, then, is that she fails to understand the relation between the flower and the veil, that she believes that the veil is something that she can dispose of as easily as her other stage costumes. Zenobia mistakenly believes that she can uphold a distinction between the flower with which she wilfully adorns herself and the veiled flower of Priscilla that is entrusted to her. This is the mistake of Hester, too, when she rids herself of the letter in the forest and expects her relation to Pearl to remain unchanged. But in contrast to what is the case in *The Scarlet Letter*, in *The Blithedale Romance* no one proves willing to instruct Zenobia to hold on to Priscilla, the way Dimmesdale makes Hester reclaim the discarded letter.

That Zenobia gives her flower to Miles Coverdale in their last scene together, instructing him to give it to Priscilla, implicitly suggests that the power of her symbolic flower is subsumed beneath the allegorical veil. Tellingly, we never see this flower again; it disappears from the romance with her death, follows her into her grave at Blithedale. For Priscilla to give her love to Hollingsworth, Coverdale ominously suggests at one point, "is like casting a flower into a sepulchre," for "Hollingsworth's heart is on fire with his own purpose, but icy for all human affection." The only person who "really cares for her," he adds, "is myself, and not even I, for her realities—poor little seamstress, as Zenobia rightly called her!—but for the fancy-work with which I have idly decked her out!" (100). If this had remained Coverdale's attitude throughout the romance, those who hold that no transformation takes place within the book would have been right; I have argued, however, that this is not the case. Through the major part of the narrative Coverdale resists stooping to a night-cap, to the thought of employing Priscilla as a means to approach an ideal, the way the toper accesses the ideal through "the muddy medium of his liquor" (175). The moral of his story, however, insists that we must come to acknowledge the necessity of accessing the ideal through the means of an imperfect medium. Coverdale, like Hester Prynne before him, learns that the desire for the perfection of symbolistic presence must be traded for the imperfect, but viable, mediation of allegory, that is, for a mode of perception in which the true object of one's desire must always necessarily remain absent from the act in which one's desire is manifested. We could thus agree with Rowe, who reads the romance from the perspective of Sartrean phenomenology, that Coverdale's narrative is an example of imaginative rather than perceptual consciousness. As Rowe explains, for Sartre the "primary distinction between the perceptual and imaginative consciousness depends upon the *presence* of the object required for perception and the *absence* of the referential object that characterizes the imaginative act."[41] The imaginative consciousness thus is always in need of some kind of spiritual stimulation: alcohol of some sort, in short, is necessary.[42] When Coverdale sets out for Blithedale once more, in the final section of this book, he has finally come to accept the necessity of approaching the ideal through the aid of an allegorical medium. Tellingly, he has also found the means to spiritualize "the muddy medium" of alcohol into its figurative counterpart, finding that the very atmosphere "had a spirit and sparkle in it" and that each "breath was *like* a sip of ethereal wine" (204; my emphasis). But as he arrives at this conclusion too late to benefit from his new-won understanding of the importance of flaunting the body in order to reach through to the spirit, his willingness to fuse his desire with an acceptance of death comes to nothing, and the redemptive office of romance remains, for him, unrealized.

## 5. Translating the Spirit of Socialism

*The Blithedale Romance* is in many ways a bitter book; it is a book about failure on every level, personal and collective. Yet to the very last, Coverdale insists that he increasingly feels that in setting out for Blithedale "we had struck upon what ought to be a truth" (246). Hawthorne is careful to underline in the Preface that he does not "put forward the slightest pretensions to illustrate a theory, or elicit a conclusion, favorable or otherwise, in respect to Socialism" (1). Here, as always, we need to take Hawthorne at his word, but also be careful to observe that these words do not entail that the book has no political ramifications. What Hawthorne rejects in the Preface is not that literature has political implications, but rather the mimetic notion that such implications can be objectively illustrated. If Hawthorne refrains from eliciting a conclusion "in respect to Socialism" in his narrative, then, it is not because he shies away from ideological matters, but because the office of the romance is to show us that its political ramifications cannot be determined by the writer alone, but are to an equal degree the product of the reader's response to the narrative. In other words, for Hawthorne the truth of political theories is not an empirical but an ideal matter, and as all ideal matters, it is connected to this world via the mediation of the individual's faith. In this final section of the chapter, I shall try to measure the book's view of social reform from this perspective.

Lauren Berlant has perspicaciously identified the narrative locus at which *The Blithedale Romance*'s love plot interlocks with its historico-political plot, as the last sentence of the opening paragraph of chapter 15, "A Crisis," where Coverdale comments upon the nature of the utopian enterprise of Blithedale: "Altogether, by projecting our minds outward, we had imparted a show of novelty to existence, and contemplated it as hopefully as if the soil, beneath our feet, had not been fathom-deep with the dust of deluded generations, on every one of which, as on ourselves, the world had imposed itself as *a hitherto unwedded bride*" (128; my emphasis). This sentence, Berlant explains, makes clear that "the scene of utopian fantasy is founded on the repression of histories that would, presumably, challenge the fact of present existence: Coverdale notes that his fellow workers act as if they are the land's first tillers and, by association, the nation's first utopians." However, the bridal metaphor introduced at the end of the sentence, suggests that the utopian vision itself can be preserved only on the condition that it remains in a state of virginity: "The 'virgin' mind, mirroring the virgin body in its lack of 'knowledge,' can project itself purely into the future without limits. But when historical and sexual knowledge comes, when 'the world has imposed itself' upon us, we lose the clarity of utopian, libidinal perfection." As Berlant goes on to point out, the passage containing the metaphor of the unwedded bride follows immediately upon "Coverdale's speculation about both Zenobia's virginity and the veracity of her self-representation" at the end of chapter 14.[43] Zenobia's secret, that we traced in section 3, is thus of great importance for our understanding not only of the love plot of the romance, but of its historical plot as well. Zenobia, then, is to Hollingsworth what the "world" is to the utopian communitarians at Blithedale: a point of original virginity which is in truth already lost. Like Zenobia, the Blithedalers disown history in their attempt to create a new mode of society. Imparting "a show of novelty to existence," they make the world take on the appearance of "a hitherto unwedded bride," but are bound to find out that the world has in truth long passed out of its state of virginity.

For Coverdale, Berlant concedes, the significance of the love story of *The Blithedale Romance* is tied to the political history of America by means of the metaphor of the "hitherto unwedded bride;" in this reading, the failure of the love story "grows from the failure of American political praxis to appropriate and incorporate his and others', visionary passion." But to Berlant, as to so many other critics, Coverdale is an unreliable narrator whose perspective Hawthorne is careful to undermine. From this point of view, Berlant claims, "Coverdale's use of the analogy of the unwedded bride to describe the series of utopian failures whose histories are obliterated by a national amnesia, suggests that in *Blithedale* the bride's plot, the love plot, contains the series of buried events that would constitute American history if that history could be written."[44] This is a suggestive line of reasoning, and it will no doubt seem appealing to literary critics who delight in demonstrating how literary classics exhibit resistance to dominant ideologies. In truth, however, Hawthorne's romance supports the reading which Berlant ascribes to the limited perspective Coverdale, wherefore we must conclude that the social collective plot of *The Blithedale Romance* can only be properly understood in relation to its love plot.

Berlant argues that chapter 14 obliquely refers to one of the buried events she maintains the romance refers to, by associating Hollingsworth with "the venerable Apostle Eliot" (119), who, as we noted above, translated the Bible into the Algonquian tongue. Hollingsworth's reform project, then, must be thought of as a parallel to Eliot's mission to the Indians. Which is another way of saying that it is a grand thing destined to come to nought; in *The Blithedale Romance*, as in his historical narratives for children, Hawthorne is careful to balance his praise for the ideal efforts of Eliot, with the grim yet truthful observation that by the time Eliot's translation was completed, all the speakers of the language had been extinguished. "I have seen it in the library of the Athenaeum," young Laurence tells Grandfather in "Grandfather's Chair," speaking of Eliot's Indian Bible, "and the tears came into my eyes, to think that there were no Indians left to read it" (6: 44). Albeit with less emphasis, *The Blithedale Romance* repeats the same point: Eliot's pulpit, we learn, is located in "as wild a tract of woodland as the great-great-great-great grandson of one of Eliot's Indians (*had any such posterity been in existence*) could have desired, for the site and shelter of his wigwam" (118; my emphasis).

Drawing liberally on Berlant's article, Tony Tanner argues trenchantly that the reference to Eliot is yet another instance of Hawthorne pulling an ironic face at history:

> If he had historicized Eliot, Coverdale might have brought to mind, and written in, the fact that Eliot created in his Christianized Indians vulnerable hybrids who could never survive. They were wiped out in King Philip's War (1673–5), not least because they were not yet fully trusted by the whites, and no longer trusted by the Indians. This must be marked up as another Utopian project which ended in disastrous failure. Or rather, not marked up but left out. Coverdale takes (makes) the Romance—the saint in the wilderness;—and forgets the history—the subsequent victims. Eliot trying to convert his Indians is clearly replicated in some way by Hollingsworth dedicated to reforming his criminals [...]. It is another massive failure.[45]

It is a brilliant suggestion; but it rests on the suppression of Hawthorne's use of Eliot in *The Whole History of Grandfather's Chair*, where Hawthorne himself has already raised Tanner's suggestion through Laurence, only to have Grandfather refute it. While recognizing the utopian impulse of Eliot, Laurence tends to feel that the fact that history made his endeavours come to nought must nullify the value of his efforts:

> "My heart is not satisfied to think," observed Laurence, "that Mr. Eliot's labors have done no good, except to a few Indians of his own time. Doubtless, he would not have regretted his toil, if it were the means of saving but a single soul. But it is a grievous thing to me, that he should have toiled so hard to translate the Bible, and now the language and the people are gone! The Indian Bible itself is almost the only relic of both."

Grandfather, however, takes an opposing view, and the rhetoric is such that one can hardly doubt that it is a view which is at one with Hawthorne's own beliefs:

> "Laurence," said his Grandfather, "if ever you should doubt that man is capable of disinterested zeal for his brother's good, then remember how the Apostle Eliot toiled. And if you should feel your own self-interest pressing upon your heart too closely, then think of Eliot's Indian Bible. It is good for the world that such a man has lived, and left this emblem of his life."

> The tears gushed into the eyes of Laurence, and he acknowledged that Eliot had not toiled in vain. (6: 49)

No doubt the linking of Hollingsworth to Eliot is steeped in irony, but in this case, at least, the irony works only one way: it is designed to expose the futility of Hollingsworth's utopianism, without undermining the beauty of Eliot's attempt.[46]

While it is certainly possible that Hawthorne could have revised his views of the Apostle in the twelve-year lapse between these two books, the text offers no traces of such a revision. On the contrary, Hawthorne's avowed admiration for Eliot would seem to be as strong as ever: "(with my eyes of sense half shut, and those of the imagination widely opened,) I used to see the holy Apostle of the Indians, with the sunlight flickering down upon him through the leaves, and glorifying his figure as with the half-perceptible glow of a transfiguration" (119). It is true that the "half-perceptible glow of a transfiguration" that glorifies "the holy Apostle" is seen by Coverdale only when his "eyes of sense" are "half shut, and those of the imagination widely opened," but we must remember that to Hawthorne as romancer imagination is the most valuable faculty of all; in this instance, then, Coverdale sees Hollingsworth precisely as Hawthorne would have the reader see his romance. After all, the romance is itself to be seen as a kind of translation of the biblical truths into a language which can be understood by the heart.[47]

This is, or so it seems to me, what lies behind Hawthorne's glorification of Eliot: throughout his career, Hawthorne is aware of the possibility that his own efforts as a romancer might very well come to an end very similar to the toils of the apostle—he may be labouring over words that will be understood by no one, but he justifies his work by looking upon the toils as an end in itself. This may be a form of aestheticism,[48] but if it is, its underlying assumptions are vastly different from those governing the *l'art pour l'art* project of French *symbolisme*, or even of the aestheticism of a contemporary such as Poe. For Poe, as for Baudelaire and Mallarmé, it is the poem that is looked upon as an end in itself.[49] For Hawthorne, in contrast, it is the human activity that goes into the making of the poem that is ultimately important; the aesthetic object itself is merely the means to communicate the significance of that activity, which is precisely that it is something which is performed "for his brother's good" rather than for "self-interest."[50]

This difference is indicative of the crucial point which separates the symbolist from the allegorist. While both work primarily through a symbolic mode, the former treasures the symbols for their own sake, and for the immediacy with which they will translate into emotional experience. The latter's main interest, in contrast, is what lies beyond the symbols, wherefore he values the symbols themselves primarily to the extent that they suggest the distance between themselves and the meaning they shadow forth. The allegorist, that is, is interested not so much in the referents of the symbolic imagery he employs, as in what lies beyond figurative expression and literal referent alike. In other words, he is interested in the veiled property which is common to figure and referent alike, rather than in the symbol's capability of impressing us with its immediate emotional power. The structure of allegory, to recapitulate, is metaphorical, that is, in allegory the substitution of figure for referent is based upon their relation to a third, veiled term which constitutes the proper meaning of both. In allegory, in short, the symbol is a veil rather than a mask: it is precisely by hiding rather than making manifest its true purport that allegory communicates its transcendent message. By rejecting the possibility of an immediate transformation of the literal into the figurative (or of the material into the spiritual) that symbolism affirms, allegory comes to insist that this world can be transcended only if it is allowed to become the medium whereby transcendence is achieved. To achieve the spiritual, that is, one must affirm the corporeal form in which it is manifested. Allegory, in short, forces transcendence back into the world, by translating the symbolist's ineffable experience of transcendence into an aporetic, but nonetheless rational, concept of guilt, which in turn may be translated into a conception of transcendence which acknowledges the necessity of deferring its fulfilment to another realm of being. Transcendence is thus made available to us, only as a translation of a translation.

This circumstance underlines an important aspect of Hawthorne's allegorical project as such: that the act of translation, or interpretation, is always already a part of the text (or the events) that it seeks to represent. The historical Miles Coverdale (1488–1569), we should bear in mind, completed the first English translation of the Bible with Apocrypha in

1535, but as he did not master either Hebrew or Greek, he had to rely on translations in order to perform his task.[51] His Bible, then, is a translation of a translation; a circumstance echoed in *The Blithedale Romance* by Hawthorne's decision to insert the fictional Miles Coverdale as something of a cognitive veil between the reader and the events proper of the romance, forcing us to perform the critical task of translation on the basis of Coverdale's own translation of the events recounted. Despite characterizing himself somewhat derisively as a mere spectator of the *ménage à trois* acted out by Hollingsworth, Zenobia, and Priscilla, then, Coverdale is in every sense as determining an agent as are they in respect of the outcome of their interrelations. And so, Hawthorne would have us see, is the reader. [52]

Coverdale's effort to translate the utopian impulse underlying his youthful commitment to Blithedale into its ideal signified, is so obviously a flawed weaving together of guesses and inferences, that we may easily confuse this imperfect attempt at communicating an experience lived for a bathetic "ballad," and Coverdale for a person who has attempted to better Mankind while refusing to respond to his fellow man.[53] From such a perspective, Miles Coverdale will appear as little else than a second old Moodie, and his final moralizing on the death of Zenobia seem empty fakery: "It is because the spirit is inestimable, that the lifeless body is so little valued" (244). We may be tempted to conclude that these words amount to a forgery, for the watermark of sympathy that alone can lend true authenticity to moral value judgements is not easily detected in the textual body of Coverdale himself. I have argued, in the previous sections, that upon close inspection of the narrative discourse, that watermark is perceivable, but I have also stressed that close inspection alone will not let us see it: to perceive that watermark, we must supplement the indices of its existence with a good portion of imaginative sympathy. But if we do recognize the significance of Coverdale's "one secret"—that is, if we see that in returning to Blithedale, Coverdale was finally ready to perform the act of mediation he shied away from for so long—then we must conclude that Coverdale does finally come round to an allegorical conception of life: he realizes that if the Blithedale project shall have any chance of becoming a "practical, as well as poetical, system of human life," the transcendence of this world must be sought *in* this world, not beyond it.

Thus we must not mistake the love plot of *The Blithedale Romance* as the "folly" of its narrator, "obliterating the historical interest of his narrative," as Berlant does.[54] The love plot of the romance is not a means to displace or suppress the political issues of the historical story it also contains, but on the contrary, a vital component of that plot. For if Coverdale is transformed by his Blithedale experience, his idealism is real; and the value of true faith in the ideal, Hawthorne would have us see, here as elsewhere, cannot be compromised by the fact that this ideal cannot be realized:

> Yet, after all, let us acknowledge it wiser, if not more sagacious, to follow out one's day-dream to its natural consummation, although, if the vision have been worth the having, it is certain never to be consummated otherwise than by a failure. And what of that! Its airiest fragments, impalpable as they may be, will possess a value that lurks not in the most ponderous realities of any practicable scheme. They are not the rubbish of the mind. (10–11)

Despite ending in pain, Coverdale's vision of a better life was worth the having—the moral of the romance essentially echoes that of *The Scarlet Letter*. In *The Scarlet Letter*, be it noted, art ultimately performs its office because in Hawthorne Surveyor Pue's manuscript has found a reader who approaches it with enough sympathy to make it his own. It is through taking his predecessor's narrative of "the life and conversation of one Hester Prynne" to heart, through experiencing "a sensation not altogether physical, yet almost so, as of burning heat" (SL, 32) that Hawthorne is able to leave the appearance of the Custom-House reality "like a dream behind me," as he says, and become instead "a citizen of somewhere else" (SL, 44). As an exemplary Gentle Reader, Hawthorne transforms Surveyor Pue's fictitious historical document into a historical fiction almost of his "own invention," while being careful not to violate "the main facts" of the story which "are authorized and authenticated by the document of Mr. Surveyor Pue" (SL, 32). Reading the story of the original author impels him to tell the story again, and in so doing he comes to indicate how his situation is parallel to that of the characters he is telling us of: how in repeating the story, he is transformed from a Dimmesdale into a Hester, setting an example that the reader is invited to follow. He is transformed, that is to say, from a representative of the public life of the Custom-House into a citizen of the private "second story" (SL, 28) it lodges; from a person whose concept of guilt is so closely framed by the unequivocal morality of the normative system of society that to him the exposure of guilt can only mean death, into a person recognizing in guilt an enigmatic type of the ambiguous nature of life that the Creator has designed for our education and ultimate benefit, in order that we may learn to exchange desire for sympathy. On completing this transformation he becomes an artist willing to accept, and indeed celebrate, the distance between his private experience of desire (sexual *and* transcendental) as the one thing that makes life worth living, and the public conception of desire as a sign of sinfulness, of man's inherent imperfection, which is prescribed by the norms of society. Having accepted the role of Father of Hester's guilt, he has also found the means of becoming the Child of the redemptive vision she found her way to express, and has grown up to be a Poet giving birth to yet another avatar of the scarlet letter.[55]

The setup of *The Blithedale Romance* is remarkably similar: it shows us Coverdale's transformation from an "observer" into an artist, a transformation that takes place on account of him having realized that the drama he observed was not in fact a masquerade that he was excluded from, but one in which was staged his own story. But this time, having turned his own life into the material of fiction, Hawthorne is unable to function as a vicarious reader of the romance, wherefore it is left to us to do for Zenobia and Coverdale, what Hawthorne did for Hester and Dimmesdale. If Zenobia holds the position of the artist in the diegesis of Coverdale's narrative, and Priscilla that of the romance, in the present recounting of that diegesis the position of the artist has been displaced upon Coverdale, and the diegesis—the story itself—has become the veil, or romance, which is suggestive of a beauty it refuses to show us, unless we prove ourselves sympathetic to such an end by actively participating in its Imaginary realization.

*The Blithedale Romance*, in other words, gives us the possibility of doing for the romance what Coverdale fails to do for Priscilla: deliver it from its veil. Yet we must do so without tearing the veil apart, for that, as the example of Zenobia shows us, would simply be equivalent to replacing it with a mask. Hawthorne, however, will not let us get away any easier than Coverdale himself. By using a first-person narrator, Hawthorne puts us squarely in the position of Theodore in Zenobia's legend.

We are forced to feel the whole weight of his dilemma, for we are asked to trust a narrator who is decidedly flawed, who admits to decking out the story with his own fancies and owns up that his memory might betray him. What is more, the craft of this romance allows us to make Coverdale's concluding Confession confirm almost any interpretation of the preceding events we will, by claiming that it is in truth a lie, a mask adorned to hide the true object of his desire.[56] Indeed, by drawing on autobiographical material, Hawthorne tempts us to look upon Coverdale as a mask, that is, as a person who, like Zenobia, passes himself off as a hitherto unmarried bride, a person with no history, while there are plenty of indices to suggest that this is merely a screen raised to prevent us from seeing behind it the outlines of Hawthorne's personal history. Berlant, in contrast, would make of *The Blithedale Romance* another kind of mask, a mask of personal tragedy displacing the real historical centre of the narrative. I have argued that there is a third possibility, namely that of looking upon the romance as a veil rather than a mask. Looking through this veil, I have suggested, we may find in fiction what Actual history cannot yield: a space in which reality may be reconsidered, and from which its course may be redirected.

*

After all this, we have perhaps not advanced very far beyond Waggoner's acute observation that in *The Blithedale Romance* "Hawthorne is saying again what he had said in 'Earth's Holocaust,' that all reform is superficial so long as the heart remains unchanged" (*Study*, 203). We have merely added, that beyond this moral, the reader of *The Blithedale Romance* is challenged to perceive that the heart of the narrator did in fact change during his stay at Blithedale, although too late for the change to be of any real consequence. But if the change of emphasis is slight, it nevertheless seems to me decisive. In fact, the whole point of the romance will elude us, unless we realize that the significance of what *The Blithedale Romance* is saying is wholly dependent upon our own willingness or unwillingness to approach the romance "in holy faith" rather than "in scornful scepticism and idle curiosity." The significance of its moral, in other words, depends largely upon whether we decide that the romance must be either a *roman á clef* or a political allegory about the utopian venture of America, or if we concede that it may be necessary to read these two strains of the romance as complementary aspects of one single meaning, which looks to the love plot of the romance not as a way of displacing the historical centre of the narrative, but as the only true means to gain access to its conception of history.

If Priscilla, the Veiled Lady, is a figure of the romance itself, and if Blithedale is not Ripley's Brook Farm but rather "that Utopian community par excellence, America"—and most commentators would seem to agree that this is the case—then Coverdale's "query as to the success of our Blithedale project" in the very first chapter is allegorically analogical to Hawthorne's question as to the future of his own country, and the Lady's "response [...] of true Sibylline stamp" (6), "is *The Blithedale Romance* itself," as Michael Draxlbauer points out.[57] What is really important is that this suggests that for Hawthorne, the future of America must be measured by the way it responds to imaginative adventures such as his own romance. *The Blithedale Romance* is indeed to a certain extent a critique of utopianism, socialism included. If one tries to distil the essence of a utopian enterprise by producing a set of tenets or strict rules from which the success of the utopian project can be scientifically predicted, any utopian effort, the romance suggests, be it socialism or America itself, is bound to turn back on itself and poison its own system with an excess of (self)-righteousness. Yet despite delivering this critique, the romance is even more profoundly, if less emphatically, an affirmation of a certain form of utopianism, a form which acknowledges that any utopian endeavour must essentially be a translation of an ideal impulse inherent in every individual. Being a translation of this desire for the ideal, the utopian endeavour must necessarily be an imperfect enterprise, that is, an enterprise the success of which is dependent upon our willingness to defer its consummation, not to a later point in time, but to another realm of being. It is a form of utopianism, in other words, that insists that we must rest content with making out the Imaginary fulfilment of our utopian desires through the veil of its Actual imperfect realization in the form of human love.

Lest this strike us as a sentimental view of history, we should keep in mind that if there is one thing that Hawthorne's romances do make clear, it is that love is not a simple emotion, but the very medium which brings the contradictory aspects of human existence to the fore:

> It is a curious subject of observation and inquiry, whether hatred and love be not the same thing at bottom. Each, in its utmost development, supposes a high degree of intimacy and heart-knowledge; each renders one individual dependent for the food of his affections and spiritual life upon another; each leaves the passionate lover, or the no less passionate hater, forlorn and desolate by the withdrawal of his object. Philosophically considered, therefore, the two passions seem essentially the same, except that one happens to be seen in a celestial radiance, and the other in a dusky and lurid glow. (SL, 260)

We must bear this in mind when we try to assess Hawthorne's view of the socialistic endeavour as such. Coverdale's narrative leaves no room to doubt its actual imperfections, nor does it represent these imperfections as contingent matters, but exposes them as features that are intrinsic to the utopian enterprise as such. But the point of this exposure is not to demonstrate the vanity of such enterprises. On the contrary, the reader is challenged to hold on to a belief in the ideal, to recognize the beauty of Coverdale's attempt and to affirm his belief that the only thing short of making the dream come true, was the necessary mediation of passionate love. For while Coverdale as actor rejects the night-cap Priscilla offers him at Blithedale, as narrator he has come to understand that the ideal cannot be attained without the mediation of one medium or another. If we reject the figurative wine of passionate love, that is, literal wine may be our only remedy, as Coverdale's anti-teetotal speech in chapter 21 clearly suggests:

> Human nature, in my opinion, has a naughty instinct that approves of wine, at least, if not of stronger liquor. The temperance-men may preach till doom's day; and still this cold and barren world will look warmer, kindlier, mellower, through the medium of a toper's glass; nor can they, with all their efforts, really spill his draught upon the floor, until some hitherto unthought-of discovery shall supply him with a truer element of joy. The general atmosphere of life must first be rendered so inspiriting that he will not need his delirious solace. The custom of tippling has its defensible side, as well as any other question. But these good people snatch at the old, time-honored demijohn, and offer nothing—either sensual or moral—nothing whatever to supply its place; and human life, as it goes with a multitude of men, will not endure so great a vacuum as would be left by the withdrawal of that big-bellied convexity. The space, which it now occupies, must somehow or other be filled up. As for the rich, it would be little matter if a blight fell upon their vineyards; but the poor man—whose only glimpse of a better state is through the muddy medium of his liq-

> uor—what is to be done for him? The reformers should make their efforts positive, instead of negative; they must do away with evil by substituting good. (175)

Ironically, Sophia expunged this outpouring from the romance that was printed in Hawthorne's lifetime. Perhaps it was in anticipation of that kind of reader response that Hawthorne wrote to Whipple: "Now that the book is off my mind, I feel as if I were out of the body; but (like a great many other translated spirits, I fear) the sense of it does not exactly increase my happiness" (16: 537).

## CHAPTER SEVEN

# *The Marble Faun:* Recovering the Sacred Candlestick

I somewhat doubt whether your dull English public will quite appreciate its excellencies. It depends upon the view a reader happens to take of it, whether it shall appear very clever or very absurd.

Hawthorne on *The Marble Faun* to Francis Bennoch, January 27, 1860.

Hawthorne published only one more novel in his lifetime after *The Blithedale Romance.* Following on the productive peak of the three year period in which he wrote almost half of the published part of his collected works, this apparent retreat from writing is perhaps understandable, especially since the years of inactivity coincide with the period of his life when he held the office as American Consul in Liverpool, a great change not only for him but for his family too. In leaving his home soil of Massachusetts, it would seem he left behind his muse as well, for despite repeated attempts to plot a story of an American going back to England to claim an inheritance, no completed romance ever developed from the rambling manuscripts that now fill two volumes of the Centenary Edition, both of considerable length. Indeed, one of the most distinctive traits of these volumes is the author's own exasperated comments at being unable to bring his project to a satisfactory conclusion: "Oh, Heavens! I have not the least notion how to get on. I never was in such a sad predicament before" (12: 286). Notebooks he kept aplenty, but was apparently unable to transform these jottings into the material of fiction; instead of a romance, there appeared in 1861 *Our Old Home*, a book of sketches from England. Tellingly, the one romance that he did finish in this period, *The Marble Faun*, is so cluttered with descriptions of art objects imported from his notebooks that the story itself seems to bog down beneath the weight of the American tourist's anxiousness to pay respect to a cultural history that can be traced back well over two thousand years: ample testimony to Hawthorne's dwindling genius.[1]

Or so the story has often been told. However, if one takes the trouble to look beyond the public horizon of book publishing and twentieth-century reports of Hawthorne's struggle to mould his new materials into the shape of a romance, a very different picture emerges. Far from being a period of literary inactivity, in the ten years between 1854 and his death in 1863 Hawthorne wrote more than he had ever done before. It is true that the English romance did pose problems for him, but as Charles Swann has convincingly argued, it would seem that its final abortion was not due to an inability to come to terms with the plot, as has commonly been assumed. Rather, what seems to have happened was that the outbreak of the Civil War made his original project—which involved pitting English values against American ones—an anomaly even before the romance was completed. "With the America Hawthorne had known all his life in such dire straits," writes Swann—whose analyses of Hawthorne's unfinished romances are a rare feat in Hawthorne scholarship—"it is no wonder that he could not continue with the American claimant material—for that was [...] crucially dependent on stable if complex ideas of America and England and on their interrelationships" (*Tradition*, 184), and such a stability could not survive in the face of war. "The Present, the Immediate, the Actual, has proved too potent for me," Hawthorne wrote of his aborted romance in the dedication to Franklin Pierce that opens *Our Old Home*. "It takes away not only my scanty faculty, but even my desire for imaginative composition, and leaves me sadly content to scatter a thousand peaceful fantasies upon the hurricane that is sweeping us all along with it, possibly, into a Limbo where our nation and its polity may be as literally the fragments of a shattered dream as my unwritten Romance."[2]

The impending Civil War has often been invoked to explain not only Hawthorne's failure to complete the romances he worked on before his death, but also the warped appearance of the one romance he did manage to produce. Right from its publication, critics have been prone to comment on its aesthetic shortcomings. Henry F. Chorley, in the *Athenaeum* issue of March 3, 1860, complains that the ending of the novel is "inconclusive and hazy," adding that: "Hints will not suffice to satisfy interest which has been excited to voracity."[3] The reproof has continued ever since. In the opinion of H. H. Waggoner, *The Marble Faun* is a "rewarding failure" (*Study*, 225)—an evaluation which for a very long time remained representative of the reception of the novel.[4] Such has been the tendency up till the very present: as recently as 1992, Evan Carton in a book-length study of the romance claimed that "*The Marble Faun* is not a masterwork by virtue of the perfection of its form or the coherence of its thought. If it may be classed a masterwork at all, it is, paradoxically, by virtue of the suggestiveness of its breakdown."[5]

But if *The Marble Faun* fails, the failure cannot automatically be ascribed to Hawthorne: given that the romance must be seen as a relation between the writer and the reader rather than an object, the failure could as easily be attributed to his readers. That the romance was a considerable commercial success does not substantially alter this fact. Henry James refers to it as "the most popular of Hawthorne's four novels;"[6] but it owed no small part of its popularity to the circumstance that its publication coincided with a growing number of Americans finding the leisure and the economic resources to visit Europe as tourists. It became, Richard Brodhead points out, "a book Americans going to Europe had to have read."[7] Whether or not Hawthorne had calculated on this reaction, the appropriation of *The Marble Faun* as a virtual Baedecker of Rome by its American audience bespeaks the nature of its "failure." The book is a paean to fantasy, or rather, to the importance of recognizing that intermixture of fantasy and reality that Hawthorne always insisted was the true habitat of his romances. But instead of looking to the Italy of the romance as "a sort of poetic or fairy precinct" (3), as Hawthorne proclaimed he had intended it as in the Preface, the reading public looked to his romance for its exquisite descriptions of literal facts: when publishers began bringing out editions carrying illustrations of the places and objects described in the text the book "even became a kind of portable museum, bringing certified Italian masterpieces into the American home."[8] Thus *The Marble Faun* became an art gallery to which the reading public betook itself to get a detached view of certified masterpieces, rather than an arena of engagement and profoundly felt ethical dilemmas.

Still, it is not difficult to understand why the view of *The Marble Faun* as a failure—or more precisely, as Hawthorne's failure—has prevailed. Despite being in many ways typical of Hawthorne's writings, it remains an intriguing book, almost perverse at times in its deliberate mystifications and intentional violations of the conventional ways of handling a plot. The main outline of the story can be summarized quite easily as a variation of the biblical myth of the Fall. These overtones are made explicit near the end when Miriam says: "The story of the Fall of Man! Is it not repeated in our Romance of Monte Beni?" (434).[9] But if the story is transparent, the same cannot be said of the plot. It often seems to disrupt the story told, rather than contribute to its evolvement, and Hawthorne exhibits little ambition of turning it into anything else but a cumbersome machinery with which to pull the action forth. The many mysteries evoked are for the most part left unresolved; relations between characters that are seemingly vital are left unexplained. Near the end, Hilda mysteriously disappears, only to reappear five chapters further on in an equally puzzling fashion. Instead of making an effort to make these occurrences seem plausible, the narrator flaunts the mystification: "Whence she had come, or where she had been hidden, during this mysterious interval, we can but imperfectly surmise, and do not mean, at present, to make it a matter of formal explanation with the reader" (452). To top off what has often been perceived as an artistic fiasco, the author added a Postscript to the first American and second British edition of the novel (included in all subsequent editions) in an attempt to meet "a demand for further elucidations respecting the mysteries of the story" (463) that had been raised in reviews upon its original British publication.[10]

These aspects of the romance, however, should not be written off as signs of confusion on Hawthorne's part, but must be recognized as the products of aesthetical choices as deliberate as are those of *The Scarlet Letter*. If there is confusion, the confusion is intentional: it is one of the ways in which the romance purveys its message. The last three decades have witnessed a gradual increase of the critical appreciation of the romance. Millington's study of the narrative strategies of Hawthorne's romances in *Practicing Romance* (1992), for instance, effectively argues the need to reassess the merits of *The Marble Faun*. What has often been seen as "confusion," in Millington's view "is the product of Hawthorne's riskiest experiment in narrative form, his most insistent subversion of orthodox literary authority." To read *The Marble Faun*, Millington argues, "is to witness two quite different books engaged in frustrating one another's smooth progress toward their appointed ends." Ultimately Hawthorne aims "to bring the Gentle Reader back to life by showing us what it is like—as an individual and as a culture—to become dead to romance" (*Practicing*, 178).[11] Without wishing to contradict Millington's view, I would phrase the matter in rather different terms: *The Marble Faun* aims to show us what it is like to live in a society which gives in to the symbolistic desire of the individual—what price the individual has to pay when the culture that surrounds her proves unwilling to resist her impulse to impose a symbolic conception of truth upon the community. In other words, what *The Marble Faun* shows us is what happens if we flaunt a symbolistic rather than an allegorical truth, a truth that is grounded in a private rather than communal interpretation of socially symbolic practices such as religion, art, and literature.

It seems to me, moreover, that despite the many ways in which criticism has contributed to our understanding of *The Marble Faun*, the way the romance incorporates and draws upon art to communicate its message still has not been properly understood. Reading *The Marble Faun*, it is impossible not to be struck by the wealth of passages describing works of art of different kinds. Indeed, in the Preface Hawthorne himself claims that "In re-writing these volumes, the Author was somewhat surprised to see the extent to which he had introduced descriptions of various Italian objects, antique, pictorial, and statuesque" (3), a remark that only just masks that the amassing of these details is anything but accidental. As had been his method when writing *The Blithedale Romance*, Hawthorne made heavy use of his notebooks when composing *The Marble Faun*—large sections of the book describing places and monuments of actual Rome were clipped almost verbatim from these notebooks. This method of relying heavily on observations already generated—to some critics a mark of decline—is no empty trick to bolster fading artistic powers, nor is it an attempt to win a larger audience by masking as a Romance what amounts to a guide-book of Rome. It indicates, rather, that Hawthorne's romance approaches the problems of psychology and history alike as problems to which the solution must necessarily be of an aesthetical nature. It suggests, I will be arguing, that we must move beyond the mimetic view which conceives of the objects of art in *The Marble Faun* as descriptive passages, and recognize their performative function in an allegorical aesthetics based on a principle of creation rather than the mimetic principle of resemblance.[12]

As the British title of the novel, *Transformation*, suggests, the story depicts the transition from one state of being to another. In fact, *The Marble Faun* is equally concerned with two transformative processes that cross and eventually counterbalance each other: that of Donatello, which might be termed a transformation from art to life, and that of Hilda, which might be termed inversely a transformation—or rather, a transfiguration—from life to art. Once again, then, the plot turns on the interrelationship of two counterbalancing transformative processes, proceeding respectively from the figurative to the literal, and from the literal to the figurative. I will be concerned in the present chapter with delineating how these two processes are interrelated. Donatello and Hilda—the Faun and the Dove—I will argue, are both in a sense creations of the character which functions as a type of the artist: Miriam. The readiness of Hilda and Kenyon to give in to Miriam's symbolistic desire to suppress guilt entails that the Faun must be executed in a far too literal sense to survive other than as a spectre haunting the conscience of the artist. These are bold claims to make about a book which is notorious for its elusiveness, but I shall defend them as best I can below. Beginning with a minute analysis of the symmetrical design of *The Marble Faun* which counters the view that the romance is formless, in sections 2 and 3 I trace the ways in which the transformative processes suffered by Donatello and Hilda interact with this design. Section 4 then delineates in greater detail how the form of the romance helps us establish the significance of the Beatrice motif, and also considers how this resonates with the plot-lines of Miriam and Hilda respectively. Section 5 addresses the romance's view of history in the light of the previous discussion, and section 6, finally, discusses Hawthorne's allegorical aesthetics and its ethical implications.

## 1. The Symmetry of *The Marble Faun*

In stark contrast to the air of chance surrounding the plot of *The Marble Faun*, the symmetry of the over-all conception of the romance is immediately apparent to the attentive reader, there being exactly 50 chapters—a number too smooth and well-rounded to be entirely coincidental, especially in a work which refers explicitly to both Dante and Milton. In fact, the geometrical aspect of the romance is clearly visible to the reader even in the heading of the opening chapter: "Miriam, Hilda, Kenyon, Donatello." The first three characters are all "artists, or connected with Art" (7), while Donatello is nothing less than Art itself, a fact recognised and commented on by the other three—he "is the very Faun of Praxiteles" (7), as Miriam claims: the Marble Faun come to life.

We do well to pause a moment at the threshold of the narrative, because as always in Hawthorne, the first paragraph is in many ways a key moment in the book:

> FOUR INDIVIDUALS, in whose fortunes we should be glad to interest the reader, happened to be standing in one of the saloons of the sculpture gallery in the Capitol, at Rome. It was that room (the first, after ascending the staircase) in the centre of which reclines the noble and most pathetic figure of the Dying Gladiator, just sinking into his death-swoon. Around the walls stand the Antinous, the Amazon, the Lycian Apollo, the Juno; all famous productions of antique sculpture, and still shining in the undiminished majesty and beauty of their ideal life, although the marble, that embodies them, is yellow with time, and perhaps corroded by the damp earth in which they lay buried for centuries. Here, likewise, is seen a symbol (as apt, at this moment, as it was two thousand years ago) of the Human Soul, with its choice of Innocence or Evil close at hand, in the pretty figure of a child, clasping a dove to her bosom, but assaulted by a snake. (5)

Superficially read, this paragraph merely sets the scene, and in so doing defers the presentation of the "four individuals" that Hawthorne is careful to place at the very beginning of his narrative. In truth, however, the passage is an immediate indication of the importance of the allegorical aspect of the romance; rather than postponing the presentation of the four leading characters, the passage is designed to make us sense how the literal historical moment and the ideal moment of symbolical presence alike are tied up with, and in a sense, mediated through, an allegorical filter which makes the ideal available to us only insofar as it is absent, or distanced, from us. The four individuals are situated in the room where "stand the Antinous, the Amazon, the Lycian Apollo, the Juno," ideal counterparts of the characters which we have yet to be acquainted with. Antinous, Anthon's *Classical Dictionary* informs us, threw himself off a rock in order to protect the Emperor Hadrian, thus displaying a sense of loyalty that resonates uncannily with that which will be displayed by Donatello, who, as we shall see, can also be said to kill himself for the sake of his beloved. The Amazon's belligerent nature invokes the fierce temper of Miriam, expressed on the paintings in her studio in the form of "the idea of woman, acting the part of a revengeful mischief towards man" (44). Kenyon, like the Lycian Apollo, throughout the book displays a penchant for interpretation. Juno, the goddess of nuptials and marriage and the closest Roman mythology comes to a personification of Womanhood, is an appropriate emblem of Hilda. And in the centre of these statues is that of the Dying Gladiator, the unknown identity of whom serves to underscore its proleptic suggestion of the fate of the Model.

So the configuration of statues in effect provides an alternative ideal fashioning of the chapter's title, reading "Donatello, Miriam, Kenyon, Hilda;" these are the ideal pairings towards which the narrative strives. This ideal, however, is denied us on the literal level of the text, because when we reach the end of the narrative, we find that nothing has changed—as the heading of chapter 50, the final chapter, we find a title identical to that of the first: "Miriam, Hilda, Kenyon, Donatello." This is all the more perplexing, as the situation sketched in the final chapter could hardly be said to mimic that of the first. It is concerned primarily with Hilda and Kenyon, and their attempt at extracting a moral out of the foregoing events. Miriam does surface at a distance, but she does not speak, and Donatello appears only in the discourse of Hilda and Kenyon. Nevertheless his absence is deeply felt, all the more so for the chapter-title pointing it out to us in such a glaring fashion.

Like Hawthorne's other romances, *The Marble Faun* is founded on the structural principle of chiastic inversion, by means of which different segments of the text are symmetrically tied together. *The Marble Faun* marks Hawthorne's most consistent and by far most important employment of this principle. If we substitute the linear arrangement of the chapters for one that places them in two columns—the first ranging from 1–24, and the second inversely from 49–26—we find that it is possible to establish a one to one correspondence between most of them. Chapter 1 matches chapter 49, chapter 2 matches chapter 48, chapter 3 matches chapter 47, and so on, all the way up (or down) to the matching of the juxtaposed chapters 24 and 26. The only substantial departure from this principle is made up by chapters 25 and 50 which make up a pair of their own within this structure. Some of the more striking correspondences to be found in the symmetrical scheme appear below; their significance will be elaborated later, as it seems important first to establish the scheme as such.

Chapter 2 is entitled "The Faun" and shows us Miriam, Hilda, and Kenyon marvelling at the resemblance between Donatello and The Faun of Praxiteles in the Sculpture Gallery in the Capitol, begging him to let them see if it "extends to the very tips of the ears" (12); in chapter 48, the concluding carnival scene, Kenyon recalls how Donatello had participated in the carnival one year earlier "in all the equipment of a Faun, doing the part with wonderful felicity of execution, and revealing furry ears which looked absolutely real" (438). Chapter 3 takes place in the catacombs where Miriam encounters the Model for the first time in the book; at the beginning of chapter 47 this scene is explicitly alluded to when Kenyon is reminded of the time when all four friends "had lived so happily together, before *the mysterious adventure of the catacomb*" (426; my emphasis). In chapter 46 Kenyon digs up a marble woman from a "cellar-like cavity" (422), much as Miriam comes across the Model when she has descended into the catacombs in chapter 4. Chapter 6, "The Virgin's Shrine" has as its counterpoint chapter 44, "The Deserted Shrine." Chapter 7, "Beatrice," is instigated by a passage describing the nature of Hilda's sympathy for art, which "drew your own along with it, endowing you with a second-sight that enabled you to see excellencies with almost the depth and delicacy of her own perceptions" (62); this faculty for aesthetical sympathy is evoked once again at the beginning of chapter 43, sorely missed by Kenyon, of whom it is said that he had counted "upon Hilda's delicate perceptions in enabling him to look at two or three [...] statues," which, being "of so cold and pure a substance [...] require to be seen through a perfectly transparent medium" (390)—such as that of Hilda.

Chapters 8, 9, and 10 depict the temporary romance of Miriam and Donatello, while chapters 42, 41, and 40 inversely depict the budding romance of Hilda and Kenyon; chapter 10 painting the temporal happiness of the former pair's dance wherein each "movement had a grace which might have been worth putting into marble, for the long delight of days to come, but vanished with the moment that gave it birth" (85), in stark contrast to the life of a "marble Eden" that Kenyon imagines for the lover and his mistress of the "unchanging climate of Saint Peter's"

(369) in chapter 40. Chapter 11 submits the sole interview between Miriam and the Model related in the book and ends with Miriam kneeling to the Model, "undetected, though in full sight of all the people" (98), though we learn in chapter 12 that Kenyon is in fact watching the scene, and that he does indeed fancy "that Miriam was kneeling to this dark follower, there, in the world's face!" (108). This act of submission is repeated at the end of chapter 39, where Hilda kneels to the Roman-Catholic Father in whom she has confided the details of the murder of the Model: "as he stretched out his hands, at the same moment, in the act of benediction, Hilda knelt down and received the blessing with as devout a simplicity as any Catholic of them all" (362). At the very beginning of chapter 40, we are again informed that Kenyon witnesses this act. Other details confirm the correspondence between the situations: to observers other than the sculptor, the narrator remarks in chapter 12, Miriam probably seems to kneel "merely for the convenience of dipping her fingers into the gush of water from the mouth of one of the stone lions" (108), and we learn in chapter 38 that Hilda, too, "dipt her fingers" (351) upon entering St. Peter's. What is more, while chapter 38, "The World's Cathedral," affords us an inside view of Saint Peter's, in chapter 12 "the entire outline of the world's Cathedral, as well as that of the palace of the world's Chief-Priest, is taken in at once" (107), in a passage describing briefly its exterior magnificence. In chapter 13 Kenyon complains to Miriam that "it will be as difficult to win [Hilda's] heart, as to entice down a white bird from its sunny freedom in the sky," to which Miriam playfully remarks that the sculptor may hope to win her if Hilda would "sprain the delicate wrist" (121) Kenyon has sculpted. In a figurative sense this is exactly what has happened in chapter 37, wherein Hilda has lost her ability to look with "the eye of faith" upon paintings, and as a result has forfeited her "remarkable power as a copyist" (335) as well. Had she met Kenyon at this point, the narrator declares, "her confidence would have flown to him *like a bird* to its nest" (343; my emphasis). In chapter 14 Miriam is plagued by her secret which according to herself is "red as blood" (130); in chapter 36, Hilda is plagued by her secret and is depicted by an artist who names his picture "Innocence, dying of a Blood-stain!" (330).

Chapters 15 through 19 show the events of the evening upon which the Model is killed; chapters 31 through 35 show the events that lead up to Miriam's and Donatello's eventual reunion. In chapter 17, which extends to the chapter in which the Model falls, it is midnight (160); in chapter 34, wherein the consequences of this fall is about to be repaired through the reunion of Donatello and Miriam, it is high noon (315)—a temporal juxtaposition that serves to underline the intertextual relation between *The Marble Faun* and *Paradise Lost*.[13] Just as "Miriam seemed dreamily to remember falling on her knees" (171) before the Model is thrown off the cliff at the end of chapter 18, so Miriam is seen as "the figure of a woman kneeling" (299) in chapter 32, in which the dreamlike atmosphere is recurrently emphasized (291, 295, 299). In chapter 20 Donatello, Miriam, and Kenyon come across a dead monk who is described as an "image of wax—or clay-cold reality" and referred to by Miriam as a "clay image" (182); in chapter 30, Kenyon is seen to be working on a bust of Donatello in clay. This is of great significance, as it is discovered in chapter 21 that the dead monk is in truth identical with the Model, and as Donatello announces his intention in chapter 29 to "Turn monk" (267). Chapter 23, in which Hilda rejects Miriam's plea to remain her friend because she fears to be stained by the "blood-stain" (209) of Miriam, is linked to chapter 27, recounting a myth of a knight who was rejected by a nymph when he "tried to wash off a blood-stain" (246) in her waters. In chapter 24, finally, Kenyon refers to the "Arcadian life" and the "family history" (218) of Donatello, which is the explicit subject of chapter 26 "The Pedigree of Monte Beni."

On the opposite page I have summarized the above outline of the symmetrical pattern (my reason for giving every seventh chapter in bold type will be explained in section 4 below).[14]

50. Hilda sees "sunlight on the mountain-tops"(462).

| | |
|---|---|
| 1. Donatello as work of art. | **49. Hilda transfigured by her stay in the Land of Picture (452).** |
| 2. Donatello as Faun. | 48. Kenyon recalls Donatello as Faun (438). |
| 3. The catacombs. | 47. The catacombs recalled (426, 432). |
| 4. Miriam discovers the Model in the "sepulchral gloom" of the catacombs (30). | 46. Kenyon discovers a marble woman in "cellar-like cavity" (422). |
| 5. | 45. |
| 6. "The Virgin's Shrine." | 44. "The Deserted Shrine." |
| **7. Hilda's sympathetic perception of art (62); Kenyon longs for Hilda's "ethereal kiss" (69).** | 43. Kenyon misses Hilda's sympathetic perception of art (390); he has decided to declare her his love (394–95). |
| 8. Donatello looking forward to meet Miriam. | **42. Hilda thinking back upon Miriam.** |
| 9. Momentary romance of Miriam and Donatello. | 41. Dawning romance of Hilda and Kenyon. |
| 10. Temporal happiness of Donatello and Miriam, in Edenic setting (85). | 40. Unchanging happiness of Hilda and Kenyon, in "marble Eden" (369). |
| 11. Interview between Miriam and the Model (who is later identified as "Father Antonio [195]); Miriam kneels to the Model in the last paragraph (98). | 39. Interview between Hilda and Catholic Father; Hilda kneels to Father in the last paragraph (362). |
| 12. Outside view of St. Peter's (107); Miriam dips her fingers (108). | 38. Inside view of St Peter's; Hilda dips her fingers (351). |
| 13. Miriam longs for world to throw off "burthen of stony memories" of art (119). | 37. Hilda pines under "crumbly magnificence" of Roman art (342). |
| **14. Miriam plagued by her secret, "red as blood" (130).** | 36. Hilda plagued by her secret, figuratively represented as "Blood-stain" (330). |
| 15. | **35.** |
| 16. | 34. High-noon (315). |
| 17. The Model as pilgrim, kneeling at shrines (156). Midnight (160). | 33. Donatello as pilgrim, kneeling at shrines (303). |
| 18. Dreamlike mood (170–1); Miriam kneels (171). | 32. Dreamlike mood (291, 295, 299); Miriam kneels (299). |
| 19. Donatello kindled into a man in an instant (172). | 31. A "wonderful process" going forward in Donatello (282). |
| 20. The "clay image" of monk (Model) (182). | 30. Kenyon fashions Donatello's bust in clay (271). |
| **21. Dead Capuchin monk identified as the Model.** | 29. Donatello announces his intention of becoming monk (267). |
| 22. Miriam admonishes Donatello to go back to his owl-tower (199). | **28. "The Owl-Tower."** |
| 23. Hilda rejects Miriam's friendship on the grounds that she might be stained by her "blood-stain" (208–9). | 27. Donatello recounts myth of blood-stain (246). |
| 24. References to "Arcadian life" and "family history" of Donatello (218). | 26. The family history of Donatello, with references to Arcadia (233, 237). |

25. Sunshine of Monte Beni (224).

Should the above outline appear excessively wrought-out, it should be observed that empirical evidence supports the impression that *The Marble Faun* was composed with minute attention to the symmetry of the whole. As Fredson Bowers points out in the "Textual Introduction" to *The Marble Faun*, it can be established that Hawthorne left blanks in the manuscript wherein he later inserted the chapter numbers and titles. He concludes that "it would seem that the titles were first written and later the numbers" (4: lxiii–lxiv), though he does point out that "the similarity of ink between chapter title and text suggests that a number of the later titles were written currently with the text." He adds, however, that "the differences in inks and hence in time of inscription of the chapter numbers persist to the end even after the first package of copy [...] had been sent to the printer and Hawthorne was completing the romance" (4: lxiv). Furthermore, on the evidence of certain anomalies in the numeration systems employed in the manuscript of MF, chapter 11 "can be exposed as a complete insertion" (4: lx) while it is also very likely that "what we now know as Chapters III and IV was only one chapter" which "was expanded by seven manuscript pages and divided into two separate chapters" (4: lix). These circumstances suggest that Hawthorne deliberately deferred to decide upon the exact sequencing of the chapters until he had a clear idea of how he could make the individual parts of the narrative suggest the chiastic form I am arguing is the major structuring device of each of his romances.[15]

This symmetrical structuring of the text makes the plot understandable from an aesthetic point of view if not from a mimetic one: it insists throughout that we read not only what is at hand, but also what is not at hand; that in addition to our perception of each individual chapter, we perceive also its echo or prefiguration. It insists, that is, that in order to understand this text, it is necessary to acquire a double vision, a vision that will enable us to realize not only the given, but also at times, the opposite of what is given—and in such a manner that their intrinsic identity is recognised without eradicating the original opposition. The scheme suggests, for instance, that the transformational processes of Donatello and Hilda are somehow related to each other, as the symmetrical scheme links Miriam's unearthing of the Model in chapter 4 to Kenyon's unearthing of "a marble woman" in chapter 46, and likewise juxtaposes the mystery of Donatello's resemblance to the Faun of Praxiteles in chapter 1, with the mystery of Hilda's return from "a Land of Picture" (452) in chapter 49, which also marks the Faun's disappearance from the romance. Similarly, Hilda's successful displacement of her guilt upon a representative of an alien culture (the Roman Catholic Father) in chapter 39 is linked with Miriam's unsuccessful effort to displace her guilt upon the Model, who is likewise a figurative father. What is more, the scheme makes some of the apparently capricious movements of the plot acquire an air of necessity. For instance, from a psychological point of view Miriam's sudden decision in chapter 47 to speak "of her own life," revealing "facts that threw a gleam of light over many things which had perplexed the sculptor" (429)—and presumably the reader as well—is surprising at best, nor is it instigated by anything resembling a necessary outcome of the events. Seen within the frame of the symmetrical structure, however, her disclosure loses its apparent erraticity: it is dictated, quite simply, by the presentation of her mystery in chapter 3, in which the "many stories about Miriam's origin and previous life" (22) is originally brought up. This is important, because it suggests that the governing principle of the romance cannot primarily be understood as any form of psychological mimesis, but is grounded, rather, in purely aesthetic considerations.

I will refrain from expounding the implications of this symmetrical way of arranging the material till we have looked into the transformational processes suffered by Donatello and Hilda, respectively. As will be seen, the scheme helps us clarify how these two transformational processes are related to each other. For clarity's sake I will address them initially one at a time, first looking into the transformation of Donatello from a mythical (hence a-historical) Faun into a person who experiences to the full the temporal conditions of man. I will then consider how Hilda gradually petrifies into a marble image of purity, before expounding more directly in section 4 how these two transformational schemes interact to form a design of great complexity.

## 2. The Transformation of Donatello

The transformation of Donatello is ostensibly such a straightforward process it may seem slightly banal: the "faun" comes to the city, commits a deadly sin, experiences guilt and as a result is transformed into a man. The apparent immediacy of this transformation is underscored by the revolutionary effect the murder of the model has upon the young Italian: "It had kindled him into a man; it had developed within him an intelligence which was no native characteristic of the Donatello whom we have heretofore known" (172). Yet as Joseph C. Pattison convincingly argues, "Donatello's fall from innocence [...] is not sudden" but has taken place over a longer period.[16] In other words, it is not the crime that Donatello commits that instigates his transformation: when this takes place, change has already set in. If we work backward from the scene of the killing through the scenes in which Donatello appears in order to trace the genesis of this change, we come across several passages that make this observation indubitable. Unsurprisingly, the scene which first makes the change explicit is one in which Donatello is directly confronted with the presence of the Model: "Donatello still gazed in the direction which he had indicated; and the expression of his face *was fearfully changed*, being so disordered, perhaps with terrour—at all events with anger and invincible repugnance—that Miriam hardly knew him" (90; my emphasis).

Although Donatello obviously represents an image of fallen innocence, he is thus never fully innocent within the scope of the book. The difference, if indeed there is one, between the faces of the Faun of Praxiteles and Donatello may be attributed to the fact, Hilda supposes in the very first chapter, "that the Faun dwelt in woods and fields, and consorted with his like; whereas, Donatello has known cities a little, and such people as ourselves" (7). At the outset, then, Donatello is already contaminated by the circumstances of the present; this walking embodiment of Art is already enmeshed in Life. This proves as clearly inadequate the contention that one of the main problems of the structure of *The Marble Faun* is that "Hawthorne apparently forgot his success in *The Scarlet Letter* when he began with the fall already an accomplished fact. In *The Marble Faun* he simply takes too long to get to the fall."[17] On the contrary, in this respect the methods of the two books are identical: in both cases, the determining event (the crime, or fall) has already taken place when the story begins. Only, in *The Marble Faun* this event is not as easily identifiable as in *The Scarlet Letter*: it cannot be reduced to the personal sin of one or two individuals, but must be understood as a feature of civilisation itself. Entering the bounds of present-day society automatically entails being stained by sin.

The transformation of Donatello, then, is not from innocence to guilt, but from a state of apparent innocence into a state in which his true sinful character is painfully recognized. From an epistemological perspective, his transformation is thus from childhood to adulthood. Hence Donatello explains to Miriam that the "burning pain in my heart," is better than his innocent happiness of yore, "for you are in the midst of it" (149; we may note in this context, that Miriam has already admitted to suffering from a similar agony in chapter 14: "There is a secret in my heart that *burns* me!" [128; my emphasis]). Besides this pain, which is presumably interchangeable with erotic desire, everything else loses its significance. It is this *burning* pain that *kindles* Donatello into a man, not the crime he commits under its influence. When Donatello throws the Model over the precipice, the Fall has already taken place. Strictly speaking, therefore, it is not sin but pain that educates Donatello, yet the sin committed serves to make the pain indubitable: it literalizes what was previously merely a figurative feature of Donatello's character.

But if the Fall has already taken place, if Donatello like mankind in general has already fallen, why must the Model fall as well? We are told very little of the specific nature of this Model. He is at one point identified as Brother Antonio, but this is an identity he has assumed after joining a congregation of monks and is likely to be adopted.[18] Of his previous relations to Miriam we are told only that he was related to her, and that he was intended to be her husband, but that this agreement, in which Miriam herself had no part, ended in a "terrible event" (431). Scholar's have speculated that this event involves murder or incest,[19] but the romance only specifies that the Model is "the Evil Fate that had haunted [Miriam] through life" (432).

Despite this sparsity of information, the mystery veiling the Model is not completely impenetrable. The killing of the Model, we should bear in mind, is the narrative locus at which art and life quite literally interlock:

the literal fall of the Model signals the figurative Fall of Donatello. The first and possibly most important clue to the Model's identity is therefore his very denomination: being a *model* for a work of art, in a sense is to be the *original* of this work. It is thus hardly a coincidence that the chapter entitled "The Faun" begins with Donatello's name and ends with that of the Model—this Faun has two very different sides:

> "DONATELLO," playfully cried Miriam, "do not leave us in this perplexity!" (12)

> "Miriam," whispered Hilda, a little startled, "it is your Model!" (19)

The internal opposition of these two characters, suggested from this symmetrical positioning of their names, is lent further depth by the contrasting tones of Miriam and Hilda respectively, not to mention the obvious contrast between the two feminine figures themselves. Yet "contrast" is a somewhat misleading term to use in describing the relationship between the Model and Donatello—it would be more truthful to say that they oppose each other as does the living body and its reflected image, especially if it is observed that Hawthorne tends to employ mirrors in his fictions to reflect ideal truths, rather than actual appearances.[20]

Donatello, then, is the ideal reflection of the Model. Tellingly, they are related to each other not only by contrast but also by a number of similarities. Sheldon W. Liebman, for instance, notes that "both are bewitched by Miriam and both 'haunt her footsteps'."[21] We could add several other parallels: both pose a mystery, to the characters as well as the reader; both apparently transgress the line between art and life. The very first words describing the Model, specifies that he "looked as if he might just have stept out of a picture" (19), a remark obviously implying a similar linking to the world of art as that which in the same chapter is established in relation to Donatello. When encountered in the Catacombs, the Model is clad in "a pair of those goat-skin breeches, with the hair outward" which the narrator claims makes the peasants of the Roman Campagna "look like antique Satyrs." He then points out that: "in truth, the Spectre of the Catacomb might have represented the last survivor of that vanished race, hiding himself in sepulchral gloom, and mourning over his lost life of woods and streams" (30). Further on, in chapter 10, when the Model interrupts Miriam's wild dance with Donatello, it is stated that he "pranced before her on its tiptoes, almost vying with the agility of Donatello himself?" (89). On the basis of these correspondences, Evan Carton has argued that "Donatello's association with the model [...] suggests that his course in the novel should be plotted not as a linear progression but as a cyclical repetition." This is a perceptive observation, yet it seems to me that in order to understand the nature of this cyclical repetition we must not dismiss the importance of the theme of the Fall, as Carton does. According to Carton, the allegory of the Fall is merely "an old organizational principle—drawn from his previous works and from the cultural order that his European experience challenged—that Hawthorne hopes will grant him the 'master-word' over *The Marble Faun*. Had it effectively done so, the novel would have offered us far less to write and think about." Carton, then, repeats the assumption that *The Marble Faun* is most profoundly significant in spite of itself.[22] But we must observe, in this context, that the Model undergoes a transformation that is the inverse of that of Donatello. After his death, Kenyon, Miriam and Donatello come upon him in the shape of a dead monk, displayed in a Capuchin-church, whose features at first glance take on the aspect of an "image of wax—or clay-cold reality, whichever it might be" (182). This takes place in chapter 20: in other words, immediately after Donatello is kindled into a man, or, as is literally the case, immediately following upon "The Faun's Transformation," the Model assumes a "cunningly wrought waxen face" (182); he is transformed, in short, to an object of art. After the Model's identity has been revealed to be that of a monk, Donatello retreats to his country-house where Kenyon seeks him out. Eventually, Donatello reveals to him his intention of becoming a monk himself:

> "Would I do wisely, do you think, to exchange this old tower for a cell?"
> "What! Turn monk?" exclaimed his friend. "A horrible idea!"
> "True," said Donatello sighing. "Therefore, if at all, I purpose doing it." (267)

Kenyon's dismayed reaction further suggests how intricately interwoven Donatello's identity is with that of the Model. "A monk," he says, "is inevitably a beast!" (267); as Donatello is repeatedly characterized over the first seventeen chapters.[23]

What is more, the killing of the Model is re-enacted in the scene in which this dialogue occurs, which makes one suspect that the similar titles of the chapters in question—"On the Edge of a Precipice" and "On the Battlements"—is not entirely coincidental. At the very end of chapter 28, Donatello stoops over a shrub growing on top of the tower where this interview is taking place and says: "here was a worm that would have killed it; an ugly creature, which I will fling over the battlements" (259). The scene continues directly in the following chapter, where Kenyon—in an action mimicking Donatello's—throws down "a bit of lime." The sculptor's assertion that he feels inclined to "fling [himself] down after that bit of lime" (260) provokes Donatello into painting a verbal picture of the scene of the crime:

> "That is not the way with this kind of death!" exclaimed Donatello, in a low, horrour-stricken voice, which grew higher and more full of emotion, as he proceeded. "Imagine a fellow-creature—breathing, now, and looking you in the face—and now tumbling down, down, down, with a long shriek wavering after him, all the way! He does not leave his life in the air! No; but it keeps in him till he thumps against the stones, a horribly long while; then, he lies there frightfully quiet, a dead heap of bruised flesh and broken bones! A quiver runs through the crushed mass; and no more movement after that! No; not if you would give your soul to make him stir a finger! Ah, terrible! Yes, yes; *I would fain fling myself down, for the very dread of it,* that I might endure it once for all, and dream of it no more!" (261: my emphasis.)

This violent reaction frightens Kenyon, who is concerned for the safety of his friend, and he remarks: "what if a vivid dream should lead you up hither, at midnight, and act itself out as a reality!" (261). Unknowingly to Kenyon, these words in fact constitute a prophetic description of a scenario that has already taken place. The aesthetic company that joins the four principal characters on the night of the killing of the Model, sets out "a little past ten o'clock" (141), and at the very end of chapter 17—which immediately precedes the chapter in which the killing occurs—they are said to meet "pairs and groups of midnight strollers" (160). Finally, a mere two pages before the fatal act takes place, there is a short statement that puts beyond doubt that Kenyon's words have already come true: "'Come, come; it is midnight,' cried another artist; 'too late to be moralizing here! We are *literally dreaming* on the edge of a precipice. Let us go home!'" (169; my emphasis).[24] Significantly, it is said of Donatello that "he seemed to feel that perilous fascination which haunts the brow of precipices, tempting the unwary one *to fling himself over, for the very horrour of the thing*" (169–70; my emphasis).

It is not until the Model emerges out of the shadows that Donatello is able to fulfil this inclination: the Model is, allegorically speaking, the original of the statue of the Faun, the *idea* of which has come to life in the form of Donatello. We should recall in this context that Hawthorne has informed us in the opening chapter that the idea of the Faun "may have been no dream, but rather a poet's reminiscence of a period when man's affinity with Nature was more strict, and his fellowship with every living thing more intimate and dear" (10–11). If this is so, the innocent Faun is an imaginary construct, which, although posing as an origin, can have arisen only as a response to an already imperfect state of the world. In other words, the Faun is a reminiscence of a past that never was, a poetic attempt to negate the actual perception of Man as a fallen creature, by projecting upon the past the qualities of a desired future. From this allegorical perspective, it is no wonder that Donatello cannot tolerate the presence of the Model: his presence makes him aware of his own imperfection, that is, of the fact that he is not his own origin, but that he is modelled upon his exact opposite. For Donatello to kill himself, therefore is to kill this unacknowledged original upon which he is modelled. Significantly, in the scene of the murder, the Model is seen to approach Miriam and Donatello from "a deep, empty niche, that had probably once contained a statue" (170–1). That is, the niche that has once contained a statue now contains the Model of the Statue, who is also the Evil Fate of Miriam. Thus it is the imperfect model from which the idea of the perfect innocence of the Faun has paradoxically sprung that Donatello flings over the precipice. Tellingly, the act itself is not directly represented: the crucial moment in which their roles are reversed is left out. But that there is such a reversal is signalled not only by making explicit that Donatello has become a man, but also by the short but concise comment of Miriam that the Model is indeed "Stone dead!" (173).

The symmetrical pattern we disclosed in the previous section fixes the parallels I have traced above by incorporating them into its design: where the Model is seen as a pilgrim kneeling at shrines in chapter 17, in its symmetrical counterpart (chapter 33) Donatello is seen as a pilgrim kneeling at shrines; where the Model is seen as a clay-image in chapter

20, in chapter 30 Kenyon is at work fashioning a clay-image of Donatello; where the Model is found to be a monk in chapter 21, Donatello announces his intention of becoming a monk in chapter 29. What may seem a random course of events from the point of view of the linearly developing plot, then, from the point of view of the spatial form of the text is revealed as a carefully constructed aesthetic design. Miriam, in chapter 47, tells us all we really need to know. Donatello, she observes, "has travelled *in a circle* [...] and now comes back to his *original* self, with an inestimable treasure of improvement won from an experience of pain" (434; my emphasis). Significantly, she immediately proceeds to set out the much debated theory of the Fortunate Fall:

> "The story of the Fall of Man! Is it not repeated in our Romance of Monte Beni? And may we follow the analogy yet farther? Was that very sin—into which Adam precipitated himself and all his race—was it the destined means by which, over a long pathway of toil and sorrow, we are to attain a higher, brighter, and profounder happiness, than our lost birthright gave? Will not this idea account for the permitted existence of sin, as no other theory can?" (434–5)

We will have reason to get back to the importance of this circle imagery below. It will suffice, for now, to observe that the redemptive office evidently associated with the image of the circle and the notion of the Fortunate Fall is not fulfilled in *The Marble Faun*; as Swann has perceptively argued, the circle, "when we go beyond Miriam's version of the tale of Donatello, may be, so to speak, a vicious one."[25] Although clearly the dominant focus of the novel, the story of Miriam and Donatello is not allowed to develop unhindered from beginning to end. In fact, with the notable exception of chapter 47, we are told almost nothing of their activities or whereabouts in the fifteen concluding chapters of the novel. The subsequent breaking of the bond is all the more conspicuous, as there is no indication of its inevitability in the conclusion of chapter 35, in which they are reunited at the foot of the statue of a pope. Rather, the gesture of the bronze Pontiff seems to constitute some sort of sanction of their union: "A blessing was felt descending upon them from his outstretched hand; he approved, by look and gesture, the pledge of a deep union that had passed under his auspices" (324). Thus it is natural to infer that the cause of their split must be attributed to the development of the story-line of Hilda and Kenyon.

## 3. The Transfiguration of Hilda

If critics have complained about the way Hawthorne manages the plot of *The Marble Faun*, they have been equally prone to censure it for the way the characters are drawn. "Of the four characters," Male complains, "only Miriam and Donatello show any signs of vitality" (*Tragic*, 157–58). Male's response is characteristic of the general reception in that it is particularly the representation of the American couple that critics have had difficulties with accepting. Hilda, in particular, has been singled out as an artistic flaw by a number of critics. [26] The problem with Hilda, simply put, is that Hawthorne would seem to condone her character, while simultaneously faulting her actions, or rather, her lack of active participation in the fate of her friends. Conrad Shumaker neatly sums up the situation:

> Hilda represents in many ways [...] the apotheosis of the American girl as the nineteenth century envisioned her, and therein lies the cause of the problems she presents as a character. As the model daughter of the Puritans, the burden of history lies heavily upon her shoulders. Her purity must be unspotted, but she must be softened by a knowledge of sin. As the guardian of culture, she must be profoundly artistic yet become a copyist and finally refuse to expose herself by "publishing" the fruits of her own mind. Her pride and independence cannot keep her from becoming a household saint, yet she must retain a virgin reserve even as she falls in love. Above all, her sunshine cannot be seriously dimmed by the dark shadow that makes sexual rebels of Hester, Zenobia, and Miriam.[27]

Different critics have tried to account for Hilda's innocence, and Hawthorne's refusal to explicitly criticize this innocence, in different ways. Shumaker himself, for instance, argues that "*The Marble Faun*, like much genteel fiction, is a nostalgic work, a last attempt to affirm the upward course of American history using a symbol system that had been profoundly threatened by actual history."[28] If that were the case, the romance would indeed deserve to be called "a sort of 'May-Pole of Merry Mount' writ large," as Colacurcio puts it, and Bercovitch once more would have been justified to repeat his argument that Hawthorne's writings constitute a version of the Puritan myth that America was destined to be a city on a hill to the rest of the world.[29]

If; for although Hilda may appear a rather static character, she may well be Hawthorne's single most complex artistic creation. In a sense, she suffers a change as profound as that of Donatello—but whereas his may be termed a transformation from art to life, hers is rather a transfiguration from life to art. Donatello, that is to say, is transformed from the a-temporal subsistence of the mythic existence of Praxiteles' marble faun to the historical conditions of man, while Hilda, conversely, escapes the sense of guilt that Hawthorne argues is an inescapable feature of human history by taking on the aspect of a moral statue. If she remains, as I believe she does, throughout an embodiment of innocence, it is because *The Marble Faun* is designed to transform our perception of *innocence as such*.[30]

To understand Hilda, to put it incisively, is to understand the way *The Marble Faun* communicates its meanings. It is to realize, above all, that Hawthorne has very little interest in making his characters conform to the psychological mould that we associate with the realistic novel. Hawthorne throughout his writings is concerned with ideas rather than with persons, nowhere more so than in *The Marble Faun*; and abstract ideas are not psychological but metaphysical entities. This is not to say that the characters of the romance are devoid of psychological ramifications, but merely that we may hope to trace these ramifications only once we have perceived the allegorical connotations of the works of art that the characters are related to. Like Donatello (and Miriam and Kenyon too, albeit to a lesser extent), Hilda is not so much a person as a discursive prism in which the radiance of a number of art objects are broken and put in motion. The many versions of the Archangel, Guido's Beatrice, Guercino's Petronilla, the seven-branched candlestick of the Jews, and the bracelet composed of seven Etruscan stones—all are designed to add a dimension to our understanding of Hilda's character.

We are introduced to the special nature of her artistic genius at an early stage of the narrative. "She saw—no, not saw, but felt," it is stated in chapter 6, "through and through a picture" (56). By means of this intuitive way of approaching art "her comprehension of any picture that interested her was perfect" (57). When looking at her work, "you seemed to be looking at humanity with angel's eyes" [sic; the first English printing has "angels' eyes"] (55); it is not by chance that Miriam, in the same chapter, broaches the possibility that Hilda may be "an angel indeed"

(54). Significantly, however, Hilda completes only partial reproductions of the paintings she copies with the aid of this angelic vision: "It was not Hilda's general practice to attempt reproducing the whole of a great picture, but to select some high, noble, and delicate portion of it, in which the spirit and essence of the picture culminated" (58). Much like Miles Coverdale in *The Blithedale Romance*, Hilda can be seen to distil the spiritual essence out of the pictures she copies. Indeed, her reputation as a copyist is founded to a large degree on her ability to disclose the ideal picture inherent but only imperfectly present in the original:

> If a picture had darkened into an indistinct shadow, through time and neglect, or had been injured by cleaning, or retouched by some profane hand, she seemed to possess the faculty of seeing it in its pristine glory. The copy would come from her hands with what the beholder felt must be the light which the Old Master had left upon the original in bestowing his final and most ethereal touch. In some instances, even, (at least, so those believed, who best appreciated Hilda's power and sensibility,) she had been enabled to execute what the great Master had conceived in his imagination, but had not so perfectly succeeded in putting upon canvas; a result surely not impossible when such depth of sympathy as she possessed, was assisted by the delicate skill and accuracy of her slender hand. In such cases, the girl was but a finer instrument, a more exquisitely effective piece of mechanism, by the help of which the spirit of some great departed Painter now first achieved his ideal, centuries after his own earthly hand, that other tool, had turned to dust. (58–9)

Rather than copying paintings, then, Hilda must be said to *transfigure* them, to suppress certain features of them in order to bring out an image more congenial to "the warmth and richness of a woman's sympathy" (56), to her own "strength of heart" and "guiding light of sympathy" (57). Being wholly pure herself, she sees only that which is pure. Her vision comprehends not how things are, but how they should be. In short, it is ideal, and this ideal vision is attributed to faith: "she wrought religiously, and therefore wrought a miracle" (60).

Looking at some sketches in the company of her friends, Hilda's angelic vision enables her to make an astonishing discovery in a drawing that she concludes must be Guido's "original sketch for the picture of the Archangel Michael, setting his foot upon the Demon" (139), namely that the face of the Demon in the original sketch—where "if anywhere, you find the pure light of inspiration" (138)—is that of "Miriam's model!" (140). That Guido Reni's painting *St. Michael Trampling the Devil* holds a central position in this romance is hardly surprising considering that its very first paragraph suggests that its theme will revolve around "the Human Soul, with its choice of Innocence or Evil close at hand" (5). Nor is it surprising to find Miriam announce that Hilda takes the subject matter of Guido's painting "more religiously than I can" (139). But there is more at stake in Hawthorne's use of this picture than the mere illustration of a theme, for just as the Model is inscribed upon the painting in the role of the Demon, Hilda herself, an attentive reader may conclude, is inscribed upon it in the very form of the Archangel. Hilda's "tender sympathy," in Kenyon's words, coexists "with the remorselessness of a steel blade" (384), and an innocence which Miriam declares "is like a sharp steel sword" (66). And the sword is not the only attribute Hilda has in common with the Archangel; she is repeatedly called "terribly severe" (66; 209; 384), which suggests the "heavenly severity in the Archangel's face," in which there "is a degree of pain, trouble, and disgust at being brought in contact with sin" (183). No wonder, then, that Miriam tells Hilda that "As an angel, you are not amiss; but, as a human creature, and a woman among earthly men and women, you need a sin to soften you!" (209).

Hilda, however, stays clear of sin, even if she "loses her innocence by proxy, as it were, when she sees her friends commit a crime," as Marius Bewley has suggested.[31] Importantly, when Miriam seeks her sympathy after the killing of the Model, Hilda declares that she is unable to guide Miriam to heaven because she is *not* "one of God's angels, with a nature incapable of stain, and garments that never could be spotted" (208). Yet Hilda's effort to keep clear of the "blood-stain" (209) of Miriam is to little avail, for when the narrative returns to Hilda after having followed the story-line of the temporary estrangement and eventual reunion of Miriam and Donatello, it becomes clear that Hilda has acquired a stain of her own. Unbeknown to herself she is drawn by an artist, who elaborates on the picture to a completed portrait, entitled "Innocence, dying of a Blood-stain!" (330). This blood-stain is linked to several passages, the most important of which is the legend of a marble nymph recounted by Donatello to Kenyon in chapter 27. The legend concerns a knight, a reputed ancestor of the young Count, who becomes acquainted with a fountain-nymph, who shrinks away from him forever after he has "tried to wash off a blood-stain" in her waters. After said incident, the knight:

"never beheld her blessed face, but once again; and then there was a blood-stain on the poor nymph's brow; it was the stain his guilt had left in the fountain where he tried to wash it off. He mourned for her his whole life long, and employed the best sculptor of the time to carve this statue of the nymph from his description of her aspect" (246). In other words, it tells of a creature of innocence stained by the guilt of her lover, whose attempt to recreate her—to wash off the blood-stain, as it were—petrifies her in the form of a statue.

This is an almost exact parallel to what happens to Hilda. Stained by a guilt that is not originally hers, she tries to wash it off by pouring out her secret "under the sacred seal of the confessional" (360) in St. Peter's, "the World's Cathedral". The chapter ends with her kneeling to the priest who has received her confession, despite his refusal to look upon it as falling under the seal of the Confessional (360); much as Miriam is seen kneeling to the Model at the end of chapter 11, "beseeching him for freedom, and in vain" (98)—at which point, we must not forget, Miriam too, is stained by a guilt which is not really hers. Neither Hilda nor Miriam are able to extricate themselves from the confessor that is seen to have an influence upon their lives, but whereas Miriam becomes responsible, if but indirectly, for the Model's death, Hilda, persistently rejecting the notion that she herself is somehow involved in the guilt she has been stained with, mysteriously disappears.

Just before she vanishes, it is true, she seemingly recognizes her bond to Miriam. This happens after a discussion with Kenyon, who has tried to advance some idea of "what a mixture of good there may be in things evil" (383), illustrating his point with the case of Donatello and Miriam. At this, Hilda "grew very sad; for a reference to this one dismal topic had set, as it were, a prison-door ajar, and allowed a throng of torturing recollections to escape from their dungeons into the pure air and white radiance of her soul" (385). Tellingly, Donatello and Miriam—who have not been seen since their reunion at the end of chapter 35—make their first reappearance in the text in the very next chapter, when Hilda is gone. It becomes clear, in other words, that the narrative can no longer tolerate the co-presence of Hilda, and Miriam and Donatello: when the latter pair are allowed to sneak out through the prison-door Hilda has left ajar, she must herself be confined.

In the interval before she resurfaces, Kenyon leaves Rome and discovers what he at first mistakes for a "shapeless fragment of stone" (422) buried in the ground. It is, however, a statue, "*earth-stained*, as well it might be" (my emphasis), and all in pieces. Placing these in what proves "their true position, the poor, fragmentary woman forthwith showed that she retained her modest instincts to the last" (423). The statue, the narrator specifies, is "one of the few works of antique sculpture in which we recognize Womanhood, and that, moreover, without prejudice to its divinity" (424). Kenyon's reaction could hardly be more revealing: "What a discovery is here! [...] *I seek for Hilda, and find a marble woman!*" (423; my emphasis). The discovery of this "earth-stained" statue serves to underscore that divine Womanhood can manifest itself in the temporal existence of the realm of Becoming only in a fragmentary and imperfect manner, which requires the aid of the spectator/reader to disclose its true divinity. Significantly, however, Kenyon does not take this lesson to heart. Enraptured by his love for Hilda, who has—in her own eyes, at least—purged herself of the earth-stain of guilt by means of her confession in St. Peter's, Kenyon loses interest in the statue without becoming aware of its allegorical significance: "He could hardly, we fear, be reckoned a consummate artist, because there was something dearer to him than his art; and, by the greater strength of human affection, the divine statue seemed to fall asunder again, and become only a heap of worthless fragments" (424). The lesson of Hawthorne's allegorical art—that the ideal can only be attained through the mediation of an imperfect medium—thus is lost on him. Having rejected this chance of affirming that the ideal can be made available by means of an allegorical distance, Kenyon chooses instead to hold on to his idealized conception of Hilda as a person in whom the Ideal of Divine Womanhood is symbolically made present. The stained reality of Hilda is thus repressed for the sake of holding on to the Ideal of Divine Womanhood which can only be affirmed by Hilda taking on the aspect of a Marble Woman. And as the example of Hester as well as of Zenobia informs us, a marble woman is a woman who has suppressed her erotic sensibilities.[32]

While seemingly the passive observer, Kenyon is thus in truth instrumental to Hilda's transfiguration. It should be noted that Donatello's re-enactment of the killing of the Model at the very end of chapter 28 is immediately followed by an act of Kenyon which figuratively parallels that which Donatello has already performed. The sculptor, we learn in the first paragraph of chapter 29, "threw down a bit of lime, watching its fall, till it struck upon a stone-bench at the rocky foundation of the tower, and flew into many fragments" (260). In the same chapter, there is a short passage loading religious imagery with sexual connotations, subtly indicating that Kenyon is in a state of sexual arousal at this point:

> he felt a strange pull at his heart-strings. It could not have been more perceptible, if, all the way between these battlements and Hilda's dove-cote, had stretched an exquisitively sensitive cord, which, at the hither end, was knotted with his aforesaid heart-strings, and at the remoter one, was grasped by a gentle hand. *His breath grew tremulous.* He put his hand to his breast; so distinctly did he seem to feel that cord *drawn once, and again, and again*, as if—though still it was bashfully intimated—there were *an importunate demand for his presence.* Oh, for the white wings of Hilda's doves, that he might have flown thither, and alighted *at the Virgin's shrine*! (263; my emphasis.)

At the end of chapter 37, it is confirmed that this arousal is indeed instigated by Hilda, as she expresses a longing for Kenyon's company to help her endure her "terrible secret": "That very afternoon, as the reader may remember, Kenyon felt Hilda's hand pulling at the silken cord that was connected with his heart-strings, as he stood looking towards Rome from the battlements of Monte Beni" (343).

As we know, Hilda's "terrible secret" is her knowledge of the crime committed by Donatello and Miriam—an act which Crews has convincingly argued functions as "a kind of vicarious sexual initiation."[33] The bloodspot which she is represented as having just discovered in chapter 36, can thus be translated into an awareness of her own sexual desire. This desire is implied already in chapter 6, fittingly entitled "The Virgin's Shrine," wherein she tells Miriam that she sometimes feels "half-inclined to attempt a flight from the top of my tower, in the faith that I should float upward!" (54). Of course, we know that she would fall, and the text implicitly confirms this when she comes down from her tower at the end of the romance. When Kenyon flings down the piece of lime in chapter 29, then, what is allegorically enacted is how his conception of Hilda as a divine being is temporarily supplanted by his desire to make her a real, and hence, imperfect woman. In other words, he figuratively shoves her out of the tower—and accordingly, when he comes across the marble woman in chapter 46, he finds her all in *fragments*; his sexual desire has shattered her image of spotlessness. Yet the same passage also makes clear that Kenyon, like Hilda before him, expects that it is possible to "fall from a precipice" without experiencing pain: "if it be a great height [...] a man would leave his life in the air, and never feel the hard shock at the bottom" (260). In order to render the fall painless, Hilda's purity must be reinstated by transforming her from a living woman into an object of art.

Throughout the romance, Kenyon's remarks on works of art are much more perceptive than his comments on aspects of life. His faith in the possibility of taking a painless plunge should therefore be seen in conjunction with his critique of the Dying Gladiator in chapter 2:

> "I used to admire this statue exceedingly;" he remarked, "but, latterly, I find myself getting weary and annoyed that the man should be such a length of time leaning on his arm, in the very act of death. If he is so terribly hurt, why does he not sink down and die, without further ado? Flitting moments—imminent emergencies—imperceptible intervals between two breaths—ought not to be incrusted with the eternal repose of marble; in any sculptural subject, there should be a moral standstill, since there must of necessity be a physical one. Otherwise, it is like flinging a block of marble up into the air, and, by some trick of enchantment, causing it to stick there. You feel that it ought to come down, and are dissatisfied that it does not obey the natural law." (16)

It is in consonance with the dictum that "there should be a moral standstill" in sculptural objects that Kenyon refrains from putting into marble "a beautiful little statue of Maidenhood, gathering a Snow-drop" that he fashions in clay, "because the sculptor soon recognized it as one of those fragile creations which are true only to the moment that produces them, and are wronged, if we try to imprison their airy excellence in a permanent material" (375). Yet a moral standstill is precisely what Kenyon craves of his future wife. Though it is true that Kenyon's interest in art is seen to dwindle at the end of the book, his essentially aesthetic conception of life is not abandoned so much as replaced by one which reinstates Woman as the object of worship in art's place. Thus it is his ideal that Hilda fulfils; she becomes a statue of Innocence in order "to be herself enshrined and worshipped as a household Saint" (461). Theirs will be a life of domestic bliss, a reinstatement of Eden on earth through the consecration of marriage. In fact, Kenyon delineates in great detail the nature of their future happiness when he is first reunited with Hilda in St. Paul's Cathedral:

> "But, what a delicious life it would be, if a colony of people with delicate lungs (or merely with delicate fancies) could take up their abode in this ever-mild and tranquil air. These architectural tombs of the Popes might serve for dwellings, and each brazen sepulchral door-way would become a domestic threshold. Then, the lover, if he dared, might say to his mistress, 'Will you share my tomb with me?'—and, winning her soft consent, he would lead her to the altar, and thence to yonder sepulchre of Pope Gregory, which should be their nuptial home. What a life would be theirs, Hilda, in their marble Eden!" (369)

A marble Eden: that is the life Kenyon and Hilda create for themselves by refusing to acknowledge their involvement in the guilt of Miriam and Donatello. Of course, what Kenyon is portraying, unbeknown to himself, is a form of death-in-life which is the direct consequence of a conception of Life as Art. Denying, as Kenyon and Hilda do, that guilt is an integral part of human existence is a prerequisite for instating the ideal of pure Innocence into life, yet ridding life of this stain is also to rid it of the sole means for turning the marble image of love into the ambiguous solace of sex.

Hilda, we noted above, denies being "one of God's angels" when Miriam comes to her pleading for sympathy. Yet there can be little doubt that Kenyon, who dares "not even kiss the image [of Hilda's hand] that he himself had made" on account of it having "assumed its share of Hilda's remote and shy divinity" (122), looks upon her as an angelic creature. As much as he longs for Hilda's "ethereal kiss" (69), his desire to "draw her down to an earthly fireside" is tempered by the condition that "it be not a sin to wish it" (372). For Kenyon, Hilda's purity must be beyond question; it must not even be stained by his own desire. It is not by chance that she mysteriously disappears precisely when he is on the verge of trying "if it were possible to take this shy, yet frank, and innocently fearless creature, captive, and imprison her in his heart" (394) by proposing to her. For before she vanishes, as we noted above, Hilda recognizes that the bond between herself and Miriam is a true one, and that the wretchedness she has experienced since the killing of the Model "was but the struggle and writhing of her sensibility, still yearning towards her friend" (386). Although she has just claimed to "have survived the death-struggle that [the secret of Miriam's crime] cost me" (383), Hilda, in other words, is on the point of acknowledging having something in common with the "strong, writhing, squirming dragon, under the Archangel's foot" (140), against which the angel must fight a "death-struggle" (184). This is a sympathy that Hilda must be cleansed from in order to remain the object of Kenyon's desire. Tellingly, when she finally reappears in the midst of the carnival antics in chapter 49, she is looked upon as "if an angel were to alight" (452), and is appropriately "dressed in a white domino" (451), overtly invoking "the shining white robe of the true faith" that the Father who received Hilda's confession has previously told Kenyon that she will be wearing "when you next behold her" (416). Earlier in the story she has declared herself unable "to lead [Miriam] upward" (208), yet Kenyon still expects her to "guide [him] home!" (461). Yet it is not by her own intent that she becomes such a guide, for Hilda consistently denies owning "that white wisdom" (460) that Kenyon ascribes to her: "I am conscious of no such high and delicate qualities as you allow me" (367), she insists; "I am a poor, weak girl, and have no such wisdom as you fancy in me" (461).

But for Kenyon, Hilda must remain an angel, a person altogether beyond imperfection, in order that she may continue to be the perfect companion for himself, the novel's "Man of marble" (411), with "features finely cut, as if already marble" (116). The sculptor, in fact, embodies the novel's implicit conception of an aesthetic understanding of life, which explains his tendency throughout to comment upon reality as if he were expounding upon an object of art: he already conceives of life as art. Thus although he protests that he is "full of sympathy" when Miriam is on the verge of disclosing the secret of her bond to the Model to him, he remains always detached, and Miriam is surely right in accusing him of being "as cold and pitiless as your own marble" (129). In fact, the scene in which Kenyon rejects being Miriam's confidante is figuratively reenacted in the concluding carnival scene, in a manner that makes explicit the consequences of his reserve. Making his way through the fantastic figures, Kenyon is approached by "a gigantic female figure, seven feet high" (445), who makes "a ponderous assault upon his heart, throwing amorous glances at him out of her great goggle eyes, offering him a vast bouquet of sunflowers and nettles, and soliciting his pity by all sorts of pathetic and passionate dumb show." When her suit meets with no favour, the figure draws up "a huge pistol," which goes off "like a boy's popgun, covering Kenyon with a cloud of lime dust," whereupon other figures crowd upon him, one of whom offers "to make the last will and testament of the assassinated man" (446). Kenyon, in effect, becomes a statue himself, a man who has allowed his passions to die out of him. Sensing this coldness of heart in the sculptor, Miriam goes on to point out, in the scene where she momentarily considers divulging her secret to him, that he can do nothing for her, "unless you petrify me into a marble companion for your Cleopatra there" (129). Miriam will not allow this, but Hilda, as we have seen, will. Tellingly, in recounting her experiences in that "Land of Picture" that we are to imagine Hilda has been snatched away to during her disappearance, Hawthorne writes that "Raphael had taken Hilda by the hand, (that fine, forcible hand *which Kenyon sculptured,*) and drawn aside the curtain of gold-fringed cloud that hung before his latest masterpiece" (452–3; my emphasis). In the allegorical context we have established, the implication is clear: the Old Master has taken hold not of the hand that Kenyon once represented as a sculpture, but of the very representation of this hand. "On earth," Hawthorne goes on, "Raphael painted the Transfiguration. What higher scene may he have since depicted, not from imagination, but as revealed to his actual sight!" The time has come for the Old Master to repay his debt to his proselyte: whereas on earth, Hilda brought out the ideal of the Old Master, in the Land of Picture the Old Master conversely brings out the ideal of Hilda, and she returns to reality in the form of a statue imbued with life.

The reappearance of Hilda, it is important to note, takes place at the very moment Miriam and Donatello in their guise of peasant and contadina are arrested and brought away. At least, we infer that this is the case, because the report of this event is restricted to a paragraph stating that a small party of soldiers "were perhaps arresting some disorderly character, who, under the influence of an extra flask of wine, might have reeled across the mystic limitation of carnival proprieties" (451), followed by some brief snatches of conversation that make the inference likely:

> "Could they be really a peasant and a contadina, do you imagine?"
> "No, no," said the other. "It is some frolic of the Carnival, carried a little too far." (451)

A frolic of the carnival, carried a little too far: that is the climax the story of Miriam and Donatello builds up to, or peters out into, because just when we expect the grand finale of their story, the narrator switches focus, as does Kenyon's interest. The above conversation, he says, "might have excited Kenyon's interest;" only, "just as the last words were spoken," Hilda is on the verge of making her reappearance. The sculptor, concordantly, loses all interest in the companions with whom he formed "a linked circle of three" (448) but two pages earlier, focusing exclusively upon Hilda "in whose gentle presence, his own secret sorrow and the obtrusive uproar of the Carnival alike died away from his perception" (454).

In other words, just as Miriam's and Donatello's future destiny is to be decided, Kenyon and Hilda are completely enwrapped in each other and exhibit no interest whatsoever in the fate of their friends. More importantly, neither does the narrative; nor, it seems safe to say, does the reader, so fiendishly is this narrative contrived. For at the very moment in which, if ever, our hearts should go out to the pair, a mystic revelation attached with such a perplexing manner of "explanation" is advanced, that the reader is bound to lose himself in interpretive speculations over an object of art: "Whence she had come, or where she had been hidden, during this mysterious interval, we can but imperfectly surmise, and do not mean, at present, to make it a matter of formal explanation with the reader. It is better, perhaps, to fancy that she had been snatched away to a Land of Picture" (452). Instead of receiving the reader's empathy, Miriam and Donatello are expelled from the narrative in order that the Transfiguration of Hilda shall be recognized as the remarkable event it is. The fulfilment of this process in which Innocence assumes the "sacred character" (136) inherent in the "pure, white, undecaying substance" (135) of a marble statue, can be achieved only by suppressing the possibility that Hilda has a share in the guilt of Miriam and Donatello.

By rejecting the paradoxical lesson of allegory that insists that the ideal must be approached through imperfection, Kenyon can hold on to his conception of Hilda as a Saint beyond the reach of sin, and Hilda herself can retain "a hopeful soul" that sees "sunlight on the mountain-tops" rather than the shadows in-between. In the place of allegory, these characters, we will see, embrace a symbolism that valorizes private emotions at the expense of communal norms. If inspected closely, however, the statue of Saint Hilda is not quite as perfect as it may first appear; there is, indeed, the slightest of cracks in its surface, which indicates that it will not survive the transition to America without falling apart. In the remainder of this chapter, I will be concerned with showing how the formal aspects of the romance contribute to exposing Hilda's and Kenyon's denial of allegory, which by extension is America's as well, as futile.

## 4. The Menorah and the Bracelet

Although the transfiguration of Hilda and her marriage to Kenyon brings *The Marble Faun* to a symbolic resolution, the conclusion of the romance is filled with questions:

> And now, happy as Hilda was, the bracelet brought the tears into her eyes, as being, in its entire circle, the symbol of as sad a mystery as any that Miriam had attached to the separate gems. For, what was Miriam's life to be? And where was Donatello? But Hilda had a hopeful soul, and saw sunlight on the mountain-tops. (462)

Just as in "Rappaccini's Daughter," the reader is confronted with a conclusion that suggests that the really important questions the narrative has raised remain to be determined. The difficulty of answering these questions stems to no small degree from the paradox that *The Marble Faun* presents us with a model Gentle Reader in the form of "gentle Hilda" (33; 127; 452; 461), only to go on to show us how this model reader explicitly rejects the moral that everything in the narrative would seem to support. Indeed, as Swann has observed, when Hilda delivers her interpretation of Donatello's unfinished bust, even she can implicitly be seen to support the formula of the Fortunate Fall, although she claims to be "shocked [...] beyond words" (460) when Kenyon suggests that the crime of Donatello and Miriam might be understood in accordance with this formula.[34]

This paradoxical strategy can be better understood, I believe, by paying closer attention to the significance of the complex structural arrangement of the textual material than has yet been done. What is implied by the identical titles of the opening and closing chapters is not merely that we have come full circle at the end, but—more importantly—that we end quite literally at the beginning; that is, that the first and the last chapter of this romance should be thought of as a single unit. Hence the novel contains not 50 but 49 chapters, a circumstance which acquires significance when seen in conjunction with two images advanced in the text, that of the menorah—the seven-branched golden candlestick of the Jews—and that of the bracelet composed of seven Etruscan stones which is left to Hilda as a bridal gift. While there are only two references to the menorah and only one to the bracelet in the entire book, both are elaborated to a degree that suggests their importance. First mentioned in passing on page 159, the menorah is expatiated on to great effect by Hilda in chapter 40:

> "There was a meaning and purpose in each of its seven branches, and such a candlestick cannot be lost forever. When it is found again, and seven lights are kindled and burning in it, the whole world will gain the illumination which it needs. Would not this be an admirable idea for a mystic story, or parable, or seven-branched allegory, full of poetry, art, philosophy, and religion? It shall be called 'The Recovery of the Sacred Candlestick.' As each branch is lighted, it shall have a differently coloured lustre from the other six; and when all the seven are kindled, their radiance shall combine into the intense white light of Truth!"
>
> "Positively, Hilda, this is a magnificent conception," cried Kenyon. "The more I look at it, the brighter it burns."
>
> "I think so too," said Hilda, enjoying a childlike pleasure in her own idea. "The theme is better suited for verse than prose; and when I go home to America, I will suggest it to one of our poets. Or, seven poets might write the poem together, each lighting a separate branch of the Sacred Candlestick!" (371)

The bracelet is introduced only at the very last page, in the penultimate paragraph of the romance proper, where it, too, is expounded at great length:

> Before they quitted Rome, a bridal gift was laid on Hilda's table. It was a bracelet, evidently of great cost, being composed of seven ancient Etruscan gems, dug out of seven sepulchres, and each one of them the signet of some princely personage, who had lived an immemorial time ago. Hilda remembered this precious ornament. It had been Miriam's; and once, with the exuberance of fancy that distinguished her, she had amused herself with telling a mythical and magic legend for each gem, comprising the imaginary adventures and catastrophe of its former wearer. Thus, the Etruscan bracelet became the connecting bond of a series of seven wondrous tales, all of which, as they were dug out of seven sepulchres, were characterized by a sevenfold sepulchral gloom; such as Miriam's imagination, shadowed by her own misfortunes, was wont to fling over its most sportive flights. (462)

Seeing that this is the sole mention of the bracelet in the whole romance, it is perhaps unsurprising that it has gone largely uncommented on by critics.[35] In effect, however, the passage submits a way of reading the text we have just partaken of. The paragraph has the ring of an afterthought, and the fact that it continues on the second side of what is the last sheet of the original manuscript strengthens Arlin Turner's supposition that the two last paragraphs were a last minute addendum.[36] The extra paragraphs could very well have been prompted by a sense that the reader would need one more emphatic suggestion of the importance of the number seven in order to trace the design of the romance.

The prominence of the number seven in these images suggests that this number holds a special significance in this romance, an impression which is reinforced by a number of other circumstances. Of course it may be entirely coincidental that in exactly 14 chapters of the book the scene is located outside of Rome. But is it also a coincidence that when the narrative switches location the first time, from Rome to the Apennines where Donatello's country-mansion is located, thereby shifting the focus from the dilemma of Miriam to the troubles of her friend, Miriam reappears in chapter 31, having stayed out of view for exactly seven chapters? It could be, yet it seems rather unlikely as the split between Miriam and Donatello lasts for exactly seven chapters: they are separated at the very end of chapter 22, and Miriam is first seen to reapproach Donatello at the very end of chapter 29. What is more, when Miriam and Donatello have been reunited in chapter 35 (ensuring that the whole of their crisis is confined to two complete seven-sequence movements), the pair stays out of view for exactly seven chapters, not reappearing until chapter 43, by which time Hilda has disappeared. She re-emerges seven chapters after her disappearance, at the end of chapter 49.

Critics have not been entirely blind to the highly schematized structure hereby suggested. According to Harry Levin, the "total pattern may be roughly divided into three equal sections: the first is melodrama; the second, pastoral; and the third, carnival." Stubbs, similarly, divides the book into three main sections, consisting of chapters 1–23, 24–35, and 36–50.[37] This is indeed the overt structure of *The Marble Faun*, but we must not fail to account for the minutiae of these three main sections. In the first, the main story-line is provided by Miriam's relation to the mysterious model; that she is the only character to appear in each of its chapters should suffice to make it admissible to say that this section is ascribable to her.[38] However, the story-line of the model with which Miriam is associated is taken up only in chapter 3, chapters 1 and 2 being more accurately described as an introduction of sorts, presenting the four major characters to the reader while briefing the romance's central theme concerning the relation between art and reality. These two chapters are also set apart from the others in that they revolve almost entirely around the similarity that the three artists perceive between Donatello and the Faun of Praxiteles. What is more, when by means of an analepsis the story-line of Miriam's model is taken up in chapters 3 and 4, the narrative never returns to its point of departure in chapter 2 but continues in chapter 5 "on the morning *after* the scene at the Sculpture Gallery" (39; my emphasis). Miriam's story, then, does not run through the first section in its entirety, but only through chapters 3–23, while chapters 1 and 2 are concerned with a theme more directly associated with Donatello.

The second major section identified by Stubbs, chapters 24–35, corresponds to the narrative's switch from Rome to the countryside where it takes up the theme suggested in the opening chapters by following Donatello's transformation from an innocent faun-like creature to a man of keen intellect ridden by remorse. The third major section, finally, falls naturally into two, chapters 36–42 focusing upon Hilda, and chapters 43–49 upon Kenyon. Thus Donatello is foregrounded in the two initial chapters; Miriam's problems dominate chapters 3–23; Donatello again chapters 24–35; Hilda and Kenyon chapters 36–42 and chapters 43–49 respectively. If chapter 50 is looked upon as making up a unit with chapter 1, that leaves us twenty one chapters attributable to Miriam, fourteen to Donatello, and seven each to Hilda and Kenyon respectively. Four main sections, that is, each divisible by seven.

To fully understand the significance of these patterns, we must combine the image of the menorah—itself suggestive of a symmetrical pattern, its seven branches interlocking two and two around one central branch—with that of the bracelet, which is introduced on the last page of the romance proper. Male's recognition of the importance of this image and his attention to "the mystic number seven" (*Tragic*, 160) entails that his analysis implies a seven-section movement even if it does not explicate it. He puts down as key-chapters number 1, 7, 21, 28, 35, 42, and 49 (*Tragic*, 160–61). And indeed, if we do away with the idiosyncrasies of this scheme by dispensing with chapter 1 and inserting chapter 14 into the sequence instead, we hit upon a way of generating an understanding of aspects of the plot that might otherwise seem difficult to account for. I shall refer to this sequence of chapters as *the bracelet*. As it happens, the seven-phase movement of the bracelet can be rewardingly combined with the symmetrical scheme we generated in section 2 (see page 318 above), to create the following figure:

**The scheme of the menorah**

| A1 | B1 | C1 | D | C2 | B2 | A2 |
|---|---|---|---|---|---|---|
| **7** | **14** | **21** | **28** | **35** | **42** | **49** |
| 6 | 13 | 20 | 27 | 34 | 41 | 48 |
| 5 | 12 | 19 | 26 | 33 | 40 | 47 |
| 4 | 11 | 18 | 25 | 32 | 39 | 46 |
| 3 | 10 | 17 | 24 | 31 | 38 | 45 |
| 2 | 9 | 16 | 23 | 30 | 37 | 44 |
| 50/1 | 8 | 15 | 22 | 29 | 36 | 43 |

The above figure represents the symmetrical scheme in the shape implied by the menorah. Seven branches of course call for seven chapters to be assigned to each branch: I have assigned every seventh chapter the topmost position of each branch as a consequence of the centrality of the number seven in the book. Significantly, the bracelet sequence is found within the very lights of the menorah itself. The chapters of section A1 are chiastically related to the chapters of section A2; that is, chapter 50/1 has as its counterpart chapter 49, chapter 2 has its counterpart in chapter 48, chapter 3 in chapter 47, and so on; the chapters of section B1 and C1 are similarly tied to the chapters in sections B2 and C2. More generally, I am suggesting that the chapters at the lower half of sections A1, B1, and C1, are to be read in conjunction with the chapters of the upper half of sections A2, B2, and C2, and that the chapters of the lower half of the latter sections should be correlated with those of the upper half of the former ones. In the central branch, finally, the upper-half chapters are chiastically related to the lower-half chapters of the same branch. Importantly, chapter 22 marks a figurative low-point in Donatello's story—his break-up with Miriam—while chapter 28 marks the literal high-point of the same story, in that it shows him ascending his tower, which, in Kenyon's words, "resembles the spiritual experience of many a sinful soul, which, nevertheless, may struggle upward into the pure air and light of Heaven, at last" (253). As with so many other of the sculptor's comments, this suggestion has an uncanny ring to it, for the chapter concludes with Donatello figurally re-enacting the killing of the Model, by flinging down "a worm" (259) threatening to kill a shrub growing on top of the tower.

The significance of the chiastic structure suggested by the menorah, as I suggested in section 1, lies primarily in the way it forces the reader to view the narrative as a representation of art rather than of reality: it enforces a spatial rather than temporal perspective, a perspective suggestive of the stasis of eternal truths. Yet the presence within this static structure of the narrative sequence of the bracelet chapters, suggests that these truths nevertheless contain an essential historical movement. The importance of the bracelet sequence, then, is not that there is in every seventh chapter "a recognition scene in which an individual is transfigured by a vital bond with the past" (*Tragic*, 160) as Male contends, but that this particular sequence of chapters retells the story of Beatrice

Cenci, and in so doing allows us to see how art and history are interrelated. As we know, Beatrice Cenci was executed (along with her mother and a brother) for having plotted the murder of her father, a cruel and despotic nobleman whom she alleged had tried to commit incest with her. But besides the historical figure, her name also invokes Dante's Beatrice, and perhaps most pertinently of all, the Beatrice of "Rappaccini's Daughter," that is to say the innocent yet poisonous woman who died when her lover gave her an antidote that he thought would purge her of the venomous toxins that her father had imbued her with. We have in Beatrice, then, an image in which two seemingly contradictory strands—secular love (sexuality), and religious devotion—are combined. "Beatrice" is also the name of chapter 7, the first chapter of the bracelet sequence, which in contrast to the scheme of the menorah (of which it forms a part) does not conceive of religion and sexuality as two conflicting concepts, but rather as categories which are mutually dependent upon one another. The Beatrice of chapter 7 is an object of art: Guido's portrait of Beatrice, of which Hilda has made her own copy, so closely resembling the original that Miriam declares it her greatest achievement. Contemplating this copy, Hilda describes Beatrice in terms which would seem to be a thinly veiled statement of her own fate, proleptically envisioned:

> She knows that her sorrow is so strange, and so immense, that she ought to be solitary forever, both for the world's sake and her own; and this is the reason we feel such a distance between Beatrice and ourselves, even when our eyes meet hers. It is infinitely heart-breaking to meet her glance, and to feel that nothing can be done to help or comfort her; neither does she ask help or comfort, knowing the hopelessness of her case better than we do. She is a fallen angel, fallen, and yet sinless; and it is only this depth of sorrow, with its weight and darkness, that keeps her down upon earth, and brings her within our view even while it sets her beyond our reach. (65–6)

But Hilda is not the only one implicitly identified with Beatrice in the chapter; looking from the picture to Miriam's face, Hilda is "startled to observe that her friend's expression had become almost exactly that of the portrait; as if her passionate wish and struggle to penetrate poor Beatrice's mystery had been successful" (67). However, though Hilda and Miriam alike are aligned with Beatrice, they are aligned with different aspects of her—one might even say that they personify altogether different Beatrices. When Miriam jumps at finding Hilda declare Beatrice "sinless," Hilda immediately changes her view, claiming that she "had quite forgotten *Beatrice's history*;" in reference to the historical Beatrice she asserts that her "doom is just" (66; my emphasis). *The Marble Faun*, then, could be said to enact a conflict concerning which view of Beatrice should acquire normative status: the historical view of Miriam, or the aesthetical view of Hilda, which looks to Beatrice "only as the picture seems to reveal her character" (66).

Chapter 14 also takes its title from an object of art, this time Kenyon's sculpture of Cleopatra, at which Miriam again is deeply impressed, and likewise deeply intrigued as to how it has been in the sculptor's powers to fashion "the womanhood" interfused into the sculpture. "Where did you get that secret?" (127) she asks him, echoing the amazement she sounds when remarking to Hilda how strange it is that "an innocent, delicate, white soul, like yours, has been able to seize the subtle mystery of [Beatrice's] portrait" (67) in the first chapter of the sequence. Whatever else the concept of womanhood may involve, it seems safe to assume that to Miriam sexuality is one of its key elements: "Were you not afraid to touch her," she asks Kenyon with reference to his statue, "as she grew more and more towards hot life, beneath your hand?" (127). It is upon her recognition of Kenyon as having perceived the relation between womanhood and sexuality, that Miriam is almost moved to disclose her secret to him, but she changes her mind when Kenyon admonishes her to "speak freely, as to a brother" (128). While we learn little of the secret save that it is "not a pearl" but "red as blood" (130), we might infer from the romance as a whole and from the specific scene in question that the secret is sexuality as such: it is the recognition of sexual desire as a fundamental constituent of one's human nature. Miriam's offer to reveal this secret to Kenyon amounts to a figurative representation of a sexual invitation, as can be ascertained from the fact that if Kenyon were to accept this secret, it would be certain to "change all former relations that had subsisted between herself and the friend to whom she might reveal it. Unless he could give her all the sympathy, and *just the kind of sympathy, that the occasion required*, Miriam would hate him, by-and-by, and herself still more, if he let her speak" (129; my emphasis).

Miriam must reject Kenyon's offer to be her brother, since the acceptance of such an offer would merely amount to a repetition of the relation which she is seeking to escape from, namely that between herself and the Model, who is identified in chapter 21 as "Brother Antonio" (194), a designation which slips into that of "Father Antonio" on the very next page: a brother in crime transformed into a Father of guilt, from whose presence innocent Beatrice can escape only by willing to have him killed.[39] That is—to spell out the significance of the opaque allegorical language in which *The Marble Faun* veils its principal subject—from which the individual can escape only by taking the step from sexuality recognized to sexuality realized, from sexual invitation to sexual intercourse.[40] Taking this step involves the substitution of one mode of being for another. In Miriam's case this amounts to having sorrow replaced by sin; in Donatello's case it entails having his consciousness transformed from faun-like innocence into the guilt-ridden intelligence of a man. The owl-tower which lends its name to the next chapter of the sequence is expressly invoked as an image of the process Donatello has entered on as a result of having yielded to the desire betrayed by Miriam's eyes; it resembles, in Kenyon's words "the spiritual experience of many a sinful soul, which, nevertheless, may struggle upward into the pure air and light of Heaven" (253).

Each of the first three chapters of the bracelet-sequence thus takes its title from an object aesthetically contemplated in the chapter: "Beatrice," "Cleopatra," "The Dead Capuchin." Ostensibly, the third title is of a very different nature than are those of the other two. But the Dead Capuchin, we must remember, is the product of Miriam's literal execution of the Model, just as Beatrice and Cleopatra are the products of Hilda's and Kenyon's respective artistic endeavours:

> The effect upon her imagination was as if a strange and unknown corpse had miraculously, while she was gazing at it, assumed the likeness of that face, so terrible henceforth in her remembrance. It was a symbol, perhaps, of the deadly iteration with which she was doomed to behold *the image of her crime* reflected back upon her, in a thousand ways, and converting the great, calm face of Nature, in the whole, and in its innumerable details, into a manifold reminiscence of that one dead visage. (190; my emphasis.)

We learn in this chapter that the Model will be put to rest in the cemetery of the Capuchins, but that this will only be a temporary resting place for his bones, as the bodies of the dead Capuchins are moved after some twenty-five to thirty years in order to give place for more recently deceased brethren. Miriam finds this circumstance somewhat distressing; in these graves, she claims, one must lie down "with a nervous anticipation of being disturbed, like weary men, who know that they shall be summoned out of bed at midnight," (194)—an uncanny comment, given the interchangeable identities of Donatello and the Model that we have already discussed, as the killing of the Model takes place at midnight. In the next chapter of the sequence, 28, Donatello informs Kenyon of "a certain famous monk" that is supposed to have been confined to his tower: "There have always been stories, Tomaso says, of a hooded monk creeping up and down these stairs, or standing in the door-way of this chamber. It must needs be the ghost of the ancient prisoner. Do you believe in ghosts?" (254). Although Donatello is quick to dismiss the idea once he has advanced it ("Ghosts never rise!"), it seems nevertheless to disturb him, much as it has disturbed Miriam earlier, as can be inferred from the continuation of the scene in the following chapter, where he claims the clouds are about to "take the figure of a monk reclining, with his cowl about his head and drawn partly over his face" (265).

From the owl-tower of chapter 28, the bracelet sequence then moves on to the scene in which Donatello and Miriam are united under the auspices of the Bronze Pontiff, confirming the extent to which Donatello has benefited from the "spiritual instruction that had come through sorrow and remorse; so that—instead of the wild boy, the thing of sportive, animal nature, the sylvan Faun—here was the man of feeling and intelligence" (320). Within the span of the sequence made up by chapters 21–35, then, Donatello is transformed from a living work of art into a man, from object to subject, while his counterpart inversely is transformed from the corpse of Father Antonio (the dead Capuchin), to the benign countenance of the Bronze Pontiff, in whose image "the desolate heart, whatever be its religion, recognizes [...] the likeness of a Father," despite the fact that "it were modelled for a Catholic Chief-Priest" (316). Below this venerable statue, Kenyon delivers a sermon on the "mysterious process, by which our earthly life instructs us for another state of being" (321) to Donatello, "shuddering," and Miriam, "also shuddering" (322), who accept his words. But when Kenyon broaches the subject of his sermon to his beloved in the next chapter of the bracelet-sequence (chapter 42), Hilda—likewise "shuddering" (383)—vehemently rejects it: "there is, I believe, only one right and one wrong; and I do not understand (and may God keep me from ever understanding) how two things so totally unlike can be mistaken for one another; nor how two mortal foes—as Right and Wrong surely are—can work together in the same deed" (384). Yet Kenyon's words leave her disturbed, and in her reminiscences of Miriam she comes to recall the packet her former friend leaves her in chapter 7, and goes off to deliver them to the Palazzo Cenci, the historical home of another reputed father, whereupon she disappears.

As in the romance as a whole, Miriam rather than Hilda is the dominant figure in the bracelet sequence: she figures in five of the seven chapters, Hilda only in three. What is more, in the one chapter in which Hilda appears but Miriam does not (chapter 42), she might nevertheless be said to occupy a central position, the very title of this chapter invoking her absence: "Reminiscences of Miriam." It would seem, then, that the scheme of the bracelet gives pre-eminence to Miriam's conception of Beatrice rather than Hilda's, even though it is the latter who is most frequently associated with Beatrice in the romance.[41] Yet although Hilda delivers Miriam's packet to the "paternal abode of Beatrice" (389) at the end of chapter 42, Hilda's spectacular re-appearance at the end of chapter 49 suggests that it is not Miriam's but Hilda's conception of Beatrice who finally triumphs in the book. Hilda, the narrator enigmatically suggests, "had been snatched away to a Land of Picture" in which we are to imagine that "Guido had shown her another portrait of Beatrice Cenci, done from the celestial life, in which that forlorn mystery of the earthly countenance was exchanged for a radiant joy" (452).

Thus it may appear as if Miriam's story were ousted by that of Hilda, much as the Model is ousted by Donatello. Yet while it is indeed the case "that the successful completion of Hilda's novel depends upon the censorship of Miriam's romance" (*Practicing*, 187), the matter seems to me even more convoluted than this perceptive comment suggests. Although it seems plausible to equate the "white light of Truth" radiating from the menorah with Hilda's truth, we must not forget that Hilda's truth is not of her own making; it is, in fact, always that of an Old Master, that is to say that of an Artist. And in *The Marble Faun*, there is only one person who is never shown to relinquish her art: Miriam. That Miriam employs Hilda as her messenger should be taken to imply, it seems to me, that even though "the Hilda-novel," as Millington aptly calls it, may be said to appropriate the close of the narrative at the expense of Miriam's romance, this outcome must be seen as dictated by Miriam herself: we must imagine that it is she who plots Hilda's disappearance and subsequent return.

This scenario is corroborated in the final chapter when the narrator announces that the release of Hilda can only be accounted for "by supposing that the fitful and fantastic imagination of a Woman (sportive, because she must otherwise be desperate) had arranged this incident, and made it the condition of a step which her conscience, or the conscience of another, required her to take" (456), and even more emphatically in the Post Script where Kenyon surmises that Miriam arranged "for that sad frolic of the Carnival" (466). We could grant with Millington that "it is strongly hinted that Hilda's release from her imprisonment is bought with Donatello's internment" (*Practicing*, 187) but only if we add that it is Miriam, not Hilda, who handles the trading. That Miriam is seen to extend "her hands with a gesture of benediction" (461) in chapter 50 adds to the impression that she condones her friends' rejection of their former bond. The situation is somewhat reminiscent of how Georgiana in "The Birth-mark" is seen to admonish her husband *not* to repent having caused her dying, because she recognizes the religious impulse behind his endeavour. In this instance, however, it is the artist, Miriam, who is seen to bestow her blessing on the object of her creation rather than the other way around as is the case in "The Birth-mark." In a sense, Miriam is even more successful than is Aylmer, for she is able to achieve her desired object of creating an entity of absolute purity by maintaining a rigorous dichotomization between her historical experience on the one hand and her aesthetical desire on the other, that is, between the guilt she shares with Donatello, and the purity she takes steps to ensure that Hilda can retain: it is hardly a coincidence that there is not so much as one word spoken between Hilda and Donatello in the entire romance. But Miriam brings her aesthetical desire to a successful close only to find that she has sacrificed her love for the sake of the purity of an object which now repels her.

*The Marble Faun* thus suggests that the artist's desire to acknowledge the beauty of an idealistic conception of life such as Hilda's, threatens to make the artist complicit in the repression of passions that she meant her art to rebel against. In Miriam's case, this is equivalent to consenting to seeing her lover imprisoned for life—if not executed, which would seem a likely punishment for someone who had killed a Roman official in the mid-nineteenth century. That this was clearly perceived as a possibility by some of his earliest readers is shown by a letter to Hawthorne from his English friend Henry Bright, in which he complains that he wanted to know "a hundred things you do not tell me," among them being "whether Donatello got his head cut off."[42] On the opposite scale, another friend of Hawthorne's—John Lathrop Motley—found nothing to complain about Hawthorne's way of handling the story, and concluded by stating that "to those who complain, I suppose nothing less than an illustrated edition, with a large gallows on the last page, with Donatello in the most pensile of attitudes,—his ears revealed at last thro' a white night-cap,—would be satisfactory" (18: 258). Hawthorne replied by addressing Motley as "that Gentle Reader for whom all my books were exclusively written," and continued: "you take the book exactly as I meant it;" "You work out my imperfect efforts, and half make the book with your own imagination, and see what I myself saw, but could only hint at" (18: 256). Indeed, if we stay sensitive to Hawthorne's allegorical procedure in *The Marble Faun*, we ought not require the evidence of a literal execution to conclude that Donatello, at the end, dies. The English Post Script suppresses this circumstance, but it is indicated by Kenyon's words in the Conclusion of the American edition of the romance:

> "The Castle of Saint Angelo," said Kenyon sadly, turning his face towards that sepulchral fortress, "is no longer a prison; but there are others which have dungeons as deep and in one of them, I fear, lies our poor Faun."

Hawthorne is careful not to reveal the exact location of Donatello's confinement, yet both the reference to the Castle of Saint Angelo itself and the description of it as "sepulchral" are highly revealing. For one thing, it suggests that here, as elsewhere in Hawthorne's writings, the idea of imprisonment is all but interchangeable with that of death; just think of the way the opening chapter of *The Scarlet Letter* juxtaposes cemetery and prison, or how Clifford comes back from prison as something of a ghost in *The House of the Seven Gables*. Whether or not Donatello is actually executed, then, his confinement unquestionably consigns him to the rank of the no longer living.

Even more importantly, a passage in *The French and Italian Notebooks* which records Hawthorne's recollection of a visit to the Castle of Saint Angelo (14: 141–44) makes evident that he was well aware of its history. Originally the tomb of the Emperor Hadrian, the castle was subsequently turned into a prison; at the time Hawthorne wrote *The Marble Faun*, it functioned as a garrison for the French troops that occupied Rome. Donatello is thus consigned—if only by association—to the tomb of the person who was indirectly responsible for the death of Antinous, who as we recall from the first section of this chapter, in an allegorical sense is Donatello's ideal counterpart. In other words, as the narrative ends Donatello has come to occupy a position uncannily evocative of that held by the Model at the beginning of the romance, as that of a spectre of the catacombs. What is more, one of the rooms Hawthorne was shown in the castle was the prison cell "where Beatrice Cenci was confined before her execution" (14: 143). Crowning this building made up of a Roman tomb and a medieval fortress, is a statue of the Archangel Michael. *The Marble Faun* itself directs us to this circumstance, just after Hilda has unburdened herself of her secret under "the seal of the Confessional" (360), a vital step in her own transfiguration into an angel:

> She continually brought to Kenyon's mind the image of a child, making its plaything of every object, but sporting in good faith, and with a kind of seriousness. Looking up, for example, at the statue of Saint Michael, on the top of Hadrian's castellated tomb, Hilda fancied an interview between the Archangel and the old Emperour's ghost, who was naturally displeased at finding his mausoleum, which he had ordained for the stately and solemn repose of his ashes, converted to its present purposes.
>
> "But Saint Michael, no doubt," she thoughtfully remarked, "would finally convince the Emperour Hadrian, that where a warlike despot is sown as the seed, a fortress and a prison are the only possible crop!" (370)

By associating Donatello's imprisonment with the Castle of Saint Angelo, Hawthorne thus brings together the three leading objects of art that the narrative has been concerned with: the Faun, Beatrice, and the Archangel. Allegorically speaking, the Faun is executed in Beatrice's place, for the aesthetical view of Beatrice can win pre-eminence only if her history is suppressed; and this can come about only if the romance can be suffered to take history's place. For Beatrice to become angelic, the Faun must become human: the romance must act out the consequences of reality's suppression of history. The short reference to the Castle of Saint Angelo in the Conclusion thus alerts us to the repressive implications of the symbolistic strategy which Kenyon and Hilda have chosen to subscribe to: by raising Saint Hilda to the level of an earthly Angel, they have effectively constructed a fortress which serves to incarcerate the romance of Miriam and Donatello. But the Faun is not the only one who suffers: Hilda, as a human rather than angelic Beatrice, is imprisoned along with him in the tomb of Hadrian, in the tomb of the despotic Father, and set to guard over these prisoners is Kenyon's conception of Hilda as Angel, denying any share in the guilt of the prisoners she keeps.

It is not, of course, guilt in general that Kenyon's "Saint Hilda" (364) denies; it is the specific conception of guilt as a mediating agency of God's will which is conceptualized in the formula of the Fortunate Fall that she rejects, as does Kenyon with her. As we saw in our discussion of Donatello's transformation from art into life, Miriam suggests to Kenyon that their entire story might be a re-enactment of this Ur-story. When the sculptor repeats this suggestion to Hilda, she claims "with an expression of horrour" that he has "shocked me beyond words!" (460). This is of special interest to our investigation, as we saw in our discussion of Hawthorne's relation to allegory in chapter two that it is by means of an allegorical conception of the Fortunate Fall that Milton mends the rupture between God and mankind in *Paradise Lost* (see pp. 92–102 above).

Disobedience, Milton's poem would seem to be saying, is good, not in itself, but by implicitly paying tribute to the benevolence of the power that can allow it because it knows itself to be sufficiently powerful to inflict just punishment on the transgressor. While the poem depicts how the symbolic union of God and Man in Paradise is broken, it also shows that the union can nevertheless be allegorically reinstated through the mediation of Christ, with the additional benefit that Man is now in a position better to *understand* God's supreme goodness. What has been irrevocably lost through the Fall, however, is the immediacy that characterized the original relation between God and Man, as well as between Adam and Eve, in Paradise. Prior to the Fall, sexuality is an aspect of a greater whole, rather than a part which can be pursued for its own end. Postlapsarian sex, in contrast, is devoid of that "adoration pure/ that

God likes best" (*Paradise Lost*, IV: 737–38) which is characteristic of their original love-making. It is thus an implicit premise of the notion of the Fortunate Fall that the consummation of the union of man and woman in sexual love can shadow forth the reunion of temporal and divine existence only if it draws attention to its own inadequacy to repeat the "adoration pure" that was an inherent trait of sexual activities in Paradise. The guilt which Hawthorne associates with the sexual union of man and woman is therefore in truth a prerequisite for turning marriage into a type of the greater union between man and God which is to come, for it is this sense of guilt which suggests the distance between temporal and divine existence.

Such are the implications of the allegorical view of life Hilda and Kenyon reject. Without ever openly questioning the authority of the American couple, Hawthorne nevertheless subtly undermines their position. We have seen in section 3 above how the identities of Hilda and the Archangel can be seen to merge with each other in the romance. With this we have reached a point from which the paradox of *The Marble Faun* may finally be understood. Hilda is unquestionably the model Gentle Reader of the romance, yet as the fiercest opponent of the concept of the Fortunate Fall, she is also ultimately responsible for expelling Miriam and Donatello from the ideal realm of perfection that she and Kenyon create for themselves. Like the Archangel Michael, then, Hilda is the one who drives "remorseful Man and Woman, linked by a marriage-bond of crime" (435) out of Paradise. But while Michael is the angel who expels Adam and Eve from Paradise, he is also the one who informs Adam of the future coming of Christ, and it is upon receiving this information that Adam sets out the formula of the Fortunate Fall:

> O goodness infinite, goodness immense!
> That all this good of evil shall produce,
> And evil turn to good; more wonderful
> Then that which by creation first brought forth
> Light out of darkness! Full of doubt I stand,
> Whether I should repent me now of sin
> By me done and occasioned, or rejoice
> Much more, that much more good thereof shall spring,
> To God more glory, more good will to Men
> From God, and over wrath grace shall abound. (*PL* XII: 469–78)

The Archangel is thus indirectly responsible for the very notion of the Fortunate Fall; and the same is true of Hilda. No matter how ardently she rejects the idea that "Sin [...] like Sorrow" may be "merely an element of human education, through which we struggle to a higher and purer state than we could otherwise have attained" (460), she is herself in the process of becoming a concrete illustration of this formula. To see this, it will be necessary to look beyond the scope of the narrative of *The Marble Faun* as such, into the American future of Hilda and Kenyon which it typologically suggests. We turn now, then, to the notion of history suggested by the romance.

## 5. Appropriating Art

Considering how well the implied historical movement of *The Marble Faun*—from a mythical Etruscan period, over antiquity, to Christianity—would seem to fit a typological conception of history, it is hardly surprising that a number of critics have read the romance in terms prefiguring Bercovitch's reading of *The Scarlet Letter*. Sidney P. Moss, for instance, argues that "Donatello's metamorphoses from an innocent faun, to a guilt-ridden human being, to a man with the possibility of redemption by the exercise of moral will, incarnate the three periods of Italy's progress and, on a still larger scale perhaps, the progress of Western man."[43] I am not disputing the typological overtones Moss identifies in *The Marble Faun* per se; what I am questioning is simply that the presence of a typological pattern necessarily entails a progressive conception of history. As I have argued throughout this study, it seems to me, rather, that Hawthorne conceives of the typological pattern as something that is confined to the span of an individual life, and hence as something that must constantly be re-enacted.

While the images of the menorah and the Etruscan bracelet that we have expounded above are obviously interconnected through their emphasis on the number seven, they just as obviously make up a contrasting pair, the one emphasizing "the intense white light of truth" invoked by Hilda, and the other characterized by the sad "mystery" of "a sevenfold sepulchral gloom" (462) associated with Miriam. The contrasting qualities associated with each respective image—light, illumination and radiance in the case of the menorah, "a sevenfold sepulchral gloom" in that of the bracelet—echo the dichotomy between America and Europe that is introduced already in the Preface, where the Author asserts that:

> Italy, as the site of his Romance, was chiefly valuable to him as affording a sort of poetic or fairy precinct, where actualities would not be so terribly insisted upon, as they are, and must needs be, in America. No author, without a trial, can conceive of the difficulty of writing a Romance about a country where there is no shadow, no antiquity, no mystery, no picturesque and gloomy wrong, nor anything but a common-place prosperity, in broad and simple day-light, as is happily the case with my dear native land. (3)

What America lacks, in other words, is the spirit of Romance, which is subtly equated with history; and history is something the setting of Rome provides with a vengeance. History is thus what Hilda and Kenyon are confronted with in *The Marble Faun*, in the form of antique sculptures and other works of art, of course, but also—and just as significantly—in the form of their relationship to two people standing in a personal and painful relation to the past. Yet history to the Americans is a purely aesthetical experience; it holds no practical consequences for them. Hilda, it is true, submerges herself into the supposedly historical world of art, but she refuses to suffer the painful experience that world was meant to serve as an expression for in the first place. As is frequently suggested in the book, art to Hilda is invested with a religious aspect. Inversely, religion—or more specifically, Roman-Catholicism—is valuable to Hilda primarily as an aesthetic experience, as a cathartic device allowing relief without any personal pain. While making use of the view of truth proffered by Roman-Catholicism to bring relief to her own tortured conscience, Hilda all the same refuses to make this view her own. Instead she shoves her guilt on to the Father taking her confession by claiming that *he* "will perpetrate a great wrong, both as a priest and a man" (361) if he furthers what she has told him. By spuriously acting out the ritualized convention of an innocent child confessing her misbehaviour to a forgiving parent, Hilda is able to transfer her guilt upon a representative of a culture that she has already rejected: she denies the communal value system which is a prerequisite for an allegorical conception of life, and chooses instead to appropriate it as a vehicle through which she can symbolically purge herself of her own private feelings of guilt. Much like the tourists "who have established a peaceful usurpation over whatever is enjoyable or memorable in the Eternal City" (99), Hilda appropriates the Roman-Catholic creed by transforming it into a subjective outlet for her own overpowering sense of guilt; she is like the tourist who "fully appreciates the enjoyment, and feels nothing of the cost" of "the rule of an irresponsible dynasty of Holy Fathers" (100).

By thus rejecting any personal responsibility for the fate of Miriam and Donatello (handing it over to a cultural system of norms that she perceives as belonging to an earlier, more primitive era) she in effect rejects her association with the past, with history. And as history is a precondition for temporality, and temporality in turn for humanity, Hilda necessarily becomes inhuman: an angel, or rather, the statue of an angel. When the book ends, her rejection of history has placed her in the position held by Donatello when the book began: as the living embodiment of a work of art. This denial of history takes place in a setting in which mothers and fathers are repeatedly invoked—in the form of paternal statues from antiquity, as well as through the Roman-Catholic idolatry of the Virgin Mary (to which Hilda, significantly, subscribes)—to the effect that "Hilda's defense against guilt," as Millington states, "places her in the confining safety of psychological childhood" (*Practicing*, 183).[44] Thus we find her in the very first paragraph of the first chapter of the novel, where the story ends and begins again, petrified into "the pretty figure of a child, clasping *a dove* to her bosom, but assaulted by a snake" (5; my emphasis).

One might perhaps object that Hilda is placed less in a *psycho*logical than a *typo*logical state of childhood. It is, after all, as the petrified embodiment of Innocence that she returns with Kenyon to America. It is therefore crucial that we do not reduce Hilda—or any of the other characters that people *The Marble Faun*—to a representation of a person, but recognize her as the allegorical embodiment of an abstract idea. Some readers have wanted to see Hilda's descent from her tower as evidence of her having acquired the sin Miriam claims Hilda needs to be softened. I have argued, in contrast, that as the romance draws towards a close Hilda takes on the aspect of a marble woman, and that when it comes to an end she allegorically enacts the role of the Archangel. From this perspective, Hilda can hardly be said to have softened, nor can she be said to have sinned—yet.

We must keep in mind, however, that the angelic conception of Hilda derives almost entirely from Kenyon; the romance as such can hardly be said to privilege his view. When Hilda reappears in the Carnival, she attracts his attention by flinging him "a single rosebud, so fresh that it seemed that moment gathered" (451), and this custom, we are informed at an earlier stage of the scene, for the lover betokens "the first sweet intimation that his passionate glances had not struck against a heart of marble" (440). When the pair sets off for America, in other words, Hilda is much more alive than Kenyon perhaps had reckoned with. When Miriam parts with Hilda in chapter 23, it is made clear that Miriam senses that Kenyon will be an unfit companion for her friend, and that his love for Hilda will not survive the revelation that there is a crack in her seemingly perfect innocence. Hilda cannot confide in Kenyon, she tells Miriam, because she has "fancied that he sought to be something more" (211) than her friend. We may mistake this for a statement implying that Hilda is attracted to Kenyon and is afraid to scare him off, but the very opposite would seem to be the case. She cannot reveal her secret to him, because to confide such a secret to a person—as Miriam's proposal to reveal her secret to Kenyon shows (cf. pp. 352–53 above)—is tantamount to opening an intimate relation with that person. If she tells him, in other words, she must be ready to love him. Yet Hilda, Miriam tells her "with a strange smile," need not fear to tell Kenyon her secret, because her confession "will frighten his new-born love out of its little life, if that be what you wish" (212). As the narrative proceeds, however, it becomes clear that this is not what Hilda wishes: at one point, at least, Hilda pines for his presence, and is ready to confide her "terrible secret" (343) in him, just as Miriam has earlier been on the verge of telling the sculptor the "secret" (128) burning in her heart. While the circumstances prevent Hilda from effecting this desire, Hawthorne takes the opportunity to make plain that Hilda's true secret is precisely that she experiences feelings of desire for Kenyon: "We ought not to betray Hilda's secret; but it is the truth, that being so sad, and so utterly alone, and in such great need of sympathy, her thoughts sometimes recurred to the sculptor. Had she met him now, her heart, indeed, might not have been won, but her confidence would have flown to him like a bird to its nest" (342). Finding the means to absolve herself from her secret in the confession without the aid of Kenyon, Hilda can appear to him "softened out of the chillness of her virgin pride" (370), and impress him as a "bright, yet softened image of religious consolation," displaying a "capability of transfiguration" which "suggests how angels come by their beauty" (364), continually bringing to his mind "the image of a child" (370). The perspicacious reader, however, may note that Hawthorne prefixes the confessional scene with a short description of Guercino's *Burial and Reception in Heaven of St. Petronilla*, which suggests that Hilda's confession is in truth a form of suicide, in that it effects a separation of the body from the soul:

> Next to the shrine where she had knelt, there is another, adorned with a picture by Guercino, representing a maiden's body in the jaws of the sepulchre, and her lover weeping over it; while her beatified spirit looks down upon the scene, in the society of the Saviour, and a throng of Saints. Hilda wondered if it were not possible, by some miracle of faith, so to rise above her present despondency that she might look down upon what she was, just as Petronilla in the picture looked at her own corpse. A hope, born of hysteric trouble, fluttered in her heart. A presentiment, or what she fancied such, whispered her, that, before she had finished the circuit of the Cathedral, relief would come. (352–53)

Nevertheless, shortly after the confession, Hilda shows herself able to appreciate Kenyon's statue of the fiery Cleopatra as intensely as did Miriam. "I am ashamed to tell you how much I admire this statue," she tells her sculpting friend. For Kenyon, on the other hand, the statue has lost its power to engage him, and he tells Hilda that he "should like to hit poor Cleopatra a bitter blow on her Egyptian nose, with this mallet!" Hilda replies facetiously, yet her words take on uncanny connotations when we remember that she herself becomes something of a marble woman for Kenyon in the final chapters of the romance: "That is a blow that all statues seem doomed to receive, sooner or later, *though seldom from the hand that sculptured them*" (378; my emphasis). It is in Kenyon's eyes that Hilda takes on the angelic properties appropriate for someone who is well acquainted with the "sacred character" (136) that the narrator imputes to marble. Like Chillingworth before him, then, Kenyon is a person who imposes "the marble image of happiness" upon his beloved "as the warm reality" (SL, 177); but as we have seen above, Hilda insists that she owns none of the qualities the sculptor ascribes to her. Kenyon too, then, has reason to "tremble to win the hand of woman," for it is clear that he no more than Roger Chillingworth has won "the utmost passion of her heart" (SL, 176). How could he, when the passion of her heart comprises the one thing he obviously is not prepared to take in: pain? Donatello, we saw, treasures the "pain in [his] heart" because Miriam "is in the midst of it," and Miriam, too, testifies to bearing "a secret in my heart that burns me" (128), which she nevertheless treasures as a "carbuncle" and a "gem" (130). Kenyon, in contrast, regards the possibility of sharing the secrets of Hilda an "impiety" (365).

Hilda, then, is a rosebud bound to bloom, but as was the case with Hester Prynne, it seems highly unlikely that she will flourish with her husband. The statue of Innocence that Kenyon brings to America is destined to go through the same process of transformation that Donatello suffers in Italy. This brings *The Marble Faun* right into the historical present in which it was published, a present marked with impending signs of civil war. For when the statue of Innocence imported to America cracks upon discovering passion, revolutionary fervour will inevitably follow, at least unless it is met by a sympathy unafraid to acknowledge pain. Indeed, *The Scarlet Letter* has already shown us what must happen if the idea of Innocence sheds its inexperience only to find that its newly found insight into the contradictions of human experience is rejected by the society that surrounds it. "Much of the marble coldness of Hester's impression," Hawthorne writes, "was to be attributed to the circumstance that her life had turned, in a great measure, from passion and feeling, to thought." With no sympathy to restrain her, she imbibes the spirit of revolution:

> The world's law was no law for her mind. It was an age in which the human intellect, newly emancipated, had taken a more active and a wider range than for many centuries before. Men of the sword had overthrown nobles and kings. Men bolder than these had overthrown and rearranged—not actually, but within the sphere of theory, which was their most real abode—the whole system of ancient prejudice, wherewith was linked much of ancient principle. Hester Prynne imbibed this spirit. She assumed a freedom of speculation, then common enough on the other side of the Atlantic, but which our forefathers, had they known of it, would have held to be a deadlier crime than that stigmatized by the scarlet letter. In her lonesome cottage,

> by the sea-shore, thoughts visited her, such as dared to enter no other dwelling in New England; shadowy guests, that would have been as perilous as demons to their entertainer, could they have been seen so much as knocking at her door. (SL, 164)

But just as the outcome of Hester's revolutionary sentiments ultimately are seen to be determined by the reaction of Dimmesdale, whose flagging spirits they help revive, the outcome of the scenario typologically suggested by *The Marble Faun* depends upon how its readers—especially its American readers—respond to the discovery that Innocence has a passionate heart, a heart which is liable to bring Guilt into the world all over again. More emphatically than any of the other romances, *The Marble Faun* is inaugurated by an invocation of the Gentle Reader, "that one congenial friend—more comprehensive of his purposes, more appreciative of his success, more indulgent of his shortcomings, and, in all respects, closer and kinder than a brother—that all-sympathizing critic, in short, whom an author never actually meets, but to whom he implicitly makes his appeal, whenever he is conscious of having done his best" (1). Yet having delivered this outline of his ideal reader, Hawthorne proceeds by declaring that he has little faith in finding such a reader for the present work:

> But is he extant now? In these many years, since he last heard from me, may he not have deemed his earthly task accomplished, and have withdrawn to the Paradise of Gentle Readers, wherever it may be, to the enjoyments of which his kindly charity, on my behalf, must surely have entitled him? I have a sad foreboding that this may be the truth. The Gentle Reader, in the case of any individual author, is apt to be extremely short-lived; he seldom outlasts a literary fashion, and, except in very rare instances, closes his weary eyes before the writer has half done with him. If I find him at all, it will probably be under some mossy grave-stone, inscribed with a half-obliterated name, which I shall never recognize. (2)

This is no feigned anxiety, nor is it a veiled expression of self-importance: it is indicative, rather, of Hawthorne's undiminished concern for his culture and society, a society which had not proven responsive to the redemptive allegorical dialectics that his romances are designed to make available to us. In taking recourse to the past, *The Scarlet Letter* had provided Hawthorne's contemporary readers with a vision of a dialectical course of action which America could follow. *The Marble Faun*, in contrast, would seem to represent Hawthorne's conception ten years later of the course America actually chose. Denying, like Hilda, its blood relation to its European sister-country, America had been able to retain the appearance of "a country where there is no shadow, no antiquity, no mystery, no picturesque and gloomy wrong, nor anything but a commonplace prosperity, in broad and simple daylight," as Hawthorne claims in the Preface to be "happily the case with my dear native land" (3); but this denial had also landed America in a position where it was on the verge of repeating the violent history of Old England on its own shores. 1859 found America on the brink of the Civil War, the outbreak of which in 1861—just a year after his final romance was published—finally confirmed that the ideological course of action Hawthorne had promulgated in his romances had failed.[45]

Like Hawthorne's other romances *The Marble Faun* is designed to make available to its readers a conception of life which recognizes history as an insurmountable limit to all human endeavours yet nevertheless finds the means to spiritualize these historical conditions by realizing that they are in fact a precondition for the existence of hope. It should be clear, by the romance's treatment of the theme of the Fortunate Fall, that Kenyon is at fault in expressing the common American view that his is a "fortunate land," in which "each generation has only its own sins and sorrows to bear" (302). The complex role assigned to Hilda makes evident that this is not the case. If *The Marble Faun* is an allegory of the history of Man, Hilda is the very concept of Innocence upon which the New England of the Puritans is founded. And if this *New* England shall have any chance of fulfilling its errand of turning America into the New Jerusalem prophesied by the Bible, its founding principle of Innocence must also be something radically new, an origin wholly unstained by the depravities of the Old World. But as the romance which brings Innocence into America makes plain, the Puritan vision is founded on a dream, a dream which is in fact rooted in the aesthetics of the Old World that the Puritans would reject. Hilda, the ideal of Innocence embodied in a "daughter of the Puritans" (54, 362, 399, 466) is not a reaction against the values of the European past, but a *product* of these very values. Far from being built from a new beginning, the very idea of America is thus seen to derive from the history of fallen man.

*The Marble Faun*, then, depicts yet another instance of the conflict between an allegorical and a symbolistic view of life, the conflict between a view of life that recognizes the pre-eminence of historical values grounded in the community, and an alternative view which strives to transcend these norms by subjecting them to the private emotions of the individual. The Americans reject the lesson of history—or at any rate, the experience of pain provided by history—and in so doing paradoxically perpetuate the historical course of appropriation and repression of which the cultural remnants scattered throughout Rome and *The Marble Faun* provide ample evidence. In this context, the image of the menorah is particularly suggestive. Considering the emphasis laid on Miriam's Jewishness in chapter 5, we may safely assume that it is not by chance that the image of the candlestick is employed, as it is potentially "the most precious relic of past ages, in the estimation of both Jew and Gentile" (159). The image is well-chosen, because as we have seen the story of Hilda may be seen to appropriate the narrative at the expense of Miriam's story, just as Roman Catholicism has appropriated the spoils of Jerusalem by subjecting the images of Judaism to the interpretative authority of Christianity.

The menorah was seized from the Jews and brought to Rome as part of the spoils of Jerusalem; in Rome it was converted into an image of Christianity by the Roman-Catholic church; and now, finally, Hilda, as a representative of Puritan New England, announces that it will burn with the white light of truth—presumably the Puritan truth, for it is surely no coincidence that the image of the seven-branched candlestick is also a prominent presence in one of the most remarkable theological books to have been produced in the New World, Cotton Mather's Church History of New England, *Magnalia Christi Americana*, which, as it happens, is composed in seven books. "Since the candlestick is," as one critic puts it, "a type of holy truth, its 'recovery' in America marks the completion of a stage in the history of redemption: the shadowy light of an Old Testament / Old World type will blaze with a new radiance in its New World antitype."[46] Yet by one of those wonderfully subtle ironies that Hawthorne excels in, "the intense white light of Truth" (371) that Hilda expects to perceive upon lighting the candles of the seven-branched candlestick is in fact made up of the "sevenfold sepulchral gloom" (462) of the bracelet, for as we saw in the previous section, the bracelet sequence which retells the story of the Fortunate Fall is to be found in the very lights of the menorah. To put it most succinctly, the menorah is indicative of symbolistic appropriation, while the circular form of the bracelet suggests that the primacy of allegory will nevertheless reassert itself: that it is expressly presented as an *Etruscan* artefact suggests that Miriam's habit of using it as a vehicle for her own subjective imagination marks a kind of cultural appropriation very similar to that inherent in the image of the menorah itself. We have, then, a series of appropriations, wherein the imagery of an earlier mode of religion is employed while the original meaning, or value-context, attached to this imagery is explicitly rejected. The image of the menorah thus suggests a recurring pattern, a pattern that enforces that historical change must remain illusory as long as we insist on trying to escape the strictures of an allegorical conception of life by reverting to symbolism. By means of a symbolistic strategy, all that can change is the positions of the individual participants of the historical process, while the relations between these participants (the system itself, that is) must remain virtually unchanged through time.[47]

*The Marble Faun*, we have seen, envisions a role for the artist more painful and less rewarding than that which is allowed Hester in *The Scarlet Letter*, in that it is a role which is *not* recognized by society. By rejecting the notion of art as an allegorical medium communicating the norms of a community, choosing instead to flaunt a conception of art as a symbolistic vehicle privileging the individual's private emotions, the Americans of *The Marble Faun* reject the historical lesson of allegorical art. Under such circumstances, the only requital for the artist must be the faith that one day there might indeed be a Gentle Reader to lift the menorah of art appropriated by society, and discover in the light it dispenses the allegorical means by which a sense of fullness is achieved by the recognition, rather than the repression, of the lack inherent in all human endeavours. In the final section of this chapter, I shall outline the aesthetical properties of these allegorical means.

## 6. The Aesthetics of Revolution

If we accept the analysis of the symmetrical conception of *The Marble Faun* outlined in the previous sections as an accurate account of its structure, then—someone may reasonably argue—must we not also grant that the received view of the romance as a failure is correct, the structure being so exceedingly complex that no one has hitherto detected it? Does not the above account merely go to show that Hawthorne tried to accomplish too much in *The Marble Faun*, and that the final result, as the general critical opinion has always maintained, is a failure? I think not, and I think this position can be defended by invoking the introduction to chapter 50, in which Hawthorne addresses the reader:

> THE GENTLE READER, we trust, would not thank us for one of those minute elucidations, which are so tedious, and, after all, so unsatisfactory, in clearing up the romantic mysteries of a story. He is too wise to insist upon looking closely at the wrong side of the tapestry, after the right one has been sufficiently displayed to him, woven with the best of the artist's skill, and cunningly arranged with a view to the harmonious exhibition of its colours. If any brilliant or beautiful, or even tolerable, effect have been produced, this pattern of kindly Readers will accept it at its worth, without tearing the web apart, with the idle purpose of discovering how its threads have been knit together; for the sagacity, by which he is distinguished, will long ago have taught him that any narrative of human action and adventure—whether we call it history or romance—is certain to be a fragile handiwork, more easily rent than mended. The actual experience of even the most ordinary life is full of events that never explain themselves, either as regards their origin or their tendency. (455)

Many readers have found this evasive stance provocative. It would appear that the narrator is simply shying away from what ought to be his occupation: to tell the story properly. When Anthony Trollope stated his view of the matter in an article of 1879, he voiced a verdict which has remained the general consensus for the major part of the twentieth century as well:

> His readers will hardly be so gentle as not to require from him some explanation of the causes which have produced the romantic details to which they have given their attention, and will be inclined to say that it should have been the author's business to give an explanation neither tedious nor unsatisfactory. The critic is disposed to think

> that Hawthorne, as he continued his narrative, postponed his plot till it was too late, and then escaped from his difficulty by the ingenious excuse above given.[48]

Perhaps this excuse would have appeared less unsatisfactory, had Hawthorne not gone on to imply that he is indeed in possession of the information the reader demands, but has chosen to suppress it: "It would be easy, from conversations which we have held with the sculptor, to suggest a clue to the mystery of Hilda's disappearance" (455); 'I know', he has the text saying, 'but I will not tell *you*.' It is no wonder, then, that this reluctance on the part of the author to reveal information he constantly implies he is in possession of has been construed as a symptom of an inability to handle the narrative material properly. Hawthorne's own response to the complaints about the plot of *The Marble Faun* suggests he saw matters differently. "As for what you say of the plot," he wrote to his English friend Henry Bright, "I do not agree that it has been left in an imperfect state. The characters of the story come out of an obscurity and vanish into it again, like the figures on the slide of a magic-lantern; but, in their transit, they have served my purpose, and shown all that it was essential for them to reveal. Anything further, if you consider it rightly, would be an impertinence on the author's part towards his reader" (18: 259). If Hawthorne refuses to tell us what he knows, then, it is because he has made it his business to *show* us the relevant clues: the structure of the romance is supposed to affect us much as the pattern of a tapestry of intricate design, creating an impression of symmetry too complex for us to care to unravel it in detail. Again, then, we are asked to approach the narrative as an allegorical veil, the function of which is to suggest its deeper purport while being careful not to expose its secrets without the sympathetic aid of the reader's imagination.

*The Marble Faun*, like Hawthorne's other romances, is in this sense an intensely religious work of art: it calls for a view which invests art with the redemptive power of religion:

> A picture, however admirable the painter's art, and wonderful his power, requires of the spectator a surrender of himself, in due proportion with the miracle which has been wrought. Let the canvas glow as it may, you must look with the eye of faith, or its highest excellence escapes you. There is always the necessity of helping out the painter's art with your own resources of sensibility and imagination. Not that these qualities shall really add anything to what the Master has effected; but they must be

> put so entirely under his controul, and work along with him to such an extent, that, in a different mood, (when you are cold and critical, instead of sympathetic,) you will be apt to fancy that the loftier merits of the picture were of your own dreaming, not of his creating. (335)

*The Marble Faun* is designed to invoke precisely such a reaction. The identical titles of chapters 1 and 50 invite us to look for some kind of symmetrical pattern, and as the symmetrical principle extends to the scenes and not just the chapters of the first and last branch of the scheme of the menorah, fanciful readers like myself may well imagine that they are tracing something of the kind, but are liable to conclude—after many hours of toilsome efforts—that perhaps they were mistaken after all. Need I say that I am talking out of my own experience? Having sensed that there was some kind of contrapuntal symmetry at work, and that the seemingly inexplicable introduction of the bracelet upon the last page of the romance had to be of great significance, I laboured more than two years with trying to come up with a convincing account of the structure of this verbal sculpture, and was on the point of giving up my initial hunch altogether when I suddenly found I had been deluded by my conviction that chapters 1 and 50, being identically denominated, must also be symmetrically linked: thus the very trait of the text that suggested the symmetrical arrangement to me was also what kept me from grasping how it was conceived.

Though culled from my personal experience, I think this example is of some significance. We have seen in the previous sections how the apparently haphazard movements of the narrative discourse of *The Marble Faun* holds a verbal sculpture of great complexity. But this structure is perceivable only when the text is viewed through a retrospective perception of its spatial form. Upon our immediate impression *The Marble Faun* will seem vague, flawed, imperfect. As Auerbach points out—and as at least one of his contemporary readers realized—the author refrains from completing the text: "Hawthorne [...] depends upon the reader to complete the form, the plot of the novel, by acting out the author's suggestions."[49] It is left in a half-finished state, much like the bust of Donatello, which Kenyon on the advice of Hilda refrains from finishing. But it is left in this fragmentary state for a purpose, not in order to flaunt ambiguity itself as some commentators would have us believe, but on the contrary as a means to establish a specific meaning. It is the ultimate example of an aesthetics of fragmentation which is repeatedly alluded to in the romance itself. *The Marble Faun*, too, is a sculpture of sorts, and as such it cannot escape becoming entangled in the complexities of art and history it delineates. Hawthorne is painfully aware of this, and he strives to make the reader equally aware of it. Indeed, as Pearce has shown, this is a fundamental concern of his: to make the reader aware of his involvement with the events of the story, to establish a direct relationship between the historical realm of the reader and the fictitious sphere of the narrative (see chapter one). This concluding section is devoted to stalking out not only by what means Hawthorne achieves this relationship in *The Marble Faun*, but also why it is of such fundamental importance for Hawthorne to do so.

*

Two notions are central to the conception of aesthetic perception in *The Marble Faun*. First, that the greatest instances of art—which are equivalent to those that are most true—are as likely to be the result of chance as of intentional creative acts. And second, that any object of art is dependent upon the idealizing capabilities of its perceiver in order to display the full beauty inherent in it. Both these notions are brought to the fore in the short section of the text in which the origin of the romance is alluded to. The scene is that of Kenyon's studio, after he has been reunited with Hilda in Rome. Upon her praise of his statue of Cleopatra, he complains that he now finds it "a mere lump of senseless stone, into which I have not really succeeded in moulding the spiritual part of my idea" (378). Hilda recognizes the dilemma, yet insists that "there is a class of spectators whose sympathy will help them to see the Perfect, through a mist of imperfection. Nobody, I think, ought to read poetry, or look at pictures or statues, who cannot find a great deal more in them than the poet or artist has actually expressed. Their highest merit is suggestiveness" (379).

Kenyon then shows her a bust of Donatello, "not nearly finished" (379), which all the same bears a marked resemblance to Donatello, an effect Hilda puts down to "the chance-result of the bust being just so far shaped out, in the marble, as the process of moral growth had advanced, in the original" (380–81). Kenyon agrees, and decides to leave it thus:

> And, accordingly, Donatello's bust [...] has ever since remained in an unfinished state. Most spectators mistake it for an unsuccessful attempt towards copying the features of the Faun of Praxiteles. One observer in a thousand is conscious of something more, and lingers long over this mysterious face, departing from it, reluctantly, and with many a glance thrown backward. What perplexes him is the riddle that he sees propounded there; the riddle of the Soul's growth, taking its first impulse amid remorse and pain, and struggling through the incrustations of the senses. It was the contemplation of this imperfect portrait of Donatello that originally interested us in his history, and impelled us to elicit from Kenyon what he knew of his friend's adventures. (381)

The passage from which the above quotes have been clipped is not the only one that reads like a veiled allusion to the text itself—the pages of *The Marble Faun* are littered with them—but it is unique in explicitly pointing out the link to the story itself. Indeed, it ought to be quite sufficient to make us see the reason for the somewhat half-baked external appearance of the novel. The story originates from the contemplation of an "imperfect portrait of Donatello;" yet this imperfection is in truth imperative for its success. It is the very fact that it is to be found "in an unfinished state" that enables the bust to propound "the riddle of the Soul's growth." As Hilda claims: "A few more strokes of the chisel might change the whole expression, and so spoil it for what it is now worth" (381).

Imperfection, then, is seen to be a prerequisite for perfection. What may seem at first almost a logical contradiction turns out after some contemplation to be merely an outcome of the aesthetic approach to life that Hilda embodies (and, it should not be forgotten, which the text itself embraces). Perfected, in the everyday sense of the word, Donatello's bust would depict his outward form; it would present a realistic representation of his features. But to Hilda, as to Kenyon (and to Hawthorne himself), the outward form of reality is of very subordinate interest, compared to the Ideas contained within it. Their concern is for an idealized version of reality—not because they wish only to see what is beautiful, but because they refuse to accept the appearance of the world as its truth. It is important to remember that they are not refusing to accept the world as it is, in order to cling to a conception of the world *as it should be*; on the contrary, they refuse to embrace as a truth the way the world appears to be, in order to arrive at an understanding of the world *as it is*. Reality is in itself but the outward form of a world of Ideas, and thus necessarily must be transgressed if this latter world is to be adequately depicted.[50]

This does not mean that Hawthorne's text can be reduced to Platonic platitudes. The world of Ideas is not a higher level of reality, but simply a different aspect of it; and it is more true than the former, simply because it will allow as meaningful (not to mention observable) motifs such diverse phenomena as "the Human Soul, with its choice of Innocence and Evil" (5), "Womanhood [...] without prejudice to its divinity" (424), or "the riddle of the Soul's growth". In short, the world of Ideas is the aspect of reality under which abstract notions may be looked upon as substantial, and therefore undeniable, elements of the world: it is the phenomenal world, not of the senses, but of the mind.

It does mean, however, that to arrive at a truthful representation of the Idea, *the form enclosing this Idea must in some sense be misrepresented.* The materials of art—colours, shapes, sounds etc.—themselves pertain to that reality which encloses the world of Ideas, and consequently cannot portray the Ideas themselves; but they may be employed so as to make the finished work of art suggest the Ideas hidden in the form. *In* the form, not *by* the form; for much as this outer form is responsible for veiling its inner meaning, it nevertheless remains the sole medium through which this meaning is accessible. As we saw in chapter five, this is what Coverdale hesitated to affirm in *The Blithedale Romance*; Kenyon's decision to worship a woman who makes the idea of Love available without the mediation of an imperfect form (her sexual corporeality), presents an example of how this idea is entirely negated. This is why imperfect objects of art, such as a painter's sketches, are said to "make the spectator more vividly sensible of a great painter's power, than the final glow and perfected art of the most consummate picture that may have been elaborated from them" (138)—they constitute attempts to portray Ideas, less refined than the finished paintings; as a consequence, their concern for realistic detail is less pronounced, which is why they are likely to convey a richer sense of the world of Ideas, despite their stark outline:

> There is an effluence of divinity in the first sketch; and there, if anywhere, you find the pure light of inspiration, which the subsequent toil of the artist serves to bring out in stronger lustre, indeed, but likewise adulterates it with what belongs to an inferiour mood. [...] The charm lay partly in their very imperfection; for this is suggestive, and sets the imagination at work; whereas, the finished picture, if a good one, leaves

> the spectator nothing to do, and, if bad, confuses, stupefies, disenchants, and disheartens him. (138)

This also explains why the artists' best work is all seen to be achieved when they work from reminiscences—this way of working enforces that reality is transformed through the medium of the imagination before it can be represented.

We are afforded an excellent example of this in chapter 25. It is somewhat perplexing, to find so close to the heart of the romance that might very well be the darkest one Hawthorne completed a chapter entitled "Sunshine." It would seem to indicate a spot of happiness amid all the gloom, sufficient, perhaps, to compensate for everything else. Yet close examination of the chapter contradicts such interpretations. The Sunshine, we find, is a wine, of remarkable characteristics:

> Sipping, the guest longed to sip again; but the wine demanded so deliberate a pause, in order to detect the hidden peculiarities and subtile exquisiteness of its flavour, that to drink it was really more a moral than a physical enjoyment. There was a deliciousness in it that eluded analysis, and—like whatever else is superlatively good—*was perhaps better appreciated in the memory than by present consciousness.* One of its most ethereal charms lay in the transitory life of the wine's richest qualities; for, while it required a certain leisure and delay, yet, if you lingered too long upon the draught, it became disenchanted both of its fragrance and its flavour. (223; my emphasis.)

This singular wine is marked by a deliciousness which is better as a recollection than as an actual experience. Its fragrance, Kenyon says on the same page, "is like the airy sweetness of youthful hopes that no realities will ever satisfy!" (223); which suggests that we have here an example of the radical stance of a Holgrave (as drawn in chapter 12 of *The House of the Seven Gables*), distilled and bottled up. Significantly, it is made clear that this is a distillation that is to be enjoyed in momentary sips, which are not promotive of inebriation. A full three pages is dedicated to delineating the nature of this "wine that keeps well in the cellar [...] and gathers fragrance, flavour and brightness, in its dark dungeon" (224–5); and of which it is said that: "When once the flask is uncorked, its finest qualities lose little time in making their escape" (225). These are exceptional traits for a wine, but they call to mind several phrases and comments made in the preceding twenty-four chapters. Indeed, if these are studied it becomes apparent that the elusive qualities of the wine are equivalent to those found in objects of art. Compare, for instance the last sentence of the long quotation above, with the following comment by Hilda in chapter 2: "'Ah, the Faun!' cried Hilda, with a little gesture of impatience. '*I have been looking at him too long; and now, instead of a beautiful statue, immortally young, I see only a corroded and discoloured stone.* This change is very apt to occur in statues'" (17; my emphasis). Time and again it becomes apparent that *true* art can be achieved only when the artist works through the medium of memory: Hilda's copy of Beatrice is painted without direct access to the original (65), Kenyon's marble representation of Hilda's hand "is a reminiscence" (121), and Hilda's Transfiguration is instigated by her "Reminiscences of Miriam." What these examples imply is that the truth of Art is achieved only when the artist dismisses Actuality to work intuitively from Imagination. Yet this truth is itself an elusive thing, a fragrance almost, of a work of art, which is likely to dissolve upon too close a scrutiny:

> It is a peculiarity of this picture [Guido's "Beatrice"], that its profoundest expression eludes a straightforward glance, and can only be caught by side glimpses, or when the eye falls casually upon it; even as if the painted face had a life and consciousness of its own, and, resolving not to betray its secret of grief or guilt, permitted the true tokens to come forth only when it imagined itself unseen. (204–5)

> There is a singular effect, oftentimes, when out of the midst of engrossing thought and deep absorption, we suddenly look up, and catch a glimpse of external objects. We seem, at such moments, to look farther and deeper into them, than by any premeditated observation; it is as if they met our eyes alive, and with all their hidden meaning on the surface, but grew again inanimate and inscrutable, the instant that they become aware of our glances. (323–4)

When viewed unreflectively, when experienced rather than inspected, Art is seen to be alive. What is more, it is seen to be in possession of a *meaning* which it displays only furtively, when it imagines itself unseen. Art, then, displays its meaning only when it is seen not as art, but as life itself. It is this non-reflective vision that Hawthorne strives to bestow upon the reader: we are implored to lay aside our critical faculties in order to *experience* the work of art at hand in a moment of passionate abandon. As soon as we begin to reflect upon our experience of this object, its meaning will become hidden, growing "again inanimate and inscrutable" precisely because this view denies art a life of its own.

Yet this non-reflective moment in which art is experienced rather than critically examined, marks only the first stage of Hawthorne's conception of aesthetic perception, a stage that must eventually be transcended. For while the moment of abandon may perhaps be characterized as an intuitive experience of Truth, it must not be mistaken for the kind of moment in which a Transcendentalist such as Emerson claims to experience the intuitive oneness of Being. There is nothing like Emerson's transparent eye-ball in Hawthorne: no instant in which the individual becomes so enraptured with the moment as to assert an essential unity of spirit and world. Even in moments of intuitive insight Hawthorne's rapture is never allowed to transgress the bounds set by his ubiquitous conditionals: we *seem* to look farther and deeper into the world of external realities at such moments; it is *as if* its hidden meaning were displayed upon the surface. Rather than annulling the gap between the actual realm of Becoming and the ideal realm of Being, then, phrasings like these (which are the very lifeblood of Hawthorne's writings) are designed to make the reader sensitive to the gap itself. What Emerson's brand of transcendentalism projects, in contrast, is the prospect of building a world without a history. "Our age is retrospective. It builds the sepulchres of the fathers," Emerson complains in the first sentences of *Nature*. Properly considered, the argument in *Nature* runs, time and space are revealed to hold no autonomous existence, since in the presence of Ideas, "we think of nature as an appendix to the soul." If human perception is perfected, time and space are revealed to be "relations of matter" and hence to have no affinity "with a perception of truth, or a virtuous will."[51]

Hawthorne too, emphasizes the importance of the individual's perception in cutting through the realm of Appearances to the realm of Ideal Reality. But whereas for Emerson, the gap between the world of subjective experience and that of material facts may be closed through an intuitive perception of the world as an absolute presence, the world of material facts being essentially an extension of the mind, for Hawthorne the gap between the world of perception and the world of material facts is not something that we should strive to negate, but the very key to the Ideal; "sublime and beautiful facts are best understood when etherialized by distance" (5: 138). For Hawthorne, then, it is by recognizing the distance between a fact perceived and the subject perceiving it, that we may apprehend the ideal in the realm of the real, for the presence of this distance requires that we actively engage the facts we encounter by means of the imagination, which thus comes to fulfil a mediating office. "Facts, as we really find them, whatever poetry they may involve, are covered with a stony excrescence of prose, resembling the crust on a beautiful sea-shell, and they never show their most delicate and divinest colors, until we shall have dissolved away their grosser actualities by steeping them long in a powerful menstruum of thought" (5: 135–36). By going back to an experience that was once present but which is now past, we may come to see how this experience—ostensibly fully present in the past—was in fact separated from itself at its very conception, as it were. If the world is spiritual in essence, the material manifestation of this essence must seem to depart from this essence rather than to present it. The spiritual essence of the world cannot become fully present to the individual, it can only be intimated when its material expression is absent; that is, when an experience is *recovered* rather than when it is instantaneously apprehended.

Hawthorne, then, does not reject an analytical approach to art (of which the present study is of course itself an example). On the contrary, he is fully aware that the moment of abandon cannot be interminably suspended, but that it must soon recede and a much less exhilarating mood set in. Again, Hawthorne's account of his trip to Lichfield Cathedral may serve to illustrate our point. Having recorded the fullest intensity of his impression of the Cathedral (which I cited at the very beginning of this study), he then acknowledges how short-lived it was:

> If the truth must be told, my ill-trained enthusiasm soon flagged, and I began to lose the vision of a spiritual or ideal edifice behind the time-worn and weather-stained front of the actual structure. Whenever that is the case, it is most reverential to look another way; but the mood disposes one to minute investigation, and I took advantage of it to examine the intricate and multitudinous adornment that was lavished on the exterior wall of this great church.

Then follows approximately a page of mundane observations, before Hawthorne remarks: "It is no matter whether I ever came to a more satisfactory appreciation of this kind of architecture; the only value of my strictures being to show the folly of looking at noble objects in the wrong mood, and the absurdity of a new visitant pretending to hold any opinion whatever on such subjects, instead of surrendering himself to the old builder's influence with childlike simplicity." This passage in typical Hawthornean manner underscores the importance of approaching art in the right mood. More importantly, however, it implicitly differentiates between a first intuitive experience of art, and a second reflective experience of it. It is the "new visitant" of the Cathedral that must surrender "himself to the old builder's influence with childlike simplicity;" the accustomed visitor, it is implied, is entitled to approach it in a different manner. Indeed, while *The Marble Faun* warns us against "looking [...] too long" (17) at statues, we are nevertheless explicitly informed in the opening chapter that it is "if the spectator *broods* long over the statue" of the Faun, that "he will be conscious of its spell" (10; my emphasis).

By thus making the distance of reflection rather than the presence of intuition the condition for grasping the essence of reality, Hawthorne in a stroke overthrows a major premise of the Transcendentalist program Emerson sets forth in *Nature*, namely that the essence of reality must be conceived of as a perfect union between spirit and matter, making the "Universe" itself merely "the externization of the soul." Whereas for Emerson, the imagination is the faculty whereby we "participate the invention of nature" by dissolving the boundary between soul and world, for Hawthorne, the final product of our imaginative involvement with the world is always the discovery of the need to retain a radical distinction between self and world, by acknowledging the discrepancy between the world as materially manifested and as imaginatively idealized.[52] This is the key to the centrality afforded to death in Hawthorne's romances: in order for a moment of intuitive perception of the divinity of life not to be perverted to the symbolistic stance of an Emerson, it must be informed by an understanding of its own limitation. To experience the divinity of life therefore necessarily entails experiencing the shortcomings of life; it is to perceive the divinity of the realm of Being through the lack of the realm of Becoming. Like Holgrave and Phoebe, Miriam and Donatello are able to be "happy in the flitting moment" precisely because their joy is tied to the recognition of the "inevitable goal" (435) of death; that is, to the allegorical tenet that prescribes that our awareness of perfection must always be mediated through our awareness of imperfection.[53]

To be an adequate expression of this paradoxical situation, art must be both stained and immaculate: it must be able to make its own defects suggestive of the Ideal. Hawthorne's romances suggest that this may be accomplished if the perceiver, or reader, of art, can be brought to see that there must always be a distance between the symbolic experience of divinity, fullness, and perfection that the artist would have the work of art express, and the reader's recovery of this experience: a distance that is analogous to that which separates the world of Being from the world of Becoming. This distance is what we call *desire*. By recovering the artist's original experience, and thus in a sense repeating it, the reader may glimpse the Reality of this experience through the gap which makes manifest an inescapable distance between Origin and Reconstruction; a gap that consists precisely in the identification of guilt at the very heart of the innocent origin we presumed we were uncovering. The recognition of such a gap of guilt prevents the individual from identifying himself with the Ideal, but it does not entail that the idea of the Ideal as such need be rejected. What it does call for is the transformation of the individual's desire to attain the Ideal into the Hope that this Ideal may some day become true: for others. Thus desire is replaced by a manifestation of sympathy for one's Other, and Hope may show itself in the place of Pain and Sorrow. Hereby the individual may take the step from an innocence which he or she has in truth already lost to an adult experience showing us that the path back to God goes through an affirmation of our responsibility for the Other.

The spatial form of the text becomes especially important in this context, for as we pointed out at the outset of this study, this form can only be recovered, never instantaneously apprehended. The form does not exist in the moment of reading; it is something we generate by looking back upon our reading experience. The form fixes the temporal flow of the text, and thereby facilitates an intuitive vision of the Truth as an imperishable structure. But this experience of true beauty below a crust of imperfection is something which must be born through the agency of the perceiver, of the reader: to represent our experience of the world—the inner rather than the outward form of the world—art must reproduce our experience of the Reality of the world as something which is born through the affirmation of the distance between an experience apprehended and an experience recovered; for it is precisely by appearing "airy rather than massive," by taking on the properties of "a kind of kaleidoscopic mystery," that art may provide us with the means to pass from the "newly created structure of the passing moment," to "the half-vanished structure of the instant before," and inspire "a joyful faith in the indestructible existence of all this cloudlike vicissitude" (5: 124–25).

This is why we find *The Marble Faun* in the state it is: it is fragmentary in order that it may be possible for the reader to arrive at a notion of the Idea it strives to portray, by painstakingly piecing it together, much as Kenyon metaphorically creates Hilda in the manner he literally creates the unburied Venus de Medici. Significantly, Kenyon does not come across this "marble woman" all in one piece, but as broken fragments of a statue. What he finds, then, is not the statue per se, but the materia containing the potential form of the statue, as it were. By piecing the fragments together, the statue is realized by the sculptor. On the completion of this process, effected by the reinstallment of the statue's head, we learn that: "The effect was magical. It immediately lighted up and vivified the whole figure, endowing it with personality, soul, and intelligence. The beautiful Idea at once asserted its immortality, and converted that heap of forlorn fragments into a whole, as perfect to the mind, if not to the eye, as when the new marble gleamed with snowy lustre [...] " (423–4). The creative process as put forward in this instance bears a striking resemblance to the act of Creation itself, as conceived by the sculptor earlier on:

> Far into this misty cloud region, however—within the domain of Chaos, as it were—hilltops were seen brightening in the sunshine; they looked like *fragments* of the world, broken adrift and based on nothingness, or like portions of a sphere destined to exist, but not yet finally compacted.
>
> The sculptor [...] fancied that the scene represented the process of the Creator, when He held the new, imperfect Earth in His hand, and *modelled* it. (265; my emphasis.)

It is important not to overlook the implication of the above quotation. The broken fragments of the world out of which (in Kenyon's imagination) the Creator is seen to compound the world are represented by "hilltops [...] brightening in the sunshine", a phrase proleptically envisioning the last line of the novel proper, in which Hilda sees "sunlight on the mountaintops." Reality, to Kenyon, exists only in this distilled form of an ideal extracted out of a domain of chaos: it is logically interchangeable with Art. It is this conception of Life as identical to Art which enforces that he rejects the marble statue unearthed by Donatello, which presents an image of Divine Womanhood in fragments, opting instead to have it fully realized in the form of Hilda, who, by having the Catholic confession serve her own symbolic ends, is able to present herself as its unstained counterpart.

As we have seen, in *The Marble Faun* the recreative process inherent in Kenyon's conception of reality does not involve merely the characters of the narrative. In order to appreciate the depth of the romance, the reader, too, is forced to piece together the fragments of an "earth-stained" sculpture; we have to "find a great deal more" in the story "than the poet or artist has actually expressed" (379), as Hilda suggests. To see the ideal form of the text, then, we are forced to neglect the way the narrative is immediately presented to us: we must find a way of perceiving how the temporality of the narrative is governed by an inherent moral space. The ideal work of art is contained in the flawed reality of the narrative discourse as the potential form of a statue is inherent in a shapeless stone, but to be seen it has to be realized by the reader by his shaping the text the way a sculptor shapes his or her working material. In so doing, however, we have to become blind to reality, or at least to suppress certain aspects of reality.

Donatello is the marble faun come to life, but only so long as we perceive him as such. If we stare too long, as Hilda admits in chapter 2, the idea hardens and grows coarse—and dies. To see Donatello as the *idea* of the faun is to turn him into an allegorical object of art, and hence to take the life away from him—in a word, to kill him. This might indeed be the reason Hilda does "not quite like to think about" (13) the likeness between Donatello and the Faun. For an object of art to come alive it has to oust the original: if art is to take precedence over reality, reality has to be killed—the model has to die. In a sense, art does provide us with a truer picture of reality than does reality itself, but the price of this truth is this violation of reality, this killing of the Model. By witnessing the scene of the Model's murder, Hilda becomes aware of the sin inherent in any artistic execution. The imaginary act whereby the idea of the innocent Faun comes to life can only be achieved by denying the actual appearance of Fallen Man, upon whom this imaginary creature must inevitably be modelled: to assert Innocence, the imagination must violate reality.

Art, in other words, throws off the imperfect reality upon which it is modelled, in order to present the ideal perfection it would affirm.

In representing the Ideal rather than the Actual, art must inevitably expose how it is founded on a principle of desire rather than a principle of mimesis. And desire, as I have repeatedly called attention to in this study, is the very mark of imperfection: desire, whatever its object, is always a sign of a lack, a sign that something we crave is absent. Mimetic theories of art are founded on a correspondence theory of truth. From the perspective of such a theory, representing ideal truths—such as the truth of the human heart—must seem a matter of refining somewhat upon already existing circumstances: it will seem possible to reach the Ideal by reforming reality, as it were. If art is founded on a principle of desire, on the other hand, art is not a matter of imitating reality but must be seen, rather, as an attempt to *create* what is lacking in reality. From this perspective, nothing short of "a revolution in the sphere of thought and feeling" (SL, 217) will suffice to attain a sense of the Ideal. In contrast to a romantic such as Shelley, however, Hawthorne does not romanticize this aesthetics of revolution. Shelley's Beatrice in *The Cenci* is a full-blown revolutionary, who defends to the last the murder of her father as the just retribution on an unjust regime: "Take cheer! The God who knew my wrong, and made/ Our speedy act the angel of His wrath,/ Seems, and but seems, to have abandoned us./ Let us not think that we shall die for this." Defiantly denying ever having sinned, she insists to the bitter end that she, "Though wrapped in a strange cloud of crime and shame,/ Lived ever holy and unstained."[54] Hawthorne, in contrast, will not allow the truth about Beatrice to be reduced to an assertion of her essentially sinless character, but insists that it must be sought in the relation between her character and her history. The paradox of Beatrice is that her attempt to retain an appearance of innocence forces her to commit "an inexpiable crime," which must inevitably compromise the actual innocence of her character, which, as Hilda tells us, is that of "a fallen angel, fallen, and yet sinless" (66). Her choice is between subordinating herself to a tyrant who has shown himself capable of an outrage he might very well repeat, and turning back upon this despot by committing a sin as unpardonable as his own. For Hawthorne, then, it is clear that an aesthetics of revolution must take the form of a radical dialectics, in which contradictions are never resolved but continuously reasserted. All his writings suggest that while the moment of revolution may indeed be characterized as a moment of creation, it must also be a moment in which the original contradiction reasserts itself in another form. The killing of the Model emblematically portrays this moment of passionate revolution, in which the Actual is violated in order that the Imaginary may be asserted. In other words, if consummated, our desire for Innocence yields the deconstructive product of a moment of creation and destruction, a moment that gives birth to Innocence by murdering Guilt, only to find the offspring of this act assume Guilt's aspect.

To the very extent that art strives to present ideal truths, then, it must draw attention to the distance between the realm of the Actual and that of the Imaginary, and hence must also expose that the latter can be attained only through the mediation of desire. This is why the killing of the Model is simultaneously a moment of artistic execution—a moment in which art supplants life—and a moment of sexual passion: it is a moment that makes evident that pure love, love without the concomitant stain of sexuality, is a fabrication, an idealization exactly analogous to that of the relation between the idea and the form containing it. Sexuality is the imperfect, but actual, form holding the ideal, and hence imaginary, essence of love, which in contrast to the imperfect form of sexuality does not know desire. Art replicates this situation in being made up of an imperfect, actual outward form, and an ideal intrinsic beauty, which the form can but imperfectly suggest. This is why Hawthorne refuses to lift the veils of ambiguity off his narratives; they cannot communicate their ideas by themselves, but are dependent on the reader's active participation to come to life. The position of the Gentle Reader towards the romance, in other words, forms an exact parallel to that of Hilda towards the paintings she copies. This is yet another paradox informing *The Marble Faun*: in order to see the Idea suggested in art, we have to idealize our vision; we have to neglect the incomplete *appearance* of the work of art at hand, to "see through it", as it were, with the ideal vision of a Hilda. But accessing this truth of art is possible only by violating reality: art's sacred aspects are attainable only if we experience "a revolution in the sphere of thought and feeling" (SL, 217), yet the need of such a revolution entails that the sacredness of art must always be stained by guilt.

This becomes apparent if we consider the indisputable Miltonic overtones of the plot.[55] Miriam and Donatello are expelled from Eden, more precisely from that Eden reinstated in marble by Hilda and Kenyon. Only—what is Eden in this instance? In a sense they are expelled from reality, but reality in this case is a fiction, a fact the Postscript only helps to bring out; it is fictive also in the sense that it is a place which has been denied the presence of Sin—Hilda and Kenyon not only embrace Art, they become fictive by making their world a place of spotless innocence. In this sense, Miriam and Donatello must be said to be expelled from Fiction—as they quite literally are in the last chapter. The bracelet sequence of the romance, as we have seen, will have their story reenacted over and over again. But while this bracelet is in itself an ideal object, smooth, rounded, complete, it is but one aspect of the text—certainly not the most conspicuous one. Though the sculpture be perfect, the narrative itself cracks: as novel, it is flawed, a disheartening piece of fiction which refuses to fulfil the reader's desire for closure. For, "what was Miriam's life to be? And where was Donatello?" (462). And why will the novel not tell us? It will not, because in stating the questions, it is in effect providing the answers. The questions advanced are *the reader's* questions, who by phrasing them, answers them. Miriam and Donatello, the artist and the work of art, are *here*, in the realm of the actual reader of the novel. Having consented to being expelled from the marble Eden evoked upon the last pages of the book, Miriam's and Donatello's future destiny is dependent upon the ethical choice of the individual reader, upon whom falls the unenviable task of deciding whether to look to the book as an allegory of our own complicity in the sense of sinfulness of which the artist has made it suggestive, or yield to the artist's desire to achieve through his art what he cannot achieve in his life, a full expression of man's inherent divinity, symbolically made present. Expelled from the realm of fiction, Miriam's future life as well as the whereabouts of Donatello are dependent not upon anything within the narrative, but upon the way the individual reader responds to this narrative.[56]

Fiction will not hold Donatello; quite literally, he is transformed from a literal object of art into living anagogical reality. Reality, on the other hand, does not allow for the character of Hilda. As we have seen, her Transfiguration is a complex process indeed, which might to some extent explain (though it cannot dispel) the troubles reviewers have had with making sense of her. This is because Hawthorne while advancing the character of Hilda, who is clearly clothed as an ideal, is simultaneously subjecting the idea of this ideal character to a most incisive critique. The transformation of Hilda is a grand thing: she is transfigured, with all the religious connotations implied by that term; she is resurrected from a figurative death to appear in the "shining white robe of the true faith" (416). She is the essence of religious purity, and consequently comes to embody the religious sentiment inherent in all art by becoming a statue of Innocent Faith. Yet critics shudder at her, and either wholly dismiss the above implications or conclude that although something in this vein was indeed intended by the author, his portrayal is artistically unsuccessful. In truth, however, the romance's portrayal of Hilda suggests the beauty of an approach to life that will allow it to be rendered stainless, an approach that advocates the possibility of innocence and is willing, if necessary, to subject reality to art in order to assert itself. At the same time, however, the romance refuses to shy away from the consequences of this approach, because it realizes the extent to which it is itself entangled in the process it at once admires and finds repelling. *The Marble Faun*, too, is a work of art, a verbal sculpture that can only achieve an image of spotless purity by suppressing the guilt it is inevitably stained with; that is, by veiling its preoccupation with sexual desire and art as an allegorical representation of the myth of the Fall. This suppression of guilt is the price we pay for beauty, and Hawthorne is acutely aware that this is no mean sacrifice, one of the results being that life (in this case: the narrative at hand) becomes virtually incomprehensible unless transformed into Art. The mimetic scheme, then, is turned on its head: only Art is comprehensible, thus life can aspire to the status of reality only insofar as it imitates Art. Reality is caught up in this incessant cross-play of imitation and counter-imitation till it is on the verge of being lost altogether. The sole remaining way out of this plight lies in recognizing and seizing the loss this religious conception of Art exhibits; to affirm, that is, the guilt it has to deny in order to assert itself, because guilt is precisely the stain that will ruin the smooth completed form of the statue, that will make it crack and come alive in pain.

*

I have argued above that *The Marble Faun* is Hawthorne's most ambitious and, contrary to the received critical opinion, his most compelling attempt at delineating the problematic relation between symbolism and allegory, the aesthetic counterpart of the relation between the individual and society. Donatello and Hilda alike are transformed by their experiences in Rome, but whereas the former character acquires an understanding of the temporal conditions that enforce that man's historical experience of the Ideal must always be mediated through pain, the latter is transfigured, to the effect that she stands forth, in Kenyon's eyes, as the virtual embodiment of angelic Innocence. Having rejected the allegorical lesson that man's experience of the Ideal in this world must always be fragmentary and imperfect, the Hilda Kenyon brings to America is a symbol of the view that America constitutes a wholly new beginning, an origin untainted by the sins of European fathers. As we have seen, however, the "seven-branched allegory" that the structure of the romance as a whole embodies suggests otherwise. Incorporating within itself the circular shape of a bracelet, the complex and highly stylized structure of *The Marble Faun* makes evident that the "Recovery of the Sacred Candlestick" that Hilda looks forward to, is in truth a moment of revolution, a moment in which the individual's attempt to break free from history is revealed to us as the very moment in which the primacy of history reasserts itself.

Hawthorne's romances all portray a moment of symbolistic bliss, a moment in which the individual is at one with her passions, and past and future alike succumb to the bliss of the present. The forest-scene in *The Scarlet Letter*; Holgrave's and Phoebe's union under the auspices of the Flower of Eden in *The House of the Seven Gables*; Priscilla's conviction at Blithedale that "the past never comes back again" (76); these are moments of the same order as the sylvan dance of Miriam and Donatello in *The Marble Faun*, in which "Each varying movement had a grace which might have been worth putting into marble, for the long delight of days to come, but vanished with the movement that gave it birth, and was effaced from memory by another" (85). It is in order to transcend this inconstancy of the symbolistic moment that Hawthorne makes the Gothic cathedral, which impresses you "at every change, as a newly created structure of the passing moment, in which yet you lovingly recognized the half-vanished structure of the instant before, and felt, moreover, a joyful faith in the indestructible existence of all this cloudlike vicissitude," the model of his own art. Aided by a sympathetic viewer's recollection of it, the Gothic cathedral conveys a sense of immediate creation which nevertheless contains within itself a trace of the past, in the form of the half-vanished structure of the moment before. It is precisely by thus incorporating within itself the recollection of what has already been that the present becomes a bridge to the future, and to the "joyful faith" that despite the fact that the "cloudlike vicissitude" of the symbolistic moment renders it transient and ephemeral, its Imaginary permanence is in truth as real as the Actual persistence of pain.

**CONCLUSION**
# Hawthorne's Allegorical Dialectics

The past carries with it a temporal index by which it is referred to redemption. There is a secret agreement between past generations and the present one. Our coming was expected on earth. Like every generation that preceded us, we have been endowed with a *weak* Messianic power, a power to which the past has a claim.

Walter Benjamin, *Theses on the Philosophy of History*

Over the course of this study I have raised and disputed the argument that Hawthorne's conception of history is in keeping with the American progressive myth that has its roots in the Puritan notion of America as a city on the hill. This argument, powerfully propounded by Sacvan Bercovitch and others, presupposes that Hawthorne's narrative art is a species of symbolism that aims to eradicate the gap between the Actual and the Imaginary, to the effect that the secular realm of history is conflated into the eternal realm of spiritual truths. I have argued, in contrast, that no such conflation takes place in Hawthorne's fictions, that they are governed not by a symbolistic conception of history but by an allegorical one, which entails that the spiritual consummation that the symbolistic view of history would grant to the present world must be deferred to another realm—to the after-life, or to fiction. The consummation of desire is thus displaced to an imaginary realm beyond Actual history, but desire itself is recognized as a medium which is necessary to attain the Imaginary, and therefore as a feature of human existence that must not be suppressed.

In pursuing the relation between symbolism and allegory in Hawthorne's romances, the present study has traced the interconnections between their structural form, the notion of faith, and the role of the reader. It has highlighted how literally Hawthorne's romances play upon the relation between the Actual and the Imaginary, and how, in so doing, they invoke the reader's active participation, a participation conducive to a paradoxical faith in the true ideality of the romance.

All of Hawthorne's longer fictions, I have argued, are structured on what has been termed a principle of chiastic inversion, to the effect that the second half of the narrative in question subtly but significantly repeats the events of the first half in inverted order. Critics have long admired the symmetrical structure of *The Scarlet Letter*, in which the narrative acquires artistic form by virtue of the tri-fold location of the scaffold scenes, yet as has been demonstrated, the principle of chiastic inversion at work in *The Scarlet Letter* revives in each of the subsequent romances. We have seen, moreover, that the inversion on the formal level of the narrative's structure, in Hawthorne's romances always interrelates closely with a conceptual inversion of sexuality into death or vice versa enacted in the plot.

In *The Scarlet Letter*, both of the lovers confess by the letter; but for the letter to fulfil its office it also must be made to communicate the spirit of the individual, which by definition must be the opposite of the letter, since the applicability of the letter is universal, whereas the spirit of the individual is unique. The principle of chiastic inversion allows the romance to transcend this dilemma. The narrative structure implies some kind of repetition, a doubling, but in reverse order and with reversed results. The momentum of the romance inheres in the movement from Hester's figural expression of the lovers' sin to Dimmesdale's literal manifestation of it in the final scaffold scene—that is, in the movement from the letter as a paradoxical signifier connoting both sin *and* sexual sanctuary to Dimmesdale's revelation of the letter's unambiguous signified: death. The latter half of the narrative, an inverted sequence of the first half, thus literalizes what the first half only figuratively suggests, yet it does so without privileging either the figural or the literal mode. Dimmesdale's death expresses the Actual significance of the letter, but it does not contradict the Imaginary significance invested in it by Hester in the opening scaffold scene. At the centre of these narrative inversions stands Pearl, "the scarlet letter in another form" (102), and the narrative locus at which the play upon the figural and literal dimensions of the plot emerge most plainly into view. For while her very name suggests how Hester looks upon sexual love as a spiritual fortune, Pearl comes into literal wealth only after her mother has already witnessed her lover's death, which is another facet of that fortune. Pearl's literal wealth thus relates to her parents' willingness to acknowledge the stained, or imperfect, character of the sexual love they conceive of as their figural fortune. Indeed, sexuality almost invariably enfigures fortune in Hawthorne's romances; yet literal wealth, in turn, enfigures death or, more precisely, the inevitable recurrence of death.

This convoluted dialectic becomes an even more prominent feature of Hawthorne's second major romance. As in *The Scarlet Letter*, the principal structural device of *The House of the Seven Gables* emerges in a form of repetition by inversion. Identical events or references recur, but under conditions so altered as to amount to a reversal. Again, this pattern reinforces a play upon figural and literal meanings central to Hawthorne's romances. The figural representation of death and sexuality appearing in the early chapters of the romance couples with its literal counterpart towards its end. The sexualization of Hepzibah's venture to set up shop suggests that handling money is somehow analogous to allowing oneself to be penetrated by the desire that such a story as "Young Goodman Brown" submits as a prerequisite for entering the bounds of society, and is an analogy by contrast with the union of Holgrave and Phoebe that takes place in chapter 20, "stained" by being precipitated by the death of Judge Pyncheon. Sexuality, the romance thus suggests, is the figural counterpart of death, while death inversely is a literal condition for human love, which turns into the figural equivalent of earthly fortune.

The complex interplay between money, sexuality, and death in *The House of the Seven Gables* reappears in *The Blithedale Romance*. Here, too, this interplay reveals how intricately the romance fuses figural and literal meanings, a circumstance that an analysis of the structure of the work serves to underscore. On the basis of a reading that observes the evidence that Miles Coverdale's closing "Confession," was not part of the original manuscript but a last minute addendum, the chiastical structure found in *The Scarlet Letter* and *The House of the Seven Gables*, which enforces a dialectics of literal and figural meanings, can be seen to be operating in *The Blithedale Romance* as well. Just as Zenobia loses her literal fortune by squandering the figural fortune of her sexuality on the wrong men, Westervelt and Hollingsworth, Coverdale loses his figural fortune – the utopian community of Blithedale – by failing to respond to Zenobia's art, the figural flower she evolves out of Priscilla. Coverdale's insensitivity towards Zenobia's figural artistry, his reluctance to approach her mystery "in holy faith" rather than "scornful scepticism and idle curiousity"

(BR, 113), ultimately makes him responsible for her death. In this respect, he prefigures the reader who approaches the romance as a veil to be removed, rather than a sensuous space to be enjoyed.

Finally, in *The Marble Faun*, the structural principle of chiastic inversion turns the text into a veritable menorah. By highlighting the structuring principle, light is shed upon key aspects of the romance's notoriously inconclusive plot. It becomes clear, for instance, that the transformational processes of Donatello and Hilda are not only related to each other, but should also be seen from the point of view of their function as narrative extensions of prominent works of art enfigured in the romance. Donatello is caught in a double bind between the ideality of the Faun of Praxiteles and the reality of the Model; Hilda, similarly, is the narrative meeting place for the historical reality of Beatrice Cenci, and her transfiguration as a work of art. As children hovering at the point of adulthood and true individuality, Donatello and Hilda are thus literally caught halfway between fiction and reality. History as such is shown to be a product of this predicament, which must inevitably yield a moment of revolution – thematized, in Hawthorne's romances, as a moment of sexual passion – in which the conflict between fiction and reality is momentarily transcended, but which cannot in the long run avoid giving birth to another form of the original opposition. If consummated, *The Marble Faun* suggests, our desire for Innocence yields the deconstructive product of a moment of creation and destruction, sexuality and death; a moment that gives birth to Innocence by murdering Guilt, only to find the offspring of this act assume Guilt's aspect. The killing of the Model emblematically portrays this moment of passionate revolution, in which the Actual is violated in order that the Imaginary may be asserted.

While *The Marble Faun* brings the conflict between fantasy and reality most plainly into the open, in each of Hawthorne's romances the outcome of the plot is represented as being dependent upon how the characters conceive of their own relation to the key romantic moment in the book. This is invariably a paradoxical moment: a moment in which dream and reality become indistinguishable from each other, and which could be described equally well in terms of full presence as in terms of complete absence. Dimmesdale's nocturnal ascension of the scaffold; Judge Pyncheon sitting dead in the chair of the House of the Seven Gables; Zenobia's enactment of the legend of the Silvery Veil; the killing of the

Model: these are moments in which desire and lack of desire meet, moments which simultaneously invoke sexuality and death. Equally importantly, these are moments of mediation within the romances, moments that effect the transposition of the literal into the figurative and vice versa. This is to be seen in the structure of the romances, in which figurative suggestions in the first half of the narrative are given their literal fulfilment in the second half. The outcome of the romance as such, we have seen, is dependent upon the way we conceive of our own relation to the textual romance that mimics the sexual romance allegorically suggested by the plot. Our hermeneutic desire for meaning, thus comes to echo the characters' desire to come to terms with their own sexual desire; and in both cases, our longing for an immediate consummation of this desire is rejected on account of it being misdirected, even dangerous. The romance, in short, makes available an interactional space in which the reader ideally fulfils the office of a sympathetic medium by willingly consenting the prerogative of its author.

It is hence not a fault, but a vital component of the romance, that its structural outline must inevitably be in part of our own making. Consider once more the following passage from *The Marble Faun*:

> A picture, however admirable the painter's art, and wonderful his power, requires of the spectator a surrender of himself, in due proportion with the miracle which has been wrought. Let the canvas glow as it may, you must look with the eye of faith, or its highest excellence escapes you. There is always the necessity of helping out the painter's art with your own resources of sensibility and imagination. Not that these qualities shall really add anything to what the Master has effected; but they must be put so entirely under his controul, and work along with him to such an extent, that, in a different mood, (when you are cold and critical, instead of sympathetic,) you will be apt to fancy that the loftier merits of the picture were of your own dreaming, not of his creating. (MF, 335)

While this passage makes it clear that Hawthorne is aware of the reader's creative input in the artistic process, it makes equally clear that the role he assigns to the reader is not one of interpretive freedom. On the contrary, the interpreter's office is to subject himself to the artist's vision, to put his "resources of sensibility and imagination [...] entirely under" the Master's "controul." Art, from this perspective, requires the same devotion as religion. What is not literally present in the work of art (its "highest excellence"), the interpreter must figurally provide. Figurally, because in truth the interpreter is incapable of adding "anything to what the Master has effected," since "the highest excellence" of a work of art is always—and again, in *truth*—already present within it, albeit simply in figural form. Indeed, it is precisely because the highest excellence of a work of art exists only in figural form that we are liable to doubt its actual, literal, existence. The spatial form of the text is thus a particularly apposite perspective from which to approach the romance, since this form can never be instantaneously apprehended, but only retrospectively recovered. After all, the spatial form, or structure, of the text does not exist in the moment of reading; it is something we generate by looking back upon our reading experience. Once the structure of the discourse has been thus determined, however, it may be said to fix the temporal flow of the narrative, and thereby to facilitate an intuitive, if paradoxical, vision of the Truth as an imperishable structure already vanished.

That Hawthorne has to rely on the reader to achieve this vision entails that the principle of chiastic inversion must be seen not only as a compositional aide, but also, and equally importantly, as a device for bridging the gap between the reader and the narrative. By the means of this device, as I suggested in chapter two, the reader's capacity for sympathetically engaging the artist's work is brought directly to bear on this work, to the effect that our sympathy (or lack thereof) becomes an integral part of the very romance we read. Whether the structure we think we perceive is "really" there or not is therefore besides the point. What matters, once we have sensed that the artist *might* have entertained an Imaginary conception of some such structure as we seem to have seen, is our ability to retain our faith in its Actual existence. "Nobody," as Hilda says in *The Marble Faun*, "ought to read poetry, or look at pictures or statues, who cannot find a great deal more in them than the poet or artist has actually expressed" (MF, 379).

The office of the reader, in other words, is to literalize what the artist has already achieved in figural form. But as we have seen, the crux is that we cannot do this without simultaneously *negating* the artist's ideal aspirations. For what the artist has represented in figural form is nothing less than the ideal itself, and since the ideal per definition transcends all material forms, it goes without saying that by literalizing the ideal we can only detract from its ideality, never add anything to it. Thus we are faced with a paradox, since by realizing the ideal we are also inevitably inverting it. Literalizing the ideality of art is thus, as suggested in the discussion of *The Marble Faun*, tantamount to killing the ideal. Yet the paradox runs deeper than this, for it turns out that it is precisely—and only—through the very negation of its own ideality that the ideal can be brought into this world, for the negation of the ideal in the form of literal death carries with itself its own negation in the figural form of hope. Hope is of course related to faith, yet it does not spring directly from faith, but is the product, rather, of faith being inseminated by guilt.

I have identified the notion of the Fortunate Fall as the paradigm for this paradox. Despite its centrality in Hawthorne's writings, critics to this day grudgingly complain that Hawthorne cannot have meant us to take it seriously. Male, to take an early but representative example, refers to it as "the fallacious formula of the Fortunate Fall," objecting to it on the grounds that the formula would seem to take away "the temporal interval between sin and redemption" (*Tragic*, 9), and thus take "the narrative element out of the Christian story" (*Tragic*, 176). I will not dispute Male's conclusion that Hawthorne's "emphasis was not so much upon God's grace as it was upon man's struggle to achieve it" (*Tragic*, 177), but merely point out that the narrative element is taken out of the formula of the Fortunate Fall only if we fail to see that the formula adds up to an ongoing process in which we ourselves are taking part. As we have seen, the most explicit suggestion of the notion of the Fortunate Fall in Hawthorne's romances occurs in *The Marble Faun*, when Miriam says: "The Story of the Fall of Man. Is it not repeated in our Romance of Monte Beni?" Significantly, Hawthorne has Miriam phrase the theme of the romance as a question. Miriam is urging us to answer in the affirmative—but Kenyon finally joins Hilda in rejecting such an understanding. This is Hawthorne's way of suggesting that the answer to Miriam's question depends upon the outcome of the romance, and that this romance is not consummated until the reader has decided whether to accept it on its own terms, or to repress its most troubling implications: that its significance is dependent upon our own response to it. The notion of *felix culpa* is thus transposed from the allegorical into the anagogical level of the text, that is, it is transposed from fiction into interpretive reality.[1]

It is in this sense, moreover, that Hawthorne's writings are steeped in religion yet may remain utterly profane: they are not primarily concerned with faith in a religious sense, but invoke it, rather, as a metaphor for the kind of act the reader must prove willing to perform in order that the romance may come alive. To realize this is to perceive that the notion of *felix culpa* must not be understood solely as an existential metaphor: while it is certainly the case that the notion of the Fall designates a psychological reality for Hawthorne, the implications of this circumstance are lost on us unless we see that the concomitant notion of the Fortunate Fall prescribes a social imperative. The operability of the formula of the Fortunate Fall rests on the possibility of grasping life as a totality, and the romances make clear that this is something the individual cannot do without the aid of a sympathetic Other. The office of romance, therefore, must be to facilitate the bonding of Self and Other, Artist and Society, Writer and Reader.

Somewhat incisively, the romance could be said to perform this task by suggesting that art may be structurally analogous to the life of Christ. We should remember that the life of Christ is a sign of man's sinfulness as well as of his divinity. If Adam had not fallen, man would never have known Christ: that is the paradoxical premise of the formula of the Fortunate Fall. But the mere existence of Christ is not sufficient to fulfil this formula. Whether the Fall deserves to be deemed fortunate or not is dependent upon the way each individual acts in response to the life of Christ. Art, Hawthorne's romances suggest, fulfils its mediating office in a similar way: as a sign of sinfulness as well as of divinity, the potentially redemptive office of art can be consummated only if the reader responds to it the way the Christian must respond to Christ, that is, by recognizing that art, like Christ, is stained by a sin which it has taken upon itself out of love for us. To acknowledge the inherent ideality of art, then, we must come to see that it cannot be blamed for its shortcomings, since its lack of perfection in truth reflects a lack inherent in ourselves. If art fails to achieve ideal perfection—and Hawthorne is adamant that it must fail in this respect—it is for the same reason that Christ died: because we have been found wanting.

By bringing this structural analogy between Hawthorne's art and Christian faith to the fore, I am not suggesting that either Hawthorne or his writings must be deemed Christian. The analogy is purely structural, and as such does not say anything at all about the nature of Hawthorne's personal beliefs. What it suggests, rather, is the lasting importance of reading Hawthorne historically, that is, of considering how his writings employ the ideas and modes of thought that he could not have avoided being affected by, given his time and culture. The secularized Hawthorne we have come to know in the wake of critics like Baym and Crews is arguably no less a product of ideas that can be traced back to Christianity than the "religious" Hawthorne constructed in the present study. The critical point is not whether or not Hawthorne was religious, but which patterns of Christian thought his writings make use of, and which they dismiss. The Hawthorne of emotion and depth-psychology derives from transcendentalism, which places his writings squarely in the tradition of symbolism. In contrast, the allegorical Hawthorne I have been concerned with must be read as radically questioning the underlying values that provide the impetus for the turn towards symbolism that takes place in Western society at large in the Romantic period.

This turn towards symbolism was not, of course, a sudden phenomenon, but something that took place over a long period of time. Christian allegory, as we saw in chapter one, always involves a dialectics encompassing the individual and society as well as past and future: it is designed to function as a mediator between part and whole, to make available to the individual a notion of spatial as well as temporal totality. The principal virtue of the medieval fourfold scheme of interpretation as we have expounded it is that it operates on a diachronic and a synchronic axis simultaneously. The move away from allegory toward symbolism is not an exclusively literary movement; rather, it is part of a general tendency towards suppressing the operability of the historical component of interpretation, for supplanting diachronicity with a more elaborate version of synchronicity. By rejecting this disruption of the significance of the Scriptures into different senses or levels, retaining only a spiritual sense over and above the literal one, Protestant exegesis inevitably came to conflate the different aspects into one. The most significant outcome of this conflation, I would argue, is that the moral sense of the fourfold scheme of interpretation that had always been tied to the present (since it designates the individual's position vis-à-vis the significance of the other three senses of the text) comes to dominate the other aspects, the allegorical and the anagogical. Whereas in the fourfold scheme the present is merely a transitional mode, the significance of which is always dependent upon its relation to an allegorical key in the past and an anagogical end in the future, the Protestant insistence on an immediate relation between the individual and God makes exegesis liable to subsume the relevance of both past and future under that of the present.

Needless to say, this valorization of the present at the expense of the past and the future is intimately connected to changes in the power structures of society taking place at roughly the same time. When the Puritan settlers set out on what one of their descendants called an "Errand into the Wilderness," Perry Miller has argued, they conceived of their enterprise as "being run for the sake of Reformed Christianity." Its aim was no less than to make New England a type of the New Jerusalem which would be built when the reformation of the Church had been consummated by Europe emulating the example, set by the colony of the Pilgrims, of a form of government that was at once civil and ecclesiastical. But when the inherent tensions of the Protestant movement in Britain exploded in the Civil Wars during the 1640's, it became apparent that no such form of government would be possible in the mother countries. Having thus, figuratively speaking, "lost their audience," the second-generation colonists were left with an errand that no one took much interest in anymore. Excepting, of course, the messengers themselves, who accommodated this situation by shifting the sense of their concept of an errand from that of an errand run for the sake of someone else to that of one performed for one's own sake. "Their errand having failed in the first sense of the term, they were left with the second, and required to fill it with meaning by themselves and out of themselves. Having failed to rivet the eyes of the world upon their city on the hill, they were left alone with America."[2]

In effect, then, between the first and second generations of settlers, the concept of New England was transformed from that of a type of a future anti-type, into that of a self-fulfilling prophecy, that is, a type *already fulfilled* by means of its inherent processual nature. At least, such is the argument that Bercovitch has pleaded on the basis of his investigations of the rhetorical strategies embodied in the Puritan jeremiad, which takes its name from the Old Testament prophet whose book takes the form of an extended railing against the chosen people on account of their having broken their covenant with God. Symbolism, in Bercovitch's conception, is thus a means to enforce a continuous gap between process and closure, to the effect that process itself becomes an end rather than a means. From this perspective, Hawthorne's much celebrated ambiguity loses its ideological innocence, and becomes instead "a strategy for pluralism—issuing, on the reader's part, in a mystifying sense of multiplicity—through which each set of questions and answers is turned toward the same solution."[3] By eschewing epistemological closure, so the argument goes, Hawthorne's romance achieves an ideological closure consistent with the ideal of liberal community, to the effect that Hawthorne's conception of history turns out to be wholly in keeping with the American progressive myth that has its roots in the Puritan notion of America as a city on the hill.

I have been at pains in the previous pages to refute Bercovitch's thesis that Hawthorne's writings can be seen as yet another form of the American jeremiad, and I will return to the issue shortly. Yet while I am convinced that Hawthorne departs substantially from this rhetorical tradition, and suspect that Melville too could be seen to escape the bounds of Bercovitch's argument if read with attention to detail, I see little reason to dispute the argument as such. As already Miller observes, "the total effect" of the Puritans' jeremiads, "is not at all depressing: you come to the paradoxical realization that they do not bespeak a despairing frame of mind."[4] Bercovitch goes considerably further than this: not only are the jeremiads vehicles of castigation that paradoxically instil faith in the future rather than despair in the present, they are also rhetorical machines designed to enforce consensus. By conceiving of America as a chosen country on a divine, future-directed errand, the jeremiad in its American form, in contrast to its European manifestations, operates on a teleological conception of history which "precludes dialectics" (*Jeremiad*, 149) and hence prevents the emergence of viable social alternatives to the existing form of government. This is why Bercovitch holds that the Puritan legacy to America is a symbolic outlook that "unites sacred and secular history" (*Jeremiad*, 40) and blurs "the distinction between the historical, moral, and spiritual levels of meaning" (*Jeremiad*, 46) to the effect that first New England, and then America, has been conceived of as the New Canaan in a spiritual as well as a literal sense. In contrast to their English and European brethren, that is, the American Puritans came to think of the Promised Land as something that was given to man in this life, as well as in the after-life. This conflation of the realm of temporality with the realm of eternity enabled the Puritans to transform tensions inherent in their society into a disciplining agency, making revolt an instrument of social cohesion rather than social conflict: "The future, though divinely assured, was never quite there, and New England's Jeremiahs set out to provide the sense of insecurity that would ensure the outcome;" their rhetorical strategies "fed on the distance between promise and fact."[5]

This conflation of religious with political power, in combination with the valorization of the here and now that it gave rise to, thus enabled the leading figures of the day to conceive of their own community as fulfilling the typological prophesies of the Scriptures. Despite its typological foundation, then, the rhetoric of the Puritan community's intellectual elite nevertheless marks a decisive step towards a symbolistic mode of thinking. What is more, it does not seem unreasonable to assume that the chilliasm entertained by the Puritans—in which the imminent Second Coming of Christ was expected—set the stage for the downplaying of the importance of Christ that is such a characteristic feature of Unitarianism, the most widely influential movement of Hawthorne's own community.[6] The step from imminence to immanence may be a considerable one, but it is surely manageable within the span of a century: and it is precisely such a step that is involved in the transformation of Puritan into Unitarian doctrine that takes place in eighteenth-century New England. As is implied by the name of the movement, the most distinctive trait of Unitarianism is its rejection of the Christian doctrine of the Trinity, which is seen as an indefensible remnant of polytheism. As Ursula Brumm has shown, this doctrinal modification has important ramifications. In Unitarian doctrine Christ is in some sense inferior to God: he is, William Ellery Channing held, "a Saviour, chiefly as he is the light, physician, and guide of the dark, diseased, and wandering mind." Transcendentalism takes this devalorization of Christ's divinity one step further; in Emerson's 1838 address to the senior class of Harvard's Divinity School, Christ is reduced to a prophet, a type of the divinity inherent in every man: "One man was true to what is in you and me. He saw that God incarnates himself in man, and evermore goes forth anew to take possession of his World." Rather than the Son of God, Christ thus came to be looked upon as the Brother of Man.[7] In literary terms, this marks a transformation of God from a concept to which we are primarily metaphorically related to a concept to which we are primarily metonymically related. Remembering that Coleridge's definition of the symbol turns on the fact "that it is always itself a part of that, of the whole of which it is representative"—that it is, in other words, an instance of metonymy—whereas allegory, in contrast, presumes a "disjunction of faculties" to the effect that it "cannot be other than spoken consciously,"[8] we can thus establish that what the transition from Puritan to Unitarian doctrine entails in literary terms, is a transition from typology—a mode of thinking which forms an important aspect of the fourfold allegorical scheme of interpretation—to symbolism. But we have also seen that if Unitarianism is most often described as a reaction towards a set of Puritan tenets that had come to seem stifling, it could equally well be described as a refinement of a position inherent in Puritanism.

This becomes obvious when one turns to the Transcendentalist refinement of Unitarian doctrine. Indeed, Emerson's conflation of nature and soul ultimately amounts to an "equation of landscape and redemptive history" which is yet another manifestation of the Puritan strategy to fuse secular and sacred history. Emerson, Bercovitch observes,

> reminds Americans that they still have "a moral wilderness" to traverse "in preparation for [...] building a New Jerusalem." Then, combining the terms of Puritan and Romantic salvation, he rejects the disparity between fact and vision—dismisses all anxiety about process or incompletion—by announcing that the thousand year reign of "the truly Human hovers, now seen, now unseen, before us." The millenium, he would have us believe, *now* "exists for us, shines in on us at unawares."[9]

Like the New England of the Puritans, Emerson's America takes the form of a self-fulfilling prophecy, a type fulfilling itself by means of promising an ever-expanding mobility, rather than a specified end. As we have seen, Bercovitch holds that the social-symbolic outlook inherent in this visionary conception of history is not peculiar to Emerson, but is shared by all the major writers of the American Renaissance, Hawthorne included. In this view, Hester's scarlet letter "is the symbol of Emersonian hope—hope in prophecy [...] in the individual [...] in the future."[10]

Yet although the dividing line between Emerson's and Hawthorne's attitudes may appear slight, it is nevertheless crucial. As analyzed by Bercovitch, symbolism—at least in its American guise—is a means to dissolve ideological contradictions by providing metaphorical solutions to very real conflicts of interest. But as we have seen, the paradoxical pattern of Hawthorne's romances is not that of symbolism, but complies with the ironical structure of allegory. While Hawthorne criticism in general has tended to depreciate the differences between these two concepts, I have maintained that the distinction remains a crucial one. For allegory, as Paul de Man has shown, involves a structure in which the solution of metaphor advanced by symbolism is undermined by being applied to metaphor itself: "Allegories are always allegories of metaphor and, as such, they are always allegories of the impossibility of reading."[11]

The "impossibility of reading" of which de Man speaks, stems from the fact that our concept of "reading" implies the reification of a temporal process into an object. That is to say, in assuming that in reading a text we are disclosing its meaning, we are implicitly making a totalizing claim to the effect that what began simply as reading (an activity) ends up as a Reading—in other words, as an *object* that metaphorically expresses the temporal activity in which we have previously been engaged. The meaning of the text, whatever we take it to be, is thus always a metaphor for the reading which precedes it. More than that, it is an attempt to close off this activity, to make it come to an end. A Reading in this sense can thus be regarded as the death of reading. Allegories, however, by highlighting the process of reading as such, make plain that this death of reading is in truth an illusion, as no reading can ever live up to the totalizing, or ideal, claim by which it is motivated.

De Man therefore does not write "reading" rather than "Reading" by chance. The impossibility of reading in his view (which, one might add, is often at odds with the received view of his writings) cannot be limited to a deconstruction of the text as an object, but applies to an equal degree to the process of reading as such. From this perspective, the process of reading in which meanings are produced and disseminated is merely another metaphor for the meaning of the text. For the metaphor of the meaning of the text as a death (an object), we have thus substituted a metaphor of the meaning of the text as life (an endless production). Allegory, however, shows such a conception of reading to be equally impossible, in that it makes plain that in order for us to effect the dissemination of the text, a fixed, or dead, meaning must already be in place. In other words, the reader cannot end the text, yet cannot avoid ending it.

It is in the tension of this dual impossibility, this double negativity, that the paradoxical insight of allegory is born, an insight that is also a blindness, as de Man never ceases to remind us: the moment of understanding must also be a moment of blindness, that is, a moment which yields a figural sense of release which is in truth equivalent to a literal state of captivity. Simply put, the blindness of insight confines us within temporality, for what we call time, as de Man points out, "is precisely truth's inability to coincide with itself."[12]

Despite being founded in rhetorical rather than religious considerations, the deconstructive dilemma identified by de Man is thus clearly parallel to the situation of postlapsarian man; in effect, de Man's deconstruction presents us with something approaching a secularized version of the myth of the Fall, without prejudice to its alleged fortuity. Hawthorne's romance and de Man's deconstruction alike emphasize the aporetic nature of human desire—that is, the seemingly unsolvable dilemma that any attempt to realize the ideal, to achieve truth, must inadvertently result in the negation of the ideal. Ideologically, this may seem to lead to nihilism, but such is not the position of either de Man or Hawthorne. Unwilling to embrace any simple conception of faith, yet refusing to come to rest with scepticism, both choose instead to pass the problem on to the reader. Such a transference of the dilemma from the writer to the reader is admittedly a slender means to guard against the sceptical abyss opened up by their own discursive practices, but because of their refusal to shy away from the predicament of temporality, this dialectical involvement of the reader with the text remains in their writings the only conceivable locus of true hope.[13]

And this is precisely what the structural principle of Hawthorne's romances serves to drive home: in order to consummate the work of art's figural representation of the ideal, this ideal must first be negated by being translated into a literal, and hence specific, statement of its meaning. The desire for the ideal, we should remember, is at its deepest a desire for life and its everlasting continuation: it is the desire to make a moment marked by beauty permanent, eternal. Symbolism and allegory are parallel aesthetical modes insofar as they both make clear that the ideality of the eternal can only be achieved in a paradoxical way. For life to be everlasting, they both insist, life must have an end, but this end must have the appearance of a new beginning. Symbolism and allegory thus provide the means for a paradoxical faith in the ideal, a faith which is mediated through the recognition rather than the suppression of negation and its signifiers: death and sexuality. Bercovitch's reading of Hawthorne has the merit of producing the notion of symbolism as an ideological problem rather than an artistic triumph, yet it stumbles in mistaking Hawthorne's deconstruction of the symbolist paradigm for the very thing itself. For allegory goes beyond symbolism in suggesting that, ironically, the new beginning provided through the means of this paradoxical hope is merely apparent. A truly new beginning would be a beginning unstained by negation; and such a beginning, allegory realizes, is *in truth* impossible, for it can exist only in the figure of the very form by which it is undone: in the figurality we commonly refer to as fiction. To recognize that the very notion of an innocent beginning is fictitious, is to recognize that every *new* endeavour is in truth historically overdetermined. Whereas the symbolism of an Emerson suppresses this circumstance, the dialectical allegory of Hawthorne's romance admonishes us, rather, to turn towards the past with the ambition of finding within it the potential, if unrealized, ideal it once held. In Hawthorne's view, to paraphrase Walter Benjamin, the present has been endowed with a *weak* Messianic power:[14] Messianic, in that our present acts may indeed be said to be invested with the power of redemption; weak, in that this power extends over the past, but not over the future.

It may thus seem as if Hawthorne rejects the idea that political agency is open to us. To insist on believing in the reality of an ideal that one knows to be unattainable in this world, is not, however, to renounce politics all together. On the contrary, the fundamental question raised by Hawthorne's romances concerns the very nature of freedom. Is freedom something that can be interminably expanded, no matter how slowly, until, in some way distant future, we shall all be free, as the symbolist vision suggests? Or is it rather the case, that the freedom of this inherently imperfect world must be conceived of as a given, a *limit*, which inexorably dictates that freedom for us must be a question of distribution rather than dispersal? By privileging the anagogical sense of the text—the always present interpretive space in which the text is read—Hawthorne's romances insist that the moral responsibility for these questions resides with the reader. Regardless of the answers we come up with, his writings thus suggest that the true significance of the writer's

Imaginary vision is determined by the reader's Actual reception of this vision. In so doing, they disclose the founding principle of Hawthorne's allegorical dialectics: that we must make our interpretation of the past the means "to find the perfect Future in the present" (10: 56). No matter that our effort thus to redeem the past must necessarily be weak and imperfect, the very effort itself, Hawthorne's romances suggest, bears the traces of the Ideal.

# Notes

## Notes to the Introduction

1. Herbert Read, Collected *Essays in Literary Criticism* (London: Faber and Faber, 1938), p. 269.
2. I refer to Hawthorne's extended fictions as "romances" simply because this was how he himself designated them. The effort to understand the Romance as a specifically American genre of certain inherent qualities was instigated by Richard Chase in *The American Novel and its Tradition* (Garden City: Doubleday, 1957). For a variety of attempts to extend or modify Chase's original definition, see Joel Porte, *The Romance in America; Studies in Cooper, Poe, Hawthorne, Melville, and James* (Middletown: Wesleyan UP, 1969); Evan Carton, *The Rhetoric of American Romance: Dialectic and Identity in Emerson, Dickinson, Poe, and Hawthorne* (Baltimore: John Hopkins UP, 1985); George Dekker, *The American Historical Romance* (Cambridge: Cambridge UP, 1987); Edgar Dryden, *The Form of American Romance* (Baltimore: John Hopkins UP, 1988); Emily Miller Budick, *Fiction and Historical Consciousness: The American Romance Tradition* (New Haven: Yale UP, 1989). Of these, Dekker would seem to agree with Edwin M. Eigner in *The Metaphysical Novel in England and America: Dickens, Bulwer, Melville, and Hawthorne* (Berkeley: University of California Press, 1978)—who prefers the designation "metaphysical novel" to "romance" as a generic term—that this allegedly American genre is more rewardingly seen in conjunction with a certain British tradition of the novel. See also Nina Baym, "Concepts of the Romance in Hawthorne's America," *Nineteenth-Century Fiction* 38 (1984): 426–43; rpt. in *Feminism and American Literary History* (New Brunswick: Rutgers UP, 1992) 57–70, who argues that empirical evidence suggests "that Hawthorne's distinction between *romance* and *novel* [...] which has carried so much weight for subsequent criticism, was idiosyncratic, his own" (p. 59). For a helpful critical discussion of this debate, see George Dekker, "Once More: Hawthorne and the Genealogy of American Romance," *Emerson Society Quarterly* 35 (1989): 69–83.
3. F. O. Matthiessen, *American Renaissance: Art and Expression in the Age of Emerson and Whitman* (New York: Oxford UP, 1941), p. 180.
4. Hyatt Howe Waggoner, *Hawthorne: A Critical Study* (Cambridge: Harvard UP, 1963 [1955]), and Roy R. Male, *Hawthorne's Tragic Vision* (Austin: University of Texas Press, 1957). See also Richard Harter Fogle, *Hawthorne's Fiction: The Light and the Dark* (Norman: University of Oklahoma Press, 1952; rev. ed. 1964), which in its focus on the religious connotations of the imagery of Hawthorne's fictions set the methodological example for Waggoner and Male. In his second book on Haw-

thorne, however, *Hawthorne's Imagery: The "Proper Light and Shadow" in the Major Romances* (Norman: Oklahoma UP, 1969), Fogle's brand of close reading tends to become a rather static exercise in balancing light against darkness.

5. Frederick C. Crews, *The Sins of the Fathers: Hawthorne's Psychological Themes* (New York; Oxford UP, 1966), pp. 7–8, and 20. Oddly, or perhaps strategically, Crews makes no references to the brief but valuable study of Rudolph Von Abele, *The Death of the Artist: A Study of Hawthorne's Disintegration* (The Hague: Nijhoff, 1955)—except to the article version of its third chapter on "The Artist of the Beautiful"—which is the first to explicitly propose that there is a link between artistic activity and sexuality (p. 5). Von Abele notes that the image of the artist in Hawthorne's fictions is deeply ambiguous: throughout his writings the artistic activity is associated with various forms of taking control over other people (mesmerism/witchcraft), or alternatively, with a tendency towards isolating oneself from the rest of humanity. As the title of Von Abele's study suggests, his argument suffers to an even greater extent than was common at the time from the misconception that Hawthorne's art deteriorates from *The Scarlet Letter* to *The Marble Faun*. For an instructive example of how long-lived this view has proved, see Joseph Allard, "Nathaniel Hawthorne: A Watchman All-heeding and Unheeded," in Richard Gray, ed., *American Fiction: New Readings* (London: Vision, 1983), 38–52.

6. Nina Baym, *The Shape of Hawthorne's Career* (Ithaca: Cornell UP, 1976), pp. 9, 8, and 10. For important precursors to Baym's position, see Von Abele, *Death*; and Terence Martin, *Nathaniel Hawthorne* (New York: Twayne Publishers, 1965). Martin stresses the importance of Hawthorne's humanism and concern for the temporal aspects of existence to a much higher degree than the critics of the earlier decade, thus preparing the way for Baym's revaluation of Hawthorne's Christianity ten years later. See also Leslie Fiedler's *Love and Death in the American Novel* (New York: Criterion Books, 1960) and Porte, *The Romance in America*, both of whom discuss the importance of the sexual theme in Hawthorne at length.

   Baym deserves credit for being one of the first Hawthorne scholars to apply a fledgling feminist perspective when reading Hawthorne that has since been developed by a number of critics. The first programmatical feminist monograph of Hawthorne is Louise DeSalvo's *Nathaniel Hawthorne* (Atlantic Highlands: Humanities Press International, 1987); if rather predictable in its analyses of gender issues in Hawthorne, it nevertheless offers a useful overview of feminist approaches. Baym herself has developed her argument for Hawthorne as a proto-feminist, adumbrated in *Shape*, in a number of subsequent articles. In particular, see "Thwarted Nature: Hawthorne as Feminist," in *American Novelists Revisited: Essays in Feminist Criticism*, ed. Fritz Fleischmann (Boston, Mass.: G.K. Hall, 1982). Well-intended though it may be, it seems to me largely unconvincing. Another pioneering feminist study is Judith Fryer, *The Faces of Eve: Women in the Nineteenth-Century American Novel* (London: Oxford UP, 1976). More recently, Monica M. Elbert's *Encoding the Letter 'A': Gender and Authority in Hawthorne's Early Fiction* (Frankfurt am Main: Haag & Herchen, 1990) combines a gender perspective with investigating the role and function of science in Hawthorne's fiction. Elbert provides thorough and well-documented chapters on six of his tales and SL, the value of which, however, is compromised by a somewhat stereotypical invocation of indeterminacy as the concomitant to what she terms "Hawthorne's non-authoritarian narrator" (p. 236). In contrast to the argument of the present study, she argues that Hawthorne's "final word is doubt" (p. 20). In my view, the most seminal application of a gender perspective on Hawthorne's writings to date is Leland S. Person's *Aesthetic Headaches: Women and a Masculine Poetics in Poe, Melville, and Hawthorne* (Athens: University of Georgia P, 1988). For discussions of the genetic relations between Hawthorne and the female writers of his day, see James D. Wallace, "Hawthorne and the Scribbling Women Reconsidered," *American Literature* 62 (1990): 201–22, and John L. Idol, Jr. and Melinda M. Ponder, eds., *Hawthorne and Women: Engendering and Expanding the Hawthorne Tradition* (Amherst: University of Massachusetts Press, 1999).

7. Matthiessen, p. 337.
8. Two particularly rewarding exceptions are Michael J. Colacurcio, *The Province of Piety: Moral History in Hawthorne's Early Tales* (Cambridge: Harvard UP, 1984), and Charles Swann, *Nathaniel Hawthorne: Tradition and Revolution* (Cambridge: Cambridge UP, 1991).
9. Sacvan Bercovitch, *The American Jeremiad* (Madison: University of Wisconsin Press, 1978), p. 207. See also *The Puritan Origins of the American Self* (New Haven: Yale UP, 1975); and *The Office of* The Scarlet Letter (Baltimore: John Hopkins UP, 1991). For critical discussions of the latter, see for instance Richard Millington "*The Office of* The Scarlet Letter: An 'Inside Narrative'?" *Nathaniel Hawthorne Review* 22 (1996): 1–8; Robert Milder, "*The Scarlet Letter* and Its Discontents," *Nathaniel Hawthorne Review* 22 (1996): 9–25; Paul K. Johnston, "Killing the Spirit: Anne Hutchinson and the Office of the Scarlet Letter," *Nathaniel Hawthorne Review* 22 (1996): 26–35; Emily Miller Budick, "Sacvan Bercovitch, Stanley Cavell, and the Romance Theory of American Fiction," *PMLA* 107 (1992): 78–91; and Peter J. Bellis, "Representing Dissent: Hawthorne and the Drama of Revolt," *Emerson Society Quarterly* 41 (1995): 97–119.
10. Millicent Bell, *Hawthorne's View of the Artist* (New York: State University of New York, 1962), pp. 34 and 67. James K. Folsom—who, like Bell, is concerned with questioning the Platonic strains of Hawthorne's writings—describes the philosophical position underlying these writings as "a very loosely Platonic one," in that it "assumes two 'worlds,' that of Man's accidents, which can be empirically known, and some ultimate Real world, that of God's purposes, which is inscrutable in itself but upon which the former world depends." Nevertheless, Folsom's study gains its impetus from arguing that the most important trait of Hawthorne's idealism is that it is always concerned with the former aspect of the world, which Folsom calls the world of Becoming, as opposed to the ultimate Reality of the world of Being. If the terminology may appear somewhat high-flown, it is nevertheless a distinction that seems to me necessary to adopt, for as Folsom demonstrates, "Hawthorne is explicit in his

belief that there are two worlds, and that they are interdependent; but he insists, as well, that we have knowledge of only one of them, the world of Appearances." See Folsom, *Man's Accidents and God's Purposes: Multiplicity in Hawthorne's Fiction* (New Haven: College and UP, 1964), pp. 13–14, and 15. As for the genetic origin of this dualistic view of the world, Folsom correctly observes that Hawthorne could have picked it up from a variety of sources: Puritanism, Transcendentalism in its European and its American forms, the English romantics—all posit some form of Platonic dualism (Folsom, p. 17). Baym, *Shape*, argues in contrast that Hawthorne did in fact embrace some version of transcendentalism. For other, and even less convincing arguments to this effect, see Marjorie J. Elder, *Nathaniel Hawthorne: Transcendental Symbolist* (Athens, Ohio: Ohio UP, 1969); and Harvey L. Gable, Jr., *Liquid Fire: Transcendental Mysticism in the Romances of Nathaniel Hawthorne* (New York: P. Lang, 1998).

11. See for instance Matthiessen, p. 224; and Millicent Bell, *Hawthorne's View of the Artist*, pp. 151–72.
12. Cf. Person, *Headaches*, who likewise argues that Hawthorne habitually identified his "deepest creative impulse" (p. 144) with female characters.
13. In this respect my argument is in many ways parallel to that of Richard Millington in *Practicing Romance: Narrative Form and Cultural Engagement in Hawthorne's Fiction* (Princeton: Princeton UP, 1990). Millington conceives of Hawthorne's writings as an extended attempt to rewrite cultural authority; the romance, in this view, becomes the author's means to reshape the individual's relation to the culture and the community enveloping her. In practice, this leads to an investigation in narrative form because, Millington believes, "Hawthorne saw in the way ideology is carried by discourse [...] a way for fiction, a similarly but strategically composed form of expression, to transform it. Hawthorne, we might say, became a formidable theorist of the novel by becoming a lucid interpreter of culture" (*Practicing*, p. 10). Millington's perhaps most rewarding idea is his view that Hawthorne's romances should be looked upon as a form of interchange, that they constitute a practice which is rewardingly viewed in analogy to Freud's notion of transference: "In both techniques an interchange between an act of representation and an answering act of interpretation overturns the mind's entrapping conceptions of itself. At the center of Hawthorne's practice, as at the center of Freud's, is an aspiration to cure. And it is finally the invention of romance as a cure for the reader that makes possible its therapeutic effect on Hawthorne himself, for such a conception of his relation to his audience permits Hawthorne to forgive himself his ambitions and find a place and a presence from which to speak" (*Practicing*, 55–56). This is a perspective with which I am largely in agreement. Nevertheless, as will be seen I have found myself compelled to develop this perspective in polemical discussion with the course suggested by Millington, whose readings seem to me ultimately to celebrate the form of symbolistic interpretations that I argue that Hawthorne's romances denounce. My general point of dispute with Millington thus arises out of my disapproval of his insistence that Hawthorne's writings amount to an advocation of the interpretive freedom of the reader.

14. For Hawthorne's use of allegorical techniques, see especially John E. Becker, *Hawthorne's Historical Allegory* (Port Washington: Kennikat Press, 1971).
15. I am using the term "chiastic" in a loose sense: in all but one of the four romances the inversion involves sequences of chapters rather than individual chapters. For other studies that turn on the identification of similar principles, see for instance Douglas Brooks, *Number and Pattern in the Eighteenth-Century Novel: Defoe, Fielding, Smollet, and Sterne* (Boston: Routledge & K. Paul, 1973), and Ralf Norrman, *The Insecure World of Henry James: Intensity and Ambiguity* (London: Macmillan Press, 1982). Brooks' study identifies a series of numerological patterns in the eighteenth century British novel of the kind that we will ascribe to Hawthorne's romances, arguing that this kind of symmetrical ordering of the material is "a reflection of that order which was traditionally synonymous with Divine Providence" (p. 19). Norrman argues that the principle of chiastic inversion is a key to understanding Henry James in terms that suggest his affinity to Hawthorne: "Chiasticists dream of synthesis, but they visualize it in terms of a middle between two extremes so that the very idea nevertheless presupposes the poles, and therefore constantly defeats itself" (p. 192). Unfortunately, however, Norrman focuses only on the static aspects of the chiasmus. A full account of the functionality of the chiastic principle must look upon the chiasmus not only as a state in space, but also as a movement in time. Such an account may, I think, help us to understand how change is possible within the bounds of a static system, and conversely, how a series of dynamic movements may be said to constitute the foundation for a static system.
16. Cf. Hawthorne's contention when struggling with the unfinished manuscript of "The Ancestral Footstep": "If I could but write one central scene in this vein, all the rest of the Romance would readily arrange itself around that nucleus" (12: 58). His avowed aversion to writing a serialized novel also bespeaks his concern for the formal dimensions of his writings: "it would be excruciating to me to have a story dragging itself, for six months or a year, before the public, like a half-torpid snake out of its hole, and becoming defunct at one end before the other had seen the light" (16: 612).

    The pioneering discussion of spatial form in literature is that of Joseph Frank, "Spatial Form in Modern Literature," in *The Widening Gyre: Crisis and Mastery in Modern Literature* (New Brunswick: Rutgers UP, 1963), 3–62; originally appeared in *Sewanee Review* 53 (1945). For a critique of this notion, see Frank Kermode, *The Sense of an Ending: Studies in the Theory of Fiction* (New York: Oxford UP, 1966), pp. 176–80. See also the essays collected in Jeffrey R. Smitten and Ann Daghistany, eds., *Spatial Form in Narrative* (Ithaca: Cornell UP, 1981).
17. The earliest study to systematically pursue these formal aspects is that of Leland Schubert, *Hawthorne, the Artist: Fine-Art Devices in Fiction* (New York: Russell & Russell, 1963 [1944]).
18. W. K. Wimsatt and Monroe Beardsley, "The Intentional Fallacy," *Sewanee Review* 54 (1946): 468–88.

19. Paul de Man, "Form and Intent in the American New Criticism," in *Blindness and Insight: Essays in the Rhetoric of Contemporary Criticism* (New York: Oxford UP, 1971), 20–35, p. 25. The structural intention must not be mistaken for Wayne C. Booth's concept of the *implied author*, which—as defined in *The Rhetoric of Fiction*, second ed. (Chicago: University of Chicago Press, 1983)—has the unfortunate consequence of making the author out to be an entity with no body in historical space. For a stringent critique of Booth, see Gerard Genette, *Narrative Discourse Revisited*, tr. Jane E. Lewin (Ithaca: Cornell UP, 1988), pp. 137–145.
20. Paul de Man, Allegories of Reading: Figural Language in Rousseau, Nietzsche, Rilke, and Proust (New Haven: Yale UP, 1979).

**Notes to Chapter One**

1. Roy Harvey Pearce, "Hawthorne and the Sense of the Past, or, The Immortality of Major Molineux," *ELH*, 21 (1954): 327–349, pp. 330, 333, 348, and 347.
2. Colacurcio, *Province*, pp. 31, 33, and 34.
3. To Colacurcio, any attempt to transfer the specificity of his historical themes to the generality of psychological themes must be looked upon as unjustifiable reductionism. See for instance his discussion of "Molineux," where he insists on the importance of distinguishing between the coming of age of Robin, and the coming of age of America which are both figuratively depicted in the story and might therefore lead us "to propose that perhaps it has been Hawthorne's intention so to join tenor and vehicle that we cannot assign primacy to either the individual or the social passage" (*Province*, p. 150). The most powerful counterstatement to Colacurcio's general argument about the importance of a historical consciousness to Hawthorne is that of Leon Chai, *The Romantic Foundations of the American Renaissance* (Ithaca: Cornell UP, 1987). Without denying the importance of history to Hawthorne, Chai argues that "what Hawthorne is progressing toward, ultimately, is perhaps best described as a transcendence of the historical perspective through one that has no 'historical' element at all and whose values are the immanent ones of life itself" (p. 270).
4. Hawthorne's religious views are conscientiously if somewhat tendentiously presented in Leonard J. Fick, *The Light Beyond: A Study of Hawthorne's Theology* (Westminster: Newman Press, 1955). Fick's study is marred by an unwillingness to confront the ambivalent note that rings through many of Hawthorne's comments on religion, a fault which is aggravated by his considering these passages out of context, yet some of his more general points still bear repeating, such as the humanistic drift of Hawthorne's faith, his antiunitarian stance, and the importance of accepting the inscrutable ways of God. For other considerations of Hawthorne's faith, see for instance Henry G. Fairbanks, *The Lasting Loneliness: A Study of the Sources of Alienation in*

*Modern Man* (Albany: Magi Books, 1965); John T. Frederick, *The Darkened Sky: Nineteenth-Century American Novelists and Religion* (Notre Dame: University of Notre Dame Press, 1969), pp. 27–78; and Waggoner, "Art and Belief," in Roy Harvey Pearce, ed., *Hawthorne Centenary Essays* (Columbia: Ohio State UP, 1964), 179–187.

5. See for instance James R. Mellow, *Nathaniel Hawthorne in his Times* (Boston: Houghton Mifflin, 1980), p. 21. On Hawthorne's reading habits in general, see Julian Hawthorne's essay *Hawthorne Reading* (Cleveland: The Rowfant Club, 1902). Even more valuable is Marion Kesselring's *Hawthorne's Reading 1828–1850: A Transcription and Identification of Titles Recorded in the Charge-Books of the Salem Athenaeum* (New York: The New York Public Library, 1949).

   There are several source studies of Hawthorne's indebtedness to Spenser; see especially Buford Jones, "Hawthorne and Spenser: From Allusion to Allegory," *Nathaniel Hawthorne Journal* 1975, 71–90, which, besides tracing how Hawthorne transforms Spenserian allusions in his tales into full-blown allegorical structures in HSG and BR, includes a complete listing of the specialized studies up to that point (p. 88, n. 3). Articles that have since appeared on Hawthorne's relation to Spenser include: Gary Scarnhorst, "Hawthorne and the Poetical Works of Spenser: A Lost Review," *American Literature* 61 (1989): 668–73; John Hollander, "Observations on a Select Party," *Spenser Studies* 3 (1982): 193–98; David M. Van Leer, *Emerson Society Quarterly* 27 (1981): 73–84; Karen Jacobs and Edward Craney Jacobs, "The Doves of Venus in Hawthorne and Spenser," *American Notes and Queries* 18 (1979): 2–5. As interesting as these are, what is really important to observe is not the episodic echoes of Spenser in Hawthorne, but the extent to which he can be seen to make use of Spenser's allegorical practice. Hawthorne's predilection for Spenser is particularly noteworthy, since so much in Spenser depends on punning. See for instance Martha Craig, "The Secret Wit of Spenser's Language," in *Elizabethan Poetry: Modern Essays in Criticism*, ed. Paul Alpers (New York: Oxford UP, 1967), 447–72; Angus Fletcher, *The Prophetic Moment: An Essay on Spenser* (Chicago: Chicago UP, 1971), p. 105; and Maureen Quilligan, *The Language of Allegory: Defining the Genre* (Ithaca: Cornell UP, 1979), pp. 25–96. Quilligan would make punning the defining trait of the allegorical genre as such, a step I think we had better refrain from taking, since puns are to be found in almost any given form of literature. Nevertheless, Quilligan may well be right in arguing that puns are an especially prominent feature of the canonical works we recognize as allegorical.

6. Matthiessen, pp. 242–315. The concept of the American Renaissance has since become a staple of American literary criticism. See for instance: John T. Irwin, *American Hieroglyphics* (New Haven: Yale UP, 1980); Larzer Ziff, *Literary Democracy: The Declaration of Cultural Independence in America* (New York: Viking Press, 1981); Donald Pease, *Visionary Compacts: American Renaissance Writings in Cultural Context* (Madison: University of Wisconsin Press, 1987); Chai, *The Romantic Foundations of the American Renaissance*; Donald Reynolds, *Beneath the American Renaissance: The Subversive Imagination in the Age of Emerson and Melville* (New York: Knopf, 1988); Larry J. Rey-

nolds, *European Revolutions and the American Literary Renaissance* (New Haven: Yale UP, 1988); and David Leverenz, *Manhood and the American Renaissance* (Ithaca: Cornell UP, 1989). For a rewarding critical discussion of the concept of the American Renaissance and a wide array of works in which it is operating, including several of the above mentioned, see Michael J. Colacurcio, "The American-Renaissance Renaissance," *New England Quarterly* 64 (1991): 445–93.

7. Matthiessen, pp. 248 and 249–50. See also Richard J. Jacobson, *Hawthorne's Conception of the Creative Process* (Cambridge: Harvard UP, 1965), who argues—elegantly yet in my view ultimately unconvincingly—that Coleridge's distinction is replicated by Hawthorne himself.
8. Matthiessen, pp. 279, 276, 277, 248–9, and 291. The last citation contains a quote from Robert Penn Warren, "John Crowe Ransom," *The Virginia Quarterly* (January, 1935).
9. Hawthorne criticism has long since reached proportions that defy attempts at quick summaries. Helpful bibliographical tools include: Gary Scharnhorst, *Nathaniel Hawthorne: An Annotated Bibliography of Comment and Criticism before 1900* (Metuchen: Scarecrow, 1988); Walter Blair, "Hawthorne," in Floyd Stovall, ed., *Eight American Authors: A Review of Research and Criticism* (New York: Norton, 1963), 100–52 (see also J. Chesley Mathews' bibliographical supplement on Hawthorne in the same volume, 428–34); Buford Jones, *A Checklist of Hawthorne Criticism, 1951–1966* (Hartford: Transcendental Books, 1967); Maurice Beebe, and Jack Hardie, "Criticism of Nathaniel Hawthorne: A Selected Checklist," *Studies in the Novel* 2 (1970): 519–87; Theodore L. Gross, and Stanley Wertheim, *Hawthorne, Melville, Stephen Crane: A Critical Bibliography* (New York: The Free Press, 1971); Jeanetta Boswell, *Nathaniel Hawthorne and the Critics: A Checklist of Criticism 1900–1978* (Metuchen: Scarecrow, 1982); Lea Newman, *A Reader's Guide to the Short Stories of Nathaniel Hawthorne* (Boston: G. K. Hall, 1986); David Callaway, "An Annotated Select Bibliography of *The House of the Seven Gables*," in Bernard Rosenthal, ed., *Critical Essays on* The House of the Seven Gables (Boston: G. K. Hall, 1995).

    Newcomers to the field may also find some of the following critical discussions helpful: Buford Jones, "Hawthorne Studies: The Seventies," *Studies in the Novel* 2 (1970): 504–17; Michael J. Colacurcio, "The Symbolic and the Symptomatic: D. H. Lawrence in Recent American Criticism," *American Quarterly* 27 (1975): 486–501; and "The Sense of an Author: The Familiar Life and Strange Imaginings of Nathaniel Hawthorne," *Emerson Society Quarterly* 27 (1981): 108–33; Dennis Berthold, "From Freud to Marx: Recent Directions in Hawthorne Criticism," *Emerson Society Quarterly* 22 (1976): 107–19; Jonathan Arac, "Reading the Letter," *Diacritics* 9 (1979): 42–52; Leland S. Person, "Hawthorne and his Culture: Three Recent Views," *Studies in the Novel* 24 (1992): 434–41; and Evan Carton, "Millenial Letters; or, Monsieur Hawthorne, C'est Nous," *Emerson Society Quarterly* 44 (1998): 199–224.

    In the last three decades or so, Hawthorne has also received considerable attention from Japanese scholars of American literature. This is a body of criticism that I have not had the opportunity to review. For a general account, however, see David Cody, "Hawthorne in Japan: Some Recent Studies, 1975–1991," in *Nathaniel Hawthorne: The Introduction of an American Author's Work into Japan* (Salem: Peabody Essex Institute), 49–95.

10. Charles Feidelson, Jr., *Symbolism and American Literature* (Chicago: University of Chicago Press, 1953), pp. 9, 15, 14–15, and 15. Cf. Daniel G. Hoffman, *Form and Fable in American Fiction* (New York: Oxford UP, 1961), who claims that Hawthorne and Melville "transformed allegorism into a symbolic method which exemplified the transcendental aesthetic of Emerson, far though either romancer was from accepting Emerson's ethics or his view of nature" (p. 5). For an instructive example of the way in which Feidelson's view is upheld even as it is being questioned, see for instance Michael Davitt Bell, *The Development of American Romance: The Sacrifice of Relation* (Chicago: University of Chicago Press, 1980), who discusses the matter under the heading "Allegory and Symbolism," and claims that Hawthorne "adopts the allegorical mode in order to turn it against allegorical intentions" (p. 134). For further arguments in the same vein, see Robert Kimbrough, "'The Actual and the Imaginary': Hawthorne's Concept of Art in Theory and Practice," *Transactions of the Wisconsin Academy of Sciences, Art, and Letters* 50 (1961): 277–93; Seymour Katz, "'Character,' 'Nature,' and Allegory in *The Scarlet Letter*," *Nineteenth-Century Fiction* 23 (1968): 3–17; Daniel J. Schneider, "The Allegory and Symbolism of Hawthorne's *The Marble Faun*," *Studies in the Novel* 1 (1969): 38–50; Dennis Grunes, "Allegory Versus Allegory in Hawthorne," *American Transcendental Quarterly* 32 (1976): 14–19; Joel Pfister, *The Production of Personal Life: Class, Gender, and the Psychological in Hawthorne's Fiction* (Stanford: Stanford UP, 1992), pp. 47–8; Brian M. Britt, "The Veil of Allegory in Hawthorne's *The Blithedale Romance*," *Literature & Theology: An International Journal of Theory, Criticism and Culture* 10 (1996): 44–57; and Terry J. Martin, "Anti-Allegory and the Reader in 'Young Goodman Brown'," in *Rhetorical Deception in the Short Fiction of Hawthorne, Poe, and Melville* (Lewiston: Edwin Mellen Press, 1998), 19–31. For important precursors to my own position on this question, see in particular Folsom, pp. 71–93; Becker; and Pease. Folsom argues perceptively "that Hawthorne uses the term 'allegory' not as a statement of artistic means, in some sense roughly equatable with 'symbolism,' but rather as a statement of artistic ends, in some moralistic sense. An allegory for Hawthorne is a *moral tale*, and an equivalent for the term would be closer to 'didactic' than to 'symbolic'" (p. 77). Male, *Tragic*, likewise seems to me exemplary in his unbiased appreciation of Hawthorne's allegorical practice.

11. Edgar Allan Poe, "Tale Writing—Nathaniel Hawthorne," *Godey's Lady's Book* 35 (November 1847): 252–56; Henry James, *Hawthorne* (London: Macmillan, 1879), pp. 62–63. Tony Tanner interestingly argues that the influence of Hawthorne on James is pervasive, "particularly with regard to the symbolism in James's late work;" see the "Introduction," in *Hawthorne*, by Henry James, (London: Macmillan, 1967), 1–21, p. 2. For studies of the influence of Hawthorne on James, see for instance Robert Emmet Long, *The Great Succession: Henry James and the Legacy of Hawthorne* (Pittsburgh:

University of Pittsburgh Press, 1979); and Elissa Greenwald, *Realism and Romance: Nathaniel Hawthorne, Henry James, and American Fiction* (Ann Arbor: Univ. Microfilms Internat. Research Press, 1989). Hawthorne's influence upon a broader spectrum of American literature is studied in Richard H. Brodhead, *The School of Hawthorne* (New York: Oxford UP, 1986). See also Kristie Hamilton, *America's Sketchbook: The Cultural Life of a Nineteenth-Century Genre* (Athens: Ohio UP, 1998).

12. Wellek, René, and Austin Warren, *Theory of Literature*, third ed. (New York: Harcourt, 1956), p. 189.
13. Richard H. Fogle, *Hawthorne's Fiction: The Light and the Dark*, rev. ed. (Norman: University of Oklahoma Press, 1964 [1952]), pp. 13–14.
14. Thus H. H. Waggoner, for instance, is careful to disassociate himself from Matthiessen's view that Hawthorne was an allegorist in The Spensarian mould (*Study*, p. 72). While nominally accepting that Hawthorne often declared his commitments in "allegorical form" (*Study*, p. 264), Waggoner is careful to imply that the signified of this allegory is always undermined by its deeper symbolic purport: "the meanings of the images are partly determined by their analogy with historic myth, mostly Christian, and partly determined internally, by context. And always, again when he is writing at his best, they are to some degree ambiguous" (*Study*, p. 260). This is so, because in Waggoner's view "Hawthorne's religious belief was existentially oriented, not institutional or traditional. He found in his own *experience* reason for looking at life as the 'old time' writers had, reason for believing the Scriptures would never be destroyed by bonfires or reform. But religious experience—not doctrine or dogma but experience—is always, and necessarily, ambiguous" (*Study*, p. 264).
15. Berek, Peter, "The Transformation of Allegory from Spenser to Hawthorne," *Amherst Honors Thesis* 10 (1962), pp. 36, 38, 48, and 38.
16. Jenny Franchot, *Roads to Rome* (Berkeley: University of California Press, 1994), pp. 351 and 352.
17. Deborah L. Madsen, *Allegory in America: From Puritanism to Postmodernism* (New York: St. Martin's Press, 1996), pp. 3 and 4; my emphasis.
18. How representative Madsen's reappraisal of allegory is, I cannot say, but the critical reception of her books suggests that her tendency to substitute a postmodernist conception of allegory for a new critical conception of symbolism is the aspect of her writings that reviewers are least prone to question. See for instance Brian Harding's review of *Allegory in America* in *Modern Language Review* 93 (1998): 805–6.
19. See Crews, *Sins*, pp. 7–8; and Kenneth Dauber, *Rediscovering Hawthorne* (Princeton: Princeton UP, 1977), pp. 12–13.
20. Northrop Frye, *Anatomy of Criticism* (Princeton: Princeton UP, 1957), p. 89.
21. Angus Fletcher, *Allegory: The Theory of a Symbolic Mode* (Ithaca: Cornell UP, 1964), p. 13. See also René Wellek, *A History of Modern Criticism*, vol. I (New Haven: Yale UP, 1955) p. 200; and Edward Honig, *Dark Conceit: The Making of Allegory* (Evanston: Northwestern UP, 1959), pp. 39–50, upon whom Fletcher draws.

22. Samuel Taylor Coleridge, *The Statesman's Manual*, ed. W. G. T. Shedd (New York: Harper & Brothers, 1875), 437–438. Cited in Fletcher, *Allegory*, p. 16.
23. Feidelson, pp. 69, and 68. As Feidelson speaks of "dialectic" rather than "dialectics," it is possible that his critique is aimed primarily at a logical procedure rather than a philosophical one, but it is questionable whether these two fields can be held entirely separate from each other.
24. Cf. Paul de Man, "The Rhetoric of Temporality," in *Blindness and Insight: Essays in the Rhetoric of Contemporary Criticism* (New York: Oxford UP, 1971), 187–228.
25. Coleridge, *Miscellaneous Criticism*, p. 29. Cited in Fletcher, *Allegory*, pp. 16–17.
26. Feidelson, p. 116. Feidelson is citing Ralph Waldo Emerson, *Works*, volume III (Boston: Fireside ed, 1909), pp. 76–7.
27. Quintilian, *The Institutio Oratoria of Quintilian*, vol. 3, tr. H. E. Butler (London: W. Heinemann, 1922), p. 326 [tr. p. 327].
28. Fletcher, *Allegory*, pp. 2, and 8.
29. Quilligan, pp. 278 and 31.
30. de Man, "Rhetoric," pp. 191, 192, and 207.
31. de Man, "Rhetoric," pp. 214, 209, and 226.
32. Gordon Teskey, "Allegory," in *The Spenser Encyclopedia*, ed. A. C. Hamilton (Toronto: University of Toronto Press, 1990), 16–22, p. 18.
33. J. R. R. Tolkien, for instance, testifies to his dislike of allegory in the preface to the second edition of *The Lord of the Rings*: "I cordially dislike allegory in all its manifestations, and always have done so since I grew old and wary enough to detect its presence. I much prefer history, true or feigned, with its varied applicability to the thought and experiences of readers. I think that many confuse 'applicability' with 'allegory;' but the one resides in the freedom of the reader, and the other in the purposed domination of the author." *The Fellowship of the Ring* (London: George Allen and Unwin, 1966), p. 7.
34. See Jean Laplanche and Jean-Bertrand Pontalis, *The Language of Psycho-analysis*, tr. Donald Nicholson-Smith (London: Hogarth Press, 1973), pp. 292–293.
35. Fredric Jameson, *The Political Unconscious: Narrative as a Socially Symbolic Act* (Ithaca: Cornell UP, 1981), p. 17; henceforth cited in the text as *PU*.
36. Jameson is responding to the critique of psychoanalytic master codes mounted by Gilles Delueze and Felix Guattari in *Anti-Oedipus: Capitalism and Schizophrenia*, tr. Robert Hurley, Mark Seem and Helen R. Lane (New York: Viking Press, 1977).
37. Karl Marx and Friedrich Engels, "The Communist Manifesto," in K. Marx, *On Revolution*, ed. and tr. S. K. Padover (New York: McGraw-Hill, 1971), p. 81, cited in Jameson, p. 20.
38. See Wilhelm Reich, *Sex-pol: Essays, 1929–1934*, ed. Lee Baxandall, tr. Anna Bostock, Tom DuBose, and Lee Baxandall. (New York: Random House, 1972). Freud too, of course, undertakes such a transposition in his later writings—most notably, perhaps, in *Civilization and its Discontents*—but as he retains sexuality rather than politics as the operating principle of society, the effect is that of transforming society into an in-

dividual of gigantic proportions, rather than of turning the individual into a social system (a transformation which Freud, with some justification, could of course claim already to have performed).

39. The main authority on the medieval scheme is Henri de Lubac, *Exégèse Médiéval: Les Quatres Sens de l'Ecriture* (Paris: Aubier, 1959–1964, 4 vols.). (Recently translated by Mark Sebanc as *Medieval Exegesis* [Edinburgh: T&T Clark, 1998]). See also A. C. Charity, *Events and their Afterlife: The Dialectics of Christian Typology in the Bible and Dante*, (Cambridge: Cambridge UP, 1966), pp. 171–178; and Beryl Smalley, *The Study of the Bible in the Middle Ages* (Oxford: Clarendon Press, 1941).
40. "Epistola X," in *A Translation of the Latin Works of Dante Alighieri*, tr. A.G. Ferrers Howell and Philip H. Wicksteed (London: J. M. Dent, 1904), 343–368.
41. Jameson advances the scheme in his attempt to dispute Althusser's critique of the notion of "expressive causality," that is, the notion deriving from Leibniz that the part may be expressive of the totality of which it forms a particle because the whole in question is reducible to a particular inner essence (in effect, a version of the commitment to metonymy signalled by the Romantics' preference for the symbol). See Jameson pp. 23–49, especially p. 24, pp. 28–9, and p. 34.
42. See for instance Marx' "Critique of the Gotha Program," in which he criticizes the Program for not having stated "that with the abolition of class distinctions all social and political inequality arising from them would disappear of itself." In *The Marx-Engels Reader*, ed. Robert C. Tucker (New York: Norton, 1978), p. 535.
43. Henri de Lubac, "Christianity and History," in *Henri de Lubac, S.J.* (London: Sheed and Ward, 1972), 9–36, p. 26
44. Jean Daniélou, *From Shadows to Reality: Studies in the Biblical Typology of the Fathers*, tr. Wulstan Hibberd (Westminster: Newman Press, 1960), p. 287.
45. Charity, p. 159.
46. Frye, pp. 77 and 78.
47. Frye, p. 99.
48. Frye, pp. 116 and 119. Jameson seems to have overlooked the fact that Frye is working with five phases rather than four: in his review of Frye he mistakenly merges the literal and the descriptive into one (*PU*, 71). Considering the fact that Frye treats these two levels under the same heading and devotes less space to the two of them together than to any of the other phases individually, this is perhaps understandable. There can be no doubt, however, that Frye intends them as separate (if complimentary) phases: "We have now established a *new sense* of the term 'literal meaning' for literary criticism, and have *also* assigned to literature, as one of its subordinate aspects of meaning, the ordinary descriptive meaning that works of literature share with all other structures of words" (Frye, p. 82; my emphasis. [see also pp. 115–116]).
49. Frye, pp. 126, 117, 80, and 78.
50. See for instance Gérard Genette, *Narrative Discourse: An Essay in Method*, tr. Jane E. Lewin (Ithaca: Cornell UP, 1980).

51. Kermode, *The Sense of an Ending.*
52. Paul Ricoeur, *Time and Narrative,* vol. 2, tr. Kathleen McLaughlin and David Pellauer (Chicago: University of Chicago Press, 1985), p. 23.
53. I am suggesting, in other words, that the relationship between what we normally call "reality" and "fiction," could be seen as analogous to the way Lacanian psychoanalysis conceives of the relation between the Real and the Symbolic spheres of human consciousness. Without getting into technicalities, we could say that the literal sense constitutes our Imaginary point of departure, the allegorical sense our Symbolical point of departure, whereas our Real starting point is always the anagogical sense which is also the projected end of the reading process. See Jacques Lacan, *Écrits* (Paris: Seuil, 1966); and Frederic Jameson, "Imaginary and Symbolic in Lacan: Marxism, Psychoanalytic Criticism, and the Problem of the Subject," *Yale French Studies* 48 (1972): 338–95.

**Notes to Chapter Two**

1. Fredrick Newberry, *Hawthorne's Divided Loyalties: England and America in his Works* (Rutherford: Fairleigh Dickinson UP, 1987), p. 112.
2. Newberry, *Divided,* p. 132. Apart from Newberry, *Divided,* pp. 111–133, the only other extensive treatments of this work are John W. Crowley, "Hawthorne's New England Epochs," *Emerson Society Quarterly* 25 (1979): 59–70, and Laura Laffrado, *Hawthorne's Literature for Children* (Athens: University of Georgia Press, 1992), pp. 6–40. Laffrado attempts to read Hawthorne's work for children in relation to his work for an adult audience, but her adherence to a notion of criticism as a means for performing "a reenvisioning of [Hawthorne's] life" (p. 5), rather than a means to further our understanding of his texts makes for a rather treadmill-like run through of his four collections of children's stories; symptomatically, she does not even seem aware of Newberry's discussion. See also Baym, *Shape,* pp. 85–96, and Colacurcio, *Province,* pp. 419–21 and 521–22.
3. Colacurcio, *Province,* p. 419.
4. Newberry, *Divided,* p. 133.
5. Bercovitch, *Puritan Origins*; *Jeremiad*; and *Office.*
6. It is customary to make a sharp distinction between allegory and typology on the grounds that while the former mode of interpretation concerns a relation between a literal and a spiritual fact, the latter always concerns a relation involving two historical events. On the grounds of this historical foundation, typological interpretation, it is claimed, avoids the arbitrariness that has always been seen as a damning mark of allegorical interpretation. For the classic expression of this view in literary criticism, see Erich Auerbach, "Figura," in *Scenes from the Drama of European Literature: Six Es-*

*says*, tr. Ralph Manheim (New York: Meridian Books, 1959), pp. 11–76. James Barr, however, argues convincingly that the sharp distinction between typology and allegory is a false one; see *Old and New in Interpretation: A Study of the Two Testaments* (London: S.C.M. Press, 1966), pp. 103–48.

For an extensive reference list of typological writings, see the annotated bibliography in Sacvan Bercovitch, ed., *Typology and Early American Literature* (Amherst: University of Massachusetts Press, 1972); for a less impracticable reading list, see the essays collected in Earl Miner, ed., *Literary Uses of Typology: From the Late Middle Ages to the Present* (Princeton: Princeton UP, 1977). On the typological aspects of *Paradise Lost*, see William G. Madsen, *From Shadowy Types to Truth: Studies in Milton's Symbolism* (New Haven: Yale UP, 1968), esp. pp. 54–166. The pioneering study of typology in American literature is Ursula Brumm's *American Thought and Religious Typology*, tr. John Hoaglund (New Brunswick: Rutgers UP, 1970), originally published in 1963. As Karl Keller points out, however, the value of Brumm's discussion is somewhat compromised by the fact that she "follows the term 'type' through American literary history as opposed to following the concept or structure of typology itself" ("Alephs, Zahirs, and the Triumph of Ambiguity: Typology in Nineteenth-Century American Literature," in Miner, *Typology*, 274–314, p. 282). For alternative accounts of Hawthorne's typology, see Gretchen Graf Jordan, "Hawthorne's 'Bell': Historical Evolution through Symbol," *Nineteenth-Century Fiction* 19 (1964): 123–29; and Becker. Becker argues that the aim of Hawthorne's allegory is "to reject the allegorical 'findings' of Puritanism as arbitrary and narrow, and to create, by means of his own historical vision, a rival allegorical world, independent of both the opaque realities of the contemporary and the schematized realities of the Puritan past" (p. 163). While I think Becker is right in maintaining that Hawthorne was not a neo-Puritan in disguise, his downplaying of the didactic dimension of Hawthorne's writings seems to me to tip the scale too far in the opposite direction. Hawthorne may have deplored many aspects of Puritanism, but each of his romances nevertheless constitutes an effort to resuscitate the Puritan notion that any shared value system must be founded on the recognition of guilt as an ineluctable inheritance of man.

For discussions of Hawthorne's ambivalent view of Puritanism, see J. Golden Taylor, *Hawthorne's Ambivalence Toward Puritanism* (Logan: Utah State UP, 1965); and Joseph Schwartz, "Three Aspects of Hawthorne's Puritanism," *New England Quarterly* 36 (1963): 192–208.

7. Colacurcio, *Province*, p. 20.
8. Colacurcio, *Province*, p. 30.
9. Alison Easton places "Rappaccini"—published, and presumably written, in the winter of 1844 —among the last seven tales he wrote in her chronological listing of the tales. Barring introductory sketches, the other six pieces are "A Book of Autographs" (likewise published in 1844), "P's Correspondence" (1845), "Main-street" (1849), "The Snow-Image," "The Great Stone Face," "Ethan Brand," (1850), and "Feathertop" (1852) (Easton omits "A Good Man's Miracle"—also published in

1844—from her list). See Easton, *The Making of the Hawthorne Subject* (Columbia: University of Missouri Press, 1996), p. 251. For discussions of the specific nature of Hawthorne's writings in this period, see for instance Richard P. Adams, "Hawthorne: The Old Manse Period," *Tulane Studies in English* 8 (1958): 115–51; John J. McDonald, "The Old Manse Period Canon," *Nathaniel Hawthorne Journal* 2 (1972): 13–39; and "'The Old Manse' and Hawthorne's Mosses: The Inception and Development of *Mosses from an Old Manse*," *Texas Studies in Literature and Language* 16 (1974): 77–108; Baym, *Shape*, pp. 98–116; and Easton, pp. 131–88.

10. In *The Darkened Sky: Nineteenth-Century American Novelists and Religion* (Notre Dame: University of Notre Dame Press, 1969), John T. Frederick succinctly expresses a widely held preference for the tales of the first period over those of the eighteen-forties. In Frederick's view, those of the latter period "are intellectual in their origin rather than emotional. They are fabrications rather than creations. Not only is the intellectual purpose and meaning of each story perfectly obvious, but all too often it is overtly stated, to the reader's embarrassment and distress, as at the ending of 'Rappaccini's Daughter.' [...] the stories written at the Old Manse [...] came from the head, not from the heart" (pp. 47–48). That this blunt statement would seem to be representative of the received opinion is suggested by the fact that while there exists a number of studies exclusively devoted to Hawthorne's historical tales, his Old Manse period still has not received a monograph. The most extensive account of this later period is that of Easton, who covers the whole of Hawthorne's literary output, up to and including SL. For historicist studies of the early tales, see Neal F. Doubleday, *Hawthorne's Early Tales: A Critical Study* (Durham: Duke UP, 1972); and Colacurcio, *Province*. For a primarily narratological study of the same period, see G. R. Thompson, *The Art of Authorial Presence: Hawthorne's Provincial Tales* (Durham: Duke UP, 1993); and Alfred Weber, *Die Entwicklung der Rahmenerzählungen Nathaniel Hawthornes:* The Story Teller *und andere frühe Werke (1825–1835)* (Berlin: E. Schmidt, 1973). For a study relating the tales of *Tales* to the possible influence of the aesthetic theories of contemporary Scottish and English critics, see Melinda M. Ponder, *Hawthorne's Early Narrative Art* (Lewiston: E. Mellen Press, 1990).
11. It is hardly a coincidence that "Young Goodman Brown" is placed immediately before "Rappaccini's Daughter" in *Mosses from an Old Manse*. For the sexual contents of the former tale, see for instance Crews, *Sins*, pp. 98–106, who backs up his claims by citing Male, *Tragic*, p. 78, and Hoffman, pp. 165–66.
12. In what amounts to a general pattern in Hawthorne criticism, the very trait that critics of the fifties found objectionable, has become, in the last two or three decades, what modern critics as a rule find most praiseworthy about it. If recent critics have not repeated Newton Arvin's accusation in *Hawthorne* (New York: Russell & Russell, 1961 [1956]) that Hawthorne in "Rappaccini's Daughter" seems not to be fully in control of his allegorical machinery, they have certainly not been prone to translate its richly allusive texture into any specific signified. Easton claims that a majority of critics "see the tale as a consistent allegory or moral parable" (p. 281),

which may be true of criticism up till around 1970; see for instance Fogle, *Hawthorne's Fiction*, 91–103; Edward H. Rosenberry, "Hawthorne's Allegory of Science: 'Rappaccini's Daughter'," *American Literature* 32 (1960): 39–46; Oliver Evans, "Allegory and Incest in 'Rappaccini's Daughter'," *Nineteen-Century Fiction* 19 (1964): 185–95; and Sheldon W. Liebman, "Hawthorne and Milton: The Second Fall in Rappaccini's Daughter," *New England Quarterly* 48 (1968): 521–35. However, since these critics wrote the pendulum has definitely swung to the opposite extreme: the view of Hawthorne's use of allegory as a means against allegory itself is firmly entrenched in the scholarship of the last two or three decades. See in particular Carol Marie Bensick, *La Nouvelle Beatrice: Renaissance and Romance in "Rappaccini's Daughter"* (New Brunswick: Rutgers UP, 1985), who argues vehemently if unconvincingly that "Rappaccini's Daughter" can only be properly understood if it is re-inscribed into the context of its sixteenth-century Italian setting. See also John N. Miller, "Fideism vs. Allegory in 'Rappaccini's Daughter'," *Nineteenth-Century Literature* 46 (1991): 223–44, according to whom the story itself becomes a critique of the "wonder-working fancy" and a denial of its own allegorical premises; John O. Rees, Jr., "Hawthorne's Concept of Allegory: A Reconsideration," *Philological Quarterly* 54, 2 (1975): 494–510; Deborah L. Jones, "Hawthorne's Post-Platonic Paradise: The Inversion of Allegory in "Rappaccini's Daughter," *Journal of Narrative Technique* 18 (1988): 153–69; and Dennis Pahl, "The Poison of Interpretation: Giovanni's Reading of Rappaccini's Daughter," in *The Architects of the Abyss: The Indeterminate Fictions of Poe, Hawthorne, and Melville* (University of Missouri Press: Columbia, 1989), 59–77. For a reading that is closer to my own position, see Beverly Haviland, "The Sin of Synecdoche: Hawthorne's Allegory against Symbolism in 'Rappaccini's Daughter," *Texas Studies in Language and Literature* 29 (1987): 278–301; Hawthorne's allegorical practice, however, seems to me much more totalizing in its ambitions than Haviland would allow.

13. Thomas F. Walsh Jr., "Rappaccini's Literary Gardens," *Emerson Society Quarterly* 19 (1960): 9–13, p. 10. Walsh also points to the similarities between Hawthorne's depiction of the garden and the Bower of Bliss in Spenser's *The Fairy Queene* Book 2, chapter 12, stanzas 50 and 74–5. For a succinct account of the criticism on "Rappaccini's Daughter," see Newman, *A Reader's Guide.*
14. Deborah L. Jones, p. 163. The argument can be traced back at least to Fogle, *Hawthorne's Fiction*, p. 99, and has been repeated almost verbatim a number of times. See for instance Crews, *Sins* p. 133; Pahl, p. 63; and Madsen, *Allegory in America*, pp. 103–21.
15. The Riverside edition of Hawthorne's works misprints the question mark that concludes "Rappaccini" as an exclamation mark; see *The Riverside Edition of the Works of Nathaniel Hawthorne*, volume 2, *Mosses From an Old Manse*, ed. George Parsons Lathrop (Boston: Houghton Mifflin, 1882), p. 148. This has led more than one prominent critic to provide a Poe-esque impact to the tale in quoting these words; see for instance Honig, p. 136; and Waggoner, p. 123. Sam J. Lundwall, the tale's Swedish translator, makes the same mistake; see Nathaniel Hawthorne, *Rappaccinis*

*dotter: en skräckberättelse*, tr. Sam J. Lundwall (Bromma: Lundwall Fakta & Fantasi, 1991).

16. John Downton Hazlett, "Re-reading 'Rappaccini's Daughter:' Giovanni and the Seduction of the Transcendentalist Reader," *Emerson Society Quarterly* 35 (1989): 43–68, suggests that Giovanni could be seen as a representation of the unbelieving reader; as Hazlett observes, the fact that we are told already in the first paragraph of the tale proper that Giovanni "was not unstudied in the great poem of his country" (10: 93) suggests that he is quite literally a reader. For earlier arguments to the same effect, see Don Parry Norton, "Rappaccini's Garden of Allegory," *American Literature* 50 (1978): 167–86; and Michael T. Gilmore, *American Romanticism and the Marketplace* (Chicago: University of Chicago Press, 1985) who argues that Giovanni embodies "Hawthorne's hopes for a sympathetic audience," (p. 67).
17. Hawthorne and his Wife, vol. 1, p. 360.
18. See John N. Miller, p. 226.
19. As H. Bruce Franklin reminds us in his anthology *Future Perfect: American Science Fiction of the Nineteenth-Century*, rev. ed. (New York: Oxford UP, 1978 [1966]), "Hawthorne draws no sharp line between Art and Science or Artist and Scientist." In *Keywords: A Vocabulary of Culture and Society* (New York: Oxford UP, 1976), Franklin continues, Raymond Williams has shown that "the modern term 'scientist' was coined only in 1840, and attempting to distinguish between 'the scientist' and 'the artist' became a major intellectual task in the eighteenforties" (pp. 18–19).
20. Cf. Walsh: "The irony is not that the flowers are poisonous *and* beautiful, but poisonous *because* beautiful" (p. 11). For other arguments that approach an adequate understanding of the radical doubleness of Beatrice, see in particular John Caldwell Stubbs, *The Pursuit of Form: A Study of Hawthorne and the Romance* (Urbana: University of Illinois Press, 1970), pp. 60–65; and Liebman, "Hawthorne and Milton." According to Liebman, we may want to observe, "Rappaccini's theory—'that all medicinal virtues are comprised within those substances which we call vegetable poisons'—is another way of expressing Milton's theory of 'areopagitica'" (p. 533).
21. Hazlett, pp. 50 and 52. For an influential precursor to the position of Hazlett, see Waggoner, who stresses the duality of Beatrice's nature, claiming that "she is evil only in so far as she shares the poison of the plant. She is both a creature of nature and an immortal spirit" (*Study*, p. 120). Easton likewise claims that the poison in Beatrice "is symbolic evidence of the split between inner and outer identities" (p. 163).
22. As Honig points out in *Dark Conceit*, this circumstance should be seen in context with the Biblical allusions of the story, for "If Rappaccini is like Adam, Beatrice is like Eve in that her body was produced out of his" (p. 135).
23. It has been argued recently that for Hawthorne Beatrice functions as a "distaff Christ." It seems to me, however, that it is not so much Beatrice as such who fulfils the mediating function of Christ in the story, but rather the story itself. See Gaye Brown, "Hawthorne's 'Rappaccini's Daughter': The Distaff Christ," *Nathaniel Haw-*

*thorne Review* 22, 1996: 21–59. Brown reads the story as a redaction of the gospel according to John. While one willingly agrees that for Hawthorne, as for the Evangelist, "the paramount issue is faith" (p. 30), Brown's identification of Beatrice with Christ, Giovanni with John (and the Antichrist), Rappaccini with God, and Baglioni with Satan seems to me unconvincing.

24. Whatever has been said of him in the past, there is little in the story itself to support the common custom of referring to Beatrice's father in terms of a "diabolical scientist" (Crews, *Sins*, p. 117). For a different position, see M. Thomas Inge, "Dr. Rappaccini's Noble Experiment," *The Nathaniel Hawthorne Journal* (1973): 200–01. Unfortunately, Inge emphasizes the medical utility of Rappaccini's project rather than its spiritual ramifications, which unintentionally gives a somewhat comical bent to his argument. For a more convincing, but also more tempered, recognition of Rappaccini's idealism, see Terence Martin, pp. 97–8. Perhaps the best statement of Rappaccini's position that remains within the bounds of psychological realism, is that of M. D. Uroff, "The Doctors in 'Rappaccini's Daughter'," *Nineteenth-Century Fiction* 27 (1972): 61–70. Pointing out that "Rappaccini operates on the homeopathic principle of *similia similibus curantur*," Uroff suggests that the scientist has calculated on curing Beatrice by poisoning Giovanni, for "If like cures like, these two should be able to cure each other by bodily contact" (pp. 65 and 66).
25. Schubert, pp. 29–30, divides the story into seven scenes rather than segments, on the grounds that there are four garden scenes proper and that these are interspersed with three meetings between Giovanni and Baglioni. As reasonable as such a division is, I do not think that it speaks against my own division, which relies less on an identification of scenes than on the identification of repetitive signifiers and incidents.
26. Fogle, *Hawthorne's Fiction*, p. 220.
27. Male, "Hawthorne's Literal Figures," in G. R. Thompson and Virgil L. Locke, eds., *Ruined Eden of the Present: Critical Essays in Honor of Darrel Abel* (West Lafayette: Purdue UP, 1981), 71–92, p. 75.
28. Significantly, the letter to his future wife (written February 27, 1842) from which the above words are clipped begins with the apostrophe "Thou dearest Heart." It is written in response to Sophia's understandable vexation at Hawthorne's unwillingness to reveal to his mother and sisters that they were engaged to be married, and contains several phrases that may be suggestively read against the story under consideration: "I do not think thou canst estimate what a difficult task thou didst propose to me—not that any awful and tremendous effect would be produced by the disclosure; but because of the strange reserve, in regard to matters of feeling, that has always existed among us. We are conscious of one another's feelings, always; but there seems to be a tacit law, that our deepest heart-concernments are not to be spoken of. I cannot gush out in their presence—I cannot take my heart in my hand, and show it to them. [...] doubtless this incapacity of free communion, in the hour of special need, is meant by Providence as a retribution for something wrong in our

early intercourse" (15: 611–12). All this goes to show that Hawthorne—unsurprisingly, perhaps, yet nevertheless significantly—conceives of his art as a vicarious way of exposing his heart.

29. Cf. Donald A. Ringe, "Hawthorne's Psychology of the Head and Heart," *PMLA* 65 (1950): 120–32.
30. The first article to expound the sexual significance of the flower imagery is that of Charles Boevre, "Rappaccini's Garden," *American Literature* 30 (1958): 37–49, but the argument is most commonly associated with Crews, *Sins*, pp. 117–135. Crews' reading of the tale marks an important step towards a full acknowledgement of the importance of the sexual themes of Hawthorne's works, but it also marks the beginning of the unhappy practice of looking upon Giovanni as the psychological focalizer of the story. It is simply not true that "we see the world of this tale through the medium of Giovanni's imagination, not his eyesight" (p. 124); every perception of Giovanni is clearly mediated to us through the narrator. This is commonly seen as a strategy to undermine the reliability of Giovanni's sense perceptions, but this is hardly Hawthorne's aim, as Giovanni's sense perceptions turn out to be completely adequate: Beatrice *is* poisonous. (Some critics stubbornly refuse to see this—Bensick, for instance, argues that a "historicized" reading of the tale conclusively shows that Beatrice in truth has syphilis… We shall leave them with those other unbelievers in the shed of C. S. Lewis's *The Last Battle*: as Lewis makes clear, there is simply no point in arguing with a dwarf who has made up his mind.) Tellingly, Crews refers to the tale not as a sexual, but a "psychological allegory" (p. 124).
31. Male is surely correct in maintaining that the "last four books of *Paradise Lost* remain the best introduction to Hawthorne" (*Tragic*, 162); for another notable discussion of the relation between Hawthorne and Milton, see Matthiessen, pp. 305–12. The first succinct formulation of the paradox in question is that of Arthur O. Lovejoy, "Milton and the Paradox of the Fortunate Fall," *ELH* 4 (1937): 161–79, who argues convincingly that Milton endorses the formula. As Lovejoy points out, Milton was in good company in making use of the concept of the Fortunate Fall: it can be traced to many of the leading authorities of the day. St. Ambrose, Leo the Great, Gregory the Great, Francis de Sales, Du Bartas; all have adhered to some version of *felix culpa*. For diverging views, see for instance Millicent Bell, "The Fallacy of the Fall in *Paradise Lost*," *PMLA* 68 (1953): 863–83; and Dennis Richard Danielson, *Milton's Good God: A Study in Literary Theodicy* (New York: Cambridge UP, 1982). See also Earl Miner, "*Felix Culpa* in the Redemptive Order of *Paradise Lost*," *Philological Quarterly* 67 (1968): 43–54, which includes a bibliographical note on the subject.
32. The guilty gaze that is bestowed upon Adam and Eve as a consequence of their experiencing sex as an isolated issue gives us an immediate example of the effects of this partialization of experience:

    But let us now, as in bad plight, devise

> What best may for the present serve *to hide*
> *The parts* of each from other, that seem most
> To shame obnoxious, and unseemliest seen,
> Some tree whose broad smooth leaves together sewed,
> And girded on our loins, may *cover round*
> *Those middle parts*, that this new commer, shame,
> There sit not, and reproach us as unclean. (IX: 1091–98; my emphasis.)

In the postlapsarian experience of sexuality, the sexual organs are recognized as parts that are somehow independent from the rest of their bodies; they stand out from the whole as shameful signifiers that need to be repressed.

33. I analyse "The Paradise of Children" in chapter five below.
34. The centrality of the concept of sympathy in Hawthorne's thinking is well-established in Hawthorne scholarship; see for instance Roy R. Male, "Hawthorne and the Concept of Sympathy," *PMLA* 68 (1953): 138–49; and "Sympathy: A Key Word in American Romanticism," *Emerson Society Quarterly* 35 (1964): 19–23; Darrel Abel, "'A Vast Deal of Human Sympathy': Idea and Device in Hawthorne's 'The Snow-Image'," *Criticism* 12 (1970): 316–32; William Manierre, "The Role of Sympathy in *The Scarlet Letter*," *Texas Studies in Literature and Language* 13 (1972): 497–507; David W. Pancost, "Hawthorne's Epistemology and Ontology," *Emerson Society Quarterly* 19 (1973): 8–13; John G. Bayer, "Narrative Technique and the Oral Tradition in *The Scarlet Letter*," *American Literature* 52 (1980): 250–63, esp. p. 257; John Michael, "History and Romance, Sympathy and Uncertainty: The Moral of the Stones in Hawthorne's *Marble Faun*," 103 (1988): 150–61; and Gordon Hutner, *Secrets and Sympathy: Forms of Disclosure in Hawthorne's Novels* (Athens: University of Georgia Press, 1988), who convincingly demonstrates how veiling the significance of the narrative is Hawthorne's method for eliciting the reader's sympathetic response. I am arguing, simply, that the function of this concept cannot be properly explained unless we consider the dialectical relation involving the reader and writer; for a useful adumbration of such a consideration, see Mary Gosselink De Jong, "The Making of a 'Gentle Reader': Narrator and Reader in Hawthorne's Romances," *Studies in the Novel* 16 (1984): 359–77.

According to Easton, Hawthorne's understanding of the concept of sympathy derives from Scottish common sense philosopher Adam Smith's use of the concept in *Theory of Moral Sentiments* (1759). Crucially, Easton argues that Hawthorne develops a Smithian conception of imaginative sympathy only in the Old Manse period; see pp. 155–57. Smith's concept of sympathy, as Easton does not fail to point out, "is closely connected to mimesis; imaginative sympathy is related to the process of imitation that gives the spectator/reader a sense of the subject" (p. 157). As I hold allegory to be essentially an anti-mimetic mode of discourse, I am not convinced that Smith's concept of sympathy can be paired with that of Hawthorne, unless we allow for the possibility that the nature of the concept of sympathy undergoes a transubstantiation in being adopted by the latter. For a different view of Hawthorne's relation to Smith, see Lester H. Hunt, "*The Scarlet Letter*: Hawthorne's Theory of Moral Sentiments," *Philosophy and Literature* 8 (1984): 75–88.

35. In his discussion of MF, Millington likewise argues that it "demands that its reader sacrifice the comforts of intellectual reconciliation and choose." I depart from Millington, however, in my conviction that there is indeed, for Hawthorne, something that must be characterized as "a right choice" (*Practicing*, p. 201).

**Notes to Chapter Three**

1. Millicent Bell, "The Obliquity of Signs: *The Scarlet Letter*," *Massachusetts Review* 23 (1982): 9–26, pp. 9 and 26. For a subtle application of a linguistic perspective on SL from a psychoanalytic perspective, see Michael Ragussis, "Family Discourse, and Fiction in *The Scarlet Letter*," *ELH* 49 (1982): 863–88.
2. Jonathan Arac, "The Politics of *The Scarlet Letter*," in Sacvan Bercovitch and Myra Jehlen, eds., *Ideology and Classic American Literature* (Cambridge: Harvard UP, 1986) 247–266, pp. 249, 248, and 258. For the semiotic rectangle, see A. J. Greimas and Francois Rastier, "The Interaction of Semiotic Constraints," *Yale French Studies* 41 (1968): 86–105, and Fredric Jameson, *The Prison-House of Language* (Princeton: Princeton UP, 1972), pp. 162–68, and *The Political Unconscious*, pp. 46–49, 165–69, and 253–56.
3. Arac, "Politics," p. 259.
4. Michael Bell argues in somewhat the same vein in contending that the purpose of Hawthorne's prefaces is to allow him "to conceal the nature of romance even as he seems to explain it." See "Arts of Deception: Hawthorne, 'Romance,' and *The Scarlet Letter*," in Michael J. Colacurcio, ed., *New Essays on The Scarlet Letter* (Cambridge: Cambridge UP, 1985), 29–56, p. 36.
5. Joel Porte, *The Romance in America*, rpt. in Seymour Gross, Sculley Bradley, Richmond Croom Beatty, and E. Hudson Long, eds., "Essays in Criticism and Scholarship," in *The Scarlet Letter* by Nathaniel Hawthorne, third ed. (New York: W. W. Norton, 1988), 179–440, 375–84, pp. 378, 376, and 378. Porte's argument precludes my own on a number of issues, the most important of which perhaps being his assertion that by "sin" Hawthorne "means sexual knowledge and passion" (p. 376). My primary point of dispute with Porte arises from his dismissal of the importance of the religious theme in SL, which hinges upon our divergent readings of Dimmesdale. To Porte, Dimmesdale's experience in the forest scene results in "Guilty passion" which "turns him into a romancer, not a religious prophet" (p. 382); thus the Revelation is really a coda to his Election Sermon, in which he specifies "that he is one of the Elect!" (p. 383). The "fantastic pride" thus displayed "is the final sign of his utter

damnation" (p. 383), and "the 'mystery' of why heaven should use the energy of dark passion to express religious truth has been solved—it does not. The truth of romance is a human one, and it is dark indeed" (p. 384). By thus discrediting the achievement of Dimmesdale, Porte may be said to lay the foundation of an argument mounted in some fairly recent commentaries, in which Dimmesdale's revelation of the letter tends to be reduced to a means of subjugating Hester—see for instance Nina Baym, "The Significance of Plot in Hawthorne's Romances," in Thompson, *Ruined Eden*, 49–70; and David Leverenz, "Mrs. Hawthorne's Headache: Reading *The Scarlet Letter*," *Nineteenth-Century Fiction*, 37 (1983): 552–75. Baym is polemicizing against the view of Darrel Abel—shared by many subsequent critics—that the plot of SL moves from the partial revelation of Hester to the full revelation of Dimmesdale. See especially Darrel Abel, "Hawthorne's Hester," *College English* 13 (1952): 303–9; but also "Hawthorne's Dimmesdale: Fugitive from Wrath," *Nineteenth-Century Fiction* 11 (1956): 81–105, "Hawthorne's Pearl: Symbol and Character," *ELH* 18 (1951): 50–66, and "Hawthorne's *Scarlet Letter*," *North American Review* 71 (1950): 135–48, by the same author (all articles reprinted in *The Moral Picturesque: Studies in Hawthorne's Fiction,* [West Lafayette, Indiana: Purdue UP, 1988]). Baym's advocacy of Hester as the principal character of SL, is implicit in Terence Martin's exposure of how Henry James reading of SL through the lens of *Adam Blair* distorts his perspective: "James reads *The Scarlet Letter* as if it were a novel entitled *Arthur Dimmesdale*;" it is because he views Dimmesdale as central to the narrative, "with Hester largely 'an accessory figure'" that "James is able to see a fundamental analogy between Hawthorne's romance and *Adam Blair*" (p. 110; Martin is citing James, p. 112). In contrast to Baym, Martin, following Feidelson, wisely insists that it is the scarlet letter itself which defines "the dramatic contours of the narrative" (p. 111). Baym's line of reasoning has been important in bringing to the fore the repressive aspect of the final scaffold scene, yet its value as a corrective to the "orthodox" view of the critics of the fifties and sixties is seriously compromised, it seems to me, by the refusal of Leverenz as well as Baym to acknowledge the extent to which the orthodox view of the scene remains valid even after such a revaluation. After all, whatever we may think of Dimmesdale's "triumphant" revelation, it can hardly be denied that it is depicted as possessing no small amount of grandeur by the narrator. (I would instruct the reader who remains sceptical on this point to try reading the passage aloud—which is, after all, the way Hawthorne read it to Sophia: it is almost impossible not to be taken in by Dimmesdale's plight in this scene through the sheer pathos of the narrator's tone, echoing that of Dimmesdale himself.) Even more importantly, it is shown to be a necessary as well as sufficient condition for the humanization of little Pearl, enabling her to cease to "do battle with the world, but be a woman in it" (256).

6. Johnston, p. 31. See also Emily Miller Budick, "Sacvan Bercovitch, Stanley Cavell, and the Romance Theory of American Fiction," *PMLA* 107 (1992): 78–91; and James Walter, "The Letter and the Spirit in Hawthorne's Allegory of American Experience," *Emerson Society Quarterly* 32 (1986): 36–54. Walter argues interestingly that

"the deepest structure of [Hawthorne's] own writing is a kind of allegory that attempts to overcome allegory's faults by at times exaggerating allegory's arbitrariness" (p. 39), and predates my own argument in stressing that it is finally "the faith of the reader, forced to make choices while following a labyrinth of possible interpretations, that must determine the novel's meaning" (p. 37). See also Frederick Newberry, "Tradition and Disinheritance in *The Scarlet Letter*," *Emerson Society Quarterly* 23 (1977): 1–26; rpt in Gross et al., 231–48, whose argument implicitly counters Bercovitch's thesis by convincingly arguing that Hester, Dimmesdale, and Pearl act out an ideological position rooted in a British past that the Puritans and their descendants have repressed. More recently, and in my view more effectively, Bercovitch's view is countered in Brook Thomas, "Citizen Hester: *The Scarlet Letter* as Civic Myth," *American Literary History* 13 (2001): 181–211.

7. Several critics have pointed out how the problems of SL are prefigured and paralleled in the introductory sketch. See for instance: Marshall Van Deusen, "Narrative Tone in 'The Custom-House' and *The Scarlet Letter*," *Nineteenth-Century Fiction* 21 (1966): 61–71; David Stouck, "The Surveyor of 'The Custom-House': A Narrator for *The Scarlet Letter*," *The Centenniel Review* 15 (1971): 309–329; and Nina Baym, "The Romantic *Malgré Lui*: Hawthorne in 'The Custom-House'," *Emerson Society Quarterly* 19 (1973): 14–25; rpt. in Gross et al., 265–272.
8. See in particular Robert L. Berner, "A Key to 'The Custom-House'," *American Transcendental Quarterly* 41 (1979): 33–43 (rpt. in Gross et al., 272–278), who argues that an analysis of the structure of the sketch shows that "the movement of the sketch [...] resembles that of the romance itself "(p. 273), and that this implies that the theme of the sketch, as in his longer fictions, is "the nature of freedom in general and of the independence of the artist in particular" (p. 276).
9. Baym, "The Romantic *Malgré Lui*," p. 267.
10. T. Walter Herbert, Jr., "Nathaniel Hawthorne, Una Hawthorne, and *The Scarlet Letter*: Interactive Selfhoods and the Cultural Construction of Gender," *PMLA* 103 (1988): 285–97, pp. 285 and 287.
11. T. Walter Herbert, Jr., "The Erotics of Purity: *The Marble Faun* and the Victorian Construction of Sexuality," *Representations* 36 (1991): 114–132, p. 116.
12. Baym, "The Romantic *Malgré Lui*," p. 266. Bercovitch repeats her point without credit, stating that "this act of identification" also serves to link Hester's art of needlework "to his own role as writer" ("Hawthorne's A-Morality of Compromise," *Representations* 24 (1988): 1–27; rpt. in Gordon Hutner, ed., *American Literature, American Culture* (New York: Oxford UP, 1999), 516–537, p. 535, n. 7).
13. Baym, "The Romantic *Malgré Lui*," p. 269.
14. See note 5 above.
15. See for instance Seymour Gross, "'Solitude, and Love, and Anguish': The Tragic Design of *The Scarlet Letter*," *College Language Association Journal* 3 (1968): 154–65.
16. Schubert, p. 139–40.

17. Besides Schubert, structural analyses of SL can be found in John C. Gerber, "Form and Content in *The Scarlet Letter*," *New England Quarterly*, 17 (1944): 25–55; Malcolm Cowley, "Five Acts of *The Scarlet Letter*," *College English* 19 (1957): 11–16; and Nina Baym, *The Scarlet Letter: A Reading* (Boston: Twayne Publishers, 1986), pp. 19–29.
18. Cf. note 5 above.
19. Von Abele, it could be noted, also talks of "the contrapuntal symmetry so firmly maintained by Hawthorne in the development of the novel." See "*The Scarlet Letter*: A Reading." *Accent* 11 (1951): 211–27; excerpted in Seymour L. Gross, ed., *A "Scarlet Letter" Handbook* (Belmont: Wadsworth, 1960), 137–40, p. 138. Admittedly, several of the images and motifs that I am arguing reinforce the structural pattern of the narrative appears at many places in the narrative discourse, and generally do not arrange themselves in neatly symmetrical patterns. But as I have already stressed, what is contended for is merely the authenticity of the outline. For a fine discussion of the parallels between the characters, see Gary Lane, "Structural Dynamics and the Unknowable in *The Scarlet Letter*," *Nathaniel Hawthorne Journal* (1977): 323–30.
20. Even if we allow that the composition of the unfinished romances may have involved somewhat more revising than what was typically the case, there is substantial evidence for the hypothesis that each one of his romances went through at least one extended revision before it went to print. See the Textual Introductions to CE 1, 2, 3, 4, 12, and 13.
21. James, p. 117. James is not alone in complaining; as recently as 1980 Mellow tried to explain "the overuse Hawthorne made of his basic symbol" by turning it into a compulsive symptom of his "troubled state of mind" (*Nathaniel Hawthorne in his Times*, p. 305).
22. James, p. 119.
23. See also Anne Maria McNamara, "The Character of Flame: The Function of Pearl in *The Scarlet Letter*," *American Literature* 27 (1956): 537–53.
24. See for instance Baym, "Plot in Hawthorne's Romances:" "For society to accept Hester at her own valuation means that it has begun to make a place for the human heart and its private needs. For Hester to return at all, however, means that she has abandoned her radical forest thoughts, when she brooded on the overthrow of society, and come to accept the human community, however imperfect, as the necessary habitat of the individual" (p. 58). Bercovitch, *Office*, argues more subtly that it bespeaks "her self-conscious manipulation of the townspeople" (p. 6).
25. See in particular Baym, "The Significance of Plot," and Leverenz, "Mrs Hawthorne's Headache."
26. Gross, "'Solitude, and Love, and Anguish'," p. 338. That adulterers were in truth sentenced to wear the letters AD strengthens the impression that Hester's letter is a veiled pun; see Charles Boewe and Murray G. Murphey, "Hester Prynne in History," *American Literature* 32 (1960): 202–4.
27. Cf. Walter, "The Letter and the Spirit in Hawthorne's Allegory of American Experience," who like me finds "symbolism in the very first perspective on Hester"

and believes "that allegory is a structure of signification governing relations and play among all signifiers in the novel" (p. 52).

28. See our discussion of Arac, "Politics," in the introduction to this chapter. For readings that relate the passage to revolutionary activities in Europe, see Larry J. Reynolds, pp. 79–96; and Bercovitch, *Office*, pp. 73–112.
29. Millington, *Practicing*, p. 89.
30. See note 5 above.
31. Cf. Gordon Hutner, "Secrets and Sympathy in *The Scarlet Letter*: Hawthorne's Confessional Strategies," *Mosaic* 16 (1983): 113–24, who rewardingly discusses Hawthorne's use of the "formula of alternative possibilities"—Winters' term for the strategy that Matthiessen later called the "device of multiple choice"—as a means to elicit "the reader's sympathetic apprehension" (p. 123) of the purport the narrative is designed to communicate. See also Yvor Winters, "Maule's Curse, or Hawthorne and the Problem of Allegory," in *Maule's Curse* (Norfolk: New Directions, 1938); rpt. in *In Defense of Reason* (New York: Swallow, 1947).
32. George E. Woodberry, *Nathaniel Hawthorne* (New York: Houghton Mifflin, 1902), p. 201. Cited in Frederick, p. 53.
33. Ursula Brumm, "Christ and Adam as 'Figures' in American Literature," in Sacvan Bercovitch, ed., *The American Puritan Imagination: Essays in Revaluation* (London: Cambridge UP, 1974), 196–212 and 239–40. See also Michael J Colacurcio, "A Better Mode of Evidence—The Transcendental Problem of Faith and Spirit," *Emerson Society Quarterly* 54 (1969): 12–22, who convincingly argues that a distinctive trait of Transcendentalism is its conception of faith as a faculty of the Self which perceives "proper good with intuitive immediacy" (p. 16), but misreads "Rappaccini's Daughter" as a tale which is compliant with this denial of the need of mediation.
34. Sacvan Bercovitch, "The Scarlet Letter: A Twice-Told Tale," *Nathaniel Hawthorne Review* 22 (1996): 1–20, p. 15.
35. Matthiessen, pp. 276 and 277.
36. St. Augustine, *The City of God*, ed. Vernon J. Bourke; tr. Gerald G. Walsh, Demetrius B. Zema, Grace Monahan, and Daniel J. Honan (Garden City: Doubleday, 1958), p. 383.
37. Bercovitch, *The American Jeremiad*, especially pp. 31–61.
38. We owe the recognition of this "Dante-esque fantasy of condemned love" to Leverenz, "Mrs. Hawthorne's Headache," p. 418.
39. The concluding motto's resemblance to the last line of Marvell's poem was first noted by Robert L. Brant, "Hawthorne and Marvell," *American Literature* 30 (1958): 366. In full, the concluding stanza of Marvell's poem runs:

    This is the only Banneret
    That ever Love created yet:
    Who though, by the Malignant Starrs,
    Forced to live in Storms and Warrs;

Yet dying leaves a Perfume here,
And Musick within every Ear:
And he in Story only rules,
In a Field Sable a Lover Gules.

See: Andrew Marvell, *Poems*, ed., Hugh MacDonald (Cambridge: Harvard UP, 1963), p. 25.

40. Pearce, "Hawthorne and the Sense of the Past," p. 347.

**Notes to Chapter Four**

1. *Graham's Magazine* (May, 1851); rpt. in J. Donald Crowley, *Hawthorne: The Critical Heritage* (London: Routledge and Kegan Paul, 1970), 197–201, p. 197.
2. Matthiessen, p. 332; and Anthony Trollope, "The Genius of Nathaniel Hawthorne," *North American Review* 129 (September, 1879): 203–222; rpt. in David B. Kesterson, ed., *The Merrill Studies in The Marble Faun* (Columbus: Charles E. Merrill Publishing Company, 1971), 10–13. Others who pronounce the ending a failure include Hoffman, pp. 187–201; Marius Bewley, *The Eccentric Design: Form in the Classical American Novel* (New York: Columbia UP, 1959), pp. 175–83; Claudia Johnson, *The Productive Tension of Hawthorne's Art* (Alabama: University of Alabama Press, 1981), p 77; Dauber, p. 148. For an important contrasting view, see Francis Joseph Battaglia, "*The House of the Seven Gables*: New Light on Old Problems," *PMLA* 82 (1967): 579–90; and "The (Unmeretricious) House of the Seven Gables," *Studies in the Novel* 2 (1970): 468–73.
3. Michael Bell, "Introduction," in *The House of the Seven Gables* by Nathaniel Hawthorne (Oxford: Oxford UP, 1991), vii–xxi, p. xxi. Milton R. Stern, "Introduction," in *The House of the Seven Gables* by Nathaniel Hawthorne (London: Penguin, 1981), vii–xxxiii, argues to the same effect: "The absolute nature of the happy ending is, in effect, denied by all the rest of the book, and the ending arises not from the directions of the romance's energy but from the conventions of Hawthorne's literary marketplace and—in 1850—his unaccustomed happiness and his relatively complacent and willing participation in those conventions" (p. xxxii). See also Gilmore, pp. 96–112.
4. This group includes William B. Dillingham, "Structure and Theme in *The House of the Seven Gables*," *Nineteenth-Century Fiction* 14 (1959): 59–70; rpt. in Seymour L. Gross, ed., *The House of the Seven Gables* by Nathaniel Hawthorne (New York: Norton, 1967), 449–59.; Edgar A. Dryden, "Hawthorne's Castle in the Air: Form and Theme in *The House of the Seven Gables*," *ELH* 38 (1971): 294–317; Baym, *Shape*, p. 171; and Swann, *Tradition*, pp. 116–17.

5. Waggoner provides a lucid account of how the imagery of line and circle permeates the whole of the romance. For a discussion of "the contradiction between the linear and cyclical views of history" from a more outspoken historicist perspective, see Michael Bell, *Hawthorne and the Historical Romance of New England* (Princeton: Princeton UP, 1971), p. 213–214. In HSG, Bell argues, Hawthorne attempts to synthesize these two contradictory views, but ultimately fails in doing so. Bell, too, takes note of the image of the ascending spiral curve without referring to Waggoner's discussion, but dismisses it on the grounds that Clifford lacks narrative authority (pp. 223–5).

   To date, the most convincing argument concerning the ending is that of Brook Thomas, "*The House of the Seven Gables:* Reading the Romance of America," *PMLA* 97 (1982): 195–211; rpt. in Brian Harding, ed., *Nathaniel Hawthorne: Critical Assessments: Volume III The Critical Response, Assessments of Individual Woks Since 1900* (Mountfield: Helm Information, 1998), 347–72, who predates my effort to show how Hawthorne's romance escapes the accusation of "affirming the widespread American belief in democratic progress" (p. 367). See also *Cross-examinations of Law and Literature: Cooper, Hawthorne, Stowe, and Melville* (Cambridge: Cambridge UP, 1987), pp. 45–90, by the same author. Thomas, however, is a notable exception among recent critics, who have tended, rather, to side step the question of the problematical ending of HSG in an effort to define its ideological centre in the discourse of its contemporary historical context. Thus Pease, *Visionary Compacts*, sees it as formulating a political alternative to the prevalent discourse of revolution; Pfister, *The Production of Personal Life* unsurprisingly finds that Phoebe personifies the domestic ideal of the nineteenth-century cult of domesticity; T. Walter Herbert, *Dearest Beloved: The Hawthornes and the Making of the Middle-Class Family* (Berkeley: University of California Press, 1993), likewise reads the book as an example of middle-class strategies, fraught with tensions, for coming to terms with material and sexual desires; and Millington, *Practicing*, argues that in HSG "Hawthorne is providing American middle-class culture with the means and the occasion for its own reimagining" (p. 153). Unfortunately, this shift in critical emphasis has come with that peculiar brand of a-historicism with which new historicist writings are often paradoxically marked: on the evidence of these critics, it would seem that the solution to old problems is simply to replace them with new ones. Millington, for instance, claims that the identification of the "play of voices" which he argues the narrator engages in solves the interpretive problems of HSG (p. 114), when his exposition in truth silently neglects the critical points of the earlier debate.
6. Arac, "Politics," p. 254.
7. Gilmore, p. 100, also notes the similarity between the situations, as a preliminary to establishing a parallel between the venture of Hepzibah and that of Hawthorne himself: Hawthorne, Gilmore argues, "is using Hepzibah to explore his own ambivalence about courting the public in order to make money" (p. 102). It is a neat suggestion that surely has some truth to it, yet it seems to me that Gilmore squanders

the potential of the argument in giving in to the view that holds the ending of the novel to be a concession to the demands of the marketplace. See Gilmore, pp. 96–112.

8. The view that the house is an image of the human psyche has been advanced by a number of critics; see for instance Donald Junkins, "Hawthorne's *The House of the Seven Gables:* A Prototype of the Human Mind," *Literature and Psychology* 17 (1967): 193–210; Curtis Dahl, "The Architecture of Society and the Architecture of the Soul: Hawthorne's *The House of the Seven Gables* and Melville's *Pierre*," *University of Mississippi Studies in English* 5 n. s. (1984–1987): 1–22.
9. On the House itself as the central symbol of HSG, see for instance Bruce Michelson, "Hawthorne's House of Three Stories," *New England Quarterly* 57 (1984): 163–83. See also Richard Gray, "'Hawthorne: A Problem': *The House of the Seven Gables*, in A. Robert Lee, ed., *Nathaniel Hawthorne: New Critical Essays* (Totowa: Vision, 1982), 88–109, pp. 96–100, for a discussion of the relationship "between architectural and fictional structures—the habitation of the major characters and the space inhabited by author and reader for the duration of the tale" (p. 96).
10. Cf. Alan Trachtenberg, "Seeing and Believing: Hawthorne's Reflections on the Daguerreotype in *The House of the Seven Gables*," *American Literary History* 9 (1997): 460–81, pp. 468–69. For other discussions of HSG in relation to the history of the daguerreotype, see Susan S. Williams, *Confounding Images: Photography and Portraiture in Antebellum American Fiction* (Philadelphia: University of Pennsylvania Press, 1997); and Alfred H. Marks, "Hawthorne's Daguerreotypist: Scientist, Artist, Reformer," *Ball State Teachers College Forum* 3 (1962): 61–74.
11. It is hardly a coincidence that chapter 12—as we shall see in section 2 of this chapter—in which this delusion of Holgrave is delineated, is the symmetrical counterpart of chapter 8, "The Pyncheon of Today," which presents us with the Judge, that other great believer in the reality of the deed.
12. Kermode, *The Classic* (Cambridge: Harvard UP, 1975), p. 92.
13. For an illuminating discussion of the significance of the Pyncheon-hens, see Kermode, *The Classic*, pp. 99–104.
14. Richard H. Brodhead, *Hawthorne, Melville and the Novel* (Chicago: University of Chicago Press, 1976), p. 85.
15. For previous critical attempts to account for the stucture of HSG, see in particular Schubert, pp. 35–36; Darrel Abel, "Hawthorne's House of Tradition," *South Atlantic Quarterly* 52 (1953): 561–578; rpt. in *The Moral Picturesque: Studies in Hawthorne's Fiction* (West Lafayette: Purdue UP), 1988, 251–69; Maurice Beebe, "The Fall of the House of Pyncheon," *Nineteenth-Century Fiction* 11 (1956): 1–17, and Waggoner, *Study*,, pp. 176–87; Dillingham; Carol Schoen, "The House of Seven Deadly Sins," *Emerson Society Quarterly* 19 (1973): 26–33; and Arthur E. Waterman, "Dramatic Structure in *The House of Seven Gables*," *Studies in the Literary Imagination* 2 (1969): 13–19, according to whom the romance has a five-act structure.

16. The arched window, in Male's view, is an emblem of Hawthorne's conception of the present as something through which the relation between the past and the future must be seen; see *Tragic*, p. 137.
17. The technical definition, as given by Genette, is that an analepsis is an "evocation after the fact of an event that took place earlier than the point in the story that we are at any given moment." Gérard Genette, *Narrative Discourse*, tr. Jane E. Lewin (Ithaca: Cornell UP, 1980), p. 40.
18. Von Abele, *Death*, p. 69.
19. Again, I stress that the parallels are between sequences rather than between the individual chapters of the sequences, even though it often is the case that one can identify examples of this more minutely wrought-out parallelism as well.
20. As we shall see in the last section of this chapter, the inversion of this dialogue on the final appearance of the pair in chapter 21 is one of the key moments for understanding Hawthorne's attempt to expose the inability of money to function as an allegorical sign along the lines of the letter in the Puritan community.
21. His corpse, it is true, is present in three more chapters—16, 18, and, as daguerreotype, 20—but this circumstance merely serves to underscore the non-presence of the actual Judge. Paradoxically, it is in the absence of this actual Judge that his real character can be revealed, as the actual Judge is a man of appearances.
22. As chapter 13 is presented as an intradiegetic fiction, it cannot be considered an analepsis proper, even though it, too, is concerned with events that have taken place at an earlier temporal stage.
23. On the sexual implications of the garden scene, see for instance Porte, p. 117; on its importance from the point of view of the plot, see Battaglia, "New Light."
24. On the various modes of the present tense in HSG, see Magnus Ullén, "The Bygone Present: Change in Tense in Nathaniel Hawthorne's *The House of the Seven Gables*," unpublished essay, (Stockholm University, 1995).
25. Which is not to say that the scene is not central to the romance; see for instance Peter J. Bellis, "Mauling Governor Pyncheon," *Studies in the Novel* 26 (1994): 199–217. Some critics have manufactured a scenario in which the scene would seem to be of vital importance from the point of view of the plot as well. Thus Baym, *Shape*, refers to chapter 18 as "the night [Holgrave] spends with the corpse," and even more implausibly seems to assume that Holgrave is the murderer of the Judge: "Having committed the fatal deed, he cannot return to his earlier free state" (p. 168). I find these assertions so astonishing I am frankly unable to respond to them. Herbert, *Dearest*, too, seems to assume that Holgrave is present in this chapter, claiming that he "watches obsessively as Pyncheon sits dead in his chair" (p. 100); like Baym, Herbert fails to substantiate this assumption by reference to the text.
26. The allegorical connotations attached to Hawthorne's conception of wealth and property makes me wary of accepting Walter Benn Michaels' convoluted ideological reading of HSG, which maintains that it is a tract that defends "social stability [...] individualism, and the rights to property." See "Romance and Real Estate," in

Michaels and Donald E. Pease, eds., *The American Renaissance Reconsidered* (Baltimore: John Hopkins UP, 1985), 156–82; rpt. in Harding, *Critical Assessments: Volume III*, 373–91, p. 390, note 3.

27. That Phoebe's and Holgrave's union emblematically represents the consummation of erotic love, can be ascertained by the intertextual connotations of the Flower of Eden to Spenser's *The Faerie Queene*, book 3, canto 5, stanzas 51–55.
28. See Magnus Ullén, "Dante in Paradise: The End of Allegorical Interpretation," *New Literary History* 32 (2001): 177–99.
29. It needs, perhaps, be said that our equation of Phoebe with the position of the reader does not invalidate Person's observation that "Hawthorne uses Phoebe [...] to test the 'reading' ability of his male characters" (*Headaches*, p. 140). On the contrary, the fact that both Clifford and Holgrave can be seen to "read" Phoebe, serves to underscore the transmutability of writer into reader and vice versa, which is a prerequisite for the operability of the allegorical dialectics Hawthorne's romances envision.
30. See for instance Von Abele, *Death*, pp. 64–5; Baym, *Shape*, p. 164; and Edwin Haviland Miller, *Salem is my Dwelling Place: A Life of Nathaniel Hawthorne* (Iowa City: University of Iowa Press, 1991), p. 333.
31. I am thinking in particular of the textbook Freudian Oedipal "explanation" first suggested by Crews, *Sins*, p. 188, and still at work in Edwin Miller, pp. 331–32.
32. Taylor Stoehr, *Hawthorne's Mad Scientists: Pseudoscience and Social Science in Nineteenth-Century Life and Letters* (Hamden: Archon Books, 1978), p. 98.
33. Samuel Coale, *Mesmerism and Hawthorne* (Tuscaloosa: University of Alabama Press, 1998) argues more generally that "the structure of Hawthorne's shadowy stuff of romance constitutes a form of mesmeric expression" (18). For mesmerism in Hawthorne, see also Taylor Stoehr, "Hawthorne and Mesmerism," *Huntigdon Library Quarterly* 33 (1969): 33–60.
34. Frank Kermode, *The Classic*, p. 113.
35. Von Abele, *Death*, pp. 66–67.
36. For HSG as a "radical" manifesto gone stale, see in particular Baym, *Shape*, pp. 152–72.
37. Cf. Clark Griffith, "Substance and Shadow: Language and Meaning in *The House of the Seven Gables*," *Modern Philology* 51 (1954): 187–95.
38. See for instance Claudia Johnson, pp. 67–82 .
39. John Gatta, Jr., "Progress and Providence in *The House of the Seven Gables*," *American Literature* 50 (1978): 37–48, pp. 38–9, and 45. Cf. Waggoner, *Study*: "we are invited simply to hope that their love will last and prove redemptive" (p. 185).
40. Thomas, "Reading the Romance of America," p. 369.
41. That Hawthorne was keenly aware of a parallel between the endeavour of his hero and his own artistic practice is suggested by the last paragraph proper on the document: "All through, represent Septimius as visited by frequent fits of despondency as to the pursuit he is engaged in, perception of its utter folly and impracticability;

but after an interval, without any apparent reason why, he finds himself in full faith again—just as in writing a poem or romance" (13: 530).

42. Cf. the contention of Thomas that Hawthorne's conception of hope in *The House of the Seven Gables* "seems very much like the view of hope within history that Walter Benjamin puts forth in his attack on Social Democracy's concept of progress through 'a homogeneous empty time.' Starting his essay by urging historical materialism to enlist the services of theology, Benjamin ends it by evoking the sense of history in which 'every second of time was a strait gate through which the Messiah might enter.' Hawthorne's 'this very now' is not empty time but *Jetztzeit*, a moment projecting a possible future" ("*The House of the Seven Gables*: Reading the Romance of America," p. 368). Thomas is citing Walter Benjamin, "Theses on the Philosophy of History," in *Illuminations*, tr. Harry Zorn (New York: Schocken, 1969), p. 264.

**Notes to Chapter Five**

1. Frederick suggests that the reason "for the difference" between HSG and BR "may lie in the nature of the sin: in *The Blithedale Romance* it is clearly that of intellectual pride, whereas *The House of the Seven Gables* dramatizes the comparatively venial sin of greed" (p. 57); Baym argues that the brightness of HSG "swerved aside from his intentions" (*Shape*, p. 184); Millington, *Practicing*, p. 218, suggests that writing one kind of fiction raised within Hawthorne a desire to produce something dissimilar. The list of proposed explanations could be made substantially longer, but the point, I hope, is taken: a compelling argument explaining the drastic change of tone between the two books remains to be made.
2. To R. H. Stoddard, March 16th, 1853.
3. Baym, *Shape*, pp. 208, 179, 178, and 175. For another reading that underestimates the achievement of Hawthorne's books for children, see Carol Billman, "Nathaniel Hawthorne: 'Revolutionizer' of Children's Literature?," *Studies in American Fiction* 10 (1982): 107–14.
4. Hawthorne's own principal source for the collections, the fourth edition of Charles Anthon's *A Classical Dictionary* (1848), is itself a somewhat bowdlerized version of the Greek myths; see John Lednicky, "The Myth and the Fall: Hawthorne's Critique of Democratic Literary Reform," *Emerson Society Quarterly* 41 (1995): 121–51, p. 124. Hawthorne, however, goes considerably farther than Anthon in this respect.
5. All further references to the Wonder Books are to this volume of the Centenary Edition, and will be given without repeating its number.
6. Baym, *Shape*, pp. 212–14.
7. See for instance A. R. Hope Moncrieff, *Classical Mythology: Myths and Legends* (London: George G. Harrap & Company Ltd., 1907), pp. 17–18.

8. For a general discussion of the story's relationship to Milton, see Martin K. Doudna, "Hawthorne's Pandora, Milton's Eve, and the Fortunate Fall," *Emerson Society Quarterly* 31 (1985): 164–72.
9. "Young Goodman Brown," first published in 1835, provides an early example of this logic of guilt by association, which is possibly given its subtlest treatment in the character of Hilda in MF, written in 1859. It is notable that it is still very much at work in the unfinished Septimius romance. For a sample of essays on "Young Goodman Brown," see Thomas E. Connolly, ed., *Young Goodman Brown*, by Nathaniel Hawthorne (Columbus: Charles E. Merrill Publishing Company, 1968).
10. Charles Anthon, *A Classical Dictionary* (New York: Harper, 1886), pp. 999, and 411. The sources of Hawthorne's stories are treated in Calvin Earl Schorer, "The Juvenile Literature of Nathaniel Hawthorne," (unpublished dissertation, University of Chicago, 1948), and Hugo McPherson, *Hawthorne as Myth-Maker* (Toronto: University of Toronto Press, 1969). See also Pearce, "Historical Introduction," CE 6, 287–311; and Laffrado.
11. Pearce, "Historical Introduction," CE 6, notes that "the rather complicated chain of events by which Bellerophon is led to combat the Chimaera," in the original story includes "the frustrated passions of Queen Antea and her husband's attempt to murder him by dispatching him to Lycia" (308).
12. See Crews, *Sins*, p. 217, and chapter seven below.
13. Crews, *Sins*, p. 14.
14. Lesley Ginsberg, "The Willing Captive": Narrative Seduction and the Ideology of Love in Hawthorne's *A Wonder Book for Girls and Boys*," *American Literature* 65 (1993): 255–73, pp. 264 and 263.
15. This is not to say that Hawthorne conceives of erotic relations exclusively in heterosexual terms. In SL and BR, critics have observed the homoerotic overtones between the male characters. One should bear in mind, however, that in BR these are at least in part directly related to those qualities of Hollingsworth that establish an indubitable link between him and Westervelt, that dark parody of the idealist reformer. "Had I but touched his extended hand, Hollingsworth's *magnetism* would perhaps have penetrated me with his own conception of all these matters" (134; my emphasis); the reference is brief, but the language is precise: Hollingsworth and Westervelt are both practitioners of the mesmeric arts; cf. C. J. Wershoven, "Doubles and Devils at Blithedale," *American Transcendental Quarterly* 58 (1985): 43–54. For the homoerotics of BR, see in particular Monika Mueller, *This Infinite Fraternity of Feeling: Gender, Genre, and Homoerotic Crisis in Hawthorne's* The Blithedale Romance *and Melville's* Pierre (Madison: Fairleigh Dickinson UP, 1996). In this context, see also *The Hawthorne and Melville Friendship: An Annotated Bibliography, Biographical and Critical Essays, and Correspondence between the Two*, edited by James C. Wilson (Jefferson: McFarland & Co., 1991); and Magnus Ullén, "'An Available Foothold between Fiction and Reality:' *The Blithedale Romance* as a Theatre of the Mind," unpublished essay (Stockholm University, 1996), pp. 8–18. Valerie Rohy, *Impossible Women: Lesbian Figures and Ameri-*

*can Literature* (Ithaca: Cornell UP, 2000), 13–41, studies how lesbian desire is figured in BR. See also Erlich, *Family Themes*, p. 130, who finds the assumption that Melville was a model for Hollingsworth unconvincing, arguing that Hawthorne's uncle Robert Manning is a more likely biographical source. John Dolis argues in contrast that the homosexual overtones between Coverdale and Hollingsworth are merely the concomitant of Coverdale's general jealousy of the latter ("Hawthorne's *Blithedale*: Narrative Ethos as Absence," *Arbeiten aus Anglistik und Amerikanistik* 10 [1985]: 155–164).

16. That Hawthorne took the trouble to record the order in which the stories were actually written in a notebook entry, indicates that this is not an accidental design: "The Pomegranate Seeds," "The Minotaur," "The Golden Fleece," "The Dragon's Teeth," "Circe's Palace," "The Pygmies"(8: 551).
17. "Wicked" is used several times in reference to Medea (189; 190; 194; 195). In addition to this, she is also described as "naughty" (190), and "cunning" (192).
18. Pearce, "Historical Introduction," CE 6, p. 310, suggests that Hawthorne's decision to abandon the frame may be due to him taking seriously the criticism of this device offered by an adult reader, Robert Carter. See Julian Hawthorne, *Nathaniel Hawthorne and his Wife*, vol. 1 (Boston: Houghton Mifflin, 1884), pp. 471–74; and Hawthorne to Carter, March 19, 1853 (16: 652–3).
19. Doudna, p. 170. This observation is elaborated on by Ginsberg, pp. 264–67.
20. Edwin Miller, p. 179.
21. Laffrado, p. 100.
22. On July 29th, 1851, Hawthorne wrote in his journal of Berkshire: "I detest it! I detest it!! I de-test it!!! I hate Berkshire with my whole soul, and would joyfully see its mountains laid flat" (8: 439). He later confirmed this view in a letter to Fields (Sept 13th, 1851), where he claimed to be "sick to death of Berkshire" (16: 486).
23. Which is not to say that Hawthorne was not affected by them; on this topic, see especially Swann, *Tradition*, pp. 132–84, who argues persuasively that *The Ancestral Footstep*-manuscripts remained unfinished not because of some vague psychological blockage on Hawthorne's part, as has frequently been suggested, but because the premises for the whole project in effect became extinct once it became clear that America was about to repeat the internal bloodshed that Hawthorne up to that point had associated with England. But if Swann is right—and no one has as yet provided a persuasive counter-argument to Swann's thesis—this is yet another indication that Hawthorne would not have been very disconcerted by signs of an impending civil war as early as 1852.
24. See Arlin Turner, *Nathaniel Hawthorne: A Biography* (New York; Oxford UP, 1980), pp. 190–92, and p. 272.
25. Turner, pp. 252–62.
26. The thesis that Melville made erotic advances at Hawthorne in September 1851 is primarily argued by Edwin Miller, pp. 353–65.
27. Mellow, pp. 317–18 and 363.

28. Herbert, *Dearest*, p. 27.
29. Norman Holmes Pearson, "Elizabeth Peabody on Hawthorne," *Essex Institute Historical Collections* 94 (1958): 256–76, p. 276; cited in Herbert, *Dearest*, p. 291. Herbert's book, it needs be said, is highly tendentious—as several reviewers have pointed out, he often suppresses material circumstances in his effort to strengthen his thesis that the Hawthornes were locked up in a continuous psychological warfare with each other, which supposedly has its roots in sexual anxieties and stereotypical gender-roles brought on by the ideological constraints of the cult of domesticity typical of the middle-class to which they belonged (see for instance Thomas Woodson's review in *Nathaniel Hawthorne Review* 20 [1999]: 27–29). Herbert's thesis is not implausible in itself, and taken by itself his book certainly provides a subtle and sometimes compelling reading of Hawthorne's life and relation to Sophia. But the price we are expected to pay for this revised understanding of Hawthorne's biography is exceedingly high: we are implicitly asked to reduce Hawthorne's fictions to the symptoms of more or less unconscious psychological processes. To me, at least, any psychological diagnosis of Hawthorne that is backed up by the contention that MF heralds the "collapse of Hawthorne's literary powers," and is symptomatic of "the spiritual death" (p. 271) that he eventually suffers through his marriage to Sophia, must be deemed dubious indeed. As I will argue in a subsequent chapter, textual analysis can put an end to claims along Herbert's lines that "Kenyon's detachment" in MF represents the author's "inability to penetrate the center of [Hawthorne's internal] torment, to generate a narrative order giving it meaning" (p. 269) On the contrary, Kenyon's detachment represents precisely the kind of insensitivity to fiction that Herbert displays. Nevertheless, in this particular case Herbert's speculation seems to me well-founded, if but for the fact that the Hawthornes had no more children after Rose. Thomas R. Mitchell, *Hawthorne's Fuller Mystery* (Amherst: University of Massachusetts Press, 1998) takes a more sceptical view, and maintains that Herbert's inference might be rash: "Short of a direct admission"—of sexual abstention on Hawthorne's part—"which does not exist, we can never know" (p. 174). Which is true enough; yet as far as informed guesses are concerned, this particular speculation of Herbert seems to me far more plausible than Mitchell's own thesis that the life of Margaret Fuller can be rewardingly applied as an allegorical key to Hawthorne's works.
30. Edwin Miller, p. 397.
31. Richard D. Rust, "Coverdale's Confession: A Key to Meaning in *The Blithedale Romance*," in *Literature and Ideas in America: Essays in Memory of Harry Hayden Clark*, ed. Robert Falk (Athens: Ohio University Press, 1975), 96–110, p. 99; see also William H. Shurr, "Eve's Bower: Hawthorne's Transition from Public Doctrines to Private Truths," in Thompson, *Ruined Eden*, 143–69, p. 169; and Male, *Tragic*, p. 151. For the parallels between Hawthorne and Coverdale, see for instance Randall Stewart, *Nathaniel Hawthorne, A Biography* (New Haven: Yale UP, 1948), pp. 59–60, and Von Abele, *Death*, pp. 71–72.

**Notes to Chapter Six**

1. James, p. 132.
2. Richard H. Brodhead, *Novel*, calls it "the darkest of Hawthorne's novels" (p. 111); Swann states in conclusion that in BR the "hope of transcendence to the level of transformation is tragically rejected as history asserts its authority" (*Tradition*, p. 131); Millington argues that it is "a counternovel to *The House of the Seven Gables*" (*Practicing*, p. 154); and Edwin Miller claims that "it sounds in its desperateness and ennui more ominous chords of disintegration and futility" (p. 369) than SL.
3. John Carlos Rowe, "The Metaphysics of Imagination: Narrative Consciousness in Hawthorne's *The Blithedale Romance*," in *Through the Custom-House: Nineteenth-Century American Fiction and Modern Theory* (Baltimore: John Hopkins UP, 1982), 52–90, p. 64.
4. Douglas Hill, "Narrative Form in *The Blithedale Romance*," *English Studies in Canada* 7 (1981): 388–401, p. 391.
5. Brodhead, *Novel*, pp. 96, and 110. Kenneth Dauber, who also stresses the realistic aspect of BR, goes even further in arguing that the realism of the book bring about "a valuelessness" (p. 179) that enforces that "*Blithedale* is a message with no meaning," and that whatever the book "may say, it never says it to affect us" (p. 180).
6. Kelley Griffith, Jr., "Form in *The Blithedale Romance*," *American Literature* 40 (1968): 15–26; rpt. in Seymour Gross and Rosalie Murphy, "Criticism," in *The Blithedale Romance* by Nathaniel Hawthorne (New York: Norton, 1978), 267–413, 380–89, pp. 381 and 382.
7. Charles Swann, "A Note on *The Blithedale Romance* or 'Call him Fauntleroy'," *Journal of American Studies* 10 (1976): 103–4. Swann elaborates this argument in *Tradition*, pp. 118–131.
8. The interrelation between action and seasonal backdrops is noted by Fogle, *Hawthorne's Fiction*, pp. 141–42, and Male, *Tragic*, pp. 142–44, among others. The archetypal connotations of this interplay is brought to the fore by Peter B. Murray, "Mythopoesis in *The Blithedale Romance*," *PMLA* 75 (1960): 591–96, who argues that BR constitutes a kind of half-cycle, a sequence of action prevented from coming full circle.
9. Vern B. Lentz, and Allen F. Stein, "The Black Flower of Necessity: Structure in *The Blithedale Romance*," *Essays in Literature* 3 (1976): 86–96, p. 88.
10. Ibid. The first to focus on Coverdale's role as narrator was Frederick Crews, in "A New Reading of *The Blithedale Romance*," *American Literature* 29 (1957): 147–170, who claims that "the 'story' that he [Coverdale] tells is not itself the center of attention; it is the act of telling that is important" (p. 149). Since then, the importance of Coverdale's first person narration has been pondered in innumerable articles. See for instance William L. Hedges, "Hawthorne's *Blithedale*: The Function of the Narrator," *Nineteenth-Century Fiction* 14 (1960): 303–16; Kent Bales, "*The Blithedale Romance*: Coverdale's Mean and Subversive Egotism," *Bucknell Review* 21 (1973): 60–82; James

H. Justus, "Hawthorne's Coverdale: Character and Art in *The Blithedale Romance*," *American Literature* 47 (1975): 21–36; Irvin Stock, "Hawthorne's Portrait of the Artist: A Defense of *The Blithedale Romance*," *Novel* 11 (1978): 144–56; Keith Carrabine, "'Bitter Honey': Miles Coverdale as Narrator in *The Blithedale Romance*," in A. Robert Lee, 110–130; Sang-Wha Lee, "Uncertain Narrator and the Intended Effect: A Study of *The Blithedale Romance*," *The Journal of English Language and Literature* 36 (1990): 471–489; Harvey L. Gable, Jr, "Inappeasable Longings: Hawthorne, Romance, and the Disintegration of Coverdale's Self in *The Blithedale Romance*," *New England Quarterly: A Historical Review of New England Life and Letters* 67 (1994): 257–78; and Millington, *Practicing*, who argues that "Coverdale's composition of the novel is in essence his attempt to compose a self, to locate in retrospect the traces of an authenticity that continues to elude him" (p. 155). The most perceptive discussion of the function of the first-person narrator in BR, and a valuable corrective to the view of Coverdale as an "unreliable narrator," is perhaps that of Jonathan Auerbach in *The Romance of Failure: First-Person Fictions of Poe, Hawthorne, and James* (New York: Oxford UP, 1989), pp. 71–117, 186–88.

11. Most attempts to deal with the structure of BR owe something of their failure to some such misconstruction. See for instance: Griffith, Jr., "Form in *The Blithedale Romance*;" and William E. Grant, "Hawthorne's Hamlet: The Archetypal Structure of *The Blithedale Romance*," (1977): 1–15.
12. I have myself dismissed this fact once, and would regret to do it again; see Ullén, "'An Available Foothold between Fiction and Reality:' *The Blithedale Romance* as a Theatre of the Mind," unpublished essay (Stockholm University, 1996). The speculation that chapter 29 is an addition is advanced by Bowers in the "Textual Introduction" to the Centenary Edition of BR. It is based on an entrance in one of Hawthorne's notebooks, that reads in full: "Wrote the last page (199th manuscript) of the Blithedale Romance, April 30th. 1852. Wrote Preface, May 1st. Afterwards modified the conclusion, and lengthened to 201 pages. First proof-sheet, May 14th" (8: 314). The modification was possibly undertaken on the suggestion of the critic E. P. Whipple, upon whom Hawthorne had conferred the manuscript before sending it off for printing. See also Buford Jones, "The Manuscript of *The Blithedale Romance*," *Hawthorne Society Newsletter* 11 (Fall 1985): 12–13.
13. That of SL, we remember, is (D), A, B, C, A, C, B, A, (D); that of HSG, d, A, B, C, d, C, B, A, d.
14. See Byron L. Stay, "Hawthorne's Fallen Puritans: Eliot's Pulpit in *The Blithedale Romance*," *Studies in the Novel* 18 (1986): 283–290. Stay is surely right in maintaining that "with this significant setting, Hawthorne reaffirms the power of the past to influence the present while he examines the dangers of misunderstanding this influence (p. 283). Whether we are intended to understand the references to John Eliot as an ironic contrast to the Blithedalers, who "fall short of his genuine spirituality", and ultimately come to embody the "Puritan brutality" (p. 284) that Hawthorne presumably associates with the "demonic figure" (p. 283) of John Endicott, is an open

question; there are, after all, no references to the latter in the book, which is otherwise littered with references to historical figures. It is true that Hollingsworth, as Stay observes, is characterized as "a Puritan magistrate, holding inquest of life and death in a case of witchcraft" (BR, 214) in the second scene played out at Eliot's Pulpit, and could thus possibly be seen as a figure of Endicott; but in that case we have to conclude that Hollingsworth embodies both aspects of the Puritan forefathers, since he is not contrasted, but rather associated with Eliot by Coverdale in chapter 14. See also Michael Bell, *Hawthorne and the Historical Romance of New England*, pp. 208–11, who observes that the recollections of the Puritans in BR are suggestive of a cyclical conception of history; Donald A. Ringe, "Romantic Iconology in *The Scarlet Letter* and *The Blithedale Romance*," in Thompson, *Ruined Eden*, 93–107, who argues that the Blithedale experiment represented in BR replicates the Puritan endeavour depicted in SL even down to its inevitable failure; and Lauren Berlant, "Fantasies of Utopia in *The Blithedale Romance*," *American Literary History* 1 (1989): 30–62, who suggests the centrality of the chapter by claiming that Eliot's Pulpit "is to *Blithedale* what the scaffold is to *The Scarlet Letter*: the place of sexual, juridical, and theological confrontation" (p. 43). I address Berlant's argument at greater length in section 5 of the present chapter.

15. Of the 93 uses of "veil" and its derivation "veiled" in Hawthorne's five longer narratives, 71 are found in *The Blithedale Romance*; see John R. Byers, Jr., and James J. Owen, *A Concordance to the Five Novels of Nathaniel Hawthorne* (New York: Garland Pub., 1979). It should be noted, however, that this high notation is largely due to the frequent recurrence of these words in chapters 1 ("Old Moodie"), 13 ("Zenobia's Legend"), and 23 ("A Village Hall").

    The first critic to expound the imagery of veils was Frank Davidson, "Toward a Re-evaluation of *The Blithedale Romance*," *New England Quarterly* 25 (1952): 374–83. Waggoner likewise traces this motif at length, also paying great attention to the fire imagery (*Study*, pp. 188–208). See also: Richard Harter Fogle, "Priscilla's Veil: A Study of Hawthorne's Veil-Imagery in *The Blithedale Romance*," *Nathaniel Hawthorne Journal* 2 (1972): 59–65; Bill Christophersen, "Behind the White Veil: Self-Awareness in Hawthorne's *The Blithedale Romance*," *Modern Language Studies* 12 (1982): 81–92; and Richard H. Brodhead, "Veiled Ladies: Toward a History of Antebellum Entertainment," *American Literary History* 1 (1989): 273–294.

16. For a rewarding discussion of the many fleeting references to Catholicism in BR, relating these to convent literature, see Robert S. Levine, *Conspiracy and Romance: Studies in Brockden Brown, Cooper, Hawthorne, and Melville* (Cambridge: Cambridge UP, 1989). The Catholic allusions in Hawthorne's fictions are also discussed in Franchot, *Roads to Rome*.

17. Tony Tanner, "Introduction," *The Blithedale Romance*, by Nathaniel Hawthorne (Oxford: Oxford UP, 1991), vii–xli, pp. xxi–xxii. Tanner raises a number of issues that I develop in this chapter. Of especial importance to my own discussion are his pages

on the veil imagery (pp. xx–xxii), and his important observations of how BR establishes an interrelation between alcohol and spirituality (pp. xxxvii–xli).

18. Tony Tanner, p. xx.
19. See Frank Davidson, and Waggoner, *Study*, pp. 191–95. Admittedly, Waggoner implicitly acknowledges the functional difference between veils and masks in his characterization of Zenobia and Priscilla ("one wears a veil by choice, the other by necessity" [p. 193]), yet seems nevertheless to accept the homology between veils and masks posited by Davidson.
20. On the same reasoning, the argument that Zenobia represents natural eroticism and Priscilla repressive cultural artifice seems to me as distorting as it is reductive; see Nina Baym, "*The Blithedale Romance*: A Radical Reading," *Journal of English and Germanic Philology* 67 (1968): 545–69; and Kent Bales, "The Allegory and the Radical Romantic Ethic of *The Blithedale Romance*." *American Literature* 46 (1974): 41–53. It should be noted in this context that the chiastically related chapters 8 and 17 contrast "the mask with which [Nature] mysteriously hides herself from mortals" (66) with the bit of naturalness that Coverdale testifies to seeing in the domestic scene of middle-class family life he observes from his hotel room: "I bless God for these good folks!" he comments, adding, "I have not seen a prettier bit of nature, in all my summer in the country, than they have shown me here in a rather stylish boarding-house" (151).
21. *A Mask (Comus)*, lines 75–77; in John Milton, *Poetical Works*, ed. Douglas Bush (Oxford: Oxford UP, 1966), 109–39.
22. Ibid. line 418.
23. Ibid. lines 205–20.
24. That this is how we must conceive of Coverdale's illness is made explicit in this paragraph from chapter 8: "My fit of illness had been an avenue between two existences; the low-arched and darksome doorway, through which I crept out of a life of old conventionalisms, on my hands and knees, as it were, and gained admittance into the freer region that lay beyond. In this respect, it was like death. And, as with death, too, it was good to have gone through it. [...] In literal and physical truth, I was quite another man. I had a lively sense of the exultation with which the spirit will enter on the next stage of its eternal progress, after leaving the heavy burthen of its mortality in an earthly grave, with as little concern for what may become of it, as now affected me for the flesh which I had lost" (61).
25. Hoffman, p. 159.
26. John Milton, "An Apology for Smectymnuus," (1642) cited in *Poetical Works*, ed. Douglas Bush (Oxford: Oxford UP, 1966), p. xxxi.
27. Taylor Stoehr, *Mad Scientists*, p. 210.
28. *The Divine Comedy of Dante Alighieri*, tr. by Henry F. Cary (New York: P. F. Collier & Son, 1909), p. 53. For the mistaken attribution of the Dante-allusion to the opening canto of the Comedy , see for instance the Norton Critical Edition (1978), edited by Seymour Gross and Rosalie Murphy. Rowe, p. 204, amends the mistake in a note,

but judging from its recurrence in later editions—for instance, the Penguin American Library edition (1983), with uncredited Notes (Introduction by Annette Kolodny), and the Oxford World's Classics Edition, with Explanatory Notes by John Dugdale (1991)—his observation seems to have passed unnoticed on most commentators.

29. Eric Auerbach, *Mimesis: The Representation of Reality in Western Literature*, tr. Willard R. Trask (Princeton: Princeton UP, 1953), pp. 202, and 196.
30. For the nature of the suicides' sin, see for instance the notes to lines 37–39 of Canto 13 in *The Divine Comedy of Dante Alighieri: Volume 1 Inferno*, ed. and tr. by Robert M. Durling, "Introduction and Notes" by Ronald L. Martinez and Robert M. Durling, (Oxford: Oxford UP, 1996), pp. 210–11.
31. For a convincing argument to the same effect, see Jonathan Auerbach, "Hawthorne's *The Blithedale Romance* and the Death of Enchantment;" rpt. in Harding, *Critical Assessments: Volume III*, 418–56, p. 436.
32. The flower imagery surrounding Priscilla is instigated in the very paragraph in which she is introduced, where Coverdale likens her to "a flower-shrub" (27). She is associated with flowers throughout; see pp. 59, 100, 169, 193, and 224.
33. Person, *Headaches*, also notes that "Zenobia's relationship to Priscilla resembles Hester's to Pearl" (p. 151), for as he observes, "while Hester wears the scarlet letter, Pearl *is* the letter" (p. 127).
34. Von Abele, *Death*, p. 80. Barbara F. and Allen B. Lefcowitz, "Some Rents in the Veil: New Light on Priscilla and Zenobia in *The Blithedale Romance*," *Nineteenth-Century Fiction* 21 (1966): 263–275, go a good deal further than Von Abele, suggesting—without demonstrating—that Priscilla has worked as a prostitute, that old Moodie is not really her father, but her pimp, and that Coverdale himself has bought the services of prostitutes. I think that our understanding of Hawthorne's romance is impeded rather than enhanced by speculative flights of fancy of this kind, grounded, as they are, in the aesthetic paradigm of the realistic novel rather than in that of Hawthorne's allegorical methods.
35. The parallel between Hester and Priscilla was first noted by Male, *Tragic*, p. 150.
36. See for instance Oscar Cargill, "Nemesis and Nathaniel Hawthorne," *PMLA* 52 (1937): 848–62. The most informed account, by far, is that of Mitchell. The significance of this reference must remain shrouded in mystery, but one can rest assured that it must have concerned a point of some importance to Hawthorne himself, or he would not have put it in. Personally, however, I find it very difficult to believe that Hawthorne was ever, consciously or unconsciously, sexually attracted to Fuller, as Mitchell argues.
37. John Harmon McEllroy, and Edward L. McDonald, "The Coverdale Romance," *Studies in the Novel* 14 (1982): 1–16, argue that Zenobia is murdered by Coverdale. As fantastic a scenario as that of McEllroy and McDonald may seem, a number of critics have argued along similar lines. See for instance Beverly Hume, "Restructuring the Case against Hawthorne's Coverdale," *Nineteenth-Century Literature* 40 (1986): 387–399;

DeSalvo, pp. 117–18; and Claudia Johnson, p. 86. For a much more subtle—though in my view ultimately still unconvincing—feminist argument about Coverdale's psychological urge to silence Zenobia, see Laura E. Tanner, "Speaking with 'Hands at Our Throats': The Struggle for Artistic Voice in *The Blithedale Romance*," *Studies in American Fiction* 21 (1993): 1–19.

38. Students of rhetoric will be aware that the nature of the distinction between metaphor and metonymy remains a contested area; my usage follows de Man, *Allegories*, p. 63.
39. Herbert claims that "Priscilla's power depends upon Hollingsworth's being haunted by Zenobia's accusing ghost" (*Dearest*, p. 28). As always, however, one should be careful not to yield to the temptation to distil unconscious meanings from a text before one has made certain of the width of its consciously wrought out meanings. I am wary, therefore, of Herbert's attempt to read this scene as a representation of the "covert reciprocal rage" (p. 29) with which Hawthorne allegedly countered the tactics of Sophia designed to make her husband feel "answerable for her miseries" (p. 28) in their daily life. Such an interpretation seems to me an unhappy return to the vulgar Freudianisms of Crews. What is more, it disregards the fact that Hawthorne apparently constructed this scene to give to Hollingsworth what he felt the reformer deserved. E. P. Whipple once claimed to have suggested to Hawthorne "that he had not sufficiently punished Hollingsworth for his cruelty to Zenobia," at which the writer reportedly claimed to "hate the man ten times worse" than his friend, adding that he did not know "how such a nature can feel the remorse he ought to feel." A few days later, however, he is to have reported triumphantly to Whipple that he had found a way to punish him, citing the passage on pages 242–3 of BR that begins "I have come, Hollingsworth [...] ," and ends "Ever since we parted I have been busy with a single murderer." (See 16: 537, note 2).
40. For an argument to this effect, see Alfred H. Marks, "Ironic Inversion in *The Blithedale Romance*," *Emerson Society Quarterly* 55 (1969): 95–102.
41. Rowe, p. 70.
42. Emerson, in "The Poet," symptomatically takes the opposite position: "The spirit of the world, the great calm presence of the creator, comes not forth to the sorceries of opium or of wine. The sublime vision comes to the pure and simple soul in a clean and chaste body. [...] For poetry is not 'Devil's wine,' but God's wine" (pp. 174–75). I have suggested elsewhere that in his portrayal of Coverdale, Hawthorne could be taking a veiled fling at his one-time neighbour, and these quotes certainly do not weaken the suspicion. See Magnus Ullén, "Hawthorne's *The Blithedale Romance*," *The Explicator* 59 (2001): 128–30.
43. Berlant, pp. 31, 32, and 35.
44. Ibid., p. 53.
45. Tony Tanner, p. xxvi; cf. Berlant, pp. 42–50.
46. I take issue here with Berlant, who would have us read in an ironic distance between Hawthorne and Grandfather, on the basis of him identifying "himself as a Harvard

man," which, Berlant claims, "in contrast to Hawthorne [...] locates him squarely within liberal, Unitarian ideology" (pp. 47–8). To take this circumstance as evidence of Hawthorne ironically undermining the words of Grandfather, seems to me the cry of a critic desperately seeking to sustain her argument in the face of confuting evidence. Hawthorne nowhere suggests that the calamity of King Philip's War in any way detracts from Eliot's achievement. On the contrary, while conceding that the war led to the dissolution of the community of the Christianized Indians, for Grandfather this only serves to underscore how admirable it was that Eliot's "zeal did not grow cold." In conclusion, Hawthorne has Grandfather tell the children that of all the soldiers who fought in the war, no one "did anything a thousandth part so glorious, as Mr. Eliot did, when he translated the Bible for the Indians" (50). If this is irony, then what is not?

It seems to me, then, that Berlant and Tanner alike overvalue Hawthorne's sympathy for the Indians' plight. They are, admittedly, in good company in detecting irony in unlikely places: the most consistent attempt to read Hawthorne ironically is that of Colacurcio, *Province*. Similar registrations of irony in Hawthorne include: Ely Stock, "History and the Bible in Hawthorne's 'Roger Malvin's Burial'," *Essex Institute Historical Collections* 100 (1964): 279–96; Edwin Fussell, *Frontier: American Literature and the American West* (Princeton: Princeton UP, 1965), pp.75–77: Diance C. Naples, "'Roger Malvin's Burial'—A Parable for Historians?" *American Transcendental Quarterly* 13 (1972): 45–48; Robert Daly, "History and Chivalric Myth in 'Roger Malvin's Burial', *Essex Institute Historical Collections* 109 (1973): 99–115; and John Samson, "Hawthorne's Oak Trees," *American Literature* 52 (1980): 457–61. For a convincing counter argument to this ironical mode of reading, see David Levin, "Modern Misjudgements of Racial Imperialism in Parkman and Hawthorne," *Yearbook of English Studies* 13 (1983): 145–58, and "The Province of Historical Criticism: Historical fact in Hawthorne and Colacurcio," *Early American Literature* 20 (1985): 164–72, rpt. in *Forms of Uncertainty: Essays in Historical Criticism* (Charlottesville: UP of Virginia, 1992), pp. 260–78 and 279–288 respectively. And for an argument that effectively brings out the limitations of Hawthorne's sympathy for native Americans, see Lucy Maddox, *Removals: Nineteenth-Century American Literature and the Politics of Indian Affairs* (New York: Oxford UP, 1991), 89–130. See also Anna C. Brickhouse, "'I Do Abhor an Indian Story': Hawthorne and the Allegorization of Racial 'Commixture'," *Emerson Society Quarterly* 42 (1996): 233–53.

47. See the discussion of the human heart as a synthesizing medium in chapter two, section 3.
48. For an argument stressing the aestheticsm of Hawthorne's writings, see Jonathan Arac, "Narrative Forms," in Sacvan Bercovitch, ed., *The Cambridge History of American Literature*, vol. 2 1820–1865 (Cambridge: Cambridge UP, 1995), 605–777.
49. As M. C. Saxena puts it, Poe invoked the theory of "unity of effect" "to demand autonomy for the poem or the tale itself;" see *Edgar Allan Poe: A Critical Study of his Tales* (New Delhi: S. Chand, 1978), p. 39.

50. This pragmatic thrust of Hawthorne's aesthetics is demonstrated by his saying that "The only sensible ends of literature are, first, the pleasurable toil of writing, secondly, the gratification of one's family and friends, and lastly the solid cash" (16: 407). The order in which these sensible ends are listed is not insignificant. Citing letters, journal entries etc., Mitchell argues that writing ceased to be a pleasurable toil for Hawthorne during the composition of *A Wonder Book* and HSG (Mitchell, pp. 171–72). It seems to me that even if the toil of writing would have ceased to be "pleasurable" to Hawthorne, it would have remained the aspect of his work which he valued most, because by conceiving of it as something which he did for someone else rather than for his own sake, he could indulge his poetic muse, so to speak, even to the point of abandoning the near completed Septimius romance for the sake of entering upon a venture which seemed to him more promising. Which is precisely what he did when he wrote the brilliant fragment we know as *The Dolliver Romance*, even though his family was hard up for cash at the time and he must have entertained little hopes of ever completing his new project (see Turner, pp. 382–83). Whether we should characterize this as egotism dressed up as idealism, or as pure dedication to art, I will not take it upon myself to settle; I doubt that one can really tell the one from the other.
51. Coverdale himself claimed in the dedication of his work to the king to have made his translation "out of five sundry interpreters." Subsequent scholarship has shown these to be Tyndale, Luther, the Vulgate, Pagninus, and the Zurich version of 1531. See J. F. Mozly, *Coverdale and his Bibles* (London: Lutterworth Press, 1953), p. 78. For what it is worth, we may observe in this context that Mozly points out that it is generally admitted that "Coverdale's version is inferior to Tyndale's," and that "he is to some extent at the mercy of his interpreters, cannot decide authoritatively between them, and may be misled by their errors or ambiguities" (106). If this was the received opinion in Hawthorne's day and age as well I am not competent to judge, but seeing how appositely Mozly's words fit the fictional Miles Coverdale as well, it is tempting to assume that this was the case.

    The first critic to draw attention to Coverdale's historical namesake was Male, *Tragic*. His view that Hawthorne's use of the name testifies to the irony "that during the empty religious experience" of Blithedale "no translation—moral or artistic—occurs" (*Tragic*, 154) has since been questioned by Joan Magretta, "The Coverdale Translation: *Blithedale* and the Bible," *Nathaniel Hawthorne Journal* (1974): 250–56, who points out that the fact that "the work exists in its peculiar form should immediately refute the charge that artistic translation has not been accomplished" (p. 250). I would agree with Magretta that although it occurs too late to be effectual, a translation of sorts does occur in *The Blithedale Romance*: when Coverdale returns to Blithedale, he has finally come to understand the importance of letting his love of the ideal spirit be translated into its material manifestation in the form of Priscilla. Magretta valuably sets BR in relation to the Bible, but her tendency to read the romance as a veiled exposition of Biblical fragments is unsatisfying. Much more challenging is Swann's discussion of the significance of Coverdale's name, who explores how BR pits the translator connotations of the narrator's name against the connotations of forgery implicit in Fauntleroy's name (see Swann, *Tradition*, pp. 118–131).

52. For a reading of BR that brings out this circumstance very effectively, see Louis Auchincloss, "*The Blithedale Romance*: A Study of Form and Point of View," *Nathaniel Hawthorne Journal* 2 (1972): 53–58; for a reading of "Rappaccini's Daughter" that makes a similar point, see Mary Cappelo, "'Rappaccini's Daughter' as Translation," *Philological Quarterly* 65 (1986): 263–77.
53. For a reading in this vein, see for instance Annette Kolodny, "Introduction," in *The Blithedale Romance*, by Nathaniel Hawthorne (NewYork: Penguin Classics, 1983), vii–xxx.
54. Berlant, p. 55. Berlant repeats this negative view of the love plot in her reading of SL; see *The Anatomy of National Fantasy: Hawthorne, Utopia, and Everyday Life* (Chicago: University of Chicago Press, 1991), p. 159.
55. Cf. the discussion of "The Chimaera," pp. 226-29 above.
56. The first critic to argue that the confession is a lie was Philip Rahv, "The Dark Lady of Salem," *Partisan Review* 8 (1941): 362–81. I have myself reasoned along similar lines once; see Ullén, "An Available Foothold," pp. 8–15. See also Berlant.
57. Michael Draxlbauer, "Utopia 'Re-membered': Nathaniel Hawthorne's Brook Farm Romance," in *Utopian Thought in American Literature*, eds., Arno Heller, Walter Holbling, and Waldemar Zacharasiewicz (Tubigen: Narr, 1988), 43–68, pp. 62 and 63. Examining letters and notebook entries in which Hawthorne comments on Brook Farm, Draxlbauer argues convincingly that Hawthorne displays "no sign of a disenchantment with the idea of Brook Farm" in this material (p. 61).

**Notes to Chapter Seven**

1. For a powerful statement of Hawthorne's late writings—including *The Marble Faun*—as a period in which "writing has become, for him, a severely disabled activity," see Richard H. Brodhead, *School*, pp. 67–80. Brodhead provides a lucid analysis of MF and a clear statement of the *felix culpa* motif as expressing "the faith that art can be not a likeness of already familiar things but a genuine new making," but stumbles—as so many other readers of MF have done—on the character of Hilda, and ultimately mistakes the romance for Hawthorne's abandonment of the radical values he had previously associated with his art.

   The view that the unfinished romances bear the traces of a dying genius owes a lot to Edward H. Davidson, *Hawthorne's Last Phase* (New Haven: Yale UP, 1949); some of its tenacity may be due to the fact that the manuscripts remained available to a wider audience only in his transcriptions until the publication of volumes 13 and 14 of the Centenary Edition. Despite subsequent revisions of Davidson's prejudiced view, the unfinished romances remain an understudied part of Hawthorne's works. The most ambitious attempt to rectify this state is Charles Swann's *Tradition.* Gloria Ehrlich's *Family Themes and Hawthorne's Fiction: The Tenacious Web* (New Brunswick: Rutgers UP, 1984), also devotes considerable attention to the unfinished romances, but its psycho-biographical approach somewhat restricts its value.

2. For another valuable discussion of *The American Claimant Manuscripts* in relation to Hawthorne's ambivalent attitude to the values he associated with England and America respectively, see Newberry, *Divided,* pp. 194–227. For an argument to the effect that *Our Old Home* to a considerable degree retains the plot of Hawthorne's unfinished English romance, see James A. Hijiya, "Nathaniel Hawthorne's *Our Old Home,*" *American Literature* 46 (1974): 363–73.
3. Cited in J. Donald Crowley, p. 319.
4. Early reviews were sufficiently ambivalent to allow highly divergent summations of their tendencies—Turner calls them "generally favorable" (p. 348), a phrase Mellow repeats in reference to the critical response in England, but with the additional specification that it was "also frequently apt in detailing the novel's faults" (p. 525); "American critics," he points out, "though respectful, were also put off by the vague story line and the considerable amount of travel-writing and aesthetic discussion" (p. 526). The censure has been repeated a number of times. Henry James complains that "the art of narration, in *Transformation,* seems to me more at fault than in the author's other novels. The story straggles and wanders, is dropped and taken up again, and towards the close lapses into an almost fatal vagueness" (p. 170). Male similarly contends that: "The book's almost complete failure as novel inevitably limits its worth as romance, and I think *The Marble Faun* must finally be reckoned the least successful of Hawthorne's finished works" (*Tragic,* p. 158). The tendency in the criticism of the last decades is to grant the novel a higher degree of appreciation: what was once "timid ambiguity" and "gloomy ambivalence" (Crews, *Sins,* p. 215) has become "the play of form and meaning to which there is no fixed resolution" (Graham Clarke, "To Transform and Transfigure: The Aesthetic Play of Hawthorne's *The Marble Faun,*" in A. Robert Lee, 131–147, p. 136). Even those who appreciate the novel, however, commonly comment on its defects. Thus Stubbs, despite his assertion that critics "have tended to ask the wrong questions about the work and to express dissatisfaction with it for the wrong reasons" (p. 138), complains about the structure of the work, and argues that Hawthorne overdoes the device of replacing a traditional plot with descriptions of art objects (pp. 156–57). It should be noted, finally, that in keeping with the general thesis of this study, Emerson apparently found nothing in MF of value, referring casually to it as "mere mush" (Turner, p. 358).
5. Evan Carton, *The Marble Faun: Hawthorne's Transformations* (New York: Twayne, 1992), p. 13. Despite the significant contributions of Swann and Millington to our

understanding of MF, both of which counters the view of the romance as a failure, it is a view which is still widely asserted; see for instance Coale.

6. James, p. 165.
7. Richard H. Brodhead, "Introduction," in *The Marble Faun* by Nathaniel Hawthorne (New York: Penguin Books, 1990 [1860.]), ix–xxix, p. xxvii).
8. Ibid. For a reading focusing on the Tauchnitz Edition of *The Marble Faun* (the most famous illustrated edition), see Williams, *Confounding Images*, 147–81, esp. pp. 164–81.
9. For discussions of the theme of the Fall in MF, see for instance: Fogle, *Hawthorne's Fiction*, pp. 190–21; Bernard J. Paris, "Optimism and Pessimism in *The Marble Faun*," *Boston University Studies in English*, 2 (1956): 95–112; Waggoner, *Study*, pp. 211–25; Peter G. Beidler, "Theme of the Fortunate Fall in *The Marble Faun*," *Emerson Society Quarterly* 47 (1967): 56–62; Jonathan Auerbach, "Executing the Model: Painting, Sculpture, and Romance-Writing in Hawthorne's *The Marble Faun*," *ELH* 47 (1980): 103–120, especially pp. 111–12; and Swann, *Tradition*, pp. 190–218, who holds that "Hawthorne writes the story of the Fortunate Fall as a tragedy and not as a comedy" (p. 204). Carton, *Faun*, pp. 27–44, argues in contrast that despite its apparent centrality in Hawthorne's works, "the Fall was not at the heart of Hawthorne's intellectual or imaginative life" (p. 40). See also Dorothy Waples, "Suggestions for Interpreting *The Marble Faun*," *American Literature* 13 (1941): 224–39, who pioneers a Freudian approach to the romance's treatment of the Fall, the success of which owes a great deal to the fact that Hawthorne's view of the origin of civilization is in many respects remarkably similar to that offered by Freud in *Totem and Taboo* and *Civilization and its Discontents*, which bears striking resemblances to the Biblical myth of the Fall. Freud's argument is in fact a version of the notion of *felix culpa*, in that he conceives of the slaying of the father as the original transgression that makes culture possible.
10. The decision to add the Post Script seems to have been provoked by the review by Henry Chorley in the *Athenaeum* (March 3, 1860) that is cited in the opening section of the present chapter. The very next day, Hawthorne wrote to Bennoch, his British publisher, that he planned to add to future editions "a few explanatory pages, in the shape of a conversation between the author and Hilda or Kenyon, by means of which some further details may be elicited" (18: 236). Five days later he wrote Ticknor, his American publisher, that "everybody complains that the mysteries of the stories are not sufficiently accounted for," repeating his intention "to add a few pages to the concluding chapter, in order to make things a little clearer" (18: 245).
11. Important precursors to Millington's revaluation of MF include Crews' reading in *Sins*, pp. 213–39, which, though compromised by its schematic Freudianisms, marks an important step towards acknowledging its sexual undercurrents; and, in particular, Nina Baym, *Shape*, pp. 228–50, who is the first one to effectively describe how these sexual undercurrents interact with the theme of art privileged by the book itself. A reading list for MF should also include Swann, *Tradition*, pp. 185–218.
12. It has been suggested that the length of MF can be attributed to the fact that his contract with his English publisher stipulated that he had to deliver a three volume

work; see Rosemary Mims Fisk, "*The Marble Faun* and the English Copyright: The Smith, Elder Contract," in *Studies in the American Renaissance 1995*, ed. Joel Myerson (Charlottesville: UP of Virginia), 263–75. But while this may indeed explain the unusual length of the romance, it leaves the question of how Hawthorne put that extra-length to work unanswered. For the aesthetic function fulfilled by the art objects in MF, see especially Gary J Scrimgeour, "*The Marble Faun*: Hawthorne's Faery Land," *American Literature* 36 (1964): 271–87; and Dennis Berthold, "Hawthorne, Ruskin, and the Gothic Revival: Transcendent Gothic in *The Marble Faun*," *Emerson Society Quarterly* 20 (1974): 15–32; but also Paul Brodtkorb, Jr., "Art Allegory in *The Marble Faun*," *PMLA* 77 (1962): 254–67; Stubbs, pp. 138–57; Donald G. Darnell, "'Doctrine by Ensample': The Emblem and *The Marble Faun*," *Texas Studies in Language and Literature* 15 (1973): 301–10; Rita K. Gollin, "Painting and Character in *The Marble Faun*," *Emerson Society Quarterly* 21 (1975): 1–10; and Millicent Bell, "*The Marble Faun* and the Waste of History," *Southern Review* 35 (1999): 354–70. Helpful, if disappointingly incomplete, background information on the art objects in MF is provided by Alba Amoia, "Hawthorne's Rome: The Tombs of Via Latina," *Nathaniel Hawthorne Review* 23 (1997): 1–14, and "Hawthorne's Rome: Then and Now," *Nathaniel Hawthorne Review* 24 (1998): 1–35; and Rita K. Gollin and John L. Idol, Jr., *Prophetic Pictures: Nathaniel Hawthorne's Knowledge and Uses of the Visual Arts* (New York: Greenwood Press, 1991). For a full list of cross-references between MF and the notebooks, see CE 14: 993–1008.

13. See Albert R. Cirillo, "Noon-Midnight and the Temporal Structure of Paradise Lost," *ELH* 29 (1962); rpt. in Arthur E. Barker, ed., *Critical Essays on Milton From* ELH (Baltimore: John Hopkins Press, 1969): 210–33.
14. As the reader will notice, some chapters are left out of my exposition (5/45; 15/35; and 16/34), as I have been unable to find any specific correspondences between these. Nevertheless, I hope that the above account should suffice to establish the method of composition as such: there are far too many correspondences to be written off as incidental. It is noticeable, moreover, that in the case of the first seven pairings the symmetry extends to scenes as well as chapters: chapters 1 and 2 form a single scene, as do chapters 48 and 49; chapters 3 and 4 form a unit as do chapters 46 and 47. Chapter 5 is a single unit, as is chapter 45; 6 and 7 again form an extended single scene, as do chapters 43 and 44. Admittedly, this may be entirely coincidental, but I prefer to think that it is not. Needless to say, the structural principle of a one-to-one link between the chapters of the first and the last half of MF that I expatiate on does not entail that there is not a multitude of other kinds of correspondences between the chapters. Indeed, if we allow for a slightly less rigorous chiastic structure—and I will argue in section 4 that we should—it can be seen to embrace the errant pairs above as well.
15. Fredson Bowers, "Textual Introduction," CE 4, xlv–cxxxiii.
16. Joseph C. Pattison, "The Guilt of the Innocent Donatello," *Emerson Society Quarterly* 31 (1963): 66–8; rpt. in Kesterson, 89–93, p. 90.

17. Stubbs, p. 157.
18. Through the course of the book he is given, or is associated with, a number of different appellations, among those being: "the Spectre of the Catacomb" (chapter 4), "the spectre" (97), "tyrant" (98), "Shadow" (130), "Brother Antonio" (194) [used by the characters], "Father Antonio" (195) and "Father" (186) [used by the narrator], "the Evil Fate" (432).
19. See for instance: Stacey Vallas, "The Embodiment of the Daughter's Secret in *The Marble Faun*," *Arizona Quarterly* 46 (4, 1990): 73–94, who claims that the portrait of Beatrice Cenci "embodies the otherwise unspeakable possibility that father-daughter incest is at the source of Miriam's 'very seriously compromised' happiness" (p. 81); and Male, who argues that Miriam's nameless crime is "probably, judging from the parallel with Beatrice Cenci, the murder of her father" (*Tragic*, p. 168). According to other sources Hawthorne is supposed to have told Henry Bright that Miriam was based on a Henriette Field, governess of the Duc de Praslin, who in August 1847 stabbed his wife to death and then poisoned himself when she discharged Henriette and refused to provide a letter of recommendation for her. Henriette was arrested, accused of complicity, but later released. See Robert L. Gale, *A Nathaniel Hawthorne Encyclopedia* (New York: Greenwood Press, 1991), pp. 167 and 311.
20. For mirrors in Hawthorne's fiction, see Malcolm Cowley, "Hawthorne in the Looking Glass," *Sewanee Review* 56 (1948): 545–63; and Ullén, "'An Available Foothold'," pp. 36–7.
21. Sheldon W. Liebman, "The Design of *The Marble Faun*," *New England Quarterly* 40 (1967): 61–78, p. 52.
22. Carton, pp. 39 and 44. Swann, *Tradition*, pp. 188–89, and 211–13, also suggests that the conception of the novel is circular rather than linear.
23. Donatello is likened to a hound (14, 170), a bull-dog (18), a pet spaniel (43), an animal (78), and a young greyhound (82). In addition to this he is once compared to dumb animals (81), and is twice ascribed an "animal rage" (90; 148). See also the narrator's contention that the priesthood of Rome is marked by "a grosser development of animal life than most men" (411).
24. That Miriam's perception of the scene is reduced to her seeming "dreamily to remember" (171) what took place further underscores the dream-like atmosphere of the scene, which is emphasized yet again on page 174, where it is stated that the whole thing was "so like a dream." That the killing is never actually represented in the text, but is pictured, rather, as the recollection of something which has already taken place, serves to underline the implication that the crime is not so much an act as a continuous re-enactment of an existential condition of life.
25. Swann, *Tradition*, p. 211.
26. Peter D. Zivkovic's assertion that "Hawthorne's truth [...] is an admirable one. But it is what he missed in his final complete novel; it is what he forgot when he created Hilda," would seem to express the received view; see "The Evil of the Isolated Intellect: Hilda, in *The Marble Faun*." *Personalist*, 43 (1962): 202–213; rpt. in Kesterson,

93–103: p. 98. Mellow puts it in even harsher terms: "Hilda, whose 'white wisdom' he meant to praise, is an almost monstrous character" (p. 524). A similar argument is made by Milton R. Stern in *Contexts For Hawthorne: "The Marble Faun" and the Politics of Openness and Closure in American Literature* (Urbana: University of Illinois Press, 1991). Emily Schiller rightly contests this view, yet I find her argument that the narrator of MF is "unreliable" in Booth's sense unconvincing, and her conception of Hilda somewhat too harsh; see "The Choice of Innocence: Hilda in *The Marble Faun*," *Studies in the Novel* 26 (1994): 372–91.

27. Conrad Shumaker, "'A Daughter of the Puritans': History in Hawthorne's *The Marble Faun*," *New England Quarterly* 57 (1984): 65–83, p. 82. Waggoner takes a similar view: "It is true that Hilda thought right and wrong completely distinct, never in any degree mingled or ambiguous—the error of judgement that Hawthorne's innocent young men have to grow out of, the idea they have to unlearn by painful experience. But Hawthorne thought such an error [...] charming and admirable in innocent young girls" (p. 222). Matthiessen likewise maintains that Hawthorne "clearly intended Kenyon and Hilda to be attractive [...] but the unintended impression of self-righteousness and priggishness that exudes from these characters brings to the fore some extreme limitations of the standards that Hawthorne took for granted" (pp. 356–57).

28. Shumaker, p. 83. Others have taken recourse to the well-established notion of Hawthorne's ambiguity. Thus Fogle maintains that Hilda "is the emblem of heaven, yet her limitations hints faintly at a higher simplicity which embraces all humanity, instead of, like her, rejecting much of life. Hawthorne intends to go no further; engrossed in the idea of divine perfection, he yet draws a line beyond which his speculation does not trespass" (*Hawthorne's Fiction*, p. 201). For a more tempered view, see Swann, *Tradition*, 185–218, who argues convincingly that "both Kenyon and Hilda have in effect committed themselves to the validity of the Fortunateness of the Fall, Kenyon in the form his bust takes and Hilda in her interpretation" (p. 208) of it.

29. Colacurcio, *Province*, p. 34. I address the historical implications of the romance at greater length in section 5 below.

30. Herbert, "Erotics of Purity," convincingly argues that MF can be seen to be concerned with "a nineteenth-century construction of sexuality" (p. 114) inherent in the Victorian cult of domesticity, "in which desire is pursued and elicited by its denial" and "in which the absence of knowledge is a form of knowing" (p. 123). Yet although Herbert acknowledges that Hawthorne "was intuitively aware of the dialectical process by which erotic solicitation and its denial sustain and incite each other" (p. 128) he nevertheless subscribes to the widespread misconception that in writing MF Hawthorne was "intent upon vindicating the dichotomy of childlike innocence and corrupt maturity that was intrinsic to the domestic ideal" (p. 130).

    Herbert's reading implicitly relies on his own argument in "Interactive Selfhoods and the Cultural Construction of Gender," which concludes that the "divine woman" which Hester looks forward to in her closing vision "is in fact the domestic angel of the nineteenth century, the epiphany of ethereal womanhood ordained by nature and nature's God, living happily in accordance with the inner truth of her being." This view is supported by the trenchant argument that "Hawthorne looked upon his wife as just such an angel and apostle of domestic felicity as Hester's vision describes" (p. 295). But this is letting the biographical narrative Herbert constructs take precedence over the literary text he claims it illuminates. What is more, it is to disregard the fact that Hester's vision in important respects can be seen to be parallel to that of Margaret Fuller in "The Great Lawsuit;" see Brian Harding, "Introduction," in *The Scarlet Letter*, by Nathaniel Hawthorne (Oxford: Oxford UP, 1990), vii–xlii, pp. xxv–xxvii. Rather than the vindication of the ideology of domesticity which Herbert would make of *The Marble Faun*, it seems to me that this is an ideology which *The Marble Faun* deconstructs.

31. Marius Bewley, *The Complex Fate: Hawthorne, Henry James and some other American Writers* (London: Chatto and Windus, 1952), p. 46.
32. For the ways in which the plot-line of Hilda and Kenyon serves to suppress that of Miriam and Donatello, see Millington, *Practicing*, pp. 177–206.
33. Crews, *Sins*, p. 217.
34. Swann, *Tradition*, p. 208.
35. Male, who points out that Hawthorne "seldom if ever labors a point unless it has meaning" (*Tragic*, p. 160), is an exception; as is Shumaker, pp. 79–80.
36. Turner, p. 339. There are only two more instances in the original manuscript of Hawthorne's writing carrying over to the second side of a leaf; see Bowers, "Textual Introduction," CE 4, p. liv.
37. Harry Levin, "Statues from Italy: *The Marble Faun*," in Pearce, *Hawthorne Centenary Essays*, 119–140, p. 135; and Stubbs, p. 156. For more elaborate structural readings of MF, see: Merle E. Brown, "The Structure of *The Marble Faun*," *American Literature*, 28 (1956): 302–313; Charles R. Smith, Jr., "The Structural Principle of *The Marble Faun*," *Thoth* 3 (1962): 32–38 (rpt. in Kesterson, 36–43); Liebman, "The Design of *The Marble Faun*;" Marjorie J. Elder, "Hawthorne's *The Marble Faun*: A Gothic Structure," *Costerus* 1 (1972): 81–88; and Arnold Goldman, "The Plot of Hawthorne's *The Marble Faun*," *Journal of American Studies* 18 (1984): 383–404. It seems to me worth noting that of the critics who have tried to counter the accusation of formlessness raised against the book, several have suggested some kind of seven-phase movement of the plot. Smith conceives of the structure as a seven-section movement distributed as follows: 1–8, 9–14, 15–18, 19–23, 24–35, 36–42, and finally 43–49; chapter 50 is seen basically as a conclusion, in which the theme is restated "in terms of the probable fate of each couple, and of the degree of insight which each is capable of attaining" (Smith, p. 38). Liebman argues that most of the chapters are structured on some form of opposition, a structuring device that he finds echoed in the alternation between chapters situated in high places and chapters acted out in low places (listing seven and six chapters respectively), arguing that the sarcophagus is the symbol which ties the other motifs together.

38. That Miriam's problems dominate the first section does not entail that they are always in focus. Chapter 6, for instance, for seven of its eleven pages is concerned almost exclusively with describing Hilda, but this description is instigated by Miriam paying her a visit; chapter 12 is externally devoted to a conversation between Hilda and Kenyon, but the main subject of their talk is Miriam's relationship to Donatello. Similarly, it is quite true that Kenyon is at least as prominent a character as is Donatello in the section I attribute to the latter, but the interest throughout revolves around Donatello, not Kenyon.
39. Crews, *Sins*, p. 226, was the first to observe this slippage between "Brother" and "Father;" its significance, however, escapes him, largely because of his assumption that the slippage should be seen as an unconscious symptom of Hawthorne's psyche.
40. Several critics have testified to reading the night of the killing of the Model as a night of sexual passion; see Crews, *Sins*, pp. 219–20; Goldman, p. 387; and Swann, *Tradition*, p. 275.
41. Apart from chapters 7 and 49, Hilda is aligned with Beatrice in chapters 23 (204–5), and 36 (330–1).
42. Cited in Julian Hawthorne, *Nathaniel Hawthorne and his Wife*, vol. 2, p. 240.
43. Sidney P. Moss, "The Symbolism of the Italian Background in *The Marble Faun*," *Nineteenth-Century Fiction* 23 (1968): 332–36, p. 335.
44. Millington, *Practicing*, traces the motif of parents and children on pages 179–87. He is predated in this effort by Crews, *Sins*, who argues that MF "sustains an elaborate analogy between the childhood of an individual man and the prehistory of mankind" (p. 233), a contention that holds true even if we reject the Freudian blemishes of his argument.
45. Apart from random remarks in letters and journals, the only direct statement of Hawthorne's views on the Civil War is his characteristically evasive essay, "Chiefly on War Matters." For a critical discussion of this subject, see for instance Daniel Aaron, *The Unwritten War: American Writers and the Civil War* (New York: Oxford UP, 1973), pp. 41–55; Robert E. Mossberger, "Hawthorne and the Civil War as the Unpardonable Sin," *Nathaniel Hawthorne Journal* (1977): 111–22; and Allen Flint, "Hawthorne and the Slavery Crisis," *New England Quarterly* 48 (1968): 393–408. For an interesting statement of how the anti-martial stance expressed in MF relates to Hawthorne's reading in ancient physiscs and eighteenth-century thermodynamics, see also Martin Kevorkian, "Within the Domain of Chaos?: Nathaniel Hawthorne, Lucretian Physics, and Martial Logic," *Studies in the Novel* 31 (1999): 178–201.
46. Shumaker, p. 80. The presence of the Candlestick in Mather was originally noted by Sacvan Bercovitch, in "Hilda's 'Seven-Branched Allegory': An Echo from Cotton Mather in *The Marble Faun*," *Early American Literature Newsletter* 1 (1966): 5–6. See also Peter M. McCluskey, "'The Recovery of the Sacred Candlestick': Jewish Imagery and the Problem of Allegory in *The Marble Faun*," *Publications of the Arkansas Philological Association* 18 (1992): 15–27.

47. For a discussion of Hawthorne's attitude towards the European heritage connected with Rome, see Christof Wegelin, "Europe in Hawthorne's Fiction," *ELH* 14 (1947): 219–45.
48. Trollope, p. 11.
49. Jonathan Auerbach, "Executing the Model," p. 112; the contemporary reader was John Lathrop Motley; see p. 249 above.
50. Cf. Dennis Berthold, "Hawthorne's Esthetics of the Imperfect," *Dissertation Abstracts International* 33 (1972), 2885–A; and "A Transcendentalist Aesthetics of Imperfection," *American Transcendental Quarterly* 50 (1981): 139–48.
51. Ralph Waldo Emerson, "Nature," in Merton M. Sealts, Jr. and Alfred R. Ferguson, eds., *Emerson's Nature—Origin, Growth, Meaning* (New York: Dodd, Mead and Company, 1969), pp. 5 and 27.
52. Ralph Waldo Emerson, "The Poet," in *Harvard Classics 5: Essays and English Traits by Ralph Waldo Emerson*, ed. Charles W. Eliot (New York: P. F. Collier, 1909), 161–82, pp. 167 and 173.
53. See also Patricia M. Roger, "Taking a Perspective: Hawthorne's Concept of Language and Nineteenth-Century Language Theory," *Nineteenth-Century Literature* 51 (1997): 433–54, who explores the differences between Hawthorne's and Emerson's concepts of language. Hawthorne's position, Roger claims, would seem to be complicit with the views of Horace Bushnell, who held "that physical things have a 'mysterious correspondence or analogy' to spiritual things, which language reveals in the relation between literal and figurative meanings," and "that 'we never come so near to a well rounded view of any truth, as when it is offered paradoxically; that is, under contradictions'" (p. 451); Roger is citing Horace Bushnell, *God in Christ: Three Discourses, Delivered at New Haven, Cambridge, and Andover, with a Preliminary Dissertation on Language* (Hartford: Brown and Parsons, 1849), p. 55.

    Stubbs, pp. 3–48, also discusses Hawthorne's use of artistic distance, like me relating it to the formal aspects of his fictions. I am prone to agree with Stubbs that to "find the moral thrust of Hawthorne's works, the reader must follow the abstract or 'ideal' pattern, worked out in the work as a whole and balanced against a semblance of the complexities of real experience" (p. 19). It seems to me, however, that the patterns Stubbs identifies are rather too abstract, and his formal remarks too general, to be very helpful. Thus SL, in his view, employs the form of historical romance, HSG the comic form, BR an ironic form, and MF, finally, a mythic form, each of which aims at "creating the artistic distance of romance and using artifice to probe self-consciously for meaning" (p. 138). For Stubbs, then, "distance" is more or less the same as "detachment."
54. Percy Bysshe Shelley, *The Cenci: A Tragedy in Five Acts*, 5:3: 113–15, and 5:4: 148–49; in *The Complete Poems of Percy Bysshe Shelley* (New York: Modern Library, 1994), 298–366.
55. See Kristin P. McColgan, "'By Long Perusal and Deep Love': Miltonic Parallels in Hawthorne's *The Marble Faun*," *Tennessee Philological Bulletin* 26 (1989): 20–29.

56. Millington, *Practicing*, arrives at a similar conclusion through an exposition of Hawthorne's "strategy of double narration," which "unleashes two distinct narrative voices" (p. 195), to the effect that the reader is forced "to choose one of two opposed moral perspectives," condemning us to "an ambivalent relation to our own interpretation, and thus to a subversive relation to whichever of the two novels we repudiate." Our "interpretation of this novel" thus becomes attached with "all the distress that ought to accompany difficult ethical choice" (p. 201).

**Notes to the Conclusion**

1. Waggoner, in contrast, tends to interpret the Fall as a metaphor of an existential condition: "Knowing myth to be myth, he could not confuse faith and knowledge. If Genesis was shaky history but his deepest experience made its meaning seem to him in some sense still true, there was nothing he could do but reinterpret the Fall in terms the heart could understand. Man falls, whether Adam ever lived or not" (*Study*, p. 260). See also R. W. B. Lewis, *The American Adam: Innocence, Tragedy, and Tradition in the Nineteenth-Century* (Chicago: University of Chicago Press, 1955); Melvin Askew, "Hawthorne, the Fall, and the Psychology of Maturity," *American Literature* 33 (1962): 335–43; and Berthold, "Hawthorne's Esthetics." Swann, on the other hand, comes close to my own position, though it seems to me that he somewhat over-emphasizes the extent to which Hawthorne "has secularized and generalized the seeming paradox [of the Fortunate Fall] in a way that strikingly parallels the German Romantic secularization of the Biblical story" (*Tradition*, p. 199).
2. Perry Miller, *Errand into the Wilderness* (Cambridge: Harvard UP, 1956), pp. 12, 13, and 15.
3. Ibid., p. 19.
4. Miller, *Errand*, p. 8.
5. Miller, *Errand*, p. 23.
6. On the chilliasm of the Puritans, see for instance Mason I. Lowance, Jr., "Typology and Millenial Eschatology in Early New England," in Miner, *Typology*, 228–273.
7. Brumm, "Christ and Adam as 'Figures' in American Literature," pp. 199–201. Brumm is citing *The Works of William E. Channing* (Boston: J. Munroe, 1878), p. 380, and *Complete Works of Ralph Waldo Emerson*, ed. Edward Waldo Emerson, 12 vols. (Cambridge: Riverside Press, 1903–4), vol. 1, p. 142. On Transcendentalism as an outgrowth of Unitarianism, see especially Lawrence Buell, *Literary Transcendentalism: Style and Vision in the American Renaissance* (Ithaca: Cornell UP, 1973), particularly pp. 21–76 and 102–39. For a more comprehensive understanding of the concept, see Philip F. Gura and Joel Myerson, eds., *Critical Essays on American Transcendentalism* (Boston: G. K. Hall, 1982). Despite the fact that the transcendentalist distinction be-

tween Reason and Understanding takes its cue from Coleridge's popularization of Kant's much more subtle distinction between *Verstand* and *Vernunft*, one must be careful not to reduce American transcendentalism to a poor man's version of doctrines imported from Europe. For an adumbration of the specifically American components of transcendentalism, see for instance Perry Miller, "New England's Transcendentalism: Native or Imported?" in Philip F. Gura and Joel Myerson, eds., *Critical Essays on American Transcendentalism* (Boston: G. K. Hall, 1982), 387–401; and *Errand into the Wilderness*, pp. 184–216.

8. Coleridge, *Miscellaneous Criticism*, p. 29. Cited in Fletcher, *Allegory*, pp. 16–17.
9. Bercovitch, *The Puritan Origins of the American Self*, p. 160; deletion in the original (for his citings of Emerson, see p. 238, n. 35).
10. Bercovitch, "Hawthorne's A-Morality of Compromise," *Representations* 24 (1988): 1–27; rpt. in Gordon Hutner ed., *American Literature, American Culture*, (New York: Oxford UP, 1999): 516–537, p. 531.
11. Paul de Man, *Allegories of Reading*, p. 205.
12. Ibid. p. 58.
13. This said, it should be noted that hope is much less explicitly an issue for de Man than for Hawthorne, partly, no doubt, as a consequence of the former having rid himself of the Christian paraphernalia much more radically than the latter ever did.
14. Walter Benjamin, "Theses on the Philosophy of History," p. 246.

# Bibliography

## 1. Primary sources


St. Augustine. *The City of God.* Ed.Vernon J. Bourke. Tr. Gerald G. Walsh, Demetrius B. Zema, Grace Monahan, and Daniel J. Honan. Garden City: Doubleday, 1958.

Benjamin, Walter. *The Origin of German Tragic Drama.* Tr. John Osborne. London: New York: Verso, 1998.

—. "Thesis on the Philosophy of History." In *Illuminations.* Tr. H. Zohn. New York: Schocken, 1969. 245–55.

Bushnell, Horace. *God in Christ: Three Discourses, Delivered at New Haven, Cambridge, and Andover, with a Preliminary Dissertation on Language.* Hartford: Brown and Parsons, 1849.

Channing, William E. *The Works of William E. Channing.* Boston: J. Munroe, 1878.

Coleridge, Samuel Taylor *The Statesman's Manual.* Ed. W. G. T. Shedd. New York, 1875. 437–438.

—. *Miscellaneous Criticism.* Ed. T. M. Raysor. Cambridge: Harvard UP, 1936.

—. *Biographia Literaria, or Biographical Sketches of My Literary Life and Opinions.* Ed. James Engell and W. Jackson Bate. Princeton: Princeton UP, 1983. In The Collected Works of Samuel Taylor Coleridge 7, 2 vols.

Dante Alighieri. *The Divine Comedy of Dante Alighieri.* Tr. by Henry F. Cary. New York: P. F. Collier & Son, 1909.

—. "Epistola X." In *A Translation of the Latin Works of Dante Alighieri.* Tr. A.G. Ferrers Howell and Philip H. Wicksteed. London: J. M. Dent, 1904. 343–368.

Emerson, Ralph Waldo. *Complete Works of Ralph Waldo Emerson.* Ed. Edward Waldo Emerson. 12 vols. Cambridge: Riverside Press, 1903–4.

—. "Nature." In *Emerson's Nature—Origin, Growth, Meaning.* Ed. Merton M. Sealts, Jr. and Alfred R. Ferguson. New York: Dodd, Mead and Company, 1969.

—. "The Poet." In *Harvard Classics 5: Essays and English Traits by Ralph Waldo Emerson.* Ed. Charles W. Eliot. New York: P. F. Collier, 1909. 161–82.

Fuller, Margaret. "The Great Lawsuit." *The Dial* (July, 1843).

Hawthorne, Nathaniel. *The Centenary Edition of the Works of Nathaniel Hawthorne.* 23 vols. Edited by William Charvat, Roy Harvey Pearce, Claude M. Simpson, Thomas Woodson, et al. Columbus: Ohio State UP, 1962–1997.

—. Volume 1 *The Scarlet Letter.*

—. Volume 2 *The House of the Seven Gables.*

—. Volume 3 *The Blithedale Romance, Fanshawe.*

—. Volume 4 *The Marble Faun; or The Romance of Monte Beni.*

—. Volume 5 *Our Old Home, a series of English sketches.*

—. Volume 6 *True Stories. Writings for Children 1.*
—. Volume 7 *A Wonder Book, Tanglewood Tales. Writings for Children 2.*
—. Volume 8 *The American Notebooks.*
—. Volume 9 *Twice-Told Tales.*
—. Volume 10 *Mosses From an Old Manse.*
—. Volume 11 *The Snow Image and Uncollected Tales.*
—. Volume 12 *The American Claimant Manuscripts.*
—. Volume 13 *The Elixir of Life Manuscripts.*
—. Volume 14 *The French and Italian Notebooks.*
—. Volume 15 *The Letters, 1813–1843.*
—. Volume 16 *The Letters, 1843–1853.*
—. Volume 17 *The Letters, 1853–1856.*
—. Volume 18 *The Letters, 1857–1864.*
—. Volume 19 *Consular Letters.*
—. Volume 20 *Consular Letters.*
—. Volume 21 *The English Notebooks, 1853–1856.*
—. Volume 22 *The English Notebooks, 1856–1860.*
—. Volume 23 *Miscellaneous Prose and Verse.*
—. *The Riverside Edition of the Works of Nathaniel Hawthorne.* Volume 2, Mosses From an Old Manse. Ed. George Parsons Lathrop. Boston: Houghton Mifflin, 1882.
—. *Rappaccinis dotter: en skräckberättelse.* Tr. Sam J. Lundwall. Bromma: Lundwall, 1991.
Lewis, C.S. *The Last Battle.* London: Geoffrey Bles, 1956.
Marvell, Andrew. *Poems.* Ed. Hugh MacDonald. Cambridge: Harvard UP, 1963.
Mather, Cotton. *Magnalia Christi Americana, or The Ecclesiastical History of New–England, from its First Planting in the Year 1620 unto the Year of Our Lord, 1698; in Seven Books.* London: Printed for Thomas Parkhurst, 1702.
Milton, John. *Paradise Lost.* Ed. Scott Elledge. Second ed. New York: Norton, 1993.
—. Poetical Works. Ed. Douglas Bush. Oxford: Oxford UP, 1966.
Pascal, Blaise. *Penseés: Thoughts on Religion and other subjects.* Tr. William Finlayson Trotter. Ed. H. S Thayer. New York: Washington Square Press, 1965.
Shelley, Percy Bysshe. *The Cenci: A Tragedy in Five Acts. In The Complete Poems of Percy Bysshe Shelley.* New York: Modern Library, 1994. 298–366.

## 2. Secondary sources

Aaron, Daniel. *The Unwritten War: American Writers and the Civil War.* New York: Oxford UP, 1973.
Abel, Darrel. *The Moral Picturesque: Studies in Hawthorne's Fiction.* West Lafayette: Purdue UP, 1988.
—. "Hawthorne's Hester." *College English* 13 (1952): 303–9. Rpt. in Gross et al., "Essays in Criticism and Scholarship." 300–8.

—. "Dimmesdale: Fugitive from Wrath." *Nineteenth-Century Fiction* 11 (1956): 81–105. Rpt in *The Moral Picturesque*, 225–248.
—. "Giving Lustre to Gray Shadows: Hawthorne's Potent Art." *American Literature* 41 (1969): 373–388.
—. "Hawthorne's House of Tradition." *South Atlantic Quarterly* 52 (1953): 561–578. Rpt. in *The Moral Picturesque*, 251–69.
—. "Hawthorne's Pearl: Symbol and Character." *ELH* 18 (1951): 50–66.
—. "Hawthorne's Scarlet Letter." *North American Review* 71 (1950): 135–48.
—. "'A Vast Deal of Human Sympathy': Idea and Device in Hawthorne's 'The Snow–Image'." *Criticism* 12 (1970): 316–32.
Abrams, M. H. *The Mirror and the Lamp*. New York: Norton, 1958.
Adams, Richard P. "Hawthorne: The Old Manse Period." *Tulane Studies in English* 8 (1958): 115–51
Allard, Joseph. "Nathaniel Hawthorne: A Watchman All-heeding and Unheeded." In *American Fiction: New Readings*. Ed. Richard Gray. London: Vision, 1983. 38–52.
Amoia, Alba. "Hawthorne's Rome: The Tombs of Via Latina." *Nathaniel Hawthorne Review* 23 (1997): 1–14.
—. "Hawthorne's Rome: Then and Now." *Nathaniel Hawthorne Review* 24 (1998): 1–35.
Anthon, Charles. *A Classical Dictionary*. New York: Harper, 1886.
Arac, Jonathan. "Reading the Letter." *Diacritics* 9 (1979): 42–52.
—. "The Politics of *The Scarlet Letter*." In *Ideology and Classic American Literature*. Eds. Sacvan Bercovitch, and Myra Jehlen. Cambridge: Harvard UP, 1986. 247–266.
—. "Narrative Forms." In *The Cambridge History of American Literature*, vol. 2 1820–1865. Ed. Sacvan Bercovitch. Cambridge: Cambridge UP, 1995. 605–777.
Arvin, Newton. *Hawthorne*. New York: Russell & Russell, 1961 (1956).
Askew, Melvin. "Hawthorne, the Fall, and the Psychology of Maturity." *American Literature* 33 (1962): 335–43.
Auerbach, Eric. *Mimesis: The Representation of Reality in Western Literature*. Tr. Willard R. Trask. Princeton: Princeton UP, 1953.
—. "Figura." in *Scenes from the Drama of European Literature: Six Essays*. New York: Meridian Books, 1959. 11–76.
Auerbach, Jonathan. "Executing the Model: Painting, Sculpture, and Romance-Writing in Hawthorne's *The Marble Faun*." *ELH* 47 (1980): 103–120.
—. "Hawthorne's *The Blithedale Romance* and the Death of Enchantment." In *The Romance of Failure: First-Person Fictions of Poe, Hawthorne, and James*. New York: Oxford UP, 1989. 71–117, 186–88. Rpt. in Harding, *Critical Assessments: Volume III*. 418–56.
Auchincloss, Louis. "*The Blithedale Romance*: A Study of Form and Point of View." *Nathaniel Hawthorne Journal* 2 (1972): 53–58.
Axelsson, Arne. *The Links in the Chain: Isolation and Interdependence in Nathaniel Hawthorne's Fictional Characters*. Uppsala: Studia Anglistica Upsaliensia, 1974.
Bales, Kent. "*The Blithedale Romance*: Coverdale's Mean and Subversive Egotism." *Bucknell Review* 21 (1973): 60–82.
—. "The Allegory and the Radical Romantic Ethic of *The Blithedale Romance*." *American Literature* 46 (1974): 41–53.

Barlowe, Jamie. *The Scarlet Mob of Scribblers: Rereading Hester Prynne.* Carbondale: Southern Illinois UP, 2000.

Barr, James. *Old and New in Interpretation: A Study of the Two Testaments.* London: S.C.M. Press, 1966.

Battaglia, Francis Joseph. "*The House of the Seven Gables:* New Light on Old Problems." *PMLA* 82 (1967): 579–90.

—. "The (Unmeretricious) House of the Seven Gables." *Studies in the Novel* 2 (1970): 468–73.

Bauer, Dale M. *Feminist Dialogics: A Theory of Failed Community.* Albany: State University of New York Press, 1988.

Bayer, John G. "Narrative Technique and the Oral Tradition in *The Scarlet Letter.*" *American Literature* 52 (1980): 250–63.

Baym, Nina. "*The Blithedale Romance*: A Radical Reading." *Journal of English and Germanic Philology* 67 (1968): 545–69.

—. *The Shape of Hawthorne's Career.* Ithaca: Cornell UP, 1976.

—. "The Romantic Malgré Lui: Hawthorne in 'The Custom-House'." *Emerson Society Quarterly* 19 (1973): 14–25. Rpt. in Gross et al., "Essays in Criticism and Scholarship." 265–272.

—. "Plot in Hawthorne's Romances." In Thompson and Locke. 49–70.

—. "Thwarted Nature: Hawthorne as Feminist." In *American Novelists Revisited: Essays in Feminist Criticism.* Ed. Fritz Fleischmann. Boston: G.K. Hall, 1982.

—. "Concepts of the Romance in Hawthorne's America." *Nineteenth-Century Fiction* 38 (1984): 426–443. Rpt. in *Feminism and American Literary History.* New Brunswick: Rutgers UP, 1992. 57–70.

—. *The Scarlet Letter: A Reading.* Boston: Twayne Publishers, 1986.

Becker, John E. *Hawthorne's Historical Allegory.* Port Washington: Kennikat Press, 1971.

Beebe, Maurice. "The Fall of the House of Pyncheon." *Nineteenth-Century Fiction* 11 (1956): 1–17.

Beebe, Maurice and Jack Hardie. "Criticism of Nathaniel Hawthorne: A Selected Checklist." *Studies in the Novel* 2 (1970): 519–87.

Beidler, Peter G. "Theme of the Fortunate Fall in *The Marble Faun.*" *Emerson Society Quarterly* 47 (1967): 56–62.

Bell, Michael Davitt. *Hawthorne and the Historical Romance of New England.* Princeton: Princeton UP, 1971.

—. *The Development of American Romance: The Sacrifice of Relation.* Chicago: University of Chicago Press, 1980.

—. "Arts of Deception: Hawthorne, 'Romance,' and *The Scarlet Letter.*" In Colacurcio, *New Essays.* 29–56.

—. "Introduction." In *The House of the Seven Gables* by Nathaniel Hawthorne. Oxford: Oxford UP, 1991. vii–xxi.

Bell, Millicent. "The Fallacy of the Fall in *Paradise Lost.*" *PMLA* 68 (1953): 863–83.

—. *Hawthorne's View of the Artist.* New York: State University of New York, 1962.

—. "The Obliquity of Signs: *The Scarlet Letter.*" *Massachusetts Review* 23 (1982): 9–26.

—. "*The Marble Faun* and the Waste of History." *Southern Review* 35 (1999): 354–70.

Bellis, Peter J. "Mauling Governor Pyncheon." *Studies in the Novel* 26 (1994): 199–217.
—. "Representing Dissent: Hawthorne and the Drama of Revolt." *Emerson Society Quarterly* 41 (1995): 97–119.
Bensick, Carol Marie. *La Nouvelle Beatrice: Renaissance and Romance in "Rappaccini's Daughter."* New Brunswick: Rutgers UP, 1985.
—. "His Folly, Her Weakness: Demystified Adultery in *The Scarlet Letter.*" In Colacurcio, *New Essays.* 137–160.
Bercovitch, Sacvan. "Hilda's 'Seven-Branched Allegory': An Echo from Cotton Mather in *The Marble Faun.*" *Early American Literature Newsletter* 1 (1966): 5–6.
—. Ed. *Typology and Early American Literature.* Amherst: University of Massachusetts Press, 1972.
—. Ed. *The American Puritan Imagination: Essays in Revaluation.* London: Cambridge UP, 1974.
—. *The Puritan Origins of the American Self.* New Haven: Yale UP, 1975.
—. *The American Jeremiad.* Madison: University of Wisconsin Press, 1978.
—. "Hawthorne's A-Morality of Compromise." *Representations* 24 (1988): 1–27. Rpt. in *American Literature, American Culture.* Ed. Gordon Hutner. New York: Oxford UP, 1999. 516–537.
—. *The Office of* The Scarlet Letter. Baltimore: John Hopkins UP, 1991.
—. Ed. *The Cambridge History of American Literature.* Volume 2, 1820–1865. Cambridge: Cambridge UP, 1995.
—. "*The Scarlet Letter.* A Twice-Told Tale." *Nathaniel Hawthorne Review* 22 (1996): 1–20.
Berek, Peter. "The Transformation of Allegory from Spenser to Hawthorne." *Amherst Honors Thesis* 10 (1962).
Berlant, Lauren. "Fantasies of Utopia in *The Blithedale Romance.*" *American Literary History* 1 (1989): 30–62.
—. *The Anatomy of National Fantasy: Hawthorne, Utopia, and Everyday Life.* Chicago: University of Chicago Press, 1991.
Berner, Robert L. "A Key to 'The Custom-House'." *American Transcendental Quarterly* 41 (1979): 33–43. Rpt. in Gross et al., "Essays in Criticism and Scholarship." 272–278.
Berthold, Dennis. "Hawthorne's Esthetics of the Imperfect." *Dissertation Abstracts International* 33 (1972), 2885–A.
—. "Hawthorne, Ruskin, and the Gothic Revival: Transcendent Gothic in *The Marble Faun.*" *Emerson Society Quarterly* 20 (1974): 15–32.
—. "From Freud to Marx: Recent Directions in Hawthorne Criticism." *Emerson Society Quarterly* 22 (1976): 107–19.
—. "A Transcendentalist Aesthetics of Imperfection." *American Transcendental Quarterly* 50 (1981): 139–48.
Bewley, Marius. *The Complex Fate: Hawthorne, Henry James and some other American Writers.* London: Chatto and Windus, 1952.
—. *The Eccentric Design: Form in the Classical American Novel.* New York: Columbia UP, 1959.
Billman, Carol. "Nathaniel Hawthorne: 'Revolutionizer' of Children's Literature?" *Studies in American Fiction* 10 (1982): 107– 14.

Blair, Walter. "Hawthorne." In *Eight American Authors: A Review of Research and Criticism.* Ed. Floyd Stovall. New York: Norton, 1963. 100–52.

Boevre, Charles. "Rappaccini's Garden." *American Literature* 30 (1958): 37–49.

Boewe, Charles, and Murray G. Murphey. "Hester Prynne in History." *American Literature* 32 (1960): 202–4.

Booth, Wayne C. *The Rhetoric of Fiction.* Second ed. Chicago: University of Chicago Press, 1983.

Borges, Jorge Luis. *Other Inquisitions 1937–52.* Tr. Ruth L. Simms. Austin: University of Texas Press, 1964.

Boswell, Jeanetta. *Nathaniel Hawthorne and the Critics: A Checklist of Criticism 1900–1978.* Metuchen: Scarecrow, 1982.

Bowers, Fredson. "Textual Introduction." In CE 4, *The Marble Faun.* xlv–cxxxiii.

—. "Textual Introduction." In CE 3, *The Blithedale Romance, Fanshawe.*

Brant, Robert L. "Hawthorne and Marvell." *American Literature* 30 (1958): 366.

Brickhouse, Anna C. "'I Do Abhor an Indian Story': Hawthorne and the Allegorization of Racial 'Commixture'." *Emerson Society Quarterly* 42 (1996): 233–53.

Britt, Brian M. "The Veil of Allegory in Hawthorne's *The Blithedale Romance.*" *Literature & Theology* 10 (1996): 44–57.

Brodhead, Richard H. *Hawthorne, Melville and the Novel.* Chicago: University of Chicago Press, 1976.

—. *The School of Hawthorne.* New York: Oxford UP, 1986.

—. "Veiled Ladies: Toward a History of Antebellum Entertainment." *American Literary History* 1 (1989): 273–294.

—. "Introduction." In *The Marble Faun* by Nathaniel Hawthorne. 1860. New York: Penguin Books, 1990. ix–xxix.

—. *Cultures of Letters.* Chicago: University of Chicago Press, 1993.

Brodtkorb, Paul, Jr. "Art Allegory in *The Marble Faun.*" *PMLA* 77 (1962): 254–67.

Brooks, Douglas. *Number and Pattern in the Eighteenth-Century Novel: Defoe, Fielding, Smollet, and Sterne.* Boston: Routledge & K. Paul, 1973.

Brown, Gaye. "Hawthorne's 'Rappaccini's Daughter': The Distaff Christ." *Nathaniel Hawthorne Review* 22 (1996): 21–59.

Brown, Merle E. "The Structure of *The Marble Faun.*" *American Literature*, 28 (1956): 302–313.

Brumm, Ursula. *American Thought and Religious Typology.* Tr. John Hoaglund. New Brunswick: Rutgers UP, 1970.

—. "Christ and Adam as 'Figures' in American Literature." In Bercovitch, *The American Puritan Imagination.* 196–212 and 239–40.

Budick, Emily Miller. *Fiction and Historical Consciousness: The American Romance Tradition.* New Haven: Yale UP, 1989.

—. *Engendering Romance: Women Writers and the Hawthorne Tradition.* New Haven: Yale UP, 1989.

—. "Sacvan Bercovitch, Stanley Cavell, and the Romance Theory of American Fiction." *PMLA* 107 (1992): 78–91.

—. "We Damned–If–You–Do, Damned–If–You–Don't Mob of Scribbling Scholars." *American Literary History* 9 (1997): 233–37.

Buell, Lawrence. *Literary Transcendentalism: Style and Vision in the American Renaissance.* Ithaca: Cornell UP, 1973.

Byers, John R. Jr., and James J. Owen. *A Concordance to the Five Novels of Nathaniel Hawthorne.* New York: Garland Pub., 1979.

Caldwell, Wayne Troy. "The Emblem Tradition and the Symbolic Mode: Clothing Imagery in *The House of the Seven Gables.*" *Emerson Society Quarterly* 19 (1973): 34–42

Callaway, David. "An Annotated Select Bibliography of *The House of the Seven Gables.*" In *Critical Essays on The House of the Seven Gables.* Ed. Bernard Rosenthal. Boston: G. K. Hall, 1995.

Cappelo, Mary. "'Rappaccini's Daughter' as Translation." *Philological Quarterly* 65 (1986): 263–77.

Carabine, Keith. "'Bitter Honey': Miles Coverdale as Narrator in *The Blithedale Romance.*" In A. Robert Lee. 110–130.

Cargill, Oscar. "Nemesis and Nathaniel Hawthorne." *PMLA* 52 (1937): 848–62.

Carton, Evan. *The Rhetoric of American Romance: Dialectic and Identity in Emerson, Dickinson, Poe, and Hawthorne.* Baltimore: John Hopkins UP, 1985.

—. "Millenial Letters; or, Monsieur Hawthorne, C'est Nous." *Emerson Society Quarterly* 44 (1998): 199–224.

—. *The Marble Faun: Hawthorne's Transformations.* New York: Twayne, 1992.

Chai, Leon. *The Romantic Foundations of the American Renaissance.* Ithaca: Cornell UP, 1987.

Charity, A. C. *Events and their Afterlife: The Dialectics of Christian Typology in the Bible and Dante.* Cambridge: Cambridge UP, 1966.

Chase, Richard. *The American Novel and its Tradition.* Garden City: Doubleday, 1957.

Chorley, Henry F. Review in the *Athenaeum* 3 March (1860): 296–7. In Crowley. 317–19.

Christophersen, Bill. "Behind the White Veil: Self-Awareness in Hawthorne's *The Blithedale Romance.*" *Modern Language Studies* 12 (1982): 81–92.

Clarke, Graham. "To Transform and Transfigure: The Aesthetic Play of Hawthorne's *The Marble Faun.*" In A. Robert Lee. 131–147.

Coale, Samuel. *Mesmerism and Hawthorne.* Tuscaloosa: University of Alabama Press, 1998.

Cody, David. "Hawthorne in Japan: Some Recent Studies, 1975–1991." In *Nathaniel Hawthorne: The Introduction of an American Author's Work into Japan.* Salem: Peabody Essex Institute. 49–95.

Cohen, Bernard B. *The Recognition of Hawthorne: Selected Criticism Since 1828.* Ann Arbor: the University of Michigan Press, 1969.

Colacurcio, Michael J. "A Better Mode of Evidence – The Transcendental Problem of Faith and Spirit." *Emerson Society Quarterly* 54 (1969): 12–22.

—. "The Symbolic and the Symptomatic: D. H. Lawrence in Recent American Criticism." *American Quarterly* 27 (1975): 486–501.

—. "The Sense of an Author: The Familiar Life and Strange Imaginings of Nathaniel Hawthorne." *Emerson Society Quarterly* 27 (1981): 108–33.

—. *The Province of Piety: Moral History in Hawthorne's Early Tales.* Cambridge: Harvard UP, 1984.

—. "The American–Renaissance Renaissance." *New England Quarterly* 64 (1991): 445–93.
—. Ed. *New Essays on The Scarlet Letter.* Cambridge: Cambridge UP, 1985.
—. "Introduction. The Spirit and the Sign." In Colacurcio, *New Essays.* 1–28.
—. "'The Woman's Own Choice:' Sex, Metaphor, and the Puritan 'Sources' of *The Scarlet Letter.*" In Colacurcio, *New Essays.* 101–136.
Connolly, Thomas E. Ed. *Young Goodman Brown, by Nathaniel Hawthorne.* Columbus: Charles E. Merrill Publishing Company, 1968.
Cottom, Daniel. "Hawthorne versus Hester: The Ghostly Dialectic of Romance in *The Scarlet Letter.*" *Texas Studies in Literature and Language*, 24 (1982): 47–67. Rpt. in Gross et al., "Essays in Criticism and Scholarship." 408–415.
Cowley, Malcolm. "Hawthorne in the Looking Glass." *Sewanee Review*, 56 (1948): 545–63.
—. "Five Acts of *The Scarlet Letter.*" *College English* 19 (1957): 11–16. Rpt. in *Twelve Original Essays on Great American Novels.* Ed. Charles Shapiro. Detroit: Wayne State UP, 1958.
Craig, Martha. "The Secret Wit of Spenser's Language." In *Elizabethan Poetry: Modern Essays in Criticism.* Ed. Paul Alpers. New York: Oxford UP, 1967. 447–72.
Crews, Frederick C. "A New Reading of *The Blithedale Romance.*" *American Literature* 29 (1957): 147–170.
—. *The Sins of the Fathers: Hawthorne's Psychological Themes.* New York; Oxford UP, 1966.
Crowley, J. Donald. *Hawthorne: The Critical Heritage.* London: Routledge and Kegan Paul, 1970.
Crowley, John W. "Hawthorne's New England Epochs." *Emerson Society Quarterly* 25 (1979): 59–70.
Dahl, Curtis. "The Architecture of Society and the Architecture of the Soul: Hawthorne's *The House of the Seven Gables* and Melville's *Pierre.*" *University of Mississippi Studies in English* 5 n. s. (1984–1987): 1–22.
Daly, Robert. "History and Chivalric Myth in 'Roger Malvin's Burial.' *Essex Institute Historical Collections* 109 (1973): 99–115.
—. "Fideism and the Allusive Mode in 'Rappaccini's Daughter'." *Nineteenth-Century Fiction* 28 (1973): 25–37.
Daniélou, Jean. *From Shadows to Reality: Studies in the Biblical Typology of the Fathers.* Tr. Wulstan Hibberd. Westminster, Md., 1960.
Danielson, Dennis Richard. *Milton's Good God: A Study in Literary Theodicy.* New York: Cambridge UP, 1982.
Darnell, Donald G. "'Doctrine by Ensample': The Emblem and *The Marble Faun.*" *Texas Studies in Language and Literature* 15 (1973): 301–10.
Dauber, Kenneth. *Rediscovering Hawthorne.* Princeton: Princeton UP, 1977.
Davidson, Edward H. *Hawthorne's Last Phase.* New Haven: Yale UP, 1949.
Davidson, Frank. "Toward a Re–evaluation of *The Blithedale Romance.*" *New England Quarterly* 25 (1952): 374–83.
De Jong, Mary Gosselink. "The Making of a 'Gentle Reader': Narrator and Reader in Hawthorne's Romances." *Studies in the Novel* 16 (1984): 359–77.
Dekker, George. *The American Historical Romance.* Cambridge: Cambridge UP, 1987.

—. "Once More: Hawthorne and the Genealogy of American Romance." *Emerson Society Quarterly* 35 (1989): 69–83.

de Lubac, Henri. *Exégèse Médiéval: Les Quatres Sens de l'Ecriture.* Paris: Aubier, 1959–1964, 4 vols.

—. *Medieval Exegesis.* Tr. Mark Sebanc. Edinburgh: T&T Clark, 1998.

—. "Christianity and History." In *Henri de Lubac, S.J.* London: , 1972. 9–36.

Delueze, Gilles, and Felix Guattari. *Anti–Oedipus: Capitalism and Schizophrenia.* Tr. Robert Hurley, Mark Seem and Helen R. Lane. New York: Viking Press, 1977.

de Man, Paul. *Blindness and Insight: Essays in the Rhetoric of Contemporary Criticism.* Second ed. Revised. Minneapolis: University of Minnesota Press, 1983.

—. *Allegories of Reading: Figural Language in Rousseau, Nietzsche, Rilke, and Proust.* New Haven: Yale UP, 1979.

DeSalvo, Louise. *Nathaniel Hawthorne.* Atlantic Highlands: Humanities Press International, 1987.

Dillingham, William B. "Structure and Theme in *The House of the Seven Gables.*" *Nineteenth-Century Fiction* 14 (1959): 59–70. Rpt. in Gross, "Reviews and Essays in Criticism." 449–59.

Dolis, John. "Hawthorne's Blithedale: Narrative Ethos as Absence." *Arbeiten aus Anglistik und Amerikanistik* 10 (1985): 155–164.

Doubleday, Neal F. *Hawthorne's Early Tales: A Critical Study.* Durham: Duke UP, 1972.

Doudna, Martin K. "Hawthorne's Pandora, Milton's Eve, and the Fortunate Fall." *Emerson Society Quarterly* 31 (1985): 164–72.

Draxlbauer, Michael. "Utopia 'Re-membered': Nathaniel Hawthorne's Brook Farm Romance." *Utopian Thought in American Literature.* Ed. Arno Heller, Walter Holbling, and Waldemar Zacharasiewicz. Tubigen: Narr, 1988. 43–68.

Dryden, Edgar A. "Hawthorne's Castle in the Air: Form and Theme in *The House of the Seven Gables.*" *ELH* 38 (1971): 294–317.

—. *Nathaniel Hawthorne: The Poetics of Enchantment.* Ithaca: Cornell UP, 1977.

—. *The Form of American Romance.* Baltimore: Johns Hopkins UP, 1988.

Dugdale, John. "Explanatory Notes." In *The Blithedale Romance* by Nathaniel Hawthorne. 1852. Ed. Tony Tanner. Oxford: Oxford UP, 1991.

Easton, Alison. *The Making of the Hawthorne Subject.* Columbia: University of Missouri Press, 1996.

Ehrlich, Gloria. *Family Themes and Hawthorne's Fiction: The Tenacious Web.* New Brunswick: Rutgers UP, 1984.

Eigner, Edwin M. *The Metaphysical Novel in England and America: Dickens, Bulwer, Melville, and Hawthorne.* Berkeley: University of California Press, 1978.

Eisinger, Chester E. "Hawthorne as Champion of the Middle Way." *New England Quarterly* 27 (1954): 27–52.

Elbert, Monika M. "Hawthorne's Reconceptualization of Transcendentalist Charity." *American Transcendental Quarterly* 11 (1997): 213–32.

—. *Encoding the Letter 'A': Gender and Authority in Hawthorne's Early Fiction.* Frankfurt am Main: Haag & Herchen, 1990.

Elder, Marjorie J. *Nathaniel Hawthorne: Transcendental Symbolist.* Athens: Ohio UP, 1969.

—. "Hawthorne's *The Marble Faun*: A Gothic Structure." *Costerus* 1 (1972): 81–88.

Evans, Oliver. "Allegory and Incest in 'Rappaccini's Daughter'." *Nineteen-Century Fiction* 19 (1964): 185–95.

Fairbanks, Henry G. "Hawthorne and Confession." *Catholic Historical Review* 43 (1957): 38–45.

—. *The Lasting Loneliness: A Study of the Sources of Alienation in Modern Man.* Albany: Magi Books, 1965.

Feidelson, Charles, Jr. *Symbolism and American Literature.* Chicago: University of Chicago Press, 1953.

Fick, Leonard J. *The Light Beyond: A Study of Hawthorne's Theology.* Westminster: Newman Press, 1955.

Fiedler, Leslie. *Love and Death in the American Novel.* New York: Criterion Books, 1960.

Fisk, Rosemary Mims. "*The Marble Faun* and the English Copyright: The Smith, Elder Contract." In *Studies in the American Renaissance 1995.* Ed. Joel Myerson. Charlottesville: UP of Virginia. 263–75.

Fletcher, Angus. *Allegory: The Theory of a Symbolic Mode.* Ithaca: Cornell UP, 1964.

—. *The Prophetic Moment: An Essay on Spenser.* Chicago: Chicago UP, 1971.

Flint, Allen. "Hawthorne and the Slavery Crisis." *New England Quarterly* 48 (1968): 393–408.

Fogle, Richard H. *Hawthorne's Fiction: The Light and the Dark.* Norman: University of Oklahoma Press, 1952. Rev. ed. 1964.

—. *Hawthorne's Imagery: The "Proper Light and Shadow" in the Major Romances.* Norman: Oklahoma UP, 1969

—. "Priscilla's Veil: A Study of Hawthorne's Veil-Imagery in *The Blithedale Romance.*" *Nathaniel Hawthorne Journal* 2 (1972): 59–65.

—. "Coleridge, Hilda, and *The Marble Faun.*" *Emerson Society Quarterly* 19 (1973): 105–111.

Folsom, James K. *Man's Accidents and God's Purposes: Multiplicity in Hawthorne's Fiction.* New Haven: College and UP, 1964.

Foster, C. H. "Hawthorne's Literary Theory." *PMLA* 57 (1942): 241–54.

Fossum, Robert H. *Hawthorne's Inviolable Circle: The Problem of Time.* Deland: Everett/Edwards, 1972.

Franchot, Jenny. *Roads to Rome.* Berkeley: University of California Press, 1994.

Frank, Joseph. "Spatial Form in Modern Literature." In *The Widening Gyre: Crisis and Mastery in Modern Literature.* New Brunswick: Rutgers UP, 1963. 3–62.

—. "Spatial Form: Thirty Years After." *Critical Inquiry* 4 (1977): 231–252 and 5 (1978): 275–290. Rpt. in Smitten, 202–243.

Franklin, H. Bruce. *Future Perfect: American Science Fiction of the Nineteenth Century.* Rev. ed. New York: Oxford UP, 1978 [1966].

Frederick, John T. *The Darkened Sky: Nineteenth-Century American Novelists and Religion.* Notre Dame: University of Notre Dame Press, 1969.

Freud, Sigmund. *Totem and Taboo.* Tr. and ed. James Strachey. New York: Norton, 1950.

—. *The Ego and the Id.* Tr. Joan Riviere; rev. and ed. James Strachey. New York: Norton, 1974.

—. *Civilization and its Discontents.* Tr. and ed. James Strachey. New York: Norton, 1989.

Frye, Northrop. *Anatomy of Criticism.* Princeton: Princeton UP, 1957.

Fryer, Judith. *The Faces of Eve: Women in the Nineteenth-Century American Novel.* Oxford: Oxford UP, 1976.

Fussell, Edwin. *Frontier: American Literature and the American West.* Princeton: Princeton UP, 1965.

Gable, Harvey L., Jr. "Inappeasable Longings: Hawthorne, Romance, and the Disintegration of Coverdale's Self in *The Blithedale Romance.*" *New England Quarterly* 67 (1994): 257–78.

—. *Liquid Fire: Transcendental Mysticism in the Romances of Nathaniel Hawthorne.* New York: P. Lang, 1998.

Gale, Robert L. *A Nathaniel Hawthorne Encyclopedia.* New York: Greenwood Press, 1991.

Gatta, John, Jr. "Progress and Providence in *The House of the Seven Gables.*" *American Literature* 50 (1978): 37–48.

Gay, Peter. *Freud: A Life for our Time.* New York: Norton, 1988.

Genette, Gérard. *Narrative Discourse.* Tr. Jane E. Lewin. Ithaca: Cornell UP, 1980.

—. *Narrative Discourse Revisited.* Tr. Jane E. Lewin. Ithaca: Cornell UP, 1988.

Gerber, John C. "Form and Content in *The Scarlet Letter.*" *New England Quarterly*, 17 (1944): 25–55. Rpt. in Gross et al., "Essays in Criticism and Scholarship." 283–291.

Gilmore, Michael T. *American Romanticism and the Marketplace.* Chicago: University of Chicago Press, 1985.

Ginsberg, Lesley. "'The Willing Captive': Narrative Seduction and the Ideology of Love in Hawthorne's *A Wonder Book for Girls and Boys.*" *American Literature* 65 (1993): 255–73.

Goldman, Arnold. "The Plot of Hawthorne's *The Marble Faun.*" *Journal of American Studies* 18 (1984): 383–404.

Gollin, Rita K. "Painting and Character in *The Marble Faun.*" *Emerson Society Quarterly* 21 (1975): 1–10.

Gollin, Rita K., and John L. Idol, Jr. *Prophetic Pictures: Nathaniel Hawthorne's Knowledge and Uses of the Visual Arts.* New York: Greenwood Press, 1991.

Grant, William E. "Hawthorne's Hamlet: The Archetypal Structure of *The Blithedale Romance.*" (1977): 1–15.

Gray, Richard. "'Hawthorne: A Problem': *The House of the Seven Gables.*" In A. Robert Lee. Totowa: Vision, 1982. 88–109.

Greimas, A. J. and Francois Rastier, "The Interaction of Semiotic Constraints." *Yale French Studies*, 41 (1968): 86–105.

Greenwald, Elissa. *Realism and the Romance: Nathaniel Hawthorne, Henry James, and American Fiction.* Ann Arbor: Univ. Microfilms Internat. Research Press, 1989.

Griffith, Clark. "Substance and Shadow: Language and Meaning in *The House of the Seven Gables.*" *Modern Philology* 51 (1954): 187–95.

Griffith, Kelley, Jr. "Form in *The Blithedale Romance.*" *American Literature* 40 (1968): 15–26.

Gross, Seymour. "'Solitude, and Love, and Anguish': The Tragic Design of *The Scarlet Letter.*" *College Language Association Journal* 3 (1960): 154–65. Rpt. in Gross 1988, 336–343.

—. Ed. *A "Scarlet Letter" Handbook.* Belmont: Wadsworth, 1960.

—. Ed. "Reviews and Essays in Criticism." In *The House of the Seven Gables* by Nathaniel Hawthorne. 1851. New York: Norton, 1967. 449–59.

Gross, Seymour, and Sculley Bradley, Richmond Croom Beatty, and E. Hudson Long, eds. "Essays in Criticism and Scholarship." In *The Scarlet Letter* by Nathaniel Hawthorne. 1850. Third ed. New York: W. W. Norton, 1988. 179–440.

Gross, Seymour, and Rosalie Murphy. "Criticism." In *The Blithedale Romance* by Nathaniel Hawthorne. 1852. New York: Norton, 1978. 267–413.

Gross, Theodore L. and Stanley Wertheim. *Hawthorne, Melville, Stephen Crane: A Critical Bibliography*. New York: The Free Press, 1971.

Grunes, Dennis. "Allegory Versus Allegory in Hawthorne." *American Transcendental Quarterly* 32 (1976): 14–19.

Gura, Philip F. and Joel Myerson, eds. *Critical Essays on American Transcendentalism.* Boston: G. K. Hall, 1982.

Hall, Lawrence Sargent. *Hawthorne, Critic of Society*. New Haven: Yale UP, 1944.

Hamilton, Kristie. *America's Sketchbook: The Cultural Life of a Nineteenth-Century Genre.* Athens: Ohio UP, 1998.

Harding, Brian. "Introduction." In *The Scarlet Letter* by Nathaniel Hawthorne. Oxford: Oxford UP, 1990. vii–xlii.

—. Ed. *Nathaniel Hawthorne: Critical Assessments. Volume I The Contemporary Context.* Mountfield: Helm Information, 1998.

—. Ed. *Nathaniel Hawthorne: Critical Assessments. Volume II 'Creating a classic' 1860–1900.* Mountfield: Helm Information, 1998.

—. Ed. *Nathaniel Hawthorne: Critical Assessments: Volume III The Critical Response, Assessments of Individual Woks Since 1900.* Mountfield: Helm Information, 1998.

—. Ed. *Nathaniel Hawthorne: Critical Assessments: Volume IV The Critical Response, General Assessments Since 1900.* Mountfield: Helm Information, 1998.

—. Review of Madsen, Deborah L. *Allegory in America. Modern Language Review* 93 (1998): 805–6.

Haviland, Beverly. "The Sin of Synecdoche: Hawthorne's Allegory against Symbolism in 'Rappaccini's Daughter." *Texas Studies in Language and Literature* 29 (1987): 278–301.

Hawthorne, Julian. *Nathaniel Hawthorne and His Wife.* Two volumes. New York: Harper, 1884.

—. *Hawthorne Reading.* Cleveland: The Rowfant Club, 1902.

Hazlett, John Downton. "Re-reading 'Rappaccini's Daughter:' Giovanni and the Seduction of the Transcendentalist Reader." *Emerson Society Quarterly* 35 (1989): 43–68.

Hedges, William L. "Hawthorne's Blithedale: The Function of the Narrator." *Nineteenth-Century Fiction* 14 (1960): 303–16.

Herbert, T. Walter, Jr. "Nathaniel Hawthorne, Una Hawthorne, and *The Scarlet Letter*: Interactive Selfhoods and the Cultural Construction of Gender." *PMLA* 103 (1988): 285–97.

—. "The Erotics of Purity: *The Marble Faun* and the Victorian Construction of Sexuality." *Representations* 36 (1991): 114–132.

—. *Dearest Beloved: The Hawthornes and the Making of the Middle–Class Family.* Berkeley: Universiy of California Press, 1993.

Hijiya, James A. "Nathaniel Hawthorne's *Our Old Home.*" *American Literature* 46 (1974): 363–73.

Hill, Douglas. "Narrative Form in *The Blithedale Romance.*" *English Studies in Canada* 7 (1981): 388–401.

Hirsch, E. D. "Transhistorical Intentions and the Persistence of Allegory." *New Literary History* 25 (1995).

Hoffman, Daniel. *Form and Fable in American Fiction.* New York: Oxford UP, 1961. 203–18.

Hollander, John. "Observations on a Select Party." *Spenser Studies* 3 (1982): 193–98.

Honig, Edward. *Dark Conceit: The Making of Allegory.* Evanston: Northwestern UP, 1959.

Howe, Irving. "Hawthorne: Pastoral and Politics." In *Politics and the Novel.* New York: Horizon Press, 1957. 163–75.

Hume, Beverly. "Restructuring the Case against Hawthorne's Coverdale." *Nineteenth-Century Fiction* 40 (1986): 387–399.

Hunt, Lester H. "*The Scarlet Letter:* Hawthorne's Theory of Moral Sentiments." *Philosophy and Literature* 8 (1984): 75–88.

Hutner, Gordon. "Secrets and Sympathy in *The Scarlet Letter.* Hawthorne's Confessional Strategies." *Mosaic* 16 (1983): 113–24.

—. *Secrets and Sympathy: Forms of Disclosure in Hawthorne's Novels.* Athens: University of Georgia Press, 1988.

—. Ed. *American Literature, American Culture.* New York: Oxford UP, 1999.

Idol, John L. Jr. and Melinda M. Ponder, eds. *Hawthorne and Women: Engendering and Expanding the Hawthorne Tradition.* Amherst: University of Massachusetts Press, 1999.

Inge, M. Thomas. "Dr. Rappaccini's Noble Experiment." *Nathaniel Hawthorne Journal* (1973): 200–01.

Irwin, John T. *American Hieroglyphics.* New Haven: Yale UP, 1980.

Jacobs, Naomi. "Substance and Reality in Hawthorne's Meta–Utopia." *Utopian Studies.* 1 (1987): 173–187.

Jacobson, Richard J. *Hawthorne's Conception of the Creative Process.* Cambridge: Harvard UP, 1965.

James, Henry. *Hawthorne.* London: Macmillan, 1879.

Jameson, Fredric. *The Prison–House of Language.* Princeton: Princeton UP, 1972.

—. "Imaginary and Symbolic in Lacan: Marxism, Psychoanalytic Criticism, and the Problem of the Subject." *Yale French Studies* 48 (1972): 338–95.

—. *The Political Unconscious: Narrative as a Socially Symbolic Act.* Ithaca: Cornell UP, 1981.

Jehlen, Myra. *American Incarnation: The Individual, the Nation, and the Continent.* Cambridge: Harvard UP, 1986

Johnson, Claudia. *The Productive Tension of Hawthorne's Art.* Alabama: University of Alabama Press, 1981.

Johnston, Paul K. "Killing the Spirit: Anne Hutchinson and the Office of the Scarlet Letter." *Nathaniel Hawthorne Review* 22 (1996): 26–35.

Jones, Buford. *A Checklist of Hawthorne Criticism, 1951–1966.* Hartford: Transcendental Books, 1967.

—. "Hawthorne Studies: The Seventies." *Studies in the Novel* 2 (1970): 504–17.

—. "Hawthorne and Spenser: From Allusion to Allegory." *Nathaniel Hawthorne Journal* (1975): 71–90

—. "The Manuscript of *The Blithedale Romance.*" *Hawthorne Society Newsletter* 11 (1985): 12–13.

Jones, Deborah L. "Hawthorne's Post-Platonic Paradise: The Inversion of Allegory in "Rappaccini's Daughter." *Journal of Narrative Technique* 18 (1988): 153–69.

Jordan, Gretchen Graf. "Hawthorne's 'Bell': Historical Evolution through Symbol." *Nineteenth-Century Fiction* 19 (1964): 123–29.

Junkins, Donald. "Hawthorne's *The House of the Seven Gables*: A Prototype of the Human Mind." *Literature and Psychology* 17 (1967): 193–210.

Justus, James H. "Hawthorne's Coverdale: Character and Art in *The Blithedale Romance.*" *American Literature* 47 (1975): 21–36.

Katz, Seymour. "'Character,' 'Nature,' and Allegory in *The Scarlet Letter,*" *Nineteenth-Century Fiction* 23 (1968): 3–17.

Kaul, A. Ed. *Hawthorne: A Collection of Critical Essays.* Engelwood Cliffs: Prentice–Hall, 1966.

Kay, Donald. "Five Acts of *The Blithedale Romance.*" *American Transcendental Quarterly* 13 (1972): 25–8.

Keller, Karl. "Alephs, Zahirs, and the Triumph of Ambiguity: Typology in Nineteenth-Century American Literature." In Miner, *Literary Uses of Typology.* 274–314.

Kermode, Frank. *The Sense of an Ending: Studies in the Theory of Fiction.* London: Oxford UP, 1966.

—. *The Classic.* Cambridge: Harvard UP, 1975.

Kesselring, Marion. *Hawthorne's Reading 1828–1850: A Transcription and Identification of Titles Recorded in the Charge–Books of the Salem Athenaeum.* New York: The New York Public Library, 1949.

Kesterson, David B. Ed. *The Merrill Studies in The Marble Faun.* Columbus: Charles E. Merrill Publishing Company, 1971.

Kevorkian, Martin. "Within the Domain of Chaos?: Nathaniel Hawthorne, Lucretian Physics, and Martial Logic." *Studies in the Novel* 31 (1999): 178–201.

Kimbrough, Robert. "'The Actual and the Imaginary': Hawthorne's Concept of Art in Theory and Practice." *Transactions of the Wisconsin Academy of Sciences, Art, and Letters* 50 (1961): 277–93.

Kolodny, Annette. "Introduction." In *The Blithedale Romance* by Nathaniel Hawthorne. New York: Penguin Classics, 1983. vii–xxx.

Lacan, Jacques. "L'instance de la lettre dans l'inconscient ou la raison depuis Freud." *La Psychanalyse*, 1957, III, 47–81.

—. *Écrits.* Paris: Seuil, 1966.

Laffrado, Laura. *Hawthorne's Literature for Children.* Athens: University of Georgia Press, 1992.

Lane, Gary. "Structural Dynamics and the Unknowable in *The Scarlet Letter.*" *Nathaniel Hawthorne Journal* (1977): 323–30.

Laplanche, Jean, and Jean-Bertrand Pontalis. *The Language of Psycho–analysis.* Tr. Donald Nicholson-Smith. London: Hogarth Press, 1973.

Laser, Marvin. "'Head,' 'Heart,' and 'Will' in Hawthorne's Psychology." *Nineteenth-Century Fiction* 10 (1955): 130–40.

Leavis, Q. D. "Hawthorne as Poet." *Sewanee Review* 59 (1951): 179–205, and 426–58.

Lednicky, John. "The Myth and the Fall: Hawthorne's Critique of Democratic Literary Reform." *Emerson Society Quarterly* 41 (1995): 121–51.

Lee, A. Robert. Ed. *Nathaniel Hawthorne: New Critical Essays.* Totowa: Vision, 1982.

Lee, Sang-Wha. "Uncertain Narrator and the Intended Effect: A Study of *The Blithedale Romance.*" *The Journal of English Language and Literature* 36 (1990): 471–489.

Lefcowitz, Allan, and Barbara Lefcowitz. "Some Rents in the Veil: New Light on Priscilla and Zenobia in *The Blithedale Romance.*" *Nineteenth-Century Fiction* 21 (1966): 263–275.

Lentz, Vern B., and Allen F. Stein. "The Black Flower of Necessity: Structure in *The Blithedale Romance.*" *Essays in Literature* 3 (1976): 86–96.

Leverenz, David. "Mrs. Hawthorne's Headache: Reading *The Scarlet Letter.*" *Nineteenth-Century Fiction* 37 (March 1983): 552–75. Rpt. in Gross et al. 416–423.

—. *Manhood and the American Renaissance.* Ithaca: Cornell UP, 1989.

Levin, David. "Modern Misjudgements of Racial Imperialism in Parkman and Hawthorne." *Yearbook of English Studies* 13 (1983): 145–58. Rpt. in *Forms of Uncertainty: Essays in Historical Criticism.* Charlottesville: UP of Virginia, 1992. 260–78.

—. "The Province of Historical Criticism: Historical fact in Hawthorne and Colacurcio." *Early American Literature* 20 (1985): 164–72. Rpt. in *Forms of Uncertainty: Essays in Historical Criticism.* Charlottesville: UP of Virginia, 1992. 279–288.

Levin, Harry. "Statues from Italy: *The Marble Faun.*" In Pearce, *Hawthorne Centenary Essays.* 119–140.

Levine, Robert S. *Conspiracy and Romance: Studies in Brockden Brown, Cooper, Hawthorne, and Melville.* Cambridge: Cambridge UP, 1989.

Levy, Alfred J. "*The House of the Seven Gables:* The Religion of Love." *Nineteenth-Century Fiction* 16 (1961): 189–203.

Levy, Leo B. "*The Blithedale Romance:* Hawthorne's 'Voyage Through Chaos.'" *Studies in Romanticism* 8 (1968): 1–15.

Lewis, C. S. *The Allegory of Love: A Study in Medieval Tradition.* Oxford: Oxford UP, 1936.

Lewis, R. W. B. *The American Adam: Innocence, Tragedy, and Tradition in the Nineteenth-Century.* Chicago: University of Chicago Press, 1955.

Liebman, Sheldon W. "The Design of *The Marble Faun.*" *New England Quarterly* 40 (1967): 61–78. Rpt. in Kesterson. 43–58.

—. "Hawthorne and Milton: The Second Fall in 'Rappaccini's Daughter'." *New England Quarterly* 48 (1968): 521–35.

Long, Robert Emmet. *The Great Succession: Henry James and the Legacy of Hawthorne.* Pittsburgh: University of Pittsburgh Press, 1979.

Lovejoy, Arthur O. "Milton and the Paradox of the Fortunate Fall." *ELH* 4 (1937): 161–79.

Lowance, Mason I., Jr. "Typology and Millenial Eschatology in Early New England." In Miner, *Literary Uses of Typology.* 228–273.

Lundblad, Jane. *Nathaniel Hawthorne and the Tradition of Gothic Romance.* Cambridge: Harvard UP, 1946.

—. *Nathaniel Hawthorne and European Literary Tradition.* Cambridge: Harvard UP, 1947.

Mackenzie, Manfred. "Colonization and Decolonization in *The Blithedale Romance*." *University of Toronto Quarterly* 62 (1993): 504–21.

Maddox, Lucy. *Removals: Nineteenth-Century American Literature and the Politics of Indian Affairs*. New York: Oxford UP, 1991.

Madsen, Deborah L. *Rereading Allegory: A Narrative Approach to Genre*. New York, 1994.

—. *Allegory in America: From Puritanism to Postmodernism*. New York: St. Martin's Press, 1996.

Madsen, William G. *From Shadowy Types to Truth: Studies in Milton's Symbolism*. New Haven: Yale UP, 1968.

Magretta, Joan. "The Coverdale Translation: Blithedale and the Bible." *Nathaniel Hawthorne Journal* (1974): 250–56.

Male, Roy R. "Hawthorne and the Concept of Sympathy." *PMLA* 68 (1953): 138–49.

—. *Hawthorne's Tragic Vision*. Austin: University of Texas Press, 1957.

—. "Sympathy: A Key Word in American Romanticism." *Emerson Society Quarterly* 35 (1964): 19–23.

—. "Hawthorne's Fancy, or the Medium of *The Blithedale Romance*." *Nathaniel Hawthorne Journal* 2 (1972): 67–73.

—. "Hawthorne's Literal Figures." In Thompson and Locke. 71–92

Manierre, William. "The Role of Sympathy in *The Scarlet Letter*." *Texas Studies in Literature and Language* 13 (1972): 497–507.

Marks, Alfred H. "Who Killed Judge Pyncheon? The Role of the Imagination in *The House of the Seven Gables*." *PMLA* 71 (1956): 355–69.

—. "Hawthorne's Daguerreotypist: Scientist, Artist, Reformer." *Ball State Teachers College Forum* 3 (1962): 61–74.

—. "Ironic Inversion in *The Blithedale Romance*." *Emerson Society Quarterly* 55 (1969): 95–102.

Martin, Terence. *Nathaniel Hawthorne*. New York: Twayne Publishers, 1965.

Martin, Terry J. "Anti-Allegory and the Reader in 'Young Goodman Brown'." In *Rhetorical Deception in the Short Fiction of Hawthorne, Poe, and Melville*. Lewiston: Edwin Mellen Press, 1998. 19–31.

Martinez, Ronald L. and Robert M. Durling. "Introduction and Notes." In *The Divine Comedy of Dante Alighieri: Volume 1 Inferno*, ed. and tr. by Robert M. Durling. Oxford: Oxford UP, 1996.

Marx, Karl and Friedrich Engels. "The Communist Manifesto." In K. Marx, *On Revolution*. Ed. and tr. S. K. Padover. New York: McGraw-Hill, 1971.

—. "Critique of the Gotha Program." In *The Marx–Engels Reader*. Ed. Robert C. Tucker. New York: Norton, 1978.

Mathews, J. Chesley. "Bibliographical Supplement: Hawthorne." In *Eight American Authors: A Review of Research and Criticism*. Ed. Floyd Stovall. New York: Norton, 1963. 428–34.

Matthiessen, F. O. *American Renaissance: Art and Expression in the Age of Emerson and Whitman*. New York: Oxford UP, 1941.

McCluskey, Peter M. "'The Recovery of the Sacred Candlestick': Jewish Imagery and the Problem of Allegory in *The Marble Faun*." *Publications of the Arkansas Philological Association* 18 (1992): 15–27.

McColgan, Kristin P. "'By Long Perusal and Deep Love': Miltonic Parallels in Hawthorne's *The Marble Faun*." *Tennessee Philological Bulletin* 26 (1989): 20–29

McDonald, John J. "The Old Manse Period Canon." *Nathaniel Hawthorne Journal* 2 (1972): 13–39.

—. "'The Old Manse' and Hawthorne's Mosses: The Inception and Development of *Mosses from an Old Manse*." *Texas Studies in Literature and Language* 16 (1974): 77–108

McElroy, John Harmon, and Edward L. McDonald. "The Coverdale Romance." *Studies in the Novel* 14 (1982): 1–16.

McNamara, Anne Maria. "The Character of Flame: The Function of Pearl in *The Scarlet Letter*." *American Literature* 27 (1956): 537–53.

McPherson, Hugo. *Hawthorne as Myth–Maker.* Toronto: University of Toronto Press, 1969.

Mellow, James R. *Nathaniel Hawthorne in his Times.* Boston: Houghton Mifflin, 1980.

Michael, John. "History and Romance, Sympathy and Uncertainty: The Moral of the Stones in Hawthorne's *Marble Faun*." *PMLA* 103 (1988): 150–61.

Michaels, Walter Benn. "Romance and Real Estate." In *The American Renaissance Reconsidered.* Eds. Walter Benn Michaels and Donald E. Pease. Baltimore: John Hopkins UP, 1985. 156–82. Rpt. in Harding, *Nathaniel Hawthorne: Critical Assessments: Volume III.* 373–91.

Michelson, Bruce. "Hawthorne's House of Three Stories." *New England Quarterly* 57 (1984): 163–83.

Milder, Robert. "*The Scarlet Letter* and Its Discontents." *Nathaniel Hawthorne Review* 22 (1996): 9–25.

Miller, Edwin Haviland. *Salem is my Dwelling Place: A Life of Nathaniel Hawthorne.* Iowa City: University of Iowa Press, 1991.

Miller, John N. "Fideism vs. Allegory in 'Rappaccini's Daughter'." *Nineteenth-Century Fiction* 46 (1991): 223–44.

Miller, Perry. "New England's Transcendentalism: Native or Imported?" In *Critical Essays on American Transcendentalism.* Eds. Philip F. Gura and Joel Myerson. Boston: G. K. Hall, 1982. 387–401.

—. *Errand into the Wilderness.* Cambridge: Harvard UP, 1956.

Millington, Richard. *Practicing Romance: Narrative Form and Cultural Engagement in Hawthorne's Fiction.* Princeton: Princeton UP, 1990.

— "*The Office of* The Scarlet Letter: An 'Inside Narrative'?" *Nathaniel Hawthorne Review* 22 (1996): 1–8.

Miner, Earl. "*Felix Culpa* in the Redemptive Order of *Paradise Lost*." *Philological Quarterly* 67 (1968): 43–54.

—. Ed. *Literary Uses of Typology: From the Late Middle Ages to the Present.* Princeton: Princeton UP, 1977.

Mitchell, Thomas R. *Hawthorne's Fuller Mystery.* Amherst: University of Massachusetts Press, 1998.

Moncrieff, A. R. Hope. *Classical Mythology: Myths and Legends.* London: George G. Harrap & Company Ltd., 1907. Rpt. London: Senate, 1994.
Moss, Sidney P. "The Symbolism of the Italian Background in *The Marble Faun*," *Nineteenth-Century Fiction* 23 (1968): 332–36.
Mossberger, Robert E. "Hawthorne and the Civil War as the Unpardonable Sin." *Nathaniel Hawthorne Journal* (1977): 111–22.
Mozly, J. F. *Coverdale and his Bibles.* London: Lutterworth Press, 1953.
Mueller, Monika. *This Infinite Fraternity of Feeling: Gender, Genre, and Homoerotic Crisis in Hawthorne's* The Blithedale Romance *and Melville's* Pierre. Madison: Fairleigh Dickinson UP, 1996.
Murray, Peter B. "Mythopoesis in *The Blithedale Romance.*" *PMLA* 75 (1960): 591–96.
Naples, Diance C. "'Roger Malvin's Burial'—A Parable for Historians?" *American Transcendental Quarterly* 13 (1972): 45–48.
Nawrocki, Gerard. "*The Blithedale Romance* and Charles Fourier." *Studia Anglica Posnaniensia: An International Review of English Studies* 29 (1994): 199–209.
Newberry, Frederick. "Tradition and Disinheritance in *The Scarlet Letter.*" *Emerson Society Quarterly* 23 (1977): 1–26. Rpt. in Gross et al. 231–48.
—. *Hawthorne's Divided Loyalties: England and America in his Works.* Rutherford: Fairleigh Dickinson UP, 1987.
Newman, Lea Bertani Vozar. *A Reader's Guide to the Short Stories of Nathaniel Hawthorne.* Boston: G. K. Hall, 1986.
—. "Sophia's Enduring Influence: Hawthorne's Creative Resurgence and the Genesis of *The Marble Faun.*" *Nathaniel Hawthorne Review* 26 (2000): 1–12.
Norrman, Ralf. *The Insecure World of Henry James: Intensity and Ambiguity.* London: Macmillan Press, 1982.
Oleksy, Elzbieta. *Plight in Common: Hawthorne and Percy.* New York: P. Lang, 1993.
Pahl, Dennis. "The Poison of Interpretation: Giovanni's Reading of Rappaccini's Daughter." In *The Architects of the Abyss: The Indeterminate Fictions of Poe, Hawthorne, and Melville.* University of Missouri Press: Columbia, 1989. 59–77.
Pancost, David W. "Hawthorne's Epistemology and Ontology." *Emerson Society Quarterly* 19 (1973): 8–13
Paris, Bernard J. "Optimism and Pessimism in *The Marble Faun.*" *Boston University Studies in English*, 2 (1956): 95–112. Rpt. in Kesterson. 61–78.
Pattison, Joseph C. "The Guilt of the Innocent Donatello." *Emerson Society Quarterly* 31 (1963): 66–8. Rpt. in Kesterson. 89–93.
—. "Point of View in Hawthorne." *PMLA* 82 (1967): 363–9.
Pearce, Roy Harvey. "Hawthorne and the Sense of the Past, or, The Immortality of Major Molineux." *ELH*, 21 (1954): 327–349.
—. Ed. *Hawthorne Centenary Essays.* Columbia: Ohio State UP, 1964.
—. "Historical Introduction." In CE 6, *True Stories.* 287–311.
—. "Day–dream and Fact: The Import of *The Blithedale Romance.*" In *Individual and Community*, ed. Kenneth H. Baldwin and David K. Kirby. Durham: Duke UP, 1975. 49–63.

Pearson, Norman Holmes. "Elizabeth Peabody on Hawthorne." *Essex Institute Historical Collections* 94 (1958): 256–76.

Pease, Donald E. *Visionary Compacts: American Renaissance Writings in Cultural Context.* Madison: University of Wisconsin Press, 1987.

Penelhum, Terence. *God and Skepticism: A Study in Skepticism and Fideism.* Dordrecht, Holland: D. Reidel Pub. Co., 1983.

Person, Leland S., Jr. *Aesthetic Headaches: Women and a Masculine Poetics in Poe, Melville, and Hawthorne.* Athens: University of Georgia Press, 1988.

—. "Hawthorne and his Culture: Three Recent Views." *Studies in the Novel* 24 (1992): 434–41.

Pfister, Joel. *The Production of Personal Life: Class, Gender, and the Psychological in Hawthorne's Fiction.* Stanford: Stanford UP, 1992.

Poe, Edgar Allen. "Tale Writing—Nathaniel Hawthorne." *Godey's Lady's Book* 35 (November, 1847): 252–56.

Ponder, Melinda M. *Hawthorne's Early Narrative Art.* Lewiston: E. Mellen Press, 1990.

Porte, Joel. *The Romance in America; Studies in Cooper, Poe, Hawthorne, Melville, and James.* Middletown: Wesleyan UP, 1969. Rpt. in Gross et al., "Essays in Criticism and Scholarship." 375–84.

Quilligan, Maureen. *The Language of Allegory: Defining the Genre.* Ithaca: Cornell UP, 1979.

Quintilian. *The Institutio Oratoria of Quintilian*, vol. 3. Tr. H. E. Butler. London: W. Heinemann, 1922.

Ragussis, Michael. "Family Discourse, and Fiction in *The Scarlet Letter.*" *ELH* 49 (1982): 863–88.

Rahv, Philip. "The Dark Lady of Salem." *Partisan Review* 8 (1941): 362–81.

Randel, William Peirce. "Hawthorne, Channing and Margaret Fuller." *American Literature* 10 (1939): 472–6.

Read, Herbert. *Collected Essays in Literary Criticism.* London: Faber and Faber, 1938.

Rees, John O., Jr. "Shakespeare in *The Blithedale Romance.*" *Emerson Society Quarterly* 71 (1973): 84–93.

—. "Hawthorne's Concept of Allegory: A Reconsideration." *Philological Quarterly* 54, 2 (1975): 494–510.

Reich, Wilhelm. *Sex-pol: Essays, 1929–1934.* Ed. Lee Baxandall, tr. Anna Bostock, Tom DuBose, and Lee Baxandall. New York: Random House, 1972.

Reynolds, Donald. *Beneath the American Renaissance: The Subversive Imagination in the Age of Emerson and Melville.* New York: Knopf, 1988.

Reynolds, Larry. *European Revolutions and the American Literary Renaissance.* New Haven: Yale UP, 1988.

Ricoeur, Paul. *Time and Narrative.* Tr. Kathleen McLaughlin and David Pellauer. Chicago: University of Chicago Press, 1985.

Ringe, Donald A. "Hawthorne's Psychology of the Head and Heart." *PMLA* 65 (1950): 120–32.

—. "Romantic Iconology in *The Scarlet Letter* and *The Blithedale Romance.*" In Thompson and Locke. 93–107.

Roger, Patricia M. "Taking a Perspective: Hawthorne's Concept of Language and Nineteenth-Century Language Theory." *Nineteenth-Century Fiction* 51 (1997): 433–54.

Rohy, Valerie. *Impossible Women: Lesbian Figures and American Literature.* Ithaca: Cornell UP, 2000. 13–41.

Rosenberry, Edward H. "Hawthorne's Allegory of Science: 'Rappaccini's Daughter'." *American Literature* 32 (1960): 39–46.

Rowe, John Carlos. "The Metaphysics of Imagination: Narrative Consciousness in Hawthorne's *The Blithedale Romance*." In *Through the Custom-House: Nineteenth-Century American Fiction and Modern Theory.* Baltimore: John Hopkins UP, 1982. 52–90.

Rust, Richard D. "Coverdale's Confession: A Key to Meaning in *The Blithedale Romance*." *Literature and Ideas in America: Essays in Memory of Harry Hayden Clark.* Ed. Robert Falk. Athens: Ohio UP, 1975. 96–110.

Samson, John. "Hawthorne's Oak Trees." *American Literature* 52 (1980): 457–61.

Saxena, M. C. *Edgar Allan Poe: A Critical Study of his Tales.* New Delhi: S. Chand, 1978.

Scharnhorst, Gary. *Nathaniel Hawthorne: An Annotated Bibliography of Comment and Criticism before 1900.* Metuchen: Scarecrow, 1988.

—. "R. H. Stoddard Reviews *The Blithedale Romance*." *Nathaniel Hawthorne Review* 14 (1988): 15–16.

—. "Hawthorne and the Poetical Works of Spenser: A Lost Review." *American Literature* 61 (1989): 668–73.

Schiller, Emily. "The Choice of Innocence: Hilda in *The Marble Faun*." *Studies in the Novel* 26 (1994): 372–91.

Schneider, Daniel J. "The Allegory and Symbolism of Hawthorne's *The Marble Faun*." *Studies in the Novel* 1 (1969): 38–50.

Schoen, Carol. "The House of Seven Deadly Sins." *Emerson Society Quarterly* 19 (1973): 26–33

Schorer, Calvin Earl. "The Juvenile Literature of Nathaniel Hawthorne." Unpublished dissertation. University of Chicago, 1948.

Schriber, Mary Suzanne. "Justice to Zenobia." *New England Quarterly* 55 (1982): 61–78.

Schubert, Leland. *Hawthorne, the Artist: Fine-Art Devices in Fiction.* 1944. New York: Russell & Russell, 1963.

Schwartz, Joseph. "Three Aspects of Hawthorne's Puritanism." *New England Quarterly* 36 (1963): 192–208.

Schweninger, Lee. "'In the middest of that paradise': Structure and Theme in *The Blithedale Romance*." *Markham Review* 16 (1986): 11–16.

Scrimgeour, Gary J. "*The Marble Faun:* Hawthorne's Faery Land." *American Literature* 36 (1964), 271–87. Rpt. in Kesterson. 16–31.

Sheick, William J. "The Author's Corpse and the Humean Problem of the Personal Identity in Hawthorne's *The House of the Seven Gables*." *Studies in the Novel* 24 (1992): 131–53.

Shroeder, John. "Miles Coverdale's Calendar; or, A Major Literary Source for *The Blithedale Romance*." *Essex Institute Historical Collections* 103 (1967): 353–364.

Shumaker, Conrad. "'A Daughter of the Puritans': History in Hawthorne's *The Marble Faun*." *New England Quarterly* 57 (1984): 65–83.

Shurr, William H. "Eve's Bower: Hawthorne's Transition from Public Doctrines to Private Truths." In Thompson and Locke. 143–69.

Simpson, Claude M. "Introduction." In CE 4, *The Marble Faun.* xix–xliv.

Smalley, Beryl. *The Study of the Bible in the Middle Ages.* Oxford: Clarendon Press, 1941.

Smith, Allan Gardner Lloyd. *Eve Tempted: Writing and Sexualiy in Hawthorne's Fiction.* London: Croom Helm, 1984.

Smith, Charles R., Jr. "The Structural Principle of *The Marble Faun.*" *Thoth* 3 (1962): 32–38. Rpt in Kesterson. 36–43.

Smitten, Jeffrey R., and Ann Daghistany. *Spatial Form in Narrative.* Ithaca: Cornell UP, 1981.

Stay, Byron L. "Hawthorne's Fallen Puritans: Eliot's Pulpit in *The Blithedale Romance.*" *Studies in the Novel* 18 (1986): 283–290.

Stern, Milton R. "Introduction." In *The House of the Seven Gables* by Nathaniel Hawthorne. London: Penguin, 1981. vii–xxxiii.

—. *Contexts For Hawthorne: "The Marble Faun" and the Politics of Openness and Closure in American Literature.* Urbana: University of Illinois Press, 1991.

Stewart, Randall. *Nathaniel Hawthorne: A Biography.* New Haven: Yale UP, 1946.

Stock, Ely. "History and the Bible in Hawthorne's 'Roger Malvin's Burial'." *Essex Institute Historical Collections* 100 (1964): 279–96.

Stock, Irvin. "Hawthorne's Portrait of the Artist: A Defense of *The Blithedale Romance.*" *Novel* 11 (1978): 144–56.

Stoehr, Taylor. "Hawthorne and Mesmerism." *Huntingdon Library Quarterly* 33 (1969): 33–60.

—. *Hawthorne's Mad Scientists: Pseudoscience and Social Science in Nineteenth-Century Life and Letters.* Hamden: Archon Books, 1978.

Stouck, David. "The Surveyor of 'The Custom-House': A Narrator for *The Scarlet Letter.*" *The Centenniel Review* 15 (1971): 309–329. Rpt. in Gross et al., "Essays in Criticism and Scholarship." 255–265.

Stubbs, John C. *The Pursuit of Form: A Study of Hawthorne and the Romance.* Urbana: University of Illinois Press, 1970.

Swann, Charles. "A Note on *The Blithedale Romance* or 'Call him Fauntleroy'." *Journal of American Studies* 10 (1976): 103–4.

—. *Nathaniel Hawthorne: Tradition and Revolution.* Cambridge: Cambridge UP, 1991.

Tanner, Laura E. "Speaking with 'Hands at Our Throats': The Struggle for Artistic Voice in *The Blithedale Romance.*" *Studies in American Fiction* 21 (1993): 1–19.

Tanner, Tony. "Introduction." In *Hawthorne,* by Henry James. London: Macmillan, 1967. 1–21.

—. "Introduction." In *The Blithedale Romance* by Nathaniel Hawthorne. Oxford: Oxford UP, 1991. vii–xli.

Taylor, J. Golden. *Hawthorne's Ambivalence Toward Puritanism.* Logan: Utah State UP, 1965.

Teskey, Gordon. "Allegory." In *The Spenser Encyclopedia.* Ed. A.C. Hamilton. Toronto: University of Toronto Press, 1990. 16–22.

—. *Allegory and Violence.* Ithaca: Cornell UP, 1996.

Thomas, Brook. "*The House of the Seven Gables:* Reading the Romance of America." *PMLA* 97 (1982): 195–211. Rpt. in Harding *Critical Assessments: Volume III.* 347–72.

—. *Cross-examinations of Law and Literature: Cooper, Hawthorne, Stowe, and Melville.* Cambridge: Cambridge UP, 1987.
—. "Citizen Hester: *The Scarlet Letter* as Civic Myth." *American Literary History* 13 (2001): 181–211.
Thompson, G. R. *The Art of Authorial Presence: Hawthorne's Provincial Tales.* Durham: Duke UP, 1993.
Thompson, G. R. and Virgil L. Locke. Eds. *Ruined Eden of the Present: Critical Essays in Honor of Darrel Abel.* West Lafayette: Purdue UP, 1981.
Tolkien, J. R. R. *The Fellowship of the Ring.* London: George Allen and Unwin, 1966.
Tompkins, Jane P. *Sensational Designs: The Cultural Work of American Fiction, 1790–1860.* New York: Oxford UP, 1985.
Trachtenberg, Alan."Seeing and Believing: Hawthorne's Reflections on the Daguerreotype in *The House of the Seven Gables.*" *American Literary History* 9 (1997): 460–81.
Trollope, Anthony. "The Genius of Nathaniel Hawthorne." *North American Review*, 129 (September, 1879): 220–22. Rpt. in Kesterson. 10–13.
Turner, Arlin. *Nathaniel Hawthorne: A Biography.* New York; Oxford UP, 1980.
Ullén, Magnus. "The Bygone Present: Change in Tense in Nathaniel Hawthorne's *The House of the Seven Gables.*" Unpublished essay. Stockholm University, 1995.
—. "'An Available Foothold between Fiction and Reality:' *The Blithedale Romance* as a Theatre of the Mind." Unpublished essay. Stockholm University, 1996.
—. "Hawthorne's *The Blithedale Romance.*" *The Explicator* 59 (2001): 128–30.
—. "Dante in Paradise: The End of Allegorical Interpretation." *New Literary History* 32 (2001): 177–99.
Uroff, M. D. "The Doctors in 'Rappaccini's Daughter'." *Nineteenth-Century Fiction* 27 (1972): 61–70.
Vallas, Stacey. "The Embodiment of the Daughter's Secret in *The Marble Faun.*" *Arizona Quarterly* 46 (4, 1990): 73–94.
Van Deusen, Marshall. "Narrative Tone in 'The Custom-House' and *The Scarlet Letter.*" *Nineteenth-Century Fiction* 21 (1966): 61–71. Rpt. in Gross et al., "Essays in Criticism and Scholarship." 249–255.
Van Leer, David. "Hester's Labyrinth: Transcendental Rhetoric in Puritan Boston." In Colacurcio, *New Essays.* 57–100.
Von Abele, Rudolphe. "*The Scarlet Letter:* A Reading." *Accent* 11 (1951): 211–27. Excerpted in Gross, *A "Scarlet Letter" Handbook.* 137–40.
—. *The Death of the Artist: A Study of Hawthorne's Disintegration.* The Hague: Nijhoff, 1955.
Waggoner, Hyatt Howe. *Hawthorne: A Critical Study.* Rev. ed. Cambridge: Harvard UP, 1963 (1955).
—. "Art and Belief." In Roy Harvey Pearce, ed., *Hawthorne Centenary Essays.* Columbia: Ohio State UP, 1964. 179–187.
—. *The Presence of Hawthorne.* Baton Rouge: Louisiana State UP, 1979.
Wallace, James D. "Hawthorne and the Scribbling Women Reconsidered." *American Literature* 62 (1990): 201–22.
Walsh, Thomas P., Jr. "Rappaccini's Literary Gardens." *Emerson Society Quarterly* 19 (1960): 9–13.

Walter, James. "The Letter and the Spirit in Hawthorne's Allegory of American Experience." *Emerson Society Quarterly* 32 (1986): 36–54.

Waples, Dorothy. "Suggestions for Interpreting *The Marble Faun*." *American Literature* 13 (1941): 224–39.

Warren, Austin. "Hawthorne, Margaret Fuller and 'Nemesis'." *PMLA* 54 (1939): 615–18.

Warren, Robert Penn. "John Crowe Ransom." *The Virginia Quarterly* (January, 1935).

Waterman, Arthur E. "Dramatic Structure in *The House of Seven Gables*." *Studies in the Literary Imagination* 2 (1969): 13–19.

Weber, Alfred. *Die Entwicklung der Rahmenerzählungen Nathaniel Hawthornes: The Story Teller und andere frühe Werke (1825–1835).* Berlin: E. Schmidt, 1973.

—. "The Framing Functions of Hawthorne's 'The Custom-House' Sketch." *Nathaniel Hawthorne Review* 1 (1992): 5–8.

Wegelin, Christof. "Europe in Hawthorne's Fiction." *ELH* 14 (1947): 219–45.

Wellborn, Grace Pleasant. "Plant Lore and *The Scarlet Letter*." *Southern Folklore Quarterly* 27 (1963): 160–167

Wellek, René. *A History of Modern Criticism*, vol. I. New Haven: Yale UP, 1955.

Wellek, René, and Austin Warren. *Theory of Literature.* Third ed. New York: Harcourt, 1956.

Wershoven, C. J. "Doubles and Devils at Blithedale." *American Transcendental Quarterly* 58 (1985): 43–54.

Williams, Raymond. *Keywords: A Vocabulary of Culture and Society.* New York: Oxford UP, 1976.

Williams, Susan S. *Confounding Images: Photography and Portraiture in Antebellum American Fiction.* Philadelphia: University of Pennsylvania Press, 1997.

Wilson, James C. Ed. *The Hawthorne and Melville Friendship: An Annotated Bibliography, Biographical and Critical Essays, and Correspondence between the Two.* Jefferson: McFarland & Co., 1991.

Wimsatt, W. K., and Monroe Beardsley. "The Intentional Fallacy." *Sewanee Review* 54 (1946): 468–88.

Winters, Yvor. "Maule's Curse: Hawthorne and the Problem of Allegory." In *Maule's Curse.* Norfolk: New Directions, 1938. Rpt. in *In Defense of Reason.* New York: Swallow, 1947.

Woodberry, George E. *Nathaniel Hawthorne.* New York: Houghton Mifflin, 1902.

—. *Nathaniel Hawthorne: How to Know Him.* Boston: Houghton Mifflin, 1918.

Woodson, Thomas. Review of Herbert, T. Walter, Jr. *Dearest Beloved. Nathaniel Hawthorne Review* 20 (1994): 27–29.

Yarden, Leon. *The Spoils of Jerusalem on the Arch of Titus.* Stockholm: Skrifter utgivna av Svenska Institutet i Rom, 1991.

Zapf, Hubert. "The Poetological Theme in Hawthorne's *Blithedale Romance*." *American Transcendental Quarterly* 60 (1986): 73–80.

Ziff, Larzer. *Literary Democracy: The Declaration of Cultural Independence in America.* New York: Viking Press, 1981.

Zivkovic, Peter D. "The Evil of the Isolated Intellect: Hilda, in *The Marble Faun*." *Personalist*, 43 (1962): 202–213. Rpt. in Kesterson, 93–103.

# Index